BRISTOL ROVERS

THE OFFICIAL DEFINITIVE HISTORY

STEPHEN BYRNE & MIKE JAY

AMBERLEY

To Stitch and Julie

Makiwongu kilot ('there is no end to knowledge')

Tugen proverb

'We blossom and flourish as leaves on the tree'

Walter Chalmers Smith
5 August 1824–19 September 1908

First published 2014

Amberley Publishing
The Hill, Stroud, Gloucestershire, GL5 4EP
www.amberley-books.com

ISBN 978 1 4456 3619 1 (print)
ISBN 978 1 4456 3647 4 (ebook)

British Library Cataloguing in Publication Data.
A catalogue record for this book is available from the British Library.

Typesetting by Amberley Publishing.
Printed in Great Britain.

Contents

Introduction

The chill autumnal air, a sullen, greying sky hinting at cold, wet evenings and the imposing darkness of the late afternoon were descending in equal measure all around. Above us, the eerie light from the floodlights enabled bizarrely configured shadows to play uneasily on the grass before us, while the waiting crowd jumped from foot to foot to keep circulation flowing. Out on the hallowed turf, the distinctive figure of Lindsay Parsons played a confident ball across the heart of the defence to his full-back partner Trevor Jacobs, who set off up the right wing as if he were acting the part of Sir Stanley Matthews in an amateur dramatic production. As the night closed in, the Rovers held on for another well-fought home draw and the eternal support of one young spectator.

Of such mediocre performances are lifelong interests born, and though the pedant will no doubt point out that the two named defenders did not appear together when I, as a wide-eyed seven-year-old, watched Rovers scramble to a goalless draw with Orient, their partnership remains an enduring image of my footballing infancy. So too will the crude challenge on David Pritchard, which earned Oxford United's Steve Anthrobus a red card and livened up a game noteworthy only for Jason Roberts' winning goal on the hour mark, become an abiding memory for my eldest child Toseland, only eight days after his fourth birthday. From such insignificant openings can lives appreciative of sport develop.

Every football club deserves a definitive history, and Bristol Rovers Football Club is certainly no exception. The first and longest-surviving professional club in Bristol can boast Football League status since 1920, remaining, until 2001, the only club never to have appeared in either the top or bottom division. Rovers were Southern League champions in 1905, twice FA Cup quarter-finalists, and Third Division champions in 1953 and 1990, in which year they made the first of three appearances under the celebrated Twin Towers at Wembley Stadium.

This history serves to record as full a story as space permits. Within these pages lie the tales of missed penalties and red cards, of seven-goal home defeats and a 20-0 home victory, the Conservative Member of Parliament who played for Rovers, the Lithuanian-born Irishman in the opposition, the unidentifiable spectator who fell in the river, and the sad demise of baker's boy, Fred Foot. Of such snippets of gilded cloth is the entire club history woven, and I make no excuses for allowing the cultural and demographic backdrop of East Bristol to impinge so readily and frequently into the narrative. Indeed, the opening chapter of this book is, in my opinion, an essential element in the Bristol Rovers' story. It attempts to explain and put into context why and how a sporting club, and a footballing one in particular, would have grown up amid the industry and poverty of the 1880s in this neck of the woods. It will also examine the role of the gentry, the undeniably influential increase in rail transport, the late Victorian surge in population growth, as illustrated by the building of churches throughout the area, the subsequent emergence of leisure time as a concept and how these factors led to this club's remarkable success story.

The Bristol Rovers story is written for all those who understand why I rang up from a public telephone box in Spennymoor to reserve my ticket for a Rovers game, or walked the 3 miles from Godramstein to Landau in der Pfalz railway station on Tuesday mornings to buy the single copy of a daily English newspaper that would arrive carrying the score from Rovers' weekend escapades. Such a story has a past, a present and a future. I trust this book satisfies the reader's curiosity about the past, maintains our enthusiasm about the present club, and all that is good in the 'beautiful game', and inspires Bristol Rovers to unprecedented glory in the as yet undetermined future.

1

The Early Years

1883–92

It was a brave move in a rugby playing environment, but a meeting of five young schoolmasters in September 1883 in the Eastville Restaurant in Queen's Parade, Stapleton Road, Bristol, led to the founding of a football club. This restaurant, run by John Collins, a forty-six-year-old former military man, and his wife, Annie Maria Young, stood between J. J. Bond, the grocer, and George West, a furniture broker. This was the birth of an organisation that grew into the first professional team in the city and developed into Bristol Rovers. Yet the circumstances surrounding the club's foundation were by no means unique. A group of young schoolteachers, led by James Allan, had formed Sunderland FC in 1879, and many other clubs – notably Bolton Wanderers, Everton, Leicester City and Northampton Town – also had their roots in the education system. That first meeting in Eastville, organised by Bill Somerton, a nineteen-year-old teacher born in Bicester and brought up in Summertown, Oxfordshire, who had moved to the area from Grove Street, Oxford, just a few months earlier, established a side that swiftly became known as Black Arabs FC – they wore black shirts with a golden sash and played on a pitch flanked by those of several rugby teams, one of whom went under the name of The Arabs. Rugby was flourishing in this corner of the world at the time, and The Arabs were able to attract a crowd of 2,000 when they entertained a strong Newport side on The Downs on 7 March 1885.

The following month, eight young men met at the home of Charles Davis, at No. 33 Clifton Place, Stapleton Road, near the locally famous Thirteen Arches railway bridge in Eastville. One was R. C. Conyers, a former pupil of and now teacher at St Mark's School, Easton, who was to follow Rovers beyond his retirement to Hayle in Cornwall in 1934 until his death there in August 1938. Also present were Richard Conyers, Henry Martin, Harry Phillips, William Braund, Frank Evans, Fred Hall and Edward Edgell. They began to establish a team, recruiting a number of local players. Herbie Hand, for instance, had played for Bristol St George and he and his son, Bill, were both to play for Clevedon Town. Frank Laurie, whose relatives Archie and Tony also played for the side, was a stalwart figure, elected to the Rovers' selection committee in 1893 and a supporter of the club up to his death from pneumonia in April 1925, at the age of fifty-nine. One member of the original team was Harry Horsey, a carpenter and later managing director of Octavius Hunt Ltd, match-makers of Redfield, whose allegiance to the club continued from the Black Arab days until his death in July 1938. He had served as player, committeeman, secretary, treasurer, financial secretary, director, vice chairman and chairman. Fifty-six years with the club is a level of dedication and commitment few can equal, and the history of Bristol Rovers would undoubtedly be all the poorer but for the contributions made by Henry James Horsey and fellow founder members.

A pitch was found, among those of local rugby sides, at Purdown, a mile north of the future Eastville Stadium. This first ground could well have been on the site of the current playing fields at the junction of Sir John's Lane and Lindsay Road. Ironically, St John's Lane, a near namesake across the city, was where Bristol South End, the club that grew into Bristol City, played its first game on 1 September 1894. Opposition proved harder to find, as few clubs yet existed. Two early rivals were Clifton and Warmley, which were among the first recognised football teams in Bristol, a city where boxing, cricket and rugby continued to command greater interest. Clifton Association were, like Rovers, formed in 1883, a year after Bristol St George and Warmley, who were acclaimed as the oldest football team in Bristol. Not far away, though, Paulton Rovers had first appeared in their distinctive dark maroon shirts as early as 1881.

Black Arabs soon found a wealthy patron in Henry Haughton Reynolds, Lord Moreton. Holt demonstrates how, of 740 directors of football clubs between 1888 and 1915, all but seventy-eight were businessmen who saw the potential in this lucrative, up-and-coming leisure pursuit. Along with having an undisputed business acumen, Moreton was also a Justice of the Peace and was Member of Parliament for West Gloucestershire between 1880 and 1885. Lord Moreton died on 8 February 1920, shortly before Rovers' accession to the Football League. Further patrons were found in Colonel Kingscote, Revd Thomas Henry Barnett (1843–1920), vicar of St Mark's, Easton and formerly of St Stephen's, Guernsey, Robert Brison (1812–88) of Gloucester Villa, Hill View, Bishopston, George T. Howe, proprietor of the Queen's Head, Fishponds Road, Eastville, and a Miss Osborne. Colonel Sir Robert Nigel Fitzhardinge Kingscote was, like Moreton, a West Gloucestershire Member of Parliament, serving his constituency between 1852 and 1885. He was also a Justice of the Peace, had been groom-in-waiting to Queen Victoria between 1859 and 1866 and was to serve as extra equerry, well past his seventieth birthday, to Edward VII. A Crimean War veteran, Kingscote was born on 28 February 1830, descended through a female line from the wealthy Berkeley family and lived in Gloucestershire until his death on 22 September 1908. His was indeed a distinguished family, for his great-aunt Catharine had married Edward Jenner, the introducer of the smallpox vaccine, and a great-niece, Flavia, married a nephew of the poet Siegfried Sassoon.

The club's initial set of rules stated that

> jerseys, which members are expected to wear in all matches, shall be the club colours, viz black. That for all engagements, players shall be chosen by Captain and Secretary, any gentleman wishing to join shall be proposed by a member and selected by a majority of the committee and pay the entrance fee of two shillings and sixpence. Also that no player shall leave the ground during a match without permission of the Captain, there shall be practice on Saturday afternoons and any other time when not less than six members are present.

The first president, Revd John Gage Norman (1864–1929), was the curate under Revd Barnett at St Mark's, Easton, between 1881 and 1885. He worked in Oxfordshire, Leicestershire and Nottinghamshire, and was a vicar at the Bay of Islands in Newfoundland, Canada, between 1886 and 1887. After later work in London and Suffolk, he was a curate in Shepton Mallet in 1898. It was no coincidence that church leaders were involved in the early years of the club, as they had been also at the foundation of several top sides. A new 'muscular Christianity' was encouraging physical exercise as a means to keep workers' bodies fit and minds distracted from the lure of heavy drinking and the associated potential social unrest. Aston Villa's foundation in 1874 owed much to the church, as did that of Wolverhampton Wanderers (1877), Everton (1878), Queen's Park Rangers and Southampton (both 1885) and Barnsley (1887). The historian John Latimer, writing in 1887, recorded that Bristol could boast 650 inns, taverns and beer shops in 1840, and as many as 1,250 by 1870. Beer consumption in the United Kingdom as a whole rose from 19.4 gallons per annum per adult in the years between 1845 and 1849 to 33.2 gallons between 1875 and 1879, while one survey carried out in Bristol in 1882 showed that, on a random weekend, some 104,557 people visited the city's pubs on the Saturday evening and 116,148 attended church or chapel the following morning. There were 4,277 charges against Bristolians in 1887 alone for being 'drunk and disorderly'.

L. B. Pearce and Charles Edward Marsh were vice presidents of the Black Arabs, Henry Martin the first captain, Bill Somerton vice captain, Frank Evans treasurer, Bill Braund honorary secretary and George Coopey a committee member, alongside Reynard Conyers, Harry Phillips and F. Hall.

On 1 December 1883, the Black Arabs played their first game, losing convincingly. The *Dursley Gazette* of 3 December reported:

> Football: Wotton-under-Edge v Black Arabs (Bristol).
>
> A match under Association rules has been played at Wotton-under-Edge between these clubs, resulting in the defeat of the visiting team. The home team were in every

> point superior to their antagonists and after a one-sided game Wotton were declared victors by six goals to nil.

The Purdown Poachers, as the Black Arabs became affectionately known, played ten games in their inaugural season, their opponents being Wotton, Warmley, Bristol Wagonworks and Right and Might. To their initial all-black strip, they added a golden diagonal sash to the shirt.

A number of significant changes were made prior to the start of the 1884/85 season. Now known from November 1884 as Eastville Rovers, a name that was to endure until 1898/99, the club played home matches at Three Acres at Ashley Hill and Bill Somerton was appointed captain. The change of name certainly had the desired effect of broadening the base of the club and encouraging players and interest from a much wider local area. The new pitch would have been an open field with no changing facilities. In fact, since newspaper interest in such a contemporarily unorthodox sport was scant, the precise location of this pitch remains a mystery. Three Acres was quite possibly an area off Muller Road and next to the Narrowby Hill footpath, where Fairfield High School now stands. A larger area of some 80 acres beside the County Cricket Ground, later developed into housing, was also noted around this time as a 'football ground', although this terminology will mean little more than open fields.

Rovers played at Three Acres with tapes for crossbars for one season and, from 1885–1891 and 1892–1894, at an unidentified location on the limestone plateau of Durdham Downs, where numerous pitches house regular football to this day. Early players included Fred Hodgkinson, who later became a vicar in Lancashire, while George Warne, who appeared in the game against Right and Might two months later, became the first Rovers player to pass away, dying in Bitton in 1891, aged just twenty-six. His teammate in this game, Harry Evans, who was later vice president of the Gloucestershire Football Association, once bowled W. G. Grace out for a duck and lived locally for many years with his wife Harriet Riddiford. Arthur Lawes, who played in the goalless draw with Warmley in November 1884, was a Bristol Rugby Club player. Meanwhile, Fred Channing, who became the regular left-back, was a Bristol-born defender who had played football in Nottingham and London prior to joining the Black Arabs in 1883. He was appointed Rovers' captain in 1886 and later served the club off the field. On 7 April 1885, he was Rovers' sole representative in the first competitive fixture involving Gloucestershire, a 1-0 win thanks to centre-half George Pocock's goal two minutes before half-time against Somerset at the Bedminster Cricket Ground. Channing was later a stalwart member of the board of directors until resigning through ill health in September 1919.

The first match on The Downs, in which Rovers sported their new strip of blue-and-white hooped shirts and white shorts, was against Right and Might, a works team from Jones & Company, in October 1885. The Purdown Poachers, captained by Bill Somerton, won through a single goal, although the identity of the scorer is unknown. The opposition was late in arriving and, after a 5.10 p.m. kick-off, only forty minutes' play was possible. The teams lined up:

Eastville Rovers: Bill Braund, Bill Somerton, Bill Pepperall, Fred Andrew, Bill Perrin, Charlie Forster, Harry Horsey, Fred Churchill, Frank Laurie, Walter Perrin, Sam Darlington.

Right and Might: H. G. Iles, L. Davies, W. Wiseman, W. Anderson, H. O. Ashton (capt), G. Barnes, J. Picton, L. W. Harvey, R. Wells, W. Wiles, T. K. Jarvis.

While Rovers' players apparently shuffled their positions on the field, the club played against an ever-increasing range of opponents. Rovers having refused to travel to Cardiff on the Aust–Beachley ferry the previous season, a journey through the Severn Tunnel, opened in 1886, enabled the first game against Welsh opposition in 1885/86. Matches against sides from Swindon, Trowbridge and Bath were regular features, even before Rovers entered a recognised league in 1892. In 1886, as interest in the club increased, Rovers formed a reserve side and now played in shirts of Oxford and Cambridge blue. Between 1887 and 1895, however, the club's colours were a tasty combination of claret and cream. At Clifton in January 1887, Rovers conceded an excellent goal to the home side's James Paterson, who hit home 'a wonderful screw-shot' just a few minutes into the game, from practically on the goal line. Rovers lost a close game 2-1 at Weston-super-Mare in November 1887; Jack Binyon's two second-half goals for the opposition included a very late winner. A combined Clifton/Rovers XI drew 4-4 at Warmley in March 1888, trailing 2-1 at the interval with the Old Carthusians and England brothers Arthur and Percy Walters in their side.

In addition to friendlies, Eastville Rovers competed in the Gloucestershire Cup from its inception in 1887/88. The Gloucestershire Cup was the brainchild of Clifton Association's Charles Lacy-Sweet, a noted tennis player, and grew from a meeting in September 1887 attended by Clifton and Rovers, along with Globe, a team made up of former pupils of Queen Elizabeth's Hospital, three church sides in St Agnes, St George and St Simon's and Southville, one of the components of the future Bristol City. Details of the format of the tournament were finalised at a further meeting, held on 5 October 1887 at the Montpelier Hotel. This competition was to run to ninety-nine finals before grinding to a halt in the 1990s. The first taste of cup action, on 14 January 1888, resulted in a 4-1 defeat at the hands of Clifton, who wore their distinctive 'chocolate and cardinal' shirts, in a match played at Bell Hill, St George. Rovers lost Horsey with a strained leg muscle after only two minutes, and were forced to play the remainder of the game with only ten men. Against the odds, however, outside-left Bill Bush put Rovers ahead five minutes before half-time. Arthur Beadon Colthurst equalised moments before the break and scored again after fifty-five minutes, Clifton's third of the game. Charles Wreford-Brown, the first Bristolian to play football for England and the man who, as vice chairman of the Football Association, was allegedly the first to coin the term 'soccer', had put his side 2-1 ahead on fifty minutes, and Harry Francis completed the scoring two minutes from time. It is believed that this final goalscorer was none other than nineteen-year-old Howard Henry Francis, a Bristol-born sportsman who later emigrated to South Africa, played in two cricket Test matches for his adopted country in 1898/99 and died in Cape Town in January 1936. The Rovers line-up was Edward Tucker, Bill Somerton, Bill Berry, Fred Channing (capt), Harry Horsey, Albert Attwell, Harry Cade, Claude Hodgson, Frank Laurie, Walter Perrin, Bill Bush.

However, the following season, after a 3-1 victory at St Agnes, Rovers defeated Warmley by a single goal to win their first final. The all-important goal was scored by Bill Perrin, twenty minutes from time, following a smart interchange of passes with Attwell and brought the first tangible reward to the Eastville club.

The only Rovers side to win the Gloucestershire Cup in the nineteenth century was Edward Tucker, Claude Hodgson, Bill Somerton, Albert Attwell, Bill Howe, Charlie Lawrence, Bill Taylor, Frank Laurie, Bill Higgins, Fred Channing (capt), Bill Perrin. The aforementioned Lacy-Sweet and Francis were the two linesmen. Rovers also reached the final in 1893/94, when George Gerrish, R. Lane, and Bruton all scored for a strong St George side before Horsey's late low shot brought a consolation goal in Rovers' 3-1 defeat in front of a crowd of 4,000 at The Chequers, Lodge Road, Kingswood.

During 1888, Rovers fielded Bill Quick who, born in 1853, was the first-born of all Rovers players, while Harry Cade, alongside Claude Hodgson, one of two hat-trick scorers as Rovers won 8-0 at Kingswood in September 1888, was later a Surrey doctor. The following month, goalkeeper Tom Poulson scored as the reserves ran up a formidable 15-0 victory over hapless St Thomas. Bill Vosper, who was in Rovers' side against St George in March 1890, later ran the Lord Nelson public house near the club's ground. In December 1888, Rovers led Clifton early on before three goals in ten minutes gave Association a 3-1 interval lead; goals late on from Bill Higgins and Bert Rayner, who became a surgeon, secured a draw. On the final day, Rovers arrived at Clevedon with only nine men. They borrowed the home side's Charlie Young and James Cooke to make up numbers, but crashed to a 4-1 defeat. The game at Warmley in October 1889 saw Rovers again draw 3-3 despite leading through two own goals within the first thirty-five minutes – the former Rovers full-back George Gay and Edwin Wilmot scoring past their own goalkeeper. Two months later, Rovers' defeat at St George in 'very cold, wretched conditions' (*Western Daily Press*) was watched by a club record low attendance of fifty. Despite wet and windy weather, the fixture with Bath Association on The Downs drew an unexpectedly high crowd as the match coincided with a Labour demonstration. During the 1889/90 campaign, despite Perrin's two first-half goals, which saw the sides level at half-time, Rovers lost 7-2 to Clifton Association in the Gloucestershire Cup – R. Innes-Pocock and Barlow scored twice each, with Attwell putting through his own goal for the fifth. The game was umpired, alongside Fred Channing, by the famous Gloucestershire and England cricketer W. G. Grace (1848–1915), who had been approached by the Rovers club committee to take charge of a number of matches. He and Bill Somerton had been the linesmen for the replay of the inaugural Gloucestershire Cup final in March 1888. Rovers were to win the trophy next in April 1903. From a tournament involving a large number of local sides, the competition evolved into a straightforward two-club play-off from 1908 between Bristol's two major sides.

For the 1890/91 season, Rovers could boast a fourteen-man squad. They defeated Craigmore College 5-1, with five different members of the team getting on the scoresheet, but lost by the same score at both Warmley and Trowbridge Town. Led by captain Bill Somerton, several old hands remained, among them Walter Perrin, Harry Horsey, Fred Lovett and both Frank and Archie Laurie. Other squad members included Albert Attwell, James Batchelor, Bill Brown, Tom Hardwicke, Claude Hodgson, Bill Howe, Edward Tucker and Fred Yates. The most astonishing score of the campaign was the 8-4 defeat at St George that October, where Rovers trailed 3-2 at the interval, having fallen behind to a goal from Fred Loveless within twenty seconds of the start. The following week, Rovers led Bedminster 2-0 at half-time through two Bill Perrin goals, only to crash to a 4-2 defeat. A 3-2 home defeat to the same opposition saw Rovers eliminated early from the Gloucestershire Cup. Harry Batchelor and Walter Griffiths, who both scored against Rovers, contributed the goals with which the South Bristol side beat Warmley 2-0 in the final. The 3-3 draw that autumn with Bath Association was played out in very high winds. At the tail end of the season, Lewis Frank, a Russian Jew, appeared in the side for one fixture, a 5-1 defeat at Warmley.

In May 1891, Eastville Rovers negotiated a seasonal rental of £8 to use the Schoolmasters Cricket Ground in Downend Lane, Horfield. The pitch would have been at the present site of the crossroads between Downend Road and Dovercourt Road. A surviving cricket club minute book reveals that the hire agreement stipulated that Rovers would provide a groundsman and maintain fencing at the ground, but would take all the proceeds from the gate. The summer of 1891 saw the introduction of the penalty kick into British football, but of greater concern to Eastville Rovers was the side's alarming capacity to ship goals. Rovers conceded seven twice and six in games played at Warmley, and also conceded five on three occasions, twice against Trowbridge Town and once at Swindon Town. Yet they also beat Craigmore College 10-0, after being seven goals ahead by half-time. In addition, Rovers won 3-1 at Kingswood in November, despite fielding only nine players. Indeed, the Gloucestershire Cup campaign of 1891/92 was to comprise two 7-1 scorelines. In driving rain and gale-force winds, Rovers raced to a 5-0 half-time lead over Craigmore College in January, Thomas scoring his second goal right on the interval to add to a brace from Archie Laurie. Rovers conceded a consolation goal only in the last minute of the match. Four weeks later, in a semi-final initially postponed due to frost, Tom Nelmes, J. King and J. MacKay scored twice each for Warmley, who defeated Rovers convincingly before a crowd of 700. Rovers stalwart Bill Braund was linesman for both games. The Rovers side that lost at Warmley was Albert Attwell, Claude Hodgson, Bill Somerton, Bill Wallace, Alf Purser, Fred Lovett, Archie Laurie, Bill Thomas, Fred Yates, Bill Rogers, Billy Taylor.

Warmley was also the venue for the worst result of the season. In September, with Fred Channing running the line, Rovers held the home side to a goalless first half, but with the strong wind in their favour after half-time, Warmley ran in seven second-half goals without reply. King, going one better than in the Gloucestershire Cup, scored a hat-trick. Apparently unable to extend their hire agreement at the Schoolmasters Cricket Ground, Eastville Rovers reverted to the Durdham Downs for the 1892/93 season. In what must have appeared a different world, Alf Jasper Geddes, later a Rovers player, scored in the FA Cup final in March 1892, as West Bromwich Albion beat Aston Villa 3-0. His was the opening goal after only four minutes, firing home a first-time shot, following a cross from the England outside-right Billy Bassett.

1892–95

The growing trend to formalise football fixtures reached Bristol in 1892. When the Football League was founded in 1888, the majority of the twelve inaugural sides had hailed from the industrial heartlands of Lancashire and the Birmingham area. However, football developed in the country through the late nineteenth century as the popular pastime in working-class society, and gradually replaced boxing as the major crowd-pulling sport in east Bristol. Bristol, as its motto suggests, was a city of great industry and Lesser Columbus reported in 1893 that 'there is scarcely anything that is not made in Bristol'. Social conditions were altering and the previously unheard-of commodity of leisure time slowly emerged, the introduction of half-day Saturdays encouraging many workers to go to football matches in the afternoon. These matches were, in turn, reported in newspapers for an increasingly literate population, with the first Special Saturday Football Edition of the *Bristol Evening News* appearing on 14 October 1893. In the aftermath of the Reform Act of 1884, prominent politicians took a keen interest in football as a means of wooing voters and the embryonic game was allowed to flourish.

The sport was also seen as a vehicle for boosting the general level of health within the working classes, especially in Bristol, where a cholera epidemic as recently as 1849 had killed 444 people. Moreover, scarlet fever, typhoid and smallpox were rife in the city in 1865. Typhoid reportedly killed 150 of its 1,500 victims in Bristol in 1864, there were epidemics of measles in 1885, 1898 and 1905, and scarlet fever in 1896 and 1900, in addition to a further outbreak of smallpox in 1880. A Parliamentary Report on the Sanitary Condition of Bristol in 1845 investigated the appalling squalor of the city and yet, in 1869, *The Times* reported Bristol to be one of the healthiest towns in Great Britain. In chapter 38 of Charles Dickens' *Pickwick Papers*, Mr Winkle visits Bristol, which 'struck him as being a shade more dirty than any place he had ever seen', while Virginia Woolf, in 1935, described Bristol as 'the most hideous of all towns'. Moreover, Thomas Chatterton's *Last Verses* refer to 'Bristolia's dingy piles of brick'.

While the Southern League did not come into existence until 1894, a recommendation from Percy Wyfold Stout of Gloucester led to the idea of establishing a regional league in the Bristol area. Bedminster, Clifton Association, Eastville Rovers, Mangotsfield, St George and Warmley sent representatives to the Earl Russell Hotel, Lawrence Hill, Bristol, on 30 March 1892, where it was unanimously agreed that a Bristol and District League should be set up. This league, which was a forerunner of the Western League, a name it adopted in 1895, was set in stone at a second meeting on 31 August, at which Rovers were one of nine clubs represented. Rovers were to have a side involved in this league for almost every season from 1892/93 to 1962/63.

Without a game on the opening day, Rovers kicked off their first match in this competition at 3.30 p.m. on 1 October 1892, and lost 3-1 to Mangotsfield. Although officially a 'home' game, Rovers were forced to play at their opponents' ground. After going a goal down to the future Rovers player Bill Nolan in the fifteenth minute, Rovers further conceded two second-half goals to twenty-one-year-old Courtney Punter – the first a penalty and the second just moments after Walter Perrin had briefly brought the side back into contention. Eastville Rovers won six out of sixteen games in this inaugural season, finishing sixth out of nine clubs. They put five goals past Wells, who fielded only ten men – Archie Laurie and Bill Taylor scoring twice each. They also scored five against Bedminster and Mangotsfield – Bill Rogers scoring a hat-trick – but also conceded five at Bedminster and six at Trowbridge Town, despite being level 2-2 at half-time. The 5-2 victory at home to Bedminster was an ill-tempered affair, with the visitors' second goalscorer, Scottie Milne, being sent off after a dreadful foul on Claude Hodgson. Twice behind, Rovers were indebted to Bill Rogers for two equalisers, while the aforementioned Hodgson added the home side's fourth goal. The worst defeat, however, was at Warmley on 18 February, where Rovers trailed 3-1 by half-time in a strong wind and, with Phil 'Nipper' Britton completing his hat-trick in the second half, lost 8-2. Rovers were also involved in a game with the same opposition in November, which was abandoned at 2-2 in failing light twelve minutes from time. As the season drew to a close, Rovers recorded a memorable 5-0 victory away to Mangotsfield, Sam Attwell marking his debut with a hat-trick, the third being a deft chip over goalkeeper Bob Bennett shortly after half-time. The home side were reduced to nine men near the close, with the aforementioned Nolan and Punter dismissed by referee Edward Harris Nettle. One contemporary reporter stated, 'play then turned very rough on the part of Mangotsfield, the referee a few minutes before time ordering Nolan and Punter off the field.' Warmley were champions by a point and, in a show of electioneering, were presented with the 19-inch trophy on an ebony plinth at the league dinner on 9 September 1893 by Charles Edward Hungerford Atholl Colston, the newly elected Member of Parliament for South Gloucestershire.

In 1893/94, Rovers finished second from bottom, above Mangotsfield whom Rovers defeated 3-0 and 5-2 – Archie Laurie and Bill Thompson scoring in both games. A further home victory, this time against Swindon Wanderers, was played in a temperature of 90°F, while the game at home to Warmley was decreed a friendly and had to be replayed as the pitch was saturated; indeed, the Eastville pitch had been under water on the Friday evening and it was incredible that the game took place at all. When the match was replayed, Phil 'Nipper' Britton put through his own goal for Rovers to earn a 1-1 draw. Rovers led at the interval at Swindon Athletic that Christmas through Arthur Williams' goal, only to lose 2-1, having been forced to borrow Wolverton's Tom Haycock to make up the numbers. When Rovers lost to Clifton in December 1893, they started with only six men, and 'this match was played in almost impenetrable fog. It was impossible to see from the halfway line to either goal, so thick was the fog', as the local press reported. The following season, an enlarged division, was won by newcomers Hereford Thistle, who, in their chocolate-and-sky blue shirts, twice put four goals past Rovers. Ten wins and eight defeats left Rovers in sixth place out of twelve clubs. Clevedon, bottom of the table with three points and 136 goals conceded in twenty-two games, were defeated 7-2 in October, six players scoring for Rovers – all five forwards plus left-half Claude Hodgson, with the captain and outside-right Hugh McBain opening the goalscoring after only two minutes. Rovers also took part in a six-a-side tournament at Kingswood in April 1894, beating Gloucester and Bedminster, the latter by an astonishing 21-0 margin, before losing their semi-final to Clifton, runners-up to Warmley.

The 1894/95 season was Rovers' first away from Durdham Downs, as the club played home matches a mile to the east of Eastville, on a ground variously known as Rudgeway, Rudgway or Ridgeway. It appears likely that the Ridgeway ground, home from 1894–97, was one of two fields lying between Crooked Lane, later Ridgeway Road, and Fishponds Road. Indeed, the club played on one pitch before moving to another just yards across the road that dried more satisfactorily. The first match there was a 2-2 draw with Staple Hill on 6 October 1894. Bill Rogers was credited with the club's first goal on the new ground, with Bob Horsey also scoring in this inaugural game. The following week, Hugh McBain scored a first-half hat-trick as Clevedon were defeated 7-2, and four days after Christmas, Rovers trailed Trowbridge 3-0 at half-time only to claim an unlikely 3-3 draw. In the return fixture with Staple Hill on Easter Monday 1895, the sides changed at the Red Lion Inn before Rovers succumbed to a 4-1 defeat. Staple Hill, frequent and regular visitors in late Victorian football, were to achieve their Warholian fifteen minutes of fame in January 1906, when they briefly held a 1-0 lead in an FA Cup tie away to Manchester United. Rovers' headquarters at this time was the Star Inn, which still stands at No. 539 Fishponds Road, opposite Star Lane, its landlord in 1894 being Florence King, who had taken over the reins after the untimely death of her husband, Charles King, and later married Arthur Griffin.

Three consecutive games were won at the end of October, but the club's form was patchy as the season wore on. Just after Christmas, though, Rovers were able to salvage an unexpected draw 3-3 at home, after they recovered from trailing by three goals at the interval to Trowbridge, despite being reduced to ten men with John Hodgkins off the field injured. Rovers also lost 5-3 at home to Mangotsfield in January 1895, with McBain scoring the first penalty the club had ever been awarded, and with the opposition's forward Brain scoring twice before being carried from the field with a broken collarbone. McBain also scored from 50 yards shortly before half-time during the 4-2 home victory over Swindon Wanderers that April. One star of this Rovers side was a youthful Tot Farnall, who left Rovers in the summer of 1895 to join First Division Small Heath, and was to represent Rovers in four different spells during his long career. On 26 November 1894, Fred Lovett was Rovers' sole representative in a Bristol and District XI that lost 5-0 to First Division Stoke in front of a 2,000-strong crowd at Greenway Bush Lane.

The first meeting between the clubs that were to become Bristol Rovers and Bristol City took place on 22 September 1894. Eastville Rovers lost 2-1 to Bristol South End in a friendly at St John's Lane, Bedminster, having trailed by two clear goals at half-time, Bob Horsey scoring for Rovers. South End, who were compelled to play solely in friendlies that season, were grateful to their two star names of the time, Hamlet Horatio Clements and Frank Ernest Mayger, two twenty-year-olds destined for highly successful roles with the embryonic Bristol City, who scored a goal each. The Rovers line-up for this first local derby was Bill Stone, Charles Llewellyn, Fred Lovett, Claude Hodgson, Lewis John, Albert Furse, Hugh McBain, Bill Rogers, Bob Horsey, George Hockin, Tony Laurie.

When the sides next met, once again at St John's Lane, a March crowd of 600 saw Rovers lead 3-0 at half-time before running up a 5-2 inaugural victory over their rivals, Bob Horsey scoring a hat-trick.

Bill Somerton, one of Rovers' founders, refereed a rough Western League game on 23 February 1895, where he reported ten Mangotsfield players and an official for insulting him. Nine players were suspended for three weeks, and one until September 1895. The following season, Somerton refereed a cup game between Warmley and Clifton, which was held up for a quarter of an hour after a pitch invasion when some people in the crowd attempted to attack the referee.

In the face of competition, the Bristol and District League chose to upgrade its image and, on 8 May 1895, changed its name to the Western League. The competition it faced came from the South Bristol League, which had begun operations in 1893, as well as the East Bristol League and the prestigious Southern League, which had both been started up in 1894. Rovers were allocated two places in the Western League, one in Division One for the first team and one in Division Two for the reserves. A later meeting, attended by Rovers officials and held at the Earl Russell Hotel, took place on 12 June 1895. The Western League set out its plans for the season ahead and invited further applications from any club playing within a 50-mile radius of Bristol. Eastville Rovers were among a group of ambitious local clubs heading inexorably towards the world of professional football. Some apparently successful clubs – most notably Clifton Association in December 1897 and Warmley in January 1899 – despite their continued on-field success, were to fold. Rovers would keep moving along the slow road to the Southern League and, ultimately, the Football League.

1895–99

Participation in the newly renamed Western League from 1895 was an indication of the high aspirations the club entertained. Rovers were quick to adopt professionalism as a means of gaining access to the higher levels of football available in the Southern League. When the board of directors agreed to the club joining this prestigious league in 1899, Rovers changed their kit, appointed a full-time manager and altered their name to Bristol Rovers. This was, however, merely the end product of a series of key changes that had taken place over a period of a few years from 1895.

By the summer of 1895, Eastville Rovers were based at the Star Inn on Fishponds Road, a public house built around 1860 and named after the Duke of Beaufort's coal mine, Star Pit. They played all their home matches at the Ridgeway Ground in a kit of buff and green. Prior to the first season in Division One of what was now the Western League, the club appointed George William Pay as their first trainer. Pay, though born in Bristol, was the Welsh champion over 150 yards, had raced under the pseudonym C. Lewis in important meetings at Sheffield and Manchester, and had allegedly never been beaten in a professional race. His considerable awareness of stamina training was an essential feature of Rovers' drive in the early professional years, and the players' fitness was rarely called into question. He remained with the club until 1923.

The first Western League game of the 1895/96 season, at Mangotsfield on 14 September, resulted in a 4-0 defeat. A fortnight later, in their first home game, Tony Laurie and Bill Thompson scored to give Rovers a 2-0 half-time lead over Trowbridge, Rovers completing a 7-3 victory in intense heat. Rovers were to beat

Swindon Wanderers 9-0 at the Ridgeway Ground in April 1896 (Osborne, Gallier and Brown scoring twice apiece) and inflicted 5-0 defeats on St Paul's twice and on Mangotsfield in the return fixture. An ultimate tally of fourteen wins and fifty-seven goals in twenty Western League games gave Rovers a final league position of equal second, six points behind champions Warmley. A 3-2 victory over Cardiff in December was chalked off due to the Welsh club's expulsion from the league for non-payment of fines. Rovers then defeated Staple Hill 2-1, despite being reduced to ten men when Charlie Leese left the field injured, and the two Christmas games were played on snow-bound pitches. In a play-off match for runners-up medals, Rovers drew 2-2 at Staple Hill, and the clubs were declared joint second. Rovers defeated the same opposition 14-7 in the final of a Western League six-a-side tournament at St George in April.

In October 1895, a first foray into the FA Cup led to disappointment, as Rovers lost 2-0 at home to Warmley: Phil 'Nipper' Britton, always a thorn in Rovers' collective side, and Bill Bowler, from a classic header, scoring in the space of two first-half minutes on a rain-soaked pitch. The same opposition, this time by a single first-half Bowler goal, defeated Rovers in the 1896 Gloucestershire Cup final. Bill Demmery, a future Rovers goalkeeper, played for this Warmley team, while 'Nipper' Britton was appearing in one of his five Gloucestershire Cup finals. Rovers' side in the final – watched by a crowd of 5,651, which brought gate receipts of £161 10*s* 5*d* – was Bill Stone, Bob Horsey (capt), Fred Lovett, Hugh McBain, John Ross, George Hockin, Bill Thompson, Richard Osborne, Howard Gallier, George Brown, Charlie Leese.

Rovers had beaten Bristol South End – the first meeting in this tournament with the future Bristol City – as well as St George and Bedminster to reach the final, but the 1-0 semi-final win at Greenway Bush Lane was overshadowed by tragedy. Bedminster's twenty-seven-year-old forward Herbert Edward Smith challenged Fred Lovett for the ball and received a head injury. Although he twice returned to the field, his injuries were such that he did not complete the match. Nonetheless, the serious nature of his condition went unnoticed, and Smith returned home, where he collapsed in the evening. Unconscious overnight, the young man never recovered and died around six o'clock the following morning.

Eastville Rovers also defeated a Mr T. G. Walker's League XI 2-0 in April 1896, in a match played at Ridgeway for the benefit of Eastville Cricket Club, while the friendly at Bedminster that month was the last fixture played at the opposition's Greenway Bush Lane. It had been a good season, but 1896/97 proved a tougher proposition. Despite winning a preseason friendly 8-1 at Barton Hill in their chocolate and red shirts, in which Richard Osborne scored a hat-trick, Rovers struggled in the Western League Division One. Prior to the start of the new season, Rovers played Singers, the forerunners of Coventry City, and 3-1 up by half-time, ran out 5-1 winners. One of their four goalscorers was Tommy McCairns, who was to enjoy several successful seasons with the club. He had scored six times when Grimsby Town defeated Leicester Fosse in a Second Division game the previous April. Defeat in an exciting game at Warmley in February 1897 came courtesy of Phil 'Nipper' Britton's last-minute penalty, while James McLean's hat-trick eased Rovers to a comfortable 5-0 victory over St Paul's. Until Easter 1897, home fixtures were still played at Ridgeway, including the first competitive game against the soon-to-be Bristol City, when a crowd of 3,000 saw Bristol South End win 2-0 through a first-half goal from H. Porter, and one after the interval from J. S. Ross.

This season, Rovers finished fifth out of nine clubs in Division One of the Western League, their biggest victory being 5-1 at home to Staple Hill in December. Rovers and Barton Hill also played out a 2-2 draw over Christmas in the first-ever Bristol Charity Cup fixture. This competition ran from 1896/97 to 1941/42, with clubs competing for a bowl donated by the jeweller C. H. Flooks of Bristol and Merthyr Tydfil. Rovers were finalists in 1899/1900 before the tournament developed into a league format, after which the club's reserve and 'A' sides were winners on eleven occasions, and shared the trophy in two further seasons. The FA Cup brought two close ties with Newbury, Rovers turning down the option of extra time in the initial tie to win a replay through goals from Richard Osborne and Howard Gallier. Rovers also beat St George in the FA Cup but, drawn away to Royal Artillery Portsmouth, decided they had no chance of avoiding a humiliating defeat and, saving the relatively steep travel expenses, withdrew from the competition. In the Gloucestershire Cup, victory over St Paul's was followed by defeat at Clifton Association, while Rovers went on to beat Clifton but lose to Bedminster in the Bristol Charity Cup.

Rovers arrived forty minutes late for an extraordinary New Year's Day Western League encounter at Bedminster. James McLean scored after twenty-five minutes, and regular custodian Bill Stone's goal put Rovers 2-0 ahead a minute before half-time. However, Rovers were by then reduced to nine men for, in the aftermath of a mass brawl, despite the paucity of sendings-off in Victorian football, Novello Shenton and Charlie Leese had been ordered off the field, along with the home side's former England international Dick Baugh. Rovers took to the field after half-time with one full-back and two half-backs, but were further hampered when goalkeeper Lewis John, injured earlier in the game, received a kick in the eye and was carried off. Stone reverted to his more customary goalkeeping position, and though Malachi McAuliffe pulled a goal back from Harris' pass, the eight-man Rovers held out for a 2-1 victory. Thereafter, Rovers welcomed back Albert Furse and captain Bob Horsey in the New Year and the club's form stabilised on the pitch.

Breaking even was an ongoing struggle that affected all local sides. For one Western League game with Fishponds, Rovers even charged their opponents and the referee admission to the ground. This was ruled excessive and the league ordered Rovers to refund those concerned. On another occasion, spectators supporting Rovers attempted to attack the referee, and the club was instructed to supply suitable changing quarters for match officials. The fact that Rovers survived this era to grow into a major force in football in the Bristol area is due partly to good management and partly to sheer chance. At this juncture even the league itself was, on occasions, out of pocket, and Rovers donated £10 during 1896/97 to help stave off the Western League's large £120 debt.

During the course of the 1896/97 season, Rovers purchased a site of 13 acres, two roods and one perch on heavy red clay soil, which stretched from the watercress meadows of Eastville along the River Frome to the Stapleton Gasworks and as far as the Thirteen Arches on one of two nearby Great Western Railway branch lines. The stench from the gasworks behind what was later the Tote End was a familiar experience to hardened regulars in Rovers' years at Eastville and gave rise to the popular sobriquets 'The Gas' and 'Gasheads', by which the club and its supporters have been known ever since Rovers' departure from the ground in 1986.

Eastville Stadium, formerly home to the Bristol Harlequins Rugby Football Club, was purchased for £150 from various directors, who were leasing it from Sir Henry Greville Smyth of Ashton Court, an extensive landowner in late Victorian Bristol. It was 'a ground surrounded with a gasworks, a railway viaduct and a river that always threatened to swamp the ground' (C.B. Fry, *Sports News*, 30 August 1919).

The Frome, or 'Danny' as it was fondly termed locally, was highly susceptible to flooding, and there had been terrible damage caused by rising waters in 1607 and 1703. Many had reportedly died in several weeks' of heavy snowfall from 22 January 1635. In May 1720, the Frome 'rose as high as the wall at the Ducking Stool', as Latimer reports in his *Annals of Bristol*, and there was £100,000 damage to submerged streets in January 1738. Part of Stapleton Bridge was carried away by the floodwater of 9 November 1800. In October 1882, just months before Rovers' formation, the Baptist Mills and Eastville areas were reported to be badly affected by flooding. Frederick Hunt, landlord of the 'Black Swan' on Stapleton Road, where Rovers were to be based until 1910, had stated he was ruined, as all his stock was under 5 feet of water. There was a fatality, too, as eighteen-year-old Frederick Foot, attempting to deliver bread from Williams' bakery of Lower Easton, was swept away by floodwater, along with his pony, from beside the railway bridge in Mina Road on 25 October 1882. Despite rescue attempts made by three locals and a policeman, both deliveryman and pony were drowned.

In Rovers' quarters, an area of some 200 acres was flooded in March 1889 as snow thawed and Sevier Street was reported impassable by 9 March. John Chenhall, who ran a steam engineering firm in Wolseley Road, Eastville, reported his workshop as being under 7 feet of water; living upstairs, his wife, Clara Rounsevell, and son, John Snell Chenhall, could hear furniture below bumping against the ceiling. Walter Clarke rescued forty passengers from a tramcar stuck in the Eastville floods; as he rowed home, he was taken by the current and had to jump overboard and swim to safety, while George Vince, who ran the Railway Inn on Stapleton Road with his wife, Harriett Thomas, from 1885 until his death, was also recorded as saving forty people from a separate tramcar. On 8 April 1889 it was reported that a Floods Relief Fund had raised £11,700. There were to be further problems of this nature in 1936, 1937, 1947 and 1968. In addition, there was water 7 feet deep on Rovers' pitch on 21 November 1950. The Bristol Flood Prevention Acts of 1885 and 1890 promised a series of schemes, but it was to be the Northern Stormwater Interceptor, incepted in 1962 and completed shortly after the floods six years later, that finally solved the problem. Much of the Frome is now intercepted at Eastville and taken underground to join the Avon at the Portway below Clifton Downs.

Rovers thus inherited the Stapleton Road Enclosure, or Black Swan Ground in 1897, a ground smelling of gas and which is sometimes underwater, but which included a wooden stand capable of seating 501 spectators, a press box and a small directors' box with cloth-covered seats. A prompt investment of a further £1,255 ensured cover for the north side, with the stated aim of creating a stadium capable of holding 20,000. Entry to the ground was from Stapleton Road, parallel to the pitch and the river was a rugby pitch occupied by the North Bristol Rugby Union Football Club.

On 26 March 1897, the club was registered as a public limited liability company under the name of Eastville Rovers. Just days later, on 3 April, a crowd of 5,000 watched the Football League and FA Cup double winners Aston Villa take on Rovers in the official opening game at Eastville Stadium. Villa, whose own ground at Villa Park was opened fourteen days later, won 5-0. Swindon Town also won 6-1 there before Rovers restored their self-belief by winning a friendly 6-1 at Bedminster. It had been a tough end of season, though, and a nadir was reached in the final game when Clifton arrived at Eastville with only nine men. Rovers produced a 'wretched performance', as the *Western Daily Press* described it, losing 2-0 against the reduced visiting side. Warmley defeated Bristol South End 2-1 before 2,000 spectators at Eastville in the Bristol Charity Cup final at the end of April. Rovers were, however, compelled to play one final game at Ridgeway, against Clifton Association, who fielded only nine men, nonetheless winning through two second-half goals on 24 April, while Eastville was being used for an athletics meeting. It is no coincidence that the electric tramway reached Fishponds in 1897. Since the construction of the first line in Bristol from Perry Road to Redland in 1875, this means of rapid transport and communication had moved progressively closer, with the Horfield section opening in 1880. The growth of Rovers as a club mirrored the development of east Bristol so that, by the turn of the century, Eastville could boast a thriving society, well-established links with the centre of Bristol and a professional football club competing in the Southern League.

In registering themselves as a limited company and acquiring a permanent home, Rovers were pressing their claim for a place in the newly flourishing professional Southern League, which had been formed in 1894. The Black Swan Hotel, at No. 438 Stapleton Road, was adopted as the club's headquarters and was to remain as such until 1920.

The new company was to have seven directors:

Samuel Sinclair Rinder (1854–1919, ostrich feather manufacturer, 79 Stapleton Road)
Samuel Joy (1850–1923, licensed victualler of The Waggon and Horses, 83 Stapleton Road)
William Henry Brown (1863–1914, gentleman of Chester Park Road, Fishponds)
Frederick William Hunt (1860–1943, licensed victualler, The Black Swan Hotel, 438 Stapleton Road)
Albert James Beaven (1852–1908, building contractor, Gotley Lodge, Brislington)
Henry James Horsey (1867–1938, commercial clerk, Dove Steet, St George)
Imlah Hewys (1841–1912, coal merchant, Old Market)

The company was to sell 1,500 shares at £1 each to raise capital, and its aims, as stated in its 'Memorandum of Association', were:

> to promote the practice and play of football, cricket, lacrosse, lawn tennis, hockey, golf, bowls, bicycle and tricycle riding, running, jumping, skating, physical training and development of the physical frame and other athletic sports, games and exercise of every description and any other games, pastimes, sports recreations, amusements or entertainments.

The ever improving standard of Western League football, coupled with the introduction of the electrified tram system around the city, led to a significant increase in support for football from the Bristol public. Around this time, the five major clubs in the area – Eastville Rovers, Warmley, Bristol St George, Bedminster and Bristol South End – began to pay their players. One of the first professionals at Eastville Rovers was James McLean, a Stoke-born player who earned his keep working through the summer as the club's groundsman. McLean's former professional contract at Port Vale led South End at first to query Rovers' payment to the player of 15*s* per week. Even though it was proved that South End had offered the same player 25*s* per week, the complaint was upheld and Rovers received a £1 fine and were deducted two Western League points, leaving the club with fourteen points from the sixteen Western League games played in 1896/97. Another early professional was George Kinsey, a thirty-year-old half-back who had won four England caps and an FA Cup winners' medal in 1893 with Wolverhampton Wanderers. He had also represented Aston Villa and Derby County before arriving at Eastville from Notts County. A Western League committee meeting on 26 May 1897 voted unanimously to adopt professionalism from the start of the following season. In 1900, South End and Bedminster amalgamated to form Bristol City, and as quickly as professionalism had taken root, there were soon just two professional clubs in the Bristol area.

For the 1897/98 season, Rovers sported the Duke of Beaufort's racing colours of light blue and white hoops, and were able to play league football in two leagues at their new stadium. The Western League established a Professional Division of eight clubs (four from Bristol plus Eastleigh, Reading, Swindon Town and Trowbridge Town) while Bedminster, who won all but their last game, won an Amateur Division that included Eastville Wanderers. Rovers never fully recovered from losing their first two games, and Bristol City, as South End had begun to be known, were crowned champions.

David Smellie had given Rovers a third-minute lead when the two sides met before a 4,000-strong crowd at Eastville in March, but McLean's goal five minutes from time served merely as a consolation as Rovers lost 3-2. In November, George Seeley scored a hat-trick as Rovers lost 4-3 to West Bromwich Albion reserves, becoming the first man to register three goals for the club and yet end up on the losing side. Long-serving full-back Walter Bunch scored a rare goal in March as Rovers recorded a comfortable 5-0 home victory over Kidderminster Harriers. Rovers were able to record two large home victories in April. Trowbridge Town found themselves 3-0 down after only eleven minutes as Rovers, up 5-0 by half-time, won 9-1 thanks to a hat-trick from Smellie. He scored twice more, opening the scoring after only ten minutes as Rovers, with six second-half goals, beat Eastleigh 8-1 in the final match of the season, McLean scoring three times. Bristol City, by means of contrast, had scored fourteen times in their home fixture against the Hampshire side.

The shrewd aspirations of the board were, however, best illustrated by the club's participation in the Birmingham and District League. The three seasons spent in this league, between 1897 and 1900, proved tough but essential experience as Rovers prepared for the challenge the Southern League would offer. Despite some good victories, the strength of the reserve sides of Wolverhampton Wanderers, Aston Villa and West Bromwich Albion was too much for a young Rovers side at this stage. However, Rovers were able to attract a crowd of 4,500 to Eastville in October 1897 for the visit of Aston Villa reserves. The side held on for a draw after losing left-back Bob Horsey through injury, while 4,000 paid £108 gate receipts to witness Rovers' 3-1 Christmas defeat at the hands of the reserve side of Small Heath, later Birmingham City. The biggest victory – 11-3 at home to Singers – saw Rovers compile a 6-2 half-time lead, despite trailing 2-1 early on, and score five more times while attacking the Railway End in the second half. George Green scored the eleventh, his fourth of the game, while Tot Farnall, who scored the eighth, was a twenty-six-year-old newly returned to Rovers after gaining Football League experience with Small Heath and Bradford City. Rovers also ran up five goals before half-time in defeating Halesowen 7-1 in November, while the previous week Worcester Rovers had appeared at Eastville with only ten men. Rovers could even afford the luxury of missing a second-half penalty as Hereford Thistle were defeated 3-0 that February, while Bill Turley enjoyed the rare experience of scoring twice from half-back when Worcester Rovers visited over Easter, and Bill Sawers added a hat-trick as Eastleigh were put to the sword 8-1. Goals were liberally scored, Jones contributing thirty-two in all, McLean twenty-three and Green twenty-two, while Smellie scored seventeen in only sixteen appearances.

After two Cottrell goals had helped defeat Staple Hill 5-0, Rovers lost 2-0 to the eventual winners, Bristol City, in the Gloucestershire Cup. Billy Jones and Jock Russell scored the first-half goals in front of a crowd of 6,400, which produced gate receipts of £170. City's victory over the holders Warmley in the final took place on Rovers' Eastville pitch. The most unlikely of opponents, Reading, knocked Rovers out of the Bristol Charity Cup, a tournament won by Bedminster. The South Bristol side was, however, one of four clubs Rovers eliminated from the FA Cup to earn a place in the fifth qualifying round. Twenty-three-year-old Jack Jones, a summer signing from Small Heath with thirty-five Football League games to his name, had struck an early hat-trick against Warmley. A second 6-2 victory, achieved over Cowes despite an own goal from goalkeeper Bill Stone, was secured through four George Green goals after a visiting forward, Bill Baker, had been sent off in the first half. The fifth qualifying round tie at Southampton attracted a crowd of 8,000, but the Southern League champions overwhelmed Rovers and recorded an 8-1 win, with forwards Jimmy Yates, Bob Buchanan, Watty Keay and Joe Turner scoring twice each. The Saints were to reach the FA Cup semi-finals before losing in a replay to First Division Nottingham Forest.

The 1898/99 season saw Rovers win just two out of eight Western League games and suffer early elimination from both the FA Cup and the Bristol Charity Cup. In the Gloucestershire Cup, a first-half Jack Jones goal defeated Bedminster, for whom the former Scottish international Bob Kelso appeared as captain at left-back, but Rovers lost the final to Bristol City 2-1 after a goalless first half – Robert Brown scoring for Rovers. The final, played at Bell Hill, the home ground of Bristol St George, attracted an astonishingly high crowd of 11,433, easily the largest at any game involving Eastville Rovers, and took £356. City had finished in second place in both their opening Southern League seasons, and their rivals' on-field success proved a spur to Rovers' directors in getting their club accepted into the competition.

It was, however, the strength of Rovers' performance in the Birmingham and District League that was their greatest asset. Twenty matches were won and only nine lost, just three of these at home. The squad was strengthened hugely by the signing in May 1898 of goalkeeper Dick Gray from Grimsby Town, and forwards John Paul from Derby County and Bill Fisher from Burton Swifts. All three had played in the Football League the previous season, as had the returning Tommy

McCairns, who now made a permanent move to Eastville. After Fisher's first-half goal had given Rovers a morale-boosting victory in a preseason friendly against Bristol City, the team entered the 1898/99 campaign with high hopes.

In the opening fixture, Rovers scored six second-half goals in defeating Worcester City 8-1, with Jones scoring four times, twice in each half, and Fisher contributing the final two goals. Against Dudley, McCairns scored a hat-trick in the opening fifteen minutes and a fourth on the half-hour mark. Rovers ran up an 8-0 win, McCairns scoring six times and Jones twice. After finding themselves a goal down with only five minutes on the clock, Rovers beat Kidderminster 9-1, with Smellie and Fisher both registering a hat-trick. Five goals in each half helped Rovers defeat Hereford Thistle 10-2, Paul scoring the opening three and Smellie claiming a second-half hat-trick. McCairns scored five times, including a hat-trick, in the opening twenty-six minutes, as Rovers, playing for the first time under the name Bristol Rovers, defeated Shrewsbury 9-1. He also scored three times in a 10-0 victory over West Bromwich Albion reserves. This final result, coupled with a compelling 4-4 draw with Aston Villa reserves, where second-half goals from McCairns, Farnall and Jones, his second of the game, hauled Rovers back from a 4-1 half-time deficit, showed just how far the side had progressed. Huge crowds were beginning to attend matches; 9,000 observed the game at Perry Bar when Villa reserves' goalkeeper Billy George saved a Rovers penalty, and an astonishing 14,897 watched the match with St George.

Goalkeeper Jimmy Cook left the field injured against Hereford Town that October, leaving ten-man Rovers to cruise to a 5-0 home victory over Hereford Town. His absence led to both Tot Farnall and Walter Bunch eschewing their regular outfield positions to represent the club in goal. Bob Horsey returned to first-team action mid-season as Rovers continued their free-scoring campaign. Bob Underwood, Fred Scotchbrook and Dick Allen, all Rovers players before the season was out, were in the St George side that faced Rovers on Boxing Day. Bizarrely, Rovers played in two fixtures on 8 April, Underwood appearing in both and scoring the third of five first-half goals at the Barracks Ground. The Villa game featured a goal, Villa's fourth, from the England international George Wheldon, while Hereford Thistle fielded a scratch XI, their regular side refusing to perform as they had received no pay.

Eastville Rovers had gradually become known as Bristol Eastville Rovers, especially as their reputation spread before them into the Midlands and South Wales and, on 7 February 1899, the club formally became Bristol Rovers, the name being approved by the Gloucestershire Football Association. It was under this new title that the directors applied for membership to join the prestigious Southern League. It was Rovers' good fortune that the May 1899 Annual General Meeting of this league was presided over by Samuel Rinder, a Rovers stalwart, who had joined the club's board in 1897 and was to continue to support the side until his death at the age of sixty-four. Bristol Rovers, without further ado, were admitted to the First Division of the Southern League, and a place in Division Two for the reserve side was also secured.

However, Rovers did continue to play in the Birmingham and District League for one final season, and there was one astonishing result in 1899/1900. On 2 December 1899, Coventry City, as Singers FC were gradually becoming known, were defeated 7-6 at Eastville. Rovers took a fifth-minute lead through Bill Thompson and George Webster doubled the lead three minutes later. However, three Coventry goals, including two in a minute from M. Rideout, put the visitors ahead after just twenty-one minutes. Twice before half-time, Rovers required equalisers to make the interval score 4-4. Thereafter, seventeen-year-old Jack Lewis, who had not scored previously, grabbed a quick-fire hat-trick to give the home side a 7-4 lead, which not even two late Coventry goals could overcome. The match had been refereed by Rovers' Bill Somerton until the delayed arrival of the appointed referee, Mr T. Green of Redditch, but this extraordinary scoreline was allowed to stand. Rovers also reached the Bristol Charity Cup final in 1899/1900, losing 4-1 to Bedminster before a 6,000 crowd at St John's Lane.

Rovers also continued to participate in the Western League well into the twentieth century. With the disappearance of Bedminster, who announced at the Annual General Meeting on 10 April 1900 that they would merge with Bristol City, Rovers became the only surviving side from the nine founder members eight years earlier. Rovers' first team appeared in the league until the end of the 1908/09 season, and the reserves until 1920/21, and from 1925/26 to 1947/48, winning the title on five occasions. Rovers were represented by a Colts side in Western League football from 1948/49 until 1962/63.

1899/1900

Elevation to the Southern League in 1899 brought with it a number of changes at Eastville. The club changed its name to Bristol Rovers, the new title being given its consent by the Board of Trade on 13 October 1899. Alfred George Homer was appointed as Rovers' first full-time manager-secretary, and the distinctive strip of black-and-white striped shirts was adopted. These shirts, worn by Rovers throughout their years in Southern League football, were also the Gloucestershire FA colours, and favoured the Duke of Beaufort's 'Badminton hoops'. Like the majority of fellow Southern League clubs, Rovers continued to put out a side in the Western League for many years. This situation allowed clubs to offer trial games to potential players and field reserve sides in competitive fixtures.

Alf Homer, formerly assistant secretary at Villa Park, where he worked for the well-known administrator George Ramsey, brought a number of high-profile signings to Eastville. Tommy Tait, Jimmy Howie and Jimmy Young, all of whom were to win Scottish caps later in their careers, were to join Rovers in the early

Southern League years. For the 1899/1900 season, Rovers relied on continuity, playing their opening game at Reading with George Kinsey still at centre-half and Jack Jones maintaining his position in the forward line. James Lamont, a steady right-half with Bedminster in two Western League games against Rovers in 1898/99, signed for the club and was to miss only one game all season. Arthur Rowley, who also played in that game at Reading, was a former Stoke full-back, and laid claim to being the first Football League player to have scored from a direct free-kick, his goal for Port Vale in a 3-2 defeat against Bolton Wanderers in 1903 being fired past goalkeeper Dai Davies, a Welsh rugby international. Twenty-six-year-old Bill Robertson was signed from Small Heath, while the former Derby County and Notts County forward John Leonard arrived from Bedminster. The first Southern League game ended in a 3-0 defeat at Reading. Twenty-two-year-old former Bury outside-left Michael Kelly opened the scoring after fifteen minutes, Richard 'Jammer' Evans added a second twenty minutes later, and Richard Davies the third half an hour from the end.

Two players who made their first appearances in the third game were Jack Lewis and Archie Ritchie. Inside-forward Lewis was a seventeen-year-old September signing from Kidderminster Harriers, who was to win a full Welsh cap during his second spell with Rovers in 1906. Ritchie, a right-back, had played for Nottingham Forest in the 1898 FA Cup final, and was to give Rovers a reliable season's work. However, in only their second game, Rovers trailed 3-0 by half-time at Fratton Park to lose 8-2 to Portsmouth. Pompey had beaten Ryde 10-0 in an FA Cup tie only seven days earlier, and four of their goals against Rovers came from Danny Cunliffe. It was to be April 1922 before Rovers next conceded eight goals in a competitive fixture.

Rovers were soon establishing themselves as a competent Southern League side. A 7-2 victory over Swindon Town, where Rovers led 4-2 at half-time, featured a Jack Jones hat-trick, while Tom McInnes scored three times against Gravesend United. Jones' hat-trick, along with Cowes' and Boucher's three goals in a 6-0 victory over Chatham, were expunged from the records when the respective opponents resigned mid-season.

The first game of 1900 saw Rovers fall a goal behind at home to Reading, before McInnes equalised from Brown's cross. Jones took advantage of defensive hesitancy to score the winner. Rovers beat Bedminster 5-2 in January, the only away win of the season, with Jones and John Paul scoring twice each, Ritchie contributing an own goal for Bedminster's second. Jones and Lewis both scored as Rovers drew with a strong Tottenham Hotspur side, after the initial fixture had been abandoned in the Eastville fog with Rovers a goal down after fifty-five minutes. The first 10,000 crowd at Eastville saw a solitary Bill Fisher goal, from a McInnes through ball ten minutes prior to half-time, defeat Bristol City on Good Friday.

One notable opponent in this inaugural season was Herbert Chapman, later a highly influential manager at Huddersfield Town and Arsenal. His sole Southern

League appearance against Rovers was for the Sheppey United side beaten 2-1 at Eastville in September, on the day Rovers recorded their first win in the league. In Western League football, an early season game saw opponents Bedminster field three future Rovers players in Bill Davies, Bill Draycott and the former Notts County forward Tom Boucher, while Alf Geddes played for them against Rovers in a different fixture. The Minsters also fielded the former Northern Ireland international Robert Crone and former England goalkeeper George Toone at Eastville, while Francis Becton, winner of two England caps, appeared in their maroon-and-gold shirts in the Western League draw with Rovers in September.

After an early run of four defeats, Rovers performed sufficiently well to finish eleventh in the Southern League, despite losing their final five away games. One of these came at Millwall, where one of the home side's two goals was 'fisted' past Gray by Scottish-born forward Arthur Millar in the manner of Diego Maradona in 1986; as in the World Cup match, the goal was given, and Rovers lost 2-0. Jones top scored with eleven Southern League goals, while Lamont, Lewis, Paul, Alf Griffiths, Robert 'Daddy' Brown and goalkeeper Dick Gray all missed just the occasional game. In the FA Cup, Lewis scored three times in an easy five-goal victory over Eastleigh, with George Kinsey recording his final goal for the club, before Rovers were comprehensively beaten in a replay at Portsmouth. Two locally based representative sides met at St John's Lane on 9 October 1899 in aid of Western League Funds. Two first-half Jack Jones goals gave English Players, who also included Lewis, a 2-1 victory over Scottish Players, featuring four Rovers players in Ritchie, Lamont, Brown and Paul, before a 1,911 crowd. In addition, Rovers were finalists in the Bristol Charity Cup for the only time in the club's history, losing 4-1 to Bedminster, for whom future Rovers players Tom Boucher and Alf Jasper Geddes both scored. More oddly, a Mr Pruett had paid 2*s* 6*d* per week to graze his horses on the Eastville pitch. Rovers' third Annual Report revealed that players' wages from 1 June 1899 to 30 April 1900 were £2,196, while gate money had brought in £2,496.

2

A New Century

1900/01

Rovers opened the new season with a confidence-boosting run of four wins and a draw in their opening five games. Yet the team that started the season against Queen's Park Rangers included eight new faces. Bill Draycott, the former Boltonian Bill Davies and Tom Boucher, who scored the club's first goal of the new season, had all joined from Bedminster. Inside-left Henry Griffiths had Football League experience with Burton Swifts, for whom he had scored twenty-three goals in sixty-eight matches. Jack Kifford, a July signing from Derby County, was ever-present in his sole season with Rovers, while Billy Clarke, later the winner of a Second Division championship medal in 1907/08 with Bradford City, arrived from East Stirlingshire.

This was a highly satisfying season for Alf Homer's side. Rovers never lost more than two consecutive games and recorded some convincing wins of their own. Boucher scored twice in a 4-0 win at Gravesend United. Jack Jones grabbed a hat-trick in February against a Watford side that included Tot Farnall. Jones went one better when Gravesend played their return game at Eastville just after Christmas. Rovers' 10-0 win that day was to be the side's largest victory in seventeen Southern League seasons. It took Rovers twenty-five minutes to open the scoring before Jackie Neilson scored two of five Rovers goals in fifteen minutes. Jones, who had scored the third, also added a nineteen-minute second-half hat-trick, with Gravesend reduced by injury to only ten men.

A crowd of 10,000 at Eastville for the local derby in April saw Rovers draw 1-1 with Bristol City, thanks to a goal after thirty-five minutes from Bill Williams. However, a new ground record at Ashton Gate of 15,500, bringing gate receipts of £380, had seen Rovers' 1-0 defeat to a second-half Bill Michael goal in October. When the sides drew 1-1 in the Western League on Boxing Day, City's scorer was Jack McLean, who was to join Rovers in 1902. Fred Corbett, a Rovers player only months later, scored the opening goal in West Ham's 2-0 win in March, while John

Lewis, sold to Portsmouth, fired in the only goal of the game with a low shot ten minutes after half-time when Rovers visited Fratton Park in December.

Over the New Year, immediately following the ten goals against Gravesend, Rovers hit a goal drought. It was five games before the side next scored, Boucher's headed winner five minutes from time at Swindon Town sparking a run of four straight victories. The goalless run had included 4-0 defeats at both Millwall and Tottenham Hotspur. At White Hart Lane, both sides wore armbands in respect for Queen Victoria, who had died at Osborne House four days earlier. Rovers conceded three first-half goals and a last-minute Cameron free-kick. Fred Bevan followed up his two goals in that game against Millwall with two more when the London side won 4-1 in a Western League match at Eastville five weeks later. Millwall also inflicted a 5-0 defeat on Rovers in the Western League in December, with George Henderson and Bert Banks, later a Bristol City player, scoring twice each. That same month, Rovers crashed to a 6-0 Western League defeat away to Spurs; the home side scored from three penalties before, at 5-0 down, Rovers' goalkeeper Gray was sent off for dissent, marking a dismal day for the club.

Rovers were expected to defeat Weymouth in the FA Cup but the poor attendance reflects the fact that few would have predicted the glut of goals. Henry Griffiths put Rovers ahead with a tap-in after only three minutes, while Jack Jones, with two long-range shots, and Billy Williams had scored twice each before the visitors' centre-forward Murphy pulled a goal back on the stroke of half-time. Rovers then scored ten second-half goals to record a 15-1 victory, a club record in any competitive first-team match. Billy Clarke scored a second-half hat-trick, his second goal being a spectacular long-distance strike, while Griffiths ended up with two, Williams three, Jones six, and John Paul scored the fifteenth. This was the only occasion a Rovers player has scored six goals in one game, though Jones almost repeated the feat twelve months later against the same opposition. It was also the only time three Rovers players have scored hat-tricks in the same game.

Jones scored twice more in the next round as Rovers beat Swindon Town, and once in the victory at Luton Town, before Rovers lost at Reading in the first round proper, the initial tie on 25 January having been postponed following the death of Queen Victoria. The FA Cup run had seen Rovers score twenty-two goals and concede only five. Jones' nine FA Cup goals remain a club seasonal record, though his own tally in 1901/02 and that of Jason Roberts in 1998/99 were not far behind, while Clarke and Williams both scored more Cup than League goals. The Gloucestershire Cup final was lost 4-0 to Bristol City, who gained Football League status over the following summer. At the end of their first season of professionalism, City boldly and over-ambitiously sought membership of the Football League at the Annual General Meeting of that organisation held on 20 May 1898. Now, despite a financial deficit of £2,000 incurred during the 1900/01 season, the Ashton Gate club tried again, displaying an ambitiousness that Rovers' directors were not prepared to follow, and were duly elected to Division Two in place of Walsall.

1901/02

It was a largely new-look Rovers side that lost its opening six Southern League games before consolidation brought a final placing of ninth. Tom Boucher had joined Bristol City, while Bill Clarke had moved to Aston Villa, after which he later appeared for Bradford City and Lincoln City. Right-back Jack Kifford joined West Bromwich Albion in June and played for Millwall, Carlisle United and Coventry City before joining Fred Karno's circus troupe in 1909.

Young goalkeeper Arthur Cartlidge, a key figure through the decade, arrived from Stoke. He was Rovers' only ever-present in the Southern League in 1901/02. The signing of full-back Hugh Dunn from Preston North End was inspired, since he had previously spent three successful years at West Bromwich Albion culminating in an FA Cup semi-final. Further experience was added through the re-signing of thirty-year-old right-half Tot Farnall from Watford for his third spell at the club. Conversely, younger talent was allowed to emerge, most notably in the shape of Fred Wilcox, a twenty-one-year-old August signing from Glendale. Wilcox was to score four times in Rovers' largest win of the season, a midweek 8-1 victory over Wellingborough at the end of February.

The alarm bells began to ring after six straight defeats. The worst result had been a four-goal loss at Watford, which included in their side Billy Wragg, who later appeared on stage alongside Stan Laurel and Charlie Chaplin. Homer's response was to sign two new forwards. Fred Corbett had scored West Ham United's second goal in their opening day victory at Eastville, while Alf Jasper Geddes, a former Bristol City player standing just 5 feet 4 inches tall, could boast an impressive pedigree, having scored for West Bromwich Albion in the 1892 FA Cup final when they had beaten Aston Villa by three goals to nil.

With Corbett, Wilcox and Jack Jones in the forward line, Rovers' fortunes were revived. All three were to score Southern League hat-tricks. Corbett scored all the goals in a 3-0 victory over Kettering Town in February and ended the season with eleven goals, three behind Jones. Wilcox's eight goals came in only three games, as he and Corbett both scored twice, each against Brentford on Good Friday, with Rovers three goals ahead before half-time, and against Luton Town eight days later. Going into the final game of the season, Jones and Corbett had, in fact, scored eleven Southern League goals each, but the former marked what was to be his final appearance for the club with a well-taken hat-trick, as Rovers defeated Queen's Park Rangers 4-1, to complete a third consecutive season as the club's top scorer. In so doing, he also set Rovers' Southern League goalscoring record at thirty-six goals.

Reliable at centre-half was Jackie Neilson, a Scottish Cup winner in 1905, who contrived to score in both fixtures against Northampton Town. The 2-2 draw in January came only seven days after the Cobblers had lost 11-0 at Southampton. Albert Brown, who scored seven goals that day, scored three more for the Saints when Rovers were crushed 6-0 at The Dell on Easter Saturday. The heaviness of this defeat was all the more galling since, in the midst of an injury crisis, the Saints had fielded the veteran former England inside-forward Harry Wood in goal. Rovers also relied on the strong full-back pairing of Hugh Dunn and Arthur Griffiths – when the former missed his only game of the season, Rovers lost 4-0 at Watford, while heavy defeats at Southampton and Portsmouth coincided with the latter's rare absences. At Fratton Park, Rovers trailed 3-0 by half-time to a strong Pompey side that included player-manager Bob Blyth at left-half, an uncle of the future Liverpool manager Bill Shankly.

Rovers drew both Gloucestershire Cup matches, but enjoyed a hugely successful FA Cup run, knocking out Football League sides Bristol City and Middlesbrough. It all started with Jack Jones' five goals (shades of November 1900) beating Weymouth at Eastville. Rovers then led Bristol City 2-0 with only ten minutes remaining, but when the fog descended, the match was abandoned. When the game was restaged, it was again abandoned, this time in extra time, before Rovers finally won a momentous replay at St John's Lane. It was their first competitive victory over Football League opposition, with Tom Becton scoring the winning goal. After victories over Swindon Town and Millwall, Rovers were drawn away to Middlesbrough, who were on course for promotion from Division Two that season. Rovers caused a huge shock by drawing 1-1 and proceeding to beat 'Boro in a midweek replay at Eastville. Before the rematch, Middlesbrough discovered the distance between the underside of the crossbar and the ground was 7 feet 11 inches, not the regulation 8 feet, but the Football Association was to reject their protests. Three minutes from the end of the match, Cartlidge and Dunn collided, leaving Boro's inside-left Bill Wardrope with an open goal. He missed and, within moments, Tommy Becton had scored a crucial goal to give Rovers a famous 1-0 victory. The visit of First Division Stoke brought an Eastville crowd of 19,850 and receipts of £547, both records that stood for many years. Rovers lost 1-0 after an inspired performance by Stoke's Welsh international goalkeeper Leigh Richmond Roose, later an Everton and Sunderland player. Bizarrely, an anonymous letter falsely claimed Roose had played for London Welsh in the preliminary round against Crouch End Vampires and was thus Cup tied, but Rovers' management was quick to distance itself from such rumours. Rovers played a Western League Crocks XI at Eastville on 29 March 1902 and raised 30*s* for the Western League Fund. The pitch was then used for two weeks by the Bostock and Wombwell Show.

1902/03

As if to prove that Rovers' late season form in 1901/02 had been no fluke, a run of four straight wins opened up a season that saw the club finish fifth, its highest placing to date in the Southern League. There were, of course, numerous changes of personnel. The most significant departure was the free-scoring Jack Jones, whose July move to Tottenham Hotspur preceded his tragically early death from typhoid in London in September 1903. Alf Jasper Geddes joined Bristol City and the former England international George Kinsey, now thirty-six, signed for Burton Early Closing, while goalkeeper Dick Gray moved to Burton United for six successful seasons.

A direct and immediate replacement for Jones was the inspirational Jimmy Howie, who was on the verge of a great career. A May signing from Kettering Town, he was to finish as the club's joint top scorer with Fred Wilcox, registering ten Southern League goals. The experienced full-back Dick Pudan joined from West Ham United. In the half-back line, Rovers signed Jimmy Young from Barrow, a one-cap Scottish international in 1906 who contributed an own goal at Queen's Park Rangers in March, and the former Grimsby Town and Liverpool centre-half Jack McLean from Bristol City.

The season began with a gymkhana and sports event, including archery tournaments and a 100-yard dribbling contest won by Fred Corbett. An opening-day victory at Northampton Town, Rovers' first-ever victory against the Cobblers, was down to two goals from Wilcox, with Daniel Wilson, who joined Rovers at the end of the season, scoring for the home side. Seven days later, Wilcox went one better, registering his second hat-trick for Rovers, while Corbett added two goals as Rovers put five past Watford. Brentford lost their opening nine Southern League matches and were easy prey, Howie contributing his first Rovers goal. A crowd of 11,000 then saw Rovers defeat a strong Tottenham Hotspur side at Eastville. It took a tap-in from Billy Grassam from Bill Linward's cross fifteen minutes from time to shatter the run of wins and give West Ham United a 1-0 win.

Consistently convincing wins maintained Rovers' challenge through the winter. Jimmy Howie and John Graham were on target in big wins over Luton Town, Queen's Park Rangers and Kettering Town. Rovers also won 2-0 at Millwall and Brentford, and in home games with Wellingborough and New Brompton. The away game at Brentford mirrored the Eastville game in September. The Bees, now in the middle of seven consecutive Southern League defeats, made five changes to their side but lost to goals from Harold Rowlands and Bill Marriott. They were to gain only five points from their thirty Southern League fixtures.

January saw two 3-0 defeats, at Tottenham Hotspur and at Portsmouth. In the latter, the great C. B. Fry (1872–1956) played against Rovers. A double international for England at cricket and football, and a rugby union player with the Barbarians, he had recently played for Southampton in the 1902 FA Cup final. Among numerous claims to fame, he had also held the world long jump record, stood unsuccessfully for parliament and famously declined the kingship of Albania. Rovers managed to draw 1-1 with a strong Southampton side in March, with Howie scrambling the ball across the line to give Rovers the lead after half an hour. Fred Harrison, who had scored all the goals when Saints had beaten Wellingborough 5-0 seven days earlier, contributed the visitors' seventy-fifth minute equaliser, after Howie's twice-taken penalty had been saved.

There were no ever-presents in 1902/03. Cartlidge and McLean missed only one game each, while Arthur Griffiths played in all but the final two matches. The 3-0 win against Kettering Town on Valentine's Day was the 100th Southern League game of Griffiths' Rovers career. He was the first player at the club to achieve this feat and was to play 105 games in total. The only goal of his career was a first-half penalty in the 1-1 draw with Reading at the end of February, in a match where, to avoid a colour clash, Rovers played in all white.

Four meetings with Millwall in December saw Rovers lose in an FA Cup second replay at Villa Park, though Rovers gained revenge with four second-half goals after a scoreless opening half of a Western League fixture at Eastville. Tom Lee, on Rovers' books until nine months earlier, made a rare appearance for Millwall at left-back in this final game. Graham and Wilcox had scored in the initial FA Cup tie and, after the replay was abandoned goalless in extra time due to bad light, the decider took place on a neutral ground. The Gloucestershire Cup was won for the first time since 1889, Bristol City being defeated 4-2 in a second replay through two Fred Corbett goals, one for Bill Marriott and a Hugh Dunn penalty.

As the season closed, Andrew Smith was signed from West Bromwich Albion to replace Wilcox, whose late move to Small Heath, later Birmingham City, was in time for him to score four goals in a 12-0 Second Division victory against Doncaster Rovers. A crowd of 3,000 at Eastville on 11 April saw a game of American pushball, won 10-4 by a Stapleton Road XV using a 40lb ball, 5 feet 6 inches high and costing £35.

1903/04

Rovers were challengers for the Southern League championship, and though they faded at the season's end, the potential was clear to see. Alf Homer's side, now playing with far greater consistency, was to claim the championship in 1904/05.

Several changes were made to the side that had finished fifth in the Southern League in 1902/03. Tot Farnall joined Bradford City, John McCall went to Notts County, Jimmy Lyon moved to Manchester City and Jimmy Young returned north of the border to join Celtic, with whom he won full Scottish international honours. Jack McLean joined Millwall in April and spent three years at The Den before moving to Queen's Park Rangers – McLean was in the Millwall side that drew a six-goal thriller at Eastville in March after Rovers had trailed 3-2 at the interval. The biggest name to depart was Jimmy Howie, who went to Newcastle United where he played his part in three League championships, appeared in four FA Cup finals and won three Scottish caps.

Homer signed two relatively inexperienced players from West Bromwich Albion. Although George Elmore had only three league games to his name and centre-half Ben Appleby just one, a Second Division match against Glossop North End, these players were to become regulars in a successful Rovers side. They were joined by high-profile centre-forward Billy Beats, who had played for Wolves in the 1896 FA Cup final, and who quickly established a powerful partnership with Andrew Smith. Beats had played for England against Scotland in the 1902 Ibrox game that ended in tragedy – a 50-foot bank of terracing behind the west goal collapsed without warning, killing twenty-six spectators and injuring about 500 more. He was to be the club's captain and top scorer with eighteen Southern League goals, five more than Smith. Homer also signed Tommy Tait, a Scottish international in 1911, who was, along with established players Cartlidge, Dunn and Marriott, one of four ever-presents.

A poor September was compounded by news from London of the premature death of former Eastville favourite Jack Jones. A testimonial game between Spurs and an International XI was held in December and featured the Millwall full-back and concert hall singer George Robeson.

October began with five first-half goals against Brentford, and Rovers barely looked back. Beats and Smith scored a couple each as the Bees were overrun – Rovers scored three times in five minutes immediately prior to half-time. George Parsonage scored for Brentford and added a consolation penalty in the return game, with Rovers already two goals to the good. Rovers scored four times in both fixtures against West Ham United, a Tommy Allison penalty being the only consolation goal. Walter Jack scored twice in a 5-1 win against Kettering Town, and there were five different scorers when Rovers defeated Wellingborough 7-1 at the end of December. Daniel Wilson gave Rovers a tenth-minute lead before a goal flurry put the side 5-0 ahead after just twenty-five minutes. Wellingborough lost two players through illness and were forced to change goalkeeper twice during a largely goal-free second-half.

Success on the field was reflected off it. There were 12,000 spectators at both matches with Plymouth Argyle and 8,000 for the 'home' tie with Tottenham Hotspur, even though it was staged at St John's Lane. Rovers completed League doubles over six different sides and gradually eased their way up the table. The crunch game came on 12 March, when Rovers, by now the main challengers, played the leaders Southampton at The Dell. It was a year to the weekend since Fred Harrison's goal had earned a draw against Rovers. This time, the Saints' forward scored a hat-trick, two of these coming from Harry Turner crosses, as the home side ran up a 4-1 lead by half-time. The eventual 6-1 win virtually secured the championship. Rovers, with four straight draws before final-day success at Wellingborough, had to settle for third place. One young Bristolian given a brief run-out was Billy Tout, who was to spend fifteen years with Swindon Town, winning two Southern League championship medals and twice appearing in FA Cup semi-finals, before becoming player-manager at Bath City during the 1920/21 season.

In the FA Cup, Rovers drew twice with Woolwich Arsenal before succumbing to Tom Briercliffe's sixteenth-minute goal in the second replay at neutral White Hart Lane, after Tommy Tait had conceded an own goal at Highbury. The Gloucestershire Cup final was lost 2-1 to Bristol City, the large crowd of 10,537 producing gate receipts of £296. A postscript to the Freddie Wilcox transfer was a meeting between Rovers and Small Heath at Eastville on a sunny September afternoon as part of the transfer deal. Rovers held the First Division side 1-1 at half-time and ran out 3-2 winners. George Elmore scored twice and Billy Beats once for Rovers, with Jimmy Robertson and Bob McRoberts replying for the visitors.

1904/05

Prior to the 1952/53 Third Division (South) championship, the one outstanding achievement in Rovers' history had been being crowned champions of the Southern League in 1904/05. This was achieved by fielding a highly experienced squad of professionals. Cartlidge in goal and his full-backs Dunn and Pudan were retained. In the half-back line, Tait and the dependable Appleby were joined by Gavin Jarvie, while Smith and Beats, with nineteen and sixteen Southern League goals respectively, continued to lead the line.

With Henry Griffiths appearing only sporadically, Alf Homer wisely strengthened his forward line with three astute signings. Billy 'Darkie' Clark was signed in May from Port Glasgow Athletic to play at outside-right. Inside him was Jack Lewis, who returned to the club on the eve of the new season, having spent 1903/04 on the books of Second Division Burton Albion. Lewis' subsequent selection for Wales made him the first player to appear in international football while on Rovers' books. Albert Dunkley, at outside-left, who signed from Blackburn Rovers, had enjoyed considerable football experience with Northampton Town, Leicester Fosse and New Brompton. Homer also signed wing-half Bill Hales, who had played in one league game for Bristol City in 1904, and left-back Harold Wassell from Small Heath (the future Birmingham City) a teammate of Fred Wilcox in the Blues' famous 12-0 victory against Doncaster Rovers in 1903.

Of the four players released, two joined Second Division Bristol City, Tom Darke and Andrew Hargett, having appeared in only five Southern League games between them. Hargett was a Boer War veteran who had served at Spion Kop and at the Relief of Ladysmith. Reliable outside-right George Elmore joined Glossop North End, from where he later moved to Partick Thistle and St Mirren, while Walter Jack was to spend a year with West Bromwich Albion before he too moved north of the border, joining Clyde in the summer of 1905.

On the field, after an opening day hiccup at Northampton Town, Rovers' experienced and settled side found defeat to be a rare experience. Portsmouth were beaten 5-0 at Eastville, with Jack Lewis scoring twice, and Rovers completed the double with a 2-1 win at Fratton Park after Pompey's full-back Roderick Walker had been sent off. Smith scored hat-tricks at Watford and Wellingborough – the latter conceded four goals in each meeting with Rovers and became the first club in Southern League history to give away 100 goals in a season. Rovers scored four goals or more on nine occasions. It was the 4-1 win against Fulham in November (Griffiths scoring twice) that put Rovers top of the table for the first time, and there they stayed for two months. A crushing 5-0 defeat at Queen's Park Rangers in January saw the top spot lost when Rovers were overwhelmed in treacherous conditions, Percy Skilton scoring twice in the final three minutes. But it was regained when Southampton came to Eastville in March for what effectively became a championship decider. It was bizarre that, for the second consecutive season, a crunch fixture between Rovers and the Saints ended 6-1 to the home side. Fred Harrison gave the Saints a twentieth-minute advantage, but two goals in a minute gave Rovers a half-time lead, after which Beats burst through for a solo goal and then headed another. As Rovers piled on the agony for their visitors, two goals in the final twenty minutes left the home side clear favourites for the championship.

After victory over Southampton, there was still time for a Tommy Tait own goal to contribute to a 3-1 defeat at Plymouth. However, a second draw with eventual closest rivals Reading and a second victory over Brighton thanks to an own goal left Rovers to secure the championship with a 3-0 victory at home to Brentford. Rovers were still able to lose the final match, with Fred Corbett playing for the first time in two years. Cartlidge, Dunn and Appleby were ever-presents while, of only seventeen players used, three had played in just five games between them.

In the Western League, life was not so simple. Danny Cunliffe, scorer of four goals in a game against Rovers in October 1899, scored a first-half hat-trick at Fratton Park. George Hilsdon scored four goals for West Ham United against Rovers; he also managed a Southern League goal in April against Rovers, one in each fixture in 1905/06, and a Football League record five on his debut for Chelsea against Glossop North End in September 1906. Bob Dalrymple and Jack Picken both scored in each game as Plymouth Argyle completed the double over Rovers. Fred Latham and a young Walter Gerrish scored six goals each in November as Rovers reserves ran up an astonishing 18-2 victory over HMS *Antelope*. The FA Cup brought an unlikely draw at Burnden Park, before Bolton Wanderers swept Rovers aside in a replay, Pudan putting a through ball from Sam

Marsh into his own net after only eight minutes. Dunkley's winning goal secured the Gloucestershire Cup in an end-of-season replay at Ashton Gate. The former Aston Villa outside-left Albert Fisher scored Bristol City's goal.

1905/06

If defending championships was supposed to be difficult, Rovers began as if they clearly had not read the script. A 6-0 opening-day victory, nine goals without reply in two games and four wins and a draw opened the season – were Rovers about to retain the Southern League championship? A 7-1 defeat at Luton Town, Billy Barnes completing a first-half hat-trick as Rovers trailed 5-0 at the interval, indicated they were not and precipitated a run of four straight defeats. By the season's end, eighth-placed Rovers had suffered a crushing seven-goal loss at the hands of Queen's Park Rangers. The club reported an annual loss of £595.

Yet Rovers were able to afford the luxury of opening the season with the side that cruised through much of the previous season. New signing Archie Taylor, who was to play for Barnsley in the 1912 FA Cup final, did not appear in the opening seven games. Davie Walker, who could boast two First Division matches with Wolverhampton Wanderers to his name, made the side sooner and eclipsed even the illustrious Beats – his twelve goals for the season making him runner-up behind the club's top scorer, thirteen-goal Jack Lewis. Harold Wassell had been sold to Queen's Park Rangers and Fred Corbett, at the end of his second spell with the club, to Brentford.

The champions put six goals past Northampton Town, three in each half, on the opening day of the new season. Albert Dunkley scored twice, after twelve and eighty-five minutes, the previous year's three top scorers, Smith, Lewis and Beats, grabbed one each, and there was a rare goal, after sixty-five minutes, for the imperious Ben Appleby. Lewis was to score in five of the first six games. Four days after the Northampton game, Rovers played Bristol City in a friendly at Eastville and crashed to a 6-0 defeat, the former Scottish international William Maxwell scoring a hat-trick. This was the first of several demoralising results through the season. Rovers were, however, to record large wins of their own. Clark and Walker scored three goals between them in large victories in November, Southampton being defeated 5-1 and Watford 6-1, defender Jack Richardson contributing an own goal. Four goals at Northampton saw Rovers complete ten without reply against the Cobblers.

On the other hand, Rovers suffered too many defeats. Two 1-0 defeats against the eventual champions Fulham came courtesy of Bill Wardrope, who should have knocked Rovers out of the FA Cup three years earlier, and Walter Freeman in the Cottagers' first-ever victory at Eastville. Peter Turner scored for Watford in both fixtures against Rovers. Sam Graham scored the only goal of the game, a long-range strike a minute before half-time, in the first-ever meeting with Norwich City; the return fixture was the third of four consecutive goalless draws for the Canaries. Fred Wilcox returned to Eastville in the Plymouth side in March, and scored twice as Argyle recorded a 5-1 victory. For the second consecutive season, the future Rovers forward Isaac Owens scored for Plymouth against Rovers, this time in the Western League on Boxing Day. Queen's Park Rangers scored seven times without reply in April, with George Ryder contributing two goals in a minute early on – he completed his hat-trick shortly after half-time.

In February, Rovers conceded four first-half goals in a Western League game at Portsmouth, losing 5-1 with 'Sunny Jim' Kirby scoring a hat-trick. In March, on the back of the sale of Andrew Smith to Millwall, where he gained Southern League experience before moving on to Swindon Town and Orient, Rovers crashed 4-1 in a Western League match at North Greenwich. At half-time, Rovers held a strong Millwall side, which included former Rovers players Jack McLean and Smith, but three second-half goals brought a heavy defeat. Smith got his name on the scoresheet and Alf Twigg, who was to score two more at Eastville in April 1908, scored a hat-trick.

There were no ever-presents in the Rovers side; however, Beats, Dunn, Pudan, Tait and Clark all played in at least thirty Southern League games. Beats scored the opening goal at Swindon in September to register his thirty-seventh Southern League goal, beating Jack Jones' club record. His forty-fourth goal, in the final game of the season, set a figure only surpassed by Fred Corbett on Christmas Day 1909. The 1904 League champions Sheffield Wednesday scraped past Rovers in the FA Cup at Hillsborough, George Simpson scoring the only goal with a fortieth-minute snap shot, while Bristol City scored four times without reply in a one-sided Gloucestershire Cup final. On 19 March 1906, Jack Lewis became the first player to appear for his country while on Rovers' books. He won his only cap for Wales in the 1-0 defeat against England in Cardiff.

1906/07

The summer of 1906 marked the break-up of Rovers' 1904/05 Southern League championship-winning side. In May, Billy Beats returned to the Football League with Port Vale, where he was joined by full-back Hugh Dunn. Jack Lewis moved to fellow Southern League side Brighton, and was to play for Southampton and Croydon Common in the same league. On the eve of the new season, outside-left Albert Dunkley signed for Second Division Blackpool.

Of Rovers' new signings, outside-left Bill Gould and wing-half Harold Hutchinson were regulars for the new season. Isaac Owens, who had played in five Southern and Western League games for Plymouth Argyle against Rovers, arrived at Eastville for what was to be a one-season stay. Arthur Cartlidge missed just one game in goal, while Gould was the side's only ever-present. Jack Young missed only five games and was the top scorer with fourteen league goals. For the third consecutive season, three Rovers players took their individual goal tally into double figures. Defeats against Tottenham Hotspur and Fulham attracted 10,000-strong crowds. The highest crowd to date at any Southern League game featuring Rovers (16,000) saw the 2-0 defeat at the hands of Portsmouth at Fratton Park on Boxing Day.

Rovers won at New Brompton on the opening day in temperatures approaching 90°F. However, inconsistency dogged Rovers early in the season, and after New Year the side won only three Southern League fixtures. When they did win, though, they did so in style. Bill Clark, Davie Walker and Jock Young all scored when West Ham United were defeated 3-0 at Eastville. Clark scored twice in a convincing 4-0 victory over New Brompton. Young scored three goals and Walker two as Southampton were thumped by five goals to nil three days before Christmas. Walker's hat-trick helped Rovers to a 6-1 victory against Northampton Town, with Isaac Owens adding two and Bill Gould scoring the only goal of his Rovers career.

Conversely, Rovers lost 4-0 at home to Brighton and conceded four goals at Tottenham Hotspur and Leyton Orient. However, a seasonal tally of five 1-0 defeats tells its own tale. Luton Town, in fact, beat Rovers by a single goal both home and away. Norwich City beat Rovers 1-0 at Newmarket Road in March, thanks to an eighty-fifth minute penalty following John Smart's foul on outside-right George Lamberton, which was converted by right-back Arthur Archer, his eighth successful penalty in the Southern League inside fifteen months. Goals from Clark and young Walter Gerrish gave Rovers a 2-0 half-time lead at home to Portsmouth on Good Friday, only for Pompey to score three second-half goals through Jack Bainbridge, 'Sunny Jim' Kirby and Bill Smith to snatch victory. Bainbridge was to later score for Southampton against Rovers – the opening goal in the FA Cup tie in February 1908 and a Southern League goal thirteen months later.

The accomplished violinist Bert Badger was an opponent at Eastville. He was in the Watford side that drew 1-1 in March and was to spend two years with the Hertfordshire club prior to his 1908/09 season at Brentford.

The FA Cup brought some excitement, with Woolwich Arsenal playing at Eastville in the third round. Queen's Park Rangers had drawn with Rovers, but Clark's goal had earned the Bristol side victory in London. Then Millwall were comfortably beaten 3-0 before 15,070 spectators, who produced gate receipts of £413. A large crowd in round three at Highbury, where Bristol City had lost in the previous round, saw a strong Arsenal side defeat Rovers through a solitary David Neave goal twenty minutes after half-time. Rovers were down to ten men at the time of the goal, captain Pudan receiving treatment after a collision with Tim Coleman, who had played for England against Ireland just seven days earlier;

22,000 spectators brought Rovers match takings of £772. After returning from a brief club tour of East Anglia, the Gloucestershire Cup final was lost 2-0 at home to Bristol City, Sammy Gilligan scoring twice. It was also a highly successful season for the future Rovers manager Andrew Wilson, who played centre-forward in the Sheffield Wednesday side that won the FA Cup final and won the first of his six full caps for Scotland.

The Southern League had twice supplied an FA Cup final team, with Tottenham Hotspur famously winning the trophy in 1901. There were proposals made in 1907, as there had been in 1898, for the division to be merged into the Football League. Indeed, relative performances of clubs suggest this would have been a viable proposition. However, working on plans first mooted in 1909, it was as a Third Division that the clubs finally attained Football League status in 1920.

1907/08

Several experienced players were allowed to leave Eastville in 1907, as Rovers strove to improve on a disappointing season. Dick Pudan, after five seasons at left-back, joined Newcastle United, for whom he earned an FA Cup final appearance in his first season. Although the former Rovers forward Jimmy Howie scored for the Magpies, the final score was 3-1 to Wolverhampton Wanderers. Davie Walker joined West Bromwich Albion, but was to return to Rovers in June 1911. Isaac Owens joined Crystal Palace, while stand-in forward Fred Latham went on to play one First Division game for Bristol City.

Tom Strang, an experienced centre-half who replaced Ben Appleby, the latter moving to full-back, was a close season recruit from Aberdeen. He had been a founder member of the Dons in 1903, and played in seventy-one Scottish League games, scoring once and captaining the side between 1905 and 1907. Rovers started the season with four new forwards. John Smith, from Birmingham, had spent four years previously at Wolverhampton Wanderers, while outside-left Harry Buckle, from Portsmouth, had represented Northern Ireland when on the books of Sunderland and played against Wales on 11 April 1908 while a Rovers player. Astonishingly, Smith, Buckle, inside-right Isaiah Turner and inside-left John Roberts, only three minutes into his first game, all scored on their Southern League debuts.

Rovers opened the season in style. The 1906/07 season had begun with a single-goal victory over New Brompton, but this season Rovers recorded their highest-ever opening-day win. Smith missed a penalty before contributing four goals, including a hat-trick inside twenty second-half minutes, in a memorable first appearance for the club as Rovers recorded a 9-1 win. A 4,000 crowd became 11,000 for the visit of Brentford three days later, and Smith scored twice more in a 3-0 victory. Then the bubble burst. Rovers crashed 10-0 at Tottenham Hotspur in a Western League match, after being 6-0 behind at half-time, centre-forward Jimmy Pass scoring eight times. They then lost two consecutive Southern League games. Smith was never to score more than once in a match during the remainder of his Rovers career.

With their feet back on the ground, Rovers began to put together some good runs and, by Christmas, were just three points behind joint leaders Plymouth Argyle and Queen's Park Rangers. At this point Rovers, unbeaten at home, had won five consecutive games, even if all were by close margins. Shortly after Christmas, three first-half goals gave Rovers a second 3-0 victory over Brentford, with Fred Corbett, due to rejoin Rovers in the summer, playing for the Bees. Following this result, however, Rovers won just four more league games, lost three in succession while Harry Buckle was away on international duty with Northern Ireland, and despite a 3-0 victory over Portsmouth on the final day, finished the season in sixth place.

Rovers were unable to achieve the results they required against the top sides. Queen's Park Rangers beat Rovers 5-3 in October, with Rovers a goal down in three minutes before going 2-1 up after ten. Goalkeeper Arthur Cartlidge played his 200th Southern League game for Rovers that day, a club record subsequently equalled only by David Harvie and Billy Peplow. Rangers also inflicted Rovers' first home defeat of the season as Easter approached. Reading and Portsmouth also scored five times in a game, while Rovers conceded four goals on a further four occasions. Bradford Park Avenue, who through a geographical quirk were playing in a sole Southern League season, beat Rovers 4-1, thanks to a George Reid hat-trick. Millwall won 4-0 at Eastville; Danny Cunliffe, who had scored four goals against Rovers in October 1899 and a total of fifteen Western and Southern League goals for Portsmouth against Rovers between 1899 and 1906, scored the opening goal after only four minutes, before Alf Twigg scored twice and Harry Shand once in twelve second-half minutes.

Norwich City's James Bauchop was sent off during the goalless draw at Newmarket Road in February and was banned for one game. When Norwich played at Eastville, Peter Roney, a Rovers goalkeeper in 1909, and James Young, a Rovers wing-half in 1902/03, were in the side. Jack Lewis, a veteran of two spells with Rovers, scored for Southampton at Eastville in October. In the Western League, two second-half goals in October brought Rovers a 2-0 victory over Millwall, inflicting the champions' only defeat of the season.

Remarkably, four Rovers players scored ten or more Southern League goals, while Turner, who was latterly out of the side, contributed nine. Roberts top scored with fourteen. The highlight of the FA Cup run was a 2-0 victory over Second Division Chesterfield, with Billy Clark scoring twice before an Eastville crowd of 15,000, which brought gate receipts of £380. Rovers were eliminated from the FA Cup at Southampton, and the Gloucestershire Cup at Bristol City by two-goal margins.

1908/09

The success of 1907/08 was repeated as a more consistent Rovers side completed the season in fifth place in the Southern League. Ben Appleby had retired to senior non-League football in Gloucester, and despite the additional loss of reliable outside-right Billy Clark to Sunderland and Harry Buckle and Isaiah Turner to Coventry City, manager Alf Homer strengthened Rovers' side with a number of shrewd purchases. Clark's replacement was Billy Peplow, a Derbyshire lad signed from Birmingham, who was to be a fixture in the Rovers side up until the First World War. Young reserve Walter Gerrish, who had first played for Rovers in April 1906, became Turner's permanent successor. The former Bishop Auckland wing-half Martin Higgins arrived after a successful career with Grimsby Town, reserve goalkeeper Bill Demmery signed from Bristol City where he had played in Division One after many seasons with Warmley, and Fred Corbett, rejoining from Brentford, began a third spell at Eastville.

Consistent form, especially at home, was the key to Rovers' success. After all, they were never again going to finish in the top twelve of the Southern League. Five times, 10,000 or more spectators watched Southern League fixtures at Eastville. When the champions-elect Northampton Town, under player-manager Herbert Chapman, came to visit in a temperature of 90°F, a crowd of 12,000 saw the prodigal hero Fred Corbett's twenty-second-minute goal earn Rovers a 1-0 victory. Corbett was the club's top scorer, his nineteen goals, which equalled Andrew Smith's achievement in 1904/05, was never to be beaten during Rovers' Southern League years. He scored a hat-trick early in January in the largest win of the season, 5-1 at home to Exeter City.

Rovers also scored four goals in the home matches against Millwall and Southampton, Roberts scoring twice in the former and Gerrish twice in the latter. Peplow also scored in both and these three forwards supported Corbett ably as Rovers ran up sixty Southern League goals, the most since the championship season. Half-backs Strang and Higgins scored two goals each during the season and, in each case, these were in consecutive fixtures. In the case of Martin Higgins, his penalties against Luton Town on Christmas Day and at Swindon Town on Boxing Day brought successive 1-0 victories. The return fixture at Luton Town on Easter Monday marked goalkeeper Arthur Cartlidge's final appearance for Rovers, his 258 Southern League matches for the club remaining an unbeaten record.

Isaiah Turner, sold to Coventry City, played for his new club in both fixtures against Rovers, while his teammate Harry Buckle scored Coventry's opening goal after ten minutes at Eastville in October. Both sides then scored penalties, Peplow only doing so when his initial kick, which hit the post, had to be retaken. Norwich City, with Peter Roney in goal, defeated Rovers 4-1 in March, having made seven changes to their side after a defeat at Coventry. The Canaries scored twice in each half, with full-back Charlie Craig registering his only goal for the club. When the sides met at Eastville, Norwich's Walter Rayner was sent off for head-butting Billy Peplow, who was also sent off for retaliation. Rovers held on for a late single-goal victory over New Brompton in November, with Frank Handley in goal, after Cartlidge was taken to hospital with a head injury just moments after half-time. Irishman Frank Kelly scored for Watford in both games against Rovers, while Scotsman David McKinley contributed two goals in the Vicarage Road game. There were five different scorers when Millwall beat Rovers 6-0 in a Western League game in October. Portsmouth fielded Arthur Knight in their side against Rovers, an Olympic gold medal winner for football in 1912, who appeared regularly for Pompey at Eastville between 1908 and 1922.

An exciting FA Cup draw brought Second Division Burnley to Eastville, but Rovers were outclassed. Although Billy Peplow scored for the home club, Rovers were not able to produce the result the crowd of 6,000 desired. Burnley's inside-right Arthur Ogden scored a hat-trick as the visitors progressed through the comfortable margin of four goals to one. While Rovers were out, Bristol City proceeded to the FA Cup final, where they lost to Manchester United, Sandy Turnbull scoring the only goal of the game after twenty-two minutes. With the Gloucestershire Cup final held over until 1909/10, Rovers set off for Paris in March to play in an exhibition match under floodlights against Southampton. The game finished 5-5, after Rovers had held a 2-1 lead at half-time. Corbett scored a hat-trick, and Gerrish and Gilbert Ovens claimed a goal apiece.

On the afternoon of Saturday 26 June 1909, the future (if temporary) Rovers home at Twerton Park, then known as Innox Park, was officially opened on land donated by Thomas Carr of Poolemeade, West Twerton. The ceremony began at 3 p.m. and featured a procession of scholars, the singing of hymns and a speech a was given by Robert Hope, a pattern maker who was chairman of the parish council.

1909/10

Despite retaining several key players, most notably a trio of goalscorers in Corbett, Peplow and Roberts, Rovers found the 1909/10 season more of a struggle. Ultimately, finishing in thirteenth place in the Southern League was something of a success. Martin Higgins had joined New Brompton, for whom he played twice this season against Rovers, while the inspirational Walter Gerrish and experienced Arthur Cartlidge both moved to Aston Villa, where they were to help their new side to the Football League championship in their first season. Bill Nichols, after just one game, moved to Merthyr Town. Peter Roney, a goalkeeper with a very good reputation, joined Rovers from Norwich City; he and Jackie Laurie were to be Rovers' two ever-presents. Two other players viewed as major signings, Fred

Riddell, a former Derby County player, and Charles Jones, who had played for Birmingham in Division Two, managed just five Southern League appearances between them.

Corbett set his stall out for the season with a goal in the drawn Gloucestershire Cup final and two in a remarkably one-sided opening-day victory over Portsmouth. Bristol City's success in reaching the 1909 FA Cup final had led to the regional cup competition being held over, with the result that, after two draws, Rovers had the dubious pleasure of losing two Gloucestershire Cup finals in ten weeks in the spring. Left-half Frank Handley may not have scored in ninety-three Southern League matches for Rovers, but his thirty-fifth-minute equaliser at Ashton Gate in October ensured a second replay to the initial tie – he was to die in unusual circumstances in December 1938, aged fifty-nine, falling off his ladder while cleaning the windows of Midland Bank in Burslem.

Free-scoring Northampton Town found Rovers' defensive line of goalkeeper Roney and full-backs Bill Westwood and Gilbert Ovens impenetrable. Rovers recorded 1-0 victories on both grounds to score a memorable double over the Cobblers, Corbett scoring on both occasions. On Christmas Day, the centre-forward's eightieth-minute consolation goal in defeat at Luton Town set a new Southern League goalscoring record for the club. It was Corbett's forty-fifth goal, surpassing Billy Beats' record set in 1906. One further milestone for Rovers' top scorer was that in scoring the opening goal in the final home game of the season, Corbett became the only Rovers player during the Southern League era to record fifty goals in this competition for the club.

For the most part, though, it was a fairly demoralising season. In one eight-match run in early spring, for instance, the only goals Rovers scored were two Bill Shaw penalties. Watford put four goals past Rovers, and Clapton Orient six. West Ham United had not scored in their previous six Southern League meetings with Rovers, but recorded a comfortable 5-0 victory early in October. The good news was that Danny Shea, scorer of ten goals in the opening eight games of the season, was, like George Webb, restricted to one goal. The bad news for Rovers was a Tommy Caldwell hat-trick, his first goals of the season for the Hammers. Harry Buckle returned to haunt his former club by scoring in both fixtures for Coventry City, who fielded Patsy Hendren for the February game at Eastville, the first of many appearances at the ground for the famous England cricket international. Even Portsmouth avenged their heavy defeat, their second goal in January being scored from the penalty spot fifteen minutes from time by the former Trowbridge Town outside-left Teddy Long, who signed for Rovers in 1911.

Rovers scored fewer goals (thirty-seven) than in any other Southern League season. Even Croydon Common, relegated at the end of their first season, conceded just one goal against Rovers and drew both fixtures. The final goal, and second debatable penalty of the match, in a meaningless end-of-season encounter at Queen's Park Rangers, was a penalty awarded ten minutes from time for a trip on McColl and successfully converted by Roney, who thus became the only goalkeeper to score for Rovers. In the FA Cup, Rovers earned an unlikely 2-0 shock victory at Second Division Grimsby Town, with Billy Peplow and Rodgers, who had never scored in the league, both shooting past the celebrated goalkeeper Wally Scott. Rovers were subsequently drawn at home to Barnsley but accepted a £500 offer to play the tie at Oakwell. The perhaps inevitable 4-0 defeat came through goals from Ernie Gadsby, a Bristol City player by the following summer, Wilf Bartrop, Tom Forman and George Utley.

1910/11

If thirteenth place had summed up a poor season, in 1910/11 Rovers slumped to their lowest position so far in the Southern League. Yet sixteenth in the table was to be the highest the club could manage in the final seasons prior to elevation to the Football League. Goals continued to be hard to come by, Corbett scoring only twice. Billy Peplow was the club's top scorer, but no individual player reached double figures and only large end-of-season wins against Southampton and New Brompton could bring an air of respectability to the season. In addition, the club's balance sheet on the annual report for 1910/11 showed a £381 loss.

Prior to the start of this season, inside-forward John Mason signed for Crewe Alexandra. Fred Boyle, a former Darlington wing-half, joined from Gainsborough Trinity, George Dodsley from Denaby United and Walter Hurley from Avonmouth. One major signing in June was that of the Scottish junior international inside-left George Hastie from Kilmarnock. He did not play in Rovers' opening seven league games, but his presence in the side as the season progressed enabled him to influence the its performance greatly. Another key figure was tough-tackling David Harvie from Stevenson Thistle, who arrived on the recommendation of the former Rovers defender James Young and was to play in over 200 Southern League games for Rovers prior to 1920. 'Hit Him' Harvie and his full-back partner Bill Westwood were the club's two ever-presents, in front of Peter Roney, Louis Williams, Harry Phillips and the reliable Peplow, missing just one game each.

Bill Ingham's second-half goal gave Norwich City victory at Eastville on the opening day, the Canaries giving a debut to Fred Wilkinson, who was to score an own goal in Watford's first Football League visit to Eastville in March 1921. Rovers lost their opening six games in the Southern League. The only goal in Adam McColl's first-class career was all Rovers had to show as their run included four 1-0 defeats. The side had interrupted this run with a 1-0 victory over Exeter City in the Southern Charity Cup, but even the Grecians were to record a league double over Rovers, with the future Rovers inside-forward Archie Hughes scoring in both games. It was the seventh game before Rovers gained their first points, amateur centre-forward Frank Woodhall, later a highly successful coach in New Zealand, scoring the winner at Plymouth, his only goal for the club.

Most bizarrely, Rovers conceded not one but two goals scored by opposition goalkeepers. On 17 September, Brentford won 1-0 at Eastville through a penalty from goalkeeper Archie Ling, a professional cricketer with Cambridgeshire. The penalty, conceded after twenty minutes when Westwood pushed Bert Hollinrake, was driven in off the underside of the bar. Rovers themselves had not scored all season, while Ling had scored both Brentford's goals, as he had converted a penalty against Swindon Town seven days earlier. Then, a week before Christmas, after the amateur Walter Hurley and Harry Phillips had scored for Rovers and Fred Whittaker and Fred McDiarmid had replied for Northampton Town, another goalkeeper scored the winning goal. Tommy Thorpe, who scored past Rovers' reserve custodian Edward Silvester, also scored his second goal of the year, both penalties, following one against Watford on the opening day of the season.

While Rovers took three points off champions-elect Swindon Town, who fielded the former Rovers wing-half Billy Tout, own goals lost the club points against Watford (Harvie, five minutes after half-time) and Coventry City (Phillips after eighteen minutes). Victory at home to the Robins on Good Friday was marred by a series of nasty fouls, with both captains – Bill Shaw and Charlie Bannister – being sent off by referee Pellowe two minutes from time, and the Swindon left-back Jock Walker receiving a police escort from the pitch. Corbett's fifty-second and final Southern League goal for Rovers, in an exciting 3-3 draw with Crystal Palace, was tempered by news of the death of former Rovers stalwart George Kinsey in his early forties. A run of ten games without victory ended abruptly with an unexpected 5-1 victory at The Dell, five Rovers players appearing on the scoresheet. For Southampton, normally such tough opponents, George Kimpton's goal could not prevent a second consecutive 5-1 defeat. Archie Hughes, signed from Exeter City in early February, and Jimmy Jones, from Aston Villa in part-exchange for goalkeeper Bredel Anstey, both scored their first Rovers goals that day and followed this up with three of Rovers' six at home to New Brompton. A new Eastville favourite, Jimmy Shervey, was given a few games as the season drew to a close.

A 1-0 defeat in the Gloucestershire Cup final was matched by the same score in an FA Cup replay. After two goalless games, Rovers took Hull City into extra time at Anlaby Road before being beaten by a freak goal. The home side's left-back Jack McQuillan had been injured and was hobbling at outside-left. When Tommy Nevins' through ball reached Wally Smith, his shot was only parried by Roney and McQuillan's first goal after over four years with the Tigers sending Rovers out of the cup.

1911/12

The late season form of Archie Hughes and Jimmy Jones allowed Rovers a basis upon which to build a forward line. Davie Walker returned in June from Leicester Fosse, four years after he had first left Eastville. Ted Long, a former Swindon Town outside-left, arrived just days before the new season started. The former Grimsby Town inside-forward Martin Bradley, whose brother James had won a League Championship medal with Liverpool in 1906, arrived from Sheffield Wednesday, where he had made two league appearances as a stand-in for Herbert Chapman's brother Harry. Two major absences from Rovers were George Hastie, who had joined Bath City, and Arthur Griffiths, sold to Notts County.

Rovers' main strength lay in defence, where goalkeeper Peter Roney, was joint top scorer with Billy Peplow, and George Richards was an ever-present. In front of him, David Harvie missed only one game, forging a strong full-back partnership with Bill Westwood and later Bert Bennett, while Louis Williams and Sam Morris played regularly at half-back. Until mid-December, Rovers did not concede more than two goals in any Southern League game. However, they also never scored more than two in this spell. Indeed, while four of the first five matches were drawn, it was an own goal by Southampton's goalkeeper Arthur Brown that brought Rovers' first goal of the season, as late as the third game.

Despite a paucity of goals, Rovers entered November having suffered just one defeat. The visit of Queen's Park Rangers to Eastville attracted a 16,000 crowd, the highest ever for a Rovers home match in the Southern League years, but Rovers crashed to a 2-0 defeat, only their second home defeat in the league since January. Thereafter, the season was more of a struggle, a run of eight defeats in ten matches in the spring leaving Rovers happy to settle for a final league placing of seventeenth. The highlight was a 4-1 victory over Norwich City, Peplow scoring twice, while Rovers completed the double over Southampton and Coventry City. The Sky Blues were beaten on Christmas Day and Boxing Day; on 27 December they defeated Brentford 9-0.

Rovers conceded four or more goals in five Southern League games, the heaviest defeat being 6-2 at West Ham United in March. Danny Shea and Fred Harrison, both prolific goalscorers against Rovers, scored twice each. In fact, for the second consecutive season, Shea scored in both fixtures against Rovers. He also scored a hat-trick, as did Bill Kennedy, in a 7-4 victory over Brentford just before the Bees met Rovers. However, despite the Bees' leaky defence, Rovers contrived to lose a two-goal half-time lead, and Brentford, with Patsy Hendren inspirational, drew 2-2, with goals from Billy Brawn and the former Bristol City forward Willis Rippon, who scored twice more in the return game. When Rovers crashed to a 5-0 defeat at Northampton Town just after Easter, Walter Tull, one of the first black players in British football, scored four times, and Albert Lewis once. Forty-eight hours later, the world was shocked by news that the *Titanic* had sunk. Rovers met

Bristol City in May before a 1,500 crowd at Ashton Gate in a charity game for the Titanic Disaster Fund and ,despite taking the lead through Walter Hurley five minutes before half-time, lost 3-1 to goals from Charles Gould, Ebenezer Owens and Billy Wedlock.

On the day Rovers conceded six at West Ham, two future Rovers managers were playing for Scotland against England. Centre-forward David McLean, who was winning his only cap, was to become manager of Rovers in 1929. Inside-left Andrew Wilson was Scotland's goalscorer in the 1-1 draw. The holder of six caps, he managed Rovers between 1921 and 1926. Both forwards, at this stage, were on the books of Sheffield Wednesday.

Rovers lost the Gloucestershire Cup final by a single goal at Ashton Gate, and were eliminated from the FA Cup by Portsmouth in front of an Eastville crowd of 15,000. Although Hughes got on the scoresheet for Rovers, Pompey scored twice through the delightfully named Love Jones and Lionel Louch. Fred Hunt, a Rovers director since 1897, tendered his resignation in mid-season and was replaced the following December by a former Aston Villa shareholder, Mr Allen of His Majesty's Picture Palace, the local cinema later renamed Concorde before being closed down in the 1980s.

1912/13

In recognition of its strength, Rovers' defence remained largely unchanged for the new season. Peter Roney in goal was to miss just the final game of the season, while David Harvie and Harry Bennett formed a reliable full-back partnership. Jack Nevin, a twenty-five-year-old with league experience at West Bromwich Albion, joined Sam Morris and Harry Phillips at half-back. Harry Harris was signed as cover, the former Kidderminster Harriers player breaking into Southern League football at the age of thirty. His Kidderminster teammate Harry Boxley also signed for Rovers. James Brogan and George Walker, who were to give Rovers loyal service, joined Peplow in a forward line that also boasted Billy Palmer, while Davie Walker joined Willenhall Swifts. Palmer's opening day debut meant the former Rotherham County and Nottingham Forest player became the first of Rovers' future Football League players to make the first team.

One rule change for the new season was that goalkeepers could only handle the ball inside the penalty area rather than anywhere in their half of the field. This alteration did little to help Rovers, who needed to wait until their ninth Southern League match to record their first win. When at last they did, Brogan, Shervey and Phillips scored in a 3-0 victory over Queen's Park Rangers. Rovers were to record just two Southern League doubles. Coventry were beaten home and away, with Harry Stansfield carried off injured in his debut as goalkeeper at Highfield Road and Bert Bennett appearing as a stand-in in goal. Merthyr Town were beaten twice over Christmas – Brogan, Rovers' top scorer with eleven Southern League goals, scored four times as Rovers won 7-1 at Eastville on Boxing Day. Goalscoring, though, was not Rovers' forte, and a 4-0 victory over Stoke in March, when George Richards scored his only three goals of the season, was the next largest win.

Harold Roe's first goal for Rovers, from Palmer's cross twenty minutes from time, brought a 1-0 win at Griffin Park in October and inflicted on Brentford a seventh consecutive Southern League defeat. Three days earlier, Rovers had crashed 4-0 at Exeter City, for whom Ellis Crompton, latterly a highly successful Rovers player, and Arthur Rutter both scored twice. Several players were perennial scorers against the Rovers side of the immediate pre-war period. Charlie White scored for Watford on Rovers' fourth consecutive visit to Colney Butts Meadow. George Hilsdon, who had scored against Rovers in 1904/05 and 1905/06, scored West Ham United's third goal in the April fixture. Bill Voisey, the scorer of the first goal Rovers conceded in the Football League in 1920, was in the Millwall side defeated by two Jimmy Shervey goals at Eastville in November. Rovers let slip a 2-0 half-time lead that month to draw with Portsmouth, whose goals came from Frank Stringfellow and Fred Rollinson. This was the first of Stringfellow's eight Southern League goals against Rovers; he also scored in both the 1920/21 Division Three (South) fixtures.

The FA Cup brought great excitement and success to Eastville. On 11 January, having unusually won four out of five Southern League matches, Rovers recorded a 2-0 victory over Notts County. Prior to the First World War, this was the club's only victory over a First Division club. County's record appearance maker, Albert Iremonger; was in goal, at 6 foot 5¼ inches, he was the tallest opponent to face Rovers until Stockport County's Kevin Francis in 1993. Despite eight hours of heavy rain, the match went ahead and, after five corners in quick succession, Harry Roe's low drive gave the home side the lead after twenty-five minutes. Seven minutes from time, Peplow's cross was turned in by Shervey with the aid of a deflection off County right-back Herbert Morley. A crowd of 15,000 – all five FA Cup crowds surpassed the highest League attendance – made Rovers' day complete.

It took three games to defeat Norwich City. Rovers led 1-0 at half-time in all three matches, Harry Woods scored for Norwich in both drawn games and Jimmy Shervey snatched Rovers' winner in the second replay at Stamford Bridge. Prior to this game, Rovers had made six changes to the side to play Gillingham in the Southern League, and were fined for fielding a weakened side. However, as if to prove the quality of these replacements, all six players recalled were to appear again later in the season. The deciding game with Norwich was unsavoury and the Canaries' goalkeeper William Mellor was suspended for two weeks following an incident during the match. Four Everton goals at Eastville without reply ended the Cup run, the second of four scorers being the England international

Frank Jefferis. In February 1913, the Empire Theatre, which stood where the Old Market/Temple Way underpass is found today, showed a sketch in which Rovers, uncharacteristically in red, led an Everton side by a goal to nil. After seven straight losses, the Gloucestershire Cup was won through Brogan's close-range goal five minutes after half-time. One representative honour was given to the former Rovers player Bill Tout; he was in the Southern League side that beat the Scottish League 1-0 at Millwall in October.

3

The War Years

1913/14

Hopes of finishing higher than sixteenth, ultimately dashed as Rovers completed the season one place lower, had been boosted by the summer signing of the inspirational Ellis Crompton. The former Blackburn Rovers and Tottenham Hotspur inside-forward cost £400 from Exeter City. Murray and Arthur Squires were also new names in the attack, while Rovers relied on the sturdy defensive line that had proved so successful in the past. Full-backs David Harvie and Bert Bennett were the only two ever-presents. Harry Phillips was a notable absentee when Rovers lined up for the new season, while Billy Palmer had joined First Division Everton for £800, a sizeable fee that boosted the club's finances and led to a £437 net profit for the year.

Crompton scored against Cardiff City on his debut. He also scored in the next home game, against West Ham United, for whom Tom Brandon, a Rovers player in 1919/20, was making his Southern League debut. However, Rovers picked up just one point in the opening seven fixtures, and the perennial struggle was underway. Rovers recorded a meagre nine Southern League wins, beat no individual opponents home and away and, were it not for Crompton's thirteen goals, might have been in real trouble. It was noticeable that he was absent for the Gloucestershire Cup final when Rovers, fielding Bill Westwood at left-back for his first game in over two years, lost 2-0 to Bristol City.

One particularly poor run of results for Alf Homer's side came in January. During this month, Rovers lost all four Southern League games, an FA Cup tie and a friendly 1-0 at home to Bristol City, the scorer being Tom Howarth, who played for Rovers in 1922/23. These defeats were not even by small margins. The Plymouth Argyle defeat was 4-1 at Eastville, with Fred Burch scoring a hat-trick. Preston North End scored five goals at Deepdale in the FA Cup, and West Ham United defeated Rovers 6-1. Syd Puddefoot scored a hat-trick for the Hammers at the start of an illustrious career that was to see him score for Blackburn Rovers against Rovers in an FA Cup game in January 1931. All five Swindon Town forwards had scored against Rovers on Boxing Day.

There were, of course, a number of positive aspects to the 1913/14 season. The game at Millwall in December attracted a crowd of 18,000 to The Den, the largest attendance at any Southern League game between 1899 and 1920 featuring Rovers. A 15,000-strong crowd saw the 2-1 home win over Merthyr Town, Crompton and Shervey scoring, and three other home games attracted a five-figure crowd. On Christmas Day, 12,000 spectators saw Rovers defeat Swindon Town 5-2 to record the largest win since the previous Boxing Day. Stand-in centre-forward Gallacher scored the only two goals of his brief Rovers career, Crompton and Shervey again grabbed one each and the Robins' Matthew Lochhead conceded an own goal. The ever-consistent Billy Peplow scored with a first-time shot after only five minutes at home to Reading on the occasion of his 200th Southern League appearance for the club. He was only the second player to reach this milestone.

It was no surprise when Rovers signed Henry McCann from Exeter City in the summer of 1914. On the final day of the season he had scored the Grecians' goal as Rovers drew at St James' Park. In fact, both games against Exeter City finished 1-1 and, in both cases, McCann was the goalscorer. Len Andrews achieved a similar feat as Southampton became one of four clubs to complete a league double over Rovers. He was to play for the Saints against Rovers as late as Good Friday 1922, and for Watford against Rovers in 1924/25.

The Gloucestershire Cup was not retained, as Bristol City won 2-0 at Ashton Gate. In the FA Cup, a tough away fixture at Preston North End was made all the more difficult when goalkeeper Peter Roney left the field with an injury that ruled him out for the rest of the season. Bert Bennett took over in goal, and although Jimmy Shervey scored twice, the home side ran up five goals. North End scored three goals in eight minutes early in the game, and Fred Osborne, who had collided accidentally with Roney after fifteen minutes, scored a hat-trick, including two penalties. Roney's injury prompted the signing from Fulham of Hugh McDonald, who had saved a penalty on his Grimsby Town debut against Bradford Park Avenue in Division Two in December 1911.

On 29 April, a crowd of 4,000 saw a Bristol XI lose 3-0 to FA Cup holders Aston Villa at Ashton Gate in a testimonial following the death of the Bristol City secretary E. J. Locke. Bert Bennett, one of five Rovers players present, opened the scoring with an own goal after twenty minutes. A combined Rovers and City reserve team beat a Gloucestershire XI 4-1 at Eastville that month in a benefit game for the E. J. Clarke Testimonial Fund.

1914/15

There were four new faces in the Rovers side that drew with Crystal Palace on the opening day of the season. George Davison, at centre-forward, scored Rovers' goal and ended up top scorer with fifteen Southern League goals, six more than Henry McCann, who signed from Exeter City. Joe Caddick, at inside-right, added seven goals and David Taylor, shaking off the challenge of Bert Bennett, soon made the left-back position his own. Bill Westwood returned to the side for his first Southern League appearance in almost three years. Jack Nevin had joined Ayr United, while Sam Morris, Joe Griffiths and Jimmy Shervey were conspicuous by their absence, but the world was more engrossed in events elsewhere.

Despite the outbreak of war on 4 August 1914, professional football, though much affected, was allowed to continue. It would, with hindsight, have been logical for football to take a back seat. Lessons were learnt by the time the Second World War was declared. But since the war would be over by Christmas, as Britain was assured by the unfounded but generally held myth circulated in the autumn by Field-Marshal John Denton Pinkstone French, Commander-in-Chief of the Forces, the Football League and Southern League continued as normal in 1914. Manager Homer, so certain of imminent peace, agreed a £2 contract for the duration of the war, a commitment he faithfully honoured. Of course, some players were conscripted and Rovers relied on a number of local players to make up the numbers. Walter Hurley, who 'if (he) had chosen to turn professional ... would have been famous like Stanley Matthews' (Ron Best, Gillingham School magazine, July 1960), played his first game for two-and-a-half years when Croydon Common visited Eastville on Easter Tuesday. After George Walker and Ellis Crompton (penalty) had scored, Hurley added Rovers' third past the future England goalkeeper Ernie Williamson, with left-back Arthur Hutchings replying for the Cock Robins from the penalty spot. Victory marked a final Rovers game for Billy Peplow, who had been rewarded with the proceeds of a benefit match against Coventry City on 21 February 1915. This result also effectively meant Rovers had avoided relegation.

Despite the early season form of Davison, who scored six times in his opening seven games, Rovers were to conform to their pattern of recent years and win just one of their first nine Southern League matches. Through autumn, though, came a run of good results, shattered ultimately by a 7-0 defeat at Cardiff City, where Billy Devlin scored a hat-trick and the future Rovers outside-left Jack Evans once – Davison missed a second-half penalty for Rovers. Prior to that, Rovers had won back-to-back games for the first time since Christmas 1912. One of these, a 4-2 victory over Norwich City when Rovers gave a debut to John Hardman, a former Derby County and Oldham Athletic wing-half, saw Caddick score twice for Rovers and Harry Woods twice for the visitors. McCann who, along with a Arthur Woodlands own goal, also scored in that game, added the winner at Gillingham and two more as Brighton were defeated 4-0.

Rovers were to suffer two runs of four consecutive Southern League defeats. The second of these ended dramatically at Eastville in February, when a well-struck twenty-fifth-minute Davison goal, following a fine three-man move, gave Rovers victory over West Ham United, who had previously not lost for nine games. The next time the two sides would meet was a 2-2 draw at Eastville in September 1953.

However, Rovers conceded seventy-five Southern League goals in 1914/15, more than in any other season spent in that league. Only bottom-placed Gillingham conceded more. Arthur Dominy, scorer of thirty goals in the season for Southampton, scored the Saints' opening goal as Rovers lost 3-1 at The Dell. A crowd of only 1,000 watched the return game at Eastville, a sure sign of the times as the equivalent fixture in 1913/14 had attracted 9,000 spectators. Once Harry Stansfield had replaced veteran Roney in goal, Rovers conceded seven at Cardiff City and five at Norwich City, where Danny Wilson scored twice and the Canaries ran up four second-half goals. Welsh international Wally Davies, on Good Friday and Easter Monday, scored for Millwall in both fixtures against Rovers. Albert Green had scored only once in thirteen months prior to his brace of goals in Watford's 3-2 win at Eastville in February.

Despite the ravages of war, some Rovers players continued to find success. Billy Palmer, for instance, won a league championship medal with Everton for the 1914/15 season, having appeared in seventeen First Division matches. In the FA Cup, Rovers recorded a 3-0 victory over Bournemouth in December, with Crompton, Davison and Squires all scoring. The predicted victory over Southend United, whom Rovers had recently defeated 4-1, failed to materialise, though. Taken to a replay, Rovers conceded three goals at The Kursaal and were eliminated. The Gloucestershire Cup final was cancelled and was next played in September 1919.

1915–19

It would be untrue to claim that the First World War had no effect on Bristol Rovers. The massive trail of grief and destruction touched every corner of the world, and at least 4,000 Bristolians died in the conflict. John Hardman, who had played for Rovers during 1914/15, was killed in action in France in February 1917. Walter Gerrish, an inside-forward with Rovers between 1905 and 1909 and subsequently the winner of a league championship medal with Aston Villa in 1909/10, was also killed (Major Frank Buckley described him as 'a splendid soldier, most willing and brave'), as were Harry Phillips, who had left the club in 1913, Joe Hulme and Albert Rodgers. Joseph Caddick, a Rovers player in

1914/15, served with the 13th Worcestershire Regiment and witnessed atrocities. The Memorial Gates outside the rugby ground in Horfield were erected to commemorate the 300 or so local rugby players who lost their lives during the First World War. Several players who had played against Rovers also lost their lives, among this number Bristol City's goalkeeper Tommy Ware, killed in June 1915, who had played in the Gloucestershire Cup finals of 1913 and 1914; Arthur Evans, who played at left-back for Exeter City in three games immediately prior to the war; Steve Jackson, Coventry City's right-back in October 1913; and Norman Wood, who had played inside-right for Plymouth Argyle against Rovers in October 1910, was killed in action in August 1916. James Comrie had played several times for Reading against Rovers and, serving with the Northumberland Fusiliers, was killed in action on 9 August 1916, aged thirty-five. John Hesham, who died on active service in France on 17 November 1915, had scored Croydon Common's second-half goal against Rovers at The Nest in April 1910. Leigh Richmond Roose, whose goalkeeping had done so much to eliminate Rovers from the 1901/02 FA Cup, once a medical trainee and an erstwhile pupil of the inimitable H. G. Wells, was killed on the Somme on 7 October 1916, while Walter Tull, whose four goals had helped Northampton Town defeat Rovers at Easter 1912, was killed on the battlefield on 15 March 1918. Some clubs were seriously depleted through war injuries. For instance, three Exeter City players who had appeared against Rovers – Fred Marshall, Herbert Tierney and Bill Smith – suffered such serious war wounds they never played again. In Smith's case, one of his legs had to be amputated in 1919. Two German bombs from a Zeppelin had earlier struck Hartlepool United's Victoria Ground on 27 November 1916 and destroyed the wooden grandstand.

The story of Blakey Martin, a former Derby County player, is a more positive one. He could claim a more distinguished war record that culminated in the receipt of the Military Medal and bar. Martin was to play at left-half for Southend United in both league fixtures against Rovers in 1920/21 and 1921/22. John Hughes, a Rovers player in 1911/12 and a former Welsh amateur international, received a Military Cross in April 1916 for his actions on the battlefield. Two Football League players with Rovers – Bert Blake with the Royal Garrison Artillery, and Hubert Ashton, who won the Military Cross on the Western Front – served in the First World War.

In July 1915, following a meeting of football authorities in Blackpool, all first-class football was suspended for the duration of the war. Rovers did, however, compete in the South-Western Combination of 1915/16, winning five of twelve games and finishing two points above Bristol City. Three players scored twice each in a 9-2 victory over RAMC in December, and separate players scored hat-tricks in each of two fixtures with both Newport County and Southampton. Rovers, along with a number of provincial sides, were refused admission to the London Combination for 1916/17 for reasons of restricted wartime travel, and, between 1916 and 1919, played solely in games around the Bristol area. The Bristol County Combination of 1917/18 saw Rovers win twenty-eight out of thirty-seven matches, scoring 137 goals in the process, but still miss out on the championship to Bristol City. The following season, only four sides participated in this tournament, with Rovers (eleven points) above Bristol city (nine), Bristol Docks (four) and RAVC (no points).

Rovers also played a series of friendly matches through the war, many against local cadet corps. There were several large wins, Rovers reaching double figures on nine occasions. The highest victory was 20-0 against Great Western Railway on 15 February 1919. Ted Rawlings scored four goals, Ellis Crompton, Bill Panes, Len Gyles and goalkeeper Harry Grubb, who played outfield after half-time, three each, Harry Roe twice and Bert Bennett and Percy Whitton once each. Bill Weston scored nine goals in a 12-0 win over the same opponents on 8 December 1917, and Lucas six goals when Rovers defeated Bristol YMCA 10-1 on 10 March 1917. The apparently free-scoring goalkeeper Grubb had earlier scored another hat-trick when Rovers beat Renown 5-0 in April 1917. On the other hand, the former England international Wally Hardinge scored a hat-trick when the Royal Naval Depot won 8-2 at Eastville in December 1916.

Jonah Wilcox, who scored for Bristol City in six different matches against Rovers during the war, was to be Rovers' top scorer in 1925/26. He scored a hat-trick in Bristol City's 5-1 win at Eastville in November 1916. The game against the Robins in September 1916 featured three penalties, scored by Green for Rovers and Chapman and Smith for City; Bristol City won 3-1. The second goal in Rovers' comfortable win at Ashton Gate on Boxing Day 1917 was put through his own net by City's twenty-six-time England international centre-half Billy Wedlock. Edward Skuse scored a hat-trick in the convincing victory at Ashton Gate on Good Friday 1919. Three days later, on Easter Monday, Rovers and City drew 1-1 through a penalty each, Jones putting the visitors ahead after fifty minutes from the spot, and Ellis Crompton, playing at centre-half, similarly equalised five minutes later. Crompton also scored from 40 yards in April, Rovers' fourth in an emphatic 8-0 victory over RAVC.

Rovers' penultimate fixture of the 1918/19 season was held at Eastville on 3 May. Following the contemporary fashion of such representative games across the country, Rovers played Gloucestershire in a match that finished 1-1.

4

Inter-War Years

1919/20

Twenty years after first accepting the job of manager of Bristol Rovers, it fell to Alf Homer to reconstruct a team in the aftermath of four years of war. For the first full season after the war, Rovers were in the newly reformed Southern League, devoid of West Ham United and the now defunct Croydon Common. Brentford returned to this division and Merthyr Town, Newport County and Swansea Town brought the number of clubs up from twenty to twenty-two.

Harry Grubb, a regular wartime goalkeeper with Rovers, opened the new season as first choice, although Harry Stansfield and Jesse Whatley, a signing from Trowbridge Town, were also to appear as the season progressed. David Harvie and Bill Panes, signed from Bath City in 1916, were reliable full-backs, with Percy Whitton, later an experienced Football League player at Newport County, alongside Harry Roe at half-back. The new centre-half was Steve Sims from Leicester Fosse, joined in November by David Steele, signed from Douglas Water Thistle, who won domestic honours and Scottish international caps while at Huddersfield Town. Ellis Crompton, who missed only one game all season, and George Davison were joined in the forward line by wartime goalscorer Ted Rawlings. Billy Palmer, or 'Lady Palmer' in reference to his perceived reluctance to get muddy, returned from a highly successful stint with Everton, while Joe Walter, Rovers' only ever-present, and Wally Bullock were signed from Horfield United. Two more experienced signings were West Ham United's left-back Tom Brandon and the Bristol City inside-forward Leslie Hughes, who was to return to Ashton Gate in 1920.

Just as in the five final pre-war seasons, Rovers got off to a very poor start. An opening home defeat against Queen's Park Rangers and an exciting 4-4 draw with Cardiff City set the season underway, but it was seven games before Rovers' first victory. Rovers were to struggle all year and finished in seventeenth place. Steve Sims was top scorer with nine goals, including a hat-trick in a 5-0 victory over Luton Town on Easter Tuesday, in which game Jesse Whatley saved John Elvey's penalty. Crompton and Walter scored eight each, Rawlings and Jim Hyam one fewer. Rawlings' total included three in a 4-1 victory over Southend United in October.

An exciting game at home to Norwich City saw the visitors give three players a debut. Rovers led 3-2 by half-time and won 5-3. Sims scored twice, the Canaries' George Dexter, in his only first-class appearance for Norwich, put an own goal past, as did Rovers' Brandon in the second half. Five minutes from time, trying to stop the ball as it flew out of play, an unfortunate spectator fell headlong into the River Frome. As the season drew to a close, benefit games for manager Alf Homer were played against Gillingham and Aston Villa.

The season's heaviest defeat came in January. Queen's Park Rangers, managed by Jimmy Howie, Rovers' joint top scorer in 1902/03, defeated Rovers 7-1 at Loftus Road, John Smith scoring four times while Rawlings had his sixty-fifth minute penalty easily saved by Joe Merrick. A 5-1 defeat at Norwich City featured a John Doran hat-trick. A 3-0 defeat at Brentford was precipitated by Patsy Hendren's opening goal shortly after half-time. Jimmy Broad scored for Millwall in both Southern League fixtures against Rovers. The defeat at Plymouth Argyle on Easter Saturday featured an opening goal from David Jack, a future England international who was to play in two FA Cup finals with Bolton Wanderers and two more with Arsenal.

Jim Hyam marked his home debut in December with a goal after only twelve seconds against Southampton. Unfortunately for Rovers, goalkeeper Harry Stansfield was injured, Billy Weston went in goal and ten-man Rovers held on for a 1-1 draw. Arthur Dominy scored the equaliser for the Saints. Two games later, Harvie clocked up his 200th Southern League appearance, becoming the third Rovers player to achieve this feat. However, the rugged and uncompromising full-back was to leave the club under a cloud within months, having allegedly sold his landlady's piano without her permission.

No fewer than eleven Southern League games and two FA Cup ties at Eastville were watched by five-figure crowds. Rovers progressed in the Cup after two high-scoring games with Northampton Town. Rawlings and Hyam scored in both games, as did Billy Pease for the Cobblers. Rovers then crashed 4-1 at home to Tottenham Hotspur before a crowd of 17,260, paying 1*s* 6*d* a head on the terraces and 7*s* 6*d* in the stands. The Second Division side knocked Rovers out of the Cup for the first of two consecutive seasons, thirty-seven-year-old centre-forward Jimmy Cantrell scoring a hat-trick. He was to score again against Rovers in the FA Cup in 1920/21. Tom Howarth, later a Rovers player, scored twice as the Gloucestershire Cup final was lost 4-0 to Bristol City. At the season's end, Football League and Southern League representatives met in Sheffield on 18 May 1920 and voted 19-1, with one abstention, to elevate the Southern League en bloc to form Division Three, a recommendation first proposed as early as 1909. It was a momentous decision, ratified at the Football League's Annual General Meeting eleven days later, opening up a new chapter in the history of Bristol Rovers.

1920/21

Presented with the opportunity of participation in the Football League, Bristol Rovers set on the journey that was to see league status preserved into the twenty-first century. It was certainly a fresh start for the club and required careful preparation. Sixty-year-old club chairman George Humphreys made the first move by appointing Ben Hall in July 1920 as Rovers' first full-time manager. Alf Homer, stepping down from managerial duties, became the club secretary, a post he was to hold for eight further years. Hall had enjoyed a successful playing career as a centre-half with Grimsby Town, Derby County, Leicester Fosse and South Shields, and a post-war spell as trainer at Huddersfield Town preceded his move to Eastville. He was tasked with creating a side to represent Rovers in league action and building a team spirit worthy of the club.

Four regular players from 1919/20 (club captain Steve Sims, Joe Walter, Ellis Crompton and Bill Palmer) as well as emerging goalkeeper Jesse Whatley became the backbone of the side. In all, eleven Southern League players reappeared for Rovers in the Football League. Bill Panes, who had broken into the side at left-back, formed a full-back partnership with Jock Bethune, a Glaswegian who had gained considerable experience in Division Two with Barnsley and was to represent England at indoor bowls between 1936 and 1938. At half-back, David Steele was joined at the end of 1919/20 by Scotsman David Kenny and, on the eve of the new season, by Derby County's Harry Boxley. Homer's last signings, inside-forwards Bill Bird and Joe Norton, a former Manchester United player, were joined shortly before the new season by inside-right Harold Bell. Another former Barnsley player, Bell was to play in the inaugural league game and on just one further occasion in his sole season at Eastville.

Before the season started, Humphreys held a special meeting to introduce Hall. On this occasion, he was also able to inform the gathering that the club was now out of debt. He had paid for the Eastville ground in full and the club now owned 19 acres of land, including property right up to the famous Thirteen Arches railway bridge, which overlooked the ground until its demolition in May 1968. The club was also planning to dispose of striped shirts and play in white tops with navy blue shorts, a kit to which Rovers were to adhere for the opening decade in the Football League.

Hall made one additional signing during the season, that of wing-half George Gane. A Bristolian by birth, Gane had played league football north and south of the border, once commanding an alleged transfer fee of £750, a world record at the time. He had moved into non-League football and, though now aged thirty-four, was able to make one final league appearance in the 2-2 draw at home to Norwich City in October. This game also marked the end of Billy Vaughan's Rovers career. Vaughan was to enjoy a further decade in high-quality football and was, in fact, in the Exeter City side that defeated Rovers through four Fred Dent goals in November 1927. In one final twist, Vaughan claimed Rovers' second goal in the Norwich game, his only one in Division Three for the club, even if, as the *Western Daily Press* reported, Joe Walter applied the finishing touch.

The opening game, on a sunny August afternoon, ended in a 2-0 defeat at the hands of Millwall. A crowd of 25,000 at The Den saw a goalless first half. Then, after fifty-two minutes, Bill Voisey's powerful shot from the edge of the penalty area put Millwall ahead. Only seven minutes later, goalkeeper Harry Stansfield, playing as ever in glasses, lost the flight of outside-left Jack Dempsey's cross in the late afternoon sun, and Jimmy Broad's header put the result out of Rovers' reach.

Four days later, in the first league match played at Eastville, Rovers gained their first victory. Ellis Crompton had missed the opening match, but returned to the side at inside-left to score the first goal when Rovers defeated Newport County 3-2. It is, of course, in the nature of such a season that a number of club firsts were set. Bill Bird claimed a hat-trick in a bad-tempered 3-1 win against Brighton in September. In this match, Kenny dislocated his collarbone and the visitors' centre-half Jack Rutherford, who was to join Rovers in 1922, was sent off.

Rovers won fifteen out of twenty-one home league fixtures during 1920/21. Victory over Crystal Palace in October was partly due to a last-minute penalty save by Whatley from Bert Menlove, while Merthyr Town earned a point at Eastville in April, when Rees Williams equalised with a shot so hard it broke the net. Two goals in the final five minutes earned Rovers a 2-1 victory over Southend United in March. Away from home, Rovers won only at Newport, Luton and Northampton. A typical story was the game at Swindon Town in January, when Harry Boxley gave Rovers a first-minute lead before two Albert Denyer goals gave the Robins victory. The heaviest defeat was against the divisional champions Southampton at The Dell, when four goals in twenty minutes during the second half gave the Saints a 4-0 victory. Joe Barratt, who was to join Rovers from Lincoln City in 1926, scored one of them. Defeat at Watford in February came courtesy of outside-left Tommy Waterall's goal scored direct from a corner. Crystal Palace scored three times in eight second-half minutes to beat Rovers in October.

On New Year's Day, Luton Town full-back Alf Tirrell became the first player to score for both sides in a league fixture involving Rovers. Sid Leigh's early goal had given Rovers a lead that Tirrell's well-taken free-kick cancelled out. As half-time approached, Leigh's shot was deflected by Tirrell off the greasy turf past his own goalkeeper to give Rovers a 2-1 victory. Luton were awarded a penalty kick in both league fixtures against Rovers, and on both occasions Jesse Whatley saved from the future England international Ernie Simms. The return game at Eastville on Easter

Tuesday, however, was a more one-sided affair, with Boxley scoring twice and Crompton, Leigh and Palmer once each in a straightforward 5-0 victory.

Rovers won seven of their final eight home league games, two of them by a five-goal margin. The home game with Southend United was won after Rovers trailed 1-0 five minutes from time. In the final match at Eastville, Rovers defeated Exeter City 5-0. This Exeter game was a personal triumph for Sid Leigh, who completed a first-half hat-trick and went on to score four goals in all. No Rovers player has yet scored more than four times in a league match. Leigh was Rovers' top scorer of the season, contributing twenty-one goals in thirty-six league appearances, even affording the luxury of a missed penalty in the home win over Watford. Rovers finished the season in tenth place.

One feature of Rovers' 2-1 victory at Northampton in March was the appearance for the Cobblers of thirty-nine-year-old goalkeeper Tommy Thorpe. As he was born in Kilnhurst on 19 May 1881, Thorpe is chronologically the first-born of all footballers who have played in a Football League game involving Bristol Rovers.

The Gloucestershire Cup final was lost to a first-time volley after an hour from Bristol City left-back Laurie Banfield, who was playing as a passenger at outside-left after being injured earlier in the game. The real excitement, however, came in the FA Cup. Non-League Worksop Town proved no obstacle at Eastville, where six Rovers players got on the scoresheet, although it took thirty minutes for the deadlock to be broken. Jerry Morgan, one of a handful of players to appear for Rovers in both the Southern League and the Football League, contributed a hat-trick. Rovers were rewarded for this win with a game for the second successive season against First Division Tottenham Hotspur at White Hart Lane. It was the perfect stage for Rovers to prove their worth before a crowd of 35,000. Sadly, though, Dennis Howes had to leave the field injured and, later, so too did Jock Bethune. In the days before substitutes were allowed, such misfortunes were too great to overcome. Although Walter and Norton both scored, nine-man Rovers lost 6-2. Spurs went on to win the FA Cup final that season, defeating Wolverhampton Wanderers by a solitary goal. Wolves featured Tancy Lea at outside-left, who was to become a Rovers player twelve months later.

In January, Rovers hosted a first-class rugby game at Eastville. In a bizarre twist to later developments at the Memorial Ground, Bristol entertained Cardiff, losing by eleven points to five; Bristol also lost by eight points to nil to Newport at Eastville in front of a 15,000 crowd the following month. Panes, Sims, Crompton and Walter, meanwhile, played for the Bristol XI, which beat an International XI 3-2 before an Ashton Gate crowd of 8,000 in a benefit game for Billy Wedlock. On Monday 21 February 1921, Eastville hosted a charity game, charging sixpence entry, in which the Bristol Theatres XI defeated a Music Hall XI 4-1 to lift the Bristol Theatrical Challenge Cup.

1921/22

Despite the relative success of Rovers' first league season, manager Ben Hall did not stay at the club. He left in May to take up a scouting post with Southend United, later working for the Leicestershire FA. The new manager was Andrew Wilson, a highly successful centre-forward with Sheffield Wednesday and Scotland, who was to spend five years at Eastville, with George Endicott at first assuming the mantle of club coach.

Summer signings were largely defensive. George Stockley, Sam Furniss and Tom Winsper all added to Rovers' full-back and half-back lines. With George Chance effectively ruled out of the season through injury, James Liddell, the scorer of a sensational goal just seconds into a reserve game in October, played in the forward line, but was to contribute only four league goals. Jack Ball, an inside-forward who was to win an England cap in 1927, proved a propitious signing from Sheffield United. Wally Hammond, a speedy inside-right, played in six league games in the first of two seasons with Rovers before pursuing a cricket career of legendary proportions. Hammond's debut at Brighton over Christmas saw him become the first player born in the twentieth century to play first-team football for Rovers.

The season began with four straight defeats in the league. Captain Steve Sims, successfully converted to centre-half, scored the club's only goal in this poor start. He then scored the goal that earned the first point of the season, a 1-1 draw with Portsmouth before the season's best Eastville crowd of 20,000. During the opening game, in a series of events oddly predictive of Graeme Power's injury in 1997, full-back George Stockley broke his leg. The crack was loud enough to be heard all around Eastville. With Stockley sidelined until Easter, Rovers needed extra cover at left-back. This was found in the form of Jock Kissock, who later played for New Zealand after his emigration there in 1922, and latterly by Jimmy Haydon, a young locally born defender who gave loyal service to Rovers for a decade.

On the opening day, Plymouth's Frank Richardson, making his Argyle debut, scored the first hat-trick Rovers conceded in league football. It was quickly followed by others. Bill Keen remains the only Millwall player to have scored three goals in a league game against Rovers. Then there were three hat-tricks conceded in the calendar month of April, one at Reading and two at Swansea. Rovers had been leading 3-1 at Elm Park in November when the game was abandoned after fifty-two minutes due to fog. Once replayed, the story was quite different. Reading, featuring centre-half Ted Hanney, the winner of a gold medal for football at the 1912 Olympics, stormed to a comfortable 4-0 victory. Sam Jennings scored three times. Just ten days later came the debacle at the Vetch Field.

Rovers' game at Swansea on Easter Saturday should have posed few problems. Only seven days later, Rovers were to draw with the same opposition. Going virtually full-strength into the game, though Jack Thomson had a rare game in goal, there was no hint of the goal glut to follow. However, after just fifteen minutes, Steve Sims left the field injured, Joe Walter soon followed, and Bill Panes was merely a passenger. Swansea were 5-0 up by half-time, and their 8-1 win constituted Rovers' heaviest league defeat at that time, a score kept down by Thomson's heroics in goal. Two forwards, Bill Brown and Jimmy Collins, helped themselves to hat-tricks, this being the first of three occasions when two opponents have scored three each against Rovers in the same league match. Collins, in fact, ended up with four goals (although one Welsh reporter credited one of his goals to Welsh rugby international Ben Beynon) making him the first opponent to score this many against Rovers in the league.

The fact that Rovers finished the season in fourteenth place was largely due to two successful mid-season runs. There were six consecutive wins in late autumn, and a spell of five victories in seven games into the New Year. These wins included a 2-0 victory at Merthyr in October, where the home side played for seventy minutes with only ten men after an early injury to their full-back Hugh Brown, and a 1-0 victory at Norwich thanks to Billy Palmer's last-minute goal after Whatley had saved a Gordon Addy penalty. Another 1-0 away victory, this time at Swindon, was secured only after goalkeeper Kossuth Barnes had saved a penalty from Town's Albert Weston. Rovers also won by a single goal at Newport, with Jerry Morgan scoring the only goal. Again, Rovers conceded a penalty at Somerton Park. Jimmy Haydon, thinking Barnes was injured, picked the ball up in the penalty area, the referee awarded a penalty and County's left-half Andrew Walker missed it.

Two defeats at the hands of Brighton over Christmas also featured a first league appearance for inside-right Wally Hammond. Hammond's significant contribution to sporting history was to be made in cricket, where he captained England in twenty Test matches and headed the first-class batting averages in seven separate summers. He scored 336 not out against New Zealand in the Auckland Test of 1932, and made a first-class double century on thirty-six occasions. Rovers' trainer Bert Williams maintained that he was the fastest runner in the fifty years that the veteran coach was attached to the Eastville club. In both Christmas fixtures, Brighton fielded Zechariah March at outside-left who, by the time of his death in September 1994 at the age of 101, was to be the oldest ex-professional footballer.

The 4-2 home victory over Charlton Athletic in September featured players called Steele scoring for both sides. In this game, right-back Jack Hall spent twenty-five minutes in goal after Jesse Whatley had been injured. However, Whatley recovered to return for the final minutes and, indeed, saved a penalty from Arthur Whalley in the return fixture seven days later. Injuries, of course, could be crucial in these pre-replacement days. Rovers lost 1-0 at Watford, with Ernie Wallington scoring, after being reduced to nine men once Sid Leigh and Jimmy Haydon had left the field injured. Perhaps Rovers were fortunate for, in the concurrent reserve game, the Hertfordshire club lost both Frank Pankhurst and James Short with broken collarbones.

Bill Panes, generally a highly dependable left-back and 'a usually inoffensive man' (*Western Daily Press*) became the first Rovers player to be sent off in a league game. Ten minutes after half-time during the 2-0 home victory over Luton Town in February, he overreacted to provocation by the visitors' Australian-born inside-right Harry Higginbotham, struck him in the face and was sent from the field by referee Mr Tolfree of Southampton. This was the first occasion that a Rovers player had been sent off at Eastville since 1897.

Rovers were involved in two high scoring games against Welsh opposition at Eastville in January. First, Rovers were three goals ahead after only ten minutes against Aberdare Athletic, and ended up winning 5-1, with top scorer Sid Leigh scoring a hat-trick. The following week, Rovers led 2-0 inside the first ten minutes against Newport County. Although Jimmy Liddell scored on his comeback game after a three-month absence, Newport staged a brave recovery to lead 3-2 at the interval and win 4-3, with Charlie Britton scoring twice, to record only their second away victory in the league that season. Earlier in the season, Rovers scored twice in the first seven minutes en route to a 4-2 victory over Norwich City. A collection was taken at this game for the former Rovers and Norwich goalkeeper, Peter Roney, who was seriously ill in Ashington. The Rovers directors sent him ten guineas.

An unsuccessful season was capped by an FA Cup defeat at Swansea Town and a Gloucestershire Cup defeat at Bristol City. Rovers were also under investigation following crowd trouble at successive reserve team matches against Portsmouth and Luton Town. In January, Walter's fifth-minute goal gave Rovers an early lead in a friendly with Coventry City, which, after Leigh left the field injured, was lost 6-1, Alick Mercer scoring a hat-trick. However, success lay just around the corner for two players. David Steele and Joe Walter, who had missed just seven games between them all season, joined Huddersfield Town. Huddersfield then went on to win three consecutive league championships under the management of Herbert Chapman and his assistant, the former Rovers trainer Jack Chaplin. Steele also won three Scottish caps and later managed Sheffield United, Huddersfield Town and both Bradford clubs. On Wednesday 11 January, George Osborne died in Bristol. A founder member of the Rovers Supporters' Club, he had served as treasurer during the dark years of the First World War. In early February, Phil 'Nipper' Britton, a key figure in the formative years of Bristolian football, died of pneumonia.

On 24 September 1921, Rovers' future home, newly developed from wartime allotments on the evocatively named Buffalo Bill's Field, was opened and named the Memorial Ground by G. B. Britton, Lord Mayor of Bristol, prior to Bristol Rugby Club's 19-3 victory over Cardiff. The land was purchased for £26,000 and dedicated to the memory of the 300 rugby players from the city who had been killed in the First World War. The president at that time of the rugby club was one Harry Willoughby Beloe, whose name is remembered in two street names in the vicinity.

1922/23

Andrew Wilson's side played out an extraordinarily unsuccessful season in 1922/23. The defence conceded only thirty-six goals in forty-two league games, a club record for over fifty years until the 1973/74 promotion season. In attack, Rovers scored just thirty-five league goals, a club record for even longer, broken only in the relegation year of 1980/81. As it was, mid-table Rovers won and lost matches in equal measure. The side also played out a club seasonal record of ten goalless draws, including three in succession around New Year.

While the forwards scored three goals in only four league matches and it took until April for an individual player to score twice in a game, the defence performed admirably all season. Goalkeeper Jesse Whatley and half-backs Sam Furniss and Walter Currie were ever-presents, while left-back Jimmy Haydon missed only one game. Whatley kept twenty-one clean sheets. Rovers lost 4-1 at Newport County and conceded three goals in a game on only four other occasions. It was a consistent defensive display not to be bettered by a Rovers side for half a century, but also one that highlighted a general trend towards lower goalscoring, which was to lead to a change in the offside rule in 1925.

During the summer of 1922, changes had been made to the pitch at Eastville. Four hundred pounds of grass seed were sown, and the pitch itself, susceptible as it was to flooding from the River Frome, was raised by 18 inches. Prior to this, children had apparently skated most winters on the frozen flooded pitch at Eastville. The price of the match-day programme was to remain 2*d*. The make-up of the Rovers side on the field was also largely unchanged, though Rovers bought a number of fringe players. Meanwhile, Billy Palmer had moved to Gillingham, from where he joined Doncaster Rovers, Tom Winsper had moved to Shrewsbury Town, Denis Howes had joined Bath City, and other players had moved locally.

Wilson returned to Sheffield Wednesday for a number of his summer signings. In defence, the fearless and tough-tackling Harold Armitage and Harold O'Neill were two such cases, while Ernie Sambidge was a naval architect who hailed from the Newcastle area. At wing-half, Walter Currie came from Scotland, while Harry Rose had been on the books of Reading. In the forward line, Fred Lunn, whose goals as the club's top scorer were, as was the case with David Mehew in 1989/90, all scored in separate games, was a former Wednesday player, while Arthur Wainwright, a fellow Yorkshireman, had played for the now defunct Leeds City. Jack Taylor and Tosh Parker were from non-League football, while Ken Boyes was the brother of a famous Hampshire cricketer. Tancy Lea, a new outside-left, was a veteran forward who had played for Wolverhampton Wanderers in the 1921 FA Cup final.

The first of many league local derbies was played at Ashton Gate in September. Whatley saved a sixty-fifth-minute penalty from Laurie Banfield, who had apparently not missed a spot-kick in the previous four seasons, and Tosh Parker's thirtieth-minute goal gave Rovers victory. The 30,000 attendance at this game contrasted starkly with the 2,000 who watched Rovers' final home game of the season, a 1-1 draw with Brentford. To typify the season, Rovers were beaten by Bristol City at Eastville only seven days after the first derby match, despite a goal from back-in-favour outside-right George Chance. The crowd at this game, again 30,000, was a new ground record, easily surpassing the estimated 20,000 at the match against Crystal Palace two years earlier. Incredible though it may sound, as many as 7,000 spectators saw Rovers reserves lose 1-0 at Ashton Gate in a Southern League game in April 1923.

Parker, joint second top scorer with Jerry Morgan on six league goals behind Lunn's ten, scored some vital goals. Four of his six, plus one at Reading in the FA Cup, earned 1-0 victories. Indeed, there was an identical story for Rovers' Cup and league visits to Elm Park. When Reading returned for a league fixture at Eastville, Rovers had a wonderful opportunity to secure a league double over the Berkshire side. Wally Hammond's second-minute goal set Rovers on the way, but inside-left Sam Jennings equalised for the visitors before half-time. Rovers' visit to Griffin Park in December, Lunn scoring the only goal of the game, was notable for the fact that both sides fielded an England international cricketer. Patsy Hendren was in the Brentford side while Hammond was to retire at the end of the season, after twenty league games and two goals, to concentrate on his blossoming career in cricket. He was to play eighty-five times for England, twenty as captain, and set an unequalled record by heading the first-class batting averages for eight consecutive seasons.

Quite clearly, goalscoring was a major failing of the club. In all four divisions, only Southport, with thirty-two league goals, scored fewer. Rovers failed to score in six consecutive games in the autumn, and in a run of five games in the New Year. In an attempt to counter this problem, Rovers signed a new centre-forward in November. Thirty-two-year-old Tom Howarth, a £500 buy from Leeds United, had also represented Bristol City either side of the First World War. He had scored a seventy-first-minute goal in the FA Cup semi-final of 1920, which the Robins lost 2-1 to Huddersfield Town. He later served a twelve-month ban imposed by the Football Association after re-signing for Bristol City while still on military service. However, this goalscoring scheme backfired, for the veteran Howarth scored just four times in twenty-one league appearances, and joined Western League Lovell's Athletic as player-manager at the end of the season.

In February, Luton Town held out for a 1-1 draw at Eastville, despite losing goalkeeper Tom Gibbon with an injury after only thirty minutes. Outside-right

Sid Hoar went in goal and conceded nothing, thanks in particular to Rovers' centre-half Jock Rutherford, who shot wide from a penalty. In April, a refereeing mistake meant that the game at Aberdare finished five minutes early. However, persuaded by a linesman, referee E. A. Hore resumed the match after a short break. Another error led to referee H. C. Curtis of London not arriving for the match at Swansea on the final day of the season. Linesman U. Jones of Ton Pentre took over with D. Sambrooke of Swansea running the line, and Rovers won 1-0 when Tosh Parker scored direct from a corner.

Just when goals appeared at a premium, inside-left Jerry Morgan doubled his tally for the season with an opportunist hat-trick at home to Norwich City. Morgan had a new left-wing partner in Durham-born Jack Pattison, and took full advantage of a hesitant Canaries defence to score three goals, one from the penalty spot. Joe Hannah, who had also scored at Eastville in 1921/22, scored once in each half for the visitors, his only two goals of the season.

An embryonic FA Cup run ended abruptly when Third Division (North) Stalybridge Celtic won in a replay at Eastville. Howarth scored for Rovers, but the former Stockport County forward Joe O'Kane and Edward Wordley were Celtic's goalscorers. The Gloucestershire Cup final was abandoned in bad light with Bristol City leading 3-1 only ten minutes from time. When the match was replayed, Rovers lost 1-0 to an extra-time goal from John Smith, who had scored City's opening goal in the original game. Smith was to reappear in the Rovers story later in his career with Plymouth Argyle and Aberdare Athletic, missing a penalty against Rovers in December 1925. A Rovers side also drew 2-2 with the North Somerset XI in November in a match that raised £35 for Paulton Hospital. The *Western Daily Press* of 11 July 1923 reported a proposed 350-yard New Road linking Eastville and Stapleton, which would cost an estimated £11,260. Work was created for eighty unemployed people for twenty-six weeks and the road was named in honour of the great local benefactor George Müller.

In September 1922, Rovers gave a trial in a reserve team game against Reading to an Egyptian engineering student at Bristol University, Mahmoud Mokhtar. His stated date of birth was 23 December 1907 in Cairo, though this appears unlikely as he represented his country in the 1920 Antwerp Olympics. 'Titch' Mokhtar also spent a fruitless trial with Tranmere Rovers, but enjoyed huge success in Egypt, and played in two further Olympics and the 1934 World Cup in Italy. Six times Egyptian player of the year, he spent seventeen seasons with National SC Cairo, seven times being the league's top scorer, and won six league championship medals and seven Egyptian Cup winners' medals. Despite his lack of success at Eastville, Mokhtar's legendary billing in his native country was such that, following his death in Cairo on 21 December 1965, the national stadium was renamed the 'Titch' Mahmoud Mokhtar Stadium.

1923/24

In scoring over fifty league goals, Andrew Wilson's Rovers side finished the season in the club's highest position to date, ninth in Division Three (South). Only forty-six goals were conceded in the league, where goalkeeper Jesse Whatley, outstanding as ever, played in every match for a second consecutive season. It was to be 1950/51 before so few goals were again conceded in a season. Besides Whatley, Rovers' other ever-present was Wilkie Phillips, a robust centre-forward signed in the close season after several years in non-League football in the Midlands. He was the club's top scorer with twenty-three goals, a figure that could have been higher had he not missed a penalty in a goalless draw at Swindon, and another at Exeter, where two penalties were awarded in the opening twelve minutes.

Phillips was ably supported in the forward line by Bill Woodhall, Ernie Whatmore and, once Tancy Lea had lost his place, Jimmy Lofthouse. A former Rotherham County outside-left, Lofthouse added stability to Rovers' left side. He was to be an ever-present in the side in 1924/25. Lofthouse scored twice in a week in December, continued Rovers' ill luck from spot-kicks when his penalty struck the crossbar during a 3-1 victory over Norwich City at Eastville in March (Phillips scored from a second penalty) and found his season prematurely ended by a broken elbow. Six players appeared at inside-left, Alec Smeaton and Jerry Morgan performing well, but Whatmore, again an influential figure the following season, was Lofthouse's most reliable partner. Woodhall, despite injury, was the second highest scorer with eleven league goals. The side was coached by Ted Jones, appointed on 21 July 1923, who was also to work for Bristol City and, from July 1938, Torquay United.

Rovers relied on a number of familiar names. Whatley was ably supported by Haydon and Armitage at full-back, with Furniss at right-half. Ernie Sambidge and Harry Rose had also appeared in the side before, while George Chance was back in favour at outside-right. One new face at half-back was the former Leeds United player Jimmy Walton, who missed just two league matches all season and scored in the game at Exeter. As the season progressed, he was joined at half-back by several former non-League players, notably Syd Smith, Frank Wragge and the inappropriately named Bob Scorer, who remained goalless in his thirty-seven league matches in two seasons at Eastville.

An otherwise consistent side was disrupted by injury, and Rovers were unable to mount a serious championship challenge. Wragge missed several weeks with a broken arm, Woodhall broke his collarbone in the home draw with Plymouth Argyle in January and was out for eleven games, while Lofthouse's broken elbow sustained against Luton Town on Easter Monday effectively ruled him out for the rest of the season. On the other hand, Swansea Town played most of the second half of their game at Eastville in April with only nine men. Robert Booth and Jimmy Collins, the latter having scored four goals against Rovers at the Vetch

Field in 1922, both left the field injured, and Rovers won 2-0. Harry O'Neill broke his arm after only fifteen minutes at Eastville, but his Swindon Town side beat Rovers through a second-half goal from centre-forward Arthur Ruddlesdin.

Twice during the season, Rovers faced a side with a makeshift goalkeeper following injury crises. Bournemouth's regular right-back Edgar Saxton played in goal during Rovers' 1-0 victory at Dean Court in December, and was beaten only by Lofthouse's oblique shot after twelve minutes. Griff James, the reserve left-half at Aberdare Athletic, was an emergency goalkeeper against Rovers in March. Rovers contrived to leave the stand-in largely untroubled, and Athletic were comfortable 2-0 winners. At Norwich in March, Rovers' opponents fielded the veteran former England international Albert Sturgess who, at forty-one years and five months, was to be the fifth oldest player to appear in any inter-war league fixture involving Bristol Rovers, and who remains the tenth oldest opponent the club has faced in the Football League.

Despite an opening-day defeat at Gillingham, Rovers were able to post their intentions with a run of four straight victories. New signing Phillips scored in all these matches, grabbing six of the side's eight goals. Further runs of results hinted at the club's potential, particularly three consecutive wins early in March when Phillips again scored in every game. However, this was instantly followed by three defeats in succession, in each case in matches Rovers could have easily won. Such a series of results necessarily undermines any championship challenge, yet so too does a proliferation of drawn matches. Rovers' early 1920s instinct for drawing games – another thirteen in the league that season and one in each cup competition – was again the side's undoing. One particular run of five draws in six matches in the New Year starved the club of the points required for success.

A convincing 4-1 win over Millwall just before Christmas was the first time in almost two years that Rovers had scored four goals in a league game. It was enough to persuade Rovers' highest crowd of the season (16,000) to visit Eastville four days later, only for the match against Reading to finish goalless. Rovers also scored four goals in the match with Watford a week before Easter. It was, of course, no surprise that Phillips and Woodhall scored three of the four goals between them on both occasions. Phillips scored three times – though never in one game – against Swansea Town, Queen's Park Rangers and Charlton Athletic, scoring in the first minute of the home game against Athletic, while Woodhall and Whatmore scored for Rovers in both victories over Brentford.

The home game against Bournemouth in January brought great concern to Eastville. At half-time, with Rovers trailing 3-2 in an exciting match, a drunken spectator assaulted referee R. R. Crump and knocked him to the ground. Although the assailant was promptly ejected from the ground, Rovers were faced with further disciplinary problems following crowd trouble at reserve games against Portsmouth and Luton Town early in 1922. On the pitch, despite a goal in each half from Woodhall, Rovers lost 4-3. Foster Robinson, a former

Coventry City outside-left, was tormentor-in-chief and fully deserved to claim Bournemouth's fourth goal fifteen minutes from time. It was the first time in over a year that Rovers had conceded four goals in a league game, a fate repeated in more devastating fashion at Watford on Easter Saturday.

Jesse Whatley, a dominant and influential figure in goal, saved a penalty from Jock Henderson of Gillingham, who had apparently scored all ten spot-kicks his side had been awarded during 1922/23. The defence again conceded relatively few goals, but Rovers lacked goals from all but Phillips and Woodhall. Once the latter was sidelined in January, it was clearly the lack of goals that proved to be the club's downfall. Nor was there any respite in the FA Cup, where Rovers made a swift exit. Whatmore's brace at Exeter City had earned a draw, but the Grecians won the replay at Eastville through a solitary goal from their centre-forward John Davis. The Gloucestershire Cup was also lost, Bristol City winning in a replay and Tot Walsh scoring in both games.

A Departmental Committee on Crowds issued a report on 13 March 1924 (Command Paper 2088) to Home Secretary, Arthur Henderson. It was recommended that terracing be subdivided into smaller enclosures, in view of safety following the perilous overcrowding at the first Wembley FA Cup final in 1923, and the death of a spectator in a crush at the Burnley *v.* Huddersfield Town FA Cup tie in February 1924. At Eastville, in line with the official recommendations, crowd barriers were staggered so as to prevent the existence of vertical gangways, the absence of which was ironically to contribute greatly to the thirty-three deaths at Bolton Wanderers' Burnden Park in March 1946.

1924/25

The mid-1920s was an era of growth in British football, and one that looked at means of improving the game. By 1924, talks were underway regarding changes to the offside law, a proposal that made common sense when viewed in conjunction with Rovers' miserly for and against columns for the two previous seasons. From the summer of 1924, players could now score direct from a corner, although several opponents claimed to have already scored against Rovers in this way. The new South Stand had been constructed over the summer at Eastville, a 2,000-seater including a paddock, dressing rooms and club offices, and Rovers responded with four straight home victories from the start of the season, with no goals conceded.

Sid Holcroft, a summer signing from Stourbridge, scored the winning goal against Merthyr Town in the first game, and, in fact, scored in each of the first five matches. The fifth of these was a 4-0 victory over Charlton Athletic at Eastville. Rovers scored three goals in a four-minute spell in the second half, with Ernie Whatmore completing his first hat-trick for the club. He and Wilkie Phillips, once

Holcroft's goals had dried up, were Rovers' joint top goalscorers with nine league goals each.

Jesse Whatley played his 100th consecutive league match in goal when Rovers beat Brentford 2-0 in November. He and outside-left Jimmy Lofthouse were the club's two ever-presents. Holcroft and outside-right Sam Edwards established themselves as regulars in a largely unaltered side. Billy Woodhall was sidelined, allowing Whatmore to lead the attack, while Frank Wragge's stabilising influence at centre-half was now more consistent. The mid-season arrival of Arthur Gibbs from Brierley Hill Athletic and Leicester City's William Thomson added defensive options, while the late season return to form of Jerry Morgan offered greater scope in attack.

Rovers enjoyed early success over that season's champions Swansea Town. A 2-2 draw in Wales was followed by a three-goal victory at Eastville; the triumvirate of Holcroft, Phillips and Whatmore scored in the opening fifteen minutes before Town's Lachlan McPherson missed a penalty. Several opponents were to miss penalties against Rovers before the season was out, while Jimmy Lofthouse's erratic record led to Jerry Morgan taking and scoring the final spot-kick of the season in the match at Reading. This fixture marked the sole appearance in a Rovers shirt of Hubert Ashton, elder brother of the erstwhile England football captain Claude Ashton. Hubert Ashton was to enjoy thirty-four years as a Conservative MP and was president of the MCC at the time of the South Africa crisis in 1960. At Elm Park, however, he was given the run-around by Belfast-born Hugh Davey, who scored a hat-trick in Reading's 4-1 victory, his only three goals of the season.

A crowd of 30,000 at Eastville in October, equalling the ground record, saw Rovers fight out a goalless draw with freshly relegated Bristol City. At the end of February, Rovers were to lose an ill-tempered return fixture at Ashton Gate. William Thomson was sent off for a foul, only the second Rovers player to suffer this fate in the league, and City scored through the ever-reliable Tot Walsh and Johnny Paul. City were to finish third in Division Three (South). Illegal play was also suspected at Eastville on Christmas Day. During the 2-1 defeat against Brighton, Wilkie Phillips appeared to score for Rovers with his hand. As with the infamous opening goal one Diego Armando Maradona scored for Argentina against England in the 1986 World Cup, the goal was allowed to stand.

Matches against Southend United were marked by dramatic starts. At The Kursaal in October, Rovers were a goal down in only two minutes, conceding a penalty that was converted by Jim McClelland. Rovers lost 2-1, despite Whatmore's goal. Only a fortnight later, Lofthouse scored a second-minute penalty awarded in Rovers' favour at Plymouth. When Southend visited Eastville in February, Ernie Edwards turned Lofthouse's cross into his own net off his knee to give Rovers a first-minute lead, before the visitors recovered to win 3-1. One of their goalscorers was Sammy Brooks, who stood just 5 feet 2½ inches; only three players shorter than him have appeared against Rovers in league action. Defeat at home to Southend prompted manager Wilson to make six changes to the side that was to travel to Gillingham.

In addition to the large win over Charlton Athletic, Rovers also won 3-0 on three occasions. Two of these came in the space of four days in March, with recalled inside-forward Jerry Morgan scoring twice in both matches. Rovers also lost 3-0 at Swindon Town, conceded four at Newport County and Reading, and were beaten 5-0 by Northampton Town, where the Cobblers scored three times in ten minutes. Louis Page, one of four brothers who represented England at baseball, scored two of these goals. It was Rovers' heaviest league defeat since the debacle at Swansea Town on Easter Saturday 1922. After centre-half Edmund Wood had opened the scoring with a rare goal, courtesy of a wicked deflection off Harry Armitage, the Cobblers' strike force of Colin Myers and Louis Page grabbed two goals apiece. The return game with Northampton was a 2-0 defeat in January, almost lost in the Eastville fog. Newspaper reporters disagree over whether the figure emerging from the shadows to score the opening goal was Ernie Cockle or Bill Poyntz. It was a precursor to the meeting between the sides in December 1928 that was decided, in dense fog, by a farcical own goal from the unfortunate Mick Cosgrove.

Rovers used only twenty-one players in the season, including three who made five league appearances between them. Not since 1907/08 had the club required the services of so few players. However, consistency did not translate into results. Despite promising early form, a dreadful run through the winter of three draws and nine defeats in twelve games, added to by a run of six games without a win in the run up to Easter, left Rovers in seventeenth place, their worst final Division Three (South) position to date. Several players were released, including Ernie Sambidge who had scored an own goal at Exeter on Easter Monday in his final game, when George Charlesworth scored his first goal for Rovers in a 1-1 draw.

Jesse Whatley was rewarded for his consistency by being given a place in the prestigious South side, which beat the North 3-1 at Stamford Bridge in January. The future Rovers player Tommy Cook scored one of the goals, and Jack Townrow, who was to arrive at Eastville in 1932, also played in this game. Whatley's commitment to the Bristol Rovers' cause was rewarded with a benefit game at Eastville in April 1925, in which Portsmouth was defeated 2-1. Simply playing in a trial match of this nature represented a major achievement for a Third Division player, although Whatley was not to win any full international honours.

Two future Rovers managers were also in the news. David McLean played for Dundee in the Scottish Cup final, while Albert Prince-Cox refereed the Gloucestershire Cup final and replay, which saw Rovers lift the trophy for the first time since 1913. In the FA Cup, where the future Rovers outside-left Jack Evans played for Cardiff City in the final, non-League Yeovil and Petters United were beaten 4-2, and Weymouth were seen off after a replay. Victory at Yeovil was secured despite an outstanding performance from the home side's outside-right

Jimmy Gardner. Rovers were so impressed that he was signed by the Eastville club at the end of the season. A goalless draw at home to Weymouth, captained by Steve Sims, a former Rovers centre-half, was not an ideal result, especially as the Dorset side had already beaten Third Division (South) Merthyr Town in the FA Cup, and Rovers relied on Whatley's penalty save from Walker before defeating the Southern League side in a replay. This set up a Bristol derby in January and the ground attendance record, equalled earlier in the season, was shattered. An Eastville crowd of 31,500, the highest there between the wars, watched Bristol City defeat Rovers with a goal from centre-forward Tot Walsh after fifty-five minutes.

1925/26

A fundamental rule change regarding offside meant that, from the start of the 1925/26 season, a forward now needed just two instead of three defenders between him and the goal. This adjustment brought the anticipated goal glut around the country. In the Football League, 4,700 goals had been scored in 1924/25, but 6,373 were scored in 1925/26. Several individuals were able to benefit greatly in the late 1920s, most notably Middlesbrough's George Camsell, who hit fifty-nine goals in only thirty-seven league matches in 1926/27. So it was that Rovers scored sixty-six times in the league in 1925/26, and yet finished the season in nineteenth place in Division Three (South), the club's lowest final league placing since entering the Football League.

With Wilkie Phillips contributing only three league goals, the main onus for goalscoring fell on new signing Jonah Wilcox, a May signing from New Brighton. Wilcox responded with nineteen goals, including four against Bournemouth on Boxing Day, to finish the season as the club's top scorer. Jimmy Gardner from Yeovil and Petters United, and Worcester City's Bill Wilson were also new faces in the side. A number of other signings enjoyed only brief spells in an ever-changing team. Alex Crichton, Albert Rotherham, Andrew Dick and Alf Bowers all featured in the half-back line, while Stafford Rangers' Charles Heinemann, the son of an England rugby international, started the season at inside-right.

Wilcox scored on his debut at Charlton Athletic when the club's train was held up in holiday traffic and Rovers were forced to hire a fleet of taxis to reach the ground in time. When Ernie Whatmore appeared for the third game, he and Wilcox both scored and the season was up and running. Gillingham's goalkeeper in this match was Alex Ferguson, whose final league appearance against Rovers was to be over twenty-one years later in the Bristol City side, which won 3-0 at Eastville in September 1946. Whatmore was second-highest scorer with eleven league goals, Lofthouse scored nine and both Holcroft and mid-season signing Willie Culley, a highly experienced leader of the attack who had won a Scottish Cup winners' medal with Kilmarnock, scored hat-tricks. Holcroft's three in a

5-0 thrashing of Queen's Park Rangers in October were his first for over a year. Culley, who had played in the 1920 Scottish Cup final for Kilmarnock, scoring the opening goal in a 3-2 victory over Albion Rovers, joined from Weymouth and his hat-trick led Rovers to a 4-2 victory on Good Friday over Reading, who were divisional champions that season.

The home encounter with Bournemouth on Boxing Day was the first time Rovers had scored seven in a league fixture. Two strikes in the first five minutes from Albert Burnell, who only scored three times in his Rovers career, sparked a flood of goals. Rovers, 4-1 up by half-time, won 7-2, with Jonah Wilcox equalling Sid Leigh's club record of four goals in a league game. Two of Wilcox's goals were penalties, both scored in the final ten minutes; he became the first Rovers player to score two penalties in a league match, a record first equalled by Jackie Pitt in 1948. Both Bournemouth's goals were scored by Ron Eyre, his first against Rovers. He was to score a total of fifteen league goals against the club in his long career, plus another in an abandoned game in December 1929, more than any other opponent in Rovers' history.

Rovers lost twenty-one league games that season, the heaviest being a 6-3 defeat at Gillingham, for whom Fred Brown scored a hat-trick. Former Rovers full-back Harry O'Neill, from the penalty spot, scored the only league goal of his career to give Swindon Town a 2-1 victory at Eastville. In the away fixture, Swindon Town had led 4-0 with only ten minutes remaining, before late Lofthouse and Whatmore goals lent the final scoreline a touch of respectability. Rovers, with full-back Harry Armitage off the field injured by half-time in this his final league game, lost 3-1 to a strong Newport County side. In fact, Rovers had scraped a draw at home to the same opposition after Whatley, with Newport already 2-0 ahead, saved a penalty that would have given John Davis his hat-trick.

In September, Rovers played at Luton in Mission Week and Rt Revd Michael Furse, the Bishop of St Albans, gave an address to the crowd before the match. In the return game at Eastville, Luton lost two men injured while David Richards played on for thirty minutes with a broken right leg; Rovers again fought back from two goals down, a late goal from Tom Williams earning a 2-2 draw. With Rovers a goal ahead through Whatmore after twenty minutes, Aberdare Athletic's goalkeeper Brown was injured five minutes after half-time in their December match. Tom Brophy, a full-back, went in goal, and Rovers clung on for victory after Athletic's John Smith and David James both missed penalties. It was Rovers' only league victory at the Athletic Ground, and in the return game in May, Jesse Whatley's own goal contributed to a 3-0 win for Aberdare.

One game that typified Rovers' goalscoring potential was the 4-0 home victory over Brighton, where Wilcox and Whatmore scored twice each. Whatmore and Wilcox both scored again when Rovers won the return fixture 3-2, with Brighton's Bill Little scoring twice from the penalty spot. However, there were still sufficient off days to cause concern. Successive away goalless draws at Bristol City and Millwall in November, on top of one run of eight matches and one of seven without a win, showed work needed to be done. The draw at The Den was played in somewhat sombre circumstances, both sides wearing black armbands as a mark of respect for Alexandra, the Queen Mother and widow of Edward VII, who had died twenty-four hours earlier.

A series of late season purchases improved Rovers' lot, and seven wins in the final thirteen league matches certainly staved off the ignominy of seeking re-election. Two of Culley's former Weymouth teammates broke into the side. Scotsman George Lennon, an £80 signing from the Southern League side, had previous league experience with Luton Town and Stoke City, while Welsh centre-half Ivor Stallard offered cover for Bill Wilson. Full-back Lew Griffiths was signed for £60 from Mid Rhondda United, but it was local nineteen-year-old Fred Bennett who succeeded to Armitage's right-back role. Griffiths joined with the highly experienced Tom Williams, whose long career included a dependable two-and-a-half-year stay at Eastville.

As Rovers hovered above the re-election position, Andrew Wilson attempted to rescue his inconsistent side. Inexperienced outside-left Jabez Foster, for instance, was given three games, and his goal against Charlton Athletic was greeted with genuinely warm enthusiasm. Yet only 5,000 watched this game at Eastville, poor in comparison with the 28,500 that had seen Tot Walsh's eighty-second minute penalty, awarded after Wragge had brought down Charlie Sutherland, a survivor from Rovers' inaugural Football League game in August 1920. When the season finished with Rovers safe by a point, Wilson resigned. He subsequently became manager at Oldham Athletic and Stockport County.

Rovers took little time in appointing Bradford Park Avenue's trainer Joe Palmer on 21 April 1926. Although a Yorkshireman, Palmer was the first man to manage both Bristol's professional clubs. He was a strong disciplinarian and placed great emphasis on physical fitness. During his three years with Bristol City, the Robins had reached the semi-finals of the FA Cup in 1920, and he had been immensely popular with the Ashton Gate crowd. The close season of 1926 saw the release of fifteen players who had appeared in league action for Rovers, ten to league clubs north or south of the border and five to senior non-League sides. Queen's Park Rangers, for instance, signed Bowers, Charlesworth, Lofthouse and Wilcox free of charge. The new season was to see a fresh start.

Once again, cup competitions had brought little cheer to Eastville. Rovers crashed 4-1 to Bristol City in the Gloucestershire Cup final, and by the same score to Aberdare Athletic in the FA Cup. This heavy defeat at the Athletic Ground was brought about by two former Portsmouth players, the veteran Jack Harwood scoring the first goal before Harry Burnham compiled a well-taken fifteen-minute second-half hat-trick.

1926/27

It was a busy summer for Joe Palmer as he constructed a new-look Bristol Rovers side. Four new half-backs and five forwards were signed in the close season, leaving just the defensive line retaining its familiar look. The key element in Rovers' ongoing progress, goalkeeper Jesse Whatley, as dependable and reliable as ever, was once again the club's only ever-present. In front of him, Fred Bennett and Jimmy Haydon formed a consistent full-back pairing. Of the old guard elsewhere on the pitch, only Tom Roberts, Tom Williams and Ernie Whatmore made any sizeable impact.

One familiar face in the side was Steve Sims, Rovers' captain in their first league season. His return from Bristol City was a popular one, and his winning goal at Bournemouth in October was his first for the club in over four years. Left-half Len Smith had experienced league action with Leeds United, while a combined total of £750 bought Coventry City's Joe Rowley and thirty-year-old Jimmy Forbes from Bolton Wanderers. Age was certainly no barrier, for Palmer signed two thirty-seven-year-old forwards in Stoke's Joe Clennell and the former Welsh international Jack Evans from Cardiff City. Thirty-three-year-old George Douglas from Oldham Athletic cost £100, as did Clennell. Halifax Town's Tommy Duncan, Merthyr Town's Jack Rumney and outside-left Joe Barrett, who joined from Lincoln City in an exchange deal involving Harry Armitage, could all boast considerable league experience. By the end of the season, Rovers' regular forward line of Clennell and Evans (both thirty-eight), Willie Culley (thirty-four), Douglas (thirty-three) and Duncan, a mere youth at twenty-nine, could boast a combined age of 172.

Recent changes in the offside law were slowly leading to a far higher rate of goals. Finishing the season mid-table, Rovers scored and conceded more goals than in any previous season in the Football League. While scoring at least once in sixteen out of twenty-one away league fixtures, Rovers also scored reliably at home. The 2-0 home defeat against Watford in December was the last time Rovers failed to score in a match at Eastville in any competition until February 1928. Culley's twenty-six goals in only thirty-one league appearances included three hat-tricks, while Williams and Whatmore each scored three times in a game.

Culley scored his first hat-trick of the season in a 5-2 home victory over Northampton Town in February, Joe Clennell claiming the other two. In Rovers' next home fixture, the Scottish forward went one better, scoring all the club's goals in a convincing 4-1 win against Queen's Park Rangers. In doing so, Culley equalled the Rovers' individual goalscoring record – held by Sid Leigh and Jonah Wilcox – of four goals in a league fixture. On Good Friday, with the aid of a penalty, his third hat-trick of the season helped Rovers to a 5-3 win at Swindon Town, for whom sixteen-year-old forward Charlie Jeffries scored twice in a four-minute spell before half-time. A brace of goals in the return game three days later meant Culley became the first of six Rovers players to score five league goals against any particular club in a season.

Ably supporting Culley were fourteen-goal Williams and eleven-goal Whatmore. Williams' greatest game for Rovers was the visit to Millwall in October when, recalled to the side, he scored his first three goals of the season to give the Lilywhites a 3-2 win. This was the first time a Rovers player had scored a hat-trick in an away league game, and was one of only four such cases prior to 1953. Whatmore narrowly missed out on a hat-trick at Plymouth Argyle in March, before scoring one in the final home game of the season. At Home Park, having scored twice, he ended up in goal with Jesse Whatley off injured. Rovers lost 3-2. A first-half hat-trick against Crystal Palace, the first one deflecting in off Henry Hopkins, helped the side to score four goals before half-time in both league fixtures against the London side. Rovers scored three times in a six-minute spell in the home fixture.

There were also heavy defeats. Rovers lost 5-0 at Eastville against Bristol City, a devastating result from a psychological point of view. City were to be Third Division (South) champions that season. Conceding two penalties at Brighton for a second consecutive season, Rovers lost 7-0 at the Goldstone Ground. On his sole league appearance, James Kedens, a miner's son from the Ayrshire pit village of Glenburn, almost put Rovers ahead in the opening seconds, but Paul Mooney scored from one of the penalties after Bill Little had missed the first. James Hopkins compiled a hat-trick and there was a goal for the future Rovers forward Tommy Cook.

The 3-0 defeat at Northampton Town in September saw the Cobblers field the thirty-eight-year-old former Spurs outside-right 'Fanny' Walden. At 5 feet 2½ inches, Frederick Ingram Walden remains the fourth shortest opponent to face Rovers in league football. He played football for England and, after twenty summers of cricket with Northamptonshire, was umpire in eleven Test matches between 1934 and 1939. Rovers also crashed 2-0 at Gillingham in March. In severe wind and rain, both sides agreed to forfeit their half-time break and play on. The Gills, who recalled Jabez Foster, briefly a member of Rovers' league side at the tail end of the previous season, won with two Bill Arblaster goals, the second deflecting in off the luckless Jimmy Haydon.

The season's most bizarre result was from the visit to Crystal Palace in March. Rovers rushed to a 3-0 lead inside seventeen minutes, with Culley scoring after only six minutes and Rowley four minutes later, before Williams had given the visitors an apparently unassailable lead. However, Palace retaliated with two quick goals, the future Bristol City striker Cyril Blakemore making the score 3-2 with just twenty-five minutes played. Culley's second goal of the game gave Rovers a 4-2 half-time lead, before Palace responded with five goals to win an extraordinary game 7-4.

Two missed penalties (by Barratt, who always played with a straw in his mouth, and Douglas) in the home games with Watford and Northampton Town respectively detracted from Rovers' 'goals for' total. On the other hand, four penalties conceded by Rovers were taken by players called Brown. The first, in August, was saved from Henry Brown by Whatley at Penydarren Park, but Rovers, 2-0 ahead at one stage, slipped to a 3-2 defeat, with George Pither scoring Merthyr's second against his former club. Both Rovers' goals were scored by Jack Rumney, making his club debut against his former side. Then there were three penalties in four days over the Easter period. Alfred Brown of Swindon Town scored one on Good Friday but missed one on Easter Monday, while the penalty converted by Gillingham's Fred Brown on Easter Saturday, following his hat-trick the previous season, served merely as a consolation goal, Rovers winning 2-1.

Of Rovers' seventy-eight league goals, five were scored on three occasions and four on five occasions. Two 4-0 home victories were recorded over Welsh opponents. Aberdare Athletic were comfortably defeated in November, Whatmore scoring twice. Newport County were also victims of a heavy defeat, with Tom Williams scoring two of the four goals, one within seconds of the restart after half-time. Culley's kick-off reached Douglas, also a goalscorer, whose through pass was smashed into the goal by Williams. Culley scored a brilliant winner ten minutes from time as Rovers clawed back a two-goal deficit to defeat FA Cup holders Sheffield United 3-2 in an Eastville friendly in February.

The Gloucestershire Cup final was lost 4-0, Tot Walsh scoring twice, once from a penalty, exactly as he had done for Bristol City in the league meeting at Eastville. The FA Cup saw Rovers grab a draw at Plainmoor when Barratt equalised three minutes from time. They then defeated non-League Torquay United, unbeaten in their previous twelve home games, in an untidy first round replay thanks to Williams' goal a minute before half-time. Torquay, who fielded the former Rovers outside-left Bill Pattison and future Rovers centre-half Ivor Perry, missed a penalty, given against Ashford for handball, when Whatley saved a Harry Hughes' spot-kick. A 5,000 crowd saw the Gulls' Harold Andrews sent off fifteen minutes from time. Culley scored twice past the future Rovers goalkeeper Charles Preedy in a 4-1 win over Charlton Athletic, and twice more as Rovers led First Division Portsmouth 3-1 with minutes to go. The 25,000 Eastville crowd was denied a momentous victory, however, as Pompey recovered to draw 3-3 before winning the replay – Billy Haines and David Watson scored in both matches.

Rovers were also successful in the Allan Palmer Cup, an invitation competition first staged in 1924 and set up by Brigadier-General George Llewellen Palmer and his wife Louie Madeleine Gouldsmith, in memory of their son, a captain in the 14th Hussars, who was killed at Amiens on 15 November 1916. Joe Clennell's goal brought victory over holders Bristol City and the right to defend the trophy twelve months later.

1927/28

Palmer's second season as Bristol Rovers manager saw the side plummet to nineteenth in Division Three (South). Successful runs over Christmas and Easter were enough to keep the club's collective head above water, but it was nonetheless a poor season. Rovers conceded a then club record ninety-three league goals, a figure only surpassed in the 1935/36 season. It was only in the relegation season of 1980/81 that Rovers equalled the twenty-four league defeats suffered that year. While the small tally of only four draws in 1927/28 remains a seasonal low for Rovers, fourteen league victories was a commendable total.

The side that defeated Walsall 5-2 on an encouraging opening day at Eastville, with Willie Culley contributing a cameo hat-trick, contained no new faces to Rovers fans. However, a couple of defeats prompted the introduction of several summer signings. Syd Homer, all 5 feet 3 inches of him at outside-right, was to serve Rovers well until November 1929 and Bristol City better thereafter. Full-back Jack Russell had represented Birmingham City in league football and had recently recovered from almost a year out of the game with a fractured leg. Jack Thom, who cost £175 from Leeds United, Ivor Perry, Reg Trotman and Roy Davies all had roles to play. Of the previous season's side, Joe Clennell joined Rochdale, Steve Sims moved to Newport County and Joe Barratt dropped out of league football to sign for Nuneaton Town. Club chairman George Humphreys retired in August 1927 and was elected president, a post he held until his death in 1939.

Rovers went on to concede four or more league goals in a game on ten occasions. Four different opponents scored at Brentford, who won 5-1, and at Brighton, where a 5-0 scoreline included two goals for the future Rovers centre-forward Tommy Cook. Frank Sloan scored a hat-trick in a 4-1 defeat at Plymouth Argyle, the first of three opponents to do so in ten weeks. As if indulging in some inter-war pathetic fallacy, a *Western Daily Press* reporter, at the home defeat to Brentford in September, recorded that 'it was Bristol Rovers weather last evening – that is, it was raining'. The worst defeat, however, was 6-1 on Christmas Eve at home to Millwall. Wilkie Phillips returned to his old club to score twice, while Perry conceded an own goal.

At St James Park on Guy Fawkes' Day, Fred Dent equalled the achievement of Swansea Town's Jimmy Collins by scoring all Exeter City's goals in Rovers' 4-1 defeat. Dent scored after six and twelve minutes, and although Tom Williams pulled a goal back eight minutes later, the former Bristol City forward completed a first-half hat-trick ten minutes before the break. Just nine minutes from time he completed the Grecians' scoring. On the same day, Rovers reserves had led their Exeter counterparts at half-time through a Roy Davies goal, only to lose 5-1. Culley missed a penalty, before he and Albert Rotherham both conceded own goals. The following Saturday, Rovers recovered to draw 2-2 with Northampton

Town, who had beaten Walsall 10-0 seven days earlier. Gillingham, with a quick three-goal burst, and Queen's Park Rangers, with Jonah Wilcox scoring from a Jimmy Lofthouse cross, both scored four at Eastville.

In October, the month that pre-war club favourite Alf Jasper Geddes died, Rovers conceded four goals at both Queen's Park Rangers and Norwich City. The Canaries had led 3-2 by half-time. The Rangers game, in which George Goddard scored a hat-trick, marked the debut of new £350 signing Arthur Ormston. This much-travelled centre-forward had attained almost legendary status at Boundary Park after scoring eight goals in his first two appearances for Oldham Athletic. He was to finish the season as Rovers' top scorer with fifteen league goals. Ormston scored twice in a tempestuous home debut, where Rovers had built up a seemingly unassailable 4-1 lead, with Williams and Russell scoring for the home side and inside-right Maurice Wellock replying for Torquay United. However, the final twenty minutes were chaotic, with several bookings and an official admonishment for the crowd. One particularly bad tackle earned Rovers a penalty, Ormston eschewing the opportunity of a hat-trick and leaving the kick to Russell, whose second goal earned Rovers a 5-1 victory.

Goals were plentiful, with Rovers scoring in all but one home game and not keeping a clean sheet until March. Even Jimmy Haydon's well-earned testimonial, played against Bristol City at Eastville in October, finished in a 3-3 draw. Over Christmas, Rovers completed a league double over Merthyr Town. Russell, who scored inside the first minute in the home game, and Welsh forward Albert Mays contributed goals in both fixtures. The meeting at Penydarren Park on Boxing Day was watched by only 1,000 spectators, the lowest crowd to see a league match involving Rovers.

An astonishing flurry of goals highlighted the game at Bournemouth earlier in December. There were six goals in a remarkable fifteen-minute spell before half-time. Three times Bournemouth had taken the lead, only for Rovers to peg them back. Ron Eyre scored twice for Bournemouth, although Rovers claimed his second had not crossed the line. When Patrick Clifford put the home side in front for a third time, thirty-seven-year-old Willie Culley responded almost instantly with his second goal of the game. Theophilus Pike played against Rovers on a number of occasions for Southend United, Norwich City and Bournemouth, but his second-half match-winning goal for the Cherries was the only time he scored against Rovers. Seven days later, Rovers returned to Dean Court only to concede four first-half goals and crash 6-1 in an FA Cup tie, the indomitable Eyre scoring again.

By March, Palmer was working to maintain Rovers' position in Division Three (South). Three Scottish players, Alf King, Fleming Falconer and John Paterson, were encouraged south of the border. The game against Charlton Athletic saw Rovers plunge Bristol-born fifteen-year-old inside-forward Ronnie Dix into the starting line-up. He remains the only player to have appeared for Rovers in league football before his sixteenth birthday. Although not the youngest-ever player in the league, he became the youngest to score a Football League goal – a record that stands to this day – when he scored Rovers' second goal with a rasping drive twenty minutes from the end of a convincing 3-0 home victory over Norwich City. Dix, who had also set up Ormston for the fortieth-minute opening goal, later hit the bar. The Norwich City game also represented Rovers' first clean sheet in the league for thirteen months.

On Easter Monday, Jesse Whatley made the last of his club-record 246 consecutive league appearances in goal. After the 1-1 draw with Crystal Palace, he stepped aside to allow Bert Densley to appear in the final six league matches of the season. A measure of Rovers' problems was that, apart from Whatley, only Fred Bennett, Jimmy Haydon and Jim Forbes appeared in over thirty league games. Rovers fielded an experienced but ageing side. At thirty-seven years of age, Culley was the side's second highest scorer. Jack Evans' goal in the first-half goal rush at Dean Court meant, at thirty-eight years 306 days, he became the oldest scorer of a league goal for Bristol Rovers.

Lack of success in the FA Cup was mirrored in the Allan Palmer Cup where Rovers, as holders, played Exeter City at Trowbridge. Billy Vaughan, once an inside-forward for Rovers, played for the Grecians, and his teammate Billy McDevitt scored the only goal after twenty minutes. Defeated, Rovers were nonetheless to regain this trophy on three further occasions in the 1920s. On the success side, the former Rovers half-back David Steele was in the Huddersfield Town side that reached the FA Cup final. Arthur Ormston's goal was enough for Rovers to recapture the Gloucestershire Cup, defeating Bristol City at Eastville.

1928/29

During the summer of 1928, Alf Homer stepped down as secretary, ending an association that dated back to 1899. His days as manager had seen the club achieve some success, so it is a disappointing parallel that what was to be Joe Palmer's final season in this role could not live up to expectations. There was a large element of inconsistency about Rovers. Only goalkeeper Jesse Whatley missed one game, Fred Bennett and Mick Cosgrove appeared in more than thirty league games, while twenty-eight players were used in all. Reserve goalkeeper Bert Densley suffered the misfortune of scoring an own goal against Newport County in his only appearance of the season, and Rovers conceded six at Fulham and Bournemouth as well as five on Boxing Day at Crystal Palace.

Jack Evans retired as a player in 1928, and a number of his teammates moved to other league clubs. Ernie Whatmore joined Queen's Park Rangers, Reg Trotman moved to Rochdale and Willie Culley signed up for Swindon Town, while Tom Williams made the short journey to Ashton Gate. Many more players moved into non-League football. Jim Forbes became player-coach at Workington, taking with him Jack Thom and John McKenna. Joe Rowley spent the 1928/29 season at Oswestry Town, George Douglas at Tunbridge Wells Rangers, Jack Russell at Worcester City and Roy Davies at Ebbw Vale.

Palmer turned north of the border to buy players. Three Raith Rovers players, including George Barton, a rare example of a full-back who scored on his league debut, were joined by three former Aberdeen teammates. One of these, Mick Cosgrove, was a veteran of English, Scottish and American football, while Tom Price had been Cardiff City's twelfth man for the 1927 FA Cup final. Billy Compton joined from Exeter City, Wattie White from Reading, Bert Turner from Torquay United and Maurice Dando from Bath City. The returning hero, however, was Joe Walter, who had left Eastville in 1922 to win a league championship medal with Huddersfield Town. His comeback game, on Christmas Day 1928 against Crystal Palace, attracted a crowd of 15,000, easily the club's highest home attendance of the season.

For the second consecutive season, Rovers finished nineteenth in Division Three (South). Yet, surprisingly, Rovers did the double over champions Charlton Athletic. Although Wilson Lennox scored a first-minute goal at The Valley in March, two Athletic defenders, Norman Smith and Albert Langford, scored own goals to give Rovers a 2-1 victory. Five weeks later, goals from Syd Homer, Dando and King earned Rovers a 3-0 win at Eastville. King certainly scored some timely goals. One came in the 5-3 victory over Fulham, the only time all season Rovers scored five goals in a game. He also scored the best goal of the season, finishing off a sweeping five-man move during the 4-1 victory at home to Southend United in March.

George Barton may have scored five goals from full-back, all of them penalties, but Rovers' top scorer was Jack Phillips. At the end of September, after a crushing defeat at Fulham, Rovers paid Brentford £450 for their centre-forward, and his thirteen league goals were almost double the total of any other player. Rovers had lost 6-1 at Craven Cottage to a mediocre Fulham side, hitting an uncharacteristic glut of goals – twenty-four in five games. Fred Avey, the Essex 2nd XI cricketer who was to score a hat-trick against Rovers in November 1930, scored twice.

Conceding goals was no longer a burning issue, but Rovers did concede six at Bournemouth, where the evergreen Ron Eyre scored a hat-trick and Percy Cherrett added one. Rovers also conceded five at Palace and four on five other occasions. In April, Rovers were a goal down in the opening seconds at Somerton Park, Jimmy Gittins scoring for Newport County. Harry Morris scored a hat-trick at Eastville in December, as Swindon Town won 4-1. This game, Cliff Britton's first league appearance for Rovers, was also one of three penalties missed in quick succession. In Barton's absence, Albert Rotherham missed one for Rovers. The visiting full-back Walter Dickinson then found his kick saved by Whatley, though he successfully converted the rebound. Jack Phillips then missed Rovers' second penalty. Rotherham never did score a league goal for Rovers, this being his final home appearance, but he did convert a penalty against Wellingborough in the FA Cup, after Rovers had trailed to a tenth-minute goal.

Quite apart from the Swindon game, December witnessed some unusual matches. Rovers had acquired the services of David Murray, a twenty-six-year-old South African international, who had played for Bristol City and arrived at Eastville as player-coach. At home to Norwich City, his early goal was a prelude to one from John Paterson and Rovers found themselves 2-0 ahead after only six minutes – they held on to win by the same scoreline. The next home game was won by the Cobblers 2-1 at an increasingly foggy Eastville, their winning goal coming from a bizarre mix-up. Mick Cosgrove passed gently back to his goalkeeper but, in the fog, Whatley could not see the ball and Rovers had conceded one of the most farcical of goals. In the following home fixture, it was the celebrated Ernie Toseland who gave high-flying Coventry City the lead en route to a 2-0 victory.

Another own goal conceded by Rovers led to one of the largest wins of the season. Fair-haired David McCaig, the former Raith Rovers right-half, put through his own net, but four Rovers players got on the scoresheet at the right end as Walsall were beaten 4-1 in September. Southend United were defeated by the same score, while Brighton, Charlton Athletic, Queen's Park Rangers and Merthyr Town were all beaten 3-0. A 2-0 win over Brentford in October proved to be the first of the Bees' club record nine consecutive league defeats. On Easter Saturday, Rovers drew 2-2 with Exeter City at St James' Park. The Grecians' first goal was scored by Harold Houghton, later a Rovers player, and the second by the seventeen-year-old future England international Cliff Bastin, whose shot deflected in off Murray.

Peter Holland of Watford and Norwich City's Wilf Greenwell both missed penalties against Rovers, but Newport County's Sammy Richardson was more fortunate. Having missed his penalty, he was pleased to see the referee order a retake, from which he duly scored. Southend United's Tom Brophy, who had spent forty minutes as an emergency goalkeeper against Rovers in December 1925, broke his arm during his side's single-goal victory over Rovers in November, following an accidental collision with his teammate Jimmy Frew. Merthyr fielded Jack Page over Easter, eight days short of his forty-third birthday and still the second oldest opponent to face Rovers in league action. The reserve game against Plymouth Argyle reserves in October proved eventful. The visiting centre-half Bill Pullen was sent off the field and, refusing to go, twice punched referee A. J. Attwood.

Rovers lost in the Gloucestershire Cup final 2-0 to Bristol City, Tom Williams returning to haunt his former side with the second goal. An FA Cup win over Wellingborough, during which game Len Smith broke his leg, simply led to defeat at Crystal Palace, whose third goal was scored by Henry Havelock, a brother of Jack Havelock, who joined Rovers from Folkestone in 1933. The form of young

Cliff Britton, whose eighteen league games marked the start of a glorious career, was a rare glimmer of hope in a larger, more depressing picture. Britton was 'never the most robust of men, but a football stylist' (Archie Ledbrooke and Edgar Turner, *Soccer from the Press Box*). Joe Palmer resigned as manager at the season's end and was speedily replaced by David McLean. The new Rovers manager had enjoyed many years with East Fife, with whom he had appeared in the 1927 Scottish Cup final and was later to guide to victory in the Scottish Cup final of 1938 before taking the helm at Hearts. McLean accepted a weekly wage of £10 and became the fifth full-time manager of Bristol Rovers.

1929/30

The new manager had made significant changes to his side. Billy Compton and the veteran Joe Walter joined Bath City, while Bert Turner moved to Brierley Hill Athletic. Len Smith and Albert Rotherham, the latter attracting a £100 fee, moved to Merthyr Town and Coventry City respectively. Rovers signed one Scot – Jock Hamilton from Penicuik – and two from the North East, Bob Plenderleith, a £150 buy from Sunderland, and the experienced Wally Gillespie for £300 from Newcastle United. Gilbert Shaw had league experience with Grimsby Town and the veteran left-half Tom Wolfe arrived from Charlton Athletic.

For all these transactions, it was a local nineteen-year-old, Cecil Thomas, who scored the only goal on his debut when Rovers beat Brighton. This result offered false hope. Rovers were to win only two of the opening fifteen league matches. Somehow the side was able to snatch mediocrity from the jaws of success. Merthyr Town, for instance, in their final league season, won twenty-one points and conceded 135 goals in forty-two games. Rovers drew both matches with the South Walian club. Gillingham were gifted two very late goals to snatch a 3-3 draw. Rovers lost twenty-three games in the league, conceded a then club record of ninety-three goals and finished twentieth in Division Three (South), the worst final placing to date.

Perhaps the most entertaining afternoon was when Rovers played the leaders Brentford at Griffin Park in September. The team's charabanc hit an electric standard on its way to the ground, and although no one was injured, three windows were smashed and delays were inevitable. Jack Phillips put Rovers ahead, and after Brentford's former Bristol City forward Cyril Blakemore missed a penalty, Rovers led 1-0 with ten minutes remaining. However, Bill Lane equalised and Jackie Foster, another who had previously been at the Ashton Gate club, scored direct from a corner. Rovers lost 2-1 and Brentford went on to win all twenty-one home league games that season.

Yet Rovers' struggle can be traced directly to the fact that for the second time in three years, ninety-three Division Three (South) goals were conceded. It was an uncharacteristic end to Jesse Whatley's decade in the Rovers goal. Shortly before Easter, Ted Bowen's hat-trick, which included a penalty, eased Northampton Town to a 6-1 victory over Rovers. He was to repeat this feat in 1930/31. Two weeks after the trip to Northampton, Rovers crashed 6-0 to Southend United, Fred Baron scoring twice in the opening thirteen minutes, securing a first-half hat-trick and four goals in all. Bill Haley scored a Christmas Day hat-trick as Fulham, 4-1 up by half-time, also put six goals past Rovers. Tom Wells scored three times at Eastville in November, Northampton Town forwards thus scoring hat-tricks in both league fixtures against Rovers. Exeter City scored four goals in the opening twelve minutes, the first by the future Rovers inside-forward Harry Houghton. George Guyan and Cyril Hemingway scored twice each as the Grecians won 5-2 at St James' Park.

There were some far better performances, of course. Twenty-four hours after the heavy defeat at Craven Cottage, Rovers defeated Fulham 4-1. It was the third consecutive home game in which Rovers had scored four times, Rovers scoring twenty-three goals and conceding twenty-eight in a run of nine league games. Jack Phillips, the first Rovers player to top twenty league goals since Willie Culley, scored a fine hat-trick in a 4-1 victory over Queen's Park Rangers. In the final game of the season, with safety assured, Rovers ran up an identical scoreline against Brentford, with Ronnie Dix, after a two-year gap following his celebrated goal, back on the scoresheet in these and three other games early in 1930.

Rovers, though, had an abysmal away record. They were the only club in the four divisions of the Football League not to win away all season. A poor start, including a four-goal defeat at Norwich City, led to that 3-3 draw at Gillingham in November, a match of six goalscorers – Murray and Shaw scored in both games against the Kent side. Thereafter, Rovers lost a club record thirteen consecutive away league fixtures. The run only ended in a goalless draw at Walsall in the final away game, before a club record-equalling lowest league crowd at a Rovers game of only 1,000, once the shadow of potential re-election had finally receded. During this run, Densley conceded six at Northampton and Southend, five at Exeter, four at Watford and three at Luton Town and Crystal Palace, where Rovers played the final hour with ten men after an injury to Fred Bennett. Whatley conceded six at Fulham and three at Plymouth, Newport, Bournemouth and Orient. These were dismal days for Bristol Rovers.

Watford's 4-3 victory in February was against a Rovers side who played out sixty-five minutes with only ten men after Cliff Britton's early injury. The veteran wing-half Neil McBain scored one of the goals and was to become, in March 1947, the oldest player in the history of the Football League when he appeared as an emergency goalkeeper for New Brighton against Hartlepool United at the age of fifty-one. Unsurprisingly, McBain was the only player born in the nineteenth century to appear in league football after the Second World War. The previous week, Jock Hamilton had scored for both sides in the 3-2 defeat at home to

Newport County. Frank Womack, who holds the Football League record for most appearances as an outfield player while never scoring, appeared at the age of forty-one in Torquay colours against Rovers in April.

One rare home victory, in April, was achieved over Bournemouth, despite a missed penalty from the normally dependable Jimmy Haydon. Rovers' regular left-back was, with Reay and Phillips, one of three players who missed only four games each all season. Twenty-seven players were used as Rovers struggled to find a regular combination and battled to combat their lack of success away from home. Whatley's twenty-six league appearances for Rovers brought his career total to 386 by the time of his retirement at the end of the season. He had been a wonderful servant of the Eastville club throughout the first decade of league action.

Rovers lost the Gloucestershire Cup final to Bristol City in a replay. Syd Homer, a former Rovers outside-right, scored one of the goals and was to score again in this fixture in 1930/31 and 1932/33. In the FA Cup, Rovers survived the potential banana skin of taking their dubious away record to non-League minnows, Nunhead, destined for the Isthmian League championship that season. Two George Reay goals helped Rovers to a comfortable 4-1 home victory over Third Division (North) Accrington Stanley. The Peel Park side replied with a goal from inside-right Danny Ferguson. The third-round game at Clapton Orient was a dull affair that hinged on two penalties. Ronnie Dix, Rovers' teenage inside-forward, missed from his kick, while Orient's Albert Lyons, seeing Whatley save his penalty, scored from the rebound for the only goal of the game. The FA Cup winners, Arsenal, included in their side the future Rovers goalkeeper Charles Preedy and left-back Eddie Hapgood who, rejected by Rovers as a youngster, enjoyed a long and successful career with Arsenal and England and appeared in three FA Cup finals.

Over the summer of 1930, the Stapleton Road end of the pitch was reseeded and Rovers' officials set about rebuilding the side into one that could do justice to its potential in the Football League. Wing-half Cliff Britton moved to Everton in June, where he was to become one of the leading lights of his generation, winning domestic honours and England caps before embarking on a successful managerial career. He was generally accepted as the pioneer of the slide-rule pass, and helped to revolutionise football tactics in much the same way as Don Revie was to do some twenty years later. Reliable full-back Fred Bennett was also allowed to leave the club after 128 league appearances, joining Third Division (North) side Chester, although he subsequently returned to live and work in Bristol. The biggest loss to Rovers, however, was the retirement of the veteran goalkeeper Jesse Whatley after 386 league appearances over a decade of reliable service. He was to be an active member of the club's former players' association for many years and kept in close contact with Bristol Rovers right up to his death in March 1982.

1930/31

Following Rovers' lowest final league position in a decade of Third Division football, the pressure was on manager David McLean's side to perform more consistently in the season ahead. Wholesale changes to the side gave the promise of better things to come. Indeed, only left-back Jimmy Haydon, who retired in the summer of 1931, and left-half Jock Hamilton, of the previous season's players, were to appear in the opening game of the season. Rovers also played for this season in unfamiliar blue shirts and white shorts.

Rovers, with their nine debutants, crashed to a 4-1 defeat in blazing sunshine at home to Northampton in that first game. Centre-forward Joe Pointon, highly experienced at this level with several clubs, scored Rovers' goal from the penalty spot, but it proved to be his only goal for the club. He was to miss a penalty in the game against Gillingham. On the other hand, three goals for Northampton's Ted Bowen were Rovers' undoing. It was a second league hat-trick against Rovers in five months for the twenty-seven-year-old forward. Even by the standards set in 1929/30, Rovers' defensive frailties were becoming clearly apparent.

Nine opponents registered league hat-tricks against Rovers during the season, a club record. Coventry City's Billy Lake, who had hit the post but not scored against Rovers the previous season, scored four times in a 5-1 victory in March. Southend United's Jimmy Shankly, brother of the future Liverpool manager, scored twice in the first sixteen minutes and completed his hat-trick at Eastville with an eighty-fifth minute penalty. Bill Lane not only scored three goals but also struck a late penalty against the crossbar during Brentford's crushing 5-2 victory at Eastville in January. Had Les Berry not saved Alex Stevenson's penalty at Griffin Park, Rovers would have conceded five goals in both league fixtures against the Bees.

Rovers also conceded five goals at home to both Watford, where George James scored three times, and Bournemouth, as well as six at Fulham. The Bournemouth defeat was indeed a remarkable game. Ron Eyre, a thorn in Rovers' side for many years, scored a hat-trick, and the former Rovers inside-forward Jack Russell scored twice. Arthur Attwood contributed two goals for Rovers, who were left with only ten men after an injury to Norman Dinsdale – three 'goals' were disallowed and Rovers' George Russell missed a penalty. At Fulham, Rovers had held the home side 2-2, before goalkeeper Berry conceded four goals in the final fifteen minutes. Fred Avey scored three goals in that game, but only five all season for Fulham. This was the third consecutive season in which Rovers had conceded six goals in the league game at Craven Cottage.

Despite the club's propensity to suffer heavy defeats, several of the new signings enjoyed a successful season. It was always going to be tough stepping into Jesse Whatley's boots, but Berry, despite conceding eighty goals in thirty-four league matches, was instrumental in preventing too many whitewashes. He was primarily a cricketer of great renown, who captained his county and scored over 30,000 runs between 1924 and 1951. Immediately prior to his arrival at Eastville, he had scored a career-best 232 for Leicestershire against Sussex in the close season of 1930. In October at Somerton Park, he played against the celebrated Worcestershire batsman Bill Fox, Newport County's left-back. Dinsdale was an efficient centre-half, and Bert Young a consistent performer at outside-left – he missed only one game and scored seven goals. However, Arthur Attwood's arrival was the key to Rovers finishing fifteenth in Division Three (South). The former Everton forward scored twenty-four league goals, only two short of Willie Culley's club record, and a seasonal total not equalled by a Rovers player until 1951/52. Attwood was also the club's only ever-present, and held together a much-changing forward line.

Rovers used eighteen different players in the opening five league games, and early heavy defeats led to manager McLean's resignation on 17 September, six days after ill health had forced chairman Mark Hasell to resign. McLean was later manager at East Fife and Hearts. His replacement was the charismatic Captain Albert Prince-Cox. A former footballer and boxer, forty-year-old Prince-Cox had refereed a number of Rovers matches in the 1920s. By 1935, he had refereed thirty-two international matches in fifteen countries. He had also, at one time, reported daily to Buckingham Palace, as a Fellow of the Royal Meteorological Society, to present the King with the weather forecast. He arrived at Eastville on 23 October 1930 in a red, open-topped sports car with white wheels, bringing with him an air of change. Within a week of his appointment, he had arranged a tour of the Netherlands.

Just twenty-four hours after a tough league fixture, and following an overnight North Sea crossing, Rovers defeated the Dutch national side 3-2 on Sunday 16 November 1930. This historic result was one that, it has to be said, Rovers were a touch fortunate to achieve. The intrinsic skills of the Dutch side, and notably twenty-two-year-old outside-right Adje Gerritse, were remarkable, and centre-forward Gerrit Hulsman scored twice, though the second was apparently from an offside position. Nonetheless, two goals from Ronnie Dix and one from the ever-reliable Attwood earned Rovers a notable victory. A couple of days later, Rovers defeated the top Dutch side Swallows 4-2 in a game played under floodlights. Initial plans for Rovers to tour Argentina at the close of the season sadly fell through.

Indeed, this autumnal victory over Holland is but one successful aspect of the season. The seventy-five league goals scored represented the second highest total since the club's Southern League days. For the first time since 1920/21, Rovers scored in every home game. Indeed, in the penultimate home game, Rovers scored four times in a twenty-minute burst against Clapton Orient, avenging December's defeat at Brisbane Road, which had been due to three goals from Karachi-born Reg Tricker. Attwood was ably supported by young Ronnie Dix, whose first regular run in the side brought nineteen league goals.

Prince-Cox attempted to instil greater order into his squad. One example of this was the treatment of outside-left Thomas Turnbull. A summer signing from Gainsborough Trinity, Turnbull had played in one league game in September and appeared regularly in the reserves. In January, Prince-Cox suspended him and reported him to the Football League for 'breaking the club's regulations, having not returned to Bristol after one month's absence'. Subsequently, Turnbull found his registration cancelled in February 1933. Prince-Cox was not one to tolerate professional indiscipline.

Over Christmas, Rovers suffered their customary heavy defeat at the Goldstone Ground, after John Carruthers had opened the scoring in the first minute. The Brighton forward went on to complete a hat-trick. The first visit of Thames to Eastville saw the visitors include in their side Fred Le May; at 5 feet exactly he was the shortest player ever to participate in league football. The return fixture in April was not played at Wembley, as some erroneous reports have hinted, but rather in an eerily empty West Ham Greyhound Stadium, the league newcomers' regular home venue. In January, Rovers' home victory over Crystal Palace was sealed with an own goal from Tom Crilly. Bizarrely, Crilly had also scored an own goal for Bristol City while playing for Derby County in September 1923. Not surprisingly, he is the only player to have scored own goals for both Bristol clubs.

Rovers were awarded three penalties against Queen's Park Rangers in five days in January. All three were conceded by Baden Herod, and all converted successfully by the reliable left-back George Dennis. Two came in Rovers' FA Cup third-round win, where Rovers found themselves 3-0 up inside twenty minutes, and the third in a 3-0 league victory. George Dennis scored a total of six league and cup penalties, including one in each league game against Luton Town. Later in the season, new goalkeeper Tom Boyce saved Bill Sheppard's penalty when Rovers met Queen's Park Rangers at Loftus Road on Easter Saturday. Boyce's debut was in a 2-1 home defeat against Walsall, where former Rovers forward Gilbert Shaw scored the winning goal after seventy-five minutes – his only league goal for the Saddlers. Ironically, in Rovers' other league fixture against Walsall, the future Pirate Jack Eyres scored for the opposition.

A final run of five consecutive league wins pushed Rovers to a respectable mid-table position. In the FA Cup, three comfortable home wins earned Rovers a fourth-round tie at Ewood Park in front of a crowd exceeding 25,000. Ronnie Dix, later a Blackburn player, scored for Rovers, but the home side won 5-1, one of their goals coming from Syd Puddefoot, an FA Cup winner in 1928. Puddefoot had scored a hat-trick for West Ham United against Rovers in a Southern League game in January 1914. Bristol City inflicted a third consecutive Gloucestershire Cup final defeat on Rovers, Syd Homer and Frank Townrow, both Rovers players at some point in their career, grabbing a goal apiece.

1931/32

The Lilywhites changed their colours in 1931, and Rovers opened the new season wearing the now familiar blue-and-white quartered shirts. Manager Albert Prince-Cox reasoned that such a design would make his players appear larger on the field. The quartered shirts quickly became established as a key element in the image of Bristol Rovers. Over the summer, terracing had replaced the earth banking at the Muller Road End of Eastville Stadium, as would be the case at the popular Tote End in 1935. This building work had created the familiar oval-shaped terracing, complete with banana-shaped flowerbeds behind the goal, tenderly cared for by generations of groundsmen, and brought the crowd capacity at this end of the ground to 16,900. Rovers were to finish the season in eighteenth place and conceded ninety-two league goals for the second consecutive season, including five to Watford and Crystal Palace, six against Northampton Town and Norwich City and eight at Torquay United.

For the new season, the previous season's three top scorers – Attwood, Dix and Young – started in the forward line. However, the manager's policy of bringing experienced, seasoned campaigners to Eastville meant there were a number of new faces in the side. Goalkeeper Joe Calvert, the club's only ever-present in 1931/32, had enjoyed a number of years in senior non-League football, and was to play for Watford, post-war, beyond his forty-first birthday. Fair-haired left-back Bill Pickering, half-backs Bill Stoddart and Jimmy Muir, and outside-right Eric Oakton all boasted impressive pedigrees with other league sides. Stoddart was noted for his exceptionally long and accurate throw-ins. Bill Routledge, an accomplished athlete, was excused from preseason training to compete in the prestigious Powderhall Sprint. Bert Young was the first goalscorer in quarters, while Rovers' other scorer in the opening-day draw at Bournemouth was Ronnie Dix, the only Bristol-born player in the side. Dix left at the season's end to play First Division football with three different clubs. He earned an England cap against Norway in November 1938, scoring once in a 4-0 win.

The second home game of the season was a morale-boosting 6-1 victory over Crystal Palace, who had scored ten goals in their first two league games. Dix, Attwood and Muir scored twice each. This remains one of only two occasions three Rovers players have scored as many as two goals each in the same league game. Of greater concern to the club, though, was that Attwood scored just one more goal after this win – the centre-forward joined Brighton just twenty-four hours before the home game with Gillingham. As can so often be the case, he returned to haunt his former club, as both he and Jack Eyres scored for Brighton in their 4-0 win at Eastville in February.

Attwood's place in the side was taken by veteran Tommy Cook who, in line with Prince-Cox's master plan, was enjoying one final fling in league football before retirement. Cook's 114 league goals for Brighton between 1922 and 1929 remain a record at that club, and he had earned an England cap against Wales in 1925. He was to score eighteen goals in only thirty-one league games for Rovers in 1931/32 to finish as the club's top scorer for the season. Eric Oakton, the second highest goalscorer, achieved only half that figure.

Cook's second game for Rovers was a 4-2 defeat at Brentford in October. The Bees had won six of their last seven games, and took the lead in the opening minute when England amateur international Jackie Burns shot past Joe Calvert. Regaining the initiative for his side, Cook scored twice and Rovers appeared to be taking a lead into the half-time interval. Shortly before the break, however, Brentford won a penalty, converted by George Robson and, within seconds of the start of the second half, Bill Berry put the home side in front. Five minutes from time a second penalty secured victory for the Bees. Robson was only taking penalties in the absence of Bill Lane, but he became the second of ten opponents to score two penalties against Rovers in a league match.

Matches in which Rovers have scored five goals before half-time are, naturally, infrequent. In November, though, five goals in twenty-one first-half minutes saw Rovers lead Gillingham 5-0, before conceding two goals in the second half – one scored by Les Ames, the England cricketer and subsequent Test selector. The same opposition suffered a similar fate in the first round of the FA Cup as five Rovers players got on the scoresheet in a 5-1 win. Another comfortable victory was the 4-1 home win over Bournemouth in January. Yorkshireman Joe Riley was given a league debut in this game at centre-forward, and he responded with three goals. Only Jimmy McCambridge and Bobby Gould have since equalled this feat of a debut hat-trick for Rovers. Riley himself was sold to Bournemouth in 1935, and was to score a league hat-trick against Rovers for his new club.

However, heavy defeats continued to loom large in Rovers' season. Shortly after Christmas, Northampton were 5-0 ahead by half-time, and their 6-0 victory featured two goals each from Harry Lovatt, Tommy Wells and the perennial Ted Bowen. Fred Dawes, who played in this game for Northampton, appeared against Rovers on a number of occasions over eighteen years, his final match against the Pirates being Palace's 1-0 victory in September 1949. Six weeks later, another 6-0 defeat, this time at Carrow Road, saw three opponents again scoring twice each – Oliver Brown, Sam Bell and Cyril Blakemore. Indeed Blakemore, a former Bristol City player, had earlier scored against Rovers for both Portsmouth and Crystal Palace, the latter in the extraordinary 7-4 defeat in March 1927. He had also missed a penalty in the controversial game at Brentford in September 1929. Only on three further occasions since 1932 have three opponents scored two or more goals each in a league game against Rovers.

Just when the defence was beginning to act as a unit, the Plainmoor debacle on Easter Monday led Rovers to rethink the structure of the team. The 8-1 defeat equalled the club's heaviest ever loss at that time in league football. Rovers were four goals down by half-time against a supposedly struggling Torquay side.

Although outside-left Bert Young pulled a goal back, Rovers were heavily beaten. The final whistle could not come soon enough as Bill Clayson, leading the forward line, scored three times in the final four minutes to take his personal tally for the afternoon to four. Rovers were to finish the season above Torquay in the league table, but the psychological damage inflicted at Plainmoor would take a while to recede.

In October, there was crowd trouble at Eastville. After a second-half penalty appeal had been turned down, with Rovers heading for a 1-0 home defeat against Norwich City, referee Stanley Rous, later president of the Football Association, was assaulted by a drunken spectator.

In January, dense fog meant the Rovers side arrived at The Kursaal only fifteen minutes before kick-off in the league game with Southend United. Rovers held the home side 1-1 at half-time, but fell apart in the second half, with Jimmy Shankly scoring twice in a 4-1 defeat. Against Cardiff City, a goal was conceded to the erstwhile Rovers forward Jimmy McCambridge. As the season drew to a close, Rovers visited Fulham and shocked the home side by leading at half-time, Cook having scored following a corner. Nonetheless, with the wind behind them, Fulham produced three second-half goals to secure the championship, despite Pickering's low drive late in the game. Rovers drew 1-1 at Eastville in March in a benefit game for the amateur Jack Pearce, which raised a total of £9, a significant amount in 1932; Joe Riley had given Rovers the lead in the first minute.

Rovers fell to Tranmere in the FA Cup, and a solitary second-half Sid Elliott goal gave Bristol City a fourth consecutive Gloucestershire Cup victory.

Over the summer of 1932, greyhound racing first took place at Eastville. The Bristol Greyhound Racing Association was incorporated as a Public Limited Liability Company on 4 March 1932, with a quarter of a million shares initially sold for 2*s* each. On 21 March, the club had granted a lease to the Bristol Greyhound Racing Association for £5,000 and an annual £600 rent; the first race was on 16 July. Alarmingly, the greyhound company was given first refusal should Rovers ever choose to sell the ground, and even promised the price would not exceed £13,000. Wartime needs were to lead to such a situation, and Rovers' departure from Eastville in 1986 can be traced back to this sequence of events.

1932/33

Rovers' charismatic manager, Albert Prince-Cox, led the club through an exciting season as the side finished ninth in Division Three (South). This performance equalled the club's highest final league position to date. With five former internationals on their books, Rovers played some exciting football. The manager's response was to take the club on various overseas trips: to Rotterdam in September; to Paris and Amsterdam in the New Year; and back to France once the season had finished.

To some it appeared that the manager was simply an eccentric. He arranged for a private aircraft to fly the experienced amateur centre-forward Vivian Gibbins from Romford Aerodrome to Filton in time for the 6.15 p.m. kick-off in the September game with Southend United. Gibbins responded with a goal in Rovers' 3-1 victory, and scored two hat-tricks the following month in a 5-3 win over Brighton and a 3-0 win at Clapton Orient. The Orient game was apparently ended five minutes early. Not that Rovers would have been too concerned, for the side had lost league games at Brisbane Road in the previous three seasons. Gibbins, 'one of the last great amateurs imbued with the Corinthian spirit', as a contemporary journalist for *Athletic News* described him, was Rovers' top scorer with fourteen league goals, the only amateur to achieve this feat in Rovers' league history. For this season, his tally was closely followed by that of Billy Jackson, whose eleven goals came in the first sixteen league matches.

The new season saw the usual influx of players. Left-back Alec Donald, a Scotsman signed from Chelsea, formed a successful full-back partnership with the dependable club captain Bill Pickering. George McNestry was to prove an influential figure at outside-right, while Jackson and Jack Eyres showed promise as a left-wing pairing. There were three goalkeepers employed, yet stability was clear in the fact that, in strong contrast to previous seasons, Rovers conceded four goals in a league game on only two occasions. Season ticket prices remained unchanged at 50*s* for the most expensive seats, while under-fourteens could buy a season ticket on the terraces for as little as 10*s*. Ronnie Dix joined Blackburn Rovers for £3,000, and was to play subsequently for Aston Villa, Derby County, Tottenham Hotspur and Reading. He won an England cap in November 1938, scoring in a 4-0 victory over Norway.

The ability to field as many as five former internationals was quite some achievement for a Third Division side. Sam Irving, born in Belfast of Scottish parentage, spent one year in the side as right-half. He had won eighteen caps for Northern Ireland. Due to the intrusions of war, and of playing football in Scotland and the United States in his twenty-year professional career, Irving could lay claim to a number of quirky facts. For instance, he did not score a league goal between October 1914 and March 1927. He also won an FA Cup final winners' medal with Cardiff City, but both played in and managed sides in losing Scottish Cup finals before becoming a director of Dundee United. Irving's only goal for Rovers came at Eastville in December, when Brentford replied with three goals in seven minutes to win 4-2. Alongside Bobby McKay, who had won a Scottish cap in 1927, Rovers fielded three former England internationals in Vivian Gibbins, Tommy Cook and Jack Townrow, who joined his brother Frank in the half-back line.

The veteran forward Tommy Cook, Rovers' top scorer the previous season, scored only three league goals this time before a broken collarbone, sustained in a collision with Cardiff City's former Rovers full-back George Russell, was to end his career. As one highly experienced player retired, another long and distinguished footballing career was just getting underway. Wally McArthur, who was to appear in 261 league games for Rovers before retiring in 1949, made his debut in April in a goalless draw with Brentford. The Bees were already divisional champions and should have won, but the veteran prolific marksman David Halliday missed a penalty. Rovers also drew at Southend United, who set a club record of sixteen consecutive league matches unbeaten that is as yet unsurpassed.

An exciting victory over Northampton at Eastville in October, 4-3 in Rovers' favour, featured an own goal from the Cobblers' goalkeeper Len Hammond in his 295th league game for the visitors, as well as two good goals from Jackson. The return game in early March saw the first of two league goals from local schoolmaster Bert Blake, a highly dependable centre-half and the nephew of a Spurs goalkeeper. This 1-1 draw proved to be one of seven in the second half of the season. Cardiff City converted one of two penalties awarded in their favour at Ninian Park in November. The 3-1 defeat at Reading saw a sole league appearance for Rovers of Ted Hough, a full-back who had earlier in his career joined Southampton for a fee of fifty-two pints of beer. Mick O'Brien converted a penalty against Rovers in January, seven months shy of his fortieth birthday, still the third-oldest league goalscorer against Rovers.

Rovers had four ultimately unsuccessful matches against Bristol City. The league fixture at Ashton Gate ended in a 3-1 defeat, with City's Billy Knox scoring direct from a free-kick taken from just inside his own half. A George McNestry goal then earned Rovers a 1-1 draw at Eastville in the spring. City won the Gloucestershire Cup final 4-3 after a 3-3 draw. Rovers had six different goalscorers in these two matches, while the former Rovers outside-right Syd Homer scored two of City's goals in the drawn match.

At the end of September, immediately after the home win over Reading, Prince-Cox took his team to Rotterdam, where they beat a Dutch Representative XI 7-4, with Joe Riley and George McNestry scoring twice each. Rovers also beat The Hague 1-0 and lost 3-0 to Nice, before returning for the game with Norwich City at Carrow Road. On 26 January, just two days before the home game with Cardiff City, Rovers were taken to Paris. Despite a goal from outside-left Tom Wyper, Rovers lost 3-1 to a French Select XI. With a week off in late February, Rovers played East Holland in Amsterdam, losing 3-2 despite goals from Doug Lewis and Jack Eyres.

Modern talk of fixture pile-ups appears trivial when you consider that, in a season of forty-two league and eight senior cup games, Rovers undertook three mid-season tours. The club also hosted the touring Czech side Nachod in April, winning 4-2 through three George Tepper goals and one from Joe Riley. A strong team also represented the club on Good Friday in a testimonial for full-back Ernie Sambidge; Bath City were leading Rovers 4-2 when the match was abandoned with twenty minutes remaining, Riley having scored twice for Rovers.

To cap the extravagance, Prince-Cox took the Rovers team on an end-of-season tour of southern France. On 14 May 1933, Rovers played AC Milan at the Stade St Maurice in Nice. Milan won this game 3-1; a McNestry penalty early in the second half all Rovers' reward before Mario Romani added the Italian side's third. Four days later, McNestry was again on the scoresheet as Rovers lost 3-1 to a French XI. Nonetheless, having beaten Holland in November 1930 and losing only narrowly in these two prestigious games, Prince-Cox's side was gaining experience to a degree rarely seen at a Third Division side between the wars.

The eight cup games, referred to above, comprised five FA Cup games, two Gloucestershire Cup matches and a first excursion into the Welsh Cup. A promising FA Cup run, which started with Rovers wearing red at Cardiff City, ended with defeat at Aldershot in the third round, where Rovers went down to a solitary goal from veteran outside-left Jack Lane in front of the Shots' highest crowd to that date – 9,470, generating receipts of £670. That Rovers reached round three at all was due to Sam Irving's late penalty after Rovers had trailed for eighty-three minutes at home to Gillingham. The fact that Rovers entered the Welsh Cup is explained by the eagerness of the authorities to open up this tournament. Bristol City, for instance, were to win the Welsh Cup in 1934, with two former Rovers players, Joe Riley and Syd Homer, in their side. Rovers' first foray ended in a 3-0 defeat at Swansea Town. The Rovers side wore black armbands following the recent death of club director Tommy Walker, a member of the board since 1922 and chairman of the supporters' club in 1927. Rovers also won the Allan Palmer Cup, which they had previously won in 1927, when holders Nottingham Forest were beaten 2-0 before a crowd of 3,200. The goals both came from first-half headers; first from Doug Lewis, converting a Ron Green cross after twenty-two minutes and then from McNestry, set up by McKay on the stroke of half-time.

The club's director reported a profit of £3,577 for the 1932/33 season. Bill Pickering was to repeat this achievement in 1933/34 and 1935/36. He, Donald, McNestry and Eyres, all of whom had played in at least thirty-five league games, all remained with the club, offering fresh optimism for the season ahead.

1933/34

With the backbone of the previous season's side intact, Rovers needed a goalkeeper and a goalscorer. Manager Prince-Cox made two astute summer signings, Charles Preedy in goal from Arsenal and the Northern Ireland international centre-forward Jimmy McCambridge to lead the line. The opening fixture of the new season was a local derby at Ashton Gate, and would be a good test of how the new team could shape up.

It is difficult to imagine, from the point of view of a Rovers supporter, a more satisfying opening-day result. New signing McCambridge compiled a debut hat-trick of headers as Bristol City were beaten 3-0 before a crowd of 25,500. He thus equalled Joe Riley's club record of scoring three goals on his first league appearance for the club. Two more goals in the return game at Eastville in late December were to equal Willie Culley's club record haul of five goals in one season against an individual club. The manner of Rovers' victory gave cause for great optimism.

Of course, a 1-0 home defeat four days later brought Rovers down to earth, especially with George McNestry having to leave the field after only ten minutes with a broken bone in his hand. However, Rovers were to enjoy a successful season. The final league placing of seventh constituted the highest inter-war league position. Seventy-seven league goals were scored, only one fewer than in 1926/27, while Rovers won twenty league games, an achievement not equalled until 1950/51, and only eleven games were lost. Apart from a 5-3 defeat at Coventry City in September and a 3-2 Boxing Day defeat at Gillingham, no more than two goals were conceded in any game.

One further addition to Rovers' side was centre-half Jock McLean. Signed from First Division Blackburn Rovers, McLean was a figure of stability; captain and ever-present in his first two seasons at Eastville. It was surely no coincidence that the only goal of his Rovers career was one of five by which Rovers beat Bristol City in December. Wing-halves Sid Wallington and Bill Murray came into the side as the season progressed and added support for McLean, in what developed into a fine half-back line. In front of them was Jack Havelock, a £330 signing from Folkestone Town, who had scored against Rovers in the FA Cup in November.

Clearly a characteristic of the season was the reliability of the defence, where Pickering and McLean were ever-presents, and Donald and Preedy barely missed a game. Preedy's enormous contribution to Rovers' cause was epitomised by the game at Brighton in November, where his first-half penalty save from Albion's Robert Farrell laid the foundations for a 2-0 win. The forward line began to work to great effect. Prince-Cox then arranged to transport supporters by plane to an away game at Cardiff, participants flying for 8*s* each from Whitchurch Airport, presenting the pilot, Bill Drinan, with a silver cigarette case and paying 2*s* 6*d* for a stand ticket at Ninian Park. Prince-Cox's bizarre entrepreneurial concept was rewarded with a 5-1 victory, Havelock scoring twice on this occasion. Bobby McKay scored a hat-trick in the return game with Cardiff. Jimmy Smith, who had scored a British seasonal record sixty-six goals in thirty-eight Scottish league matches for Ayr United in 1927/28 to inscribe his name in the *Guinness Book of Records*, enjoyed a high point in his brief Rovers stay with a hat-trick in Rovers' 4-1 victory over Queen's Park Rangers. In this game, after McNestry's twelfth-minute penalty, Smith scored after twenty-eight, fifty-five and eighty-six minutes, twice converting rebounds after Albert Taylor had hit the crossbar, claiming glory despite an injury time consolation goal in semi-darkness.

Consequently, it appeared wholly out of character that Rovers should have found themselves 4-0 down at half-time against Coventry City at Highfield Road.

Coventry were riding high in the table, but the dominance of City's Harry Lake and Jock Lauderdale, who scored twice each, was unexpected. The return fixture saw Rovers win 4-1, with young outside-left Jimmy Watson scoring the fourth. Coventry's consolation goal came from Arthur Bacon.

On 2 December, Rovers' game at Plainmoor attracted an attendance of just 1,000. This was the third time such a low turnout had watched a league game featuring Rovers, and remains the last such instance in the club's history. Rovers succumbed to the predictable defeat, despite George McNestry's sixty-second minute penalty following a foul on Jack Eyres. Since Torquay's elevation to the Third Division (South) in 1927, Rovers have only won seven league games at Plainmoor.

Much of Rovers' success was based on the side's propensity for turning close games into wins. Single-goal victories at Crystal Palace, Aldershot and Northampton Town bore witness to this, while the forty-seven goals conceded was the club's lowest in the league since 1923/24. Rovers were thus able to win twenty league games for the only time in the inter-war years. Indeed, only in 1955/56 has the club been able to equal this achievement in a forty-two-match season. One of these wins – the game at Brighton in November – followed an excellent solo goal by Jackson, who beat three defenders to score one of the greatest goals in the Bristol Rovers story. There was a run of three consecutive victories around early November and another in April, while Rovers only once had to endure as many as four consecutive league matches without a win. Likewise, a seasonal tally of eleven league defeats was the club's lowest since the Southern League championship season of 1904/05, and was not improved upon until 1952/53, in which season Rovers were Third Division (South) champions.

As the season drew to a close, the former Rovers goalkeeper James Harvey was in the news. Harvey, a Yorkshireman by birth, had played in just one league game for Rovers in 1932, and was spending the 1933/34 season on the books of Frickley Colliery. In April, he was charged in court with obtaining £60 by false pretences from two girls he employed at his 'University Novelty Pool' in Barnsley. He was to join Gillingham in the summer.

A successful season saw McCambridge as the club's top scorer with seventeen league goals, McNestry, McKay and Havelock all also reaching double figures. In the FA Cup, Rovers played out a goalless draw at Folkestone in a blizzard before defeating their Southern League opposition in a replay, but then fell to a goal from Accrington Stanley's top scorer Jackie Cheetham. For the sixth consecutive season, the Gloucestershire Cup final was lost, Bristol City winning 2-1 in a replay, with Joe Riley scoring against his former Rovers teammates. Rovers also entered the inaugural Division Three (South) Cup tournament but, after a 2-2 draw with Coventry City, were eliminated by the same opposition.

Rovers appeared in the Welsh Cup for the second and final time in the club's history. A Jimmy Hamilton own goal after thirty-three minutes and Jackson's finish three minutes from time proved sufficient to defeat Wrexham at Eastville. This was followed by a free-scoring draw with Port Vale, where Rovers, an early goal down, scored twice in the seventeenth minute. McCambridge, Lewis and McNestry from the penalty spot earned Rovers a 3-3 draw. In the replay at Vale Park, Joe Havelock's goal took the game into extra time before a heavily disputed goal put paid to Rovers' ambitions, the ball being allegedly 'a foot over the line' before it was crossed.

One alarming development during the course of this season was the agreement signed by football and greyhound directors to amend the lease of 21 March 1932. The modification of lease document, agreed on 23 January 1934, saw Rovers essentially lose the club's advantage in the struggle for ownership of Eastville Stadium. The Bristol Greyhound Racing Association was given the right to inform Rovers at any point if they wished to purchase the ground. Rather than remaining tenants, the greyhound company was now in a position to buy up Eastville Stadium at any stage with only two months' written notice, and at a guaranteed price within the range of a maximum £13,000 and minimum £8,000 value. By the onset of war, as financial conditions dictated, Rovers were forced to sell and thereby set up the enforced exile from Bristol that took place in the late 1980s.

Rovers' reserves were involved indirectly in the Taunton Carnival in September 1933, with Madge Coles, the Carnival Queen, symbolically kicking off the fixture at Taunton Town. The reserves, 3-0 ahead after fifteen minutes, won 7-3, with Phil Taylor, Jimmy Watson and George Tadman scoring twice each. Jimmy Smith scored five times in the return fixture, when Taunton Town were defeated 7-0 at Eastville in January 1934. In the same calendar month, Smith scored four and Tadman three as the reserves beat Cheltenham Town 12-1.

1934/35

After years of underachievement, Rovers enjoyed a second consecutive season of relative success. Manager Albert Prince-Cox was beginning to see his apparently optimistic plans for the club come to fruition. It was another entertaining season. Rovers finished eighth in Division Three (South), scoring seventy-three league goals in the process. Several large crowds were attracted to Eastville, including over 20,000 for the visit of Manchester United in the FA Cup, and 25,000 for the home league game with Bristol City. Best of all, though, was the winning of Rovers' first major trophy since the 1904/05 Southern League title.

The only inter-war trophy won by Rovers on a national scale was the 1934/35 Division Three (South) Cup. This tournament ran for a number of years up to the Second World War and was, in many respects, a forerunner of the Leyland Daf Trophy, which was to offer Rovers a first opportunity to play at Wembley in 1990. George Berry's winner saw off Reading in the first round, and Rovers needed a replay with Torquay in the second, two Jimmy Smith goals ensuring victory. Rovers were drawn at home to Exeter City in the semi-final at the end of March. The two sides had drawn in the league four days earlier, but goals from Stan Prout and top scorer George McNestry earned Rovers a 2-1 victory. Harry Poulter scored for the Grecians, who fielded the future Rovers centre-half Harold Webb.

The final was played at Millwall on 15 April before a poor crowd of 2,000. The Den had been selected as a neutral venue after Rovers and Watford had refused to toss a coin to decide home advantage. On a very wet surface, Rovers, visibly buoyed by a 4-1 victory over Bournemouth forty-eight hours earlier, were a goal ahead at half-time through Bobby McKay's twentieth-minute shot. Shortly after half-time, McNestry crossed for Charlie Wipfler to put Rovers 2-0 ahead. With captain Jock McLean leading from the back, Rovers looked in control. Even when Bill Lane pulled a goal back with eight minutes remaining, Irvine Harwood put Rovers ahead 3-1. In the dying seconds, Vic O'Brien added a second goal for Watford, but Rovers had won their first major honour in thirty years.

In the league, captain Jock McLean was the only ever-present, although goalkeeper Jack Ellis and defenders Bill Pickering, Alec Donald and Sid Wallington missed very few games. McNestry, who scored nineteen league goals from outside-right, played in all but two matches in the league. Stan Prout and Albert Taylor both figured prominently, but of the new signings, Ellis was the one to offer the most valuable and consistent service. A tall, confident goalkeeper, he was to appear for Rovers in four consecutive league seasons. Jack Allen was to make few appearances in the Rovers side, but he had been top scorer in two consecutive seasons for Sheffield Wednesday when they won the League championship in 1928/29 and 1929/30. Rovers also signed twenty-one-year-old Samuel Edward Jones from Lovell's Athletic, the winner of three Welsh amateur caps, but he was unable to break into the league side.

The season got off to an unusual start, with the 3-1 defeat at Brighton kicking off at 6.30 p.m. as Sussex were also playing the Australian cricket tourists at Hove. Rovers conceded five at Southend in only the fifth game, with Harry Lane and Harry Johnson scoring two apiece, the first time since the equivalent weekend twelve months earlier that Rovers had conceded more than three goals in a game. Yet after failing to win in the opening eight league matches, Rovers clicked into gear. Four consecutive wins set the season on its way and goals were to follow – seven against Northampton and five against Exeter, Crystal Palace and Newport. This first win of the season, 2-0 at home to Queen's Park Rangers, had seen the visitors field Jackie Crawford, an outside-left who had played for England against Scotland in 1931, and who, at 5 feet 2 inches, was shorter than any other opponent in Rovers' league history, except the diminutive Fred Le May, who had played for Thames in 1930.

Rovers drew an extraordinary home game with Exeter 5-5, thanks to a hat-trick from Jimmy Smith, one of only two ten-goal draws in the club's league history.

Rovers had led 3-0 after half an hour and 5-2 with eight minutes remaining, but allowed their opponents to snatch a draw. The future Rovers centre-back Harold Webb scored the first of the Grecians' five goals from the penalty spot. Two highly entertaining 5-3 victories soon followed. In February, Rovers led Crystal Palace 3-1 after only twelve minutes and 4-1 by half-time, but eventually held out for a 5-3 win after being reduced to ten men following an injury to Albert Taylor. Five weeks later, it was Taylor's turn to shine as his sole league hat-trick contributed to a 5-3 win. His first goal came after only two minutes, and all three before half-time as he became the third Rovers player to complete a first-half league hat-trick after Sid Leigh in 1921 and Ernie Whatmore six years later.

Rovers' largest league win between the wars was the 7-1 hammering of Northampton Town in January. Goalkeeper Ellis was missing from the side and Rovers, with four changes following defeat at Luton, gave league debuts to the Somerset cricketer Newman Bunce in goal and James Durkan at right-back. Undeterred, Rovers scored seven times, McNestry and Taylor notching two each. Northampton's Dick Brown put a penalty wide of Bunce's goal. This match, however, was watched by a crowd of only 1,500, the lowest ever at a league game played at Eastville. The Cobblers subsequently dropped seven of their side, including goalscorer Tommy Ball, for their next game.

There were also some heavy defeats. Luton's third goal of the six they put past Rovers in January was the 1,000th Rovers had conceded in league football. This goal was in fact an own goal, sliced in after thirty-three minutes by McLean as Rovers, conceding four goals in twenty-five first-half minutes, crashed 6-2. Ball completed his hat-trick after eighty-seven minutes, but Rovers maintained that his first strike, following a goalmouth scramble after a quarter of an hour, had not actually crossed the line. Southend United, Reading and Clapton Orient all put five goals past Jack Ellis before Christmas, David Halliday scoring a hat-trick for the Os. Over Easter, when Rovers conceded nine goals in a four-day spell, the side wore unconventional red shirts for the 3-0 defeat at Watford. Billy Baldwin, who scored twice in Gillingham's high-scoring victory at Eastville in the run-up to Christmas, was to win the 1965 All-England Bowls Cup.

On 13 April, for a 4-1 home victory over Bournemouth, Rovers fielded five Macs in their side. This was, in effect, the culmination of a distinct policy between the wars to cultivate scouting links in Scotland and, in some respects, reflected the cosmopolitan make-up of the side. Wing-half McArthur was a Yorkshireman, McNestry from County Durham, and McCambridge from Northern Ireland, while both McKay and McLean were born north of the border.

In the final game of the season, Rovers drew 1-1 at Gillingham in an incident-packed afternoon. McNestry scored his nineteenth goal of the season, a penalty, but the home side missed two spot-kicks through Dick Doncaster, a former Welsh Schoolboy international, and Joe Wiggins. This was the second of five league matches featuring Rovers in which three penalties have been awarded. Elsewhere, Charlton Athletic played through this season with three future Rovers managers in their squad. Fred Ford and Bert Tann could not break into the side, but Bill Dodgin's twenty-five league appearances included a 2-0 victory over Rovers at The Valley in February. Dodgin was to join Rovers as a player in 1936 and as manager in 1969. Charlton were Division Three (South) champions, finishing eight points clear of runners-up Reading.

In the FA Cup, victories over non-League sides Harwich and Dartford without conceding a goal earned Rovers a plum third-round tie with Second Division Manchester United. Harwich had held out for twenty-eight minutes, but after Smith scored, McNestry netted the rebound from his own saved penalty on the stroke of half-time, and Prout added a third after the break. A successfully converted McNestry penalty saw off a spirited Dartford performance. Rovers had conceded six at Luton in the run-up to the Manchester United game, losing goalkeeper Jack Ellis in the process with a broken collarbone. Incredibly, a low McNestry drive after twenty minutes gave Rovers a half-time lead, before three second-half goals in the space of seventeen minutes – two from Tommy Bamford and one from George Mutch – brought United a comfortable victory. Rovers beat Bristol City 2-1 in the Gloucestershire Cup final, with Jimmy Smith scoring the winning goal, to win the trophy for the first time since 1928. For the second consecutive season, City's Joe Riley scored against his former club.

Rovers retained the Allan Palmer Cup, which the club had won in 1927 and 1933, but which had not been contested in 1934. As holders, Rovers were invited to play Southampton and found themselves two goals ahead inside twenty minutes through McNestry and Taylor. Southampton pulled level through goals from Fred Tully and Johnny McAlwane, but Rovers ran out 5-2 winners, with Irvine Harwood scoring twice and Taylor adding his second of the game. Two Ted Buckley goals enabled Rovers to defeat Thornbury Town 4-3 in April in a match to raise money for the Berkeley and Almondsbury Hospitals Fund.

1935/36

Prince-Cox had brought relative prosperity to the club, but by the 1935/36 season, the effect of his undoubted charisma was beginning to wane. Rovers avoided having to seek re-election, but an erratic season contributed in part to his ultimate decision to leave the Eastville club in October 1936. Rovers conceded six goals at Aldershot and at Notts County and, infamously, twelve at Luton Town. A club seasonal record of ninety-five goals conceded left Rovers in seventeenth place in Division Three (South).

Yet the season both started and finished well, in front of the newly constructed Tote End, whose name derived from the betting totaliser clocks for greyhound racing. There was a covered section to this spectator area in the south-west corner, though the majority was not roofed until 1961. In its heyday, the Tote End was to house a crowd capacity of 12,250. Opening with three straight clean sheets, including a 2-0 win against Bristol City at Ashton Gate, Rovers lost only one of their opening eight league games. Barely twenty-four hours after the Luton debacle, Rovers defeated Torquay 3-0 at Eastville, while five different players got their names on the scoresheet as Rovers beat Exeter City 6-1 in the final home game of the season. Jack Woodman, who scored twice in both games, was the club's top scorer with fifteen league goals.

Two new faces appeared in the goalless draw with Notts County that opened Rovers' sixteenth league campaign. Outside-right Hugh Adcock was a former England international, while Archie Young could play at left-half or inside-left. Both joined from Leicester City. As the season progressed, Rovers further strengthened the forward line. Harry Barley, a signing from Scunthorpe United, had once scored for New Brighton against Darlington with a shot so hard it had burst the net and apparently floored a ballboy 25 yards behind the goal. George Crisp joined Rovers with Woodman, the experienced Harry Houghton and former Wolves left-back Jack Preece. Rovers also signed George Rounce for £150, an experienced player who had opposed the side with both Queen's Park Rangers and Fulham. He never made Rovers' first team and died of tuberculosis in Hackney on 2 October 1936, aged just thirty-one.

Rovers fielded an experienced side. Jack Ellis, behind a beleaguered defence, found himself with much to do. Right-back Bill Pickering, forming a useful partnership with Donald and later Preece, was the only ever-present. Behind Woodman, the veteran inside-forwards Harry Houghton and Irvine Harwood weighed in with nine league goals apiece. Yet two youngsters with great futures ahead of them made their league debuts for Rovers as the season progressed. Locally born forward Phil Taylor played against Gillingham on his eighteenth birthday, and scored an impressive FA Cup hat-trick against Oldham. He was sold to Liverpool in March in a deal worth £1,000 plus Bill Hartill, and subsequently captained his side in an FA Cup final as well as winning three England caps. Ray Warren, a seventeen-year-old Bristolian, played in the home defeat against Queen's Park Rangers and was later to captain Rovers to the Third Division (South) championship in 1952/53 before retiring in 1956.

When Rovers visited Northampton in September, they trailed 3-0 before scoring three times in the final twenty minutes to earn a draw. The first of these goals came from Eli Postin in his only league appearance of the season. Woodman, who scored the equaliser, missed a number of games over the winter. Tom Harris took advantage and, on his recall to the side, scored after only two minutes against Notts County, going on to complete a hat-trick. Woodman's return to the side in late January saw him score in seven consecutive league games, a club record beaten only by Dai Ward in 1956. Rovers also won 2-1 away to Watford, despite having captain Jock McLean out injured for the remainder of the season. The Hornets had won their previous three home games with a 16-1 goal average.

The defeat at Exeter in December was marked by the late appearance of referee B. Ames. A linesman refereed the opening twenty minutes of a game Rovers lost 3-1. Prior to the draw at Southend in January there was a one-minute silence in memory of King George V, who had died five days earlier. Playing Watford in October, Syd Wallington was knocked out before half-time, but returned for the second half with his head in plaster. On Christmas Day, Eddie Parris, Chepstow born of Jamaican parentage and widely regarded as one of the first black players in the Football League, scored for Bournemouth against Rovers. The 2-2 draw with Aldershot on Easter Saturday saw the visitors field a forty-one-year-old goalkeeper Willie Robb, at this time the sixth oldest opponent that Rovers had faced in the Football League.

Above all else, this season is perhaps best remembered for a string of heavy defeats. In February, Rovers conceded three goals in the opening eight minutes against Crystal Palace, yet lost only 5-3, despite losing goalkeeper Ellis to injury, with Pickering going in goal. Albert Dawes scored twice for Crystal Palace in both league meetings with Rovers. Both Notts County and Aldershot put six goals past Rovers. The former game included two goals from the veteran Arthur Chandler; at forty years thirty-one days, he was the only man to score a league goal against Rovers after his fortieth birthday. Centre-forward Bertie Lutterloch scored a hat-trick as the Shots recorded a 6-1 victory, their highest league win at the time.

The epitome of Rovers' inter-war struggle was, perhaps, the disastrous visit to Kenilworth Road on Easter Monday. There was little hint of what was to come, for Rovers had drawn their other two Easter games, including one at home to Luton Town. Rovers were unchanged, but Luton selected a reserve wing-half, Joe Payne, as an emergency striker. The experiment paid off, as Payne completed a first-half hat-trick, then added seven more in atrocious weather after half-time. 12-0 remains, by a wide margin, the worst defeat in the history of Bristol Rovers. Luton Town's achievement was the only occasion that a club scored twelve goals in any Third Division (South) fixture. Moreover, Joe Payne, who scored his final nine goals in forty-six minutes, eclipsed Tranmere Rovers' Bunny Bell's feat of nine goals in a match – his ten goals in the game stand as a Football League record to this day. Payne was to represent England as a centre-forward and enjoy a distinguished career with Chelsea. He opened the scoring with a low shot after twenty-three minutes and, after Fred Roberts had scored a second, added two tap-ins in the run-up to half-time. After the interval, the centre-forward could do no wrong and, by the eighty-sixth minute, had increased his impressive goal tally to three headers and seven shots. A minute from time, inside-right George Martin, who had initially been falsely credited with the sixth goal, added the twelfth.

If Rovers were to pick up the pieces, they could have done far worse than win three of the remaining four league fixtures. That they did reflects admirably on Prince-Cox and his team. Large home victories over two Devon sides and a hard-earned 2-1 victory at Gillingham, Hartill scoring twice, brought a positive finish to a potentially disastrous season. The opening goal against Exeter City, the only one of inside-right Les Golledge's brief Rovers career, was the 1,000th goal Rovers had scored in league football.

In the FA Cup, Rovers defeated Northampton Town 3-1 in a replay, a score that could have been greater but for two second-half penalty misses by Tom Wildsmith. Phil Taylor's hat-trick at home to Oldham Athletic set up a tie with mighty Arsenal at Eastville in round three. Arsenal were arguably the most powerful football club in the world at this time and boasted a number of household names. However, in the first half, Ted Drake was subdued, Ellis saved a penalty from Cliff Bastin and, sensationally, Houghton shot from the edge of the penalty area three minutes before half-time and Rovers were ahead. Leading the Gunners at half-time was a huge achievement, but the visitors scored five second-half goals – Bastin and Drake claiming two apiece – and went on to defeat Sheffield United in the Wembley final at the end of the season. The Arsenal tie drew a crowd of 24,234 and produced takings of £3,552, the most expensive grandstand seats costing 10*s* each and the cheapest terrace prices being 2*s*. Prince-Cox had called for 6,000 tiered chairs to be installed around the ground, which, if sold at 4*s* each, would have realised a £1,000 profit. The directors, however, erected tubular steel stands, with seats costing 1*s* each; as a result of its unwillingness to back the manager's plans, the club lost almost £700 on the scheme.

Rovers, the holders, were knocked unceremoniously out of the Third Division (South) Cup. The future Rovers inside-forward Willie White scored twice as Bristol City won 4-2. Revenge was sweet as Rovers won 3-1 in the Gloucestershire Cup final. Extra-time goals from Harry Houghton and Ted Buckley gave Rovers victory in the Allan Palmer Cup final, when holders Rovers beat challengers Bournemouth 2-1. Rovers' reserves won the Bristol Charity League for a record twelfth and final time, while Rovers also competed for the Bristol Hospital Cup in May, clawing back a 4-2 half-time deficit to earn a 5-5 draw with guest opponents Liverpool.

1936/37

The false dawn of an opening-day win at The Den gave scant indication of Rovers' prospects for the season ahead. Five players were new to the side that day, from goalkeeper Joe Nicholls, a former Grenadier Guard who stood 6 feet 4 inches tall, to outside-left Oliver Tidman. The experienced Bert Watson played at left-half, while Scotsman David Bruce and former Welsh international Tommy Mills formed a strong right-wing partnership. These players were coached by Walter Moyle, a former manager of the French side Nîmes, appointed on 30 June to replace the veteran Harry Lake.

Jack Woodman and Harry Houghton scored the goals that beat a Millwall side containing Reg Smith. Four consecutive home league games followed, and Rovers won the first three of them. Woodman was on form, continuing his rich vein of goals from the end of 1935/36 by scoring five times in these four straight wins from the start of the season. His fifth, Rovers' second in the 2-0 victory over Northampton Town, was said by many to be one of the finest ever seen at Eastville.

However, although hopes were high, the rot soon set in. Woodman was to score just once more all season, in the heavy New Year defeat at Ashton Gate, and was sold to Preston North End once the season was over. Jimmy Cookson scored a hat-trick as Swindon Town humbled Rovers in September. Rovers lost all five league games in October, using twenty different players in the process. More of a blow, perhaps, was manager Albert Prince-Cox's decision to leave Rovers after six years. He had, for a time, successfully turned the club from perennial underachievers into one with the potential to achieve, but the Luton defeat in April 1936 and a string of poor results had taken their toll, and he left to promote boxing, becoming as undeniably successful in Plymouth as he had already in Bristol.

In November, Rovers appointed Percy Smith as manager. A former Blackburn Rovers and Preston North End player, Smith had also managed Nelson, Bury and Tottenham Hotspur. His Rovers side performed creditably, and a final league position of fifteenth was a satisfactory start, but he was to last just twelve months in the post.

New players were staking claims to regular places. George Tweed and Les Sullivan, both summer signings, broke into the side during the poor run of results. So too did twenty-one-year-old former Manchester United centre-forward Bill Pendergast, who was to score in twelve consecutive league games for Chester in the final season before the Second World War. Smith's first move in the transfer market was to return to Preston for Albert Butterworth, who was to prove a shrewd acquisition and played at outside-right in each of Rovers' twenty-eight remaining league matches. He also brought Syd Wallington back to Eastville, the wing-half first reappearing in the reserves' 12-2 victory over a Monmouthshire Senior League XI in January.

Under Smith's management, Rovers achieved some creditable results. Tom Harris scored twice in each of the large wins at home to Cardiff City and Exeter City, while Bournemouth were comprehensively defeated 4-0 at Eastville. However, the turning point in fortunes was clearly the impressive 3-2 win at Southend in February. In Rovers' previous three away games, four goals had been conceded at Bristol City and Northampton Town, as well as five at Brighton on a day when there were no away wins in thirty-five Football League and FA Cup matches. However, Sullivan was the hero of the day at Southend, creating all three of Rovers' goals. Smith's protégé Butterworth, the ever-reliable Houghton and recalled centre-forward Bill Hartill were the recipients. Smith had successfully resurrected two careers and built his side around them. For the first time, he was able to play both Matt O'Mahony at centre-half and Bill Hartill as centre-forward at Southend. The former was to prove a constant in Rovers' side until the war, winning six caps for Eire and one for Northern Ireland while on Rovers' books. The latter, recapturing past glories when he had become the top goalscorer in Wolverhampton Wanderers' league history, his 162 goals being a club record until bettered by Steve Bull in March 1991, was to finish as Rovers' top scorer for the season with thirteen goals in only sixteen league matches.

Following victory at Southend, Rovers enjoyed several good wins. Hartill scored a hat-trick in a 5-1 defeat of Torquay and twice in both 4-0 wins over Orient and Luton Town. This final result was of particular note since the Hatters were divisional champions that season, and this victory went some way towards repairing the damage inflicted twelve months earlier at Kenilworth Road. Prior to the comprehensive victory over Luton Town, which attracted a crowd of 15,000, the highest since Boxing Day, Rovers Supporters' Club opened its new clubhouse, boasting billiards and skittles, along with other facilities. Hartill scored ten goals in a run of seven league games leading up to the Easter period. Yet heavy defeats at Walsall, and at Aldershot on Good Friday, gave an indication that there was still work to be done. Rovers also lost 4-3 to Notts County at Meadow Lane, where the legendary Scottish forward Hughie Gallacher scored a hat-trick. Gallacher scored twice in the opening nine minutes. Rovers then recovered well from being 3-0 down before the forward scored his third goal with a seventy-first minute run and shot. This was to be the last hat-trick conceded by Rovers in league football until January 1947.

On Easter Saturday, Rovers lost an unusual game 3-1 to Cardiff City at Ninian Park. Rovers fielded the eleven players who had appeared in the previous five games, winning both home matches 4-0 but conceding thirteen goals in the three away fixtures. There were three penalties awarded in quick succession at Cardiff, and while Arthur Granville scored for the Bluebirds, Harry Houghton converted one of his two for Rovers. This equalled the three penalties awarded in the matches with Swindon Town in 1928 and Gillingham in 1935, and subsequently repeated against Newport County in 1948 and at York City in 1971.

Potential disaster was averted at Eastville on Thursday 22 April by the prompt actions of an alert watchman called Tom Berry. He spotted a fire in a storeroom beneath a stand at 11 p.m., and though kit was lost, two fire engines had the blaze out within five hours. It was generally recognised that Berry had single-handedly prevented Rovers from suffering the fate that was to befall the club in 1980. After this drama, Rovers were left with two away games to complete a creditable total of seventy-one league goals scored, with Harris and Mills contributing eight each behind Hartill. There was also a testimonial for popular full-back Bill Pickering, who scored a penalty as Rovers lost 4-2 to Bristol City. It was the end of a long association with the club, for Pickering moved to Accrington Stanley over the summer. His full-back partner, Jack Preece, had been the only ever-present for the season.

In the FA Cup, a Harris goal in each half defeated prominent amateur side Corinthians at a sparsely populated Crystal Palace. Then victory over Southport brought Second Division Leicester City to Eastville, where Rovers fell to a crushing defeat. Leicester, who were to be champions of Division Two that season, convincingly defeated Rovers 5-2. After a 3-0 win at Swindon Town, Rovers were knocked out of the Third Division (South) Cup by Watford. While Bristol City won the Gloucestershire Cup final, Rovers gained revenge by beating the old rivals at cricket.

Rovers' long association with the Allan Palmer Cup, which stretched back to Joe Clennell's goal in 1927, finally closed with defeat at the hands of Bournemouth. The Cherries gained revenge for their loss twelve months earlier by beating Rovers, the holders, 3-1. The former Rovers forward Joe Riley scored a well-taken hat-trick, with a fiftieth-minute penalty and goals after fifty-three and eighty-eight minutes, and Hartill pulled a goal back fourteen minutes from time. It was the second hat-trick Riley had scored against Rovers that season, for he had contributed all Bournemouth's goals in their 3-0 victory at Dean Court in September. The irony of the situation was not lost on Rovers, since it had been against Bournemouth themselves that Riley had scored three goals on his Rovers debut in January 1932.

1937/38

By the summer of 1937, Bristol Rovers were in freefall and heading towards the need to apply for re-election on the eve of the Second World War. In some respects, hostilities in Europe helped save the club's bacon. The Prince-Cox years were now but a memory, and the quality players who were introduced then were not being replaced. For the new season, a season ticket on the terraces cost £1, the wing-stand 40*s* and for the centre stands 50*s*.

The only summer signing to make Percy Smith's line-up for the visit to Watford on the opening day of the season was the former Dundee United inside-left Bobby Gardiner. Though standing just 5 feet 4 inches tall, he was a formidable figure, but quality support was lacking. Rovers crashed 4-0 at Watford, with Jack Preece putting the opening goal of the season past his own goalkeeper. Rovers failed to score in the opening four league games, and when Gardiner scored the club's first league goal of the season in the fifth game, it was a mere consolation in a 4-1 defeat at Torquay United.

As results went against the club, Jack Howshall was introduced at right-half, and Smith signed Ernie Parker and the experienced Harry Roberts. The latter, known as 'The Rock of Gibraltar', was a highly dependable full-back whose career encompassed over 400 league matches. He was to give Rovers valuable service, as was Albert Iles, whose successful move from Southern League football at last set

Rovers scoring goals. Iles was by far the club's top scorer with fourteen goals in his thirty-one league games. In September, the former Bristol City stalwart Archie Annan became a Rovers scout, a path later followed by Ashton Gate favourites Wally Jennings and Bob Hewison.

As it happened, the course of the season swung on the FA Cup tie against Queen's Park Rangers at Eastville in November. The sides had drawn 1-1 only a month earlier, and though Rovers went into the match with only three league wins to their name, a home tie should have given the club every chance of progressing to round two. As it was, Rangers won 8-1, before a crowd of 8,869, producing gate receipts of £520. Incredibly, the first goal did not arrive until the twenty-seventh minute, but Rangers scored five times in seventeen minutes to lead 5-0 at the break, with Fitzgerald completing his hat-trick before half-time. Pendergast pulled a consolation goal back after fifty-five minutes, but this result remains to this day the club's heaviest home defeat in first-class competitions. Rovers were not so much outplayed as overwhelmed. As with the twelve-goal defeat at Luton and eight-goal hammerings at Torquay and Swansea in the inter-war years, the size of the defeat was unexpected and demoralising.

The immediate fall-out after this sharp Cup exit was the departure of manager Percy Smith after twelve months at the club. Rovers were managerless until January, in which period four players made their first appearances for the team. Out-of-favour Tom Harris joined Southampton in an exchange deal for Tosh Withers, who made his debut in the draw with Notts County. So too did Danny Tolland, a talented but frustrating Irish forward, bought for £550 from Northampton Town, where he had been one of the few inter-war players sent off in a league game. More controversially, the third debutant was full-back Alec Millar, a £150 signing from Margate who had previously spent two years with East Fife. His registration had been bought in July by director Fred Ashmead, while Percy Smith was on holiday, yet the defender had never figured in the manager's plans. Once Smith had left, Millar went on to stake a regular place at left-back for more than a season.

During the interregnum, Rovers' form improved. Despite the absence of Iles, Rovers recorded a 5-2 victory over Walsall on Christmas Day, their largest win of the season. Les Sullivan and Tommy Mills scored a pair of goals each, and Tolland notched his first goal for the club. As so often happened in the days of double fixtures, Walsall beat Rovers by the same score twenty-four hours later, thanks largely to the outstanding form of their seventeen-year-old goalkeeper, Bert Williams, a post-war England international. Rovers responded with a much-needed single-goal victory over Bristol City, Withers' second-half goal in a keenly fought local derby proving the zenith of his brief league career.

On 18 January 1938, Rovers appointed a new manager to succeed Percy Smith. Brough Fletcher, chosen ahead of the veteran Crystal Palace defender Bob Collyer, had enjoyed a long career with Barnsley as player and manager, and had also played for Sheffield Wednesday. His was the task of steadying the ship. In the post-war era, Fletcher might well have been sacrificed following the club's poor showing in 1938/39, but he in fact remained with Rovers a further decade, rebuilding the side after the war and laying the foundations for the future. It was he who discovered young talent such as Geoff Bradford, Harry Bamford and George Petherbridge, in so doing paving the way for the halcyon days of the 1950s.

One player given a late run in the side was Wilf Smith, a full-back signed in the summer from Clevedon Town but never given a game by his former manager. Smith was a regular in the side late in the season, when Rovers' form began to revive. Although he appeared only once the following year, he stayed with the club and became one of a handful of players to appear for Rovers in league football both sides of the Second World War.

There were 4-0 defeats at both Queen's Park Rangers and Reading. In the former, Wilf Bott claimed a brace of goals to match his FA Cup achievement, while in the latter, four different opponents got on the scoresheet in a one-sided game. However, following defeat at Elm Park, Rovers were unbeaten in their final eight league games of the season. At Dean Court, Rovers recovered from a goal down to score three times in twenty minutes, Hartill and Withers both scoring in their final matches for the club.

Centre-half Matt O'Mahony, the only ever-present, contrived to score own goals in consecutive league games in the autumn. He scored past goalkeeper Nicholls in the home draws with Reading and Notts County. Somewhat bizarrely, O'Mahony was to score again for Reading in February 1939, when he contributed to Rovers' 2-0 defeat at Elm Park.

On a positive note, Rovers completed a league double over both Gillingham and Bournemouth, and also won the Gloucestershire Cup final. Goals from Wally McArthur and Albert Iles gave the club a 2-1 victory over Bristol City at Eastville. Just under 4,000 watched this game, as compared to 25,000 for the equivalent league fixture. When Rovers next won the trophy, ten years later, McArthur again played a key role.

In July 1938, news reached the club of the death of Harry Horsey, a founder member of the Black Arabs and latterly a chairman of Bristol Rovers. Seldom has one man spent as long as fifty-five years with a club, nor have many contributed in as many ways as Horsey. As a player, financial figurehead and member of the board, he epitomised the spirit of the club in its early days and his death closed a chapter in Rovers' history.

1938/39

Being forced to apply for re-election remains the nadir of Bristol Rovers' league history. Rovers had struggled all season and the prospect of finishing in last place in Division Three (South) loomed large. After a heavy defeat at Brighton on the final day of the season, Rovers found themselves stranded below Walsall on goal average, while Orient leapfrogged them with a convincing 5-0 victory over Swindon Town the same afternoon. For the only time in the club's history, Rovers were consigned to seek re-election to the league. This they were to gain comfortably, but the future would surely offer little hope. As it was, the arrival of war meant that Rovers could re-establish themselves in Division Three (South) in the late 1940s.

Yet the season had begun with a convincing 3-0 victory over Mansfield Town at Eastville. Manager Brough Fletcher had stuck with his inherited side, and there were no new faces in the Rovers, the previous season's top scorer Albert Iles scoring twice. Transfer activity had, however, been brisk, and nine new summer signings were to break into the league side, Frank Curran in particular making a big impression. The first change to the side saw Dick Spivey in place of Albert Butterworth for the visit of Southend United. The former Hull City outside-right had scored against the Shrimpers on his Torquay United debut and he repeated this feat for Rovers, his two goals leading the way to a 4-1 win.

However, following the Southend game, Rovers endured a run of thirteen consecutive league matches without a win. This autumnal spell was a major factor in the club's end-of-season struggle. In one of these games, a 2-1 defeat at Ashton Gate, many records debit both Rovers' Ray Warren and Bristol City's Jim Pearce with own goals. During this run, Rovers briefly recalled Wilf Smith, while nine other players made league debuts, eight of the summer signings and Albert Turner, a free signing in December from Cardiff City, who had previously enjoyed a glut of goals in his four years with Doncaster Rovers. One player who never made the league side was Charlie Hurst, a regular reserve player in 1938/39, whose son Geoff famously scored a hat-trick in the 1966 World Cup final.

Two factors involved in Rovers' third win of the season should come as no surprise. When this long-awaited event finally did occur, it was against struggling Mansfield Town at Field Mill, and it came as a result of second-half goals from both Turner and Curran, as well as an angled drive after twenty minutes from the ever-consistent Albert Butterworth. Frank Curran had waited patiently for three months, following his transfer from Accrington Stanley, but he wasted no time in making the centre-forward position his own. Twenty-one goals in only twenty-seven league games included ten in a five-match spell in the run-up to Easter. He scored Rovers' final pre-war league goal and also the first after the war, when Rovers drew 2-2 with Reading in August 1946.

Curran scored twice in an astonishing game at home to Ipswich Town in February. As they had done against Northampton Town in September 1935, Rovers recovered a three-goal deficit to draw 3-3. On this occasion, Curran's goals and one from Tommy Mills, all in the last half-hour, earned Rovers a point. Curran also scored four goals when Rovers defeated Swindon Town 5-0 in March. Three of these goals came before half-time, making him the fourth player to complete a first-half hat-trick for Rovers in league football. His personal haul equalled the club individual scoring record for one game, a figure often paralleled but never surpassed.

In some respects, Rovers could consider themselves a touch unfortunate to finish the season in bottom place in the division. Champions Newport County were held to a draw, Rovers did not lose to clubs such as Ipswich Town, Walsall and Queen's Park Rangers, and the away wins at Cardiff City and Mansfield Town showed great promise. No opponent scored a league hat-trick against Rovers in 1937/38 or 1938/39. There were none of the black days, such as Luton in 1936, Swansea in 1922 or Torquay in 1932. The club had not finished bottom when the goals dried up in 1922/23, nor after losing thirteen consecutive away fixtures in 1929/30. Yet, when the pressure was on, Fletcher's side appeared unable to raise their standards.

The two heaviest defeats both left stories to relate. At Bournemouth, Rovers led through Curran's forty-second minute goal at half-time, but were forced to take to the field again without the influential Ray Warren. The ten men conceded five second-half goals to lose 5-2. At Brighton, needing a point to move away from bottom place, Rovers conceded three goals in each half. Curran scored twice, but so too did Herbert Goffey, Herbert Stephens and Robert Farrell for Albion.

Matt O'Mahony, who scored an own goal for Reading for a second consecutive season, won six caps for Eire while on Rovers' books and played for Northern Ireland against Scotland in October. This international appearance, made possible by a loophole allowing players born in Eire to participate in the Home Championship competition, made O'Mahony one of a select band to have represented two different countries. He missed only four league matches all season, with Millar, Roberts and Butterworth also regular team members. Goalkeeper Nicholls and left-half McArthur were the club's only ever-presents.

Three-goal margins were the order of the day in Rovers' Cup campaigns, beating Peterborough United, losing at home to Bournemouth in the FA Cup, where all three goals came in the final twenty minutes, and losing the Gloucestershire Cup final to Bristol City. It took just one goal at Newport County to eliminate Rovers from the Third Division (South) Cup.

Through the early months of 1939, the board of directors met regularly to discuss what was considered a serious financial situation for the football club. On 5 May 1939, secretary Sid Hawkins reported that he had informed the greyhound company, in a letter dated 26 April 1939, and sanctioned by chairman Fred Ashmead, that Rovers were now prepared to sell Eastville Stadium. Isidore Kerman, chairman of the greyhound company, offered £20,000 for the freehold. There had clearly been little or no consultation with other members of the board, for other directors had simultaneously been engaged in consultations regarding the renewal of rent payments. At the same time, the directors loaned the club £200 to pay the players' wages, with Ashmead personally providing £130 of this amount.

Both Walsall and Bristol Rovers had to suffer the ignominy of applying for re-election to the Football League. Only twelve months earlier, Gillingham, fellow founder members of the Third Division (South), had lost their league status in similar circumstances. As other clubs – such as Merthyr Town, Aberdare Athletic, Thames Association – had shown, falling through the trapdoor into Southern League football could be a road of no return. Rovers had a good deal about which to be concerned. As it was, Rovers (forty-five votes) and Walsall (thirty-six votes) comfortably survived the non-League challenge of Gillingham (fifteen votes), Chelmsford City and Colchester United (one vote each). Nonetheless, the lesson had been learnt, and Brough Fletcher and his successors were keen to ensure that such a situation would not repeat itself once football had re-established itself following the Second World War.

5

War Intervenes Again

1939–46

As war clouds gathered across the continent, Rovers returned to preseason training for the 1939/40 season. The tireless and effective Matt O'Mahony, Rovers' most capped player at the time, joined league newcomers Ipswich Town for £600 in July 1939, after the board had turned down a £750 bid from Bristol City. There were four new faces and a welcome return for Jimmy Watson, but the whole country was in the surreal position of waiting for war. Watson scored twice to give Rovers renewed optimism with an unexpected 4-0 victory over Bristol City in a Football League Jubilee Match a week before the new season. As it was, crowds were well down around the country, only 10,000 at Eastville witnessing a 2-2 draw with Reading on the opening day of the season. Watson scored for Rovers just seconds after half-time from a header, his first goal for the club since January 1934, after Ray Warren's 30-yard free-kick had equalised for Rovers. Defeats followed at Ipswich Town and Crystal Palace, the latter with Albert Iles recalled to lead the line. However, only 5,000 were at Selhurst Park, for the evacuation of children was underway and Londoners' minds were understandably elsewhere. Within hours, war had been declared on Germany.

A Football League meeting on 6 September effectively aborted the 1939/40 season, and Rovers continued to play a series of friendlies, one of which was an exciting 5-5 draw with Bristol City in October. By the end of that month, a temporary Regional League was in place – the South West League – in which Rovers were to finish third, six points behind Torquay United. Crowds, quite naturally, were poor, and only 704 saw the final game of a series of four 'home' matches played at Ashton Gate, when Rovers drew 2-2 with the Gulls. The return game in February at Plainmoor attracted only 800 spectators, and Rovers trailed after forty seconds, were 3-0 down after nine minutes and lost 5-1. Torquay United's veteran Albert Hutchinson was one of the architects of the 1932 Easter Monday massacre, putting through his own net after an hour.

Rovers fielded a largely weakened but Bristol-based side. Iles was a potent force at centre-forward, scoring four times in a 7-0 win over Cardiff City in January. Wilf Whitfield, who scored a hat-trick against Swindon Town, George Tadman, Wally McArthur and Matt O'Mahony were among the players who had represented the club in league football. However, the system of guest players, which allowed far greater flexibility in player movement, was one that left Rovers' meagre resources depleted still further. Other clubs' players did come to Eastville; Les Talbot and Bill Woodward, for instance, both scored hat-tricks in different games against Swansea Town.

Eastville Stadium became the setting for other wartime activities. The future President of the United States of America, Dwight Eisenhower, visited a wartime greyhound meeting, while the bandleader Glenn Miller and high wire act The Great Blondini also appeared at Eastville. There was also an American football final played before large numbers of servicemen and, apparently (wartime restrictions prevent the modern researcher from discovering the true identity), a member of the British Royal family. Many contemporary celebrities appeared at the stadium in a bid to boost flagging spirits in the face of continued warfare, among them the famous Joe Davis who, on the evening of 23 April 1945, gave an exhibition of pool and snooker skills.

A number of Rovers players resurfaced at the more glamorous setting of Ashton Gate. Ronnie Dix, along with the veteran Clarrie Bourton, scored for City when Rovers won the derby game 4-2 after Christmas. Frank Curran, who had scored twice for Rovers in that game, added two goals for City in an exciting 4-4 draw at Eastville in March. By the time George Tadman's goal brought victory at Ashton Gate the following month, both Albert Butterworth and Jack Preece were in City's line-up. Also of note is Jack Dugnolle, who scored Plymouth Argyle's opening goal against Rovers in November 1939, and was to score an own goal in April 1946, Rovers' third in a 3-1 victory at Brighton. Len Rich, who had played in Luton's infamous 12-0 win in 1936, scored a hat-trick for Plymouth Argyle when they defeated Rovers 4-1 in May 1940.

Unable to maintain a side, Rovers were obliged to suspend their playing commitments. Like a number of other clubs, they played no matches between the end of the 1939/40 season and the start of 1945/46. One side effect of this inaction was to prove crucial. The club had no revenue, and although at first the board had strongly opposed chairman Fred Ashmead's unilateral decision to sell Eastville to the Bristol Greyhound Racing Association, the sale eventually went through on 3 March 1940. Although the greyhound company had offered more, Eastville was sold for £12,000. Rovers were granted a lease on 8 March 1940 at £400 per year to continue playing on the ground for a further twenty-one years.

During the war years, Rovers might well have folded, had it not been for the support offered by the greyhound company. In the summer of 1942, the company had suggested to Rovers' directors that the club should begin playing matches again, and had offered to meet all financial obligations for 1942/43. On 19 September 1944, the company's managing director, Constantine Augustus Lucy Stevens, and secretary John Patrick Hare were voted on to the board, bringing with them a £3,000 cash injection. A total of 1,500 new shares worth £1 each were created and sold through a loan from the greyhound company for 1*s* per share to Con Stevens, who purchased 1,000, and Hare, who bought the remainder. As the matchless 1944/45 season progressed, Rovers' debts mounted. A sum of £600 was still owed to the bank, £700 to creditors and £4,700 on outstanding loans, and the season's inaction had cost a further £1,000. On 15 June 1945, therefore, Stevens and Hare became chairman and vice chairman respectively and Charles Ferrari was appointed secretary on 20 August 1945. Effectively, from 29 November 1944, Rovers became an undisclosed subsidiary of the greyhound company for four years. On 21 September 1945, Lew Champeny, an employee of the greyhound company and a key figure in the events of 1950, was elected to the Rovers board. Various well-wishers waived more than £2,000 of the unpaid loans, and it was with a greater sense of optimism and purpose that Rovers pieced together a scratch side in the following weeks.

A number of Rovers players had made names for themselves in wartime football. Above all others, Roy Bentley, rejected by Rovers as a schoolboy, was building a career that led to twelve England caps, a hat-trick against Wales in 1954, and captaining Chelsea to the League Championship in 1955. Ronnie Dix helped Blackpool win the League Cup in 1943. Alec Miller, now with Hearts, played for Scotland in 1943, although, outfoxed by Stanley Matthews, his country lost 8-0 to England. Bobby Gardiner, still officially a Rovers player, 'guested' for Dundee United in the 1940 Scottish Cup final. Fred Chadwick scored six goals for Norwich City, who ran up ten first-half goals in their extraordinary 18-0 win against Brighton on Christmas Day 1940. David Steele turned out for Bradford Park Avenue in 1942, at the age of forty-nine, scoring in a 3-3 draw with Sheffield Wednesday. Tadman and O'Mahony played regularly for unfashionable Aberaman. The future Rovers manager Malcolm Allison, under the pseudonym Herbert Schmidt, played for Klagenfurt and Rapid Vienna in 1945.

More unusually, the former Rovers full-back Jack Smith's career ended after his foot was run over by a bus during a blackout in Wolverhampton. Still, Rovers were very fortunate to suffer no worse in wartime. Gordon Addy, for instance, whose penalty for Norwich City had been saved by Jesse Whatley in 1921, was among those killed. John Lee, an accomplished opening batsman with Somerset, who had been in the Aldershot side that visited Eastville in 1933/34 and 1934/35, was killed in action on 20 June 1944 near Bazenville, Normandy. Sandy Torrance, who played for Bristol City in the first league derby in 1922 and scored in the 1924 Gloucestershire Cup final, died in the air raid on Bristol on 14 April 1941. Also killed were several other players who had played a number of times against Rovers, including Peter Monaghan, who had scored for Bournemouth in the March 1939 fixture, Alan Fowler, who had claimed one of Swindon Town's goals three years earlier, and the Luton Town pairing of Joseph Coen, a goalkeeper briefly on Rovers' books in 1934, and Charlie Clark. Andrew Wilson, Rovers' manager between 1921 and 1926, died on 13 March 1945 at the age of sixty-four. Locally, several children died when two bombs fell in Eastville Park on 25 November 1940, and an unexploded German wartime bomb was discovered in 1984 during the construction of the Tesco supermarket next to the stadium. The air raids of 16 and 17 March 1941 affected much of the Eastville and Easton area, including Stapleton Road gasworks and railway station. There were 1,299 civilian deaths in Bristol during the Blitz, including the former Rovers player George Berry, along with his wife and young daughter. Some 140 people were killed in the district in three air raids between September 1940 and March 1941.

And so it was that Rovers emerged from the war to participate in the southern division of the unofficial Division Three (South) in 1945/46. Eastville was unscathed, unlike Ashton Gate, where a stand had been bombed on two consecutive nights in January 1941. Plymouth Argyle and Millwall had suffered fires, Exeter City and Swindon Town had seen their grounds turned into military camps, Newport County's Somerton Park had been commissioned by the Civil Defence and Reading's club offices had been bombed. Further afield there had been similar stories to that of Sheffield United, whose Bramall Lane ground was struck by no fewer than ten bombs in December 1940.

On the pitch, young players such as Vic Lambden, George Petherbridge and Harry Bamford were offered first-team football, alongside older and more experienced heads such as Albert Butterworth and Tommy Mills. Rovers played Bristol City on Boxing Day 1944, and formed an amateur side in the spring of 1945 in preparation for the new season. Lambden scored hat-tricks in a 6-2 victory over Patchway Sports, a 5-2 win against Eden Grove, and in a defeat and a draw, after Rovers had held a 3-1 half-time lead, against army sides. Three goals from Bert 'Nobby' Clark helped defeat BAC 5-1. Rovers reappointed manager Brough Fletcher on 1 July 1945 and, on 20 August, Charles Ferrari became club secretary to replace Sid Hawkins, who had joined Charlton Athletic. Harry Boxall, who had been a club director since the spring of 1928, died in October 1945. Lambden scored a hat-trick against Reading in November 1945, while 'Nobby' Clark scored three times against Aldershot in a match Rovers lost 5-4, with the veteran Bill Hullett, whose goals knocked Rovers out of the 1946/47 FA Cup, scoring twice for the visitors. Butterworth, on the other hand, also appeared against Rovers for a Bristol City side that included Jack Preece. Jack Weare saved a twentieth-minute Terry Wood penalty at Ninian Park after Lambden had put Rovers ahead, but Cardiff City recovered to win 4-2, Ken Hollyman scoring once in each half. Rovers arrived at Plainmoor in August 1945 with their red-and-white quartered shirts by mistake, which clashed with

Torquay United's kit. Leant a set of shirts, Rovers played in all white and won 3-0. There were also some extraordinary Western League results, as Welton Rovers were defeated 14-0 and Soundwell 11-3.

Seven victories and six defeats saw Rovers finish mid-table – fifth place in their abbreviated division. Rovers also reached the semi-finals of the Division Three (South) Cup where, despite a Vic Lambden goal, Walsall ran out 3-1 winners. In the FA Cup, victory over Swindon Town through four goals in nine first-half minutes was followed by an aggregate defeat against the old rivals from Ashton Gate. Don Clark, who had scored twice when the clubs met in September, grabbed a goal in each leg of this tie. He also scored four times as City won the first post-war Gloucestershire Cup final 5-0 at Eastville. He was to continue to prove a handful for Rovers' defence in the immediate post-war years. More encouragingly, the goalless local derby at Eastville in March had attracted a crowd of over 25,000, lending optimism to the belief that the rebirth of the Football League in 1946 could lead to a golden era for football in Bristol.

6

The Golden Years

1946/47

The anticipated post-war struggle facing Bristol Rovers following several years of inaction was a very real problem in 1946, but 1947 heralded a turn in fortunes for the Eastville club. A run of ten defeats in eleven league games in the autumn included soul-destroying reversals at Cardiff City and Notts County. However, victory over Crystal Palace on 4 January was the first of thirteen in an eighteen-match run, and Rovers were able to finish the first post-war season in fourteenth place. Bland statistics indicate a clear picture of a season of two halves.

When professional football returned in its recognised format, the general public, starved of full-time sport for so long, was quick to support the new season. Attendances were high: over 30,000 at Eastville for the visit of Cardiff City, bringing gate receipts of £2,218, and 25,000 for Bristol City. Manager Brough Fletcher, retained by Rovers and nurturing young Bristol-born players, worked to build together a side worthy of the enthusiastic support the side was shown. The club's wage bill to players and officials for 1946/47 came to £9,483. The match programme rose in cost from *2d* to *3d*. Football had returned in earnest.

Frank Curran, the scorer of Rovers' final goal of the 1938/39 season, scored the first of 1946/47 with a well-placed drive after twenty minutes. The opening-day draw at home to Reading also featured a debut goal for Vic Lambden from Lance Carr's cross ten minutes after half-time, the first of 117 league goals the Bristol-born forward was to score for Rovers in a decade. The first components were being put in place for the all-conquering side of 1952/53. Harry Bamford, Jackie Pitt and George Petherbridge, mainstays of the Rovers side through the halcyon days of the 1950s, were given league debuts early in the season. Ray Warren, the captain of that championship-winning side, was one of three ever-presents in a highly changeable Rovers team. The first minute of the directors' meeting on 11 November 1946 introduced the infamous 'no buy, no sell' policy, although, notably, Con Stevens had already left the meeting, while John Hare and Lew Champeny both voted against.

Curran and Warren were just two of five players to play league football for Rovers both sides of the war. Wilf Smith, Wally Whitfield and Wally McArthur all returned to first-team action. Other players, such as Carr, an ever-present in his only season with the club, and the veteran Harry Smith had enjoyed long and successful careers with other clubs before the war. These were understandably years of great change, and it is no surprise that as many as twenty-nine players appeared in the Rovers line-up before the end of December. Indeed, the side that drew with Brighton in December showed six changes to the eleven beaten 3-0 by Northampton Town at Eastville. This constitutes the largest number of changes to any post-war Rovers league side. It is, however, no great surprise to learn that, at this stage, an own goal was Rovers' only score in seven league matches. Continuity was indeed well nigh impossible to maintain.

One new face in the side (albeit briefly) was reserve player-coach Harry Smith, a former Nottingham Forest and Darlington full-back, who became, at thirty-eight years and forty-three days, Rovers' oldest league debutant when he appeared in the Northampton Town defeat. Another was Fred Leamon, a former Royal Marine from Jersey. Leamon became the club's top scorer in 1946/47 with thirteen league goals. Rovers' third ever-present, besides Carr and Warren, was full-back Barry Watkins, who embarked on a run of fifty-two consecutive league appearances.

Heavy defeats were prominent at home and away early in the season. Teenager Jackie Sewell, a future England international, scored two of the six goals Jack Weare conceded at Notts County. With Rovers already 3-0 down after twenty-six minutes, Sewell scored twice in a minute, just past the hour mark, both times converting sweeping County moves. Weare left the field injured at Cardiff City after only seven minutes, with Rovers already trailing to a third-minute Stan Richards goal. Ray Warren played eighty-three minutes in goal, and ten-man Rovers, in unconventional red-and-white quartered shirts, crashed to a 4-0 defeat. Watford scored four times at Eastville in September, where Rovers, 3-0 down after forty-eight minutes, pulled two goals back before being defeated by a spectacular right-foot drive on the hour by debutant Johnny Usher, whose hat-trick seven days earlier had helped defeat Rovers reserves. There were six goals in a seventeen-minute spell midway through this 4-3 defeat. The Bristol City side that won 3-0 at Eastville featured a forty-three-year-old goalkeeper in Alex Ferguson, still the oldest man to appear against Rovers in league football. Mansfield Town, Southend United and Exeter City all scored three times against Rovers in games before Christmas. Southend achieved this feat with full-back Bob Jackson in goal, a secret kept hidden from Rovers after regular goalkeeper Albert Hankey had been injured earlier in the day.

After New Year, as Rovers strung together some good results, heavy defeats were less frequent. However, there were demoralising 3-0 reversals at both

Torquay United, for whom Joe Conley scored all the goals, and Leyton Orient. The 4-0 defeat at Ashton Gate in February, with Wilson Thomas and Don Clark scoring twice each, remains Rovers' heaviest loss in league action on that ground. Ironically, though, the side that played on the day remained unchanged for a club record of twelve consecutive league games. This in itself symbolises the rebirth Rovers experienced in the latter stages of this first pre-war league season.

A run of five straight wins in February and March first set the club on the right path. Rovers scored three goals in each of the first four victories, several of these emanating from Leamon, who scored twice at Bournemouth. Outside-left Carr scored the only goal of the game, a rising left-foot drive at the Thirteen Arches End after twenty-seven minutes, to defeat Cardiff City at snowy Eastville. He then scored Rovers' second at Carrow Road seven days later in an exciting 3-3 draw. One familiar face in the Aldershot side Rovers defeated in January was Alf Fitzgerald, who had scored an FA Cup hat-trick at Eastville for Queen's Park Rangers in November 1937. Victory at home to Mansfield Town proved to be the third in the Stags' club record run of seven consecutive league defeats.

Once the goals were flowing, Rovers were to lose just once in a run of thirteen league matches to move to mid-table respectability and banish the ghost of pre-war re-election. Notts County, so dominant when they had beaten Rovers at Meadow Lane in November, were humbled 4-1 at Eastville, Leamon again scoring twice. Just three days after a comfortable victory over Rovers at Brisbane Road, Leyton Orient conceded six goals on their visit to Eastville, with Len Hodges and Jimmy Morgan both scoring in each half, and Ken Wookey creating three goals as Rovers raced to a 6-0 lead on the hour mark. The stage was set for some bigger victories in the years to come.

Ray Warren scored penalties in both league games with Queen's Park Rangers; his first, Rovers' second goal at Loftus Road in October, was the centre-half's first league goal since November 1936, a club record gap of almost ten years. Wing-half Wally McArthur's goal in the defeat at Port Vale in April was his first since the opening day of the 1938/39 season. Rovers completed their season with a home game against Ipswich Town, whom they were to meet in more dramatic circumstances twelve months later. This match kicked off at 3 p.m., with Bristol City's remaining home game with Queen's Park Rangers starting at 6.30 p.m. Both matches were to result in a 1-1 draw.

The FA Cup brought Rovers no joy as, for the first time since elevation to the Football League in 1920, the club was knocked out by a non-League side. Rovers visited Penydarren Park, where a crowd of 14,000 saw Merthyr Tydfil defeat their deflated opponents 3-1. Rovers led at the interval through Lambden's twentieth-minute goal, but Bill Hullett scored with a rising shot soon after the break and with a header ten minutes from time, before George Crisp added the third. The Gloucestershire Cup final was again lost, Bristol City winning in a replay.

1947/48

However remarkably well Rovers survived having to apply for re-election, ultimate success could not entirely hide the side's shortcomings. Rovers had been a point adrift at the foot of the Division Three (South) with only two games to play. There had been one run of six consecutive defeats and eleven home defeats in total. Manager Brough Fletcher was gradually piecing together the side Bert Tann would lead to great success, but the early steps on the path were faltering ones.

The arrival of the former Fulham outside-left Harold Cranfield, a mere youth at twenty-nine, saw thirty-seven-year-old Lance Carr move to Merthyr Tydfil on a free transfer. This apart, Rovers opened the new season with an eminently recognisable side. Only twelve players were used in the first ten league games as Rovers sought greater on-field consistency. As the season progressed, Geoff Fox and Bryan Bush made their first appearances in the side Tann was to inherit. Josser Watling made his league bow on the left, while Fred Chadwick, a prolific wartime goalscorer, played in half a dozen games at inside-forward.

Jackie Pitt, the only ever-present, was level with Fred Leamon as the club's second highest goalscorer behind young Vic Lambden, who contributed eleven league goals on his return to the side following a ten-month absence. The full-back pairing of Harry Bamford and Barry Watkins continued to develop, while Ken Wookey's six goals from outside-right came at crucial moments in the season. Ralph Jones, later a successful singer who performed at Glyndebourne and at the Edinburgh Festival, was given a run in the side at full-back, but was injured in the 4-0 defeat at Exeter City and was out of football for two years.

Secretary Charles Ferrari resigned on 23 October 1947, and the greyhound company assumed responsibility for the management of Rovers' accounts, with John Gummow appointed secretary on 8 December. Gummow was to serve in this role for a year before the appointment of Ron Moules, who continued as club secretary up to his sudden death in 1967.

The Rovers director John Hare had called a meeting on 26 August 1947 to set up a supporters' club. The purpose was to back the club financially and vocally, giving a mouthpiece to the paying spectators. As football emerged from the repression of wartime, this appeared a natural step. The first chairman selected was a local solicitor, Herbert John Hampden Alpass. As a cricketer, Hampden Alpass had played in seven first-class games for Gloucestershire, where he had been a colleague of the former Rovers player Wally Hammond. At the age of forty, he now had considerable energy to put into Bristol Rovers, and he was to support the club in a number of ways for many years. He ran the supporters' club for two years before resigning in 1949, whereupon Eric Godfrey ran the organisation through the glory years of the 1950s. One early committee member was Ray Bywater, who remained on the board until January 1966. Other early volunteers included Joan Bruton, Tom Spiller, Bill Creed and Harry Stansfield, whose father had played in goal in Rovers' first Football League match. At its peak, the club was to have a membership of over 2,000.

On the field, the tally of eleven home league defeats, a club record equalled only in the relegation season of 1992/93, goes some way toward explaining why this was a season of struggle. Don Clark was again one of Bristol City's scorers as they won at Eastville, Doug Lishman scored twice for Walsall in their away victory and a Watkins own goal proved to be Southend United's winner when they visited. The most extraordinary home defeat, however, was clearly Newport County's 3-2 victory on Easter Saturday. Rovers had not scored for four games, but Jackie Pitt successfully converted two early penalties, after just five and six minutes, to equal Jonah Wilcox's achievement on Boxing Day 1925. It was a game of three first-half penalties, with County's Len Emmanuel scoring one after thirty-three minutes in his side's success. Emmanuel, once on Rovers' books and the uncle of a future Rovers midfielder, had himself scored two penalties in the sides' 2-2 draw at Somerton Park in November. Rovers conceded four penalties in three league games at this stage. Emmanuel thus became the only opponent to convert three penalties against Rovers in a league season.

To counter this argument, Rovers scored four goals at home to Brighton, as well as at Leyton Orient and Ipswich Town. In November, two goals apiece from Leamon and Len Hodges earned the side a convincing 5-1 victory at Norwich City. The largest victory, however, came at Eastville on Easter Monday. Vic Lambden scored a hat-trick inside nine first-half minutes, and a fourth after half-time as Rovers beat Aldershot 7-1 to equal the club's largest league victory at that time. Pitt scored twice, for the second consecutive game, as Rovers defeated opponents who had beaten them 2-0 only three days earlier.

After a promising start, Rovers' season began to fall away in the New Year. The Aldershot victory ended a run of six consecutive league defeats, only one short of the club-record seven straight losses that started the 1961/62 relegation season. Queen's Park Rangers and Bristol City both put five goals past Rovers. Don Clark, tormenting Rovers' defence as usual, on Valentine's Day became the only City player to score a league hat-trick in a local derby at Ashton Gate. Rovers trailed 3-0 by half-time to Norwich City, with Les Eyre scoring twice and Driver Allenby once, before Rovers rallied and almost claimed a point. Bamford's thirty-fifth minute own goal was Exeter City's second in Rovers' heavy defeat at St James' Park in March, Dennis Hutchings scoring once in each half.

There had been high-scoring games, both sides for instance scoring at least twice in four consecutive league matches in the autumn. However, with two matches to play, Rovers were fighting for survival. On the morning of Wednesday 28 April, Rovers were bottom of the table with thirty points and two games to play, both against Ipswich Town. Above them stood three clubs: Norwich City on thirty-one points, Swindon Town on thirty-two and Brighton on thirty-three. Incredibly, Rovers followed up a 2-0 home victory over Ipswich Town with a resounding 4-0 victory at Portman Road against opponents that had, not long before, harboured genuine championship hopes. Rovers had clutched a final position of twentieth from the jaws of re-election.

As Rovers completed a run of five wins in seven league games, they moved above both Norwich and Brighton on goal average. Both Rovers and Norwich won final-day games away to top-four sides to leave Brighton bottom of the table in the wake of their goalless draw at Swansea. It was, indeed, a narrow escape for Rovers and, given the need to apply for re-election in 1938/39, and the club's desperate start to the first post-war season, failure to win at Ipswich Town would have left the club's league future in a perilous state. Indeed, Gillingham, who returned to Division Three (South) in 1950, headed a plethora of viable alternatives to a struggling side like Bristol Rovers.

Nonetheless, survival had been achieved, and with it were sown the first seeds of a bright future. Bert Tann, who was to succeed Fletcher as manager in January 1950, arrived at Eastville in February and swiftly persuaded three of Rovers' staff to attend a Football Association trainers' and coaches' course in May 1948. Trainer Bert Williams, his assistant Wally McArthur and assistant coach Harry Smith were the first Rovers employees to attend such a course, and this set a benchmark for the years to follow. There was considerable hope that the future would bring success.

A free-scoring FA Cup run earned Rovers a lucrative fourth-round tie against Second Division Fulham at Craven Cottage. In fact, behind after only ten minutes and 2-1 down at half-time, Rovers had only defeated unfancied Leytonstone through Morgan's headed winner. Pre-war Rovers player Bill Pendergast was New Brighton's centre-forward in their 4-0 defeat at Eastville. Lambden and Morgan had both scored in all three previous Rovers ties and, in their new-found enthusiasm, the supporters' club took 1,000 spectators to the Fulham game. Rovers put up a brave show before a 20,000 crowd, but lost 5-2, despite goals from McArthur and young George Petherbridge. Arthur Stevens, who was to score twice in Rovers' FA Cup quarter-final on the same ground ten years later, scored a hat-trick. In April, Rovers entertained a touring Racing Club Haarlem side, winning by a single Lambden goal after ten minutes and laying the foundations for a close season tour of the Netherlands. Once survival had been achieved, a 2-1 win at Ashton Gate secured the Gloucestershire Cup, Morgan and Watkins both scoring with low shots inside the opening eighteen minutes. Barry Watkins had not scored in his first sixty-two league games for Rovers, but six league and Cup goals late in the season proved his versatility.

1948/49

Rovers' oft-discussed 'no buy, no sell' policy had its origin in the immediate post-war years. The directors decreed that the club could develop local talent and keep it at

Eastville. To this end, only free transfers, generally of peripheral players, were likely to occur. Over the summer of 1948, Fred Chadwick moved to Street and Harold Cranfield to King's Lynn, while Peter Sampson and Bill Roost arrived from local football. Fred Laing from Middlesborough and Newport County's Harry Haddon also arrived on free transfers. When Ken Wookey was sold to Swansea Town in November, the £1,000 transfer fee was put into the players' benefit fund.

Manager Brough Fletcher was continuing to build the side his successor Bert Tann was to lead into Division Two. Fifth place in Division Three (South) was a good indication that the raising of standards was under way at Eastville. Fletcher's side was becoming more consistent both in appearance and in results. Defensive players Harry Bamford, Geoff Fox, Wally McArthur and Ray Warren were all ever-presents, while a further four players missed just one league game each. The side still, however, lacked a prolific goalscorer to partner the ever-improving Vic Lambden. The imminent arrival on the scene of Geoff Bradford was to have a profound effect on Rovers' on-field success.

Preparation for the new season included a two-match visit to the Netherlands. Rovers lost 1-0 to NEC Nijmegen and beat Racing Club Haarlem 4-2, thanks to two goals from Lambden and one apiece from Barry Watkins and Maurice Lockier. However well prepared the side may have appeared, there was a heavy defeat on the opening day of the season, as Ipswich Town crushed Rovers 6-1 at Eastville. Strangely, this was a third consecutive league fixture against the Suffolk club, yet memories of the four-goal win at Portman Road in May were cast aside as Rovers collapsed to a then club-record home league defeat. Sampson, making his club debut and on his way to 339 league matches for the Eastville side, and goalkeeper Harry Liley did not play again in the league that season, while Ken Wookey was playing his final game for Rovers. Bill Jennings and John Dempsey scored twice each for Ipswich, who scored sixteen goals in their first three league games but finished the season below Rovers in the Third Division (South) table.

After the opening four games, Rovers were to suffer only one heavy defeat – a 5-0 mauling at Swansea Town where future Welsh international Frank Scrine scored a hat-trick and twenty-eight-year-old Roy Paul, later the winner of thirty-three Welsh caps, also found his name on the scoresheet. Indeed, when Noel Kinsey scored twice and Ron Ashman once for Norwich City on 4 December, it was the final time that season Rovers conceded three goals in a game. By then, Rovers had also crashed 4-1 at Notts County, whose £20,000 signing of Tommy Lawton had caused great concern over spiralling transfer prices. Lawton scored four times as County beat Ipswich Town 9-2 only twelve days later, but the bubble soon burst and Rovers completed the season six places above the Meadow Lane club.

Thereafter, Rovers enjoyed a relatively trouble-free season. Only sixteen players were used in the final forty-one league games of the forty-two-match season. The largest victory was 5-1 at Aldershot, George Petherbridge scoring twice, while Warren and the home side's Tom Sinclair both scored from the penalty spot.

Jimmy Morgan scored twice in a 4-0 victory over Bournemouth at Eastville. Bill Roost scored a couple of goals on his debut as Reading were beaten 4-1 at Eastville on Good Friday, and another twenty-four hours later as Port Vale lost by the same score, Josser Watling adding a brace of goals. Three points were taken off Bristol City, a 3-1 win at Eastville being the fourth of six straight home victories after the disastrous opening game.

The 1-1 draw with Swindon Town in October, where Lambden scored after fifty-six minutes for Rovers and Jimmy Bain from Maurice Owen's pass fourteen minutes later for the Robins, ended a remarkable run, unparalleled in the club's history – thirty-seven consecutive league matches without a draw. As is the nature of such records, Rovers proceeded to draw ten league games in the season, including four in succession in the spring. Three of these ten draws were secured through Ray Warren penalty kicks. He scored from the penalty spot in both of the last two games, the latter past his future Rovers teammate Bert Hoyle at Exeter City, to end the season with a club record of seven successful penalties in a season. This match at Exeter was watched by a crowd of 7,000, the lowest at a Rovers game all season.

The lowest attendance at a game played at Eastville was the 11,147 who saw the 2-0 defeat at the hands of Aldershot in April. Bearing in mind that Rovers did not attract a five-figure home crowd at all during the relatively successful years between April 1985 and December 1999, much can be made of the club's loyal support in the post-war period. For the third year in succession, the size of crowds had risen, heralding the golden years of the 1950s. In 1948/49, the average attendance for a league game at Eastville was 17,539, the sixth highest in the division, a figure that would increase to the club's seasonal best of 24,662 in 1953/54.

Two prolific goalscorers were able to contribute to the fifty-one league goals conceded, the fewest since 1933/34. Guido Roffi, Ynysbwl-born of Italian descent, scored for Newport County against Rovers at Somerton Park for the first of two consecutive seasons. For the third year in succession, Bristol City's Don Clark scored in both league fixtures against Rovers. Although he scored in each of the first six post-war derby matches and remains the only player to score a league hat-trick for the Robins in these games, his total of nine goals against Rovers still lags behind the figure of twelve goals in league local derbies scored by the prolific John Atyeo.

Rovers did, however, beat Bristol City in September, their first league victory over the old rivals since Christmas 1937. A huge crowd at Eastville saw Jackie Pitt and McArthur in fine form for Rovers. After twenty-five minutes, feeding off Petherbridge, Lambden beat the veteran Dennis Roberts and drove past George Marks. Five minutes later, Rovers were two goals ahead when Watling volleyed home from 15 yards. Just six minutes after half-time, Lambden's through ball sent Petherbridge through to secure a victory that was straightforward, despite Clark's headed reply from a John Davies cross five minutes from time.

Ipswich Town, having inflicted a heavy defeat on Rovers, featured prominently in the season. Rovers, in white shirts and blue shorts, won 1-0 at Portman Road in December, Jimmy Morgan scoring after sixty-five minutes from a Petherbridge cross.

There was a sharp exit from the FA Cup at Walsall, where home forwards Arthur Aldred and Phil Chapman scored as Rovers lost 2-1. This enabled Rovers to arrange a friendly with Newcastle United on Fourth Round day in January, a precursor to the epic FA Cup tie two seasons later. Sadly for the crowd of 25,855, this game was abandoned because of fog just seven minutes after half-time with the score 1-1, Petherbridge having scored for the Pirates. Goals from Lambden, the club's top scorer in the league with thirteen, and Morgan, enabled Rovers to retain the Gloucestershire Cup. Rovers won the White Hart Cup in defeating Bridgwater in May 1949, and also played a Berkeley and District XI, as well as Cadbury Heath for the Frank Loader Fund.

1949/50

One of the major turning points in the history of Bristol Rovers was the appointment of Bertram James Tann as manager early in January 1950. The new manager arrived on the personal recommendation of Sir Stanley Rous and Cliff Lloyd, later the secretary of the Professional Footballers' Association and once a Rovers reserves player. Tann, a charismatic forty-five-year-old Londoner, who had played professional football with Charlton Athletic, breathed new life into Brough Fletcher's side. He forged close working links with the local community through schools and organisations, and established preseason training camps at Uphill, Weston-super-Mare. His innovative approach even led to an appearance on the quiz show *The £1,000 Word*, on the first day (14 January 1958) that the channel destined to become ITV was on the air. His eighteen years as manager were to see Rovers reach two FA Cup quarter-finals as well as the distant dreamland of Division Two. In addition, his revival of Rovers' fortunes helped distract some of the attention away from mounting dilemmas off the field.

Over the summer of 1949, Fletcher was once again unable to break away from the board's 'no buy, no sell' policy. This was a policy that would both restrict Tann but also enable him to build a Rovers side capable of achieving success. Of six new arrivals, only Frank McCourt could claim to be a regular in Rovers' side, although Tony James, a former Brighton inside-left, contributed five league goals. Unable to sell, Rovers lost just two players through the close season, both to Trowbridge Town. Harry Haddon was to score over 200 goals and spend seven years as manager at the Western League club, while Fred Laing left after one season to work at Butlins Holiday Camp in Ayr. Bert Hawkins, who had never made Rovers' first team, left over the close season and played for Bristol City, West Ham United and Queen's Park Rangers in the Football League. Over the summer of 1949, more than £250,000 had been spent on pitch improvements and concrete terracing at Eastville, increasing the terracing capacity from 6,000 to an unlikely 27,000.

The oft-seen photograph of Bill Roost standing up to the Ipswich Town goalkeeper, Tom Brown, epitomises in many respects the Rovers of the later Fletcher era. His two goals in that game and two more against Leyton Orient in December brought rare convincing wins, but early season form was largely disappointing. Eight victories and twelve defeats prior to New Year did not inspire confidence. Some young talent had been blooded, most notably Geoff Bradford, who played in depressing defeats at Crystal Palace and at home to Watford. Generally, however, the club was waiting for the major input Tann was to contribute.

By the turn of the year, Rovers were out of the FA Cup, falling to a nineteenth-minute Maurice Owen goal at Swindon Town. The heaviest defeat had been 4-0 at Carrow Road, where Les Eyre scored twice for Norwich City. Rovers also conceded three goals in a game on four occasions in an early season fortnight. Trips to Ipswich Town and Southend United both ended in 3-1 defeats, while both Notts County and Bristol City scored three times at Eastville. County's scorers were the England international Tommy Lawton, who scored twice, and outside-left Tom Johnston, while City's victory was a demoralising blow for which Rovers were to seek ample revenge in January.

Rovers were due to meet Port Vale at Eastville on 10 December, a game that was put back seven days as Vale were obliged to fulfil an FA Cup tie on that day. Only 9,890 were present on the final Saturday before Christmas Eve as goals from George Petherbridge and Josser Watling earned Rovers a 2-1 victory. For the blank Saturday, a friendly was hastily arranged, with Millwall the visitors to Eastville. Rovers were a goal up through Jimmy Morgan after only five minutes, before succumbing to defeat before a crowd of 4,613. The final game of the Fletcher era was a tepid 1-1 draw at home to Southend United. Bill Roost, Rovers' seasonal top scorer with thirteen league goals, was the home side's scorer, following a ninth-minute run and cross from Watling, with Albert Wakefield getting his name on the scoresheet for the Shrimpers ten minutes after half-time.

On 2 January, Fletcher was dismissed and his assistant trainer Dick Mann, with the club since November 1945, followed on 31 January. Although the decision had been a unanimous one, it provoked a rift between directors that was to plague Rovers for a number of months. Fletcher himself was to spend just one brief spell in football after leaving Eastville, joining Walsall as manager in 1952; he settled in Bristol, where he died in 1972. Tann's task, as his replacement, was to convert a team of local players and free transfer signings into a side capable of holding its own in Division Three (South), and subsequently in Division Two. His first game in charge saw Rovers gain ample revenge for September's defeat by beating Bristol City 2-1 before a crowd of 33,697 at Ashton Gate. The combination of the big occasion and the feel-good factor as the new decade opened helped Tann's period as manager to start in the most positive manner possible.

Tann certainly inherited very settled defensive and half-back lines. Harry Bamford and Geoff Fox continued to be models of reliability at full-back, with Fox and centre-half Ray Warren ever-presents, and right-half Jackie Pitt missing only two games. However, no forward appeared in more games than Roost, whose twenty-eight appearances in forty-two league matches made him stand out in attack. There was obviously work to be done in this regard, and Geoff Bradford was recalled in February, scoring the opening goal in a 2-0 victory at Watford, the first of a club-record 242 in the league. Eleven wins in the first nineteen league games under Bert Tann enabled Rovers to finish in ninth place, a respectable finish to the league season. The largest win, 5-1 at home to Norwich City in April, was achieved through five separate goalscorers, and Rovers bizarrely completed the season without drawing any away games.

However, developments off the field were drawing attention away from the club's performances. Five directors, Bert Hoare, Jim Bissicks, Eric Lloyd, George Humphreys junior and Ernest Smith, were distancing themselves from the three with interests in the greyhound company: Con Stevens, John Hare and Lew Champeny. A number of disagreements, notably the role of Rovers at Eastville and the knock-on effects of the 'no buy, no sell' policy, dropped on 1 February, had been fuelled by poor on-field performances. The appointment of a new manager had brought these points to a head. Although Tann's side was now achieving more positive results, the situation with the board of directors continued to deteriorate.

The spring of 1950 witnessed two key developments in the saga. The chairman and vice chairman, Stevens and Hare, in line with their interests regarding the Bristol Greyhound Racing Association, were relieved of their positions on 21 March. The Greyhound Company had hitherto handled Rovers' accounts, and this task was now taken on by club secretary John Gummow. On 22 March, Lloyd became chairman with Hoare as his deputy. In a separate development, an FA Commission met in Bristol on the final day of the month and subsequently fined Rovers £250 after examining the club's books. The greyhound company was instructed to dispose of its controlling interest in the football club and the former secretary, Charles Ferrari, was banned from football management.

As the season drew to a close, the situation appeared to be resolved. In order to lose its controlling interest, the greyhound company sold 400 shares of £1 each, which Mr Hare held as their representative in his capacity as a private individual. In anticipation that the 'non-greyhound' directors were likely to be removed from office, the directors secured the appointment of three new board members. Hampden Alpass, a figure already well-respected in football and cricket circles, Syd Gamlin and Dr Matt Nicholson gave no promises or undertakings and were duly elected on 18 May, with Alpass as chairman. Sure enough, Jim Bissicks disposed of enough shares to disqualify him from the board, while Hoare, Lloyd, Humphreys and Smith were removed through a poll vote at a shareholders' meeting eight days later. Normal boardroom relations gradually returned, but the question of Rovers' relationship with the greyhound company continued unabated until the club's departure from Eastville in 1986.

Rovers' season was completed by defeat in the Gloucestershire Cup final to a couple of first-half goals from Bristol City's Sid Williams. The attendance of 16,560 brought gate receipts of £1,150, and represents the highest crowd ever to watch a Gloucestershire Cup tie at Ashton Gate. Blackburn Rovers attracted a crowd of 13,349 to Eastville for a January friendly, in which Tony James and George Petherbridge scored twice apiece. On 31 July 1950, Rovers reported an annual profit of £2,574.

1950/51

While Rovers' financial affairs continued to come under scrutiny, the side's performances on the field under manager Bert Tann still impressed. Sixth place in Division Three (South) was a fine end-of-season position, and a first-ever FA Cup quarter-final, through a Cup run that earned the club £5,754 was a major achievement. Rovers' exploits fired the imagination of the success-starved Bristol sporting public. During the summer of 1950, the board had waived its 'no buy, no sell' doctrine to allow two transfers to take place. Goalkeeper Bert Hoyle was signed from Exeter City for £350, while Frank McCourt was sold for £2,000 to Manchester City, where he won six Northern Ireland caps. Len Hodges moved on a free transfer to Swansea Town, while veteran wing-half Wally McArthur retired to become assistant trainer.

This season is, of course, primarily remembered for the scintillating FA Cup run that took the club further in the competition than ever before. It was slow in starting; Rovers required three games to dispose of obdurate non-League Llanelli in the first round. Rovers and Llanelli each played in eleven FA Cup matches in 1950/51, more than any other competing club. The Welsh side boasted Jock Stein, later an influential international manager with Scotland, at centre-half, while their right-half, Len Emanuel, was well known to the Eastville crowd. Once Rovers had won the second replay 3-1 at Ninian Park, they still required three more games before disposing of Gillingham 2-1 in appalling weather at White Hart Lane, with Ray Warren converting a penalty five minutes from time. The Gills were enjoying their first season back in the Football League after failing to be re-elected in 1938.

Rovers' lowest home crowd of the season (10,000) saw the third-round clash with Aldershot. Once Vic Lambden had given Rovers the lead after only eight seconds, it was plain sailing, and the 5-1 victory incorporated a Lambden hat-trick. Over 26,000 saw Rovers win at Second Division Luton Town in the next round, George Petherbridge scoring the winning goal. Cup fever gripped Bristol and a new ground record of 31,660, producing receipts of £2,600, gathered at Eastville for the visit of Hull City. The Second Division visitors fielded the veteran former England international Raich Carter and the future England manager Don Revie as their inside-forwards. Two goals from Josser Watling helped give Rovers a convincing 3-0 victory and a place in the quarter-finals for the first time in the club's history. Watling's first followed a goalmouth scramble after twenty-six minutes, and his second, ten minutes after half-time, crashed in off the crossbar. A quarter of an hour from time, victory was sealed when Roost set up Lambden for the third.

On 24 February 1951, Rovers ground out a goalless draw with Newcastle United in the FA Cup quarter-final at St James' Park. The attendance at this game, 62,787, which produced £7,561 in gate receipts, remains the largest ever at a Bristol Rovers match. Around 5,000 Rovers supporters had witnessed this momentous game, but some 100,000 queued at Eastville two days later for tickets for the Wednesday afternoon replay. A line of policemen was deployed to keep around 50,000 people out of Eastville car park as soon as it became evident how over-subscribed the game had become, while His Majesty's Cinema was turned into a medical treatment station. As it was, a number of businesses shut, supporters tuned in to live wireless commentary and 30,074 crammed into Eastville for the game itself. Fifteen minutes in, amid scenes of incredulous delight, Geoff Bradford scored a fine opportunist goal to give Rovers a surprise lead, prompting strains of the crowd's favourite song, 'Goodnight Irene', to echo around the ground. By half-time, however, goals from Ernie Taylor, whose shot deflected in off Geoff Fox, Charlie Crowe and the legendary Jackie Milburn, gave the Magpies victory, despite a spirited second-half Rovers revival. Newcastle United went on to win the Cup, the same eleven players who had faced Rovers twice in four days defeating Blackpool at Wembley.

Off the field, Rovers were subjected to a lengthy Board of Trade enquiry under Section 164 of the Companies Act of 1948 into the club's affairs since 1932, published as a report in 1951. This document gives evidence of investigation into serious allegations regarding the relationship between the football club and greyhound companies. In particular, the modification of the 1932 lease in January 1934 and the subsequent hasty sale of Eastville to the greyhound company came in for close scrutiny. Inspectors interviewed Sir Stanley Rous, the secretary of the Football Association and Isidore Kerman, the chairman of the British Greyhound Racing Association, in London on 14 September 1950. There was also criticism concerning a written report by Hampden Alpass and John Hare, submitted at a board meeting on 17 August 1950, into Rovers' rights as tenants at Eastville. It was clear that no such report had been requested, and Syd Gamlin expressed astonishment that this had taken place secretly. Gamlin wished for it to be put on record that 'he considered it improper for this to have taken place without a definite resolution by the Board' (Board of Trade report, 1951, P20, Section IV ii). As in 1940, rash decisions by individual directors had serious repercussions for the club. The Board of Trade enquiry found sufficient irregularities for the football and greyhound companies to be separated and Gamlin was removed from the board on 25 April 1951. Rovers claimed the greyhound company owed them £844, but the auditors declared that, of a total of £2,675 payable on work to the stadium, including turnstiles, plumbing and levelling of the car park, Rovers should pay £2,111.

Throughout the 1950/51 season, one key to Rovers' success was their ability to retain a consistent side. Apart from half a dozen players who appeared in no more than seven games each, Rovers relied on just twelve relatively regular players. Goalkeeper Bert Hoyle, half-backs Ray Warren and Peter Sampson, and top scorer Vic Lambden, the first post-war Rovers player to reach twenty league goals for the season, played in all fifty-eight league, FA Cup and Gloucestershire Cup games. A settled defence was completed by full-backs Harry Bamford and Geoff Fox and right-half Jackie Pitt, missing just nine league games between them all season. In the forward line, Geoff Bradford and Bill Roost ably supported Lambden, with Petherbridge, Watling and Roost competing for the remaining places. Jack Weare, once a fixture in the Rovers goal, could not break into the side and was allowed to join Swansea Town in March 1951.

In completing the season in sixth place, Rovers fell back on an excellent autumnal run of nine wins and three draws. Following defeat at Norwich City in September, the side was unbeaten until going down to the veteran Fred Kurz's 15-yard drive after half an hour at Crystal Palace in January. One November victory was over Orient, for whom the future Rovers left-half 'Chic' Cairney was making his first league appearance. Eastville was developing into a stronghold, where Rovers won thirteen and drew three of their first sixteen home league matches. Rovers' proud unbeaten home record finally fell to runaway champions Nottingham Forest. Between November 1949 and April 1953, only five home league games out of eighty-one were lost. There were five-figure crowds at every home match in 1950/51 at an average of 17,763 – the highest at a league game being the 31,518 that saw Lambden's double strike defeat Bristol City in December.

With Colchester United newly elected to the Football League, Rovers had the honour of being the first visitors to Layer Road, where they fought out a goalless draw. It was the same result when Rovers and Port Vale met at Stoke City's Victoria Ground on Christmas Day. Swindon Town were then beaten 2-1 after Jimmy Bain's goal had put the Robins in front. The home game with Norwich City in February was abandoned after an hour with the pitch waterlogged, after a Lambden brace had put Rovers 2-1 ahead. When it was replayed in April, Rovers overcame a half-time deficit to claim a point in an exciting 3-3 draw, thanks to second-half goals from Lambden and Bradford. Rovers' final five games were all at home – Nottingham Forest, through first-half headers from Johnny Love and Tom Johnson, being the only away side to win.

For the home draw with Ipswich Town in March, when Peter Sampson scored his first goal for the club, Rovers faced their third oldest league opponent in history – goalkeeper Mick Burns, at forty-two years 239 days. A familiar face came back to haunt Rovers in January, for the scorer of Torquay United's twentieth-minute goal at Eastville in a 1-1 draw was Wilf Whitfield, who had made his Rovers debut in November 1938 and had last scored on that ground in league football almost twelve years earlier.

On 4 November, Plymouth Argyle arrived at Eastville with an accordion player, who performed contemporary songs around the edge of the pitch prior to the start of the match. One of these songs was the Huddie William 'Lead Belly' Ledbetter record 'Goodnight Irene', an old folk song emanating from 1880s Cincinnati, Ohio. It was first recorded in July 1933, and sung by Argyle supporters by dint of the fact that The Weavers, featuring Pete Seeger, had released their own version in 1951. As Argyle took a first-half lead, their supporters used the song to taunt home fans. Three Rovers goals in eight second-half minutes provoked a rendition of 'Goodnight Argyle', and the song soon caught on. When Rovers played at Newcastle in the FA Cup quarter-final, the Magpies bowed to pressure and played the Jo Stafford rendition of the song during the pre-match build-up. As Rovers' FA Cup run gained momentum, 'Goodnight Irene' had been swiftly adopted as a club anthem, sung by generations of Rovers supporters ever since.

All in all, 1950/51 was a season to offer encouragement to Bristol Rovers. A consistent and efficient team was riding high in Division Three (South) and had reached the FA Cup quarter-finals. Manager Bert Tann had successfully taken on the task of maintaining Rovers' post-war promotion push. Despite the traumas of the Board of Trade enquiry, financial irregularities appeared to be a thing of the past as the club sailed into less choppy waters. The considerable support at Eastville was looking forward to many enjoyable years ahead. They were not to be disappointed.

1951/52

On the back of FA Cup success, Rovers built a side that would fulfil its potential in the spring of 1953. The advantage of hindsight is, of course, the wisdom to see what a springboard the 1951/52 season gave to the championship-winning side. Harry Liley, the veteran goalkeeper, had joined Bath City, while Howard Radford and Andy Micklewright were the only signings to make a sizeable impact on Rovers' promotion push. Radford was initially Bert Hoyle's understudy, but became a key ingredient in Rovers' Second Division side, playing in the league team until 1962. Micklewright played sporadically in this and the promotion season, scoring from inside-right in the large win over Walsall in April 1952. Harry Bamford retained his place in the side following his powerful defensive play during the summer Football Association tour of Australia, where he scored three goals. Following an inspection by a team from St Ives Research Centre, Bingley, on 6 February 1951, the pitch at Eastville was treated with nitro-chalk at the rate of half an ounce per square yard to counteract the acidity of the turf and allow for an improved playing surface in 1951/52.

Football was on the up in Bristol, with Bristol City also building a side that would reach Division Two. In addition to defeating First Division Preston North End in the FA Cup, Rovers scored an unprecedented and still unequalled sixty goals at home in league matches that season. Only three times in the club's history has a Rovers team scored five goals in two consecutive league games, and two of these instances took place in 1951/52. Rovers scored a club record twenty-two league goals in the calendar month of April, more even than the twenty of October 1982. With both professional clubs performing well in an era of high attendances, it is little surprise that the derby at Eastville in January drew the highest crowd at any game at any Third Division (South) ground that season. The 34,612 constituted a new ground record, bettered only once, and saw goals from Geoff Bradford and George Petherbridge give Rovers a 2-0 victory.

The season began slowly for Rovers. Single-goal defeats at Walsall, to a Hugh Evans header after just twenty-six minutes, and at home to Watford were interspersed with draws. When Shrewsbury Town visited Eastville in August, Harold Robbins became the first opponent for over twenty years to score a league hat-trick on that ground, but Rovers still scrambled a 3-3 draw. Tommy Docherty scored Norwich City's goal at Eastville to earn a draw, the second of three consecutive seasons he scored against Rovers. Although Rovers had, in forty-eight hours in September, beaten Aldershot 5-1 and Crystal Palace 4-0, Vic Lambden scoring twice in each game, there was little sign of the success to come. A draw at Millwall on 10 November was the seventh consecutive league game without a win, and left Rovers with just five victories in their opening seventeen matches.

Manager Bert Tann was not one to panic, and it is no coincidence that Rovers fielded an unchanged side for the following game. The side had not won at home for over two months, but consecutive five-goal victories were to turn the season on its head. With a predominantly Bristol-born and Rovers-bred line-up, the club was to enjoy a hugely successful eighteen months, taking the club to previously unattained heights.

In front of the hugely popular Bert Hoyle, whom fans showered with oranges after he rashly admitted his fondness for them, was the ever-reliable pairing of Harry Bamford and Geoff Fox. It is unlikely that Rovers will ever again find such a dependable full-back partnership. Captain Ray Warren, at centre-half, was flanked by Jackie Pitt and Peter Sampson. Crucially, Fox, Pitt and Sampson were ever-presents in 1951/52, and the entire back five appeared in every game in the championship season. Also an ever-present was George Petherbridge, whose dazzling right-wing skills were switched to the left the following year. Inside-forwards Bill Roost and Barrie Meyer made significant contributions to the side in both seasons. Josser Watling played well but did not score, and his replacement, John McIlvenny, was to be the only major change.

Undeniably, the fact that Rovers could boast two hugely prolific goalscorers was a key factor in the side's success. Lambden had proven his pedigree, and continued in fine style. His four goals against Colchester United made him the only player to have scored so many times twice in the league for Rovers. His club-record twenty-nine league goals in 1951/52 were followed by twenty-four more the following year, when, as an ever-present, he helped Rovers towards great success. Bradford, on the other hand, was just beginning to prove his worth, and his twenty-six league goals, including ten in the final eight games, serves as a prelude to his thirty-three in 1952/53.

Indeed, goalscoring was not generally a problem for Rovers, who scored eighty-nine when finishing seventh in Division Three (South). The visit of Brighton on 17 November saw Lambden and Bradford on the scoresheet in a 5-0 win. In the very next game, when Rovers defeated Torquay United by the same scoreline, Petherbridge scored four times, becoming the sixth Rovers player to achieve this feat in the league. He opened the scoring after four minutes, and scored with a header and three right-footed shots. Rovers also beat Port Vale 4-1 and scored three times at both Aldershot and Watford – Lambden and Bradford scoring in all these games – before again hitting a purple patch over Easter. Roost scored twice on Easter Saturday, with Lambden, Bradford and Petherbridge getting one each, as Gillingham were beaten 5-0. Two days later, Colchester United, who had that week beaten Rovers at Layer Road, were taken apart by a rampant Rovers forward line. Lambden opened the scoring in the first minute, completed his hat-trick after fifteen minutes and grabbed a fourth after half-time, with Bradford adding two more in a highly convincing 6-0 victory.

That Rovers did not achieve greater success in 1951/52 must be put down to a lack of consistency. The autumnal run of seven matches without a win was followed by a run of three points in six games around February and two straight defeats after the Colchester game. After November, Rovers still lost at home to the top two sides – Plymouth Argyle and Reading. In February, the side even went two games without scoring. Despite scoring five or more goals in six home matches, Rovers finished fourteen points behind eventual champions Plymouth Argyle. There were some clear lessons to be learnt and Tann would ensure that all that was required would be done.

Prior to the game at Brisbane Road on 6 February, Rovers and Leyton Orient observed a one-minute silence in memory of King George VI, who had died at Buckingham Palace the previous day. The match itself was very exciting, with Geoff Bradford scoring twice for Rovers, and Orient's thirty-five-year-old left-half

Jackie Deverall contributing an own goal as the sides shared six goals. Another player to share his goals was the ubiquitous Vic Lambden, who, not content with the hatful he contributed, contrived to score for both sides in the 1-1 draw at Brighton in April. Only Jock Hamilton had managed previously to score at both ends, and only Tim Parkin and Geoff Twentyman have repeated this feat since, as Rovers players in league action.

Lambden also scored in both games as Rovers saw off non-League FA Cup opposition in Kettering Town and Weymouth. The visit of the Dorset side attracted a crowd of 27,808, encouraged by the fact that the two previous league games at Eastville had finished 5-0 to Rovers. In the third round, Rovers drew the mighty Preston North End at home. Not only were the Lilywhites founder members of the league, but they were also able to field players of the calibre of Tommy Docherty and Charlie Wayman. On paper, at least, Rovers should not have been able to beat their illustrious opponents. Preston were to finish the season seventh in Division One, above FA Cup winners Newcastle United, but Rovers defeated them 2-0 with an efficient display. Before a 30,681 attendance, Bradford, with an angled first-half drive, and Lambden thirteen minutes from time – after goalkeeper Jim Gooch had saved his initial header – grabbed their customary goal apiece for a famous victory. In round four, Rovers stumbled at Southend United, losing 2-1, and the Gloucestershire Cup final was lost to Bristol City in May by the same scoreline.

1952/53

Comparisons between Rovers' promotion seasons are perhaps inevitable. In both 1952/53 and 1973/74, Rovers enjoyed a twenty-seven-match unbeaten run before suffering a very shaky patch. Whereas Don Megson's side had a nine-point lead in 1974 and still did not win the championship, Bert Tann's team almost let slip a ten-point margin over their nearest rivals. In April 1953, Rovers won only two points in a potentially disastrous run of six matches. The goal averages (1.97 in 1973/74 and 2.02 in 1952/53) are also incredibly similar. Like the 1989/90 championship side, Rovers won twenty-six league games in 1952/53, then a club record; the 2006/07 campaign was entirely different.

This was, however, the first time since elevation to the Football League in 1920 that Rovers had gained promotion, and the first championship since the Southern League in 1904/05. One by one, many of Rovers' fellow Third Division (South) founder members had sampled life in Division Two, and now it was to be Rovers' turn. Success was achieved through an ever-present back five, and the firepower of Geoff Bradford and Vic Lambden. Bradford's thirty-three league goals, twenty-four of which were scored at Eastville, constituted a club record and went some way towards creating the his legendary status to this day. It was typical of his season that he should score a hat-trick on the day promotion was finally secured.

The one significant change in personnel was the addition of John McIlvenny from Cheltenham Town. Although he scored just twice, McIlvenny at outside-right, like George Petherbridge on the left, was instrumental in creating many of Rovers' club record ninety-two league goals. Rovers began the season well with a run of four convincing victories early in September. Bradford and Lambden both scored in a 5-3 win at Walsall and a 3-1 home victory over Gillingham. Bradford scored a hat-trick of right-foot shots in a 3-0 victory over Torquay United, and Rovers won by the same score at Colchester United. After defeat at Millwall, Rovers embarked on a club record twenty-seven-match unbeaten run, after which the championship appeared won.

This incredible run began with a 3-1 victory over Colchester United, where familiar goalscorers Lambden, Bradford and Petherbridge helped complete the double over the Essex club. It was to run from mid-September to the end of March. In October, Rovers had trailed 2-0 at Northampton Town before injury-time goals from Bradford and Bryan Bush had reclaimed an unlikely point. This was the spur for Rovers to set off on an extraordinary run of twelve consecutive league wins, from 18 October to 17 January. Not only is this run easily a club record, it was also achieved in spectacular fashion. Rovers conceded just five goals in this run, yet scored seven against Brighton, to record the club's largest league win at the time, five at Ipswich Town and four each past Gillingham and Reading. In every one of these twelve games, Bradford, Lambden or Bush got on the scoresheet. It was an awesome display of the capabilities of Tann's side, and one that no Rovers team is likely to repeat.

In two separate matches in November, Rovers scored four goals in eighteen minutes. At home to Reading, McIlvenny's fifteenth-minute goal was followed by further strikes from Bradford two minutes later and Lambden after twenty-five minutes. Warren's penalty, incredibly his final goal for the club, preceded a goalless second half. Two home games later, Rovers repeated the feat against Brighton. After Petherbridge's eighteenth-minute opener, Rovers scored six second-half goals, a tally equalled only in the game at Reading in January 1999. Roost scored twice, after forty-eight and seventy minutes, either side of the predictable goals from Lambden on fifty-three minutes and Bradford seven minutes later. Petherbridge claimed his second goal with a quarter of an hour remaining, before the luckless Reg Fox put through his own goal two minutes from time.

Thereafter, Lambden and Bradford scored twice each in a 4-1 victory over Aldershot, and again when Coventry City were defeated 5-2. Rovers were involved in a six-goal draw at Brisbane Road for a second consecutive season, and beat Ipswich Town 3-0 at Eastville in March in the twenty-seventh successive league game without defeat. After Reading had put paid to this proud record, Rovers proceeded to beat Bournemouth and Swindon Town. The former game followed a one-minute silence, as Queen Mary, the widow of King George V, had died four days earlier, and featured goals from Bryan Bush and Bournemouth's Jack Cross, both of whom had also scored in the game at Dean Court in November.

It seems implausible, but Rovers won just one of their final nine league games. One of these matches, a draw with Newport County, was (remarkably) the ninth consecutive visit to Somerton Park in which Rovers had conceded exactly two goals. The sole victory, however (3-1 win at home to County) secured promotion to Division Two. With impeccable timing, Geoff Bradford, having established a new club seasonal record at Somerton Park, scored a majestic hat-trick to send Rovers up to the heady heights of Division Two. His first-minute sidefoot was followed by headers after forty and seventy minutes, while beleaguered County, who had at one stage equalised through George Beattie's shot off the underside of the crossbar, lost goalkeeper Harry Fearnley to a broken collarbone.

After the victory over Newport County, club chairman Hampden Alpass addressed the ecstatic crowd of 29,451 from a microphone in the directors' box:

> My first feeling is one of gratitude to players, manager and staff. Being on top of the table since the middle of September has meant that every club has been out to beat us and every match has been like a Cup tie. The strain on the players has been terrific. Secondly, I have a feeling of pride that, after all these years, the club has succeeded in reaching the Second Division.

Alpass received the Championship Shield and thirteen medals at a Football League meeting held at the Café Royal in London on 13 June. The players split a £275 bonus between them for their achievements. No small part, of course, had been played by Bert Tann, whose dynamic approach to management had inspired Rovers. Supporters, thrilled by the 1950/51 Cup run and now promotion, seemed to view him with an awed reverence. Never before or since has one individual held such a magnetic sway over Bristol's sporting public.

This final success was achieved without the services of goalkeeper Bert Hoyle. Rovers contrived two goalless draws each with Bristol City and Exeter City, and the Ashton Gate encounter drew a crowd of 35,372 – the highest at any Third Division (South) ground that season. That evening, in Devon, Hoyle suffered serious injuries in a motor accident and his career with Rovers was sadly and abruptly ended. Howard Radford gamely took over in goal but, as the promotion push began to falter, Tann persuaded the directors to breach their 'no buy, no sell' policy. Bob Anderson, signed from Crystal Palace, played in the final seven games and went on to appear in Bristol City's Third Division (South) championship side of 1954/55. No other player has won two championships from the same division with two clubs from the same city.

A first-minute goal from Roost proved decisive in an FA Cup first-round replay against Leyton Orient, after Warren had missed a penalty in the original tie, and

Lambden's goal earned victory over Peterborough United at Layer Road. The previous two seasons' FA Cup campaigns had earned Rovers plum draws, and this was no exception. Rovers faced a third round tie at Huddersfield Town, who were promoted to Division One at the end of the season, and the task was made still tougher when goalkeeper Hoyle left the field injured and the versatile Lambden finished the game in goal. Ten-man Rovers lost 2-0, to goals from Jim Watson and Jim Glazzard. In the Gloucestershire Cup final, first-half goals from John Atyeo and Alec Eisentrager gave Bristol City a 2-0 win.

Tann's projection of the club had much to do with the on-field success of 1952/53. The average attendance of 23,411 was the highest in the division, and reflects the close affinity felt between the team and its supporters. A largely Bristol-raised side of local men, led by an eloquent and enthusiastic Londoner, had brought long-awaited success to a delighted public. Now the team of local heroes was to face the new and welcome challenge of Second Division football.

1953/54

The promised land had been reached. The fears of those who felt Bert Tann's home-grown side would struggle in their inaugural season in Division Two were proved unfounded, as Rovers finished in ninth place, just twelve points behind the two promoted sides, Leicester City and Everton. Tann had nurtured the team spirit and commitment that had driven the club so far and was now developing it to create a high quality side. The golden years in the Bristol Rovers story were the days when this largely Bristol-born team came so close to that still elusive place in the top division.

Rovers' arrival in Division Two was announced with a hugely entertaining 4-4 draw with Fulham at Craven Cottage. In predictable fashion, Geoff Bradford opened the scoring after thirteen minutes and marked the occasion with a hat-trick, while Geoff Fox, four minutes after half-time, scored only his second goal in over 200 appearances. Bobby Robson, later manager of England, scored the first two of Fulham's three equalisers. Arthur Stevens, whose hat-trick put Rovers out of the FA Cup in 1948, and the future England forward Johnny Haynes, with only the second goal of his embryonic league career, scored once each before Bradford pulled Rovers level fifteen minutes from time. A crowd of 28,173 saw the first home game, when Doncaster Rovers spoiled the celebrations by winning through a solitary Eddie McMorran goal after sixty-six minutes from Len Graham's defence-splitting pass, although Rovers won seventeen corners to Doncaster's three. Rovers began the season with a side composed entirely of players who had helped the club to the Division Three (South) championship.

The star attraction, once again, was the phenomenal goalscorer Geoff Bradford. He followed up his club record thirty-three league goals in 1952/53 with twenty-one goals in only eighteen league appearances. Quite what Rovers might have achieved if he had remained injury-free remains a moot point, for a career-threatening leg injury, suffered after he had scored the opening goal at Plymouth Argyle in November, was to rule him out for almost six months. In true heroic fashion, he made a dramatic comeback in the final match of the season, his knee heavily strapped, and scored a hat-trick as Rovers defeated Stoke City 3-2 at Eastville – his fifth hat-trick of the season. After Rovers had trailed 2-1, two dramatic Bradford headers inside sixty seconds brought an unlikely victory. Although Rovers as a team scored five hat-tricks in 1926/27, Bradford's feat is a clear club record.

Bradford's injury, coupled with the winding-down of Vic Lambden's long career – he scored just twice this season – meant Rovers had to search for adequate free transfer replacements. Three of the players given first-team opportunities were to play a significant role over the next few years. Peter Hooper was to enthral Rovers supporters for a decade with his close control and powerful shot. Remarkably, he had apparently played for Kenya against Uganda in 1951 while on National Service, but it was at Eastville, with his 35-yard drives and over 100 league goals for Rovers, that the young Devonian was to make his mark. Frank Allcock appeared in fifty-nine league games for Rovers before a knee injury ended his career. The player who made the biggest immediate impact, however, was Paddy Hale, who was in effect Bradford's deputy.

Hale's goalscoring record for Rovers is certainly unorthodox. In nineteen league appearances in 1953/54, he scored twelve times, never more than one per game, to finish as the club's second-highest scorer. Thereafter, he appeared predominantly as centre-half and never scored again in over 100 further league matches, before joining Bath City in 1959. On his debut, Hale, the recalled John McIlvenny and Gloucestershire cricketer Barrie Meyer all scored as Rovers defeated eventual champions Leicester City 3-0 at Eastville – one of the highlights of this first season in Division Two.

Rovers recorded a number of comfortable wins early in the season. Bradford scored all the goals as Rovers won 3-0 at Brentford, while Derby County were defeated by the same score. Bill Roost, Josser Watling and Bradford all scored in consecutive games, as Rovers won 5-1 at Notts County and 4-2 at home to Hull City. Bradford's hat-trick at Meadow Lane was the start of a personal run of eleven goals in seven games prior to his injury. After November, Rovers were to only score three times in a match in the home games against Plymouth Argyle, when Alfie Biggs, a name for Rovers' future, scored his first goal for the club, and Stoke City.

October was a month for draws, with Rovers registering three 3-3 draws in four weeks. First, Rovers went to Elland Road to face a Leeds United side deprived of the league's top scorer, John Charles. Bob Forrest scored a hat-trick, but two Bradford goals earned Rovers a draw. The roles were reversed three weeks later, when Bradford scored an Eastville hat-trick against Luton Town, but did not finish on the winning side. The third six-goal draw was the one in which the club's top scorer was injured on 7 November. Rovers also drew 1-1 at home to Birmingham City in October, Bradford scoring past international goalkeeper Gil Merrick, while Ted Purdon scored against his future club. The attendance broke the ground record and remains, at 35,614, the largest ever at a home league game. It was also the highest at any Rovers game all season, home or away, marginally ahead of the 34,015 at the goalless draw with Everton three days after Christmas. For six consecutive years, 1952/53 to 1957/58, the club's average home crowd topped 20,000. In a mood of optimism and enthusiasm, the seasonal average of 24,662 in 1953/54 remains the highest in Rovers' league history.

Urged on by large crowds at home, Rovers produced several notable victories. Away from home, there were not many bad defeats, though Everton were 4-0 winners on Christmas Day, with David Hickson scoring twice before a 27,484 crowd in Rovers' only visit in league football to Goodison Park. A first-ever league visit to Boothferry Park saw Rovers lose 4-1 to Hull City in April, with Sid Gerrie scoring three times and Viggo Jensen, the holder of fifteen full Danish caps, converting a penalty. What is remarkable about a Rovers side deprived of their key goalscorer is the number of low-scoring results through the winter and spring. In a run of twelve league games between December and early April, five were 1-1 draws and two goalless, while four others featured just one goal each. It was a series of mid-table results, but the lack of a consistent goalscorer was abundantly clear.

Promotion to a higher division not only brought a host of new opponents, particularly northern clubs, but also meant Rovers faced a number of high-profile players. Four well-known future managers were in the West Ham United side that drew 2-2 at Eastville in September. Dave Sexton, a goalscorer, Frank O'Farrell and Noel Cantwell were joined in the Hammers' line-up by Malcolm Allison, for the first of eight league appearances against the side he was to manage in 1992/93. In April, a Jack Froggatt header fifteen minutes from time earned the points for a Leicester City side that also included Stan Milburn, Derek Hines and the Football League's all-time top goalscorer, Arthur Rowley. Mel Charles, the experienced Welsh international, scored against Rovers in both meetings with Swansea Town, who also fielded both Len and Ivor Allchurch in the game at the Vetch Field on Easter Saturday. These new experiences were invaluable to the East Bristol boys as their team established itself in Division Two.

Ultimately, the demise of the Bradford-Lambden partnership and lack of adequate replacements hindered Rovers' chances of progressing above mid-table. However, ninth place in this new division was a major achievement upon which to build. While the stability of the side remained relatively intact, it is worth noting that no individual player was an ever-present. The back five, each one a permanent fixture in front of the goalkeeper in the championship season, all missed sporadic games for a variety of reasons. There was no success in the FA Cup where, for a second time inside a month, Blackburn Rovers won at Eastville. Eddie Quigley, once Britain's most expensive footballer, scored the only goal with a low, hard drive after fifteen minutes. The Gloucestershire Cup final was drawn 2-2 with Bristol City, Rovers being indebted, in Bradford's absence, to veteran club captain Ray Warren's only goal of the season.

1954/55

The bubble was certainly not about to burst. Rovers had spent twenty-six seasons trying to get into Division Two and were now proving they could stay there. Manager Bert Tann had instilled a confidence and sense of belonging into this homely club, and on-field performances indicated the side was capable of holding its own. Even an uncharacteristic lean spell from the prolific Geoff Bradford late in the season and humiliating defeats at Rotherham United and Blackburn Rovers, could not dent the infectious enthusiasm at the club. Those who feared a decline was setting in and Rovers were heading back to Division Three (South) were to be proved wrong as 1955/56 found the club just four points away from promotion to Division One.

Consistency on the field was mirrored in the large crowds that flocked to Eastville every matchday. With an average home crowd of 23,116, Rovers were the third best supported Division Two side, behind Liverpool and Blackburn Rovers. For a third consecutive season, the average was not only above 20,000, but also higher than that at Bristol City, who were Division Three (South) champions. A new ground record of 35,921 in January saw Rovers defeat First Division Portsmouth 2-1 in the FA Cup third round, with Bradford and Bill Roost scoring past the Northern Ireland international goalkeeper Norman Uprichard to record a famous victory. This ground record did not even see out the month. In round four, Chelsea, league champions that season for the only time in the club's history, drew a crowd of 35,972 to Eastville. With former Rovers schoolboy Roy Bentley in fine form, Chelsea were able to win 3-1. Even the Gloucestershire Cup final was watched by its highest-ever crowd, home or away, when 20,097 saw Rovers win 2-1 at Eastville – Bristol City's Ernie Peacock deflecting the winner into his own net from Biggs' right-wing cross seven minutes after half-time.

Rovers continued to boast a strong defence, with Howard Radford in goal. Right-back Harry Bamford was supported initially by Geoff Fox, who played his 274th and final league game for Rovers in April, and from November by Frank Allcock. Pitt, Warren and Sampson remained the usual half-back line, though Jimmy Anderson, a signing from Army football, enjoyed an extended run in the side at left-half. Of the forwards, only Bradford, Roost and Petherbridge enjoyed any consistency in a side again lacking an ever-present. Young Peter Hooper offered glimpses of his potential, and Barrie Meyer, Alfie Biggs, Paddy Hale, John McIlvenny and Josser Watling all appeared in the forward line.

Vic Lambden, given one final run in the side, contributed seven goals late in the season. He scored the only goal of the game after sixty-five minutes at Plymouth Argyle on Easter Monday, from Geoff Bradford's through pass, in what proved to be his final appearance for the side. In almost a decade, he had scored 117 times in 269 league matches and remains the fourth highest goalscorer in Rovers' Football League history. He subsequently joined Trowbridge Town, where he scored over 150 goals in six highly successful seasons in the Western League. Bryan Bush's career was also to end, his final appearance in a Rovers shirt coming in the debacle at Blackburn Rovers. One new face, though, was Dai Ward, who played at inside-left against Nottingham Forest in April, and was to give Rovers many years of valuable service. Over the summer of 1954, William Cowlin and son had erected new gates and railings at a cost of £203 and a stand season ticket for 1954/55 cost six guineas.

The season started in a frenzy of goalscoring from Geoff Bradford. He scored the only goal against Port Vale and was to score nineteen goals in fourteen league games by 23 October. Ultimately, he was easily the club's top scorer with twenty-six Second Division goals. In the first week of September, he scored two hat-tricks in forty-eight hours; the first in a 4-1 home victory over Derby County and the second as Liverpool were defeated 3-0 at Eastville. The goals against Derby came in a frantic eighteen-minute spell in the opening half hour, with Peter Hooper adding the first of his many Rovers goals, while the Liverpool game was the seventh in succession in which Bradford had scored, a new club record that was to last just eighteen months. At this stage, in fact, he had scored in each of his last nine league appearances, if his final games before injury in November 1953 are taken into consideration.

Rovers also recorded a 5-1 home victory over Leeds United, a fourth consecutive game in which Bradford had scored twice, and a 4-0 win at home to Ipswich Town, thanks to a brace of goals from George Petherbridge. The largest victory, though, was when Swansea Town visited Eastville in the first week of October. Mel Charles, having scored in both fixtures against Rovers the previous season, put through his own net after only six minutes, and Bradford doubled Rovers' lead nine minutes later. After half-time, Bradford scored again after fifty-five minutes, Hooper scored on the hour mark, Ron Burgess became the oldest man ever to concede a league own goal against Rovers twelve minutes later, and Roost added a sixth with a quarter of an hour left. Hooper's second goal, in the last minute, meant Rovers had equalled the club record 7-0 league victory. It was also the second of only three occasions that opponents had contributed two own goals in a league match.

On 12 September 1954, Jack Lewis, Rovers' inside-right in the 1904/05 Southern League championship season and the winner of a Welsh cap while on

Rovers' books, died at the age of seventy-two. Around this time, Rovers' defensive frailties were being exposed. In two consecutive games, Rovers conceded five. All the West Ham United forwards, including the future Manchester United manager Dave Sexton, got on the scoresheet in a game played in torrential rain and a thunderstorm. Four days later, Rovers scored three times at Anfield, only for John Evans to score all Liverpool's goals in their 5-3 win. It was a devastating show of goalscoring from an underrated forward, finding the net after seven, thirty-nine, forty, seventy and eighty-five minutes, and his achievement remains a Liverpool record equalled only by Andy McGuigan and Ian Rush.

The Upton Park game was the first time since October 1948 that Rovers had conceded five goals in a league game, yet Rovers proceeded to lose 6-2 at Rotherham United and let in four at home to Notts County and West Ham United. Seventy goals were conceded in the league, the club's worst defensive record since 1947/48. The heaviest defeat came at Blackburn Rovers in a match Rovers had led 3-2 at half-time. Roost had put Rovers ahead after only six minutes, and Lambden twice restored the lead after Eddie Crossan and Tommy Briggs had equalised. However, in a one-man second-half, Briggs scored six more for a personal tally of seven, consigning consign Rovers to an 8-3 defeat.

Briggs was a powerful and strong centre-forward, exactly the type of player Rovers struggled to contain. His first goal had come from a low drive twelve minutes before half-time, and his second, Blackburn's third equaliser, was a header from Crossan's free-kick after forty-eight minutes. Fourteen minutes later, he converted Bobby Langton's cross to put the home side ahead. With twelve minutes remaining, Rovers trailed 4-3, but Briggs was to score four times with his right foot in those final minutes, the last as a reluctant penalty-taker to establish a club record. He also hit a post, but Briggs had scored seven goals in fifty-six minutes to inflict Rovers' heaviest league defeat since April 1936.

Seven days later, Rovers responded with their largest win of the second half of the season. Fulham, appearing in the snow in red-and-white quarters, as opposed to Rovers' blue-and-white quarters, were beaten 4-1 at Eastville, with the future England forward Johnny Haynes scoring their goal. A series of low-scoring games saw Rovers' second season in Division Two end with the club in ninth place. On the long trip to Elland Road, where Rovers lost 2-0 to Leeds United, Bob Forrest's opening goal after eleven seconds constitutes the fastest goal scored in a league match involving Rovers. It had been a long season, and many lessons had been learned. Rovers set off for Devon, where the season was rounded off by an extraordinary friendly, won 10-6 at Dawlish, with Bradford contributing four of the goals.

1955/56

In the history of any football club there is a key moment where fate can determine success or failure. In the case of Bristol Rovers, bereft of their injured talisman, Geoff Bradford, two late defeats meant missing out narrowly on promotion to Division One. The club has still never attained the dizzy heights of the top division. Rovers missed out by four points, the thin line between success and mediocrity.

With Geoff Fox, Vic Lambden and Bryan Bush having departed, the championship side of 1952/53 was finally breaking up. Ray Warren, after twenty years with the club, played in his 450th and final league game in December, while Bill Roost, John McIlvenny and Josser Watling were being used less frequently in the side. With Howard Radford a pivotal figure in goal, Harry Bamford was now accompanied at full-back by the promising talent of Frank Allcock. Bamford, the only ever-present, again did not score, though he was debited with an own goal against Bury in November. Peter Sampson, George Petherbridge, Barrie Meyer and newly appointed club captain Jackie Pitt remained of the old guard, with Paddy Hale now assuming the mantle of centre-half and the talented Peter Hooper at outside-left. Alfie Biggs, who scored twice in victories over Nottingham Forest and Sheffield Wednesday, was fast emerging as Bradford's new sidekick. Fred Ford, the new coach, was to share in five excellent seasons, and later returned to Eastville in 1968 as manager.

The role of Geoff Bradford in the Rovers story cannot be underestimated. He scored in all but four of his first seventeen matches of the season, scoring twice in a game seven times. Potentially key games at Stoke City and Hull City were both won 2-1, Bradford scoring the goals on both occasions. On 2 October 1955, he became the only player to appear for England while on Rovers' books. The supporters' club chartered an aeroplane to take thirty-four Rovers fans to the game in Copenhagen, including in their number Mrs Betty Bradford as a guest of the club. For the majority of the travellers, this was the first time that they had been in an aeroplane, and their memories of the occasion were to prove priceless. Characteristically, in a 5-1 victory over Denmark, Geoff Bradford scored England's fifth goal, with a low right-foot shot eight minutes from time from Jackie Milburn's flighted cross pass. It was to be his only England cap. Then, having scored a hat-trick in the return fixture with Hull City, Bradford was seriously injured in an FA Cup game at Doncaster Rovers in January. With their star player out for the rest of the season, Rovers' promotion push foundered on the rocks of inadequacy.

The Hull game was the ninth and final time Rovers had scored four or more goals at Eastville in league and FA Cup football in 1955/56. Bradford had scored at least once on all nine occasions. The Hull City side included the veteran Stan Mortensen, scorer of a hat-trick in the 1953 'Matthews FA Cup final' and the holder of twenty-five England caps, but it was Bradford who stole the show with three goals. Promotion rivals Leeds United had been defeated 4-1 at Eastville in October, Bradford claiming a pair of goals on that occasion. The largest victory, however, was a 7-2 mauling of Middlesbrough in November.

Rovers went into the home game with Middlesbrough, having scored sixteen goals and conceded ten in their previous four league matches. The crowd of 23,728 anticipated a feast of goals and was duly rewarded. This remains one of only two post-war league fixtures where three Rovers players have scored two or more times each. Bradford opened the scoring after thirteen minutes, and two Ward goals meant Rovers led 3-0 with only eighteen minutes played. Charlie Wayman pulled a goal back just before half-time, Bradford and Hooper put Rovers 5-1 ahead and Lindy Delapenha scored the visitors' second. Hooper's second goal, after seventy-eight minutes, and one from Petherbridge six minutes later left Rovers in the ascendancy.

The euphoria of this 7-2 victory lasted just a week. The following Saturday, at Notts County, Rovers crashed to a 5-2 defeat, their heaviest of the season. Ron Wylie, later manager of West Bromwich Albion, was to score only five goals all season, but claimed a hat-trick for County. Bradford-less Rovers later crashed 4-1 at home to Rotherham United with Ian Wilson, the scorer of one of the six at Millmoor in October 1954, weighing in with three goals. Tommy Briggs, after his seven goals the previous season, scored just the once at Ewood Park in February, while Johnny Haynes scored at Eastville for a second consecutive year, playing for a Fulham side that included Jimmy Hill at outside-left.

The first all-ticket game ever to be staged at Eastville was the local derby with Bristol City in March. The sides had drawn 1-1 at Ashton Gate in the autumn before a then record Ashton Gate crowd of 39,583, and the first Second Division clash of these sides in East Bristol was expected to attract a large turnout. Rovers had, prior to this fixture, scored in forty-three consecutive home league games, but faced a proven goalscorer in John Atyeo. The attendance of 35,324, though not a ground record, remains in perpetuity as the highest ever at a league game at Eastville. These were the days when thousands flocked into the Tote End, which boasted a maximum capacity at one point of 12,250, and the Muller Road End, where up to 16,900 spectators gathered behind the trademark flowerbeds that, carefully maintained by the Rovers groundstaff, formed a colourful if unorthodox backdrop to the goalnet at that end of the pitch. However, despite the massive support in the cauldron of one of Britain's most keenly fought local derbies, Rovers were to lose 3-0, with Atyeo scoring twice.

A new goalkeeper, Ron Nicholls, played his first few games in the winter months. Like Meyer, he was a county cricketer, the fourth-highest scoring batsman in the history of Gloucestershire and, although potential training clashes between the sports lay ahead, both players contributed well to Rovers' on-field success. Meyer scored a hat-trick at Fulham, as Rovers recorded their largest away win of the season. He was also instrumental in Rovers ' defeat of Liverpool 2-0 at Anfield through Bradford's header three minutes before half-time from Meyer's cross and a low shot from Biggs cutting in from the right after fifty-nine minutes, on the ground that was to see such undiluted success in the years to come.

The fixture at Elland Road on 21 April 1956 was one of the more crucial league matches in Rovers' history. With Sheffield Wednesday virtual champions, Rovers lay second with forty-eight points and two games remaining. Leeds United, with three games left, had forty-six points, one more than Blackburn Rovers and Nottingham Forest. Victory for Rovers would leave the Eastville side requiring a point at home to Liverpool for promotion to Division One and, in eager anticipation, the supporters' club once again chartered an aeroplane for the trip. Dai Ward had scored crucial goals in recent weeks and his goal at Elland Road set a club record – scoring in an eighth consecutive league game, eclipsing Bradford's seven in succession earlier in the season that had equalled his own record. Dramatically, from a Petherbridge cross, Ward headed Rovers into the lead after only two minutes. Before half-time, though, John Charles had headed home a George Meek cross and set up Jack Overfield for what proved to be Leeds United's winning goal. The Elland Road crowd of 49,274 remains the largest league crowd in front of which Rovers have played. Once the bubble had burst, Rovers also lost to Liverpool. Wednesday were champions with fifty-five points, Leeds United promoted with fifty-two, while Liverpool, Blackburn Rovers and Leicester City all inched above Rovers on goal average. So close to their target, Rovers were left to wonder what might have happened if twenty-five-goal top scorer Bradford had not been injured, and why no adequate replacement was found. A final placing of sixth in Division Two remains the highest in Bristol Rovers' history.

The FA Cup brought, as the *Bristol Evening Post* described it, 'Rovers' finest hour'. Matt Busby's Manchester United played at Eastville before a crowd of 35,872 and were defeated 4-0. Although Duncan Edwards was injured, the United side was packed with household names, five of whom were to perish in the Munich air crash in 1958. An opportunist goal from Biggs put Rovers ahead after only ten minutes, and Meyer, at the second attempt, doubled the advantage before half-time. Creative and surprisingly confident against such talented opponents, Rovers scored again through Biggs and a late penalty from Bradford, after England left-back Roger Byrne had handled. Rovers were the '£110 team with the million-dollar touch of class', according to Desmond Hackett in the *Daily Express*. It seemed hardly just that Rovers should exit in round four, falling to an angled drive ten minutes before half-time from inside-right Bert Tindill in a replay at a snowy Doncaster Rovers, which was overshadowed by Bradford's horrific injury. Meyer's first-half goal at Ashton Gate enabled Rovers to retain the Gloucestershire Cup.

1956/57

Bert Tann's home-grown side had come close to an unlikely promotion to Division One and had produced an England international in Geoff Bradford, but reality lay around the corner. Season 1956/57 saw some large victories and heavy defeats as the side had to settle for ninth place in the Second Division. It was largely an unchanged Rovers side that opened the season with a home victory over Grimsby Town, thanks to a Dai Ward fifty-sixth minute reaction shot. With Frank Allcock's enforced retirement casting a shadow over the previous season's success, Les Edwards partnered the evergreen Harry Bamford at full-back, Ron Nicholls appeared regularly in goal and young wing-half Norman Sykes made the first of numerous league appearances.

Rovers scored in each of the first fourteen league games of the new season to complete a run of twenty-four consecutive matches dating back to March 1956. Two more games would have equalled a club record established in 1927, but Rotherham United held Rovers to a goalless draw at Millmoor. The early season run included a 4-2 win at Doncaster Rovers, Bradford scoring twice, and a 4-0 home win over Stoke City, as Rovers remained unbeaten in their opening five league fixtures. There were equally convincing 4-0 victories at home to Huddersfield Town, which included a blitz of three goals in five minutes, and against a Fulham side boasting the England international and former Rovers schoolboy Roy Bentley, as well as Elton John's uncle Roy Dwight. In March, two Bill Roost goals contributed to a 4-2 home win over Rotherham United.

The two largest wins, however, came in consecutive home fixtures over Christmas. On 22 December, Rovers defeated Doncaster Rovers 6-1 at Eastville. Dai Ward, who scored after seventy-seven, seventy-eight and eighty minutes, recorded the fastest league hat-trick by a Rovers player, and Barrie Meyer, for the second consecutive Saturday, scored twice. This was the first time Rovers had accumulated ten league goals against any opposition in a season. The anomalies of post-war football left Rovers to be crushed 7-2 by Bury at Gigg Lane on Christmas Day, before repeating their 6-1 scoreline over the same opposition on Boxing Day. Peter Hooper, the eighth player to score three times before half-time for Rovers in a league game, scored a hat-trick against Bury, with Meyer again weighing in with two goals. Hooper gave Rovers a sixth-minute lead and completed a thirty-minute first-half hat-trick when he scored from the rebound after his thirty-sixth minute penalty had been saved.

Such a convincing home victory stands in direct contrast to Rovers' heaviest defeat for almost two years. Bury had led 3-1 after seventy-nine minutes before five goals in eleven minutes, four of them to the Lancashire side, distorted the scoreline beyond recognition. Stan Pearson, now almost thirty-seven and a member of Manchester United's 1948 FA Cup winning side, became the oldest opponent ever to register a League hat-trick against Rovers, while Tom Neill and

Eddie Robertson added two goals apiece. Outside-left Norman Lockhart's missed penalty saved Rovers from further embarrassment. Incredibly, within weeks, Rovers had lost by the same 7-2 scoreline at Leicester City where, for the fifth and most recent time in Rovers' league history, three opponents had scored twice each. One of these, Arthur Rowley, who had also scored at Eastville in September, remains to this day the record aggregate goalscorer in Football League history.

While these two defeats stand out, an extraordinary 5-3 defeat at Ashton Gate in September similarly exposed Rovers' defensive frailties. John Atyeo and Cyril Williams scored twice each for Bristol City and Dai Ward twice for Rovers. Middlesbrough and the three Ls – Leicester City, Lincoln City and Liverpool – all won at Eastville but, to counter this, Rovers won six away games, including victories over Notts County at Meadow Lane and West Ham United at Upton Park. At Vale Park, Rovers led 2-0 after eighty-six minutes, but after a frenetic final four minutes, were left clinging on for a 3-2 win, afforded by two Geoff Bradford goals. This was Port Vale's seventh consecutive league defeat en route to a club record nine in succession.

That there was no shortage of goalmouth excitement at Rovers games is amply illustrated by the fact that the local derby with Bristol City at Eastville in February was only the club's second goalless draw since April 1954. Yet this game provided an incident that, in many respects, epitomised the spirit of Bristol football in those glorious days of the 1950s. Local derbies never have been for the faint-hearted, and two tenacious battlers, Rovers' Jackie Pitt and City's Ernie Peacock, were sent off for their misdeeds in a robust game. As they left the field together, the players linked arms, a symbol that rivalry does not necessarily mean enmity, and a sign of what football meant to those at the chalkface in the immediate post-war era.

Four minutes from the end of the 2-1 home defeat against Leicester City in September, Hooper's penalty was struck with such ferocity that, rebounding off a post, it set the opposition on the attack. With Rovers players pushed forward for the penalty, Ian McNeil sent Tommy McDonald through to score past an unprepared defence. Three weeks later, Sheffield United took a first-minute lead at Eastville through John Wilkinson, only for Rovers to recover to win 3-1. Similarly, an apparently convincing 3-0 home victory over Notts County in February concealed the fact that County's Gordon Wills missed a penalty. In December, Tommy Briggs revisited the Rovers defence, scoring both Blackburn Rovers' goals in a 2-0 win. He had now scored a total of ten goals in Rovers' three most recent visits to Ewood Park. All of this hides a surfeit of 3-2 results, which threatened at times to reach epidemic proportions. Rovers won by this score against Leyton Orient, Swansea Town, Nottingham Forest and Port Vale, and lost 3-2 at Middlesbrough, Grimsby Town and Fulham. Three consecutive games in the run-up to Easter finished this way. What with 7-2 defeats and 6-1 victories, the team from East Bristol was due a run of unusual results, and so it was to prove in 1957/58. This would have to be achieved without left-back Les Edwards, whose place was taken by a rejuvenated Josser Watling, and forward Bill Roost, whose goal at home to Swansea Town in March marked his final game in a nine-year association with the club.

In the FA Cup, Rovers were 3-0 up at Hull City after only nine minutes, and held on to win 4-3. Shades of 1981 at Preston, perhaps. Sure enough, victory at Boothferry Park attracted North End and a 32,000 crowd to Eastville. Preston were to finish the season third in Division One, and boasted two future Manchester United managers at wing-half, Tommy Docherty and Frank O'Farrell. Rovers had just lost 7-2 at Leicester City, while Preston were to beat Portsmouth 7-1 in Division One only a week later. Although Hooper scored from the penalty spot after just five minutes, the form book was not rewritten as North End ran out 4-1 winners. Tom Finney, now thirty-four and already the holder of sixty of his career total seventy-six England caps, scored twice and shot wide from a sixty-fifth minute penalty after Paddy Hale had fouled England international Tommy Thompson. The Gloucestershire Cup final was also lost, 2-1 at home to Bristol City.

1957/58

The FA Cup is a tournament filled with excitement and expectation, although, in Rovers' case, early disappointment is all too frequent an occurrence. In 1957/58, for the second of three occasions in the club's history, however, Rovers reached the quarter-finals. Unlike 1950/51, they only had to progress from round three by dint of Second Division status but, like the previous quarter-final appearance, the run was to end in a 3-1 defeat.

The FA Cup journey began with a convincing 5-0 victory over Third Division (North) side Mansfield Town, four Rovers forwards getting on the scoresheet. The reward for this was a home tie with high-riding Burnley, and a crowd of 34,229 was attracted to Eastville. Burnley, finalists four years later, were to finish sixth in Division One, and boasted famous names such as England captain and centre-half Jimmy Adamson and Jimmy McIlroy, an inside-forward who won fifty-five caps for Northern Ireland. For the second time in three years, Rovers were to defeat top division opponents. Rovers led through Paddy Hale after twenty-five minutes until a flurry of mid-second-half goals left the tie all-square. A 2-2 draw meant a potentially tough replay at Turf Moor, but Rovers emerged 3-2 victors, Norman Sykes scoring his first goal for a year and Dai Ward adding a couple. This was a staggering achievement for Rovers to have accomplished. It remains the only occasion that the club has won any fixture before a crowd of over 40,000 and was, until January 2002, the only time Rovers had won away to a top division club in the FA Cup.

Supporters of football in Bristol could not believe their luck as Rovers and City were drawn together in the fifth round. An attendance of 39,126 at Ashton

Gate brought gate receipts of £5,439, and witnessed arguably the most exciting of all Bristol derby matches, with seven goals, a missed penalty and a highly controversial Geoff Bradford winner seven minutes from time. Rovers should have taken a first-minute lead, but it was Barry Watkins who scored against his former club three minutes later to give City an early lead. By half-time Sykes, Ward and Barrie Meyer had scored, Ron Nicholls had saved a penalty from Watkins, and Rovers led 3-1. However, City recovered to level at 3-3. With a quarter-final place up for grabs, Ward's through ball to Bradford, looking suspiciously offside, brought Rovers a 4-3 victory.

The second quarter-final in Rovers' FA Cup history was a Second Division affair. However, despite a Bradford goal to parallel the one he had scored in February 1951, Fulham ran out clear winners. George Cohen, an England World Cup winner in 1966, played alongside the old guard of Roy Bentley, Roy Dwight and Johnny Haynes. Jimmy Hill put Fulham ahead from a rebound after his ninth-minute shot had been blocked, and Arthur Stevens, whose goals had knocked Rovers out of the FA Cup in 1948, added close-range goals after twelve and thirty-five minutes. At the kick-off, a Rovers supporter had run onto the pitch, dribbled the ball and scored, but all Rovers had to cheer was a classic Bradford header from Sykes' sixty-eighth minute free-kick.

Rovers approached season 1957/58 with no new personnel, and converted forwards Josser Watling and Paddy Hale filled the troublesome left-back and centre-half positions respectively. This was to be the final season goalkeeper Ron Nicholls and forward Barrie Meyer were to spend at Eastville, while half-back Jackie Pitt retired at the season's close after 467 league appearances, a figure only bettered by Stuart Taylor and Harry Bamford. Full-back Bamford, who turned thirty-eight in February, was the club's only ever-present, while Geoff Bradford top-scored with twenty goals in thirty-three league matches. In another high-scoring season, Rovers scored eighty-five and conceded eighty in finishing tenth in Division Two, goalless draws at Huddersfield Town and Notts County sticking out from among a glut of goals.

If FA Cup attendances were high, then so too were those in the league, where the golden years of post-war football coupled with Rovers' years of relative success combined to boost crowd figures. For a sixth consecutive season, the average attendance at Eastville topped 20,000 but this was also the final such season in the twentieth century. On the opposite side of the equation, a crowd of 5,687 watched Rovers' 2-0 victory over Cardiff City at Ninian Park in March, the lowest gathering all season for any Second Division fixture.

In a season of unusual results, one of the most remarkable was a 6-4 defeat at Swansea Town in Rovers' final Christmas Day fixture. Despite being bottom of the table, the Swans were two goals ahead after half an hour through Mel Charles and a Cliff Jones penalty, and 3-1 up through Ivor Allchurch after thirty-eight minutes. Peter Sampson's first goal for over two years and Dai Ward's seventh goal of the season left the score 3-2 at half-time. Alfie Biggs equalised two minutes after the break, and Meyer made the score 4-4 with twenty minutes remaining, after Jones had scored his second. However, Charles scored his second of the game and, with twelve minutes remaining, Jones completed his hat-trick to give Swansea Town a 6-4 win they fully deserved. Twenty-four hours later, with George Petherbridge scoring twice, Rovers made a mockery of this result by defeating the Swans 3-0 at Eastville.

Rovers then contrived to concede five or more goals twice in the space of four days – six at the Vetch Field and six at Upton Park. In becoming the youngest league hat-trick scorer against Rovers, eighteen-year-old John Smith scored three times as West Ham United won 6-1, just as his teammate Billy Dare had scored a hat-trick in the Hammers' 3-2 win at Eastville in August. Alan Peacock scored three goals in Middlesbrough's 4-3 victory over Rovers at Ayresome Park in March, the other goal claimed by Brian Clough. Ally McLeod, later Scotland manager, scored the opening goal as Rovers crashed 2-0 to Blackburn Rovers at Ewood Park in January 1958.

The heaviest defeat of the season was at Eastville in December when, in Jackie Pitt's penultimate game for Rovers, Grimsby Town won 7-0 to inflict Rovers' heaviest ever home league defeat. At one stage, the Mariners scored four goals and missed a penalty in the space of eighteen second-half minutes. In fact, Hooper, unmarked in front of goal, and Biggs had both spurned opportunities to put Rovers ahead, before Ron Stockin, after six minutes, and Gerry Priestley, two minutes later, put the visitors 2-0 up when goalkeeper Nicholls twice lost control of the ball. Priestley's cross was converted at the second attempt by Johnny Scott, a minute before half-time, before Grimsby's four late goals. After seventy minutes, Ron Rafferty scored from the penalty spot after Sampson had fouled Priestley. Seven minutes later, Jimmy Fell's solo goal made him the fifth Grimsby forward on the scoresheet, and his next run led to a second penalty, blasted over the bar by Rafferty. Late goals for Scott and Stockin, their second each of a bizarre game, meant Rovers had lost a league game by seven clear goals for the first time since April 1936. On the other hand, in addition to a successful FA Cup run, Rovers enjoyed some memorable victories of their own. In November, nineteen-year-old Bobby Jones was given a league debut against Middlesbrough, opened the scoring after just two minutes and later added a second in a 5-0 win. Two Bradford goals helped defeat Blackburn Rovers 4-0, while Leyton Orient were defeated by the same score in a match where Rovers' Hooper and the visitors' Johnny Hartburn both missed penalties. Barrie Meyer's second hat-trick for Rovers enabled them to defeat Derby County 5-2 in August. A fortnight later, the first hat-trick of Alfie Biggs' blossoming career earned Rovers a 5-3 victory at Stoke City. More bizarrely, in beating Notts County 5-2 at Eastville, Rovers were indebted to own goals from Frank Cruickshank and John McGrath.

The season drew to a close with high-scoring home draws. On Good Friday, Fulham earned a 2-2 draw at Eastville through goals from Roy Dwight and the celebrated Jimmy Hill. Twenty-four hours later, another Bradford double eased Rovers towards a 3-3 draw with Bristol City, where all six goals were scored in an extraordinary first half. The sides met again in the Gloucestershire Cup final, where City won 4-1, as well as hitting the woodwork twice, after Bradford had put Rovers in front from a Biggs pass after only six minutes. The four meetings of the sides had produced a total of twenty-three goals.

1958/59

Towards the end of his long and successful career as a full-back with his only league club, Harry Bamford had begun to give back to the community that had supported him for so long. The 3-2 defeat at Derby County in September was his 486th for Rovers, a club record at the time and since bettered only by Stuart Taylor. In the meantime, he coached schoolboys at Clifton College, and it was on his way home from a training session that his motorcycle was involved in a collision with a car. For three days, his life hung in the balance before he died of his injuries on 31 October 1958. At a memorial service in St Mary Redcliffe church, manager Bert Tann said that 'a part of Bristol Rovers died with him'.

Not only had Rovers lost a gifted player, but a pivotal figure in the club's history had died at a point when his career was still not quite over. His influence on the spirit of Rovers in the 1950s was instrumental in the club's success. An annual memorial trophy for sportsmanship among local footballers was set up, awarded on four occasions to Rovers players and won in 1967/68 by Alfie Biggs' brother Bert. On 8 May 1959, a combined Bristol XI featuring six Rovers players defeated Arsenal 5-4 in a testimonial fixture, Geoff Bradford scoring twice, before an Eastville crowd of 28,347, which contributed to the Harry Bamford Memorial Fund. A total of just over £3,709 was raised. It is no coincidence that the days of FA Cup quarter-finals and promotion challenges were over. Following Bamford's death, Rovers fell into a decline that climaxed with relegation in 1961/62, and the scary proximity of Division Four twelve months later.

Over the summer of 1958, Divisions Three and Four were created out of the old geographical leagues. As early as 30 November 1944, the Rovers secretary Sid Hawkins had written to the Football League to say the club directors 'strongly deprecate the suggestion that Third Division clubs should be divided into Third and Fourth Divisions. Within the Rovers camp, trouble was brewing as the two county cricketers, Ron Nicholls and Barrie Meyer, unable to make preseason training because of commitments with Gloucestershire, put in transfer requests amid disputes. On the eve of the new season, the goalkeeper joined Cardiff City in an exchange deal involving John Frowen. He later played for Bristol City, and was to appear in 534 matches for Gloucestershire between 1951 and 1975. Meyer, after 139 league games for Rovers in almost a decade, joined Plymouth Argyle in a deal worth £4,500 plus the services of John Timmins. Another player who later resurfaced at Bristol City, Meyer played 406 times for Gloucestershire and also served as a Test umpire.

Eastville had a 3,000-capacity North Stand constructed through the close season at a cost of £76,000, of which the supporters' club, then numbering 6,931 members, paid £10,000. This new stand was officially opened in August, prior to the first home game of the season. Following an away win, this first of five in the league being completed when Orient's George Wright conceded an own goal on his club debut, Rovers defeated Scunthorpe United 4-0 in this fixture, with four forwards getting their names on the scoresheet. By the time the sides met at the Old Show Ground in January, the Iron had scored in twenty-one consecutive league games, but Rovers were able to hold them to a goalless draw.

It was a mixed season for Rovers, for they neither won three league matches in succession nor lost three consecutive league fixtures all season. Rovers scored four at home to Scunthorpe United, Rotherham United and Swansea Town, as well as at Cardiff City and, in November, seven times at home to Grimsby Town. The heaviest defeat came in the final away game of the season; 5-2 at Sheffield United. In addition, Rovers lost an exciting game at Charlton Athletic 4-3, and by 4-1 at Lincoln City.

The greatest personal performance, however, came against Rotherham United at Eastville in March. Geoff Bradford had scored eleven league hat-tricks for Rovers, but never before four times in one match. He had missed the 3-3 draw at Millmoor in October and, returning from injury only a week before this return fixture, had not scored since Boxing Day. However, a first-minute goal set him on his way, and he contributed all his side's goals as Rovers recorded a 4-1 victory. The first Rovers player to score four times in a match in this division, he was also the first to achieve this feat since Vic Lambden on Easter Monday 1952. Not only did this equal a club record as yet unsurpassed, but Bradford also remained, until Rickie Lambert in October 2008, the most recent Rovers player to score four league goals in a home fixture – Robin Stubbs, Alan Warboys and Jamie Cureton all having done so away from home in the meantime.

The team performance of the season was against Grimsby Town at Eastville in the middle week of October. A masterful 7-3 victory, the only occasion Rovers have won by this scoreline in league football, made light of the fact that Rovers had lost their two previous home games. After a quiet start, the match exploded into life just before half-time, as Dai Ward, after twenty-eight minutes, and Peter Hooper, eleven minutes later, gave Rovers a 2-0 lead. Tommy Briggs, whose seven goals for Blackburn Rovers had sunk the Eastville side in February 1955, then managed to pull one back a minute before half-time. Ward extended Rovers' lead, and Mike Cullen replied for Grimsby before two Hooper goals in four minutes completed his hat-trick and left Rovers 5-2 ahead. Undeterred, Ron Rafferty, scoring against Rovers in both fixtures for the second consecutive season, registered a goal fourteen minutes from time. Geoff Bradford, however, scored twice in five minutes – three Rovers players had registered doubles and Rovers had avenged the 7-0 drubbing of eleven months earlier.

On Easter Monday, Rovers and Swansea Town served up a goal feast at Eastville. Rovers led 3-2 at the interval, and though Bradford had restored the two-goal cushion just after the hour mark, the home side was forced to settle for a 4-4 draw. The Pirates had taken a fourth-minute lead through Ward, Hooper had added a second ten minutes later, and though Welsh international Len Allchurch reduced the deficit after eighteen minutes, it took Hooper just seven more minutes to put Rovers 3-1 ahead. Once the Swans had scored twice in four minutes midway through the second half, Rovers were resigned to a second consecutive home draw.

In November, goals from Geoff Twentyman, whose son was to be a doyen of the Rovers side, and Jimmy Melia gave Liverpool a tight victory at Anfield. Although Huddersfield Town took just one point off Rovers, their forward Kevin McHale scored in both fixtures, as did the ubiquitous John Atyeo of Bristol City. In January, Bert Tann fielded virtually a first team for a Football Combination game against Portsmouth reserves, Rovers winning 9-1. In that month, Rovers gave a league debut to Ray Mabbutt, a local wing-half who, like his younger son after him, was to give sterling service to the club for many years. Outside-right Granville Smith also impressed, as did Graham Ricketts at half-back, full-back Doug Hillard and goalkeeper Malcolm Norman. As the old guard began to move on, a number of players with sizeable contributions to make to the club's story began to seize the moment.

In finishing sixth in Division Two, there was indeed ground for optimism. Rovers won their final three home games, each time defeating sides with larger reputations and greater spending power and which had beaten Rovers earlier in the season. Two goals from Hooper, the only ever-present, and one from Ward earned a 3-0 victory over Liverpool, before Rovers ended the campaign with 2-1 home wins over Charlton Athletic and Sheffield Wednesday. In the latter, Rovers fielded Tony Gough, whose second league appearance was to be for Swindon Town a remarkable eleven years later. He did not play at all in the league during the 1960s. Wednesday were defeated by a Bradford goal, struck venomously from Doug Hillard's through ball after eleven minutes – it was the 200th goal of his Rovers career and his twentieth of the season to leave him the club's second highest scorer, behind twenty-six goal Ward.

Despite the FA Cup glory of the previous season, Rovers found themselves a goal down after nineteen seconds, and lost 4-0 at home to Charlton Athletic in the third round. This very early goal, the first of two by South African international Sam Lawrie, was followed by goals from John Summers and Ron White. Rovers took a sensational lead in the Gloucestershire Cup final with the fastest goal in the club's history. Sweeping forward from the kick-off, Ward scored after only seven seconds, but Bert Tindill's second-half equaliser for Bristol City left the score all square.

1959/60

With the benefit of hindsight, the end of the 1950s can be seen to have drawn to a close the golden years in the Bristol Rovers story. The 1959/60 season opened with a six-match unbeaten run, but entailed several heavy defeats. Four or more goals were conceded on six occasions as Rovers finished the season in ninth place in Division Two. Relegation in 1961/62 and a long struggle, ultimately successful, the following season to avoid the unprecedented drop into Division Four, lay just around the corner.

It is still difficult for any Rovers supporter to admit this, but Geoff Bradford was no longer the prolific, potent goalscorer he had once been. The five hat-tricks in 1953/54, the two goals in each of four consecutive games in October 1954 and the England cap were a thing of the past. That season he scored twelve league goals, two against Stoke City in February being his only brace. While Alfie Biggs had recovered from his poor goal return in 1958/59, and was top scorer with twenty-two league goals, Bobby Jones did not score at all this year. Granville Smith did not pose the threat at outside-right that his early performances had promised. The veteran Peter Sampson's appearance in the opening-day draw with Leyton Orient was his only game of the season.

On the other hand, Bert Tann was beginning to weave together a team of young, predominantly Bristolian footballers. A lack of funds hampered his progress, but his task was to glean every nugget from the local football scene. Ray Mabbutt, a prime example of this policy, was the club's only ever-present in 1959/60. Doug Hillard, David Pyle and Graham Ricketts continued to establish themselves in the side, while local teenage inside-forward Ian Hamilton scored his first goals for the club. Victory over Swansea Town on Boxing Day marked the league debut of twenty-year-old Harold Jarman at outside-right – a Rovers player until 1973, a county cricketer with Gloucestershire and an essential ingredient in the long-running recipe of football in Bristol.

Having drawn three of their opening four games, Rovers' first home win came against Ipswich Town in September. The new floodlights at Eastville were used for the first time in this Monday evening game, artificial lighting allowing for greater flexibility over kick-off times. Four 134-foot-high pylons had been installed at a cost of £16,000, paid for by the Rovers Supporters' Club, whose chairman, Eric Godfrey, had been one of the committee that first proposed the concept in April 1959. Prior to the game, Rovers' chairman, Hampden Alpass, expressed his gratitude and added that 'our supporters' club is second to none in the country in its support of the parent club'. Although the home side lost Doug Hillard with a dislocated shoulder just seven minutes after half-time of the first fixture under floodlights, two goals from Peter Hooper gave Rovers victory, while Ted Phillips scored for Ipswich Town in both league fixtures against Rovers. For the following game, at Sunderland, Brian Doyle was given a first appearance of the season and responded with the only goal of his Rovers career.

Rovers lost just three home league games, 2-0 defeats to both Liverpool and Middlesbrough and an astonishing 5-4 defeat against Brighton in October. Prior to the game at Colchester United in January 2000, this was amazingly the only occasion Rovers had lost in the league by this score. Alfie Biggs was in the middle of a goalscoring run, in which he had scored Rovers' first in five consecutive fixtures. His eighteenth-minute goal cancelled out Tommy Dixon's opener. Peter Hooper then twice gave Rovers the lead, with Adrian Thorne, who was to score four times against the Pirates in August 1960, levelling the score at 2-2 on the stroke of half-time. Hooper's second, seven minutes after the break, should have left Rovers in control, but within twelve minutes, two quick-fire goals from Bill Curry put Brighton 4-3 ahead. George Petherbridge scored Rovers' second equaliser after seventy-two minutes, only for half-back Jack Bertolini to pop up with the winning goal thirteen minutes from time.

Five-goal defeats were also the order of the day at Middlesbrough and Plymouth Argyle in consecutive away matches before Christmas. At Ayresome Park, Brian Clough scored a hat-trick in a 5-1 result. He scored again in April when Middlesbrough completed a comfortable double over Rovers. Colin Grainger, the talented musician playing outside-left for Sunderland, Eddie Brown of Leyton Orient and Rotherham United's Brian Sawyer all scored in both league fixtures against Tann's side. So too did Graham Moore, as Cardiff City, fielding future Rovers players in Brian Jenkins, for the Ninian Park tie, and John Watkins, drew both games. For the trip to Ninian Park, Rovers Supporters' Club chartered the steamboat *Glen Usk* to travel from Hotwells to Cardiff. Rovers also lost 4-1 at Villa Park and 4-0 at Anfield.

Portsmouth were defeated 2-0 at Eastville in September, while Swansea Town, Sunderland, Stoke City and Rotherham United all lost 3-1. Rovers scored three times in a glorious twelve-minute spell in the opening half-hour to defeat a strong Sunderland side. Towards the end of April, Huddersfield Town and Plymouth Argyle both suffered two-goal defeats at Eastville. Away from home, Rovers won five league games, all by a single goal. Victory at Scunthorpe United, in an extraordinary game that finished 4-3, was largely due to Hamilton's first two goals for the club. Rovers had gone ahead after only eighteen minutes when Bradford scored following a neat interchange of passes with Hooper, but conceded a goal either side of half-time before Mabbutt equalised. Hamilton's brace, either side of Barrie Thomas' second goal of the game, were both confidently taken, the first from a 15-yard strike on the hour, and the winning goal, nine minutes from time, after goalkeeper Ken Jones had only parried a rasping drive from Hooper.

The most remarkable victory, though, was a 5-4 win at Fratton Park, which mirrored the home defeat against Brighton. Portsmouth conceded a second-minute own goal through Ron Howells, the earliest own goal in any Football League match involving Rovers, only for Ron Saunders to equalise fifteen minutes later. Dai Ward's twenty-third minute goal gave Rovers a 2-1 interval lead, and when he scored again two minutes after the break, Rovers appeared to have some breathing space. Not so, for Saunders grabbed a second within a minute, and although Hooper put Rovers further ahead, Derek Harris reduced the margin to 4-3, with seventeen minutes remaining. Eight minutes from time, Biggs handballed, and Reg Cutler drove home the equaliser from the penalty spot. With all to play for, Rovers swept forward and, on eighty-eight minutes, Hooper claimed his second goal of the game to give Rovers a memorable victory.

In the FA Cup, held to a goalless draw at home by Doncaster Rovers, the Eastville side won 2-1 in the replay at Belle Vue. Both Biggs and Ward found their customary way on to the scoresheet, with Albert Broadbent replying for the home side. The reward for this victory was that, for the second time in three years, mighty Preston North End were drawn to play Rovers at Eastville. This fixture against one of the most powerful sides in the country drew a record crowd of 38,472 to Eastville. This figure stood the test of time and remains the largest attendance ever to assemble at the old stadium. The huge gathering was not to be disappointed either, as the sides served up a six-goal thriller. Biggs scored twice for Rovers, while the legendary Tom Finney was one of North End's scorers. Gordon Milne, later a very successful manager, was in the Preston side, while Jim Smith, who was to play for Stockport County in both league fixtures against Rovers in 1969/70, conceded an own goal. The replay at Deepdale drew a crowd of 33,164, Preston running out 5-1 winners, with Finney and Sam Taylor, scorers of a goal apiece in the first game, claiming two each.

The Gloucestershire Cup final was lost. Bristol City had finished last in Division Two and been relegated but, despite trailing at half-time, defeated Rovers 3-2 to win the trophy, the evergreen John Atyeo scoring twice. Rovers also played Bristol Rugby Club on 4 May in an experimental game of Socby. After a goalless first half, Bradford scored twice and Hooper once to give Rovers a 3-1 win, with the rugby club's captain John Blake scoring a consolation goal. Coach Fred Ford, a pivotal figure in five excellent seasons, left Rovers to become manager at Ashton Gate.

Dai Ward was rewarded for his talent at club level by representing Wales in their 1-1 draw with England at Cardiff on 17 October 1959. He was, after Jack Lewis in 1906, the second player to play for the full Welsh side while on Rovers' books, and he was to win a second cap as a Cardiff City player three years later.

7

The 1960s

1960/61

It is all too often the case with a relatively small club that the threat of relegation is never too far away. While Rovers had finished in the top ten in Division Two for seven consecutive seasons, there was now no money to purchase replacements for older players. As a younger generation of Bristolians came through the ranks, the club slipped to a final league placing of seventeenth, and two long, trying years lay ahead. Twenty league defeats was the club's worst record since 1947/48, and ninety-two goals conceded the most since 1935/36. Rovers finished the season just four positions and four points above relegated Portsmouth.

Once the season had opened with an unexpected defeat at home to Middlesbrough, in which Rovers twice equalised before falling to Alan Peacock's winning goal at seventy-nine minutes, it was clear a troublesome year lay ahead. Within weeks, Rovers had lost 6-1 at Brighton and 4-0 at Rotherham United. Rovers were to concede four goals at Luton Town, Southampton and Huddersfield Town, and five in both encounters with Plymouth Argyle. At home, in addition to Argyle's visit, Rovers were to concede four to Leeds United and three on a total of three occasions in the league.

With the familiar names of George Petherbridge, Alfie Biggs, Geoff Bradford, Dai Ward and Peter Hooper, the sole ever-present, in the forward line, it was a very recognisable Rovers forward line that began the season. With the retirement of Brian Doyle, John Frowen became the regular left-back, working behind Ray Mabbutt and in partnership with the solid Doug Hillard. However, lack of early season success prompted two departures. Dai Ward left to pursue his career with Cardiff City and the deal, worth £10,000, brought John Watkins to Eastville; the prospect of him and the emerging talent of Harold Jarman on opposing wings certainly filled supporters with optimism. At the season's end, after missing the last fifteen games with a fractured leg, Biggs joined Preston North End for £18,000, though he was to return in fifteen months.

Above left: 1. Alan Ball, a World Cup winner in 1966 with England signed for Rovers in 1983 at the age of thirty-seven and enjoyed a tremendous last season of League football; his career spanned twenty-two years.

Above right: 2. Arthur Griffiths made over 100 Southern League appearance for Rovers between 1899 and 1904. He was a member of the championship side of 1904.

3. Rovers supporters at Bristol City in 1959.

4. Rovers forward Barrie Meyer challenges Bristol City goalkeeper Bob Anderson in the thrilling FA fifth-round tie at Ashton Gate in February 1958, which Rovers won 4-3 with a late Geoff Bradford goal.

Above left: 5. Manager Bert Tann, who joined Rovers in 1950 and enjoyed success with the club's first championship in 1953. He remained in charge until 1968, he then became the club's general manager until his death in 1972.

Above middle: 6. Bobby Jones, another Bristolian who enjoyed a long career as a winger at Eastville. Jones scored 101 League goals for Rovers in 421 games.

Above right: 7. Captain Vaughan Jones holds aloft the Third Division championship trophy at his testimonial game.

8. Cheers Rovers fans at Eastville before the memorable FA Cup defeat of the Mighty Busby Babes (Manchester United) in 1956. Rovers beat the eventual First Division Champions 4-0.

9. Carl Saunders tries a shot in the 4-0 defeat of Bristol City at Twerton Park on 13 December 1992. Rovers enjoyed a remarkable short spell with Malcolm Allison in charge as manager.

10. Dick Sheppard saves one of the penalties in July 1972 during the 7-6 penalty shoot-out win to ensure Rovers won the Watney Cup after a goalless final against First Division Sheffield United.

11. Stuart Campbell, inspirational Rovers captain who guided Rovers to the JPT final and play-offs in 2007. He had a brief spell as caretaker manager in 2011, but he could not stop the club being relegated to League Two.

12. Chic Bates heads a fine goal against Sunderland on 19 April 1980. The goal in the 2-2 draw contributed to Rovers avoiding relegation under the caretaker manager Harold Jarman.

13. David Clarkson scores a late Rovers goal at Wycombe Wanderers on 26 April 2014 to try and ensure the club retains its League status, but it was not enough after they were beaten at home to Mansfield.

Above left: 14. Dai Ward, Rovers' Welsh international goalscorer. He scored eight goals in a club record spell of consecutive matches in the spring of 1956. He netted ninety goals for Rovers in 175 League games between 1954 and 1961.

Above right: 15. David Williams was a creative midfielder who made 342 League appearances in a decade at Rovers before becoming Rovers' youngest-ever player-manager, at age twenty-eight in 1983.

16. Rovers' squad for season 1974/75, who had won promotion to the Second Division. Back, from left: Bater, Williams Moore Crabtree, Aitken, Powell, Stephens. Middle: B. Jones, Stanton, Green, Taylor, Lewis, Sheppard, Eadie, Warboys, Rudge, Prince, Parsons. Front: Campbell (trainer), Jacobs, M. John, Fearnley, Megson (manager), Bannister, D. John, Britten, Dobson (player-coach).

Above: 17. Rovers' Eastville Stadium from the air in 1926.

Below: 18. Craig Hinton in action in the 2007 JPT final at the Millennium Stadium, Cardiff, when Rovers were beaten 3-2 by Doncaster Rovers.

19. Geoff Bradford opens the scoring for Rovers in the Newcastle United FA Cup replay in 1951 to the cheers of 30,000 fans. United came back to win 3-1 and went on to win the Cup.

20. Geoff Fox battles for possession with Newcastle United's Jack Milburn in the quarter final FA Cup tie, watched by 63,000 fans at St James' Park. A goalless draw resulted in a 3-1 defeat for Rovers in the replay at Eastville.

21. Harold Jarman scored 127 goals in 452 League games for Rovers between 1958 and 1973.

Above left: 22. Harry Bamford, a classy full-back, who made 486 League appearances until his tragic death in October 1958. A memorial sportsmanship trophy was started in his name.

Above right: 23. Don Megson, Rovers manager from 1972, gaining promotion in 1974 before leaving to manage in the USA in 1977.

Below: 24. Ian Holloway scores from the penalty spot in the 3-0 victory over Bristol City on 2 May 1990. The win ensured promotion and, four days later, the Third Division championship.

Above: 25. Rovers' talented left winger Peter Hooper, who had a tremendous shot. He scored a remarkable 101 goals in 297 League games.

Top left: 26. Gary Mabbutt, son of Rovers' Ray Mabbutt. Gary was in the first team at seventeen, but was sold to Tottenham Hotspur in 19822. He enjoyed legendary status in his sixteen years at Spurs, gaining sixteen full England caps and making over 600 appearances and being awarded an MBE.

Middle left: 27. Geoff Bradford, Rovers' record goalscorer – 242 goals in 462 League games between 1949 and 1964.

Bottom left: 28. Jesse Whatley, Rovers' long-serving goalkeeper, who enjoyed over a decade at Rovers (1919–30) appearing in 371 League games.

29. Rovers reached the Second Division play-off finals at Wembley in 1994/95. Justin Skinner tries a shot against Huddersfield Town, who won 2-1, watched by 59,175 fans.

30. Manager John Ward and chairman Nick Higgs at the end of the 2012/13 season, celebrating Rovers maintaining their League status after a fine last month of the season.

31. Rickie Lambert celebrates with Rovers fans after his dramatic late goal at Hartlepool in May 2007 to ensure Rovers reached the play-offs.

Above left: 32. Manager Paul Trollope holds aloft the play-off trophy after the exciting 3-1 victory over Shrewsbury.

Above right: 33. Paul Randall enjoyed two spells with Rovers and scored ninety-four goals in 240 League games. He was sold to Stoke City, but returned three years later.

Below: 34. Rovers mascot Eastville Ernie draws his sword on Bristol City mascot Ashton Alf, much to the amusement of the fans at Ashton Gate before the 1958 FA Cup tie.

35. Rovers manager Gerry Francis leads out the team at Wembley in the Leyland Daf final against Tranmere Rovers on 20 May 1990.

36. Gerry Francis and players on the team coach, Wembley-bound. Gerry Francis returned to Rovers for a second spell as manager in June 2001, but left in December after just a further thirty-one games in charge.

Above left: 37 Ray Warren, Rovers' long-serving captain, who joined the club in 1936 until 1956, making 450 League appearances.

Above right: 38. Richard Walker celebrates his first goal at Wembley in the 2007 play-off final victory.

39. Team photo 1964/65. From left: Ronnie Briggs, Lindsay Parsons, Dave Stone, Doug Hillard, Gwyn Jones, Alex Munro, Terry Oldfield, Joe Davis, Ray Mabbutt, John Brown, Roy McCrohan, Roger Frude, Bernard Hall, Bobby Jones, Ian Hamilton, John Petts, Chris Weller, Harold Jarman, Alfie Biggs.

Above left: 40. Ian Holloway enjoyed three spells as a player at Rovers, making almost 400 League appearances for the club and then became player-manager, guiding the club to the 1999 Second Division play-offs.

Above right: 41. Stuart Taylor holds the club record for League appearances, making 546 appearances before joining Bath City in 1980.

42. Rovers 1984/85. Back, from left: Kendall (kit man), Dolling (physio), White, Bannon, Cashley, Kite, Parkin McCaffrey, G. Williams, Jarman (youth coach), Jones (coach). Front: Bater, Slatter, B. Williams, D. Williams (player-manager), Holloway, Stephens, Randall.

43. Team photo 1969/70. Back, from left: Lindsay Parsons, John Petts, Dick Sheppard, Laurie Taylor, Tom Stanton, Frank Prince. Middle: Bobby Campbell, Bryn Jones, Phil Roberts, Stuart Taylor, Gordon Marsland, Alex Munro, Bill Dodgin (manager). Front: Ray Graydon, Wayne Jones, Robin Stubbs, Bobby Jones, Bobby Brown, Harold Jarman.

44. Rovers' full squad who were Third Division South Champions in season 1952/53.

Above: 45. Rovers players celebrate promotion after the 2007 play-off final at Wembley against Shrewsbury Town.

Below: 46. Rovers captain leads out the team at Eastville in 1950, with mascot Tony Spiller.

A final nine league matches brought to a conclusion the long and reliable career of wing-half Peter Sampson, leaving just Bradford and Petherbridge of the championship-winning side. After 339 league games for Rovers, Sampson spent two further seasons as captain of Trowbridge Town. However, young Bobby Jones continued to progress and two players for the future, Joe Davis and Terry Oldfield, broke into the side for the first time. The side's only ever-present, Hooper, was top scorer with twenty league goals. Another departure was secretary John Gummow who retired five days before Christmas and was replaced by Ron Moules.

The second home game of the season featured the greatest comeback in Rovers' history. Four goals behind at the interval, Rovers staged an exceptional second-half recovery to draw 4-4 with Leeds United at Eastville. Don Revie, later an England manager, had been in the Leeds side that drew 1-1 with Rovers at Elland Road five days earlier, but this Monday fixture still found Rovers facing strong opposition, including centre-half Jack Charlton, a 1966 World Cup winner. Leeds were 4-0 up inside forty-one minutes. Colin Grainger, a thorn in Rovers' side while with Sunderland in 1959/60, scored after ten minutes. John Hawksby scored twice, the second after Noel Payton had hit a post, and John McCole snapped up a rebound off goalkeeper Malcolm Norman. Rovers, however, approached the second half with renewed vigour and scored three times in twelve minutes: through Petherbridge, after an interchange of passes with Hillard, Hamilton, from a Mabbutt free-kick, and Hooper. A very tense half-hour passed until Hooper hit a dramatic equaliser from a Biggs cross with two minutes remaining. Even then, Graham Ricketts had an opportunity to score, but an entertaining game finished with honours even.

Despite the heavy defeats, Rovers were to achieve some very creditable results. The first win of the season, against Rotherham United in the eighth game, was the first of four in six games, and there were three straight victories just before Christmas and four in five games in March. Leyton Orient, Swansea Town and Southampton were all beaten 4-2 at Eastville, Hooper scoring on each occasion. Hooper scored again in a 4-1 victory over Luton Town, and added a further goal in an extraordinary 4-3 home win over Liverpool, where Bobby Jones scored twice for the first of two consecutive league matches. Liverpool's Kevin Lewis scored three times, one from a penalty, in so doing becoming the first of four opponents to score a league hat-trick against Rovers and yet end up on the losing side.

Indeed, Rovers won their last seven home games of the season. Portsmouth, ultimately relegated, were beaten 2-0 in a key fixture in March, Hooper and Bradford both scoring. Sheffield United, already promoted and having reached the FA Cup semi-finals with Len Allchurch in majestic form, were seen off 3-1 in the final home match to complete an improbable league double. From New Year onwards, Rovers were unbeaten at Eastville and recorded a second away win, two Hooper goals defeating Lincoln City at Sincil Bank. A potential win at Swansea Town in February was thwarted by an early injury to goalkeeper Howard

Radford, which ended his season and saw Mabbutt play the final seventy-two minutes in goal. A flurry of goals in January was epitomised by the 3-3 draw with Scunthorpe United, for whom Barrie Thomas scored twice in each of the league meetings with Rovers.

While the club's home record was good, Rovers contrived to lose ten of the last eleven away games. As the season drew to a close, these defeats became steadily heavier. Rovers lost 3-0 at Liverpool and Portsmouth, and 5-0 at Plymouth Argyle, George Kirby and Wilf Carter scoring twice each. Ominously for 1961/62, these results left Rovers scrapping for points to ensure the retention of Second Division football. This achieved, Rovers crashed 4-0 to Huddersfield Town at Leeds Road on the final day of the season, the home side requiring at least a point to guarantee survival. As it was, Derek Stokes scored twice after thirty-eight and seventy-eight minutes before Hamilton struck a consolation goal six minutes from time.

The signs for 1961/62 were bleak. With minimal funds for player recruitment, Bert Tann was able to sign just Brian Carter and John Hills over the summer of 1961. Rovers lost every game in which either of these players appeared. Eighteen players were used in the opening four games, but Rovers lost the first seven, the Huddersfield game at the end of 1960/61 creating a club record eight in succession. Ward and Biggs had left, but young talent in the form of Mabbutt, Jarman and Jones was coming to the fore. Over the close season, though, Bobby Campbell, later Rovers' manager between 1977 and 1979, joined Rovers as trainer. In July 1961, Tann brought Bill Dodgin to Eastville as chief scout. A wing-half with Rovers in 1936/37, he had played alongside Tann and Fred Ford at Charlton Athletic. Dodgin was to be Rovers' manager between August 1969 and July 1972, and his return to Eastville at this point must be viewed as a highly positive move. Mention must also be made of the social club, which put together a busy first full working year for its 2,000 members. Tombola, often run by the son of former goalkeeper Harry Stansfield, and dancing evenings proved highly popular, while there was a darts night every Monday and whist on Tuesdays. Sunday evenings were show night, where Bill McMullen presented a variety of acts, including a fire-eater, an Indian fakir and a troupe of performing cats. Brian Jones hosted an increasingly successful rock 'n' roll evening every Wednesday.

Rovers made history in September by hosting and winning the first game ever played in the newly created League Cup. By dint of a 7.15 p.m. kick-off, fifteen minutes earlier than other ties, Fulham's Maurice Cook is credited with the tournament's first goal, and Rovers, with Jarman scoring for the club for the first time, with the first victory. Hamilton scored twice as Rovers ran up a 5-3 victory at Reading before succumbing to Rotherham United. It was the first match ever played under floodlights at Millmoor, and the home side won through goals from Alan Kirkman and Ken Houghton. In the FA Cup, First Division Aston Villa were held to a draw at Eastville, but won the replay convincingly, with two goals apiece from Bobby Thompson and England international Gerry Hitchens. Dai Ward was accused by many of lacking interest in this game and, indeed, never appeared in a Rovers shirt again. Two Biggs goals helped defeat Chelsea 3-1 in a friendly in January before an Eastville crowd of 5,245. Rovers gave a debut to David Stone in the Gloucestershire Cup final, but after a goalless first half, lost 3-1 at home to Bristol City. John Atyeo, who had scored a hat-trick against Brentford forty-eight hours earlier in the final league game of the season, scored two of the goals.

1961/62

After nine seasons in Division Two, Rovers were relegated to Division Three. It was the end of arguably the most glorious chapter in the club's history. The first seven games of the season were lost, and there were twenty-two league defeats in total, the most since 1936/37, though not as many as in the relegation campaign of 2010/11. A tally of thirteen league victories was, at the time, the lowest since 1947/48. Rovers scored fifty-three league goals, the lowest figure in the Second Division years, where the club had reached eighty in four consecutive seasons.

In truth, the minimal funds at Bert Tann's disposal, meant it was inevitable the club would struggle. John Hills and Brian Carter, the latter having played for Portsmouth in the nine-goal thriller in February 1960, arrived on free transfers, and Micky Slocombe was the only local player to break into the side in the early part of the season. Geoff Bradford began the season at centre-forward, but by Christmas was playing at right-back with the ever-reliable Ray Mabbutt leading the line. Although a tireless worker and key figure in the side, Mabbutt was to score just twice all season. The only ever-present was left-back John Frowen, who completed a run of sixty-six consecutive league appearances, while Bobby Jones, with one more than Bradford and Peter Hooper, was top scorer on thirteen league goals.

It is not just that Rovers lost their opening games, though, but the manner of these defeats that set the stage for the season ahead. A bumper crowd of 19,438 at Eastville on the opening day of the season earned the players a £6 bonus each, but Liverpool, destined to be runaway champions, took the points. This was the first fixture with the newly roofed Tote End, where the greyhound totaliser clocks had now been placed prominently on the roof fascia. Bury completed a league double and Rovers crashed 4-0 at Rotherham United before Rovers managed to score their first goal of the season. Bradford scored twice at home to Sunderland, but Rovers still lost, and did so again at Scunthorpe United and Stoke City, in Josser Watling's final game for the club. Doug Hillard's broken leg at Scunthorpe ruled him out of football for seven months. Seven straight defeats, or eight if the final game of 1960/61 is included, constituted an unwanted club record and left Rovers adrift at the foot of Division Two.

Through the middle of September, the revival got underway. Consecutive 2-1 victories were followed by a decisive 4-0 win against Leeds United, Hooper scoring twice against a side who were, in fact, to finish just three points above Rovers. A draw at Norwich City followed, but this encouraging run was ended by none other than Alfie Biggs, who scored the only goal of the game from 6 yards out two minutes from time as Preston North End defeated his home town club. Whereas in the relegation season of 1980/81 only five league matches were won, this Rovers side certainly proved it could win key games on occasions. A Jones hat-trick contributed to a 4-1 win over Swansea Town, a fifth consecutive home victory and the third of four occasions that Rovers scored as many as four times in a home match. Astonishingly, Rovers completed league doubles over Leyton Orient, who were promoted to Division One, and over sixth-placed Southampton.

On the other hand, though conceding fewer goals than the previous season, Rovers suffered a number of heavy defeats. Their situation is best summarised through the experiences of Keith Havenhand, who only scored fourteen goals for Derby County, but became the only player to register two league hat-tricks in a season against Rovers. Derby won both matches 4-1. Len White also scored three times, with Len Allchurch claiming one of the others, as Newcastle United defeated Rovers 5-2. Although Jarman gave Rovers a fourth-minute lead at Roker Park, Rovers trailed by half-time, and conceded three goals in the final quarter of an hour to lose 6-1. Roger Hunt and Ian St John were Liverpool's scorers as Rovers lost 2-0 at Anfield to a side featuring Ron Yeats, Ian Callaghan, Jimmy Melia and Gordon Milne, which was to win the league championship in 1963/64. Future Rovers players John Williams and John Brown both scored for Plymouth Argyle at Eastville, though Rovers won 4-3, and Alfie Biggs scored in both league meetings for Preston North End.

However, own goals proved to be something of a problem. When Rovers lost at Brighton in December – the final league appearance of George Petherbridge, who had played in 452 league matches and scored in the first sixteen consecutive post-war seasons – it was to a David Pyle own goal after twenty-nine minutes, from Bobby Laverick's low cross. Norman Sykes somehow contrived to concede own goals home and away to Sunderland, a feat paralleled in August 1977 when Phil Bater scored against his own side in both legs of a league Cup tie with Walsall. However, Pyle and Sykes both scored own goals in a bizarre 2-0 home defeat to Stoke City in January. Dennis Viollet, who had scored for England against Luxembourg just four months earlier, made his Stoke debut but Rovers contributed both goals by deflecting harmless-looking crosses from Don Ratcliffe into their own net, Pyle six minutes before half-time and Sykes after sixty-six minutes. In Sykes' case, it was just seven days after his own goal at Roker Park.

On 21 October, Rovers suffered a crushing 4-1 defeat at Huddersfield Town, which were soon followed by heavy defeats against Derby County and Newcastle United. The home game against Middlesbrough at the end of November was watched by the first home crowd under 10,000 for many years. Esmond Million, later a Rovers goalkeeper, was injured in this game, but the visitors still inflicted one of Rovers' seven league defeats at Eastville. Seven days later, a goalless draw at Walsall was the first Rovers league match with that scoreline since the game at Barnsley in March 1959, a club record run of 114 league fixtures. The Devon hypnotist Henry Blythe, whose teenage son was on Rovers' books, at that time running a psychology course at Ruskin College, Oxford, offered his services to prevent Rovers from suffering relegation; Bert Tann rejected the offer.

Rovers went to Middlesbrough on 14 April, out of the relegation zone with five matches to play. Brighton were apparently virtually relegated and the race to avoid the second position saw Leeds United on thirty points, Rovers and 'Boro on thirty-one and Swansea Town, with just four games left, on thirty-two. It had not been Rovers' season in the North East, what with a 5-2 defeat at Newcastle United and 6-1 hammering at Sunderland, but the 5-0 loss at Ayresome Park left Rovers with much to do. On Good Friday, Rovers drew with a Charlton Athletic side forced to play inside-forward John Hewie in goal. Twenty-four hours later, Bradford's two goals earned a draw with Walsall and left Rovers and Leeds United, with two matches remaining, on thirty-three points, above Swansea Town, now with a game in hand, on thirty-two and a rejuvenated Brighton on thirty-one.

On Easter Monday, as Rovers and Brighton lost, Swansea picked up a point. Twenty-four hours later, Leeds United drew with Bury and the Swans beat Plymouth Argyle 5-0. Brighton were relegated and Swansea safe while, with one game left, the remaining relegation place was to be taken by Leeds, on thirty-four points, or Rovers, a point below them. As Leeds faced the daunting task of visiting Newcastle United, Rovers had to beat Luton Town, a side they had earlier defeated at Eastville. At Kenilworth Road, however, Gordon Turner put the Hatters ahead after three minutes, following a poor goal-kick by Howard Radford. Alec Ashworth's shot, twelve minutes later, was deflected in off Dave Bumpstead so that Rovers, in losing 2-0, were relegated with Brighton to Division Three, three points adrift of Leeds United who had unaccountably won 3-0 at St James' Park. Above Leeds and Swansea Town were an incredible eight clubs on thirty-nine points. Crucially, Rovers had won only twice in the sixteen fixtures against these sides.

League performances were reflected in Cup results. Oldham Athletic, a Fourth Division side, held Rovers in the FA Cup before winning a replay through two John Colquhoun goals at Boundary Park. Rovers beat Hartlepool United 2-1 in the League Cup and held Blackburn Rovers to a draw before the First Division side recorded a straightforward replay victory, Eddie Thomas scoring all four of their goals. Roy McCrohan, later a Rovers player, was a member of the Norwich City side that defeated unfashionable Rochdale 4-0 on aggregate in the League Cup final. Rovers had latterly strengthened their side with the signings of Dave Bumpstead, from Millwall, and Keith Williams, a £6,500 move from Plymouth Argyle. It was the latter who scored Rovers' goal in a demoralising 3-1 defeat in the Gloucestershire Cup final at Ashton Gate. Rovers led at half-time, but

Brian Clark's splendid second-half hat-trick won the trophy for Bristol City. The Football League defeated the League of Ireland 5-2 in a representative game at Eastville in October before a crowd of 31,959, with Bryan Douglas of Blackburn Rovers scoring two of their goals.

1962/63

Although the 3-0 defeat at Hull City in August 1962 was officially Rovers' first game in Division Three, the realigning of the divisions in 1958 had led to a distortion of statistics. The reality was that Rovers were back in the division they had occupied between 1920 and 1953, and in which they have spent the bulk of their league existence. The reality was also that, devoid of financial support, the club was to struggle and, indeed, came within minutes of a disastrous second consecutive relegation into the uncharted waters of Division Four.

Manager Bert Tann made strenuous efforts to avoid such a calamity. He had appointed Bill Dodgin in 1961 as chief scout and now, in July 1962, he promoted Bobby Campbell to the post of coach. A fast raiding winger with Chelsea and Reading, Campbell had won two Scottish caps and was manager at Dumbarton before joining Rovers. Both Dodgin and Campbell were to manage Rovers in their own right but, for now, their role was to rebuild the club from the ashes of relegation. There was clearly insufficient talent on Rovers' books and no money to purchase replacements, so their task was to work with the many mediocre local footballers, searching for the rare glimpse of raw skill or character that would enable a young player to break into league football. Long, dark winter evenings were spent carefully building up the skills of numerous players under the dim floodlights of the Muller Road car park ash practice pitches.

The departure of George Petherbridge to Salisbury City left Geoff Bradford as the sole survivor of the Division Three (South) days. Doug Hillard, Norman Sykes, Ray Mabbutt, Harold Jarman and Bobby Jones were all by now experienced Rovers players. The new goalkeeper, with Howard Radford retired, was Esmond Million, signed for £5,000 from Middlesbrough. The same fee bought the accomplished left-back Gwyn Jones from Wolverhampton Wanderers, an excellent musician and alert defender who, in missing only two league games in 1962/63, played more times than any other Rovers player. These two players were purchased with the money raised by the sale, after 297 league games and 101 goals, of Peter Hooper to Cardiff City. John Watkins joined Chippenham Town. Rovers also eschewed their quartered shirts in favour of a short-lived white top with blue pinstripes.

Rovers were able to benefit from the experience of the previous season's signings: Keith Williams, top scorer with seventeen league goals, and Dave Bumpstead. This complemented the slow influx of local talent such as Micky Slocombe,

Joe Davis, Tom Baker and David Hurford. All eight of Graham Muxworthy's league appearances, including defeat at Ashton Gate where Rovers trailed 3-0 by half-time, were in the calendar month of April. Glaswegian Alex Munro arrived, initially on trial, and Jimmy Humes joined from Preston North End on the recommendation of Alfie Biggs. Finally, the great man himself returned in October for £12,000, Biggs coming back to Eastville after fifteen months away.

Prior to the new season, a Bristol Combined XI lost 2-1 at Ashton Gate against Arsenal in a match to raise funds for the St Mary Redcliffe Restoration Appeal. Williams scored, while Million, Bradford, Jones and Sykes also played. Life in Division Three soon proved uncomfortable, as a string of poor results testify. An early season 5-2 defeat at Wrexham, where Williams missed a penalty, was followed by a catastrophic October. Rovers lost 3-0 at Swindon Town and equalled an unwanted club record, set in April 1922, by conceding three hat-tricks in a calendar month. In losing 7-2 at Shrewsbury Town, Rovers suffered their heaviest defeat since December 1957. Frank Clarke and Jim McLaughlin scored three times each, the second of three occasions on which two opponents have each scored hat-tricks against Rovers in the league. Arthur Rowley, the league's all-time top scorer, hit the third goal from 25 yards and later hit the crossbar with a free-kick, while the Shrews also fielded Ted Hemsley, who was to play a key role in Rovers' Watney Cup final triumph in 1972. Two goals down inside ten minutes, after Million twice spilled long-distance shots, Jarman pulled a goal back, Biggs headed against the bar, Hamilton missed an open goal and Williams saw a good shot saved. Rovers then conceded two more goals to trail 4-1 at half-time. A fortnight after defeat at Shrewsbury, Rovers lost 3-2 at Southend United, for whom John McKinven scored the first of his two hat-tricks against Rovers.

The season, however, got no easier. Eddie O'Hara scored three times as Rovers lost 4-0 to Barnsley at Oakwell, four Carlisle United players got on the scoresheet at Brunton Park and five Hull City players at Eastville. Bristol City completed a league double over Rovers, and Coventry City won 5-0, with Willie Humphries and Ron Rees scoring twice each. On the other hand, two Terry Oldfield goals steered Rovers to a 5-2 victory at home to Halifax Town, and the resurgent Biggs scored twice in a 4-1 home win over Brighton. Rovers also won at home to Barnsley, who fielded their youngest-ever player in league football, at sixteen years 226 days, in goalkeeper Alan Ogley. On Good Friday, Rovers recorded a 5-3 win at Queen's Park Rangers, with Williams and Jones scoring twice each. Rovers had led twice but responded to Mark Lazarus giving Rangers a 3-2 lead after seventy-six minutes with three goals in nine minutes for a well-earned victory. Another encouraging sign was the emerging talent of inside-forward Ian 'Chico' Hamilton, whose ten league goals made him joint second highest scorer alongside Jones.

The winter of 1962/63 was one of the worst in the twentieth century as far as the weather was concerned, with snow lying for weeks. The game at Reading on Boxing Day was abandoned after an hour because the pitch was frostbound, with Rovers a goal down. As a result, Rovers did not play between 15 December and 9 February, when the side began a run of three consecutive victories. Great goalscorers of the 1960s, such as Notts County's Tony Hateley and Jeff Astle, both on the threshold of long and successful careers, scored against Rovers in 1962/63. So too did Dai Ward for Watford at Eastville. Another former Rovers forward, Barrie Meyer, celebrated his final game in professional football with a hat-trick in Bristol City's 6-3 victory over Southend United in March; Bobby 'Shadow' Williams, a future Rovers player, scored City's other three goals that day.

In April 1963, *The People* newspaper alleged that goalkeeper Million had accepted a £300 bribe to enable Bradford Park Avenue to beat Rovers. He had allowed a back pass to slip past him and let a cross go, leaving the innocent Kevin Hector to score twice. Hector was to score against Rovers in the FA Cup in 1975. The match had been drawn 2-2, so Million and his accomplice Williams received none of the money. Suddenly, Rovers were making national headlines for all the wrong reasons. The press uncovered details of how they had unsuccessfully tried to persuade full-back Jones to join them. Mansfield Town defender, Brian Phillips, a former teammate of Million's at Middlesbrough, was named as the 'fixer', working on behalf of a syndicate of professional gamblers, and was later sentenced at Nottingham Assizes to fifteen months' imprisonment.

Rovers had invested £11,500 in transfer fees for Million and Williams, and the battle against relegation had not yet been won. However, the club wasted no time in suspending both players. They and Phillips were fined £50 each at Doncaster Magistrates Court in July 1963 and banned from football for life by the Football Association. Williams was to resurface in South African football, which, at that time lay outside the remit of FIFA, the world governing body. The image of professional football had been tarnished, but Rovers' immediate response to the crisis and the way the club had responded and helped bring the culprits to justice came in for high praise. Rovers were left to survive the relegation dogfight without two key players, but with a clear conscience that the club was working hard to stamp out all that was unsavoury in the game.

By dint of the atrocious winter weather, Rovers extraordinarily played nine league games in April and five in May. Bradford and Biggs had scored to beat Colchester United, leaving Rovers requiring victory over Halifax Town at The Shay to avoid relegation, prior to the final game that was lost 2-0 at Port Vale. A narrow 3-2 win at Halifax avoided the prospect of double relegation, and Rovers never did appear in Division Four. Yet, it was a close call. A miserly crowd of 2,126, albeit boosted by some 500 enthusiastic Rovers supporters, saw Rovers a goal ahead after two minutes through Jones' shot, and 2-0 up ten minutes later when Hamilton headed home Bradford's cross. However, already relegated Halifax recovered after half-time and equalised through shots from Paddy Stanley and Dennis Fidler. With just fourteen minutes remaining, Rovers won a corner and Jones' kick found Hamilton's head to ensure Third Division survival.

FA Cup defeat at Port Vale contrasted with victory over the same opposition in the League Cup. However, after brushing aside Cardiff City, Rovers lost 3-1 in the third round at Second Division Bury. Goals from Hamilton and Jones earned Rovers a 2-1 victory over Bristol City at Eastville in the Gloucestershire Cup final.

1963/64

In comparison with the relegation dogfight of 1962/63, the second season in Division Three gave cause for great optimism. Identical tallies of wins and defeats left Rovers in twelfth place in the table, and seven of the next ten seasons were to see top-six finishes. While seventy-nine league goals were conceded, the ninety-one scored had only been bettered in the 1952/53 championship season. Alfie Biggs became the first Rovers player since then to score thirty league goals. The total of 170 goals by both sides in Rovers' forty-six league matches constitutes a club seasonal record.

One crucial element in this relative success was the benefit of a settled side. After two seasons as a reserve goalkeeper, Bernard Hall was an ever-present, and full-backs Doug Hillard and Gwyn Jones missed just one league game between them. In the forward line, Biggs and Harold Jarman were ever-presents; Bobby Jones, Ian Hamilton and John Brown, a free signing from Plymouth Argyle, were all regulars. Brian Jenkins, recruited from Exeter City, and the veteran Geoff Bradford also appeared. With a settled half-back line, Rovers could continue to experiment with youth, Roger Frude and Lindsay Parsons both making a league debut in April. The pinstriped shirt had not been a success, and Rovers took to the field in 1963/64 in blue-and-white striped shirts.

John Frowen, after eighty-four league games, had returned to Wales to sign for Newport County. After sporadic appearances, several other players had moved on, including Allen Wood to Merthyr Tydfil, Hugh Ryden to Stockport County, Jimmy Humes to Chester, Tom Baker to Dover and Graham Muxworthy to Bridgwater Town. After appearing in the first three winless games of the new season, Dave Bumpstead announced his retirement from football to work in industry, though he later returned to manage Brentwood and Chelmsford City. As Bert Tann cultivated a side fit to survive in Division Three, there was no scope for sentiment, and Bradford and Norman Sykes were both dropped. A new-look side was beginning to emerge, with goalkeeper Hall embarking on a run of 115 consecutive league games and Brown, Jarman and Hamilton supporting free-scoring Biggs.

In winning nineteen league matches, Rovers scored seven times at home to Shrewsbury Town, five at Brentford and four on five other occasions. In December, the sixth time Rovers scored four times proved insufficient for victory. Two first-half Hamilton goals were mirrored by a brace each from Tony Richards and Jack Mudie, as Port Vale drew 4-4 at Eastville. Richards had put the visitors ahead after only thirteen minutes, but Rovers three times threw away the lead, with five goals being scored in the space of sixteen minutes midway through the second half. A Hamilton hat-trick earned a 5-2 win at Griffin Park, while Hull City, Bristol City and Notts County all lost 4-0 at Eastville. The win against Bristol City, which started with a Mike Gibson own goal, was rounded off with Geoff Bradford's final goal for Rovers. The crowd of 19,451 was bettered only by Rovers' visits to Ashton Gate and to champions Coventry City.

Rovers also recorded 4-3 victories after being 3-1 down away to Southend United and to bottom club Notts County. At Roots Hall, Rovers were a goal down after four minutes, 2-1 down inside ten minutes and were 3-1 behind following a sixty-fifth minute defensive mix-up. Biggs reduced the deficit ten minutes later, Hamilton equalised with three minutes remaining and a great comeback was completed when Peter Watson, under pressure from Biggs, steered the ball into his own net to give Rovers victory. At Meadow Lane, sixteen-year-old Bob Woolley claimed the second goal to become the youngest player ever to play and score against Rovers in league football. Keith Fry then scored twice, once from a penalty awarded for handball against Stone, as Rovers trailed 2-1 by half-time, and the second seven minutes after the break. The stage was set for Biggs, whose goals after sixty-two, sixty-nine and eighty minutes, the winner from a volley, completed his second hat-trick for the club and earned Rovers an unlikely victory. Notts County must have dreaded the sight of Biggs for, following his hat-trick at Meadow Lane, he scored twice in a 4-0 win at Eastville to take his seasonal tally to the magical thirty mark. Rovers scored a club record thirty-nine away league goals in 1963/64 and, in January and February, won five consecutive matches away from home to equal a club record set in the 1952/53 championship year.

The biggest win of all, though, was a seven-goal demolition of Shrewsbury Town at Eastville in March. Four forwards scored, with Jones and Jarman striking twice each and Biggs, from a penalty, and Brown once. Centre-half Dave Stone scored his first goal for the club. Five goals ahead by half-time for only the second time in the club's history, Rovers equalled their largest-ever league win with comparative ease. Seven days later, though, they were brought down to earth when John O'Rourke's hat-trick gave Luton Town a 4-2 victory. O'Rourke was to score five of the six league goals the Hatters scored against Rovers that season.

There was another 4-2 defeat at Coventry City, though revenge was gained in the FA Cup, while John Atyeo's final league goal against Rovers and one from the former Eastville favourite, Peter Hooper, gave Bristol City an opening-day 3-0 win. With the England manager Alf Ramsey in the stand, apparently running the rule over Jarman, Denis Coughlin scored Bournemouth's winner after half an hour at Dean Court and, four days later, Coughlin added two more goals at Eastville as Rovers followed up their 7-0 win with four straight defeats. Similarly, high-flying Crystal Palace were indebted to Peter Burridge, who scored the winner at Selhurst

Park and twice at Eastville as his side, en route to promotion, completed a league double over Rovers. The season was completed with heavy defeats at Reading and at Crewe Alexandra. Rovers played their final game at Gresty Road on 25 April against a Crewe side that had to win to avoid relegation. Their 4-1 victory condemned Wrexham, 5-0 losers before a paltry crowd of 4,497 at Port Vale, to the drop.

Although only nine league games were drawn, four of these finished 2-2. Both matches with Peterborough United were four-goal draws, winner of forty-three Northern Ireland caps Derek Dougan scoring on both occasions. Joe Haverty, a Rovers player the following season, scored for Millwall in their 2-2 draw at Eastville. When Rovers visited Boundary Park, goals from Hamilton and Jarman were not enough, as Bobby Johnstone became the fourth opponent to score two penalties in a league game. The Gloucestershire Cup final was also a 2-2 draw, with Alex Munro scoring his first goal for the club and the future Rovers forward Bobby Williams scoring Bristol City's second goal.

At the close of the season, Rovers were informed of the death, at the age of sixty-nine, of David Steele, who had played in Rovers' first league game. He had won league championship medals with Huddersfield Town and, as a scout, had been credited with the 'discovery' of Len Shackleton. There was a loss on the field, too, with the retirement of Geoff Bradford, the last survivor of the 1952/53 championship-winning side. In 461 league appearances, he had scored a club record 242 goals, including twelve hat-tricks. After leaving Rovers, he worked as a tanker driver in Avonmouth and continued to take an interest in the club's progress. In his testimonial game in April, a Bristol United XI lost 4-1 to an International XI. Recalled for the final home game of the season, however, Bradford had been overshadowed by Reading's Dennis Allen, who scored a hat-trick as his side won 5-2. In the previous game, Bert Tann had given a debut to Lindsay Parsons and, thus, a member of the 1973/74 promotion side was in the team prior to the final game of the longest survivor of the 1952/53 line-up.

Hamilton, perhaps harshly labelled 'the inside-forward who never seems to score goals', claimed the first four at home to Shrewsbury Town in the League Cup, with two first-half headers and two shots after the interval. The visitors, managed by Arthur Rowley, scored twice in ninety seconds to pull the score back, the second when Gwyn Jones' clearance ricocheted into the net off George Boardman, before Biggs added a couple of goals in the last seven minutes. Rovers' League Cup ended in a replay at Gillingham, where Ron Newman scored twice. In the FA Cup, Rovers won at Bournemouth, after Hall had saved Stan Bolton's penalty, and Coventry City, before defeating Second Division Norwich City at Eastville. Round four saw Rovers at Old Trafford, before a crowd of over 55,000, facing Bobby Charlton and George Best in a very strong Manchester United team. Rovers lost 4-1, with Denis Law's hat-trick including two second-half headers, and David Herd scoring once and creating two others, while Scottish international

Paddy Crerand headed the ball into his own net for Rovers' seventy-first minute consolation goal. While Bristol Rovers reported an annual loss of £41,000, the supporters' club reported a £10,000 profit.

1964/65

In retaining the shape of the previous season's side, Bert Tann introduced just one close season signing. Roy McCrohan had played in 385 league games for Norwich City and joined Rovers in a £400 deal from Colchester United. Unable initially to break into a well-drilled side, he appeared in ten league matches for Rovers, scoring in the draw at Brentford, before working as Bobby Robson's assistant at Ipswich Town. Otherwise, it was a consistent Rovers line-up for the 1964/65 season. Although goalkeeper Bernard Hall was the only ever-present, six other players appeared in over forty league matches. Alfie Biggs scored eighteen league goals, with Ian Hamilton top-scoring on twenty-one.

The mid-table position obtained twelve months earlier had raised the level of optimism and Rovers, with eighty-two league goals and more points than in any season since 1952/53, finished in sixth place. Rovers completed the season with consecutive away wins to end up with twenty league victories. This final flourish took the club within four points of promoted rivals, Bristol City. Although City finished with three straight victories to pip Mansfield Town on goal average, the reality was that Rovers were outsiders in the race. A desperate seven-match winless run in February had cost the club dearly, during which time Rovers lost three games in succession to potential promotion rivals, Hull City, Brentford and Bristol City. Defeat at Hull City was preceded by one minute's silence in memory of Sir Winston Churchill, the former prime minister, who had died six days earlier at the age of ninety.

Rovers had, in fact, begun the season in sparkling form. The first four home games were all won, with eighteen goals scored. Only one point was dropped in the opening five league fixtures. Alfie Biggs scored the second hat-trick of his Rovers career as Peterborough United were defeated 4-0 at Eastville in September, and fifteen goals in the first fourteen matches. However, his season was curtailed by injury, and with Ian Hamilton also sidelined with a troublesome knee, Rovers' goal flow could not be maintained. As it was, Harold Jarman and Bobby Jones both contributed significant goals later in the season.

On the opening day of the season, Biggs, Hamilton, Jarman and the impressive John Brown all scored against a strong Mansfield Town side that was ultimately only denied promotion on goal average. In the next two home games, in the space of a few days, Rovers put five goals past Grimsby Town and champions-to-be Carlisle United. The former game finished 5-3, Rovers leading 3-0 after thirty-two minutes and 5-1 with fifteen minutes to play; seven separate players appeared on the scoresheet and the future England manager Graham Taylor played at left-half for the Mariners. Carlisle had led after eighteen minutes, only for Rovers again to lead 5-1 with a quarter of an hour left. This was the third and most recent occasion, after two such runs during the 1950/51 season, that Rovers have scored five times in consecutive league fixtures. Rovers were to beat Bournemouth 4-2 in October and record 4-0 victories at home to Workington and Port Vale.

Unusually, Rovers could also claim to have completed a league double over the champions Carlisle United, Jarman and Hamilton both scoring in the 5-2 victory in September and in the 2-1 victory at Brunton Park at New Year. Rovers also led at Ashton Gate, when Joe Davis' second-half penalty, his only goal of the season, threatened to derail Bristol City's promotion push. City recovered to win 2-1. Promotion rivals Gillingham were comprehensively beaten twice, with Jarman scoring one of Rovers' three goals on each occasion. On the other hand, relegated Colchester United claimed two draws with Rovers, lowly Walsall won at Eastville, and struggling Exeter City and Southend United both drew on their travels. In addition to the champions, Rovers also completed league doubles over Luton Town, Gillingham and Barnsley.

In October, the local derby at Eastville attracted a crowd of 25,370, the highest at any Rovers league or Cup game all season. Later in the campaign, only 2,300 were to see Rovers lose to a 25-yard Dixie Hale volley and an eighty-third-minute Jimmy Morgan winner at Workington. However, later in October, there was an astonishing match at Roots Hall, where Southend United defeated Rovers 6-3. Hamilton's third minute opener could not prevent Rovers from trailing 4-1 by half-time, Jimmy McKinven having scored twice. Hamilton scored again after fifty-eight minutes, but the home side led 5-2 with eleven minutes to play. Moments after McKinven had completed his hat-trick, so too did Hamilton for Rovers. It was Hamilton's second hat-trick for the club, and the only occasion a Rovers player had scored three goals and ended up on the losing side in a league match. McKinven had previously scored three times when Southend United had beaten Rovers 3-2 in October 1962. This remains one of only two league games featuring Rovers when both sides have included a hat-trick scorer.

As the season progressed, Tann looked to strengthen his squad. The December signing of Irishman Joe Haverty from Millwall went some way towards achieving this. A diminutive figure at 5 feet 3½ inches, the second shortest player to appear for Rovers, Haverty was a highly skilful acquisition and he was to score in the large win against Port Vale. He also played for Eire against Spain while on Rovers' books. Another player to break into the league side was local inside-forward David Hudd, who picked up a career-threatening ankle injury at Barnsley and never appeared in a Rovers shirt again. In Biggs' enforced absence, it was Hamilton who was to lead the way with seven goals in four games over Christmas, including his second hat-trick of the season as Luton Town were beaten 3-2 at Eastville. However, a team that had started so confidently in front of goal now scored just eleven goals in a run of twelve league games between the end of January and Good Friday.

It was, with the benefit of hindsight, probably just as well that Rovers did not gain those four extra points and promotion to Division Two. In the absence of Biggs, the side was no match even for average Third Division sides. The most successful Rovers sides could boast a string of well-known local characters, and although Biggs, Mabbutt and Jarman were household names by 1965, this particular side still lacked depth. The patient work of Tann and his sidekicks continued, work that would ultimately lead to success under Don Megson in 1973/74. One key member of that side, Lindsay Parsons, once again made a few league appearances, while another, the giant Stuart Taylor, was waiting in the wings.

The FA Cup offered Rovers a tantalising glimpse of glory. Victory at Walsall, where David Stone scored his only goal of the season, drew Southern League Weymouth at Eastville. Eschewing a repeat of the 15-1 victory in November 1900, or even the five-goal win twelve months later, Rovers were perfectly satisfied with a 4-1 scoreline. There then followed a tie that features largely in any perusal of the annals of Stockport County. The Cheshire club was now languishing in the bottom position in Division Four, where they were destined to end the season and, though outplayed, left Eastville with a goalless draw.

By the time of the replay, both sides knew that an away tie at First Division leaders Liverpool awaited the winners. An expectant crowd of 19,695 at Edgeley Park saw County take the lead after half an hour through Derek Hodgkinson, with Frank Beaumont adding a second within a minute. Stung into action, Rovers responded with goals from Mabbutt and Jones in a six-minute second-half spell. With just four minutes remaining, to the delirious delight of the home faithful, Ean Cuthbert's free-kick was knocked home by Ian Sandiford, and Rovers' Cup dreams were over. County, though, were to take the lead in front of a 51,000 crowd at Anfield and hold out for a respectable draw before losing in a replay. The key to this opportunity, victory over Rovers on a Monday night at Edgeley Park, is still viewed by many Stockport County supporters as a defining moment in their club's history.

Luck was not on Rovers' side in the League Cup, where goals from Ralph Hunt and Peter Stringfellow gave Fourth Division Chesterfield a 2-0 victory over Rovers at Eastville. On the other hand, after a goal apiece before half-time, Rovers beat Bristol City 3-2 in the Gloucestershire Cup final at Eastville, Hamilton scoring the winning goal. Arnold Rodgers scored three times for a Bristol City Old Players side that defeated their Rovers counterparts 6-3 at Eastville, with Geoff Fox, George Petherbridge and Geoff Bradford scoring. Further afield, Bath City lost 4-2 to Arsenal in December in a match to mark the official opening of the floodlights at Twerton Park, a ground destined to become Rovers' home in 1986.

1965/66

Ever the shrewd tactician, manager Bert Tann was slowly moulding a side that was to reap further success in the early 1970s. With the help of men such as Bill Dodgin and Bobby Campbell, a group of players was being honed at minimal expense. Season 1965/66 saw a team of experienced local players, such as Alfie Biggs, Harold Jarman and Doug Hillard, combined with younger Bristolians, such as Dave Stone, Ray Graydon and Stuart Taylor. The cornerstones for the years to come were being put carefully in place.

Season 1965/66 was one of great change nationally. The introduction of substitutes brought a new dimension to the game. Rovers' first nominated substitute, Roy McCrohan, remained unused and was never to appear for the club again. The first time a substitute was used by Rovers was the appearance of Joe Davis in a 3-0 home victory over Walsall in October. This was also the season in which England hosted the World Cup and won the Wembley final. Geoff Hurst, whose father Charlie Hurst had played for Rovers reserves in 1938/39, scored a memorable hat-trick in the final, while Alan Ball, a Rovers player himself in 1982/83, ran the engine-room in midfield.

Despite having finished as high as sixth in 1964/65, Rovers, albeit never appearing to be at risk of dropping into Division Four, completed the new season in sixteenth place in Division Three. The total of sixty-four goals scored in league football was, with the exception of the 1961/62 relegation year, the lowest seasonal total by the club since 1949/50. The absence of goalkeeper Bernard Hall from three league matches, and an FA Cup defeat in November not only ended a run of 115 league appearances, but also left Hillard as the club's only ever-present. Six players played in over forty league matches, but twenty-three were used in all; Harold Jarman being the top scorer with thirteen league goals, three more than Alfie Biggs and Bobby Jones.

What above all transformed Rovers' season into one of mediocrity was a demoralising club record run of fourteen consecutive league games without a win. This depressing statistic was to be repeated in the relegation season of 1980/81, and in the club's first season in the basement division, 2001/02. Following victory over Oldham Athletic in the middle of October, Rovers were not to win again until the defeat of Grimsby Town at the end of January, which sparked a revival of sorts, as Rovers won six out of ten games. Yet, this previous run of fourteen games had included seven draws, two of these against Millwall, who were promoted to Division Two at the season's end. There were also three 1-0 defeats and a 2-0 loss at struggling Oldham Athletic, whose goals came from Albert Quixall, who converted a penalty, and Jim Frizzell. Oddly, the only heavy defeat of this dreadful run was a 6-1 mauling at the hands of champions-elect Hull City at Boothferry Park in December, when five opponents found the net.

When heavy defeats arrived, they came just as Rovers were playing well. After a positive run of results, Rovers lost 4-1 at third-placed Queen's Park Rangers on Good Friday. Revenge victory over Rangers was followed by a 5-2 capitulation at Peterborough United. Two big wins in September preceded a 3-0 defeat at Swansea Town, and Rovers lost by the same score at Scunthorpe United, as well as losing 4-3 both at Swindon Town and at Brighton. On a Tuesday night at Swindon Town in October, Rovers led 2-0 after only twenty-four minutes, Jones and Jarman having scored. Eric Weaver and Roger Smart drew the home side level by half-time but, just four minutes after the break, Rovers regained control with Jarman's second of the game. However, two goals in four minutes, scored by Dennis Brown and Keith Morgan, consigned Rovers to defeat.

Defeat at Brighton came as a result of what the *Bristol Evening Post* described as 'an abysmal display by Rovers' defence'. Charlie Livesey scored Albion's opening goal after thirteen minutes, and he was to equalise after Brown and Jarman had scored for Rovers shortly after half-time. Livesey then turned provider, creating a goal for Brian Tawse twenty minutes from the end. Oldfield pulled the scores level after eighty minutes, but with only five minutes remaining, Hall misjudged Bob Baxter's free-kick, leaving Wally Gould with a simple tap-in, and his goal left Rovers smarting from another high-scoring defeat.

As the season progressed, a number of new signings were able to contribute to Rovers' later success. John Petts, a former England international at schoolboy level, became a regular choice at right-half, and scored in the large victory over struggling Mansfield Town. Chris Weller and Dick Plumb were both tried in the forward line, the latter scoring twice in a 4-0 victory over lowly Oldham Athletic, while Scottish inside-forward Ken Ronaldson scored two league goals as the season drew to a close. Rovers scored three or more goals on eleven occasions in the league. Bottom of the table York City lost their goalkeeper Tommy Forgan injured and, with right-back Alan Baker in goal for seventy-five minutes, lost 5-1 to Rovers. It was the club's largest away win since an identical scoreline at Notts County in September 1953. A week later, Rovers met Oxford United for the first time in league action, a Jones hat-trick past goalkeeper Harry Fearnley, who apparently smoked his pipe whenever his side was attacking, giving Rovers a comfortable 3-1 victory.

The two biggest wins, though, came in February. Having beaten Grimsby Town to end their fourteen-game spell without a victory, Rovers' goalscoring went berserk as they recorded a 5-0 win at Brentford, Alfie Biggs scoring a hat-trick. It was the first time Rovers had ever won an away league game by such a decisive margin. A fortnight later, the goal machine went one better, as Mansfield Town were defeated 6-0. Biggs, with two more goals, in the first and thirty-ninth minutes, was one of five Rovers scorers, Roger Frude contributing a rare goal, Jones scoring for the first time in four months and Petts completing the scoring three minutes from time. It was to be September 1971 before Rovers next won a league match by six clear goals. As would befit Rovers' season, though, York City visited Eastville seven days later and fought out a goalless draw.

Don Rogers, whose goals were to win a sensational League Cup final for Swindon Town in 1969, scored the only goal of the game at Eastville in September with a terrific 25-yard drive. Keith Burkinshaw conceded an own goal at Eastville at the end of March as his Scunthorpe United side was defeated 2-0. The goalless draw at Workington in April marked the first of a club record 546 league appearances made by Stuart Taylor between 1965 and 1980. At 6 feet 5 inches, Taylor was, at the time, the tallest player to represent Rovers in league action. The inclusion of the Bristol-born central defender, as well as Lindsay Parsons in defence, marked the first stage in the construction of the side Don Megson would lead to promotion in 1973/74.

The FA Cup brought Rovers no joy, and they did not progress beyond round one in the League Cup either, but West Ham United were in fairness more glamorous opponents than Reading, and there were two epic matches. A large Eastville crowd saw Hurst open the scoring after only two minutes, and though Brown equalised with a long-range left-foot drive, England striker Johnny Byrne set up another Hurst goal and then scored off the far upright to put West Ham 3-1 ahead after half an hour. Before the interval, Petts reduced the arrears when his low shot arrowed in off a post and he started the move from which Jarman equalised after fifty-eight minutes. Although Peters later fired against his own post, the Hammers survived. In the replay, Byrne and Hurst gave them a 2-0 half-time lead. Again there was a spirited Rovers revival, Petts volleying home after fifty-four minutes after Jarman had created an opportunity, and Jones equalising two minutes later when Eddie Bovington slipped. Then, ten minutes from time, Petts lost control, Hurst fed Byrne and he grabbed the decisive goal. In the Gloucestershire Cup final, a first-half Jarman goal gave Rovers victory over Bristol City at Ashton Gate.

1966/67

On paper, finishing fifth in Division Three represents the highest final position achieved by Rovers since their return from Division Two five years earlier. In reality, however, missing out on promotion was a bitter blow. Bert Tann's side suffered four straight defeats in the run-up to Christmas, yet still harboured genuine promotion hopes after a run of seven wins in nine games. Entering March, leaders Queen's Park Rangers and Rovers still boasted a six-point gap over the chasing pack. Yet Rovers then endured a run of nine matches without a win to finish, after a final-day defeat, just two points behind promoted Middlesbrough.

Rovers rejected stripes and turned out in 1966/67 in an all-blue strip. In contrast, it was not a Rovers side that showed many changes from the previous season. Gwyn Jones, having lost his left-back berth to Joe Davis, had joined

Porthmadog, and a familiar line-up drew 3-3 with Swansea Town on the opening day, with young Stuart Taylor at centre-half. The season kicked off in a wave of optimism, for England were world champions. The optimism sweeping Eastville emanated from the successful youth policy, whereby Rovers were able to field Bristol-born players such as Ray Graydon, Alfie Biggs, Doug Hillard and the side's only ever-present, Harold Jarman. Laurie Taylor, Wayne Jones and Vic Barney, all products of the youth scheme, broke into the league side as the season progressed, while Larry Lloyd played his first game in the Gloucestershire Cup final.

Success was based around a strong home record. Of the top eight sides, only Watford avoided defeat against Rovers. In fact, their decisive 3-0 victory at Eastville in December was only Rovers' second home league defeat in fifteen months. The other home defeat came, bizarrely, at the hands of bottom-club Workington, whose second away win of the season was assured through a Brian Tinnion shot after twenty-eight minutes. This home success was gained through the prolific goalscoring of Biggs, with twenty-three goals, and nineteen-goal Jarman. Although no other player contributed more than five league goals, a total of fifteen Rovers players, the most since 1949/50, made the scoresheet. Rovers completed a league double over five clubs and won away against Reading and Middlesbrough, both of whom finished above them in the table.

Rovers dropped just one point in their opening four league games. Despite defeat at Colchester United, the first five-figure home attendance of the calendar year saw a convincing 3-0 victory over Swindon Town, with Hillard, Jarman and Ian Hamilton scoring. It was the first in another run of three consecutive victories. After five straight home wins, the last being another 3-0 win, this time against Darlington, Mansfield Town were the visitors at Eastville in mid-October. This was a highly entertaining eight-goal draw. The visitors were 2-0 ahead after thirty-five minutes, only for Ken Ronaldson to reduce the margin three minutes before half-time. John Rowland's second goal put Mansfield 3-1 up after sixty-five minutes, and this sparked a Rovers recovery. Biggs, after seventy minutes and Jarman after seventy-five and eighty-five minutes, contributed three goals in a quarter of an hour and Rovers were dramatically in front. As the seconds ticked away, Stuart Brace equalised for the Stags and Rovers had to settle for a 4-4 draw.

Three days later, Rovers again scored four times at Eastville, Jarman again scoring twice in a 4-1 victory over Gillingham. Walsall, Colchester United and Doncaster Rovers, the latter fielding the former Rovers wing-half Norman Sykes, all conceded four goals at Eastville. Rovers also beat Shrewsbury Town 4-3 in a dramatic game at Gay Meadow in November. Rovers already led 2-0, through Biggs and Jarman, when the home side was awarded a thirty-sixth minute penalty against Ray Mabbutt for handball. Bernard Hall saved Trevor Meredith's kick. Seconds after half-time John Manning reduced the arrears only for John Brown, on forty-nine minutes, and Jarman again, just nineteen minutes from the end, to give Rovers a 4-1 lead. Two goals in three minutes set up a tight finish, but Rovers held out to complete a league double over the Shropshire club.

As Christmas approached, and seeing his side lose its way with four consecutive league defeats, Tann splashed out £6,500 to bring the highly experienced right-half Johnny Williams to Eastville. A veteran of over 400 league appearances with Plymouth Argyle, Williams was in fact Bristol-born and the son of a journalist with the *Bristol Evening World*. He was to play in the final twenty-one league games, scoring the opening goal at home to Oldham Athletic. Bobby Williams, well known in Bristol circles after many years at Ashton Gate, then arrived in a £16,000 move from Rotherham United in March to act as understudy to Ronaldson and the emerging talent of eighteen-year-old Wayne Jones.

Rovers suffered three 3-0 defeats and lost 4-1 at Oxford United, still their heaviest defeat at the Manor Ground. A young Ron Atkinson orchestrated this defeat, with his brother Graham grabbing two of the goals. What cost the side dearly, though, was a club record run, since equalled in 1975/76, of five consecutive league draws over Easter. Three of these came in home matches, at a time when Rovers required victory to push for promotion, while there were two drawn games with Bournemouth in the space of three days. In addition, Rovers lost several games they should have won, going down 3-2 to soon-to-be relegated Doncaster Rovers, for whom the former Pirate Graham Ricketts played and the former Rovers apprentice Laurie Sheffield scored twice. Rovers also lost at Torquay United, whose second goal was scored after fifty-six minutes by Robin Stubbs, a Rovers player in 1969. Stubbs had hit the crossbar in the opening seconds of the second half, with Ron Barnes equalising Bobby Williams' thirteenth-minute opening goal from the subsequent rebound.

On New Year's Eve at Eastville, during the 2-2 draw with Middlesbrough, Johnny Williams' back pass stuck in the mud and goalkeeper Bernard Hall and Boro's John O'Rourke, who had scored a hat-trick against Rovers in March 1964, collided sickeningly. Hall was rushed unconscious to Frenchay Hospital, with Ray Mabbutt continuing in goal. The injury was more serious than many believed, however, and Hall spent sixteen days unconscious. Ultimately, with the best wishes of all football supporters across the country, he was able to return to normal life but not to football. After 163 league games, he was forced to retire on medical grounds and was granted a testimonial game in October 1967 against West Ham United.

Though some matches were comfortably won, Rovers were obliged to miss out once again on promotion. At Workington in February, Biggs scored in first half injury-time with Hamilton adding a second eight minutes from the end. In the final home game, two Biggs goals defeated runaway champions Queen's Park Rangers. Defeat at Watford meant Rovers, having finished their fixtures, still lay in the second promotion place, but could only watch helplessly as other clubs overtook them. Reading won at Workington to go above Rovers on goal average, Watford drew both their games in hand to finish a point higher and Middlesbrough, in defeating both Peterborough United and Oxford United, overtook all three to gain promotion. Back in fifth place, Rovers were left to rue wasted opportunities.

The extent of Rovers' participation in the League Cup was a single-goal defeat at Cardiff City. The Gloucestershire Cup final was lost 3-0 at home to Bristol City, for whom Tony Ford, later a Rovers full-back, converted a second-half penalty.

In the FA Cup, Rovers had to rely on a Joe Davis penalty and an own goal from left-half John Lamb to earn a draw with Isthmian League Oxford City. Four goals in the replay, three from the talismanic Biggs, brought Rovers a comfortable victory. Fourth Division Luton Town, conquerors over Exeter City, were no walkover, but Rovers won through the odd goal in five to set up a third-round tie at home to Arsenal. A crowd of over 35,000, the highest at Eastville for seven years, saw Rovers take on an Arsenal side that boasted Frank McLintock, captain of their 1970/71 double-winning side. Rovers were easily beaten 3-0.

1967/68

Despite having ended up so close to promotion in 1966/67, Rovers finished the following season in sixteenth place, albeit a comfortable six points clear of the relegation zone. Bert Tann's final summer as Rovers manager saw few changes in playing personnel. Joe Davis had joined Swansea Town for £1,000 at the tail end of the previous season, so Doug Hillard and Alex Munro were full-backs behind goalkeepers Laurie Taylor and Ronnie Briggs, who played in twenty-three league matches each. Johnny Williams, Stuart Taylor and Dave Stone formed the half-back line.

The forward line included top scorer Alfie Biggs, who scored eleven times before joining Walsall in March, Wayne Jones, Harold Jarman and Ken Ronaldson. The veteran Ray Mabbutt, an occasional utility player, weighed in with ten goals, one more than Johnny Williams and the returning Bobby Jones. His signing, just days after an opening-day defeat at Bournemouth, could have inspired the club to a successful season. There were no ever-presents, and five players wore the No. 9 shirt. Ian Hamilton's recurring injury problems restricted him to one final game for the team. In league football, only the visits of Peterborough United in November, Reading on Boxing Day and Torquay United on Good Friday drew five-figure crowds at Eastville. In comparison with the preceding years, these were not the best of times, and reshuffling in April was Rovers' method of dealing with the situation.

In a season of great inconsistency, Rovers never won more than two league games in succession. The best runs were one of three wins in four games in the autumn and a similar spell in December, when two Johnny Williams goals in the final five minutes contributed to a 4-1 victory over Shrewsbury Town. In contrast, the worst run was one of three consecutive defeats around January.

Rovers scored five times at both Northampton Town and Oldham Athletic and four times each at home to Oldham Athletic, Shrewsbury Town and bottom-of-the-table Scunthorpe United. The Pirates also contrived to beat both sides promoted at the end of the season – Oxford United and Bury. Indeed, the first victory of the season was 2-0 away to eventual champions, Oxford United. Even in losing 3-1 at home to Southport, there was a goal from Ronaldson after only twenty-eight seconds. However, just three days after his final Rovers appearance, ironically against Walsall, top-scorer Biggs moved to join The Saddlers in a £10,000 transfer. Rovers had been stripped of a proven goalscorer.

The most remarkable victory came at Northampton Town in October. A 1-0 win over Barrow gave little indication of what was to come against a side that had won five of its previous six matches, especially as Mabbutt was drafted in as an emergency inside-forward for his first game in two months. As it was, Mabbutt scored a hat-trick, there were six first-half goals – a hat-trick scorer for each club – and an astonishing 5-4 win for Rovers. In the first half, the Cobblers led twice and Rovers once, with home centre-forward Frank Large scoring twice and winning the penalty converted by John Mackin, who scored two penalties when York City visited Eastville in October 1971. Mabbutt had scored when Johnny Williams had his shot parried, while Bobby Jones, against his former club, and Williams had also found the net. Level 3-3 at half-time, Rovers took the lead again through Mabbutt and, after Large scored his third of the game, so too did Mabbutt to record the only hat-trick of his career and give Rovers a 5-4 win. Amazingly, Mabbutt was to score twice more as Rovers drew 3-3 at Tranmere Rovers in the next fixture.

Rovers were also involved in two high-scoring wins over Oldham Athletic. In February, after falling behind to an Ian Towers goal after fifteen minutes, Rovers took control and Johnny Williams' penalty, his second goal of the game, put Rovers 3-1 up with only eleven minutes to play. However, Towers scored again and, five minutes from time, former Rovers trainee Laurie Sheffield equalised. In the final seconds, from a Williams free-kick, Biggs headed his second goal of the match to give Rovers a dramatic victory. The return game in May was even more unlikely, as Rovers recorded their first away win since victory over Northampton over six months earlier.

In winning 5-3 at Oldham Athletic on the final day of the season, Rovers completed only a second league double. Wayne Jones, after eleven minutes, and Bobby Jones, fifteen minutes later, had given Rovers a comfortable half-time lead, only for Ian Wood, after fifty-three and fifty-eight minutes, to pull the Latics level. Within seconds, Taylor had put Rovers ahead again, before Wood completed his hat-trick twelve minutes from the end. Once again, Rovers replied instantly, Bobby Jones scoring his second goal of a fluctuating game, with Jarman adding the visitors' fifth three minutes later. By scoring what were, in fact, his only three league goals of the season, Wood became the third opponent to score a league hat-trick against Rovers and end up on the losing side.

On five occasions, at Peterborough United, Watford, Northampton Town, Bury and Swindon Town, Rovers conceded four league goals, the heaviest defeat being 4-0 at Vicarage Road, where Watford's star-in-the-making Tony Currie scored twice. The only hat-trick in Rovers matches during 1967/68 was scored by Stockport County's Jim Fryatt in April, when Rovers lost 3-1 at Edgeley Park. The future England manager, Graham Taylor, scored in Grimsby Town's 3-2 victory over Rovers in February, while Dennis Rofe, later a Rovers manager, was a teenage goalscoring substitute when Leyton Orient won at Eastville in April.

In the final weeks of the season, Bert Tann was elevated to the post of general manager and secretary. On 1 April 1968, the directors appointed fifty-two-year-old Fred Ford as the new Rovers manager. A former teammate at Charlton Athletic of fellow Rovers managers Bill Dodgin and Bert Tann, Ford had also played for Tottenham Hotspur, Millwall and Carlisle United before coaching Rovers between 1955 and 1960. Thereafter, as manager, he had led Bristol City back into Division Two in 1965, before taking over a coaching job at Swindon Town. At Eastville, Fred Ford attempted to cobble together a young side, starting with the introduction of Frankie Prince in April 1968. It was a team that would ultimately earn promotion to Division Two in 1973/74.

Rovers' 1967/68 FA Cup run began in Nottinghamshire, where Midland League Arnold were defeated 3-0. Even after their merging with Arnold Kingswell in 1988, this first of two appearances by Arnold in round one of the FA Cup is preserved in the record books for having attracted a ground record attendance of 3,390 to the King George V Playing Fields. After a 4-0 win at Southern League Wimbledon, Rovers were drawn to play Bristol City at Ashton Gate. A well-earned goalless draw before a crowd of 37,237, was followed by a disappointing match at home in the replay. Rovers were defeated 3-0 at Reading in the League Cup.

1968/69

While the club's youth policy had been the starting point for much of Rovers' post-war development, new manager Fred Ford appreciated that it represented the best hope for the future. With the backing of Douglas Mearns Milne, the new chairman after five years on the board, Ford added new vigour to the development of young local talent. Rovers fielded a particularly young side in 1968/69, yet reached an FA Cup fifth round tie at Everton. Although there were many knocks along the way, the production of the 1973/74 promotion season side was under way.

Ford encouraged his younger players to play a pivotal role in the club's fortunes. Nineteen-year-old Larry Lloyd made his league debut on the opening day against Watford and, regardless of results, played in the first forty-three league matches of the season. He and a youthful Stuart Taylor, tall and dominating in defence, were fondly known as the 'Twin Towers'. Taylor's two league goals included an excellent headed winner after fifty-one minutes against Oldham Athletic in October. Other players who came through the ranks and broke into the side were eighteen-year-old left-winger Peter Higgins, Bobby Brown, a forward who was a year older, and goalkeeper Laurie Taylor. Glaswegian Tom Stanton, a signing from Mansfield Town, was just twenty, a year younger than the former Millwall utility player Trevor Rhodes, once a Wimbledon tennis junior finalist. Rovers lost the experience of Dave Stone and Ronnie Briggs, who both moved to Southend United, and Doug Hillard, who joined Taunton Town, while John Brown's contract was reluctantly terminated as the talented inside-forward was increasingly required to work extra shifts on the family farm in Cornwall. At a meeting on 29 August 1968, the supporters' club committee, including Eric Godfrey, chairman for twenty years, resigned en masse as a protest aginst the continued losses of the social club.

There was a new twist, too, in the continuing development of the M32 near Eastville Stadium. The M32 motorway was to be constructed to link the city centre with the conveniently close interchange of the north-south M5 with the M4 to London and South Wales. The motorway would end up cutting across the corner between the South Stand and the Muller Road terraces, and the hard shoulder was to attract a steady supply of cars with mysterious ailments on match days. Eastville's dubious distinction of being the closest league ground to a motorway meant that the noise level became increasingly intrusive.

The highlight of the league season was a large home victory over Mansfield Town in March. Rovers had defeated Gillingham 5-1, with the indefatigable Ray Mabbutt scoring twice, and recorded 4-2 home wins against both Barrow and Barnsley. However, Mansfield's visit to Eastville was to culminate in the first 6-2 win in Rovers' league history. There was a four-goal flurry in six minutes midway through the first half, starting with Ken Ronaldson's eighteenth-minute opener. No sooner had Malcolm Partridge equalised than Harold Jarman and Larry Lloyd, with the only goal of his Rovers career, gave the home side a 3-1 half-time lead. Bobby Brown added a fourth goal after fifty-four minutes, and when Johnny Petts also scored, eight minutes later, victory was sealed. Although Jim Goodfellow pulled a goal back after seventy minutes, Jarman added his second of the game ten minutes from the end to complete a comprehensive victory.

By means of contrast, the heaviest defeat of the season was a 6-1 defeat at the hands of unfashionable Crewe Alexandra at Gresty Road. Gordon Wallace put the home side ahead after half an hour and Keith Stott doubled the lead moments before half-time, only for Wayne Jones to fire an instant reply. As the second half started, Kevin McHale added a third, and the home side provided three more goals before the end. John Regan's goal twenty-two minutes from the end was followed by two in the final six minutes, an own goal from the unfortunate Lindsay Parsons and a second goal from Regan. Crewe were relegated at the end of the season, and Rovers' next visit to Gresty Road was to be in the 1989/90 Third Division championship season.

While Rovers lost on their travels to each of the bottom three clubs in the division, they also defeated Swindon Town, destined for promotion to Division Two at the season's end. Rovers never won three consecutive league games, but lost four in succession in the spring, including a 4-2 defeat at Barnsley. Only the visits of Swindon Town and Orient drew five-figure crowds to Eastville, where the season's average attendance was 7,118. Of twenty-three players used, Taylor and Jarman missed just one league game each, with the latter top-scoring with fourteen league goals, four more than Bobby Jones. Ray Mabbutt's appearance as centre-forward at Oldham Athletic on Boxing Day, in which he scored Rovers' goal in defeat, was the final one of almost 400 in which this highly dependable player had figured. The England international goalkeeper Eddie Hopkinson was in Bolton's side, which met Rovers in January 1969.

In November, towards the end of the convincing 4-2 home victory over Barrow, Ronaldson became the first Rovers substitute to score in league football. Just five days later, Kit Napier's hat-trick, the only one conceded all season by Rovers, earned Brighton a 3-1 victory at the Goldstone Ground. Rovers swiftly got into the habit of losing at regular intervals and by narrow margins. At no point in the season did the club put together a run of more than four consecutive matches without defeat, yet all but nine of the nineteen league defeats were by a single goal. This record was tarnished somewhat by the fact that, once clear of relegation worries, Rovers lost both their last two matches 3-0 away to sides destined to lose their league status within a decade.

Towards the end of the season, two former Rovers trainees who had never made the first-team at Eastville, returned to haunt their former club. John Tedesco scored for Plymouth Argyle, who drew 1-1 at Eastville, while Laurie Sheffield claimed one of three goals Luton Town put past Rovers at Kenilworth Road. When the Bedfordshire club visited Eastville twelve days later, Rovers had Alex Munro sent off but held out for a goalless draw. Phil Sanderock of Torquay, aged eighteen years thirty-nine days, became the youngest man ever to concede an own goal against Rovers in the league. In a late flurry of matches, Rovers won twice in a week against Stockport County and drew with promoted Swindon Town before a crowd of over 20,000 at the County Ground, before crashing to a heavy defeat at Holker Street, Tony Morrin scoring twice for Barrow.

A Swansea Town side inspired by the veteran Mel Nurse won 2-0 at Eastville to knock Rovers out of the League Cup. The Gloucestershire Cup final was disastrous from a Rovers point of view, with five Bristol City players scoring a second-half goal apiece at Eastville to inflict the club's heaviest defeat in the tournament since a 7-1 thrashing at Warmley in February 1892. All this was forgotten, though, as Rovers enjoyed a run of seven FA Cup games, losing only to a solitary goal at Everton in the fifth round.

As is often the way, a stuttering FA Cup run slowly gathered momentum as it progressed. Peterborough United were beaten 3-1 at Eastville and Rovers held out for a goalless draw at Bournemouth, before scraping through in a replay through a solitary Graydon goal. The same player saved Rovers with the club's equalising goal in round three as non-League Kettering Town held on to a 1-1 draw at Eastville. It was with some trepidation that Rovers went to Rockingham Road, where league sides had struggled before, but despite going a goal down and relying on Laurie Taylor to save a sixty-fifth minute penalty, victory was secured when Kettering player-manager Steve Gammon conceded a very late own goal. Rovers were drawn away to Second Division Bolton Wanderers, and fell behind to Gareth Williams before two goals from substitute Wayne Jones brought an unexpected win and a snow-delayed fifth round tie before a crowd of 55,294 at Goodison Park. Everton, beaten finalists in 1967/68, fielded Alan Ball, later a Rovers player, and Ray Wilson, both World Cup winners with England in 1966, and won through a Joe Royle goal after thirty-three minutes, set up by Ball's astute through pass.

One side effect of the long FA Cup run was national attention on a number of players in the young Rovers side. The Liverpool manager Bill Shankly watched the Everton Cup tie and was to pay Rovers a club record fee of £55,000 for Larry Lloyd before the season was out. Although Lloyd had appeared in only fifty-one league and Cup games, Shankly had no hesitation in putting his faith in the centre-half's potential. Lloyd was to share in much of the success experienced on Merseyside in the 1970s, winning European Cup winner's medals with Liverpool and Nottingham Forest as well as playing for England. The profit from his sale was swallowed up by the club's overdraft.

1969/70

On the eve of the new season, manager Fred Ford left Rovers after eighteen months to accept the vacant post of manager at Swindon Town. This was a blow to Rovers, whose youth policy, inspired by their former coach, was developing further. Ford was to coach at Torquay United and Oxford United, continuing to instil his football experience in his young protégés up to his death in October 1981. In a surprising yet highly effective move, the Rovers directors appointed Bill Dodgin from within. The fifty-eight-year-old former Rovers wing-half had managed Southampton, Fulham and Brentford, though he had not held a full-time job as manager for twelve years. His appointment, temporary at first, was made permanent on 19 December 1969, and he stayed in the job until July 1972.

Rovers' supporters were in for some exciting years; Dodgin's football philosophy was attack-minded and Rovers managed top-six finishes in each of his years in charge. Rovers started the new season with three new faces: Bristol-born goalkeeper Dick Sheppard, a free transfer from West Bromwich Albion, wing-half Gordon Marsland, who arrived in a £6,000 deal from Carlisle United, and the £10,000 centre-forward Robin Stubbs, a legendary figure for many years at Torquay United. Stubbs was top scorer for two seasons, scoring fifteen league goals in 1969/70, though Ray Graydon, Harold Jarman and Carl Gilbert all reached double figures. Another new name was Phil Roberts, a nineteen-year-old former Rovers apprentice, who was to win four Welsh caps after his high-profile move to Portsmouth in 1973.

Some more familiar faces had left, with Ray Mabbutt joining Newport County, Joe Gadston Exeter City and Trevor Rhodes Bath City. Dick Plumb was to become the second highest goalscorer in Yeovil Town's history. After Rovers had lost 1-0 to Gilbert's fiftieth-minute goal at Gillingham in September, the twenty-one-year-old striker moved to Eastville in an exchange deal that saw Ken Ronaldson make the opposite journey. At this stage, Rovers also found £4,000 to attract the experienced Bristol City full-back Tony Ford to move across the city. Dodgin's intention was to build a side capable of returning to Division Two and, in truth, his team came very close to achieving this aim.

Rovers adopted white shorts from the summer of 1969 to their otherwise all-blue kit. At the start of the season, Rovers hosted the American touring side Dallas Tornado, coached by the former Portsmouth centre-forward Ron Newman. A crowd of 4,313 saw Stubbs and Bobby Jones score in the five minutes prior to half-time, and a further burst of goals, from Harold Jarman and Stuart Taylor after sixty-five and sixty-eight minutes respectively earned Rovers a comfortable 4-0 win. This form was carried over into league action, where Rovers opened with a goalless draw at Southport, where they had suffered a heavy defeat in their previous game. Rovers dropped just two points in their opening five league matches, and suffered only three defeats in the first sixteen. By the end of October, the club was riding high in Division Three and promotion looked a realistic proposition.

In the opening fourteen league fixtures, Rovers scored at least three goals on eight occasions. Stubbs scored twice in a 3-0 win against Tranmere Rovers, when Bryn Jones was given a league debut, and there were identical wins against Brighton and at home to Rotherham United. Rovers drew with Mansfield Town, who lost Jim Goodfellow with a fractured jaw after a collision with Lindsay Parsons. There was also an astonishing 3-3 draw at Eastville in the first-ever league meeting with Rochdale, Tony Buck scoring a hat-trick for the visitors and still not ending up on the winning side. Rochdale followed up this result with eight consecutive league victories, still a club record run, yet drew their first four meetings with Rovers. However, Rovers' largest win of the season came at Reading where, in a forerunner to the fixture in January 1999, they won 5-1. Rovers led 3-0 after eight minutes, through Ray Graydon, a Colin Meldrum own goal and Bobby Jones, with Graydon adding his second of the game two minutes before half-time. Stubbs put Rovers 5-0 ahead after forty-eight minutes with Les Chappell, who also scored at Eastville in the return fixture, adding a consolation goal eighteen minutes from time.

The good run could not last, however, and Rovers won just the once in their final nine league games of 1969. Bizarrely, in each of the last eight league matches of the calendar year, Rovers scored exactly one goal. This run was finished by a convincing 4-1 home win against Mansfield Town, Frankie Prince, a product of the youth scheme, opening the scoring after ten minutes from Bryn Jones' pass, and Jarman adding a solo second a minute later. The third goal was an own goal attributed to Sandy Pate, who also put through his own goal at Eastville in March 1972, thus becoming the only opponent to score twice in the league for Rovers. Thereafter, Rovers were able to record 4-2 and 5-2 wins over Bradford City and Bournemouth respectively to finish the season with eighty league goals to their name, the highest total for five years.

After Christmas, Rovers drew four consecutive away matches. One of these was a goalless draw at Millmoor, whereby Rotherham United set a club record as it was their eighteenth game undefeated since they had lost at Eastville in October, the first six matches in this run having resulted in draws. At the same time, Rovers embarked on a run of six consecutive home league victories, which propelled the side towards the top of the division. The first of these was a 3-0 win against Luton Town, in which both Rovers' full-backs, Ford and Alex Munro, scored penalties, the first occasion that two Rovers players had done so in a league game, a feat equalled in 2005 by Junior Agogo and Richard Walker. This match acted as a form of revenge, as Luton Town, promoted at the end of the season, had exacted a 4-0 defeat in September.

Going into the final few games, Rovers had not conceded three goals in a league game since mid-December. Back-to-back 2-1 wins over Barrow, for whom Jim Mulvaney scored in both meetings with Rovers, and Torquay United, for whom Alan Welsh did likewise, as did Stubbs, against his former club, and Gilbert for the Pirates, left Rovers in a strong promotion position. The situation was further enhanced by two astute signings in March. Dodgin bought veteran Sheffield Wednesday captain Don Megson as player-coach, who rapidly emerged as the man being groomed to succeed in time as manager, and Sandy Allan, a proven goalscorer in European football with Cardiff City.

Promotion was now a realistic target and a crowd of 22,005 – the highest at Eastville, local derbies with Bristol City apart, since October 1959 – saw a first-minute Gilbert goal earn Rovers victory over the leaders Orient. This was followed by three straight draws, but another huge crowd saw Allan's twenty-fourth minute goal defeat already relegated Stockport County 1-0 and leave Rovers still in the promotion frame. With two games to go, Rovers had fifty-six points, sitting two points behind Orient and one ahead of Luton Town, both of whom had three matches left, including home fixtures with Southport, who desperately needed the points themselves in their battle against relegation. Two victories would, in all likelihood, earn promotion to Division Two.

As it was, a frustrated crowd of 18,978 saw Rovers attack with huge spirit but lose 2-1 at home to Gillingham. A 5-2 defeat at Tranmere Rovers represented a hugely disappointing end to a season of great promise. Both their rivals beat Southport, who were relegated by one point, and Rovers, with only themselves to blame, finished in third place on fifty-six points, behind Luton Town on sixty and Orient with sixty-two. Nonetheless, the enthusiasm with which Dodgin's attack-minded side had pushed for promotion gave enormous hope for the years to come. Young Stuart Taylor, the only ever-present, was developing into a pivotal figure at the heart of a side with vast potential.

In the FA Cup, a convincing win at Telford United was followed by defeat at Aldershot, who fielded the veteran Jimmy Melia and for whom Jack Howarth scored twice. Participation in the League Cup was even more short-lived. Ted McDougall scored twice as Rovers lost 3-0 at Bournemouth. He also scored twice when Rovers drew 2-2 at Dean Court in October, and once when Rovers recorded a 5-2 win at Eastville in February, though the Dorset club was relegated to Division Four. For a fourth consecutive year, Rovers were unable to win the Gloucestershire Cup.

8
The 1970s

1970/71

Heartened by the previous season's success, Bristol Rovers approached 1970/71 with vigour and enthusiasm. Bill Dodgin's side harboured real belief in its capabilities but, perhaps, sixth place, nine points away from promotion, represented a disappointing return. The first-team squad had barely changed. Gordon Marsland spent time on loan at Crewe Alexandra and Oldham Athletic before joining Bath City at the end of the season. Tony Ford was forced to retire after rupturing his spleen in the game at Preston North End in August. While Rovers received £4,000 insurance compensation, Ford carved out a career in coaching at Plymouth Argyle and Hereford United. Slowly but surely, a team worthy of promotion to Division Two was being constructed. Stuart Taylor, once again an ever-present, Lindsay Parsons, Frankie Prince and Bryn Jones would all star in the temporarily all-conquering 1973/74 side. They were joined by two free transfer recruits – Walsall's Kenny Stephens and midfielder Gordon Fearnley, previously a teammate of player-coach Don Megson at Sheffield Wednesday. In the meantime, the side was built around the goalkeeper and centre-backs, the only three to play in every match. Seven players missed fewer than seven league games each and only twenty-one players were used in total.

By the season's end, Dick Sheppard had played in goal in the previous eighty-two competitive matches. In front of him, Phil Roberts, Megson, Taylor and Parsons were a sturdy defence, with Prince joined by at least one Jones – Bobby, Bryn or Wayne. Ray Graydon, scorer of thirteen goals from the right, and Harold Jarman, who contributed twelve from the left, provided the crosses for seventeen-goal top scorer Robin Stubbs. Sandy Allan had a poor season by his standards, scoring only twice, while Carl Gilbert joined Rotherham United in mid-season. Once again, relative success brought good crowds to Eastville, the second highest being 18,875 for the visit of Fulham in February, while 25,836 watched the January visit of Aston Villa, the highest-ever crowd for a Third

Division game at Eastville. Bruce Rioch, on the threshold of a successful career that won him many Scotland caps, scored the winning goal in this, the fourth meeting of these two clubs that season and, astonishingly, the one watched by the lowest attendance of the four fixtures.

Off the field, Eastville Stadium was undergoing further change. Increasingly hemmed in by developments, it now had the M32 'Parkway' motorway crossing the corner of the ground between the Muller Road End and the South Stand. As traffic levels increased, the incidence of apparent breakdowns on the eastbound hard shoulder during home matches grew dramatically and Rovers' games were played to a background din of traffic.

Rovers scored four times in a league game on five occasions. Four second-half goals at Oakwell over New Year, where Stubbs opened the scoring before Stephens, Graydon and Wayne Jones all scored in the final fourteen minutes, helped defeat Barnsley 4-0. Reading and Bradford City were beaten 4-0 and 4-2 in consecutive games in November. Four different scorers saw off the Royals, while Jarman scored his first hat-trick in a decade with Rovers to see off Bradford City, for whom Bruce Bannister, later such a pivotal figure at Eastville, scored twice to accompany his goal in the return fixture. There were also two 4-1 away victories: at Shrewsbury Town, where Stubbs scored twice in the final three minutes after Graydon had twice put Rovers in front; and at Gillingham, where Stubbs scored all Rovers' goals, the first occasion that a Rovers player had scored four goals in an away league match. In fact, Jarman was Rovers' star man as the Pirates overcame a half-time deficit following Kenny Pound's excellent thirty-fifth minute goal after a one-two with Andy Smillie. Stubbs scored four second-half goals with his right foot – after forty-six, fifty-eight, seventy-eight and eighty-two minutes – set up on each occasion by Jarman. Gilbert, a summer signing from Gillingham, replaced Graydon as a substitute against his former club, who were relegated.

In fact, Rovers were to complete a league double over three of the four relegated clubs. On the other hand, relegated Bury beat Rovers 1-0 at Eastville, with the former England winger John Connelly scoring two minutes before half-time, and 3-0 at Gigg Lane. Connelly scored in both games and Terry McDermott also scored in the away fixture. Rotherham United's Neil Hague scored both his side's goals in their 2-0 win at Eastville in February, and a thirty-fifth minute opener when the sides drew at Millmoor. Rovers claimed a point off champions Preston North End before the BBC *Match of the Day* cameras, but lost both fixtures with equally promoted Fulham and ultimately finished well in arrears of both clubs.

Despite starting the season with an impressive fourteen-match run, where the only defeat had been at the hands of Preston at Deepdale, Rovers never seriously challenged for a place in the top two. The decisive blow came in the form of an eight-match winless run in the New Year, which included the 3-0 defeat at Bury and a 4-1 deficit at Mansfield Town, where Parsons conceded an own goal. Finishing the season with straight defeats, Dodgin's side had not achieved its preseason aspirations in terms of league football, but the League Cup was to provide enormous excitement, as Rovers reached the fifth round for the first time in the club's history.

Rovers had been knocked out of the League Cup in the first round in consecutive seasons, so there was considerable satisfaction when Graydon's fifty-sixth-minute goal helped defeat Brighton 1-0 in the opening round. A home tie followed with Newcastle United, evoking the vivid memories of Rovers' epic 1951 FA Cup matches. The attraction of a major First Division side, boasting household names in Frank Clark, Bobby Moncur and Pop Robson, drew a crowd of 16,824 to Eastville. The many Rovers supporters were not disappointed, as the veteran Bobby Jones scored twice and the Magpies were defeated 2-1. Jones scored again in the next round, as Rovers drew at Carrow Road against Second Division Norwich City. The Canaries held Rovers in the Eastville replay until extra time, when Rovers opened up a 3-1 lead.

In addition to one First Division side, Rovers knocked three Division Two sides out of the 1970/71 League Cup. The third was Birmingham City when a total of 22,189 spectators gathered at Eastville as Cup fever gripped the Rovers camp. There was every possibility that Rovers could make real progress in the competition, and a dominant display in round four left many believing in Rovers' potential. Following an own goal from centre-half Roger Hynd, Gilbert and Stubbs both scored to give Rovers an apparently comfortable 3-0 lead and send them into the quarter-finals for the first time in this tournament.

It was ironic that, having progressed so far, Rovers would be locked in an all Third Division clash with Aston Villa. However, the weather dictated much of the play at Eastville, where a draw was a fair result and brought about a replay at Villa Park. Rovers, who were by now in a run that would see them lose only three times in thirty games in all competitions, held Villa for eighty-nine minutes before 36,483 spectators, both sides playing very well in a spectacular game. In the final seconds, Pat McMahon, who had scored in the first meeting, claimed the decisive winning goal to end Rovers' dreams.

In the FA Cup, high-flying Fulham were beaten by two Gilbert goals, manager Dodgin masterminding victory over the side controlled by his son. Having drawn at Aldershot, Rovers were brought down to earth in the replay, the veteran Jimmy Melia among the goalscorers. A Stephens goal from Graydon's pass after sixty-seven minutes and a drawn Gloucestershire Cup final ended Rovers' losing streak in that tournament, while in May goals from Ian Hamilton and Alfie Biggs enabled Rovers Old Players to defeat City Old Players 2-0. In May 1971, Rovers' Wayne Jones earned a full international cap for Wales in a 1-0 European Championship victory over Finland in Helsinki.

1971/72

A very similar Rovers line-up experienced a feeling of déjà vu for, as in 1970/71, Rovers reached a quarter-final and finished sixth in Division Three. The main absentee was Ray Graydon, whose move to Aston Villa set him on the way to three League Cup final appearances and, ultimately, a successful career in management. Alex Munro, who had appeared in nine consecutive seasons, emigrated to South Africa in the summer of 1971, while Don Megson retired as a player to concentrate on his full-time role as coach. Graydon's place was taken, through an exchange deal with Villa, by the highly experienced former Welsh international midfielder Brian Godfrey, while Mike Green, Rovers' captain in the 1973/74 promotion season, appeared in the side following his summer move from Gillingham.

A number of other players appeared in occasional games for Rovers. Three young goalkeepers, Malcolm Dalrymple, Richard Crabtree and loan signing Allen Clarke, as well as twenty-two-year-old forward Malcolm John each made a league debut. Another product of the South Wales nursery organised by Stan Montgomery, seventeen-year-old Peter Aitken made his way into the squad as an unused substitute. As the season progressed, manager Dodgin improved his hand with the signing of two strikers who were to see Rovers into Division Two. Bruce Bannister had built up an excellent reputation at Bradford City as a brave, busy forward, and it took a club record £23,000 fee to bring him to Eastville in November. Three months later, in exchange for Robin Stubbs, who had not scored all season, Rovers signed the vastly experienced John Rudge from Torquay United.

Once again, it was the League Cup that sparked Rovers' season into life. A relatively straightforward three-goal victory at Exeter City was followed, for the second consecutive season, by three wins against Second Division opposition. Sandy Allan and Billy Hughes exchanged penalties in two mid-second-half minutes as Rovers defeated a strong Sunderland side by 3-1 at Eastville. Then Stuart Taylor and Harold Jarman scored to put out Charlton Athletic. When Jarman scored again to earn a draw at Queen's Park Rangers, for whom Rodney Marsh scored and both Terry Venables and Gerry Francis played, a crowd of 24,373 was attracted to Eastville to see an Allan goal, driven home after a three-man move twelve minutes from time, earn Rovers a second consecutive League Cup quarter-final. These remain the only two seasons that Rovers have progressed so far in this tournament.

The quarter-final tie drew a crowd of 33,634 to Eastville, Rovers' highest ever for a home League Cup tie. Rightly so, for Stoke City brought a star-studded side, the First Division club including most notably Gordon Banks, a World Cup winner in 1966 and believed by many to be the best goalkeeper in the world. Banks was kept busy early in the game, but once the veteran George Eastham stamped his authority on the game, Stoke began to dominate. The visitors ran up a four-goal lead, with Jimmy Greenhoff, an FA Cup winner with Manchester United in 1977, and the future Bristol City manager Denis Smith among the goalscorers. With the job done, the visitors relaxed, and both Stubbs and Godfrey, the latter from a penalty, were able to score past Banks. Once more, though, Rovers had shown their qualities as Cup fighters.

Rovers prepared for the new season with the usual flurry of friendlies. One game prior to the 1971/72 season was Rovers' 1-1 draw with Hereford United at Edgar Street on 2 August, Green scoring for Rovers five minutes before half-time and Billy Meadows equalising nine minutes from the end. This game marked the Hereford United debut of David Icke, who saved well from Wayne Jones and Allan, a competent goalkeeper and national television sports anchorman who courted national fame in March 1991 by declaring himself to be the son of a 'Godhead'.

It did not take Rovers long to post warning of their goalscoring potential. After victory over Tranmere Rovers, Bradford City were the second league visitors to Eastville. Rovers were a goal up in the first minute, five ahead inside twenty-five minutes, and scored seven in total for only the eighth occasion in the Pirates' league history. It was Godfrey who opened the scoring early on, and his hat-trick in the opening twenty-five minutes included two stunning long-range volleys. Although the visitors scored before the break, a 5-1 half-time lead was a healthy return, and the 7-1 victory was Rovers' largest since March 1964. Bruce Bannister, in the Bantams' attack, was to finish the season as Rovers' top scorer, while the return fixture saw Bradford give a debut to David Bairstow, later England's wicketkeeper. Just a week after the 7-1 victory, two Jim Fryatt goals condemned Rovers to defeat at Oldham Athletic.

There was a flurry of penalties at Eastville. Both Allan, against Tranmere Rovers, and Bannister, when Rovers beat Blackburn Rovers 3-0, joined a select band of seven Rovers players to have scored two penalties in a league game. When York City visited in October, John Mackin became only the fifth visitor to convert two penalties in a league fixture with Rovers. A crowd of 6,876 witnessed an extraordinary game that featured six goals before half-time. Kenny Stephens and Jarman put Rovers 2-0 up in nine minutes, and Jarman's second left Rovers 3-1 ahead, but Mackin's first penalty, awarded on the stroke of half-time for a foul by Lindsay Parsons, left the scores level at the break. Stephens put Rovers ahead again after fifty-seven minutes and, four minutes later, Jarman completed the second hat-trick of his Rovers career to put the Pirates 5-3 ahead. Rovers held on for victory, despite a second Mackin penalty after handball against Bobby Brown, in his penultimate start before a transfer to Weymouth, eighteen minutes from time.

After a few initial concerns, Rovers put together some good runs of results. Between November and February, there was a nine-match unbeaten run, while Rovers also ran up convincing victories over Barnsley, Allan scoring twice in a 3-0 win, and Rochdale, where a 5-2 win included a brace from Bannister. Perhaps crucially, there were just four away wins, enabling Rovers to do the double over

Tranmere Rovers, Blackburn Rovers and Chesterfield. Aston Villa, for whom Willie Anderson's goal at Eastville sent his side to the top of Division Three, and Bournemouth completed doubles over Rovers. Kevin Randall, having scored in both of the first-ever meetings between Rovers and Chesterfield, also scored in the third as Rovers won 3-1 at Saltergate.

Defensively, Rovers gave little away. From October onwards, there was no league game in which three or more goals were conceded. Roberts, Taylor, Lindsay Parsons and Frankie Prince were ever-presents, while Bannister's two final-day goals made him the club's top goalscorer. Roberts scored an own goal for Notts County in September to match one he was to score for them on Portsmouth's books in February 1974. Five straight wins in March, with only two goals conceded, gave a hint of a late promotion challenge. The key fixture was the Easter Monday trip to leaders Aston Villa, where Rovers, in an injury crisis, selected apprentice goalkeeper Crabtree just a few weeks after his seventeenth birthday. The crowd at Villa Park was 45,158, the second highest for a Rovers league game, but despite an inspired performance from the young goalkeeper, Rovers lost 2-1. Even after winning the final four matches, Rovers finished well adrift of second-placed Brighton.

After convincing 3-0 wins at home to Telford United and Cambridge United, Rovers played an FA Cup third-round tie at Elland Road. Before a crowd of 33,565, Leeds United scored three times in seventeen first-half minutes and defeated Rovers 4-1, with Peter Lorimer scoring twice and creating two goals for Johnny Giles, household names such as Terry Cooper, Billy Bremner, Joe Jordan and Norman Hunter also playing. With Stoke City winning the League Cup, Rovers had thus been knocked out of both major cup competitions by the eventual victors. The Gloucestershire Cup final was drawn.

The new M32 motorway overhanging the corner of Eastville Stadium was closed for a week after a fire on 14 April on the Eastville slip road; a ten-year-old boy and his twelve-year-old accomplice were suspected, although charges were not pressed. Of more immediate concern to Rovers was that, in July, manager Bill Dodgin handed over the reins to his coach Don Megson. While Rovers had not achieved immediate success, the bricks were in place for future Rovers triumphs, and progress in League and League Cup football had given time for the younger players to mature. Dodgin remained as chief scout until 1983, keeping a watchful eye on tomorrow's stars through the twilight years of his career, and retained a healthy interest in Rovers' fortunes up to his death, at the age of ninety, in October 1999.

The former Rovers manager Brough Fletcher, who had 'discovered' young talent such as Harry Bamford and Geoff Bradford in his time in charge of the club either side of the Second World War, died in Bristol on 12 May 1972, aged seventy-nine.

1972/73

In July 1972, with Bill Dodgin reverting to his post as chief scout, Rovers appointed from within to make Don Megson the new manager. A relative youngster at thirty-six, the former Sheffield Wednesday full-back had displayed considerable talent as a player and it was hoped he could translate his expertise into good management. Rovers were not to be disappointed. After Andrew Wilson, Brough Fletcher and David McLean, he was the fourth Wednesday player to become manager at Eastville. Megson brought a touch of class to Rovers. He would gather the team for a pre-match lunch at a motel outside Bristol prior to every home game to generate a greater feeling of team spirit. Unlike his predecessor, Megson believed in solid defending and quick counter-attacking, believing in the merit of 1-0 victories and, despite his critics, he succeeded in overseeing the return to Division Two in 1974 and establishing Rovers in this higher division.

While new hope arose at Eastville, there was considerable mourning for Bert Tann, who died in Bristol on 7 July 1972. Tann had managed Rovers between 1950 and 1968, during which time he gained widespread recognition for his shrewd tactical awareness. In 1971, the Football Association had awarded him a medal to commemorate twenty-one consecutive years with Rovers, in which period he had masterminded the club's first spell in Division Two. A key figure in the history of the club was gone.

Megson had an early opportunity to test his managerial ability in the preseason Watney Cup. Ironically, for a tournament designed to reward the top-scoring non-promoted sides from the previous season, there were just four goals in Rovers' three matches. Rovers strolled to apparently easy 2-0 victories at home to First Division Wolverhampton Wanderers and away to Burnley, who were destined to be Division Two champions that season. Bruce Bannister scored in both games. A crowd of 19,380 gathered at Eastville in sweltering heat for the final between Rovers and First Division Sheffield United. The visitors fielded teenage goalkeeper Tom McAlister, later a Rovers player himself, and his fine display kept the final scoreless, though many felt Rovers had deserved to win. The match went to a penalty shoot-out, the first thirteen penalties were scored and, with Dick Sheppard saving a crucial spot-kick from the veteran Ted Hemsley, Rovers recorded a 7-6 win. In only his third game in charge, Megson had led the club to its first major cup competition success since 1935.

On the back of this preseason success, Rovers embarked on a third successive giantkilling run in the League Cup. Two Second Division clubs were beaten: Cardiff City in a replay after Rovers had grabbed a 2-2 draw at Ninian Park, and Brighton. This second-round 4-0 win, in which four different players scored, gave Rovers ample revenge, for it was only four months since the Sussex club had beaten Rovers to the second promotion place. More immediately, victory earned Rovers a prestigious home tie against Manchester United. The attraction of high-profile names such as George Best and Bobby Charlton drew a crowd of 33,597, the highest ever for a League Cup tie at Eastville. John Rudge's goal after an hour earned a 1-1 draw and the opportunity of a replay at Old Trafford, secured only by United through Willie Morgan's equaliser three minutes from time.

Rovers faced a team including nine full internationals in the Old Trafford replay, and the veteran winger Bobby Jones was recalled to add experience to the Third Division side. After Sheppard had saved well from Bobby Charlton, Rudge put Rovers ahead after thirty minutes when he headed home a corner taken by Lindsay Parsons. Midway through the second half, the home side was awarded a controversial penalty when Ian Storey-Moore fell under a challenge from Frankie Prince, but Sheppard saved George Best's kick. Good fortune could not last forever, though, and substitute Sammy McIlroy headed an equaliser from a Morgan corner with ten minutes left. Sensationally, four minutes later, a third header from a corner, Bannister's goal created by Kenny Stephens, gave Rovers one of the greatest victories in the club's history.

Despite achieving the impossible, Rovers did not reach the League Cup quarter-finals for a third consecutive season. The 4-0 defeat at Molineux was as comprehensive as the result suggests. Jim McCalliog scored twice as Wolverhampton Wanderers, orchestrated by the future Rovers player-coach Kenny Hibbitt, exacted revenge for their earlier Watney Cup humiliation. Nor was there any place to hide for Rovers in the FA Cup. Just five weeks after victory at Manchester United, Rovers suffered the indignity of losing at Isthmian League Hayes. The Middlesex side fully deserved the victory obtained through Bobby Hatt's goal nine minutes into the second half, and the infamous maverick Robin Friday, then a twenty-year-old on the verge of a highly entertaining career, stood out as a player to watch.

It was the unlikely figure of Danish-born midfielder Preben Arentoft who set Rovers on their way in 1972/73, his own goal sealing Blackburn Rovers' 3-0 opening-day defeat at Eastville. Whereas many of the leading sides lost when they visited Bristol, where only unfancied Southend United and York City recorded victories, Rovers' away form was poor. Ultimately, Rovers finished only four points behind promoted Notts County, but the side had lost away to many in the challenging group. Indeed, a paltry figure of three league wins away from home, which did not even hint at promotion potential, enabled just two league doubles over two relegated clubs, Scunthorpe United and Swansea City. The defeat at Grimsby Town featured four disallowed 'goals', two for Alan Gauden and one for Stuart Brace for the Mariners, as well as one for Bannister for Rovers.

However, Rovers were able to score freely at home. Bannister scored twice in a 5-1 win against Shrewsbury Town and Stuart Taylor twice as Scunthorpe United were beaten by the same score. Rovers also defeated Halifax Town and Port Vale 4-1 and recorded two 3-0 wins. Bannister scored from the penalty spot in both fixtures against Rotherham United. While Rovers recorded eight straight home wins through the winter, five away fixtures ended in goalless draws. Both matches with Rochdale were goalless, Stuart Taylor being sent off on Rovers' visit to Spotland, as was Southend United's 1,000th home league fixture, when Rovers played at Roots Hall on a Friday night in November. Dick Sheppard's thirty-fifth minute own goal gave Brentford victory in September, while Stuart Houston, on the verge of a long and successful career, scored the Bees' consolation goal in the return fixture.

This match at home to Brentford in November marked the end of Wayne Jones' promising career. A knee injury was revealed to be a rare bone condition that forced the Wales under-23 international midfielder to retire from playing the game. Just two months later, goalkeeper Sheppard's career was effectively ended when he suffered a depressed fracture of the skull, diving at the feet of Tranmere Rovers' Eddie Loyden, with Tom Stanton finishing that particular game in goal. Megson made just one major signing, procuring his former Sheffield Wednesday colleague, the erstwhile England under-23 winger Colin Dobson on a free transfer as player-coach. Now he was forced to strengthen Rovers' squad, and the two highly astute purchases he made ensured Rovers would be serious promotion contenders in 1973/74. Goalkeeper Jim Eadie and striker Alan Warboys, who had experienced European football together at Cardiff City, were to be essential ingredients in Megson's successful cocktail. Warboys, a former teammate of Rovers' manager at Wednesday, became the club's record signing as his move from Sheffield United cost a reputed £35,000.

Suddenly, Rovers' promotion aspirations once again flickered into life. Eadie did not concede a goal in his first five games. All realistic hope disappeared, however, in the space of three days in mid-March as Rovers crashed 4-2 at Shrewsbury Town and 4-3 at Walsall. In the latter game, Rovers trailed to a ninth-minute Bobby Shinton goal at half-time, but after Bannister and Warboys, with his first goal for the club, had put Rovers ahead, a second Warboys goal appeared to seal a 3-2 victory. Referee Jim Whalley of Southport, though, added on seven minutes of injury time. Chris Jones scored his second goal of the night after ninety-two minutes, while Barnie Wright's header five minutes later condemned Rovers to a further season in Division Three. However, four wins in the last five games left Rovers in a morale-boosting fifth position. Parsons, the only ever-present, had now appeared in 135 consecutive league matches, while Bannister's twenty-five league goals was the most by a Rovers player since Alfie Biggs in 1963/64. A late flurry of goals – Warboys and Bannister both scoring in four league games and the Gloucestershire Cup final, which was lost to Bristol City on a penalty shoot-out – ensured qualification again for the Watney Cup. Rovers' prospects for 1973/74 looked highly encouraging.

The final home game also marked the farewell appearance of the North Enclosure's favourite son, the winger Harold Jarman, who had appeared in well over 400 league matches for Rovers since his debut in 1959 and had attained cult status in his later years at Eastville; Jarman was rewarded with a testimonial game against Liverpool, and he joined Newport County along with Brian Godfrey. As he left, so too did Phil Roberts, a club record £55,000 sale to Portsmouth, where he won four full caps for Wales, and Sandy Allan, who emigrated to South Africa. Bobby Jones, who had also surpassed 400 league games for Rovers, retired in May 1973, and was justly rewarded for his long and loyal service with a testimonial game against West Ham United.

1973/74

On the evening of Friday 19 April 1974, Rovers drew 0-0 at Southend United to regain Second Division status. Over 1,000 Rovers supporters had made the journey to Roots Hall for this game, and the resultant pitch invasion reflected the sense of relief and pride at the club's achievement. Don Megson, building on the groundwork of Bert Tann, Bill Dodgin and Bobby Campbell, had generated a team spirit that would guide the homely club back out of Division Three. Rovers had also reverted to blue-and-white quartered shirts in 1973, and these old, trusted tops restored the golden years to Eastville with instant effect.

Much of the success was due to the stability of Megson's side. Ever-present goalkeeper Jim Eadie improved on his feat of the previous season by playing a club record 707 minutes in the autumn without conceding a goal. In fact, Rovers conceded only five goals in the opening sixteen league matches. Dependable left-back Lindsay Parsons, whose missed games in March ended a run of 167 consecutive league appearances, was partnered by Phil Roberts' replacement, the tough-tackling former Bristol City right-back Trevor Jacobs. Ever-present Stuart Taylor and captain Mike Green were dominant centre-halves, while Frankie Prince and another ever-present, Tom Stanton, were forceful figures in midfield. On the wings, Kenny Stephens and Colin Dobson created the opportunities on which forwards Alan Warboys and Bruce Bannister were able to thrive. Beyond these eleven players, only John Rudge and Gordon Fearnley enjoyed extended runs in the side.

Megson's influence on the side was primarily to tighten Rovers' defence. Only thirty-three goals were conceded in forty-six league matches, fewer than any other Third Division club, and overtaking the club record thirty-six in forty-two league games in 1922/23. With a strong defence, Rovers could embark on a long unbeaten run. In attack, player-of-the-year Warboys, top scorer with twenty-two league goals, was muscular and strong, while Bannister was quick, the pair becoming known nationally as 'Smash and Grab'. Indeed, when Warboys was sidelined in the spring with a hamstring injury, Rovers began losing games, though it would be wholly unjust to blame his highly competent replacements, Rudge and David Staniforth, a £20,000 March signing from Sheffield United.

The new season opened with a Watney Cup tie against West Ham United. Rovers outplayed their First Division opponents but had to rely on victory in a penalty shoot-out after a 1-1 draw. Disappointingly, Hull City then won by a single goal in the Eastville semi-final, while a solitary Harry Redknapp goal at Bournemouth knocked Rovers out of the League Cup. Division Three, though, presented an entirely different proposition, as Rovers swept all before them, remaining unbeaten for the first twenty-seven games of the season. This achievement equalled a record for the division, also set by Rovers in winning the championship in 1952/53. It would, however, be just to accept that Rovers had set a new record in remaining undefeated for thirty-two matches between 31 March 1973 and 2 February 1974.

On the opening day of the season, Rovers played away to Bournemouth, whom many believed would be promotion candidates. A morale-boosting 3-0 victory, with Warboys and Bannister both on the scoresheet, set Rovers on track for the success that was to follow. Although Hereford United, Port Vale, York City and Grimsby Town held out for draws at Eastville, Rovers looked increasingly awesome. There were three consecutive 2-0 victories in September, Tom Stanton scoring twice against Halifax Town. Two Warboys goals helped Rovers towards an impressive 4-2 win over Plymouth Argyle on Boxing Day. The machine kept rolling as Rovers held out for draws at Charlton Athletic and Halifax Town, ran off another 3-0 victory over Bournemouth (Bannister and Warboys both scoring again) and won 3-2 at Aldershot in the first Sunday Football League game in which Rovers participated.

Rovers hit a purple patch just before Christmas. Warboys scored a hat-trick to beat Southport 3-1 in mid-November, the first of three hat-tricks he claimed in four weeks. The Pirates then arrived at Brighton for a 2 p.m. kick-off on 1 December, an hour earlier than usual to save electricity during the Miners' Strike. Rovers had a poor track record at the Goldstone Ground, but the league leaders were facing a side knocked out of the FA Cup only three days earlier by Walton and Hersham. However, few could have predicted an 8-2 win for Rovers, a club record victory and the only occasion two Rovers players had scored three times or more in the same league fixture. To follow this up, Warboys scored three more goals and Jacobs his first for the club as Rovers demolished Southend United 4-0 at Eastville seven days later.

The Brighton win, broadcast on national television, was a demoralising blow to their young manager, Brian Clough. Bannister put Rovers ahead after four minutes, following an excellent move involving Parsons, Dobson and Warboys. Fearnley put Rovers 2-0 up eight minutes later and, though the Welsh international Peter O'Sullivan pulled a goal back, Rovers were 5-1 ahead by the break and Bannister had already completed what was to be the only hat-trick of his Rovers career. After half-time, Warboys took over, adding three more to his first-half goal to become only the second Rovers player to score four goals in an away league game. He could have had more, too, had he not been forced to leave the field at one stage to have stitches inserted in a cut above his eye. Ronnie Howell's eighty-seventh minute consolation goal could not deprive Rovers of a record league win, on the day the reserves won 6-1 against Bristol City reserves. No other Division Three fixture has ever finished in an 8-2 win for the away side.

Once February arrived, Rovers' dreams of going undefeated for an entire season were shattered. Indeed, the Aldershot game in January, a club record seventeenth consecutive unbeaten away league game, which left Rovers seven points clear at the top, marked the last time until August 1976 that Warboys and Bannister both scored in the same league fixture. A single-goal defeat at Wrexham, to Arfon Griffiths' strike a minute after half-time, was followed by a 3-1 loss at Port Vale, when Green ended the match in goal after Eadie had been stretchered off with concussion. Although two Jacobs goals helped defeat Blackburn Rovers 3-0, the defeats continued, the first at home coming at the hands of Walsall. Stephens and Walsall's Doug Fraser had both been sent off when Rovers visited Fellows Park in November, and now in March, two Alan Buckley goals inflicted a first loss at Eastville since March 1973.

Rovers played at second-placed York City on 16 March in blustery conditions. Chris Jones had put York ahead seven minutes after half-time and, when Bannister was sent off nine minutes from time, overreacting to a Chris Topping foul, it looked all over for Rovers. Remarkably, four minutes later, Stephens equalised with a low left-wing cross shot, but he was then also sent off for disputing a penalty five minutes into injury time that gave the home side victory. Referee Jim Whalley had crucially also allowed seven minutes of injury time at Walsall twelve months earlier, while York's first goalscorer, Chris Jones, had ironically scored twice in the Walsall game. The upshot was that York now stood just three points behind Rovers with a game in hand, and the pressure was back on Rovers.

The worst setback of all, however, was a 2-1 defeat on Easter Saturday at home to promotion rivals Oldham Athletic. Rovers' healthy seven-point lead had been whittled away as the Latics had won ten consecutive league games. Oldham had beaten Southport 6-0 just twenty-four hours prior to their game at Eastville. Then a long-range shot from George McVitie and an opportunist goal from top scorer Colin Garwood earned a crucial victory over Rovers. Oldham Athletic, promoted when they beat Huddersfield Town 6-0 a week later, were champions with sixty-two points, just one point ahead of second-placed Rovers and York City, both promoted under the new 'three-up' rule. The point gained at Southend not only ensured promotion, but enabled Rovers to claim a club record, equalled only in 1989/90, as only five away games had been lost. A happy crowd of 19,137 at Eastville saw Rovers recover from Lammie Robertson's nineteenth-minute goal to draw with Brighton in the final match, Bannister converting a penalty five minutes from time after Prince had been fouled by Ron Welch.

'Megson's Marvels' had held out, despite growing pressures, and Rovers were to return to Division Two after an absence of more than a decade. It had been a season of hard work and of numerous club records, most notably the thirty-two-match unbeaten league run. Moreover, many early season points had been ground out week by week to form a platform for success. It was also a season of milestones, for the draw with Port Vale in October had been Rovers' 1,000th home league game, and the draw against York City seven days later Rovers' 2,000th match in the Football League. Yet, what many observers regarded as one of the best performances came in the FA Cup. Rovers had won confidently at Bideford, who fielded only two players who experienced league football, namely the Exeter City pair of Steve Morris and Graham Moxham, and subsequently at Northampton Town. The following 4-3 defeat at Nottingham Forest, for whom Neil Martin scored twice and the future Rovers player Miah Dennehy played a key role, showed the club could compete with higher division sides. There was much to gain from season 1973/74, and Megson's next challenge would be to maintain the club's newly regained Second Division status.

1974/75

By the turn of the century, many clubs greeted promotion by splashing into the transfer market and forking out millions of pounds on strengthening their squad. The return to Division Two after twelve seasons away saw no such reaction from Don Megson's Rovers. Despite the sale of captain Mike Green to Plymouth Argyle, where he repeated his success by helping the Pilgrims up from Division Three in his first season, the Rovers manager stuck with his successful side. Perhaps this attitude was reflected in Rovers' season-long struggle to avoid relegation, a situation repeated almost annually until the relegation season of 1980/81.

The previous season's success was rewarded with a summer tour of Australia, New Zealand and Thailand. It was a largely familiar-looking Rovers side that took a point off Notts County before what was to be the largest opening day crowd for a home game until 1999. There was a brief honeymoon period, Rovers remaining unbeaten for three games, with Gordon Fearnley scoring against his former club at Hillsborough and also in the home win over Hull City. Reality soon struck, however, when a rampant Sunderland side scored five times at Roker Park. A hat-trick in that game from Billy Hughes was the first conceded in the league by Rovers for over four years. Rovers responded with a fine home victory over a strong Aston Villa side. Phil Bater, a debutant at full-back, subdued the former Eastville favourite, Ray Graydon, and two shots from Alan Warboys, set up by Peter Aitken on fifty-four minutes and by Gordon Fearnley five minutes from time, brought about a memorable victory.

There followed sufficient heavy defeats for Rovers to spend the remainder of the season looking anxiously over their collective shoulders at the relegation zone. Bolton also scored five times, with John Byrom only denied a hat-trick when his manager Ian Greaves credited his third goal to Stuart Lee, and Rovers lost 3-0 to York City, Southampton and Portsmouth. In the game at The Dell, all the goals were scored by England international forward Mick Channon, who was to play for Rovers briefly during 1982/83. He and Joe Riley remain the only two players to have appeared in league football for Rovers and scored a league hat-trick against them. Southampton also won at Eastville, when Eadie pulled back a misdirected Channon lob, sixteen minutes from time, into his own net.

A tough season is always made harder by marginal decisions. Single-goal defeats at home to Southampton and in four tough away games, notably at Villa Park, reflected the fact that results were not going Rovers' way. When Fulham won 2-1 at Eastville in March, Colin Dobson, in his first home league appearance of the season, missed a penalty. Rovers won a right-wing corner in the dying seconds of the goalless draw at home to Orient in November, but the final whistle was blown before substitute John Rudge's flying header hit the goal net.

The long-awaited local derby at Eastville proved to be a disaster from Rovers' point of view. Having lost three consecutive games in the run-up to the match, Rovers were also deprived of the services of the ever-reliable goalkeeper Jim Eadie. His absence through injury after eighty-four consecutive league games enabled a one-match recall for Dick Sheppard, who had not played for almost two years since his sickening injury against Tranmere Rovers. Rovers, in fact, led at half-time through Fearnley, before being buried by an avalanche of City goals past the beleaguered Sheppard at the Muller Road end.

That relegation was ultimately avoided came about as a result of several well-earned victories. After considerable pressure, it took a last-minute header from the dependable Stuart Taylor, following a corner in front of the Tote End, to beat Oxford United in February. Nottingham Forest were beaten 4-2 at Eastville, while two Alan Warboys goals defeated Sunderland. Rovers also completed a memorable double over old rivals Oldham Athletic. In a remarkable game at Boundary Park, Rovers won 4-3 after a goalless first half and a bizarre final forty-five minutes. Jeff Coombes gave Rovers a forty-sixth minute lead, and the visitors were 3-0 ahead within twenty minutes. Once Ian Robins and Maurice Whittle, from a penalty, had cut their lead, Rovers were grateful for Gordon Fearnley's second goal of the game, five minutes from time, which gave them a cushion that Robins promptly halved. Rovers have appeared in other league games featuring seven or more second-half goals, but never after a scoreless half-time. Five weeks later, goals from Warboys and Taylor brought victory in the return game.

The introduction of two new faces in March, in young Bristol-born centre-back Graham Day, replacing the injured Taylor, and experienced midfielder Wilf Smith, brought a string of more positive results. Dobson and the ever-combative Frankie Prince both scored in consecutive fixtures in April. Rovers drew four of their final five away league matches, including the local derby at Ashton Gate. courtesy of a thirty-third-minute own goal when Dobson's high cross deflected in off Gary Collier's shoulder. Manchester United visited Eastville at Easter, having suffered the ignominy of relegation from Division One twelve months earlier. Rovers, having lost 2-0 at Old Trafford in September, gained a point through substitute Bruce Bannister's last-minute close-range equaliser.

Although able to field a side predominantly unchanged from 1973/74 and largely stable through the season, Rovers undeniably struggled on their much-awaited return to Division Two. Warboys, clearly top scorer for the club with twelve league goals, and the versatile Peter Aitken both played in every league fixture. Warboys and Bannister never scored in the same game. For an attacking partnership that had yielded so many goals (both players had scored in seven different league matches the previous season, both scoring hat-tricks at Brighton) this year was a great disappointment. The following season brought little further joy, and it was August 1976 before both scored in the same match again.

Rovers players past and future featured, at least nominally, in both major domestic Cup finals. Bobby Gould, a Rovers player by 1977, was an unused substitute for West Ham, who beat Fulham 2-0 in the FA Cup final. The only goal in the League Cup final was scored by the former Rovers outside-right Ray Graydon as Aston Villa defeated Norwich City. Graydon had also scored the winning goal after an hour on Boxing Day, capitalising on Taylor's misdirected back pass, as Rovers lost narrowly at Villa Park.

In contrast to these players' achievements, Rovers were not able to feature largely in cup competitions. A solitary Warboys drive four minutes from time disposed of Plymouth Argyle on aggregate in the League Cup, before Luton Town defeated Rovers at Kenilworth Road. Second Division status meant Rovers did not enter the FA Cup before the third round, and victory at Blackburn gave Rovers a first appearance for six years in the fourth round. Third Division champions-elect Blackburn Rovers had proved easy prey, but reigning League champions Derby County beat Rovers comfortably through a goal from Kevin Hector and a Bruce Rioch penalty. The crowd of almost 28,000 at the Baseball Ground was bettered all season only by the 30,000 who saw the local derby at Ashton Gate and the remarkable 42,948 that witnessed Rovers' first league visit to Old Trafford. Rovers retained the Gloucestershire Cup by defeating Bristol City 2-1 with goals from Prince and Warboys.

On 25 February, an Eastville crowd of 3,000 saw England Youth draw 1-1 with Spain Youth in a Youth International qualifying match. The English side contained three future full internationals in Bryan Robson of West Bromwich Albion, Ray Wilkins of Chelsea and Peter Barnes of Manchester City.

1975/76

Second Division football was proving tough for Don Megson's side. A difficult 1974/75 season was followed by another of struggle and ultimate success in avoiding relegation. Once again, with limited funds available, the only new names were those nurtured carefully in the club's rapidly growing South Wales nursery. John Rudge's departure was offset by the continued emergence of David Staniforth, of whose five league goals four earned Rovers a point. The average home crowd, despite dropping to 10,022, was nonetheless the final five-figure average attendance at Rovers' home matches in the twentieth century.

Defeat at Oldham Athletic on the opening day, when Peter Aitken scored an own goal, marked the league debuts of two of the new influx of young Welsh players. One was David Williams, initially a left-back, later an accomplished midfield general and ultimately player-manager, and the holder of a very belated Welsh cap. The other was Andrew Evans, who showed immense promise on the left-wing before an exciting career was cut cruelly short by injury in 1977. Tony Pulis, Wayne Powell and Paul Lewis were not far behind. Pulis made his league debut in the cauldron of a local derby at Ashton Gate, where he was later manager. Powell became the first Rovers player to score as a substitute on his league debut, as Rovers recorded a second consecutive 4-2 win over Nottingham Forest, while Lewis deputised for Jim Eadie in the final match of the season.

Eric McMordie's fifty-seventh-minute own goal earned victory over York City and, after two creditable draws, Alan Warboys scored both Rovers' goals in a 2-0 victory over Fulham at Craven Cottage, the first away league win since December 1974. Rovers were to record a league double over the previous season's beaten FA Cup finalists. After a promising start, a relegation dogfight was not high on the club's list of expectations. Most surprising of all was that, after his goals at Fulham, Warboys was not to score again in the league until the final game, his tally of three being a highly disappointing return from such a proven goalscorer.

In November, Rovers drew five consecutive league games, thus equalling a club record set in 1966/67, starting with a 1-1 draw with Blackburn Rovers. The most remarkable of these draws was at Roker Park, where Rovers belied their poor record at Sunderland and earned a point through David Williams' first goal for the club. The crowd of 31,356 was the largest at a Rovers game all season. At this stage, after a twelve-match unbeaten run, Rovers had in fact only lost two of their opening eighteen league matches. Ten of these games, however, had been drawn, and the loss of points through the club's inability to turn good performances into victories was to prove a major factor as the season progressed.

In the spring, four consecutive away games were lost 3-0 as Rovers looked over their shoulder at the trapdoor back to Division Three. Rovers failed to score in five consecutive league games away from Eastville prior to the now customary victory at Blackburn Rovers. Mick Channon, later a Rovers player, and Bobby

Stokes, scorer of the winning goal in that season's FA Cup final, were among Southampton's scorers at The Dell. Derek Hales scored twice for Charlton Athletic, while one of three scorers for Plymouth Argyle, led by the former Rovers captain Mike Green, was Paul Mariner, later an England international striker. The Plymouth game marked the final appearance in a Rovers shirt of Colin Dobson, who became youth coach at Coventry City prior to working in footballing circles in the Middle East.

Three consecutive wins in October, against Sunderland and at Portsmouth and Blackpool, proved the highlight of the season. Bruce Bannister scored in all three, and the fine 4-1 win at Bloomfield Park also saw Fearnley's first two goals for almost a year and Smith's first league goal for the club. It was to be December 1976 before Rovers next won two consecutive league games. From November to the end of the 1975/76 season, only five further league games were won and only two of those by two clear goals. Martyn Britten's eighteenth-minute goal, his first for the club, paved the way for a 2-0 victory over Portsmouth, while Southampton were defeated at Eastville by two Frankie Prince goals. Ultimately, Rovers' final four away games of the season resulted in heavy defeats.

What made Rovers' continuing struggle all the more galling was the success experienced across the city at Ashton Gate. Excitement levels rose as the season progressed, and a lone goal from Clive Whitehead in April was enough to defeat Portsmouth and propel Bristol City, with West Bromwich Albion and Sunderland, into Division One. Top-flight football had returned to Bristol after an absence of sixty-five years. Yet this merely emphasised the gulf between the haves and the have-nots. Before, during and after season 1975/76, Don Megson was unable to delve into the transfer market to strengthen Rovers' squad. Another summer's inaction was to be followed by the mid-season sale during 1976/77 of both Warboys and Bannister, the very names that had brought the club to where they were. They were to be replaced, ultimately, not by new signings, but by home-grown talent in the form of Paul Randall and Steve White.

A crowd of over 35,000 saw Rovers earn a highly creditable 1-1 draw in the third round of the FA Cup at Stamford Bridge. Peter Bonetti, Charlie Cooke, Ray Wilkins and Ron Harris were among Chelsea's star names. It took a Bill Garner equaliser from Wilkins' thirty-fourth-minute free-kick to earn a replay after Warboys' eighteenth-minute header from a Williams cross had given Rovers an unlikely lead. Forty-eight hours later, a solitary Kenny Swain goal handed Chelsea a 1-0 replay victory.

There was more success in the League Cup. Cardiff City were disposed of in the first round, with Warboys and Bannister, free from the shackles of Division Two expectation, both getting on the scoresheet in the away leg. Substitute Gordon Fearnley's eighty-third-minute goal at The Dell, after Mick Channon had shot wide from a penalty, brought a third-round tie at home to Newcastle United. Rovers had chances to win, but were taken to a replay that was lost in front of a crowd of over 25,000 at St James' Park to the eventual finalists. Irving Nattrass and Tommy Craig, from a penalty, scored the replay goals, with considerable help from the instrumental Stewart Barrowclough, later a Rovers player. An exciting Gloucestershire Cup final was lost 3-2 at Ashton Gate, despite goals for Rovers from David Williams and Stuart Taylor.

The implications of the 1975 Safety of Sports Grounds Act led to £70,000 being invested in Eastville Stadium. However, this served simply as a reminder to Rovers that their lease of the ground was due to expire in 1979. With hindsight, it is easy to see what steps could have been taken at this stage concerning the club's future in Bristol.

1976/77

As Bristol City embarked on their much-heralded return to top flight football, Bristol Rovers attempted to steady the ship and attain at least mid-table status in Division Two. Yet, it was difficult to see how this could be achieved. With the exception of emerging young Welsh talent, a struggling team was now ageing. Without the arrival of new faces, it was clearly going to be another long, hard season.

The players who appeared in the Rovers side on the opening day of the season constituted, broadly speaking, the side that had won only five of its final twenty-nine league matches in 1975/76. Blackpool were the visitors to Eastville and, with Bob Hatton scoring twice, they ran out comfortable 4-1 winners, Warboys scoring his first goal at home in sixteen months. However, Megson had few options in team selection. Money was still not available for buying new players, and all he could attempt was a reshuffle. Wilf Smith, David Williams and Peter Aitken were all tried in defence and midfield, and young full-back Phil Bater was recalled on the right and later on the left.

In comparison with certain seasons earlier in Rovers' league history, there were no disastrous results. It was just as well, for goal average had replaced goal difference as a means to calculate league tables. By their own standards, though, Rovers were dealt several crushing blows. Blackpool scored four times when Rovers visited Bloomfield Road and another 4-0 defeat, this time at Oldham Athletic, featured a hat-trick from Vic Halom. In addition to the FA Cup defeat, where losing was no embarrassment but the one-sided scoreline was, Rovers were also crushed by Wolves at Eastville over Christmas. The Wolves side, heading for the Division Two championship, was certainly a strong one, but to go five goals behind before David Williams' last-minute consolation goal indicated the extent of work required on the team.

On a positive note, Rovers won their first away game, with both Alan Warboys and Bruce Bannister scoring at Cardiff. For 'Smash' and 'Grab', a partnership that had terrorised defences at will during the early part of 1973/74, this represented the first time since January 1974, a period of over two-and-a-half years, that both had scored in the same league match. A huge win over Notts County in September, where both David Staniforth and the recalled Gordon Fearnley scored pairs, their first goals of the season, was the biggest victory at Eastville since October 1972. A significantly comfortable 3-0 win against Hull City in November featured a first Rovers goal for the highly promising Andrew Evans, after six minutes, and Alan Warboys' 100th league goal just two minutes before half-time.

The home fixture with Hereford United in November summed up, in many ways, the intense frustration of the season. Both Warboys and Bannister were able to score very early on, with Rovers leading 2-0 inside ten minutes. It was the first-ever league meeting of the clubs and newly promoted Hereford seized their opportunities to lead 3-2 after just eighteen minutes. Steve Davey scored twice, affording the luxury of a missed penalty from Dixie McNeil, whose shot four minutes from time, following a foul by Taylor, went wide of the post. Although a Wayne Powell goal, after David Staniforth's shot seventeen minutes from time had been blocked, earned a draw at Edgar Street, Rovers never gained the opportunity for revenge, as Hereford were relegated that season and never returned to Division Two. Bannister's goal proved to be his last for the club, as the old guard from 1973/74 was dismantled.

Two mid-season sales were to radically alter the make-up of Rovers' side. Bruce Bannister had scored only four goals in eighteen games and was sold to Plymouth Argyle in December in a deal that brought Jimmy Hamilton to Eastville; Hamilton was to score just once in his Rovers career. Alan Warboys left for Fulham, his sixth league club, in a deal worth £30,000. The pair met up again later at Hull City before both embarked on successful business careers, Bannister's sports shoe manufacturing company in Bradford proving particularly lucrative. By the season's end, when Jim Eadie joined Bath City and Kenny Stephens moved to Hereford, only the ever-reliable Stuart Taylor was left from the promotion season. These players were not replaced by experienced footballers, but by teenage stars-in-the-making and, at least in the meantime, Rovers were destined to continue to struggle in Division Two.

There was, though, some hope. Seventeen-year-old Martin Thomas, who replaced Eadie in goal for January's game at Charlton Athletic, and Vaughan Jones, who was to captain Rovers in the 1989/90 championship season, both made their first league appearances. Rovers regularly fielded five young Welsh-born players in the side, products of the club's nursery system. On the other hand, they were not ready to deal with some of the more experienced names in football. Chelsea, Nottingham Forest and Southampton all brought big-name players to Eastville. The legendary maverick Robin Friday was in the Cardiff City side that drew 1-1 at Eastville in January, while George Best scored the only goal of the game, with a first-minute mishit shot, when Fulham defeated Rovers at Craven Cottage in September.

At least the season finished on a high note, with Rovers reaching fifteenth place in the table following a late seven-match unbeaten run. Young Wayne Powell, belatedly recalled to the side, scored six goals in this run. His eighty-fifth minute far-post header at home to Sheffield United completed a memorable hat-trick, the first in the league by a Rovers player since December 1973. He had been given just one league start in 1975/76, and this spell in the spring of 1977 represented the high point of his Rovers career. With Rovers safe from relegation, there was a final 2-2 draw with Bolton Wanderers, who were reduced to ten men by the sending-off of Paul Jones. Special mention should also be made of late wins at Hull City and Carlisle United, the latter through substitute Hamilton's sole league goal for the club after Rovers had earlier trailed 2-0.

There were many changes through the season. No player appeared in every game. Top-scorer Warboys and his sidekick Bannister had left the club. However, for a third consecutive season, Rovers survived relegation, achieving league doubles over Hull City, Sheffield United and Carlisle United along the way. Elsewhere, former Rovers player Larry Lloyd, in the Anglo-Scottish Cup final, and Ray Graydon, in the League Cup final, were achieving greater success. Rovers' scouts were busy monitoring the progress of young Paul Randall, whose mid-season transfer from Glastonbury to Frome Town had brought him goalscoring success. On his shoulders much of Rovers' immediate future was to rest.

Once again, cup competitions brought little joy for Rovers. Larry Lloyd's Nottingham Forest were held to two 1-1 draws, but Rovers capitulated in the second replay at Villa Park. Forest scored six times without reply, with England international Tony Woodcock scoring twice. Four other household names – Viv Anderson, Ian Bowyer, John O'Hare and Peter Withe – also featured on a decidedly one-sided scoresheet. At this point, Rovers conceded fourteen goals in a run of three league and cup matches. In the League Cup, Warboys and Bannister both scored penalties against Cardiff City, one in each leg, but Rovers were eliminated 6-5 on aggregate after Tony Evans had scored all the visitors' goals in an exciting 4-4 draw at Eastville. Rovers had led 4-2 on the night and 5-4 on aggregate, with just over twenty minutes remaining, before Evans headed past Eadie to complete his hat-trick. His fourth goal, eight minutes from time, sealed the visitors' overall victory. No other opponent has scored four goals in a League Cup tie against Rovers. Bristol City won the Gloucestershire Cup final with a single goal victory at Eastville.

1977/78

It was the form of teenage striker Paul Randall that stood out in the 1977/78 season. The summer signing from Frome Town scored twenty goals in twenty-eight (plus three sub) league matches, the first Rovers player since Alan Warboys in

1973/74 to break into the magical seasonal tally of twenty league goals. Yet it was not simply the goalscoring that marked Randall out, but his all-round contribution to the team. With him in the side, despite some heavy defeats, Rovers were to finish the season in eighteenth place in Division Two.

Promoted Cardiff City were Rovers' opening day opponents. Rovers fielded just the one new face in Randall, though Martin Thomas, Eadie's long-term successor in goal, had only one league match under his belt. Randall's debut goal at Ninian Park was one of four in his opening five games. After drawing the first three games, Rovers were not to win until the ninth, when David Williams scored twice against Mansfield Town. Randall's absence from that match meant that he was not on the winning side in a league fixture until Guy Fawkes' Day.

As the new season unfolded, Don Megson entered the transfer market in search of big-name players to bolster his side. With Bristol City temporarily on top of Division One, it was clearly time to build up Rovers' stature. The experienced former Crystal Palace full-back Tony Taylor arrived on trial and quickly gained a regular place in the side. Mike Barry joined Rovers from Carlisle United in an exchange deal that took Jimmy Hamilton to Brunton Park, while the former Birmingham City footballer Paul Hendrie arrived on a free transfer. The biggest-name signing, however, was the highly experienced forward Bobby Gould. Gould joined Rovers, his seventh league club, for a £10,000 fee the day before they were due to meet Blackburn Rovers at Eastville.

It was very much a new-look Rovers side that opposed Blackburn on 15 October. Eighteen-year-old Glyn Jones was in goal, Taylor, Barry and Hendrie all played and, in the absence of Randall, Gould made his club debut. It was an opening game to remember; Gould scored a first-half hat-trick after three, thirteen and thirty-five minutes, and David Staniforth added another midway through the second half as Rovers ran up a convincing 4-1 win. Only Joe Riley and Jimmy McCambridge, in Rovers' long Football League history, can match Gould's achievement of three goals on his debut. Rovers, it was said, had turned the corner and the tough away fixture at White Hart Lane seven days later was anticipated with relish.

Tottenham Hotspur's relegation to Division Two meant a first-ever league meeting with Rovers, and television cameras were there to record the game. It turned into a living nightmare for Rovers, who crashed to their heaviest post-war defeat. For all the pre-match optimism, Rovers were three goals behind by half-time, conceded four goals in a nine-minute spell and ended up beaten 9-0. Bristolian Colin Lee scored four goals and Ian Moores three in twenty-six second-half minutes, only the third occasion that two opponents had scored hat-tricks in a league game against Rovers. Future England international managers scored in the last minute of each half; Peter Taylor on the stroke of half-time and Glenn Hoddle the soul-destroying ninth in the dying seconds. One player who was singled out for praise was goalkeeper Jones, who was largely credited with keeping the score down to single figures. He played again on the same pitch only nine days later, this time helping the reserves to a 1-1 draw.

It took Rovers just seven days to recover sufficiently to manage a goalless draw at home to a strong Southampton side and to return to winning ways, once Randall was back against Millwall. The Southampton game, though, marked the end of winger Andrew Evans' career. Just days after his twentieth birthday, Evans broke his right ankle in this game and a career of great promise was brought to a sad and premature end. Nor were Rovers able to shake the Spurs defeat wholly from their collective systems. Sunderland put five goals past the recalled Martin Thomas, Steve Taylor scored a hat-trick in Oldham Athletic's 4-1 win, and three goals from Malcolm Poskett led Rovers to an embarrassing 4-0 home defeat at the hands of Brighton. For the first time in fifteen years and the last time in the twentieth century, Rovers had conceded four league hat-tricks in a season. The seventy-seven league goals conceded in finishing eighteenth in Division Two also constituted the club's worst defensive record for a decade.

The major after-effect of these results was the departure in November of manager Don Megson, who took over at Portland Timbers in the North American Soccer League. Rovers promoted from within, with the former Scottish international Bobby Campbell, the club's trainer since May 1961, being swiftly appointed manager, a post he held for two years. He was the third Scottish international footballer to manage the club. Under his leadership, results improved to a certain degree. There was a morale-boosting 3-2 home win over Sunderland, featuring Stuart Taylor's first goal in almost two years, and Rovers put three goals without reply past Crystal Palace. Late-season 4-1 wins over Sheffield United and Stoke City, for whom Garth Crooks scored in both meetings with Rovers, saw Randall and his fellow teenager Steve White score three times between them in each game. White weighed in with four goals in his first eight league appearances.

Randall, however, was not to be outdone. A rich vein of goalscoring through the spring saw him score in eight consecutive league games. From late December until early April, he was to score in thirteen out of fourteen league appearances. This included a goal in an exciting 2-2 draw with Charlton Athletic, when Bobby Gould converted an eighty-seventh minute penalty and the visitors had Phil Warman sent off. Randall also scored in a 3-1 victory over Millwall in a match played at Fratton Park, as The Den had been closed following crowd trouble. It was significant that Randall should score the only goal of the final game of the season in a victory at Hull City to give an element of hope for Rovers' prospects in the forthcoming season.

Short-lived participation in the League Cup was compounded by the fact that Phil Bater contrived to score own goals for Walsall in both legs of a 3-1 aggregate defeat.

There was an attendance of over 20,000 at every one of Rovers' four FA Cup ties. Rovers were drawn to play Sunderland at Roker Park, only weeks after their 5-1 defeat there. Despite missing David Williams, Bobby Gould's twenty-first minute lobbed goal after Staniforth had flicked on Day's free-kick earned an outstanding 1-0 win. Southampton were the visitors to Eastville in round four, and a memorable pair of goals from Paul Randall brought a comprehensive victory. When Ipswich Town visited snowy Eastville in February, two David Williams goals seemed to be leading Rovers to their third-ever FA Cup quarter-final appearance. However, deep into injury time, Robin Turner equalised to break Rovers' hearts. Ipswich won the replay at Portman Road with ease and went on to win the Cup that season, the only time in the club's history.

Bristol City retained the Gloucestershire Cup, a crowd of 10,178 at Ashton Gate witnessing their comfortable three-goal victory over Rovers. There was also a 3-1 defeat on the same ground in the Anglo-Scottish Cup, in which competition Rovers also lost to a single goal at home to Plymouth Argyle and drew with Birmingham City to find themselves eliminated at the end of the group stage. A Rovers Old Players side defeated Bristol City Old Players 1-0 on 28 February, thanks to a Geoff Bradford goal. The introduction of speedway to Eastville, where meetings were held between 1977 and 1979, meant the pitch was necessarily reduced to 110 x 70 yards, making it, along with those of Halifax Town and Swansea City, the smallest in the Football League.

1978/79

Bobby Campbell's preseason plans, like those of so many managers before him, were heavily restricted by the absence of spending power. For all the major transfer fees ahead (Barrowclough's fee in 1979 was to remain a club record until Rovers were back in the Second Division over a decade later) Campbell's structuring was slow and quiet. Youngsters such as Vaughan Jones, Gary Clarke, Gary Mabbutt and Paul Petts were allowed to develop and break into the league side. The only significant summer signing was that of the former Eire international winger Miah Dennehy, a £20,000 signing from Walsall at the end of July. He had scored the first-ever hat-trick in an Irish Cup final when playing for Cork Hibernian against Waterford in 1972, but he did not manage a goal in his first season at Eastville.

Before the season could begin in earnest, Rovers participated for a second consecutive year in the Anglo-Scottish Cup. Dennehy and Clarke both played in a 1-0 home victory over Cardiff City, and young striker Alan Hoult replaced goalscorer Paul Randall near the end. Rovers then lost embarrassingly 6-1 at Bristol City and 2-1 at Fulham and were eliminated. The League Cup followed a similar pattern, with Peter Aitken scoring a rare goal with a 25-yard drive as Rovers led Hereford United 2-0 and missed a penalty in the first round first leg, before conceding a late strike and then crashing 4-0 at Edgar Street to lose 5-2 on aggregate.

Revenge over Fulham was swift as Rovers, with Dennehy making his league debut and six Welsh-born players in the side, defeated the Cottagers 3-1 at Eastville. The first goal was scored after a quarter of an hour by Paul Randall, who was to enjoy continued early season success. Bobby Gould scored in the first two league matches before joining Hereford United as player-coach. A run of two early away defeats was arrested by a confidence-boosting 4-2 home win over Cardiff City; a sixth-minute Steve Grapes own goal from Mike Barry's inswinging corner put Rovers on their way, with Paul Randall scoring and David Staniforth adding two close-range finishes. John Buchanan scored a penalty in both fixtures for Cardiff City against Rovers.

The 3-0 defeat at Charlton Athletic in August had marked Stuart Taylor's 487th league appearance for Rovers, surpassing Harry Bamford's club record. His 500th game, a 2-1 home win over Sheffield United, came just seven days after the extraordinary return tie with Charlton. Rovers had won all seven of their home games prior to the London side's visit, including an impressive victory over Blackburn Rovers 4-1, with Randall scoring his first league hat-trick, and over Newcastle United 2-0, when Randall claimed both goals. A winning goal from Staniforth had defeated a strong Orient side featuring, in Tunji Banjo and John Chiedozie, two Nigerian international midfielders. Equally, Charlton boasted an unbeaten away record, but nothing indicated the ten-goal thriller that was to unfold.

After Dick Tydeman had put the visitors ahead on fifteen minutes, Randall responded with two quick goals so that Rovers led by the half-hour mark. In the four minutes leading up to half-time, though, Keith Peacock created goals for Martyn Robinson and Mick Flanagan, and Rovers trailed 3-2 at the break. Flanagan put Charlton two goals ahead after forty-nine minutes, and though David Williams, shooting through a ruck of players eight minutes later, narrowed the gap, Robinson's second goal, after sixty-three minutes, restored the visitors' two-goal lead. After Peter Aitken's shot was saved just three minutes later, Randall completed his hat-trick and Williams equalised from the penalty spot after a sixty-eighth-minute foul on substitute Paul Hendrie. Rovers' second 5-5 draw in league football, the first being against Exeter City in November 1934, had seen ten goals in a frenetic fifty-three-minute spell in the middle of the match.

December, however, brought a turnaround in fortunes. A 5-0 defeat at Roker Park, where Wayne Entwhistle grabbed a hat-trick, was followed by a dramatic end to Rovers' unbeaten home record. Full-backs Brian Chambers and Nick Chatterton both scored penalties as Rovers lost 3-0 at home to Millwall. Rovers were to win only two more home league games all season. It was time for action on the transfer front, and Campbell, having earlier secured Norwich City's eighteen-year-old winger Phil Lythgoe on a month's loan, succeeded in buying the midfielder he required in Gary Emmanuel. The nephew of a former Rovers trialist, Emmanuel commanded a club record fee of £50,000 as he joined Rovers from Birmingham City.

At the end of December, to the major disappointment of Rovers fans, Paul Randall was sold to Stoke City for a club record fee of £180,000. He had scored thirty-three goals in forty-nine (plus three sub) league matches over an eighteen-month period and was not easily replaced. Steve White scored twice at Luton and twice more in the win at Millwall, the latterly ironically by the same 3-0 margin as the Eastville fixture, yet the goals no longer flowed so freely. Prior to the Burnley game, where Vaughan Jones, from the penalty spot after thirty-five minutes, recorded his first league goal for Rovers, the side had gone four matches without a goal. It was to be a year after Randall's departure before Rovers next scored four times in a league match.

Relegation was staved off, by Rovers' immediate standards, with great ease. Sixteenth place in Division Two reflected much of the early season success. The reserves, meanwhile, finished ninth in the Football Combination, their highest final position since 1968/69, and a height never again attained in the twentieth century. After three straight defeats, Rovers rested Stuart Taylor for the final game of the season, leaving Martin Thomas and David Williams as the club's only ever-presents. Williams scored the only goal at Wrexham in the final game of the season, with a 20-yard drive from Keith Brown's pass twelve minutes from time, to end as the club's second highest scorer behind Randall. This last match saw Rovers field the youngest side in the club's history. Brown, Martin Shaw, Dave Palmer and Mike England were given their first full league appearances; England was to wait over six years for his second league match. Gary Emmanuel, at twenty-five, was the oldest player in a side with an average age of twenty.

The FA Cup saw Rovers record 1-0 wins at Swansea City and at home to Charlton Athletic before losing at Portman Road to Ipswich Town for a second consecutive season. Steve White scored in all three matches. Charlton had defeated Southern League Maidstone United in round three despite floodlight failure in the replay, after their strikers Mick Flanagan and Derek Hales had been sent off in the initial tie for fighting each other. Rovers' round four victory was to be Flanagan's only appearance for Charlton in the second half of the season. The crowd at the fifth round game, 23,231, was the largest to watch Rovers all season, and spectators saw Rovers overwhelmed by an Ipswich Town side destined to finish sixth in Division One. The Cup holders won with two goals from Alan Brazil and one each from Arnold Muhren, Paul Mariner, Mick Mills and substitute David Geddis.

Rovers also hosted testimonial games at Eastville for midfielder Frankie Prince, 0-2 against Bristol City, and goalkeeper Dick Sheppard, which West Bromwich Albion won 3-2. The most unusual match, though, was against the touring Zambian national side on 24 October. A crowd of 4,000 saw Rovers beat Zambia 4-1 at Eastville, with goals from Paul Randall, Phil Lythgoe, Miah Dennehy and David Williams.

1979/80

Two highly experienced players were signed in the summer of 1979 to add strength to the Rovers side. At the end of July, Bobby Campbell paid £100,000 to Birmingham City for the services of Stewart Barrowclough, a former Barnsley and Newcastle United winger who had won five England under-23 caps. This figure represented a record fee spent by the club and was to remain unsurpassed until 1991. Two weeks later, Terry Cooper arrived from Bristol City as player-coach. Cooper had won twenty England caps while on Leeds United's books and was to be Rovers' manager before the season was out.

Within days of Cooper's arrival, Rovers were knocked out of the League Cup on aggregate by Torquay United when they let an away lead slip. League form, however, appeared more consistent. Two consecutive home wins were followed by a highly creditable draw at Birmingham City. The speedy and dependable Barrowclough scored from the penalty spot in three consecutive league games, a club record later equalled by Ian Holloway in October 1990, and scored six penalties all season, including one in each game with Orient.

All illusions, however, were shattered by a heavy defeat at Cambridge, which set Rovers on a run of poor results through the autumn. Floyd Streete gave the home side a first-minute lead, and Lindsay Smith and Alan Biley added goals either side of half-time. Although David Williams pulled a goal back after an hour, Cambridge United's 4-1 victory was sealed nineteen minutes from time. This was the first of nine defeats in fourteen games that sent Rovers tumbling down the table and ultimately lost Campbell his job.

While Bobby Campbell stayed in Bristol, working outside professional football, Rovers appointed youth coach Harold Jarman as his temporary successor. Not only was Jarman the first Bristolian to manage the club, but he was also a figure who had gained huge respect in his fourteen years as a Rovers player. Within days of his arrival, successive home wins over Oldham Athletic and Swansea City led the side to believe it could pull clear of relegation. Under his guidance, Rovers beat Chelsea 3-0 and secured enough points to avoid Third Division football. It was, therefore, scant reward for Jarman when, with just two matches remaining, his application for the full-time manager's job was turned down and Terry Cooper was appointed.

In October, an easily distinguishable character in English football, Brian Kilcline, had appeared at Eastville on his league debut. His first professional club, Notts County, won this particular game 3-2. Kilcline's most famous day was perhaps that of the 1987 FA Cup final, where he and Spurs' Gary Mabbutt, who was in the Rovers side against Notts County, both got on the scoresheet. Three days later, Rovers were undone by Bob Hatton, who scored a first-half hat-trick as Luton Town won 3-1 at Kenilworth Road, Gary Emmanuel's only goal of the season reducing the deficit after half-time. It was Luton who paid £195,000 on

Christmas Eve for the signature of Rovers' exciting young forward, Steve White. It was a club record transfer fee received by Rovers, but the two main strikers had now been sold in the space of twelve months.

No sooner had White left than Rovers ironically ran up their largest win of the season. Swansea City were beaten 4-1 at Eastville.Welshmen Alan Waddle scored for both sides either side of half-time before Miah Dennehy, set up three times by Barrowclough in thirty-four second-half minutes, scored a memorable hat-trick. They were to be the mercurial winger's last three goals for the club for, after a trial with Cardiff City, he began the 1980/81 season at Trowbridge Town. Frankie Prince, who had won four Welsh under-23 caps during a long association with the club, played his last game for Rovers in the heavy defeat at bottom-of-the-table Charlton Athletic, while centre-half Stuart Taylor made the last of his club record 546 Football League appearances in the 3-3 draw with Preston North End at Eastville in March. There were six goals in twenty-nine second-half minutes, as Rovers, 2-0 up just after the hour mark, dropped a point thanks to Peter Aitken's own goal three minutes from time. Young Tony Pulis, who scored Rovers' third goal against Preston after eighty-two minutes, also scored in the victory over Chelsea. In a fine team performance, where Aitken was outstanding, Shaun Penny grabbed two goals to give Rovers a convincing win. This victory, however, was marred by the disgraceful behaviour of some spectators at the Chelsea end, who pushed down a wall supporting the Muller Road terraces.

Bobby Campbell had taken an untried teenager, Noel Parkinson, on loan. Jarman's approach was to go for experience, and thirty-year-old Chic Bates arrived at Eastville in March. He played in the final eleven league games of the season and scored in consecutive home draws with Sunderland and Leicester City, two of the promoted clubs. Youth was also given a go as the season drew to a close, with Paul Petts and Mike Barrett being offered league experience. The former was the son of Eastville favourite Johnny Petts and, like his father, was an England Youth international. The latter was a natural ball-playing wingman, whose close control and ability to beat opponents was to endear him to an adoring Eastville public. New manager Cooper gave debuts to two young Welsh players – Mark Hughes, a cousin of the England defender Emlyn Hughes, and Ashley Griffiths – in the meaningless final game of the season at home to West Ham United. The Hammers treated the game as a warm-up for the FA Cup final seven days later, where Trevor Brooking's thirteenth-minute header proved enough to defeat Arsenal.

Martin Thomas in goal had played a key role in maintaining Rovers' Second Division status. Rovers only conceded four goals in a game twice, and Thomas was able to keep five consecutive clean sheets in early spring until he was finally beaten by a Teddy Maybank goal at Fulham. Thomas was one of a number of Welsh players in the side; indeed, eleven out of the twenty-five players used in League Football during 1979/80 were born in South Wales. Bristol-born goalkeeper Phil Kite was given his club debut in the Gloucestershire Cup final, while the unfortunate Andrew Evans was granted a testimonial game against Southampton at Eastville. Prior to Geoff Merrick's testimonial game at Ashton Gate on 12 May, Rovers Old Players played out a goalless draw against Bristol City Old Players.

Rovers were to experience no joy in any of the cup tournaments. Goals from Gordon Cowans and Gary Shaw earned FA Cup success at Eastville for a very talented Aston Villa team, while Les Lawrence scored in both legs as a struggling Torquay United side put Rovers out of the League Cup. It was the same story in the Gloucestershire Cup, where Rovers, having lost the first two games under Cooper's management, lost to a second-half goal from Howard Pritchard at Ashton Gate.

A temporary extension to Rovers' tenancy at Eastville enabled the club to remain in east Bristol into the 1980s. However, fears continued to grow for the long-term future, and what the club could not afford was to suffer as disastrous a season as the one that now lay ahead. In the meantime, along with all other Second Division venues, the stadium was brought under the provisions of the 1975 Safety of Sports Grounds Act, the brief of which was now extended beyond the top division. This act specified that all grounds with a capacity exceeding 10,000 were to be 'designated' and therefore hold a safety certificate issued by the local authority. Eastville Stadium fell into this bracket and, amid spiralling costs and falling attendances – a late 1970s phenomenon – Rovers were forced to comply with legal requirements. This the club clearly did not, for Rovers were later fined £200 for making unauthorised changes to the layout of the stadium.

9

The 1980s

1980/81

This was a season of record lows. Only five league wins all season, only four wins at Eastville in any competition, just thirty-four league goals, including twenty-one at home; all these were unwanted club records. It was Valentine's Day before Rovers recorded their second win of the season. The previous victory had been the first in seventeen matches under Terry Cooper. Overshadowing this was the South Stand fire in August, and Rovers' enforced absence from Eastville. Relegation, after seven seasons in Division Two, became inevitable. Rovers finished seven points adrift of Bristol City, who were also relegated.

There were huge restrictions imposed on Cooper as he attempted to convert his vast playing experience into managerial success. Funds were being used to develop the Hambrook training ground, and there was no money available for the much-needed introduction of new players. Meanwhile, the directors were unable to forge an agreement with the Bristol Stadium Company over the lease of Eastville. A new licence for the stadium to comply with the Safety of Sports Grounds Act was to reduce the ground capacity from 30,000 to 12,500. Repercussions from the ill-advised sale of Eastville in 1940 were now placing Rovers in the downward spiral that would lead to the move to Twerton Park in 1986. The long-serving club secretary Peter Terry retired on 5 October to be replaced by Marjorie Hall. Self-made businessman Barry Bradshaw joined the board and, over the summer, youth team development officer Gordon Bennett became chief executive, in which role he would make a huge contribution to staving off bankruptcy over the next few years. Bennett had donated his prize of £1,000, after being named Britain's top football fan in 1968, to the club to enable the establishment of a youth side, and he had undertaken a series of fundraising events across the years. Now he was able to put into action much of what he believed.

The next major blow to Rovers was not too far away. Overnight, following Rovers' opening day draw with Orient, David Williams and John Chiedozie scoring in the opening sixteen minutes, a mystery fire badly damaged the South Stand at Eastville. The club's administrative offices and changing rooms were destroyed. Nonetheless, there had been no loss of life. Eastville was left as a shell, with seating only in the North Stand and the traffic noise from the M32 motorway now increasingly evident. It was a depressing situation. Cooper's young, inexperienced side was forced to play three league games and two League Cup ties at Ashton Gate and, when they returned to their damaged home in October, were so deeply into their club record run of twenty league games without a win that relegation appeared the only possible outcome.

Exile at Ashton Gate was fraught with problems. The thought of playing on 'enemy territory' put off a number of spectators, and only 3,808 saw the game with Oldham Athletic and 3,047 the League Cup game with York City. Even the potentially lucrative visit of fallen giants Newcastle United drew only 5,171 to the borrowed stadium. Rovers drew all three league games there, and the only League Cup win was as a result of an own goal. Indeed, own goals accounted for two of Rovers' miserly three goals at Ashton Gate. Kevin Moore of Grimsby Town, who scored in the first game there, was later a Rovers player, and his goal against Birmingham City in October 1992 was therefore his second for the club, after a gap of over twelve years.

One other aspect to the Rovers story may have its roots in this era. Although it came into regular use in 1986/87, after Rovers' enforced exile at Twerton Park, several Rovers supporters mention the 1980/81 season as when they recall first being described as a 'Gashead' and the club being referred to as 'The Gas' in deference to Eastville Stadium's historic proximity to the gasworks. Steve Slade recalls Bristol City fan Andy Johnson calling him a 'Gashead' as he waited on Redcliffe Hill for a bus in 1980, and regulars in the Princes Bar and Wheatsheaf pubs remember the term 'Gas' in popular usage in the same year. While Rovers made temporary use of Ashton Gate, the phrase 'no Gasheads' was scrawled above one of the turnstiles, and certainly the popular song 'Proud to be a Gashead' was sung from the first match in Bath. At Wrexham in April 1981, Rovers supporters sang 'You'll Never Get Rid of the Gas', and Trevor Francis apparently wrote an article for a football magazine in 1979, in which he described Eastville as the worst ground he had ever played at, on account of the pervading smell of gas. The *Evening Post* first used the word 'Gashead' in 2001, and Harper Collins approved the word 'Gashead', meaning 'people dwelling north of the River Frome in Bristol, supporter of Bristol Rovers Football Club' for its various dictionaries from February 2005.

Cooper signed three experienced players in Aiden McCaffrey, Donnie Gillies, for two seasons of dependable play, and Bob Lee. McCaffrey, a one-time pupil of the Olympic athlete Brendan Foster, had represented England Youth while on Newcastle United's books and, following a £50,000 move from Derby County, was promptly made Rovers' captain. Though a centre-back, he was the club's top scorer with five league goals, level with the defensively minded Gary Mabbutt, who had scored his first goal for the club in the 3-1 defeat at Notts County in October. Mabbutt was one of a vast number of young players who were being blooded in Division Two. Vaughan Jones and Mark Hughes were claiming places in the side on merit, and young Geraint Williams became increasingly essential to Rovers' midfield cause as the season progressed. Mike Barrett scored his first league goal for Rovers in an eventful 3-3 draw with Sheffield Wednesday at a subdued Eastville in October. Each side scored in the opening six minutes, and Barrett's seventy-fifth minute-equaliser followed, two minutes later, by a Chic Bates goal put Rovers ahead, only for David Grant to equalise for Wednesday after eighty-four minutes. Stewart Barrowclough contributed just two league games and returned to his hometown club Barnsley at the end of February.

On 4 November, Rovers finally ended their club record run of ten home league games without a victory. This first win of the season, 3-1 over Watford, where Rovers were 2-0 up inside twenty-seven minutes, with Mabbutt adding a third nine minutes after the interval, brought little respite for it was followed by another run of fourteen league matches without a win. John Ward, later Rovers' manager in two stints, scored for the Hornets in the return fixture. At this stage, too, Ian Atkins and Steve Cross, two future Rovers managers, both scored for Shrewsbury Town against Rovers. Through December, Rovers picked up just one point in eight league games. This was achieved at home to Notts County when, with a sixty-fifth-minute equaliser to Iain McCulloch's goal, Steve Williams became, at seventeen years and 236 days, Rovers' youngest post-war goalscorer in league football. It was the only goal he ever scored for Rovers. Another of Ronnie Dix's pre-war records was challenged but remained unsurpassed, as Neil Slatter made his debut in the home game with Shrewsbury Town, at the age of sixteen years and 216 days.

Amid this run of poor results, Rovers never quite suffered the humiliating defeats that threatened. West Ham United, Second Division champions, won just 1-0 and 2-0, the latter before a crowd of 23,544 at Upton Park. Only Queen's Park Rangers, Sheffield Wednesday and Luton Town scored four goals in a game. The Hatters won 4-2 after Christmas at Eastville.

The big news on 29 January was that the crowd's favourite, Paul Randall, was returning to Rovers. The out-of-favour Chic Bates had moved to Shrewsbury Town, and supporters clubbed together to help raise the £50,000 required to bring Randall back from Stoke City. He returned in time for the local derby with Bristol City, which drew the season's only ten-figure crowd to Eastville for a second successive goalless draw with the equally struggling rivals. The Mabbutt brothers, Kevin and Gary, who played in both derby games this season, remain the only pair of brothers to oppose each other in matches between Rovers and City. A collection was made at the next home game, in mid-February against Bolton Wanderers, no doubt boosted when Randall scored a first-minute goal and later added a second in Rovers' second win of the season. He scored again, from Penny's pass a minute before half-time, at Cambridge United as Rovers ended a run of twenty-three away league games without a victory, second only to the twenty-nine winless away matches between March 1929 and September 1930, and Rovers also beat Chelsea and Preston North End. Randall's arrival was followed by the departure of winger Stewart Barrowclough, who returned to his first club, Barnsley.

Chelsea was one of the clubs involved in the battle developing above the two Bristol clubs for the third relegation spot. Two sides managed by World Cup winners played against Rovers in 1980/81, and while Jack Charlton's Sheffield Wednesday scored seven times in two games, Geoff Hurst's Chelsea side was less successful. It had taken sixty-eight minutes at Stamford Bridge before Chelsea took the lead, when Rovers' striker Bob Lee, who scored just twice for the Pirates in an entire season, scored a spectacular 30-yard own goal. A minute later, Clive Walker had secured a 2-0 victory. Chelsea's single-goal defeat at Eastville in March was the first of nine consecutive league games in which the Pensioners had failed to score, and as Chelsea hovered precariously above the relegation drop, wags inevitably pointed out they were saved only by a pair of drooping Bristols. As it was, Preston North End, albeit on goal average, was the third club to drop into Division Three.

Rovers somehow contrived to play six League Cup ties. Exeter City were beaten on penalties and York City on the away goals rule before Rovers lost in a replay at Portsmouth, Steve Perrin and David Gregory scoring the goals that took Pompey through to the fourth round. Bristol City were Gloucestershire Cup final winners through an extra-time goal from Kevin Mabbutt. In the league, the only ever-present was the ever-improving Gary Mabbutt, with McCaffrey and Hughes also regulars. A late substitute at Wrexham in April was debutant Ian Holloway, beginning a long and fruitful association with the club. He had become Britain's first Associate Schoolboy when he signed for Rovers on his fourteenth birthday.

The real excitement came in the FA Cup where Rovers, on 3 January, with only one league win all season, found themselves 4-0 up by half-time at Preston. Rovers were two goals ahead inside six minutes through Mabbutt and Stewart Barrowclough, with Barrett adding a third after thirty-eight minutes, and Geraint Williams a fourth on the stroke of half-time. Graham Houston and Alex Bruce pulled goals back, and when Dublin-born substitute Paul McGee made the score 4-3, it left debutant seventeen-year-old goalkeeper Phil Kite and his defence nervously seeing out time. With this remarkable away win behind them, Rovers, with 4,000 travelling fans supporting them, lost 3-1 at Southampton in the fourth round.

1981/82

A combination of events had led to Rovers' future at Eastville becoming the major talking point in the summer of 1981. New safety regulations, which had seriously reduced the ground capacity, financial problems within the club and belt-tightening in the aftermath of the devastating South Stand fire were all critical factors. In July 1981, the Stevens family, who had been key shareholders for forty years, lost control of the club to Martin Flook and Barry Bradshaw, who had been able to benefit from the directors' £75,000 new-share issue.

At the same time, Rovers were taking the decision to go to the High Court regarding compensation for losing their rights as tenants at Eastville. Discussions over a new lease had broken down and Rovers demanded £700,000 from the Stadium Company if they were to accept a move from their established 'home' since 1897. Rovers also wanted a twenty-one-year lease on a sliding scale. The Stadium Company offered £100,000 compensation and a three- or five-year lease involving profit-making schemes through gate receipts and takings from the bars and car parks. At the High Court in London in November 1981, Rovers were awarded £280,000, a figure that the club's directors reluctantly accepted.

The impending loss of a home base, a departure in fact delayed until 1986, sparked a renewed search for a stadium elsewhere. The Rovers chairman Martin Flook offered Bristol City £450,000 to buy Ashton Gate, an apparently audacious bid, which, given City's perilous financial state as the club plummeted towards Division Four, was not as outrageous as it would at first appear. However, the creation of Bristol City (1982) plc on 15 February scuppered Flook's plans. As the season drew to a close, Rovers were investigating a £45,000 groundsharing scheme at Ashton Gate, and were, indeed, offered a similar scheme with Bath City at Twerton Park at an annual rent of £15,000. As it was, Rovers' directors finally worked out a five-year lease for £52,000 with their landlords at Eastville.

Financial problems, however, though minimal in comparison to those experienced at this time at Ashton Gate, would not disappear entirely. Rovers recorded a loss for the year of £335,146, a figure partly attributed to transfer fees and the introduction of several expensive player contracts, while gate receipts continued to fall. The club had also purchased, in March 1982, an artificial pitch for the Hambrook training ground for £125,000, albeit with some aid from Sports Council grants. Rovers approached their centenary year with a great deal of uncertainty hanging over their immediate future.

On the pitch, a largely unchanged side faced the first season back in Division Three. Two new faces were the experienced Brian Williams, once the youngest player to appear for Bury and now signed from Swindon Town, and the Melksham Town striker Archie Stephens, a relatively late entrant to League Football at the age of twenty-seven. Another was the former Blackburn Rovers centre-half Tim Parkin, who had played for Malmö in the World Club Championship final, and who, to comply with Swedish transfer regulations at that time, was technically an Almondsbury Greenway player for half an hour during his £15,000 move to Eastville. With three Williamses controlling the heart of the team, young Phil Kite commanding in goal and a burgeoning attacking partnership in Stephens and Randall, ably supported by Mike Barrett, Rovers got off to a good start. Stephens scored twice on his full debut at home to Burnley, and followed this up with two more at Reading seven days later. There were also wins at Preston and Exeter. Therefore, it came as some surprise when, just days after the death of the former Rovers manager Fred Ford, manager Terry Cooper was dismissed on 19 October, following a defeat at home to Swindon Town. He was replaced temporarily by Rovers' chief scout, the former Chelsea and Exeter City full-back Ron Gingell. Cooper signed for Doncaster Rovers as a player before, at the season's end, becoming manager of Bristol City.

The new permanent manager was another high-profile former player, Bobby Gould, who had signed for Rovers as a player four years earlier and had latterly been on the books of Aldershot. He retained Cooper's squad and began to work it into the side that would achieve significant on-field success in the autumn of 1982. Yet one major problem was home defeats – six in total in 1981/82, including one in December against Carlisle United in what was to be player-coach Gary Pendrey's only league game for the Pirates. By the end of the season, Rovers had secured a mid-table finish. Randall was the club's top scorer with twelve league goals, Stephens and David Williams contributing eleven each, while Brian Williams was the sole ever-present.

Following Ford's death on 16 October, three other key figures in the history of Bristol Rovers were to die during the season. Dr Douglas Mearns Milne, who passed away on 14 January at Abbots Leigh, aged sixty-five, had served on Rovers' board from 1962 and as chairman from 1968 to 1978. At a meeting of directors on 22 July, his 5,404 shares in the club were devolved to his son Alastair. On 19 March, at the age of eighty-seven, goalkeeper Jesse Whatley, who had played in a club record 246 consecutive league games between 1922 and 1928 and in 386 in all, died in Chipping Sodbury. Forty-eight hours later, Bert Williams, Rovers' groundsman in 1918, and long-time trainer from 1920 to 1962, died in Bristol at the age of eighty. The board of directors resolved on 25 March to donate £50 in regard to Williams to the Friends of Frenchay Hospital and £50 in Whatley's memory to Dr Barnardo's.

There were some ponderous games – forty free-kicks were awarded in the first half as Rovers ground out a 1-0 victory over Chesterfield at Eastville in January, thanks to Randall's goal ten minutes after half-time. However, generally the season was far more positive. Rovers recorded some well-earned victories, most notably the doubles recorded over Exeter City and Huddersfield Town. For the 3-2 home win against the Grecians, Rovers introduced a seventeen-year-old midfielder Steve Bailey, and it was his appearance that led to the club being deducted two league points. An oversight meant that he had not been registered with the league and the loss of these points, though not seriously affecting the club, slightly distorted Rovers' league standing by the end of the season.

March saw a succession of unusual events. At Swindon Town, having earlier lost 4-0 at both Burnley and Plymouth Argyle, Rovers crashed to a 5-2 defeat, the

Robins thus totalling nine league goals in two games past Phil Kite. Tim Parkin became only the fifth Rovers player to score for both sides in the same game, while the future Rovers midfielder, Roy Carter, from a penalty and Paul Rideout added a goal apiece. Three days later, referee Tony Glasson abandoned the game with Oxford United at a waterlogged Eastville after sixty-four minutes, shortly after Keith Cassells had equalised Paul Randall's first-half opener. It was the first home game abandoned since February 1951. Only four days later, despite losing Kite injured (Vaughan Jones playing in goal) Rovers defeated Huddersfield Town 2-0, their first win at Leeds Road since April 1960. Earlier in the campaign, Chester's Alan Oakes scored against Rovers three days short of his thirty-ninth birthday, the fourth-oldest League scorer against the Pirates since 1920.

Two of Rovers' opponents this season were to feature in England's semi-final defeat against Germany in the 1990 World Cup finals in Italy. Trevor Steven was in the Burnley side defeated by two Stephens goals at Eastville in September, while twenty-year-old Peter Beardsley was to reappear against Rovers in the Fulham side in November 1998, after a record gap of almost seventeen years between league appearances against Rovers. Bristol City's goalkeeper for the local derby in December was the Swedish international Jan Möller. At the opposite end of the spectrum, David Smith played in the final ten minutes of the 2-1 win against Walsall in April to record the shortest league career of any Rovers player.

In the League Cup, aggregate victory over Crewe Alexandra was followed by defeat against Northampton Town, who scored five times over the two legs. Tony Mahoney scored his first-ever goal for the Cobblers, while left-back Alex Saxby scored for the first time for more than a year. The FA Cup brought no joy either, with two goals from Dean Coney earning Fulham victory at Eastville. The future Rovers player Gary Waddock was a losing FA Cup finalist with Queen's Park Rangers. There was, however, a ray of hope from the unlikely source of the Gloucestershire Cup final, where Aiden McCaffrey's far-post goal, after Barrett's forty-eighth minute centre had been flicked on by Gary Mabbutt, brought what was the first of four consecutive victories over Bristol City in this competition. The season concluded with the high-profile transfer of Martin Thomas to Newcastle United, where the genial goalkeeper was to earn a well-deserved full international cap with Wales.

1982/83

An air of uncertainty hung over Eastville as Rovers approached their centenary year. Amid groundsharing talks with both Bristol City and Bath City, the board of directors made another concerted attempt to buy Eastville back from the Stadium Company. It was an audacious bid, given Rovers' perilous financial state, and one promptly dismissed. The Eastville site was one with huge commercial viability for developers, standing so close to the M32 motorway and thus within easy access of the M4 and M5, and the case put forward by Bristol Rovers was deemed relatively insignificant. With hindsight, there was little hope that the club could remain at Eastville beyond the end of the current lease in 1987. Attention was now turned to a green-belt site at Stoke Gifford, to the north of the city, where Rovers' directors now began seeking planning permission for a £10-million sports complex including a football stadium.

On the pitch, the tide was turning. In the wake of relegation in 1980/81, new manager Bobby Gould was now building a side that could realistically challenge for a return to Division Two. Extra revenue was generated through a shirt sponsorship deal, Great Mills DIY becoming the first name emblazoned on Rovers' tops. The team made a successful preseason Scottish tour, winning at Partick Thistle, Falkirk and Ayr United. Yet the side would have to battle without Gary Mabbutt, a Rovers favourite like his father before him, whose £105,000 move to Tottenham Hotspur preceded sixteen England caps during a hugely successful career. Once the season got underway, a series of large wins, incredibly six league and one League Cup victory before Christmas being by four-goal margins, raised the level of excitement around Eastville. Gould added to this shrewdly by adding some high-profile names to his close-knit and largely locally based squad.

Arguably, the two biggest footballing names to have, albeit briefly, graced the Rovers side were signed by Gould. In October, the highly experienced forward Mick Channon was signed from Newcastle United. He had won forty-six full caps for England, scoring twenty-one goals, and had enjoyed a hugely successful career, largely with Southampton, where he remains the all-time record aggregate goalscorer. His infectious enthusiasm for the game inspired the Rovers side, but his trademark windmill goal celebration was never seen at Eastville for, kept out of the side by Ian Holloway, he departed goalless in December to join Norwich City. Red-haired Alan Ball, who arrived in January, ended a momentous career with seventeen league appearances and two memorable goals for Rovers. The winner of seventy-two full England caps, he had once attracted a record British transfer fee when he moved from Everton to Arsenal in December 1971 for £220,000, and was an eminently recognisable figure on the football circuit. 'I'm not a believer in luck,' he is credited as saying, 'but I do believe you need it.' His position in midfield in England's 1966 side meant that he is the only World Cup winner to have played football for Rovers. Ball's tremendous 30-yard goal, following a left-wing throw-in, to defeat Huddersfield Town in April was a wonderful way to end a twenty-one-year professional playing career, and was the final league goal scored by any of England's 1966 side.

Rovers enjoyed an astonishingly successful first half of the season. Despite a crushing opening day defeat by Brentford at Griffin Park, and a potentially demoralising home defeat against Lincoln City, the string of good results through the autumn gave very real hopes of promotion. Two 4-0 wins in Devon, in the

League Cup at Torquay United and the league at Plymouth Argyle, set Rovers scoring seemingly at will. Despite the sending-off of the veteran Roy McFarland at Eastville, Bradford City would not have anticipated a 4-1 defeat, Randall scoring a brace of goals for the second consecutive game. Later the same month, Rovers defeated Wigan Athletic and Millwall 4-0 each and Reading 3-0, as well as winning 5-1 at Orient. It was an awesome display of firepower.

The first-ever visit of Wigan Athletic to Eastville marked the return of the former Rovers centre-back Larry Lloyd. Sadly for him, he and his teammate Alex Cribley were both sent off, the first time two opponents had been sent off against Rovers in a league game. Graham Withey, a £5,000 summer signing from Bath City, became the first Rovers substitute to score twice in one game, a club record subsequently equalled in May 2001 by Mark Walters. Indeed, Withey proved to be a real thorn in Wigan's side for, recovering from a mid-season ankle injury, he and Paul Randall both scored twice, once each either side of half-time, in February as Rovers won 5-0 at Springfield Park to record what remains the heaviest home defeat in Wigan's league history. Randall and Withey both scored in three minutes midway through the first half, and the latter's second goal in the final minute sealed a memorable victory. It remained the Latics' worst league defeat of all time until Carl Saunders inspired Rovers to a 6-1 victory at Twerton Park in March 1990.

Perhaps the most encouraging result was the 5-1 home victory over a Portsmouth side heading for the Third Division championship. In a totally one-sided encounter, five Rovers players (sequentially shirt numbers five to nine) were to score before Billy Rafferty's very late consolation goal. The players wore black armbands to the memory of Jimmy Dickinson, the Portsmouth legend who had died four days earlier. This match clearly highlighted Rovers' potential, even against stronger opposition. The side was also devastatingly ruthless, as illustrated by the three goals in three minutes on the hour, which helped defeat Wrexham 4-0 in December. Three players called Williams scored in this game.

As Bristol City slipped temporarily to the foot of Division Four, it appeared Rovers were destined for great things. However, inconsistency set in and, ultimately, seventh place in Division Three was an acceptable final league position. At Cardiff City, Brian Williams was sent off and Rovers lost a televised game 3-1, despite a goal from the veteran Les Bradd, still Notts County's all-time record goalscorer, in his sole league appearance on loan from Wigan Athletic. Young Keith Curle, a major discovery, scored against Millwall after only twenty-five seconds, but was then sent off and Rovers drew 1-1. As a gesture of goodwill by the Rovers Board of Directors, free coach travel was arranged to take Rovers fans to Walsall in April, only for the side to lose 5-0. Rovers also played eighty-five minutes of the game at Bradford in February with an orange ball, before conceding two very late goals when a flatter, white ball was substituted, to lose 2-0. The defeat at Bramall Lane in May, despite being Sheffield United's ninth consecutive home league victory, was watched by the lowest post-war league crowd at that ground.

Rovers also conceded eight goals in three days after Christmas. The 4-2 defeat at Oxford United was a psychological blow against promotion rivals, while the eight-goal draw with Exeter City at Eastville was quite simply a dropped point. Bristol-born Peter Rogers had twice put the Grecians ahead, but Paul Randall's second equaliser, five minutes before half-time, followed swiftly by a goal from Ian Holloway and a Keith Viney own goal gave Rovers a commanding 4-2 half-time lead. However, Exeter were let off the hook as George Delve, after fifty-one minutes, and Stan McEwan, twenty minutes from time, earned the visitors a draw. The first half of this game had featured a mercurial display from Mike Barrett, whose fine run and shot, saved by Len Bond, had rebounded into the net off Viney on the stroke of half-time. The unfortunate defender was himself to play for Rovers in a loan spell in September 1988.

Rovers won a number of key games in the spring, but the impetus for promotion had been lost. The big win at Wigan was the first of three consecutive victories, Randall scoring a first-minute goal against Orient, and Withey scoring five times in this run to end up as second highest scorer with ten goals. Top scorer Randall scored his twentieth of the season in a storming second-half display as Rovers swept aside Preston North End at Eastville in April. Rovers crushed Chesterfield 3-0, the side's only ever-present Phil Kite keeping a clean sheet. Despite the consistent form of individuals in key positions, Rovers never challenged seriously for promotion, and manager Bobby Gould resigned in May 1983 to rejoin one of his other former clubs, First Division Coventry City.

There had been limited success in cup competitions. Nick Platnauer, a close-season signing from Bedford Town, had scored on his debut as Rovers beat Torquay United 4-0 at Plainmoor. Rovers then lost a League Cup second-round tie on aggregate to Swansea City. Despite the high-scoring league form, a solitary Archie Stephens goal defeated non-League Wycombe Wanderers in the FA Cup. Rovers then lost in a replay to Plymouth Argyle, over whom they were to complete a league double. Ian Holloway's curling right-wing strike retained the Gloucestershire Cup, while Spurs won 3-2 at Eastville in April's centenary match.

One footnote to 1982/83 is that Rovers used a substitute in forty-three league games, an English record for all clubs in the era 1965–87, when only one replacement per team was allowed each game.

1983/84

As Rovers' directors continued negotiations regarding the club's long-term home, the centenary year was rounded off by the first months in charge for a new manager. Bobby Gould was succeeded from within the club by David Williams. In fending off the applications of Alan Ball, who became coach at Portsmouth, and Larry Lloyd, who joined Notts County, Williams became the league's youngest manager at twenty-eight. He appointed Wayne Jones as his assistant and retained much of the squad that had served Rovers so well in 1982/83.

Graham Withey, Nick Platnauer and Errington Kelly rejoined their former manager at Coventry City, where Bobby Gould's appointment had led to Rovers receiving £30,000 compensation. Jeff Sherwood moved to Bath City on a free transfer. Williams initially brought just one new player to the club, although, as the season progressed, the experienced goalkeeper Ray Cashley joined from Bristol City, and Carlisle United's Paul Bannon was signed in an £8,000 deal. The 'new' player was an old hand, Steve White, who returned to Eastville from Charlton Athletic in a deal worth £35,000. So it was that a very recognisable Rovers side lost the first game of the new season at Newport County. Archie Stephens, who scored a consolation goal in this match after coming on as a substitute, was initially out of favour but became the club's seasonal top scorer with thirteen league goals.

Once again, a successful preseason tour of Scotland prefaced a promising opening to a new season. Rovers were unbeaten against Airdrieonians, Hamilton Academical and Kilmarnock, but lost 2-0 at Morton to goals from Bobby Houston and Mungo MacCallum. As the league season got underway, Rovers won ten of their opening sixteen fixtures, and gave promise of a return to the previous season's form. Although the goals never flowed at the rate seen the previous autumn, Rovers were to finish fifth in Division Three and were, in fact, to lose only three of forty-six home league games under Williams' management.

In stark contrast to 1982/83, Rovers scored four goals in a game on only three occasions. Newport County were convincingly defeated 4-0, but Rovers required own goals to beat Scunthorpe United and Walsall. The latter game was notable for the unlikely fact that both sides' player-managers scored – Williams contributing Rovers' second and Alan Buckley replying for the Saddlers. On the other hand, Rovers conceded four goals in only two league games: at Lincoln City, where the future England international John Fashanu grabbed a hat-trick, and, at the season's end, to promotion-bound Sheffield United after a goalless first half.

What bore an uncanny resemblance to the previous season was how Rovers' form crumbled in December. Yet again, it was defeat at Oxford United over Christmas that was a huge psychological blow. In this instance, though, it followed hot on the heels of a first home defeat of the season, in which Hull City could afford the luxury of Brian Marwood's missed penalty and still beat Rovers 3-1. This defeat finally shattered all illusions of Rovers' invulnerability, which had been strengthened earlier by the convincing nature of the side's performance in defeating Burnley and enhancing their growing early season reputation.

Rovers endured one late winter run of four league games without a goal, but were nonetheless more consistent across the season. However, while home form was undeniably strong, the team lacked a certain cutting edge in away matches. Six away league wins was no poor record, but equally was not one that suggested a promotion challenge in earnest. These away wins came in pairs. There were 1-0 wins at Orient and Bournemouth at the end of September, the latter after Phil Kite had saved a penalty from the future Rovers striker Trevor Morgan. There were 2-1 wins in January at Southend United and Exeter City, where Rovers supporters invaded the pitch, six policeman were injured and there were twenty-four arrests. Finally, late wins at Gillingham and Bradford City, through Archie Stephens goals, brought Rovers to a seasonal total of four league doubles.

Rotherham United's Mick Gooding became only the sixth opponent to score two penalties in a league game against Rovers. He had put his side ahead at Millmoor in the second minute, but the game was to finish 2-2, with Rovers' only ever-present and unlikely candidate as second-highest scorer, Brian Williams, also scoring from the spot in a match of three penalties. Rovers' winning goal at home to Wigan Athletic in March was a fifty-second-minute headed own goal by Steve Walsh.

One huge disappointment was Randall's inability to follow up his twenty league goals with a meaningful contribution in 1983/84. He scored just six goals in the league, while Steve White was also unable to reach double figures. Stephens was never consistently in Rovers' starting line-up, while the side grew to depend increasingly on Mike Barrett. Not only did Barrett contribute nine league goals, but his presence was hugely important to those around him, and his rare ability to beat even the most dogged defender enthralled the crowd. In the last home game of the season, Millwall had led 2-0 before Barrett had inspired a comeback, also scoring the sensational last-minute winning goal.

In defence, Rovers possessed a developing star in full-back Neil Slatter. He had earned a first full international cap for Wales against Scotland in Cardiff in May 1983, and was to play on ten occasions for the full Welsh side while on Rovers' books, and twenty-two times in all. His full-back partnership with Brian Williams flourished through the reliability of both players and a good tactical understanding. Rovers conceded just fifty-four league goals, the fewest since the 1975/76 season.

In the League Cup, Rovers defeated Bournemouth 4-3 on aggregate, despite Brian Williams scoring a penalty and an own goal in the home leg. It is rare indeed for Rovers to win at Dean Court, but this season the feat had been achieved in league and cup before the end of September. Second Division Brighton were stretched in round two, with the influential Barrett scoring in both legs as Rovers clawed back a 4-2 deficit to take the tie into extra time. Sadly, the only goal added in this period was scored by the visitors' Terry Connor. Rovers avoided a potential banana skin in the FA Cup by drawing with non-League Barnet at Underhill, before a comfortable replay victory set up a mouth-watering tie with Bristol City. It was the first meeting of the sides in this competition since 1968, but the Fourth Division side snatched victory at Eastville through Tom Ritchie's eighty-eighth minute winning goal.

Rovers also participated in the newly formed Associate Members Cup, winning three times before losing at Bournemouth, the inaugural winners. The early disinterest in a tournament designed for lower division clubs was apparent in the attendances. For instance, only 1,480 turned out to see Rovers win at Southend United on a Tuesday night in April, but they witnessed dramatic events as Aiden McCaffrey swallowed his tongue in an accidental collision with Phil Kite. His life was saved by the prompt action of the club physiotherapist, Roy Dolling. This competition was used as a vehicle for blooding new talent, with Paul Vassall and Wayne Noble playing against Port Vale, Mike Adams, who headed the winning goal six minutes after half-time, and Carl Metcalfe at Southend.

November saw a testimonial at Eastville for the unfortunate Steve Bailey, whose career had been cut short by a knee injury. Bobby Gould's Coventry City supplied the opposition, and the former Rovers striker Graham Withey scored the winning goal. The following month Rovers returned to the scene of their first fixture to play a centenary game against Wotton Rovers, which Rovers, in distinctive Black Arabs shirts with a yellow sash, won 4-0, Barrett scoring twice. Two days later, Newcastle United visited Eastville for another centenary match, Randall's hat-trick leading Rovers to a 5-4 victory.

On 4 February 1984, the supermarket chain Tesco announced plans to start work on an 82,000-square-foot outlet on 18 acres at the site of the stadium, including parking for 1,200 vehicles; this deal included the construction of a new road and bridge from Muller Road to the store.

1984/85

That player-manager David Williams' side was consistent and settled is abundantly clear from the paucity of close season transfer deals. Mark Hughes and Tony Pulis joined South Walian sides, the defender on a free transfer to Swansea City and the midfielder moving to Newport County for £8,000. Until events on the eve of the new season sadly rendered it inevitable, the manager did not venture into the transfer market for new players. Off the pitch, the promotion of Gordon Bennett to managing director on 25 June 1984 was a significant advance, as it was he who steered the club into financially less choppy waters towards the end of the decade.

Just days before the new season, however, the club was rocked by tragic news. Mike Barrett was dead. Rovers' inspirational winger had struggled in preseason training, entered hospital for tests and died of cancer on 14 August, aged only twenty-four. The entire Eastville camp shared the grief felt by his pregnant wife, and his funeral six days later was well attended. Rovers swiftly organised a game against Aston Villa for the benefit of his family, goals from Tim Parkin and David Williams giving Rovers a 2-1 win. From the angle of team selection, the player-manager delved hurriedly but wisely on the transfer front to sign Mark

O'Connor from Queen's Park Rangers for £20,000. O'Connor, despite the unenviable task of stepping into Barrett's shoes, played at least a part in every game of the season and contributed eight league goals.

Rovers started the season as if on a mission to secure promotion at the earliest possible opportunity. Of the opening seven league games, six were won, while Rovers also gained a creditable goalless draw at Burnley. Archie Stephens and Paul Randall, forming a productive forward partnership, appeared to be scoring goals frequently enough for Rovers to mount a serious challenge. An autumnal blip saw Rovers draw three consecutive home matches and lose three in a row away, the worst being 3-0 before a seasonal best league crowd of 18,672 at Ashton Gate, with Glyn Riley scoring twice for Bristol City. However, still unbeaten at home, Rovers hit a golden patch in December.

The Randall-Stephens partnership was flourishing, and once O'Connor started to score too, Rovers won four consecutive games in the league. O'Connor scored in all these games and Randall in all but one. It may have been the first away win since September, but the 4-1 win at Orient was achieved through a masterful team display and was followed by comfortable home victories over Newport County and Swansea City. When Rovers went 3-0 ahead at Brentford on Boxing Day, O'Connor, Randall and Stephens having scored, the side appeared in absolute control, but was about to hit a brick wall. Stephens was involved in an incident with the home side's Steve Wignall and both players were sent off. Bizarrely, this event seemed to set off a chain of events.

Following the victory at Griffin Park, Archie Stephens' final league goal for Rovers could not prevent the side crashing to a 4-1 defeat at Gillingham. Soon out of favour, Stephens moved to Middlesbrough in March for £20,000. Despite the efforts of his replacement, Paul Bannon, there was no return to the pre-Christmas form. Rovers lost four consecutive league games in the New Year and won only one of the final seven matches of the season. While only Bolton Wanderers and Orient, clubs Rovers had beaten on their travels, won at Eastville, Rovers conversely won just one away game after Boxing Day. It was the lack of success away from Eastville that led the promotion charge off the rails, Rovers finishing in sixth place.

This sole away win in the latter half of the season came at Cambridge United, where defenders Tim Parkin and Neil Slatter both scored, watched by the lowest crowd since January 1935 at a league game involving Rovers. It was the second of four consecutive wins, a beacon of hope as the season drew to an end. At this time, goalkeeper Ron Green, on loan from Shrewsbury Town, kept five consecutive clean sheets. It was eight home games before an opponent managed to get one past him, Orient's Ian Juryeff doing the honours after fifty-two minutes. Bristol City were beaten in a gale by a twentieth-minute Ian Holloway goal in front of the last five-figure crowd ever to watch league football at Eastville. The next time Rovers attracted a crowd of over 10,000 to a home league game was to be on

Boxing Day 1999. Burnley were defeated 4-0 for Rovers' largest league win in fifteen months. Brentford conceded two penalties at Eastville, both converted by Brian Williams, only the fifth Rovers player to achieve such a feat in the league, and many observers considered Rovers unfortunate not to be awarded a third penalty late in the game.

Goalkeeper Jon Hallworth and midfielder Paul Raynor, both of whom went on to enjoy long footballing careers elsewhere, appeared briefly on loan. At Newport County in May – where Brian Williams, who later missed a penalty, scored his side's first goal in 315 minutes – Rovers gave a full league debut to Gary Penrice, a home-grown talent who was to serve Rovers well for many years. It was Penrice who scored with a strong twenty-sixth-minute header in the 1-1 draw with York City on the final day of the season. He was to become, in due course, the only player to score for Rovers on four home grounds. Winger Chris Smith, who had represented the Gloucestershire Youth XI, was granted a solitary league appearance in the York game. David Williams, chaired off the field despite gifting the visitors an injury time equaliser in that game, moved to Norwich City within weeks for £40,000, where he was to appear in First Division football and won a first full Welsh cap against Saudi Arabia in February 1986.

Rovers had survived a relatively successful season with a largely unchanged side. Cashley and Green had shared goalkeeping responsibilities, Vaughan Jones had returned to his first club from Cardiff City and was to play a momentous role in Rovers' near-term future, and the influential Geraint Williams had joined Derby County for £40,000. A solid defence, with Brian Williams again the club's only ever-present, had conceded only forty-eight league goals, the lowest since the 1973/74 promotion season. Williams' 100th consecutive league game was Rovers' 2,500th match in the league; a 2-1 win at Walsall in March, where Randall's two goals took his seasonal league tally to eighteen.

In the League Cup, two goals each from Randall and David Williams gave a forceful Rovers side a 5-1 lead from the away leg against Swindon Town, a very safe margin despite an unconvincing and ultimately disappointing second leg display. This set up a lucrative tie with Arsenal, for whom the legendary Northern Ireland goalkeeper Pat Jennings played in both games. A crowd of over 28,000 at Highbury saw a first leg in which Rovers' hopes were killed off by three goals in the final quarter of an hour. Steve White's goal a minute after half-time earned a draw on the return leg, which drew over 10,000 to Eastville. Cashley conceded an unfortunate own goal after twenty minutes when Tommy Caton's header rebounded to him off the crossbar, but he redeemed himself by saving a Tony Woodcock penalty after sixty-six minutes.

An apparently straightforward first-round FA Cup tie with King's Lynn nearly turned disastrous. Four minutes after half-time, the Linnets took a shock lead when Richard Johnston's shot rebounded off the crossbar for Clive Adams to score. It took four minutes for David Williams to equalise, but the winning goal took a long time to materialise. Four minutes from time, Brian Williams' cross was turned into his own net by the unfortunate Adams to nullify his earlier goal. This set up a second-round tie before a crowd of 19,367 at Ashton Gate, where Rovers gained ample revenge for the previous season's result by beating Bristol City 3-1. O'Connor scored Rovers' first, and Randall added two more before half-time to complete a noteworthy victory. First Division Ipswich Town were the visitors in round three, and despite a volleyed goal from Ian Holloway, ran out worthy winners.

Participation in the Freight Rover Trophy ended promptly, as a result of Geraint Williams' own goal from a Chris Marustik cross four minutes prior to half-time and substitute Dean Saunders' fifty-third-minute penalty for Swansea City. A fourth consecutive Gloucestershire Cup final victory was secured when Rovers scored twice in extra time. White's goal had put Rovers ahead by half-time, only for Bristol City to equalise through an Alan Walsh penalty. Nineteen-year-old Nicky Tanner, on as a substitute for his club debut, scored an astonishing 30-yard extra-time goal before the revitalised Paul Bannon added a third in his final game for the club. An October 1984 charity game for the Mike Barrett Fund saw Rovers defeat Shirehampton Sports to the tune of 11-2.

At the close of the season, just weeks before a £80,000 move to Oxford United, Neil Slatter played in his tenth international for Wales, marking the occasion with an own goal in a 4-2 defeat in Norway, to set a record for international appearances by a player on the books of Bristol Rovers, which was to stand until 2001.

1985/86

The previous two seasons had been successful and, but for an inconsistent away record, Rovers might have found their way back into Division Two. Nonetheless, manager David Williams decided his job was done and moved to Norwich City and later Bournemouth as a player. Away from Eastville, his playing career hit new heights and he was rewarded with five full international appearances for Wales in 1986 and 1987. Williams was replaced by Bobby Gould who, in his two years away from Eastville, had struggled to create a team to his liking at Highfield Road, but had kept Coventry City in the First Division.

Gould's reappointment was the last major decision made by club directors Martin Flook and Barry Bradshaw. Both men had provided Rovers with loans at crucial times since taking control of the club in the summer of 1981, but resigned when pleas to build a new stadium at Stoke Gifford finally collapsed. Discussions about a multi-sports complex on this site had dragged on for two years, but Rovers had faced considerable opposition from residents as well as the local authority planners. The decision not to proceed was to leave Rovers with little option but to leave Eastville and groundshare with Bath City from the end of the season. The Popplewell Report, delivered in January 1986 (Command Paper 9710) in the aftermath of the Bradford fire and Heysel tragedy, ordered that Twerton Park should be incorporated within the stadia covered by the 1975 Safety of Sports Grounds Act. Geoff Dunford and Roy Redman bought up chairman Flook's shareholding in the club. At times through 1985/86, they held three board meetings a week simply to keep the club afloat. The Stadium Company frequently placed injunctions on Rovers playing at Eastville and, on one occasion, this was lifted only on the Friday evening prior to a Saturday fixture.

Not only did Rovers approach the new season with new directors and a restored manager, but in order to tackle the ever-increasing losses, many of the more experienced players were released. A squad of considerably younger players reduced the wage bill but led to a tougher season on the pitch. Rovers finished the season in sixteenth place in Division Three. Fifteen of Rovers' twenty-three home league games were played before crowds of under 4,000, and these attendance figures fell away as the club recorded just two victories in the final nineteen league games of a miserable season.

The season opened with a misleadingly exciting six-goal draw with Darlington at Feethams. Rovers were giving club league debuts to five players, two of whom (Steve Badock and Byron Stevenson from the penalty spot) were able to mark the occasion with a goal. The full-back pairing of Andy Spring and Ian Davies, the latter once Norwich City's youngest-ever player, did not last long. Phil Bater, an own goal scorer against all-conquering Reading, was given a run in the side, as were promising young defenders John Scales and Nicky Tanner. Mike England, back in the side in September, over six years after his only previous game in a Rovers shirt, ended the season at left-back. Tim Parkin completed another successful season before moving to Swindon Town in a deal worth £28,500 in June 1986.

It took Rovers seven league games to record their first win of the season, and it was October and the fifth home game before Rovers scored a league goal at Eastville. That first victory, an astonishing 4-3 victory over Wolverhampton Wanderers on a Tuesday night at Molineux, was achieved through two Badock goals, his final ones for the club, after Paul Randall and Steve White had both put their names on the scoresheet against the future England goalkeeper Tim Flowers. Indeed, Rovers also won at Swansea City before recording the elusive first home league victory.

As the season unfolded, Rovers tried and rejected a number of players. John Vaughan came on loan from West Ham United in goal, while Allan Cockram, Tony Obi and Richard Iles made just one appearance each in the league. Other players with a role to play in years to come made their league bows – David Mehew and Tim Carter were joined by Gary Smart, Wayne Noble and Darren Carr. Two new signings, however, stood out from the pack. Gerry Francis, the former England captain and the holder of twelve full international caps, joined as a non-contract player in September 1985, and his influence in twenty-eight league appearances undoubtedly helped Rovers retain their Third Division status. Trevor Morgan, a £15,000 buy from Francis' former club, Exeter City, was the architect of Rovers' late autumn revival in fortunes.

It was Morgan's goal, a far-post header from Gary Penrice's eighty-third minute free-kick, which brought about victory at Swansea City in his first full appearance. Thereafter, a purple patch of seven goals in three games endeared Morgan to the Rovers supporters and began to restore some belief in a youthful side's ability. His convincing hat-trick against Rotherham United in mid-October brought the long-awaited first victory at Eastville, and this was followed up by two first-half goals at Doncaster Rovers seven days later. Indeed, on the stroke of half-time at Belle Vue, as Gary Smart, on as an early substitute for his debut, rounded goalkeeper Paul Allen, it appeared Rovers might be about to repeat their prolific goalscoring of the previous week. As it happened, Smart hit the side netting, the goal for which he would forever remain a hero in Rovers' hearts would not be scored until New Year's Day 1987.

Clearly, the season was saved by a run of ten wins in sixteen league games between mid-October and February. White's hat-trick against Darlington in January was the first by a Rovers player at Eastville since Boxing Day 1979, and his goal seven minutes before half-time from Mark O'Connor's centre against Doncaster Rovers completed a league double. Severe weather conditions meant Rovers played no away league games between Boxing Day and 4 February, when they won at Bolton Wanderers. Yet this more positive mid-season spell also included a 6-1 defeat at Bournemouth and a 4-0 loss at Wigan Athletic. Rovers were to lose 4-0 at York City and in the FA Cup at Luton Town as well as 6-0 at Walsall. The total of seventy-five goals conceded in the league was only exceeded once since 1967/68.

Rovers played nine games in March and did not win any. April opened without Paul Randall, who joined Yeovil Town on a free transfer, but with a full league debut for Phil Purnell, another player set to figure prominently in years to come. Despite his presence and a fifty-seventh-minute lead over Wigan Athletic through Stevenson's shot, an instant equaliser from a Graham Barrow header deprived Rovers of a much-needed victory. When Rovers did win, it was at the unlikely setting of Derby County's Baseball Ground, Morgan and White scoring after Alan Buckley had missed a penalty for the home side. Purnell scored twice at Lincoln City in the penultimate fixture when Morgan, easily top scorer with sixteen goals compared to White's twelve, ended up in goal after Ron Green had been injured.

White's goal at Chesterfield in November had been expunged when the game was abandoned due to fog with the score 1-1 at half-time. When the game was replayed in April, it drew a crowd of 1,800, the lowest at a Rovers game all season, with Tony Reid and Phil Walker scoring for the home side, who won 2-0. The return game eleven days later was to be the final game ever played at Eastville. A crowd of only 3,576 saw Morgan's goal earn a 1-1 draw, Brian Scrimgeour scoring for Chesterfield. Few of those present suspected that this really was a final farewell to Rovers' home since 1897. A moment of history passed by and events over the summer led Rovers towards a decade of exile from the city of Bristol. With Rovers' departure, a fourth weekly greyhound meeting could be added to Eastville's schedule, rendering it the busiest greyhound track in the United Kingdom. Twelve acres were sold to a supermarket chain for £2,000,000 plus an annual income of £150,000, leaving a once-glorious stadium a very sorry sight.

The newly sponsored Milk Cup saw Rovers defeat Newport County over two legs, before two Tommy Wright penalties at St Andrew's helped ease First Division Birmingham City through over two legs. Randall scored in three of the four games in this tournament. Early exit from the Freight Rover Trophy was coupled with defeat in the Gloucestershire Cup final. Bristol City's Steve Johnson did not score in the league all season for his club, but his second-half penalty at Ashton Gate in September enabled the Robins to regain the trophy.

In the FA Cup, Gerry Francis scored his only goal for Rovers to seal a 3-1 victory at Brentford, and a win at Swansea City was set up by Morgan's first-minute penalty. Round three brought First Division Leicester City and a 9,392 crowd to Eastville for the last big occasion the old stadium was to host. Forty-four-year-old goalkeeping coach Bob Wilson came within a whisker of being called into the side, but it was a recognisable Rovers side that matched Leicester in an evenly contested first half. Five minutes after half-time, after Tanner had been fouled by Russell Osman, Stevenson fired in a 30-yard free-kick to put Rovers ahead. Three minutes later, with the crowd still buzzing, Morgan scored a second in off a post, and he repeated the feat sixteen minutes from time, rounding the goalkeeper after exchanging passes with Mark O'Connor. Despite Gary McAllister's penalty, following a foul by Tim Parkin, Rovers had secured a major FA Cup victory, their first over top division opposition for twenty-eight years. Parkin, who played in more games than any other Rovers player in 1985/86, conceded an own goal as Rovers crashed out of the Cup 4-0 on Luton Town's artificial pitch.

1986/87

In May 1986, to save the club an annual cost of £30,000 plus expenses to hire Eastville, Rovers' board of directors took the historic decision to leave the club's spiritual home. A groundsharing scheme was drawn up with Bath City, whereby Rovers paid £65,000 per year to play home matches at Twerton Park. This ground, constructed on recreation land donated in 1909 by Thomas Carr and opened as Innox Park on 26 June of that year, had been the hosts' home since 1932, and was built on the side of a hill on the edge of the city, some 15 miles from the traditional hotbed of Rovers support in east Bristol. Rovers by name, Rovers by nature, it appeared. It was a revolutionary move, in that a league club was sharing with a non-League side in a different city but, in 1986, it was an integral part of Rovers' immediate survival. An emergency meeting of the Western League committee on 23 July 1986 discussed the knock-on effects of the move, with Bath City reserves due to play at Hambrook, Rovers' training ground, though they later began a groundsharing scheme with Radstock Town. Rovers' identity was questioned, support was down 25 per cent on the previous season and financial hardships continued, but the club survived. Ultimately, success, as epitomised by the championship season of 1989/90, was to lead to the club's return to Bristol after a decade of groundsharing.

Rovers rented Twerton Park from Bath City for an annual fee of £20,000 plus a percentage of gate receipts, while the club's offices remained in Keynsham. Twerton Park was an unlikely setting for league football, with a stand of 780 black-and-white seats built into the hillside. Cliftonhill, home of Albion Rovers, was the only similar example in British first-class football. 'The views are spectacular and it is well worth the ... walk up the steep Landsdown hill' (Fanny Charles, *Blackmore Vale*, 12/5/2000, p. 60). It would take some getting used to.

Bobby Gould's side opened the season with a 3-0 win at Walsall. It was a poor indication of results to follow, as Rovers lost twenty-one league games, conceded seventy-five goals for a second consecutive season, and finished in nineteenth place. Even Walsall were to gain revenge by defeating Rovers 3-0 in the return fixture. Four new faces appeared in the side for the opening day: Kenny Hibbitt, who scored the opening goal, and Tarki Micallef added experience to a side boasting many young players developed at Eastville, such as Tanner, Scales, Carter, Penrice and Smart. Other youngsters were given opportunities, Gerry Francis appeared just five times in the league, and the only really consistent newcomer to emerge was Geoff Twentyman.

Nonetheless, the first bricks for the 1989/90 championship season were being positioned. Twentyman, an August signing from Preston North End, missed only three league games, and Gary Penrice only four. Vaughan Jones, Ian Alexander and Phil Purnell enjoyed protracted spells in the side, while seventeen-year-old Steve Yates made his league debut on Shrove Tuesday at Darlington. As in the championship season, David Mehew was Rovers' top scorer, his tally of ten league goals giving him two more than Trevor Morgan, who joined Bristol City in January.

The start of the new season coincided with the death of George Endicott at the age of ninety-two, a well-respected club trainer through many generations of Bristol Rovers players. The first home league game at Twerton Park, or the 'Azteca Stadium', as Gould termed it, resulted in a 1-0 victory over Bolton Wanderers, despite the sending-off of Nicky Tanner. The win sent Rovers briefly to the top of Division Three. A crowd of 4,092 saw Trevor Morgan, the scorer of the club's final goal at Eastville, register the first league goal on the new ground from a seventeenth-minute penalty after he had been fouled by Mark Came. However, both the crowd and the result were misleading. Attendances dropped, Rovers lost seven times at Twerton Park in the league alone and survival was not assured until the final game of the season. In a bid to boost funds, the home game with Swindon Town over Easter was held at Ashton Gate, and an inflated crowd of over 8,000 saw Rovers lead 3-1 shortly after half-time, before losing 4-3.

In moving to Bath, Rovers had lost a considerable proportion of the traditional support. Season 1986/87, amid poor on-field performances and before a new generation of supporters could be found in the new surroundings, marks the lowest point in league attendance in Rovers' history. The seasonal home average of 3,246 remains the lowest the club experienced in the twentieth century. On their travels, only 1,206 saw the defeat at Doncaster Rovers in May, the lowest attendance at a post-war league game involving Bristol Rovers. There were also some crushing blows, with Port Vale, Gillingham and Wigan Athletic all emulating Swindon Town's four goals. Rovers lost 5-0 at Mansfield Town in January, with Keith Cassells, who scored after three, nine, fifty-three and fifty-six minutes, becoming the eighth opponent to score four goals in a league game, and 6-1 at Blackpool.

A 2-2 draw with Newport County in December (Rovers' fourth consecutive home draw in league and Cup) marked a new experiment, as it was Rovers' first home league game on a Sunday. The attendance was 2,660, and this well-intentioned plan was soon scrapped. It survived long enough, however, for Rovers to beat York City through a Gary Penrice goal on a Friday night in January, and to stage the Swindon Town game at Ashton Gate on a Sunday. The concept was to attract spectators at a time when there was no competition from Bristol City or the rugby clubs of Bristol and Bath. Not only did this imply Rovers were settling for second best, something the 1989/90 season was to strive to contradict, but it was a scheme to which supporters did not readily respond. Only 2,597 saw the victory over York City, and Rovers reverted to losing or drawing home matches on Saturdays.

Rovers were involved in two league fixtures in the North East within four weeks of each other in the spring. The game at Ayresome Park was won for Middlesbrough by the future England international Stuart Ripley's sixtieth-minute goal, in a game where Boro's full-back Brian Laws slipped in taking a penalty in first half injury time, sending the ball shooting away for a throw-in and leaving him in a crumpled heap, out injured for the rest of the season. A 1-1 draw at Darlington on Shrove Tuesday featured two goals in a minute during the second half. Rovers' directors generously rewarded travelling fans with a half-time urn of tea. By the end of the match, the dregs in the plastic cups had frozen in the chill north-eastern wind. The Darlington game was one in which seventeen-year-old Steve Yates, a name for the future, made his league debut in a side that included experienced journeymen David Rushbury and Bob Newton.

Undeniably, the game of the season was at Ashton Gate in an early kick-off on New Year's Day. Rovers were clearly underdog, and a strong Bristol City side pounded Tim Carter's goal. City had eleven shots on target to Rovers' two and, in addition, Paul Fitzpatrick and Steve Neville both hit the Rovers bar. To make matters worse, an injury to Carter meant David Mehew spent the final fifteen minutes of the first half in goal as ten-man Rovers attempted to stem City's flow. Then, incredibly, three minutes from time, Gary Smart's 20-yard shot dipped under the bar to give Rovers an unlikely victory. It was results such as this, and the four wins in the last eight league games, that kept Rovers in Division Three. The largest was 4-0 at home to Carlisle United, even though Jeff Meacham, a new signing from Trowbridge Town, who had opened the scoring with his first goal for the club, ended up in goal with the veteran Paul Bradshaw off the field injured. Meacham scored five goals to help keep Rovers alive, two of them at home to Chester City, when Rovers clawed back a 2-1 deficit to win after Graham Barrow, scorer of the visitors' second goal had been sent off before half-time for a foul on Rovers' match-winner John Scales. Ultimately, Rovers required a point at Newport County on the final day to retain their Third Division place, a mission accomplished with Phil Purnell scoring the game's only goal.

For the second year running, Rovers drew Brentford in the FA Cup. This year, after poor weather saw the tie called off several times, Brentford won in a replay, the second of three meetings of the clubs in December, with Ian Weston becoming the first Rovers player ever to be sent off on his club debut, a record matched by Wayne Carlisle in March 2002. Reading put six goals past Rovers in a two-legged League Cup tie, with Trevor Senior scoring a hat-trick and substitute Dean Horrix once, as Rovers crashed 4-0 at Elm Park. The Gloucestershire Cup final was held over to the following season as fixtures piled up towards the season's close, but Bristol City nonetheless effectively knocked Rovers out of the Freight Rover Trophy. Their 3-0 victory, through goals from David Moyes, Rob Newman and Alan Walsh, remains Rovers' heaviest ever defeat in this competition.

1987/88

Three games into the new season, with Rovers sitting on top of Division Three, the trials and tribulations of 1986/87 seemed a thing of the past. Rovers won their first two home games of 1987/88 by convincing margins. By February, Rovers hovered precariously above the relegation zone. However, March saw the side's first back-to-back wins of the season, and nine victories in the final fourteen league matches saw the team rise from twentieth to the heady heights of eighth in the table.

It had been a summer of significant change among the playing staff. In truth, Rovers could not afford the larger wage demands of more experienced professionals, and the emphasis was very much on untried youth, especially as two substitutes were now required for every league game. While Kenny Hibbitt remained at the club, it was John Scales who left, joining Wimbledon in a £70,000 deal. Bobby Gould left the club for a third time, ending his second two-year spell as manager by moving back to the capital, taking Scales as an integral part of his Wimbledon side that would stun the footballing nation by winning the FA Cup. Gary Smart moved to Cheltenham Town and Wayne Noble, the last player released by Gould, joined Yeovil Town. Two veterans, David Rushbury and Bob Newton, the latter indirectly, transferred to Goole Town.

The replacement for Gould was Gerry Francis, already a well-known face at Bristol Rovers. It was an inspired decision to appoint him, as he was to lead Rovers to continuing success. Under his guidance, there was to be the Third Division championship, a first Wembley appearance and a return of self-belief to the side soon known by elements within the media as 'Ragbag Rovers'. Francis had a 'fascinating style of management' (Roy Dolling), and is quoted as saying, with regard to one particularly inept first-half performance, 'what I said to them at half-time would be unprintable on the radio.' He inherited a side boasting the experience of Kenny Hibbitt and already featuring several key figures in the success to come: Vaughan Jones, Ian Alexander, Geoff Twentyman, David Mehew, Gary Penrice and Phil Purnell, to name a few. These were soon joined by midfielder Andy Reece, a smart acquisition from Willenhall.

During August 1987, three masterstrokes from Francis altered the Rovers side considerably, and paved the way for future glory years. First, he signed goalkeeper Nigel Martyn on a free transfer from the Cornish side St Blazey. The tall, confident Cornishman proved to be a shrewd acquisition and one of the most popular figures at the club. His transfer to Crystal Palace in November 1989 was to make him Britain's first £1-million goalkeeper, and he went on to play for England. Next, Francis paid just £10,000, initially as a loan from himself to the club, to bring Ian Holloway back from Brentford to his home club, where the influential midfielder was to play such a pivotal role in the club's success. Finally, to fill the need for a goalscorer, Devon White arrived, a few days into the season, from Shepshed Charterhouse to make an immediate impression.

White stepped into the breach at the eleventh hour, when Robbie Turner missed the train from his Cardiff home, and scored the second goal as Rovers raced to a 3-0 half-time lead over Aldershot. His reputation was made. Even though Mike Ring pulled a goal back, Rovers' second consecutive 3-1 home victory, and Penrice's fourth goal in three games, put the side top of Division Three, above preseason favourites Sunderland on goal difference. Indeed, Rovers had already earned a draw at Roker Park and were to embarrass the eventual divisional champions still further in February. Devon White's powerful, physical presence was to be a major factor in Rovers' success. His goals against Bristol City in May 1990 to seal promotion and at Wembley against Tranmere Rovers were to earn him an undisputed place in Rovers folklore.

Reality soon returned, of course, as Rovers lost 2-1 at Blackpool to be knocked off top perch. All three goals came in a four-minute spell midway through the second half, the winner coming from a controversial penalty, calmly converted by the veteran Tony Cunningham for his second goal of the game. But it was to be the side's away form that produced greatest concern. Rovers managed to draw at Sunderland, Bristol City, Notts County and Walsall, all of whom were in the top eight at the time, but lost to a range of lower-table and apparently beatable opposition. It was not until 5 March, when goals from White, Purnell and Mehew earned an emphatic 3-0 win at Chester City, that Rovers recorded their first away win of the season. By then, though, the side was in twentieth place in the division and alarm bells were ringing.

Rovers' home form, on the other hand, was reasonably good. Fourteen out of twenty-three league matches, plus all three League Cup and FA Cup ties, were won, and Rovers remained unbeaten at 'Fortress Twerton' from mid-December. The three sides automatically relegated were all beaten; Doncaster Rovers and Grimsby Town both conceded four goals at Twerton Park, with Purnell and White on the scoresheet on both occasions. The leaders Sunderland visited Twerton Park and, in a game that altered the flow of Rovers' season, were crushed 4-0. Manager Francis gave David Mehew a first league start, and he scored the third goal. Holloway had rifled Rovers ahead six minutes before half-time, and the top two scorers, Penrice and White, also hit the target. The Rokerites were knocked off top spot and Rovers' season was back on track. This game, however, was marred by a robust challenge from Sunderland's Gordon Armstrong, which broke Kenny Hibbitt's leg and effectively ended his twenty-year professional career.

Seven days after the visit of Sunderland, new leaders Notts County were held 1-1 at Twerton Park, Geoff Twentyman bizarrely scoring his only two goals of the season, becoming only the fourth Rovers player to score for both sides in a league match. Early season heavy defeats at Gillingham, Southend United, Bury and Aldershot now behind them, Rovers embarked on a glorious run of results to rescue their season. Twice Nigel Martyn kept six consecutive clean sheets as Rovers conceded goals in only one of thirteen league matches between early March and early May. During this run, Rovers were able to complete league doubles over Doncaster Rovers, York City and Chesterfield. The victory at Saltergate was won through a Penrice goal created by debutant Christian McClean. Sadly, though, Chesterfield's Dave Perry fractured his right knee in a collision with Purnell, an injury that was to end his career. Bury were in the middle of a five-match goalless spell when they earned a draw at Twerton Park. A forty-eighth minute Penrice goal, the penultimate of the eighteen that rendered him the club's seasonal top scorer, was enough to beat Bristol City, with whom Rovers had shared six goals at Ashton Gate in mid-September.

Behind Penrice and White, Rovers were competently served by eight goals each from Purnell and Mehew. While Purnell's goals were predominantly early in the season, Mehew started only the final seventeen games of the season. His contribution to the run of victories and Rovers' resultant surge up the divisional table should not be underestimated. Three of his goals came in the space of twenty-nine minutes during a highly convincing 4-0 victory at York City, watched by only 1,834. A mere 1,311 saw the single goal victory at Doncaster, the lowest crowd of the season at a Bristol Rovers league match. By way of contrast, 19,800 were at Brighton on the final day of the season, where Billy Clark's first league goal, toe-poking home an Andy Reece corner after sixty-eight minutes, could not prevent the Seagulls gaining the win they required for promotion to Division Two.

Stewart Phillips scored in successive 2-0 victories for Hereford United, which knocked Rovers out of the Littlewoods Cup and Sherpa Van Trophy. In the FA Cup, Rovers recorded their largest win since 1900, when a Penrice hat-trick helped defeat Merthyr Tydfil 6-0. It took two attempts, but Rovers eventually beat VS Rugby with ease, before losing 2-1 at Second Division Shrewsbury Town, for whom a former Eastville favourite, Brian Williams, scored a second-half winning goal.

Despite a goal from Andy Reece after sixty-eight minutes, Rovers lost the Gloucestershire Cup final, held over from 1986/87, 2-1 at home to Bristol City. Three months later, Rovers lost again, when the 1987/88 final was also won by City. Marco Carota, who never appeared in league action for Rovers, scored a consolation goal nineteen minutes from time, after City had run up a 3-0 lead before half-time.

1988/89

A position in the Division Three play-off final and missing out on promotion by one goal offered a glimpse of what was to follow the previous season. In many respects, the promotion push had begun in earnest in March 1988, and Rovers' form through 1988/89 reflected that of the latter stages of 1987/88. Gerry Francis stuck largely to this side, which was beginning to gel as a unit capable of great success. Gary Penrice scored twenty league goals and, alongside ever-presents Nigel Martyn and Geoff Twentyman, five other players appeared in at least forty-two of Rovers' forty-six league fixtures.

Nigel Martyn once again proved what a crucial figure he was to Rovers' success. Promoted sides excepted, no Third Division side conceded so few league goals, while defeat at Bramall Lane in September 1988 was the last time until February 1992 that Rovers conceded four goals in a league game. Although Simon Stapleton appeared in the opening game, converted winger Ian Alexander recovered from swallowing his tongue in an FA Cup tie against Fisher Athletic to form a strong full-back partnership with captain Vaughan Jones. First Billy Clark and later the consistent Steve Yates, his wages paid by the Rovers President's Club in Rovers' perilous financial situation, appeared alongside the dependable Geoff Twentyman in central defence. Mehew, Holloway, Reece and Purnell continued as the midfield quartet, each supplying a regular supply of goals, with Penrice partnering Devon White in attack.

If one cog was missing from the success story to come, it was perhaps Devon White's good luck in front of goal. His five league goals were not a fair reflection on his commitment to the side's cause and it was significant that his stand-in, Christian McClean, fared no better at first. White and McClean, both well over 6 feet tall, complemented perfectly the style of Penrice and latterly loan signing Dennis Bailey, who scored in eight of his first eleven league matches for Rovers.

Rovers were trailing at half-time in their first four league matches, yet lost just one of these. Penrice, White, Reece and Purnell scored twice each in home matches as, by mid-November, Rovers had won six out of eight home league games and lay fourth in the table. Bizarrely, no Rovers player was to score twice in a game at Twerton Park for the remainder of the season, though only Brentford, Bury and Cardiff City recorded away victories on the ground. The fixture against Bury featured a Reece own goal as well as two goals for the Shakers from their thirty-year-old striker, Steve Elliott. This remains the only occasion Bury have won an away league game against Rovers. Reece also scored an own goal early in the home game with Aldershot.

A successful season is perhaps best illustrated by matches played against mid-table Huddersfield Town and divisional champions Wolverhampton Wanderers. Rovers recorded their largest win of the season, 5-1, against the Terriers at the end of October, and fought their way to a goalless draw with all-conquering Wolves at Twerton Park on Boxing Day. Once the return fixtures were played, Bailey had arrived on loan from Crystal Palace. He scored twice as Rovers, overturning a half-time deficit, beat Huddersfield 3-2 at Leeds Road. When Rovers visited on Easter Monday, Rovers kept at bay Steve Bull and Andy Mutch, with thirty and eighteen league goals respectively already to their names, and became the only club to win at Molineux all season. It was a superb turn and shot after forty minutes from Bailey that earned Rovers perhaps their greatest result of the season.

On-field success quite naturally led to an increase in attendances. A crowd of 8,480 turned out for the Rovers on Boxing Day, and 8,676 for the local derby, while over 20,000 watched Rovers' 1-0 victories at Ashton Gate and Molineux. Penrice's goals in both derby games against Bristol City earned four points, and Rovers repeated, albeit less dramatically, the New Year exploits of two seasons earlier at Ashton Gate. At Twerton Park, City's Rob Newman saw his well-struck penalty saved by Martyn, who continued to prove his worth in Rovers' goal.

In addition to Huddersfield Town, Rovers also completed league doubles over Chester City, Chesterfield and Gillingham. At Priestfield, Rovers trailed at half-time to a Steve Lovell penalty before recovering to beat Gillingham 3-2. A home victory over Swansea City in April, Rovers' ninth consecutive league game without defeat, was achieved against opposition fielding former Rovers player Paul Raynor and, as a substitute, Stewart Phillips, whose goals for Hereford United had knocked

Rovers out of two cup competitions the previous season. Rovers also recorded a 2-1 victory away to then high-flying Northampton Town, with Paul Smith, an able and bustling stand-in for David Mehew, scoring his only goal of the season.

It speaks volumes for Rovers' consistency that a five-match winless run and no goals in the final four league games of the season did not prevent the Pirates from reaching the promotion play-offs. Their rivals in the play-offs – a system into its third season devised to increase late season mid-table interest – would include Fulham and Port Vale, both of whom played Rovers during this last barren run. A second-half Penrice goal was all Rovers had to show from a semi-final first-leg at Twerton Park, but this slender lead over Fulham was ample. At Craven Cottage four days later, four second-half goals earned Rovers a convincing 5-0 aggregate victory. Clark, Holloway, Bailey and Reece all scored against a Fulham side boasting future Rovers midfielders Ronnie Maugé and Justin Skinner.

Rovers were left to face Port Vale over two legs for promotion to Division Two. A record Twerton Park crowd of 9,042 saw Penrice score again, as Rovers led 1-0 at half-time in the first leg against a side that had finished the season with ten points more than Rovers. However, Robbie Earle scored a crucial second-half equaliser to leave the Pirates with a mountain to climb. Earle had scored for Vale in both league fixtures against Francis' side, and his second-half far-post header before a crowd of 17,353 in the second leg at Vale Park consigned Rovers to a further season in Division Three. Nonetheless, the seeds of hope had been sown and were to come to fruition over the forthcoming twelve months.

Cup competitions brought Rovers little joy in 1988/89. Eliminated early from the Littlewoods Cup through Trevor Aylott's second-half goal in the first leg at Bournemouth, Rovers also suffered the humiliation of an FA Cup defeat at Kettering Town. A comfortable win over Fisher Athletic, who fielded a young Ken Charlery, set up a tricky away tie, which, after a goalless first half, Rovers lost 2-1 at Rockingham Road. All Rovers had to show for their efforts was an Andy Reece consolation goal after seventy minutes. Kettering featured several experienced players, including Lil Fuccillo and Ernie Moss, and the former Peterborough United and Brentford striker Robbie Cooke scored both their goals. Nonetheless, it was a demoralising and embarrassing result in front of the BBC *Match of the Day* cameras.

The Sherpa Van Trophy at least gave a hint of Rovers' Cup run of 1989/90. A first-half Reece goal saw off Bristol City, and Cardiff City were also beaten before Rovers fell to Mark Loram's goal for Torquay United in the quarter-finals. Two second-half Mehew goals and a third in the final minute from White brought Rovers a 3-0 victory over Bristol City in the Gloucestershire Cup final, the club's most convincing victory in this tournament since the game against Staple Hill in January 1898.

1989/90

Thirty-seven years after topping Division Three (South), Rovers were crowned Third Division champions in 1989/90 with a club record ninety-three points. It was a momentous achievement for Gerry Francis' 'Ragbag Rovers' at their temporary home outside Bristol. The elusive promotion was achieved on a glorious if tense Wednesday night when Bristol City were defeated at Twerton Park. Then, with the championship secured, Rovers could enjoy the icing on the cake provided by the club's first-ever appearance at Wembley Stadium.

The side that earned this success was largely that which had shown such potential already. Francis stuck with the tried and tested formula, bringing in Ian Willmott, New Zealand international Paul Nixon and Tony Sealy to play sporadic but crucial roles. Sealy scored twice in the win at Shrewsbury Town in November that took Rovers back to the top of the table, while Nixon's five goals included the final one as Rovers sealed the championship at Blackpool in May. It was, however, the experienced hands that held the side together. Twentyman, Mehew, player of the year Holloway and captain Vaughan Jones were all ever-presents, while Alexander, Yates, Reece and White appeared in over forty league matches.

In securing the Third Division championship, Rovers remained unbeaten at home for the only season in the club's history. There were scares, of course, with Sealy's last-minute equaliser earning a November draw with ten-man Blackpool, and Rovers trailing to Cardiff City before two injury time goals earned an unlikely 2-1 victory. Rovers lost just five times in forty-six games, a Division Three record, and equalled the club's tally of twenty-six league victories in 1952/53. There were twenty-seven clean sheets, as opposed to the thirty achieved during the 2006/07 season. Yet, it was achieved the hard way. Rovers, in fact, trailed at half-time in three games and only once scored more than three goals in a match. The exceptional game was a 6-1 victory over Wigan Athletic in March, where Carl Saunders, a February signing from Stoke City to replace Gary Penrice, scored the first league hat-trick seen at Twerton Park. This was the Latics' record league defeat, eclipsing the 5-0 loss suffered when Rovers visited Springfield Park in February 1983.

An August Gloucestershire Cup final victory over Bristol City set the tone for the season. On a hot August afternoon, David Mehew's thirty-seventh-minute goal defeated Brentford, and Rovers followed this up with a first post-war league victory at Field Mill – the first of a club record eleven away league wins. Three first-half goals against Notts County in a third narrow victory sent Rovers to the top of Division Three. In the next home game, when Preston North End visited Twerton Park, three more first-half goals sealed a comfortable victory, with Twentyman heading the opener against his former club. Bristol City were hovering ominously close, and the sides met at the end of September with two points separating them in the league. The highest crowd to see Rovers all season,

17,432, witnessed a goalless draw, as Francis' side held on with ten men following the dismissal of Alexander eleven minutes before half-time.

Nigel Martyn's impressive goalkeeping displays were beginning to attract the attention of larger clubs. This burgeoning reputation was enhanced still further by a run of 645 minutes without conceding a goal, just short of Jim Eadie's club record 707 minutes set in 1973/74. The run ended with Mark Kelly's eightieth-minute equaliser for Cardiff City at Twerton Park in mid-October, in a match in which Ian Holloway missed a penalty. The following game epitomised the season for, after trailing 1-0 at half-time to an ultimately relegated Northampton Town team, Rovers were 2-1 down with eleven minutes to play. Then Nixon grabbed an equaliser, Holloway converted a penalty and the unfortunate Trevor Quow put through his own net to give Rovers a 4-2 victory.

With Gary Penrice moving to Watford for £500,000, Rovers were further depleted when Nigel Martyn became Britain's first £1-million goalkeeper, his transfer to Crystal Palace smashing Rovers' club record. Before the season was out, he appeared for his new club in the FA Cup final where Lee Martin, himself a Rovers player in 1996, smashed a rising left-foot volley past him in the replay to win the cup for Manchester United. Martyn was to break his own transfer record in a move to Leeds United in July 1996, which led to international recognition with England. In exchange, Palace's reserve goalkeeper Brian Parkin moved to Bristol to appear in the final thirty league games of the season, kick-starting a career that saw two Wembley appearances with Rovers even before an unlikely comeback in the 1999/2000 season.

Early promotion rivals, Birmingham City were the Boxing Day opposition for the first imposed all-ticket game. Rovers then saw off the threat of Tranmere Rovers, but only after David Fairclough had been stretchered off. Rovers then gave a trial to Sunday football, playing three home games on spring Sundays, won at Preston North End, where Mehew's goal after an hour gave the side its only win in four league matches played on artificial pitches, and faced, in Swansea City's forty-two-year-old Tommy Hutchison, the fourth oldest opponent in the club's league history. The real threat, however, came from Ashton Gate, where Bristol City had put together an impressive run of results and claimed top spot in the division. Rovers, with a game in hand through the spring, were waiting for City to slip.

Even the calmest of Rovers supporters was put on the emotional treadmill as the side, with the scent of promotion in its nostrils, recorded six consecutive 2-1 victories in the run-up to Easter. Devon White's two goals earned victory at Craven Cottage, even after Fulham had equalised sixteen minutes from time, when Clive Walker's shot deflected in off Yates, Jones and a post. In the next five games, Rovers went a goal down each time, but won them all. Cardiff City, eventually relegated by a point, were perhaps the hardest done by. After losing Sealy with a broken right leg, Rovers scraped home with two goals in eleven nail-biting injury-time minutes. In White's absence, the unorthodox yet distinctive figure of Christian McClean scored decisive goals in each of the next three games. At Brisbane Road, Mehew's goal earned a victory after Rovers had arrived at the ground only twenty minutes prior to kick-off. Rovers also recovered a two goal deficit, which would have been worse if referee Philip Wright had awarded a penalty at 2-0 for a clear trip by Willmott on Birmingham City's Robert Hopkins. Instead, Rovers rallied to draw 2-2, with the former Eastville favourite Martin Thomas conceding an own goal.

As Bristol City stuttered, the local derby on 2 May assumed gargantuan proportions. If Rovers won to preserve their unbeaten home record, promotion to Division Two would be assured, but defeat would hand the championship to City. It was certainly not a night for the faint-hearted. A glorious two-goal display from White, one in each half, and a late Holloway penalty sealed the promotion push and Rovers were back in Division Two. First, White put Rovers in front after twenty-five minutes when Andy Llewellyn's slip allowed Mehew to cross the ball, then he doubled the lead after Saunders beat Rob Newman to cross. When Llewellyn handled Purnell's shot after sixty-two minutes, Holloway sent Ron Sinclair the wrong way from the penalty spot. A night of high drama before a record home crowd for a game at Twerton Park, 9,831, will live long in the memory. Yet, to ensure that Bristol City, also promoted, could not steal the championship away, victory was essential at already relegated Blackpool in the final game. Over 5,000 Rovers supporters made the trip to Bloomfield Road, where a second successive 3-0 victory – Phil Purnell scoring in the final minute of the first half and substitute Paul Nixon in the final minute of the second half – saw Rovers secure the championship in a carnival atmosphere. Vaughan Jones was able to lift the trophy at his own testimonial game a week later.

Early exits from the Littlewoods Cup, at Portsmouth, and FA Cup, to Reading, for whom Trevor Senior scored a seventy-first-minute winning goal in a first-round second replay, merely highlight the club's success elsewhere. A draw with Torquay United and victories over Exeter City and Gillingham earned Rovers a Leyland Daf Cup quarter final meeting with Brentford. This was won in a penalty shoot-out, as was a semi-final with Walsall, Brian Parkin saving three kicks in each shoot-out. Rovers now faced Notts County over two legs for the right to meet Tranmere Rovers in a Wembley final. A fifty-eighth-minute header from David Mehew in the first leg and a strong rearguard action at Meadow Lane, as well as County having a last-minute 'goal' controversially disallowed, earned Rovers a first-ever visit to the Twin Towers. Mehew's eighteen league and three cup goals had, bizarrely, all come in separate matches.

There were some 32,000 Rovers fans at Wembley in the 53,317 crowd on 20 May and, despite the result, it was a wonderful day of celebration. A veterans' warm-up game saw Rovers and Tranmere draw 1-1, Alan Warboys and Frank Worthington scoring the goals in a show that also featured George Best, Bobby

Moore OBE, four members of the pop group Spandau Ballet and the England rugby international Wade Dooley, and which was refereed by the veteran Jack Taylor. Just ten minutes from the start of the final, the former Rovers defender Mark Hughes crossed and, from Chris Malkin's flick-on, Ian Muir scored. Six minutes after half-time, substitute Nixon's cross found White who, at the second attempt, shot right-footed high into the net for the equaliser. However, seventeen minutes from time, Jim Steel's header consigned Rovers to defeat; the winning goal was fervently contested as a push on by Rovers' Geoff Twentyman by Steel, but it was overruled by controversial match referee Vic Callow. Nonetheless, it was a major achievement for a club of the stature of Bristol Rovers to reach a Wembley final. The season had brought much greater success than any realistic Rovers fan could have dreamed of.

10

The 1990s

1990/91

It is perhaps typical of Bristol Rovers that the long-awaited return to Division Two should be overshadowed by events off the field. The all-conquering side of 1989/90 understandably found the going considerably harder in the higher division, and a final league placing of thirteenth, the club's highest since 1959/60, was commendable. However, the actions of arsonists and further rebuffs to Rovers' hopes of a move back to Bristol provided many of the overriding memories.

The continued search for a stadium nearer Rovers' fan base in east Bristol was still encountering problems. With the proposal for a move to Stoke Gifford rejected, much emphasis had been placed on a potential move to Mangotsfield. With the huge success of the 1989/90 season, the club now appeared more likely to interest the local authorities, who seemed keen to jump on the bandwagon, given the on-field success and aspirations of both Bristol clubs. Suddenly, Bristol was being touted as a sporting city. Yet disappointment was to strike on two fronts in September 1990. First, the plans for a stadium at Mangotsfield were rejected and secondly, a week later in the early hours of 16 September, a serious fire damaged the Main Stand at Twerton Park.

There was little doubt as to the perpetrators of the stadium fire. Seven so-called 'supporters' of Bristol City, returning from a 2-1 defeat at West Bromwich Albion, went back to the scene of their side's disappointment in May, attempted to burn down the stand and, in court, were found guilty of arson. Repair costs to the Main Stand were to run to £800,000, although Rovers did receive financial aid from Bath Rugby Football Club as well as a £300 donation from Sheffield Wednesday supporters following their visit in October. Moreover, there was a prearranged commitment to a £90,000 family stand, which opened in December. Yet again, precisely at the point when Rovers promised on-field success, politics and finance interfered in the club's affairs.

At the same time, Rovers were obliged to comply with the increasing legal requirements imposed following the tragedies at Bradford, Hillsborough and

Heysel. The 1985 Sporting Event (Control of Alcohol) Act had prevented those being suspected of drunkenness gaining access to the ground, and the 1986 Public Order Act enabled clubs to impose exclusion orders for 'hooligan related offences'. This was followed by the 1991 Football Offences Act, which banned obscene and racially offensive chanting and forbade spectators from entering the field of play.

Why make alterations to a winning side? Apart from the departure of stand-in Peter Cawley and the arrival of the exciting Tony Pounder, it was largely the championship-winning side that attained a perfectly respectable mid-table finish. Some argued it was a return to the halcyon days of the 1950s, with Rovers' paltry financial clout virtually necessitating a return to the 'no buy, no sell' policy that dictated the early post-war years. Others argued that the club stood to suffer almost immediate relegation if, in this era of huge spending, a number of key positions were not filled by expensive signings. As it was, 'Ragbag Rovers' retained their Second Division standing with relative ease.

If life in a higher division was to prove difficult for Rovers, as many claimed, there certainly was little sign of it. A narrow defeat at Leicester City, with Ian Alexander contributing a bizarre own goal and Vaughan Jones scoring the club's first goal back in Division Two, was followed by victory at home to Charlton Athletic, the visitors' eighth in a club record run of ten consecutive league defeats. Devon White, on sixteen minutes, and David Mehew, after forty-nine minutes, put Rovers ahead before Robert Lee scored for the Addicks four minutes from time. As early as mid-October, Rovers won back-to-back away games at Swindon Town and Middlesbrough. Ian Holloway scored from penalties in both games and coolly converted another after forty-two minutes of a 1-0 home victory over Oxford United. He had equalled Stewart Barrowclough's club record from 1979 of scoring penalties in three consecutive league matches, but Holloway never scored again from the penalty spot for Rovers.

On a Wednesday night in September, Blackburn Rovers recorded a 2-1 victory at Twerton Park to end Rovers' proud run of thirty-four home league matches unbeaten. Three days later, Sheffield Wednesday also won at 'Fortress Twerton'. On 6 October, Rovers only avoided dropping into the relegation zone – reorganisation having meant only two clubs would be relegated – because of the three second-half goals Oxford United conceded at Barnsley. Nonetheless, by the first week in December, Rovers lay in ninth place in the table, the highest placing in an encouraging season. At this stage, the club was in the middle of a morale-boosting nine-match unbeaten run, which ended abruptly when Jimmy Quinn scored West Ham United's sixty-eighth-minute winning goal on New Year's Day. However, enough had been done to satisfy the claim that Rovers were in this division by right.

As the season wore on, Francis briefly recalled Willmott, and Billy Clark played in his first games since October 1988, after many substitute appearances and missing the entire promotion season through injury. Clark first played in March in the cauldron of a local derby and, before the month was out, he had contributed an own goal in a 2-1 defeat at Hillsborough. Adrian Boothroyd and Gavin Kelly both broke into the league side and, two years on, Dennis Bailey enjoyed a second, if less prolific, loan spell with the club.

Over Easter, Rovers' Jekyll and Hyde character came to the fore. Goalkeeper Parkin was sent off in a 3-1 defeat at home to Brighton, with stand-in Ian Alexander saving the subsequent penalty from John Byrne. Forty-eight hours later, before a crowd of 17,509, second-half goals from Devon White and Tony Sealy earned a notable 2-0 victory at Newcastle United. Rovers then finished the season with demoralising 3-1 defeats at Oxford United, where Vaughan Jones' second own goal of the season left Rovers three down by half-time, and Portsmouth, for whom John Beresford opened the scoring after only thirty-eight seconds. In depriving West Bromwich Albion of a final-day win, Tony Pounder contributing his third goal of the season nineteen minutes from time following Jones' near-post corner, Rovers effectively relegated the Hawthorns club.

Osvaldo Ardiles, a World Cup winner with Argentina in 1978, was the manager of Rovers' opponents in three of Rovers' league victories. Pounder's first goal for the club helped Rovers record a 2-0 victory at Swindon Town in October. A 2-1 win against the same opposition completed the first of Rovers' two league doubles, but only after Nestor Lorenzo had hit a Twerton Park post. Shortly afterwards, Ardiles took over the reins at Newcastle United in time to suffer a third defeat at the hands of Gerry Francis' side.

Once again, relative success was based on a consistently settled side. Twentyman, Holloway and Reece were ever-presents, but in truth the team virtually picked itself for much of the season. Parkin proved himself an adept goalkeeper and an experienced defence was not in the habit of shipping goals regularly. Carl Saunders, after enjoying a mid-season purple patch of nine goals in ten league matches, finished the year as the club's top goalscorer with sixteen goals in league action. David Mehew's two goals in a 3-2 home victory over Bristol City in January 1991 constituted the first occasion since November 1988 that the talented midfielder, top scorer in 1990/91, had contributed more than one in a league game.

There was disappointment in the FA Cup. Third Division Crewe Alexandra won 2-0 at Twerton Park, with the former Rovers defender Darren Carr scoring one of the goals. Bob Bloomer had been forced into goal once Parkin was carried off the field injured, but this is no excuse for a humiliating experience. There was also an early exit from the Rumbelows Cup where, although full-backs Alexander and Twentyman both scored, Rovers lost on aggregate to Third Division Torquay United.

One benefit of being in Division Two was qualification for the Zenith Data Systems Cup. Rovers played in just two games in this tournament, taking a half-hour lead through Tony Pounder before losing to Crystal Palace, who went on to win the Wembley final with the former Rovers goalkeeper Nigel Martyn in their side. Bristol City scored twice in each half, Nicky Morgan contributing half their goals, as Rovers were beaten 4-1 in the Gloucestershire Cup final.

1991/92

After the disappointments regarding proposed stadia in Stoke Gifford and Mangotsfield, Rovers at last appeared on the verge of finalising plans for a move nearer its spiritual home in east Bristol. The new site was at Hallen Marsh, a 70-acre site in close proximity to the proposed M49 motorway, which was due to open in 1996. Good road and rail links would, of course, be essential, as Rovers attempted to build on the fact that Bristol boasted two Second Division sides. The new stadium was also seen as a means to attract major national and international sporting events to a West Country arena.

Plans to develop the Hallen Marsh site into a multi-sport complex were drawn up by Severnside Sportsworld, an organisation effectively run by the Rovers directors Denis and Geoff Dunford. Spectator, a leading American facilities management company, was called in to advise and, by December 1991, the local authorities appeared to be in favour. Yet, the Bristol Rovers story is not so straightforward. No sooner were plans being tabled than it was revealed that the site was too close to a chemical plant to satisfy safety regulations. The deal was off, the Dunfords had lost an alleged £300,000, already invested into the scheme, and Rovers' increasingly desperate search for a new Bristol home continued.

It was inevitable that Gerry Francis' success at Rovers on a shoestring budget should lead to interest from larger clubs. Sure enough, he left Rovers in the summer of 1991 to become manager at Queen's Park Rangers. While at Loftus Road, he accumulated a number of players who had served him so well at Twerton Park, with Ian Holloway, Dennis Bailey, Devon White, Gary Penrice and Steve Yates all rejoining their former manager. On the other hand, a large number of Queen's Park Rangers players were to make the opposite move, untried youngsters such as Graeme Power and Steve Parmenter, as well as record signing Andy Tillson. For his part, Francis was later manager at Tottenham Hotspur before returning for a second spell as manager at Loftus Road, the ground where he had made his name as a player.

The new manager was Martin Dobson, an erstwhile, classy midfielder with Burnley, Everton and Bury, and the winner of five full England caps. He had been manager at Northwich Victoria and had spent five years in charge of Bury prior to his arrival at Twerton Park. While Holloway followed Francis to London in a £230,000 deal, Rovers also lost Tony Sealy to Finnish football and the distinctive Christian McClean, who joined Swansea City prior to many years as a peripatetic striker in Essex non-League circles. Dobson was able to call upon the services of two experienced signings in Fulham's Justin Skinner and Derby County's Steve Cross. While Richard Evans and the former Manchester United midfielder David Wilson started in the side, it was Lee Maddison and Gareth Taylor who, both selected by Dobson, began careers that would bring success with Rovers and beyond.

In starting the season without the suspended Carl Saunders, Dobson also unleashed the talents of eighteen-year-old Marcus Stewart, already the winner of twelve England Schoolboy caps, who had worked his way up through the youth system. After a header and a left-foot volley in a meeting with Ipswich Town, in which Ian Alexander saw his forty-seventh-minute penalty saved by Craig Forrest, Stewart scored twice at Tranmere Rovers in his second game, becoming in the process Rovers' youngest penalty scorer when he converted a last-minute equaliser. Over the coming seasons, Stewart established himself as one of the brightest prospects produced by Rovers in recent years. His excellent first touch and ability to take on opponents soon drew the attention of larger clubs, but Rovers were to retain him long enough for him to score the side's goal at Wembley in the 1995 play-off final.

Yet Dobson's side lost six of its first nine league games, and the manager's brief tenure was over. He later returned to football as youth development officer at First Division Bolton Wanderers. The one victory, 2-1 at home to Oxford United, marked the first game of the season for captain Vaughan Jones. His return lasted all of sixty seconds before he suffered a broken leg, which ruled him out for a further fourteen months. Coach Dennis Rofe was quickly elevated to the post of manager on 10 January 1992. He too enjoyed a long professional career, winning one England under-23 cap and enjoying almost a decade as Leicester City's left-back after making his league debut as a goalscoring substitute in Orient's 2-0 win at Rovers in April 1968.

The season had started dramatically with Rovers repeating their feat of February 1939 by recovering a three-goal deficit at home to Ipswich Town. As on the previous occasion, the centre-forward scored twice, Devon White's brace of goals earning an unlikely point after Ipswich had led 3-0 with twenty-six minutes left. In the next home game, Justin Skinner scored a last-minute consolation goal after coming on as substitute for his debut. He was a £130,000 club record signing from Fulham, a transfer deal finally exceeding the fee paid for Stewart Barrowclough in 1979. The Rovers midfield now added the craft of Skinner to the efforts of Mehew, Reece and Pounder.

There were some high-scoring games at Twerton Park, notably a 3-3 draw with Port Vale and a second consecutive 3-2 victory over Bristol City. A similar win at home to Millwall came courtesy of Devon White's last-minute winning goal. Away from home, Rovers lost 1-0 at Portman Road in Ipswich Town's 2,000th league game and 1-0 at Derby County, for whom the most-capped England international, Peter Shilton, played in goal. At forty-two years 151 days, he is the fifth oldest opponent to face Rovers in league football. Amid all the changes, no single Rovers player appeared in every league game.

The heaviest defeat of the season, indeed Rovers' worst loss since February 1987, came at the Abbey Stadium on a Friday evening in February. Cambridge United, who scored four goals in an eleven-minute second-half spell, went second in the table by beating Rovers 6-1. Earlier, Cambridge had earned a draw at Twerton Park in December, when the future England international Dion Dublin and his fellow striker John Taylor had both scored equalisers. At the Abbey Stadium, five opponents scored against Rovers, Neil Heaney became only the third opponent to score for both sides in a league game, and both the opposition's substitutes scored. One of these substitutes was John Taylor, later Cambridge United's all-time top goalscorer, but at that stage struggling to score regularly. Within weeks, Taylor was a Rovers player and a very astute signing he proved to be, his eight goals in as many appearances leaving him just behind Saunders and White on ten, and Mehew on nine goals. Taylor scored twice against Southend United and three times against Brighton as Rovers recorded two 4-1 victories in April. His goals were to prove invaluable the following season, despite Rovers suffering relegation.

Rovers' cup games in 1991/92 were certainly not dull. The season began with a Gloucestershire Cup final defeat at Ashton Gate, where two Rovers defenders, Ian Alexander and Geoff Twentyman, were sent off. All the goals in a 3-2 defeat were scored before half-time. In the League Cup, the sides met again and, having lost the Twerton Park leg 3-1 to Bristol City, Rovers appeared dead and buried. However, at Ashton Gate, a crowd of 9,880 saw Rovers score three times in a strong second-half display as they won 4-2 to defeat the local rivals on the away goals rule. On a night of typically high passions, old heads White and Mehew scored twice each. Despite fears of a rerun of the 1977 FA Cup tie, Rovers lost just 2-0 in the next round to a Nottingham Forest side featuring Stuart Pearce and Teddy Sheringham. Two goals from Ipswich Town's David Lowe sent Rovers out of the Zenith Data Systems Cup at the first hurdle, while a former Pirate, Kevin Moore, scored for Southampton as they lost the Wembley final in March.

In the FA Cup, Ian Alexander gave Rovers an early lead in the third-round tie with West Country rivals Plymouth Argyle, who featured in their side Rob Turner and Steve Morgan, both Rovers players at some point in their career. Then Carl Saunders took over, scoring two minutes before half-time and adding a second-half hat-trick. His feat of four goals in twenty-seven minutes was the first occasion since Jack Jones in November 1901 that a Rovers player had scored so many in an FA Cup tie, and it was Rovers' largest win in this tournament since 1987/88. Rovers thereby earned a plum home game with Liverpool, and a then ground record of 9,484 watched a thrilling 1-1 draw, players called Saunders scoring for both clubs. Dean Saunders, however, hit the headlines after receiving a three-match ban for elbowing Alexander, an offence missed by the referee but captured by television cameras. Extraordinarily, Carl Saunders' powerful long-range right-foot volley gave Rovers an interval lead at Anfield but, before a 30,142 crowd, Liverpool won through goals from Steve McManaman and Dean Saunders and progressed to beat Paul Hardyman's Sunderland side in the final.

1992/93

Amid the disappointment of continued rebuffs in their attempts to return to a home ground in Bristol, Rovers lost their position in the newly renamed First Division, relegated with Cambridge United and Brentford. The nomenclature is deceptive. This apparent first season for Rovers in Division One came as a result of a renaming process, stemming from the creation of a Premier Division, first won in 1992/93 by Manchester United. In reality, Rovers continued their slow nomadic bounce between the old Second and Third Divisions.

Rovers began the new season without Adrian Boothroyd, who had joined Heart of Midlothian, and Bob Bloomer, now with Cheltenham Town. However, the side bore a strong resemblance to that which had finished mid-table in 1991/92, and attacking options looked exciting, with John Taylor, Carl Saunders and Marcus Stewart all in contention for places. Taylor and Stewart scored fluently early in the season, but Saunders, starting as first choice, only got onto the scoresheet in October after being relegated to substitute. Goalscoring was not a problem for Rovers. The side relegated in 1980/81 had scored only thirty-four times in the league, whereas fifty-five goals were scored this time round, Taylor contributing fourteen of them.

The real problem in 1992/93 was the frequency of League defeats. Rovers lost a club record twenty-five League games in being relegated, and the total of eleven home defeats equalled the tally set in 1947/48. In the first home game of the season, having previously been unbeaten in sixteen matches at Twerton Park, Rovers conceded four goals for the first time on that ground. Then, on 3 November, Rovers lost 5-1 at home to Barnsley, the heaviest home defeat since December 1976. This was followed by a 5-1 defeat at Wolverhampton Wanderers, Rovers conceding five goals in consecutive games for only the third time in the club's League history. They were staring relegation in the face.

Another worrying feature of the early part of this season was the club's propensity for conceding penalties. There were five penalties given away in the first four League games. During the third match, in which Rovers recorded their only win in the first thirteen League fixtures, Brentford were awarded two, Gary Blissett scoring from one seven minutes after half-time before Mickey Bennett squandered the second, nineteen minutes from the end. At Watford, Jason Drysdale scored a penalty after only five minutes. Gavin Kelly, replacing Brian Parkin in goal, saved penalties, one from Dean Saunders at Villa Park and one from Ray Houghton at Twerton Park, in each of the FA Cup ties with Aston Villa. John Byrne, who had missed a penalty for Brighton against Rovers eighteen months earlier, missed another as Rovers scrambled a 1-1 draw at Sunderland. Julian Dicks, Bristol-born, scored penalties for West Ham United in both their League games against Rovers.

Dennis Rofe suffered a traumatic start to the season as Rovers manager. Rovers conceded four goals in four of their twelve opening games, and also suffered a demoralising 3-0 home defeat to Grimsby Town. West Ham United's visit to Twerton Park saw hapless Rovers lose 4-0, and Paul Hardyman, a summer signing from Sunderland following a Cup final appearance, was sent off as the first was conceded. Clive Allen created one goal and scored the fourth five minutes from time, after Mark Robson's shot had rebounded off the crossbar. After only seventeen wins in fifty-three League games, Rofe's tenure came to an end, and he subsequently worked as a coach to Stoke City and Southampton. He was succeeded from within the club by a man initially appointed to work alongside him.

On Tuesday 10 November 1992, as a last throw of the dice, Rovers appointed a larger-than-life figure as the new manager. If Albert Prince-Cox had been the figurehead for the 1930s revival, so too could Malcolm Allison in the 1990s. During a long playing career, he had played on eight occasions against Rovers in league football. Among the litany of achievements with the many clubs he had served as manager, the 1967/68 league championship with Manchester City stood out. He is the only Rovers manager who has led a club to this honour. Allison's side was strengthened by two players signed shortly before his arrival – Gary Waddock and the club's new record signing for £370,000 Andy Tillson. Both players had joined from Queen's Park Rangers just hours before the 5-1 defeat at Molineux, in which they had appeared.

Initially, Allison's arrival instigated a change in Rovers' fortunes. Vaughan Jones returned to the side after an absence of over a year and a run of four straight victories without conceding a goal offered fresh hope. During the first three of these, recent arrival Justin Channing, a £250,000 signing, contrived to score in the twenty-fifth minute of each game, his only three goals of the season. The third was easily the brightest moment of a gloomy season, as Rovers won 4-0 against a Bristol City side boasting the future England striker Andy Cole. Three goals in thirteen second-half minutes helped Rovers to record their largest victory in a local derby since December 1963. However, this great run ended at Fratton Park, where Portsmouth beat Rovers 4-1, the first of three straight wins. In scoring all Pompey's goals, Guy Whittingham became only the twelfth opponent to score four or more times in a League game against Rovers. It was a record-breaking season for Whittingham, who set a club seasonal record with his forty-fourth goal of a productive season, scored at Twerton Park in April. Then Stan Collymore inspired Southend United to victory at Twerton Park after Ian Alexander had been sent off.

By then, though, despite a 3-0 win at Brentford and a creditable goalless draw with champions-elect Newcastle United, before a crowd of 29,372 at St James' Park, Malcolm Allison had left, ending a long, largely successful and enigmatic association with Football League management. Coach Steve Cross, who had appeared in his last game as a player in October, took temporary charge for three games, prior to the appointment on 15 March 1993 of John Ward. It was too late to prevent the inevitable relegation, but it was a positive move. A player himself of great experience, Ward had spent sixteen months as manager at York City and had served as assistant to Graham Taylor at Watford, Aston Villa and England, and soon proved himself to be a progressive and enthusiastic leader. Over the next three years, under Ward's leadership, Rovers were able to re-establish themselves as a force in Second Division football and return to Wembley in 1995. With relegation apparent, he took the opportunity to blood young talent, with Gareth Taylor, Andy Gurney and Mike Davis among those promoted to the first-team squad before the season was over.

Under Ward there was little change at first. A dull, goalless draw in driving rain with Leicester City, where the visitors' David Lowe had hit a post before his thirty-fifth-minute red card, was followed by derby day defeat at Ashton Gate, with Ian Alexander sent off again. Despite taking a second-half lead at Upton Park in April through Billy Clark's first goal of the season, defeat against West Ham United saw Rovers relegated for the third time in the club's history. There was frenetic action nine points above Rovers on the final day, with all sorts of relegation permutations possible before Brentford and Cambridge United finally dropped with Rovers. In 1920, Rovers had appeared in the first league game at The Den, and now they appeared in the last, spoiling Millwall's final day at their old ground with a 3-0 win. The game was twice held up by pitch invasions before Mike Davis, on as a substitute for his debut, registered Rovers' last First Division goal.

Rovers' only season in the short-lived Anglo-Italian Cup saw only matches in this country against Southend United and West Ham United, with the club being eliminated by virtue of a toss of a coin, conducted over the telephone. The Gloucestershire Cup final, by contrast, was won through Marcus Stewart's last-minute goal, after the future England striker Andy Cole had given Bristol City a half-time lead. In the League Cup, Rovers held out for a goalless draw at Maine Road but, despite the hilarity of the Manchester City substitute Flitcroft being announced as 'Gary Flipflop', were defeated at Twerton Park by the First Division side, Lee Maddison conceding an own goal. Likewise, in the FA Cup a well-earned draw at Villa Park before a crowd of 27,040 earned a lucrative home replay. Rovers, though, collapsed under pressure and Aston Villa could even afford the luxury of a missed penalty in running out 3-0 winners.

1993/94

The return of Second Division, or former Third Division, football to Twerton Park renewed the call for a new stadium in Bristol. Having lost out in recent years on proposed sites at Stoke Gifford, Mangotsfield and Hallen Marsh, the search was becoming increasingly intense. Several other league clubs, Brighton and Chester City being arguably two examples, played home matches in towns other than their own, but as Rovers approached a decade's tenancy at Twerton Park, fears grew that the club would have lost the support of a whole generation in east Bristol.

The clamour for such a move became embodied in the work of the Bristol Party, a political group formed in October 1993. There had been a precedent, for the Valley Party, which stood for elections in May 1990, had helped hasten Charlton Athletic's long-awaited return to their spiritual home. The Bristol Party, lent support by Tom Pendry, the Labour Party's Shadow Minister for Sport, strove to recreate in Bristol the perceived superior leisure facilities of other cities. Partnership with housing and community organisations was demanded in order to restore a sense of pride in all aspects of Bristol life. In the local elections of May 1994, the Bristol Party polled 4,000 votes and won no seats, although its call for a healthier political attitude to sports as well as Rovers' return had been heard loud and clear.

In December 1993, as the party's work grew, Rovers expressed interest in a fourth potential site for a new stadium. The proposed spot comprised 60 acres within the ICI complex at Pilning, again within easy access of the planned M49 motorway. A stadium here could house 20,000 spectators, as well as offering a greyhound track, that recurring leitmotif through the Rovers story since 1932, an exhibition centre and a School of Excellence. Discussions began to the backdrop of the increasingly politicised demands for Rovers' return to the Bristol area. Such a call from the club's supporters was one that would not go away.

On the field, the season opened with a disappointing single-goal victory at home to Bournemouth. Unbeknown to the crowd, this was to be the final Rovers appearance for Steve Yates, who rejoined Gerry Francis at Queen's Park Rangers shortly afterwards in a deal worth £750,000. Three other key members of the 1989/90 championship side – David Mehew, Andy Reece and Geoff Twentyman – had slipped out of League football over the summer. It was also the first time Nationwide League sides had been able to use up to three substitutes. Rovers selected a substitute goalkeeper for every league game, and this paid off in the return game at Bournemouth. The home side, very convincing at times, had led by three first-half goals before the highly controversial sending off of Rovers' goalkeeper Brian Parkin. Rovers promptly took off Gary Waddock, replacing him with Martyn Margetson, so that, although a man short, they at least played on with a recognised goalkeeper.

After five games, Rovers had scored four goals, all by John Taylor. He was to score twenty-three League goals, including goals in a run of four consecutive matches in the autumn. This spell included a first-minute goal that led to victory over Cardiff City at Ninian Park, and goals in exciting home victories over Burnley and Bradford City. Burnley found themselves three goals in arrears when Worrell Sterling, an exciting and skilful winger signed in the close season for £140,000 from Peterborough United, created the second before scoring the third with a spectacular 35-yard volley on the stroke of half-time. This game also featured a new centre-back partnership between debutant defender Ian Wright and Ian McLean, a Scottish-born player who scored his first goal for Rovers that day and won his first full cap for Canada in January 1995 while on Rovers' books. Against Bradford City, Rovers trailed 3-2 before two late penalties by Marcus Stewart gave the home side an unlikely victory. He thus became the sixth Rovers player to convert two penalties in a league match.

In September, Rovers lost 3-0 at Hull City, all of whose goals were scored by Dean Windass, only the third league hat-trick conceded by Rovers since 1983. Astonishingly, Brentford players managed to score hat-tricks in both games against Rovers, equalling the achievements of Northampton Town in 1929/30 and Derby County in 1961/62. In January, Denny Mundee scored all Brentford's goals in a game at Griffin Park, which Rovers won 4-3. Joe Allon then became the first opponent to score a hat-trick at Twerton Park. Rovers' captain Gary Waddock suffered a broken nose in the build-up to the first goal, but the side was easily defeated by Brentford, running up three first-half goals before Allon ran through a ragged defence after half-time to complete his hat-trick.

In November, the former Rovers goalkeeper Tim Carter was in the first Hartlepool United side to meet Rovers since the 1968/69 season. His side almost left Twerton Park with a win, too, denied only by Justin Skinner's last-minute equaliser. In their next League game, Rovers travelled to top-of-the-table Stockport County and left Edgeley Park with a fine 2-0 win. John Taylor and Lee Archer were Rovers' scorers, while Jim Gannon missed a penalty, found the referee ordering it to be retaken following an infringement and promptly missed again. County fielded 6-foot 7-inch striker Kevin Francis, the tallest player ever to appear against Rovers in League action. Rovers drew with Reading in January, thanks to Billy Clark heading in off the crossbar before half-time from Justin Skinner's free-kick – a match that saw Marcus Browning sent off after forty-nine minutes and the visitors' Uwe Hartenberger after sixty-seven minutes for violent conduct, just four minutes after his arrival as a substitute.

A series of fine end-of-the-season results eased Rovers into a comfortable final League position of eighth. A run of five straight defeats was halted when relegation-bound Barnet came for their sole League visit and were despatched 5-2. Justin Channing had, until a week earlier, gone fifteen months without a goal, but contributed a hat-trick to defeat the Bees. Worrell Sterling's first-minute goal was enough to defeat Blackpool. Tony Pounder's first two goals for over a year helped defeat Wrexham 3-2, while Taylor's brace against his former club, Cambridge United, gave Rovers a convincing away victory on the final day of the season.

The process of rebuilding the side had begun. Lee Maddison was a consistent performer at left-back, and the acquisition of Telford United's right-back David

Pritchard offered the prospect of another solid full-back partnership. Justin Skinner and Marcus Browning were developing as reliable midfielders, while Taylor's goals had brought relative success. There were still changes to be made, however. Wright and McLean never started again in the same side while, following Carl Saunders' mid-season move, Taylor joined Bradford City in a £300,000 summer move. Rovers needed a new striking partner for Marcus Stewart. Off the field, Rovers lent weight to the 'Let's Kick Racism out of Football' campaign, run by the Commission for Racial Equality, the Professional Footballers' Association and the Football Trust. Meanwhile, the old Eastville Stadium suffered another fire on 13 February 1994, caused by a mouse gnawing through wire, necessitating 100 firefighters and four months of repair work.

Rovers retained the Gloucestershire Cup 5-3 on penalties after a 1-1 draw, the winning kick being taken by Browning. A goalless ninety minutes had been followed by extra time, in which Clark, from Stewart's cross, scored for Rovers and Matt Bryant equalised for Bristol City four minutes from the end. Kit man Ray Kendall was also granted a testimonial at the end of the season, when a 1,500 crowd raised £4,000. Rovers, with Pounder and the substitute Sterling scoring, drew 2-2 with Premier League Coventry City, whose goals came from Julian Darby and Peter Atherton.

That success in the major cup competitions was not forthcoming is a major understatement. Home defeats at the hands of West Bromwich Albion and Wycombe Wanderers brought Rovers' interest to a swift conclusion. Albion's convincing 4-1 League Cup first-round first-leg win at Twerton Park rendered the second leg practically meaningless. Third Division Wanderers ended Rovers' FA Cup aspirations, with Dave Carroll's second-half winning goal earning them a home tie with Cambridge United. After victories over Torquay United and Cardiff City in the Auto Windscreens Shield, Rovers drew 2-2 at home to Fulham, Lee Maddison conceding an own goal, and were eliminated from the tournament after a penalty shoot-out.

1994/95

Ultimately, a season has to be assessed on achievement. Rovers appeared at Wembley Stadium in May 1995 for the second time in the club's 112-year history. Though they were unsuccessful in their attempts to regain the First Division place lost two years earlier, a positive feeling about Rovers' on-field potential was beginning to return. Moreover, by the end of the season, Northavon District Council was showing signs of being in favour of the club's proposed move to Pilning. So, despite the disappointment of final-day defeat against Huddersfield Town in the play-offs, hopes were high in the Rovers camp.

The one major addition to the Rovers squad was Paul Miller, an experienced striker signed from Premier League Wimbledon for £100,000 in August. Miller added a cutting edge to the side, contributing sixteen league goals to finish the season as the club's top scorer. The extra-time goal at Crewe Alexandra, which took Rovers to Wembley, was not his best of the season, but was arguably his most crucial. Tom White and goalkeeper Marcus Law came through the youth scheme to make first-team appearances, while Carl Heggs' loan spell included a Tuesday night consolation goal at Bradford City in February. Andy Collett arrived in a £100,000 move from Middlesbrough on transfer deadline day in March to act as goalkeeping cover for Brian Parkin.

The relative success of 1994/95 was achieved despite the absence, for long stretches of the season, of the highly influential Marcus Stewart. In one purple patch through the winter, he scored twelve goals in ten league matches and scored in eight consecutive League and Cup games in which he played between November 1994 and Valentine's Day 1995. It is also fair to record that, prior to an eleven-match unbeaten run, starting in March, Rovers stood in eleventh place in their division. Player of the year Worrell Sterling was the club's only ever-present, and scored his only goal, with a forceful left foot drive from 20 yards, in a 1-1 draw at Huddersfield Town's new Alfred McAlpine Stadium in February.

Although Rovers were unbeaten for the first eight league matches of the new season, they found themselves in seventh place in Division Two. Five of these games had been drawn, three of them being goalless draws, while Rovers had beaten York City 3-1, Rotherham United, through three first-half goals at Millmoor, and Wrexham. The Welsh side put up a strong fight at Twerton Park before succumbing to a 4-2 defeat. Billy Clark's second-minute header from Justin Skinner's corner and Gareth Taylor's first goal for the club twice put Rovers ahead, only for Wrexham to equalise both times. However, Karl Connolly's eighty-fifth-minute goal served only to spur Rovers on, with another Clark header and Miller's burst through the Robins' defence giving Rovers all the points. Clark, with six league goals in the season, more than doubled his career total with the club.

When the unbeaten record went in the ninth game, Shrewsbury Town's Ian Stevens scoring the winning goal before half-time, it was to the first goal conceded away from home all season. Rovers' bubble had burst, and despite recovering a two-goal half-time deficit at home to Crewe Alexandra, Taylor scoring twice, the heaviest defeat of the season was to follow. With Marcus Law an unlucky debutant in goal, Rovers found themselves 2-0 down at Griffin Park after only five minutes, Brentford's Nicky Forster's two early goals leading Rovers to a 3-0 loss. Brentford were to finish second in the division, while Rovers, from this lowest seasonal placing of fifteenth, slowly climbed the table into a play-off position.

A run of seven wins and a draw between 5 November and 4 February began to propel Rovers back up the table. The first win, 4-0 against Bradford City, showed the potential of a revitalised Rovers side, Marcus Stewart scoring twice in this game and twice again in three of the next four matches. Four straight home matches either side of Christmas were won, Lee Archer scoring twice in a 3-0 victory over Chester City on New Year's Eve. In poor weather, the only League fixture honoured in January was an exciting 3-2 victory over Oxford United, who had led through Mark Druce goals after twelve and fifteen minutes. The arrival of Taylor as substitute sparked Rovers into life and his seventy-third-minute goal was the first of three in seven minutes, Miller and Stewart helping Rovers snatch an improbable victory from the jaws of defeat.

The sad news in Rovers circles at this time was the death of Geoff Bradford on 30 December 1994. Although more than a dozen players have represented their country while on the books of Bristol Rovers, Bradford remains the only one to have appeared for England. His name became synonymous with the club through the halcyon days of the 1950s, when he scored for Rovers in two FA Cup quarter-finals and helped establish the club as a force in Second Division football. His career total of 242 league goals remains a club record and, in his 461 league appearances for his only club, he scored a Rovers record twelve hat-tricks. It is highly unlikely that, as the image of football continues to develop with the years, any player will quite capture the hearts of Bristol Rovers supporters as Geoff Bradford was able to do.

After four consecutive home games, all five fixtures in February took place away from home, the only victory coming at Brighton. March brought a second 4-0 home victory, with four different players getting on the scoresheet against Shrewsbury Town. Following defeat at Stockport County, Rovers were to lose just once in the last fifteen games of the scheduled season. Among nine victories in this run, Rovers completed league doubles over Rotherham United and Leyton Orient, and recorded commendable wins at Blackpool and at Cardiff City. Orient's defeats were part of a series of nine in succession that led to the London side's inevitable relegation. There was an almost-victory over a strong Birmingham City side to add to this list, after Rovers led at half-time through an own goal from Chris Whyte, whose gentle backpass had trickled bizarrely past goalkeeper Ian Bennett. Birmingham, who won the only automatic promotion slot as champions, equalised seventeen minutes from time when substitute Steve Claridge headed home a cross from Portuguese winger José Dominguez.

With Rovers and Brentford already assured play-off places, the Pirates thanks to Stewart's eighty-seventh minute goal at Cardiff after Miller's header had thudded against the bar, the sides played out an exciting 2-2 draw. This included a towering headed goal from Taylor, his second of the game, before a seasonal best home crowd in regular League fixtures of 8,501. Even more saw the goalless draw with Crewe Alexandra at Twerton Park in the play-offs and, with the aggregate score remaining goalless, the second leg at Gresty Road went into extra time. The stakes were high, a game at Wembley against Huddersfield Town, who had beaten Brentford on penalties, with the winners promoted to Division One. Substitute Darren Rowbotham put Crewe ahead in extra time, but Miller's scrambled equaliser saw Rovers through on the 'away goals' rule.

On 28 May 1995, before a crowd of 59,175, the second highest to watch a Rovers game, the club made the second Wembley appearance in its history. Behind to an Andy Booth goal, Marcus Stewart's equaliser just seconds before half-time offered renewed hope. Stewart also hit the bar with a 35-yard shot and Andy Gurney hit his own crossbar, while Gareth Taylor missed an open goal. But it was Chris Billy's diving header that brought Huddersfield Town victory. Rovers were to remain in Division Two for the time being, but they had performed well in an exciting game. Gurney and Pritchard, in particular, had formed a powerful full-back partnership, and Lee Maddison's £25,000 transfer to Northampton Town therefore came as little surprise.

Although initially leading through Andy Tillson's goal, an early Coca-Cola Cup exit against Port Vale included a goal in each leg from Lee Glover. Likewise, after draws with Oxford United and Bournemouth and four goals against Cambridge United, Rovers were knocked out of the Auto Windscreens Shield in a penalty shoot-out at Leyton Orient, youngster Martin Paul missing the vital kick. Rovers won the Gloucestershire Cup final for the final time in the club's history, defeating Bristol City 11-10 on penalties after a goalless draw at Twerton Park.

The FA Cup threw up an intriguing tie, with Rovers drawn to play away to their landlords Bath City. Stewart put Rovers ahead after eighteen minutes via a post, after Justin Channing's shot had hit the crossbar. Bath, who fielded former Rovers players in Vaughan Jones and Gary Smart, had Grantley Dicks sent off for a foul on Pritchard, before Miller scored four goals in twenty-three second-half minutes, registering with a header and shots with both feet. Miller's goals, emulating those of Carl Saunders three years earlier, gave Rovers a convincing 5-0 victory. Two Stewart goals defeated Leyton Orient, and only a John Hartson goal prevented Rovers winning at First Division Luton Town in the third round. The Hatters, with Gary Waddock in midfield against his former club, won the Twerton Park replay through a second-half Dwight Marshall goal.

1995/96

Hopes had been high that Rovers could be successful in 1995/96, but high achievement was not forthcoming. After reaching Wembley through the play-offs, a final League placing of tenth in Division Two was a relative disappointment. A second route to Wembley, the Auto Windscreens Shield, turned abruptly into a cul-de-sac when Rovers, requiring only a draw at home to Shrewsbury Town in order to return to the Twin Towers, inexplicably lost to the Third Division side. More humiliating by far was the FA Cup exit at Hitchin Town, the type of banana skin all League clubs dread. In addition, local government reorganisation meant the proposed stadium site at Pilning was now in the administrative district of South Gloucestershire, and the new councillors were not in favour. As with numerous schemes before it to bring Rovers back home to Bristol, the plan was reluctantly shelved.

At the end of an exhausting and demoralising season, John Ward left Rovers after three years as manager. Under his guidance, the club had won sixty-four out of 149 league matches, re-established itself in Division Two, played in the Southern final of the Auto Windscreens Shield and reached a play-off final in May 1995. Within a year of leaving Rovers, Ward was to return to management with Bristol City, leading the Robins to promotion to Division One in 1997/98, and was later assistant manager at Wolverhampton Wanderers. His successor as Rovers manager, in the summer of 1996, was to be a very familiar face, and Ian Holloway's return coincided with Rovers' reappearance in Bristol.

Eight players made a Rovers debut in 1995/96, yet only one – Peter Beadle – could claim to be a regular in the side. Josh Low appeared in the team in four consecutive seasons, Jon French and Matt Hayfield in three each, yet none was picked consistently by Ward, nor indeed by Holloway. Three players arrived at Twerton Park on loan, Damian Matthew and Steve Morgan having both played top division football. Beadle, a £50,000 signing from Watford, joined Rovers in the aftermath of the Hitchin Town debacle and became the tall target man Rovers had missed since the departures of Devon White and John Taylor. His two goals at Ashton Gate secured a confidence-boosting 2-0 victory over his future club Bristol City in January.

Twice in the opening five home League games, Rovers' opponents found themselves reduced to nine men; only once before had two members of the opposition been sent off in a league game. However, Rovers could only draw 2-2 with Swansea City after Steve Torpey, later of Bristol City, and the former Rovers striker Carl Heggs had both been sent off. Then, with Martin Paul scoring on his first start of the season, Rovers defeated Brentford 2-0, with the visitors having centre-backs Martin Grainger and Jamie Bates sent off. Rovers also suffered an uncharacteristic 4-1 home defeat at the hands of Swindon Town, for whom Kevin Horlock scored a hat-trick. The only other opponent to score a hat-trick at Twerton Park had been Joe Allon on the previous occasion Rovers had conceded four goals in a league match. The Cameroonian international Charlie Ntamark was another recipient of a red card when Rovers met Walsall in February.

On 29 September 1995, Gareth Taylor, with four goals to his name already, was sold to Crystal Palace for a club record £1,600,000. He was replaced in November by the prolific Beadle, who was to score in four consecutive league matches in the spring. Of greater immediacy was Marcus Stewart's renewed goalscoring form. He scored after only twenty-six seconds of the home game with Hull City, and added a goal in eight of nine consecutive games in the spring to compile an impressive seasonal total of twenty-one league goals, ending the year as the highest individual goalscorer in Division Two. It was no surprise when, after a career total of fifty-seven goals in 137 (plus thirty-four sub) League appearances for Rovers, Stewart joined Huddersfield Town in a £1,200,000 deal at the end of the season.

Rovers used their full allocation of substitutes for the first time when they visited Brighton in October. Ian McLean, Martin Paul and Tom White all played their part, but Rovers lost 2-0 after conceding a farcical goal to George Parris after fifty-one minutes. Goalkeeper Andy Collett, who gradually ousted Brian Parkin from his long-held position, had not seen Parris waiting by the goalpost as he shaped to take a goalkick. The Brighton player waited for Collett to ground the ball, tackled him, rounded him and scored a perfectly justifiable goal. At this stage, following an excellent win at Bradford City, Rovers endured a run of seven matches without a win. This ended when Stewart scored twice in a 2-0 victory over Oxford United, which set Rovers off on a club record twenty-three consecutive League matches in which the side scored. Although there had been twenty-six consecutive games between March and December 1927, this spell constituted the longest run within a season.

There were three games of note in a ten-day patch in mid-February. Rovers celebrated the club's 3,000th Football League fixture since election to Division Three (South) in 1920 with a 3-1 win at Hull City, Marcus Browning after sixty-three minutes joining the ubiquitous Beadle and Stewart on the scoresheet. Seven days later, Rovers scraped a single-goal victory at home to Rotherham United, even though the visitors, bereft of injured goalkeeper Matthew Clarke, had played the entire second half with full-back Gary Bowyer in goal. The following Tuesday, Andy Tillson's first goal for fifteen months was not enough as Rovers lost 3-2 at Wrexham. Some records debit Justin Channing with two own goals, and he would certainly be the only Rovers player to have achieved this feat. The first, after twenty-five minutes, resulted from Barry Hunter's header, which pinballed off both Clark and Channing, while the second, thirty minutes later, was a more clear-cut diversion of Peter Ward's cross. 'Two were own goals attributed to … Channing' (Kevin Fahey, 'Rovers' own goal horror', *Western Daily Press*, 21/2/96), '[Rovers] contributed to their downfall by conceding two own goals' (Mark Currie, 'Battle of Nerves', *Daily Post*, 21.2.96), reported the press. Yet the national papers, Wrexham FC and the general consensus of opinion awarded the first goal to Hunter.

Despite a late flurry of victories, including six 1-0 wins in the New Year, five in a run of seven home matches, Rovers lacked the consistency to challenge seriously for a play-off place. A 4-2 defeat at home to Bristol City proved particularly demoralising, and four goals were also conceded at Notts County. Ultimately, all play-off hopes were killed off in a 2-0 defeat at Stockport County where John Jeffers, later to score in the first game at the Memorial Ground, created both goals. The final position of tenth, though commendable, was not enough to hold on to Ward or Stewart. However, the summer of 1996 heralded a new era in the history of Bristol Rovers, the return of the prodigal son, Ian Holloway, on

13 May as manager, a return to an east Bristol home and the prospect of prosperous days ahead.

In the Coca-Cola Cup, a first-minute Stewart goal helped Rovers towards a 4-2 second leg and 5-3 aggregate victory over Gillingham. Stewart completed his hat-trick, while the visitors' opening goal was scored by Dennis Bailey against his former club. In the second round, a single first-half John Moncur goal gave West Ham United victory at Twerton Park, before three second-half goals at Upton Park saw Rovers eliminated 4-0 on aggregate. Exit from the FA Cup was far more nightmarish. As if being drawn away to Hitchin Town was not enough to strike anticipatory fear into the mind of any Rovers supporter, the ICIS Premier Division side took the lead through a Steve Conroy header after only forty-seven seconds, and went even further ahead when Lee Burns chipped an outstanding second in the ninth minute. Rovers were able to pull one goal back through Lee Archer, but it was clearly an afternoon to forget, as Hitchin Town held on for a thoroughly deserved victory.

Elsewhere, victory over Brighton, Cambridge United and Bournemouth earned Rovers a tough tie at Fulham. The Auto Windscreens Shield had adopted the 'Golden Goal' rule, whereby the first goal scored in extra time would be the winner, and Stewart's second goal of the night proved just that. His penalty then defeated Peterborough United, and Rovers just had to overcome Shrewsbury Town over two legs to reach Wembley. After Damian Matthew's goal at Gay Meadow, a goalless draw would have taken Rovers through. However, Stewart's fifty-sixth-minute penalty was saved by Paul Edwards and, seventeen minutes from time, Ian Reed crossed for Ian Stevens to notch the goal that killed off Rovers' hopes.

1996/97

The history of any football club involves a series of crossroads at which future direction is determined. One of the crucial moments in the history of Bristol Rovers came in the summer of 1996. The ten-year wait for a return to a home base in north Bristol was at a dramatic end. The prodigal son returned to manage his former club. No fewer than fourteen players were to make a Rovers debut in 1996/97, while the prolific Marcus Stewart was sold. It was a moment of great anticipation and hope.

Bristol Rugby Football Club, operating at the Memorial Ground in Horfield, was running into ever-deeper financial waters. In April 1996, it became a limited company, but only 278 of its 2,000 founder shareholders invested further. In a desperate situation, the rugby club offered Rovers the opportunity to buy half the ground for £2,300,000. It was the moment Rovers' dreams of moving back to Bristol came to fruition. The ground, bought by the rugby club in 1921 for

£26,000, had seen some development, though much more would be necessary in order to house League football. The pitch, at 101 by 68 metres, was the smallest in the Football League, and there was room for only 740 away supporters on the Centenary Stand Terrace, a figure increased to 1,161 by August 1998. The Centenary Stand, constructed in 1988 and then rebuilt at the constructors' expense following renewed fire safety regulations in the wake of the Bradford fire, represented merely a first step in the redevelopment of the stadium. The Cambridge United website 'Moosenet' (in reference to The Mem) announced 'its quaint architecture unique in that it boasts one stand that would look more at home at Newmarket racecourse [and] one temporary effort ... more suited to polo'. Ever since, discussions have raged as to Rovers' next step, with stadia in various locations being mooted down the years. As discussions mounted with regard to stadia to host the 2012 London Olympics, one John Hart of Sunderland wrote a letter to *The Observer* criticising 'building a new national stadium for a couple of thousand Bristol Rovers fans and some rugby-loving farmers out of geographical tokenism' (*The Observer*, 25/2/07, sports letters, p. 20).

John Ward's successor, Ian Holloway, as Rovers manager in May 1996 was a hugely popular choice. Holloway epitomised the spirit of the club. A local player, returning for a third spell with a club with which he had experienced triumph and despair, Holloway now brought his vast resources of enthusiasm and commitment into his first management job. The inevitable sale of Marcus Stewart, who joined Huddersfield Town in a £1.2 million deal, injected much-needed cash into the club and was to generate a further £260,000 when the player moved on to Ipswich Town in February 2000. Of Holloway's recruits, the greatest impact was made by Jamie Cureton, a Bristol-born striker who arrived from Norwich City and soon acquired the knack of scoring Second Division hat-tricks. Transfer fees apart, Rovers were able to announce a turnover of £1,374,000 for the 1996/97 season.

Over the summer, a once prolific Rovers goalscorer, Vic Lambden, died in Bristol. Lambden had served his only league club with distinction, scoring on his debut in the first post-war game in 1946 and remaining an integral part of the side until 1955. Latterly a very successful foil for the indispensable Geoff Bradford, who predeceased him by eighteen months, Lambden scored 117 goals in 269 league matches before spending six free-scoring seasons in Western League football with Trowbridge Town. He remains the fourth-highest goalscorer in the club's history.

The opening game of the season, billed as the first game back in Bristol, proved instead to be the last one in Bath, with Andy Gurney's eleventh-minute strike earning all three points. Peterborough United, in this game, fielded one former Rovers defender in Aidy Boothroyd and future strikers in Giuliano Grazioli, who signed for Ray Graydon's Rovers in the close season of 2002, and Scott McGleish, who joined Rovers in the summer of 2011. This game marked the first appearance, as Keith Valle's successor, of long-term match-day announcer Nick Day. The long-awaited return to Bristol took place a fortnight later, when Stockport County were the visitors. Although Lee Archer's goal put Rovers ahead after twelve minutes, an equaliser seventeen minutes from time by John Jeffers ensured that, as in the final Eastville game a decade earlier, the match finished 1-1. The first victory in a home match in Bristol since April 1986 was to follow, as Rovers clawed back a half-time deficit to defeat Bournemouth 3-2.

With new-signing Cureton scoring twice against Chesterfield on his home debut, and following this up with further strikes, Rovers moved slowly up the table. In early October, a 2-0 home victory over second-placed Crewe Alexandra, with long-range second-half goals from Cureton and Gurney, put Rovers into ninth place, which was to be their highest placing of the season. The fact that the side recorded just two wins in the following seventeen league games explains why Holloway's first season in charge brought no immediate success. In one of these games, captain Andy Tillson was booked after only twenty seconds for a foul on Richard Cresswell, from which Nigel Pepper put York City ahead from the penalty spot. One of these two victories, however, followed Marcus Browning's goal two minutes after half-time in farcical circumstances, when Brentford goalkeeper Kevin Dearden reacted to a phantom whistler in the crowd, while the other was an extraordinary 4-3 success at home to Bury in November. Peter Beadle scored a nine-minute hat-trick shortly before half-time, only for Bury to pull back two goals in first half injury time. Billy Clark's only goal of the season, just seconds after the interval, was the sixth goal inside sixteen minutes. Bury were Second Division champions this season, this defeat being the only league game in which the Shakers conceded four goals. Yet, three days later, Rovers lost tamely to a Walsall side inspired by Sierra Leone international John Keister. Rovers also squandered a 3-1 lead at home to Wycombe Wanderers. The visitors' players had been told by manager John Gregory prior to the game that they faced a fine for any shots from outside the penalty area, but three long-range goals steered them to a 4-3 win.

On 19 October 1996, for the first time, Rovers and the rugby club played home matches on the same day. At 3 p.m., Rovers took on Blackpool, with a crowd of 5,823 witnessing a goalless draw. With the posts hastily changed, Bristol RFC were able to kick-off at 7.30 p.m., in a European Conference Group B game, which was lost 18-16 to Narbonne before a crowd of 2,000. In the early days, the longer grass required for the fifteen-a-side game drew some criticism from opposition managers, but six sides, including relegated Rotherham United, recorded League wins at the Memorial Ground. The new £2,000,000 West Stand, which increased the ground capacity to 9,173, was opened prior to Bristol's game with Auckland Blues in February, and reopened forty-eight hours later before an extraordinary game with Luton Town. Tony Thorpe, later a Bristol City player, was fouled after ten minutes by Tom White and converted the penalty himself. Midway through the first half, seconds after Paul Miller's equaliser for Rovers, the Bulgarian international Bontcho Guentchev was sent off for a foul on David Pritchard. Andy Tillson and Ian Holloway gave Rovers a commanding lead, before Gary Waddock pulled a goal back against his former club ten minutes from time.

There were some excellent Rovers performances, giving optimism for the task ahead. In particular, Rovers played astonishingly well to hold table-topping Brentford to a goalless draw in a hugely entertaining match at Griffin Park in January. However, when Rovers lost at Watford that March, a Watford website commented that the Pirates 'appear to be cack on a scale that only people who bought the St Winifred's School Choir single can really comprehend' (Ian Grant). Yet there were also unsavoury moments, such as the crowd disturbances at the derby match in December, with pictures being broadcast live on Sky Sports. With Rob Edwards sent off, ten-man City appeared to be holding on for a single-goal victory until Beadle's last-minute equaliser sparked a confrontation between rival supporters on the pitch. It was generally appreciated that the action of Rovers fans had been predominantly celebratory, but Bristol City, for the lack of adequate crowd control, were handed a suspended two-point deduction.

If the Ashton Gate crowd of 18,674 was more than double any other attendance all season at a Rovers game, the 8,078 for the return fixture constituted an embryonic football record at the Memorial Ground. Sadly, Rovers were two goals down to Bristol City before Julian Alsop scored with nine minutes remaining, Beadle becoming the first player to miss a penalty in a Bristol League derby, and hovered one place above the relegation zone. Consecutive victories over Preston North End, Peterborough United and Wrexham averted the danger and enabled Holloway to look to the future, with Tom White, Frankie Bennett, Josh Low and Lee Zabek making appearances.

In an unsettled side, Holloway himself was the only player to start both the first and last games of a disappointing season. While Beadle and Cureton scored twelve and eleven league goals respectively, the final league placing of seventeenth owed much to the lack of goalscoring support. After his heroics of 1995/96, Miller scored just twice, as did regular midfielders Skinner, Archer and Marcus Browning. At Luton Town in November, where Rovers lost to a last-minute Tony Thorpe penalty, Jason Harris, on loan from Crystal Palace, became only the fourth Rovers player to score a debut goal as a substitute. He scored past Ian Feuer, Luton's American-born goalkeeper who, at 6 foot 7 inches, emulated Kevin Francis in 1993/94 as the tallest opponent at that time to face Rovers in League football. Rio Ferdinand played in the Bournemouth side on Boxing Day at the start of a long career in top-flight and international football.

A first-round exit from the Coca-Cola Cup at the hands of Luton Town, for whom David Oldfield scored in both legs, mirrored Rovers' early departure from the Auto Windscreens Shield, beaten at home by Brentford. Likewise, the FA Cup brought scant consolation for Rovers, who lost at home to Third Division strugglers Exeter City, who had scored twice in the second half before the Rovers substitute Steve Parmenter pulled a goal back in the dying seconds. The former Rovers defender Darren Carr was in the Second Division Chesterfield side that led 2-0 before losing in a replay in an FA Cup semi-final against Middlesbrough. Two years after the penultimate game, the ninety-ninth and last Gloucestershire Cup final was decided in August in Bristol City's favour by substitute Shaun Goater's second-half goal.

1997/98

Rovers' second season back in Bristol saw the side qualify comfortably for the play-offs, but not regain First Division status. In an eventful year, Rovers scored seventy league goals – a figure the club had not exceeded since the championship season of 1989/90, and higher than that scored by any other club in the division – and were involved in several high-scoring matches. Ultimately, the reward of a visit to Wembley for Ian Holloway's side came within reach before disappearing entirely in an uncharacteristic display in the play-off second leg at Northampton Town.

The vastly experienced Billy Clark moved to Exeter City, and Paul Miller, after only two league goals in a disappointing 1996/97 season, joined Lincoln City, whom he helped to promotion from Division Three. With the enforced retirement of Lee Martin and Lee Archer's belated transfer to Yeovil Town, Holloway needed to strengthen the side prior to the new season. This was achieved primarily on 20 May 1997, when the club spent £150,000 on Woking Town's Steve Foster and £200,000 on Barry Hayles from Stevenage Borough. Rovers had purchased two of the most talented players on the non-League circuit. Hayles' control, strength and powerful running were a key factor in the club's success and he scored twenty-three goals in his first season. Foster brought a calm authority to the defence, where he ably replaced Clark alongside club captain Andy Tillson. Holloway also recruited the combative and highly experienced Cardiff City full-back and captain Jason Perry on a free transfer.

On the opening day of the season, Graeme Power dislocated his shoulder during the 1-1 draw with Plymouth Argyle at the Memorial Ground, and was out of first-team football for six months. This was the start of a season's toils to fill the troublesome left-back position. Rovers fielded seven different players in the apparently jinxed No. 3 shirt during the season, including Luke Basford, who made his debut in a disastrous 4-0 home defeat against Grimsby Town just weeks before his seventeenth birthday. In a bizarre way, Power's unfortunate injury reflected that of Jack Stockley, also against Plymouth Argyle on the opening day of the season, who had been out of the game for eight months some seventy-six years earlier.

Rovers were involved in a number of high-scoring games. In September, they were 3-0 down at Oldham Athletic after twenty-four minutes, Stuart Barlow scoring twice, before Peter Beadle scored a couple of goals in three minutes and created an equaliser for Barry Hayles on the stroke of half-time. After such an outstanding first half, Oldham's fourth goal was cancelled out by Jamie Cureton's penalty three minutes from time, after handball by Scott McNiven, for a 4-4 draw. There were also six first-half goals when Rovers won 4-2 at Luton Town in December and, eight days later, Rovers again scored four goals before half-time in beating Bournemouth 5-3. Beadle, who completed a first-half hat-trick in this game with a fine 30-yard shot, also scored three goals in eleven minutes when Rovers defeated Wigan Athletic 5-0 in April. Bournemouth's Steve Robinson became only the fourth opponent to score a penalty in both League games against Rovers, one in the 5-3 defeat and one in a 1-1 draw at Dean Court in September, preceded by a two-minute silence in memory of Diana, Princess of Wales, who had died in Paris two days earlier.

Sendings-off proved to be a talking point of the season. Millwall's Brian Law was sent off in both League games against Rovers, and the Lions had players dismissed in both fixtures in 1998/99. Basford, at seventeen years eighty-seven days, became the youngest Rovers player to receive a red card in a League game, late in the 1-1 draw with Gillingham, who had taken the lead through Iffy Onuora after only thirty-eight seconds. However, nothing could prepare Rovers for the five red cards issued on a frosty evening in Wigan in December by referee Kevin Lynch. David Pritchard received a second yellow card only seconds before half-time and was promptly joined by Jason Perry, Andy Tillson and Wigan's Graeme Jones for alleged pushing while the resultant free-kick was about to be taken. These decisions were viewed by many as harsh, as was Josh Low's second-half dismissal for a second booking, in a game generally considered fair and clean. Nonetheless, seven-man Rovers, only the second league club to suffer this fate, after Hereford United in November 1992, made the headlines for all the wrong reasons.

Gary Penrice, back in the side after a popular summer transfer from Watford, became the only Rovers player to have scored a league goal on all four of the club's home grounds. His goal in a 3-1 victory over Carlisle United in August was his first for the club since October 1989, a gap between Rovers goals only exceeded by Ray Warren and Wally McArthur. Among the good wins were some poorer results. Ian Stevens, for instance, scored a hat-trick when Carlisle United gained revenge by beating Rovers 3-1 at Brunton Park in January, while Carl Heggs played well against his former club in March, a foul on him by David Pritchard leading to the second goal in Northampton Town's 2-0 victory. As Rovers moved towards the play-offs, David Whyte arrived on loan, and Lee Jones, destined for many games in Rovers' goal, joined as cover for Andy Collett.

In addition to his consistent goalscoring, Hayles missed just one league game, the demoralising 2-0 local derby defeat at Ashton Gate before the highest crowd, 17,086, to watch Rovers in League action all season. It was a fifth consecutive league defeat for Rovers. No Rovers player appeared in as many games this season as Hayles.

Cureton scored in five consecutive league matches early in the New Year, and he and Beadle both scored highly respectable seasonal goal totals. Ultimately, Rovers needed to win at home to Brentford on the final day to relegate their opponents and secure a play-off place. These targets were achieved, even though Penrice was sent off early in the match and despite the fact that Cureton broke a leg late on. Amid great tension, the reliable figure of Barry Hayles scored a winning goal six minutes from time in front of a record ground attendance at the Memorial Stadium. Even more spectators (9,173, who produced record takings of £74,952) saw Beadle and Frankie Bennett give Rovers a two-goal lead inside thirty-seven minutes of the play-off semi-final second leg. When Hayles added a third just seconds after half-time, Wembley beckoned, but Northampton Town grabbed a late John Gayle goal. In the second leg, Rovers' dreams fell apart as the Cobblers scored three times, the first by Carl Heggs, for a demoralising 4-3 aggregate win.

After a goalless draw at Ashton Gate, Rovers crashed out of the Coca-Cola Cup to Junior Bent's extra-time winner for Bristol City at the Memorial Stadium. Victories over Cambridge United and Exeter City counted for nothing as Walsall's French striker Roger Zokou Boli scored a 'Golden Goal' just seconds into extra time to knock Rovers out of the Auto Windscreens Shield at the quarter-final stage. In the absence of the now defunct Gloucestershire Cup, Rovers fielded a reserve team in the county Senior Challenge Cup, a tournament dating back to 1936, beating Mangotsfield United but losing 6-0 to Bristol City reserves in a semi-final in which Colin Cramb scored all the goals. In the FA Cup, Rovers required an eighty-seventh-minute equaliser at home to Gillingham before winning the replay comfortably in Kent. Having to travel to Wisbech Town in round two brought back uncomfortable memories of Hitchin Town in 1995. However, Rovers were better prepared and won professionally through goals from Beadle, seven minutes after half-time, and Hayles, eleven minutes from the end, against a side fielding a thirty-nine-year-old Jackie Gallagher. The third-round draw paired Rovers with Ipswich Town, who fielded the popular former Rovers midfielder, Geraint Williams. Rovers might have beaten their First Division opponents in a gale and hailstorm at the Memorial Stadium, leading from Beadle's thirty-sixth-minute goal, but Mick Stockwell grabbed a deserved equaliser nineteen minutes from time. David Johnson's low shot three minutes before half-time in the replay at Portman Road ended Rovers' FA Cup aspirations for another year. The former Rovers chairman Herbert Brown died in October, and the National Football Programme Directory voted Rovers' match-day magazine as the best in Division Two.

As an eventful season drew to a close, dramatic developments ended Rovers' fifty-eight-year wait for a home of their own. Their hosts at the Memorial Ground, Bristol Rugby Club, had forged a deal early in January 1998 to sell the ground to the parcel carrier firm Amtrak for just over £1 million, a good deal less than the £2.2 million at which it had been valued in 1996. Rovers would continue to pay an annual rent of £90,000. Then, when the buyers withdrew their offer, the rugby club was placed in receivership on 17 April 1998, and Rovers invoked a buyout clause that enabled the 12-acre ground to be bought up for £100,000. A newly formed Memorial Stadium Company made the purchase in the names of both clubs, but since Geoff Dunford was chairman of the new organisation, it was abundantly clear Rovers held the upper hand. While it was obvious that considerable work would be required on improvements to floodlighting and cover, as well as seating at the South End, both clubs were quick to point out their future could lie elsewhere. Plans for a multi-sport stadium near Pilning were rejected at the end of April by landowners ICI, with developers valuing the newly renamed Memorial Stadium at £6 million.

Shortly before these momentous events, Eastville Stadium, Rovers' home between 1897 and 1986, finally closed. The last greyhound meeting on 27 October 1997, where entry fees were sentimentally waived, signalled the end of the road for a ground so integral to the club's history. Eastville was 'now sadly obliterated by a sprawling furniture store [replacing] the smell of gasholders which loomed, grimly but somehow hospitably' (Ivan Ponting, *The Independent*, 7/5/12). The arrival on site in March 1999 of furniture giants Ikea did, however, have one saving grace, for the Swedish firm often uses a tall local landmark to advertise its store, and a solitary floodlight was left standing as a poignant reminder of the good and bad memories the old stadium would forever hold.

1998/99

The 1998/99 side promised much, lacked consistency and, after hovering a little lower in the table, finished in thirteenth place in Division Two. Rovers were without Jason Perry and Graeme Power, who had moved to Lincoln City and Exeter City respectively, and Tom Ramasut, who joined several clubs on trial before signing in November 1998 for Merthyr Tydfil. On the eve of the new season, Peter Beadle made a surprise £300,000 move to John Rudge's Port Vale, while November saw Fulham pay Rovers a record £2 million for Barry Hayles. This income helped outweigh an operating loss of £664,791 in the year to June 1999 and leave Rovers with a £1,014,784 profit. Nonetheless, supporters were left to wonder where the side would find sufficient goalpower.

They need not have worried. At one stage over New Year, Rovers scored twelve goals in three games. Jamie Cureton, whose three league hat-tricks were all registered away from home, scored twenty-five goals in the League, and Jason Roberts, a Grenada international who overcame the tag of being a 'replacement' for Hayles, added sixteen, in addition to a record-breaking seven in the FA Cup. Rovers also made a large number of other summer signings, notably Marcus Andreasson from Swedish football and Cameroonian Guy Ipoua from Spain. Ipoua, whose elder brother Samuel had played for Cameroon in the 1998 World

Cup finals, contributed just three League goals, plus the only goal when Rovers unveiled Mangotsfield United's Cossham Street floodlights in March. Frenchman Stéphane Léoni, Trevor Challis, Rob Trees, Jamie Shore and Michael Meaker all made significant contributions, as did mid-season signings David Hillier, a league championship winner with Arsenal, and seventeen-year-old striker Nathan Ellington, the Surrey county high-jump champion.

After conceding a second-minute goal to Andy Payton in the opening day defeat at Burnley, Rovers overcame Reading 4-1, Meaker scoring against his former club and Cureton converting one of two penalties. Controversy struck at Gillingham, where both sides were reduced to nine men. Goalkeeper Lee Jones was sent off with Challis and the home side's Barry Ashby and Adrian Pennock as referee Matt Messias of York dealt with a twenty-one-man injury-time flare-up. Mark Smith made his debut in that game and, astonishingly, Rovers were reduced to nine men in each of his first three league appearances. Roberts and Trees were sent off as Rovers held on for a 1-0 home victory over Bournemouth in October, followed seven days later by Meaker and Challis in defeat at Northampton Town, for whom Carl Heggs was again on the scoresheet. Lee Thorpe, a future Rovers striker, was in Lincoln City's side against Rovers that September.

By Christmas, Rovers lay seventeenth in the table, with just five home wins to their name. A first away win should have been forthcoming at Wycombe, where Wanderers brought on a last-minute substitute, Dannie Bulman, for his League debut and the nineteen-year-old scored an equaliser after being on the field for just twenty-six seconds. He was also to score the goal in May 2001 that consigned Rovers to basement division football for the first time in the club's history. A single-goal defeat at champions-elect Fulham saw Rovers face the former England international, Peter Beardsley, who had previously faced the Pirates a club record sixteen years 232 days earlier, while on the books of Carlisle United. It was not until 28 December that Rovers recorded the first of their five away league victories.

Home form could be suspect, too. Three second-half goals saw off struggling Lincoln City, but Macclesfield Town drew 0-0 at the Memorial Stadium in the sides' first-ever meeting, yet were to lose nine of their next ten league matches. David Gregory, who had scored for both sides in a chaotic first half against Stoke City seven days earlier, earned Colchester United a share of the points with a last-minute penalty. Rovers also threw away a two-goal half-time lead for a 2-2 draw with Preston North End, who were becoming, after Notts County, only the second club to appear in 4,000 League games. Strangely, an identical scoreline in the return game at Deepdale meant Preston were the first League club to draw 1,000 League matches.

Both Walsall and Burnley won 4-3 at the Memorial Stadium. Rovers led Walsall 2-0 after only four minutes through Cureton and Hayles, but were pegged back by half-time, Mark Smith conceding an own goal. Andy Rammell and the Icelandic midfielder Bjarni Lárusson both scored in the last ten minutes, with Rovers a man short after Trees had been stretchered off. Burnley, on the other hand, took the lead four times, with all three Rovers equalisers arriving before half-time. It was only the tenth time in the club's League history that as many as six goals had been scored in the first half of a League game involving Rovers.

In December, Rovers drew 0-0 at Maine Road before a crowd of 24,976 in the first League meeting with Manchester City. This was followed by the first away victories of the season, a convincing 3-0 win against Colchester United and a powerful 6-0 success at Reading. Rovers also dominated Stoke City to record a memorable 4-1 victory at the Staffordshire side's newly christened Britannia Stadium, and came from behind for wins at Blackpool and Macclesfield Town. With Roberts scoring freely in the FA Cup, Cureton, the side's only ever-present, hit a rich vein of goals in the New Year. He hit four second-half goals at Reading and a hat-trick after half-time at Walsall, who had led 2-0 and were heading for promotion to Division One. On the final day of the season, Cureton's third hat-trick of the season brought Rovers a win at Macclesfield Town, where they had trailed 3-1 just two minutes after half-time.

The most incredible result was undeniably the victory over Reading in the new Madejski Stadium. Eighth-placed Reading had just beaten Wrexham 4-0, and gave a debut to the former Rovers player Andy Gurney. A crowd of 13,258 saw a goalless first half before Rovers scored six times without reply in the space of forty-one minutes for their largest away win since December 1973. The irrepressible Cureton scored the first four in twenty-one minutes, only the eleventh occasion that a Rovers player had scored as many in a league match, while Roberts added two goals in the final couple of minutes. Rovers had scored ten goals in the season against Reading, a figure only previously achieved against Doncaster Rovers in 1956/57. Cureton's penalty, his second goal, made him the sixth Rovers player since 1920 to score from the penalty spot in both fixtures against the same opposition.

Lior David scored twice as a substitute for Swansea City reserves as they defeated Rovers reserves 4-2 in a South West Trophy game in September. Rovers' reserves gave trials that month to the Nigerian international Ben Iroha, who later joined Watford, and Icelandic under-21 goalkeeper Ólafur Gunnarsson, though neither made the first team. The reserves also lost to a goal in each half at Forest Green Rovers in the Gloucestershire Senior Challenge Cup. Rovers' match-day programme was nominated the best in the division by *Programme Monthly* magazine and in the League Programme of the Year survey commissioned by the Wirral Programme Club. The former club director Hampden Alpass, a one-time Gloucestershire cricketer, died on 16 March 1999 at the age of ninety-two.

Rovers' FA Cup exploits more than made up for early exits from the Worthington Cup, to an extra-time goal for Third Division Leyton Orient from substitute Mark Warren, and the Auto Windscreens Shield, where Rovers threw away a two-goal lead at Walsall before losing in a penalty shoot-out. The FA Cup was an altogether more successful competition from a Rovers perspective. A second-half Roberts hat-trick saw off the challenge of non-League Welling United, and Rovers twice equalised at Exeter City before demolishing the Grecians 5-0 in a one-sided replay. Three goals in ten second-half minutes, two by Shore, set up a comfortable victory with Roberts scoring the fifth, a goal his supreme performance merited. Léoni's first goal for the club, after a swift interchange of passes with Roberts on the stroke of half-time, brought victory in a potentially awkward third-round tie at Rotherham United.

As the FA Cup campaign gathered pace, so did expectations. Matt Lockwood was in the Leyton Orient side Rovers were expected to brush aside in the fourth round. Revenge was gained for the Worthington Cup defeat, but it was a real struggle before a capacity crowd, and it was only after Roberts broke the deadlock with fourteen minutes remaining that Rovers visibly relaxed to run out 3-0 victors. Of all the possible fifth-round opponents, Barnsley might have offered Rovers the easiest passage to a third quarter-final, but Craig Hignett scored a sparkling hat-trick and Rovers crashed to a 4-1 defeat. Roberts' consolation goal, seven minutes from time, made him the overall top scorer in the 1998/99 tournament, the first Bristol Rovers player ever to achieve this feat. No Rovers player had scored as many FA Cup goals in a season since Jack Jones in 1901/02.

1999/2000

It was a very bitter pill to swallow but, at the close of an eventful, topsy-turvy season, Rovers let a clear opportunity of promotion slip, sank through the play-off places and finished seventh in Division Two. Ultimately, a late run of only six points out of a possible thirty was to undo all the positive early season form. Yet the side bore great similarity to that of 1998/99. Despite Guy Ipoua joining Scunthorpe United, Ian Holloway retiring from playing to focus on management and Jamie Shore out all season to undergo pioneering knee surgery, Rovers' side retained a familiar appearance.

Four international players were welcome additions to the side, while promising youngsters Bobby Zamora and Simon Bryant, the latter being the club's youngest post-war debutant, broke into the team. The Latvian international captain Vitalijs Astafjevs and former England midfielder Mark Walters were to prove inspirational mid-season purchases. Nigel Pierre, a Trinidadian striker, showed promise until his application for a work permit was rejected on the grounds that Jack Warner, who owned his former club, had tried to bribe governmental officials in return for the promise of his vote for England's bid to host the 2006 World Cup. Early in the season, Ronnie Maugé proved to have been an astute signing, but the experienced midfielder broke a leg playing in a Gold Cup match for Trinidad and Tobago against Mexico in February, and his absence precipitated Rovers' late season demise.

Early season success engendered great optimism in north-east Bristol. A preseason testimonial for Lee Martin drew a ground record of 10,534 to the Memorial Stadium to see Rovers draw 2-2 with European champions Manchester United – David Beckham and Paul Scholes in midfield – after falling behind to an Ole Gunnar Solskjaer strike. The best opening-day crowd since 1974, 8,514, watched Rovers' 800th League draw, a match in which Brentford, whose central defender Hermann Hreiðarsson was sent off for a 'professional foul' two minutes from time, set a club record of seventeen League matches unbeaten. On Boxing Day after a lunchtime kick-off, Rovers' sixth consecutive victory was watched by the first five-figure crowd at a home League game for fourteen years. The highest of four such attendances was the 11,109 to witness the draw with Wigan Athletic in March. Amid such optimism, a £100,000 roof at the Blackthorn End, formerly the clubhouse terrace, was opened prior to a convincing 3-0 victory over Luton Town in November, after man-of-the-match Andy Thomson and Walters, with a glorious free-kick, had put Rovers two goals ahead after only nineteen minutes.

There was a player sent off in each of the first six League games to add to one at Macclesfield Town on the final day of 1998/99. Ronnie Maugé, after twenty minutes at Priestfield, and Trevor Challis against Burnley were dismissed in August, but Rovers received no further red cards. By contrast, no fewer than ten opponents were sent off. Slowly but surely, Rovers climbed the table, with Jason Roberts scoring freely and victory at Notts County left the side top of Division Two through much of October. Surviving a stutter in late autumn, a run of six straight victories – Walters' first six appearances for the club – left Rovers positively placed at the turn of the millennium. The side had kept seven clean sheets in the first ten away league fixtures.

After Jamie Cureton had scored the club's first goal of the New Year, Rovers' tightly knit defence, with Thomson, Steve Foster and captain Andy Tillson prominent, fell apart in an extraordinary game at Layer Road. A goal up after eleven minutes, when Roberts took five attempts to force the ball over the line, Rovers conceded an equaliser to Colchester United before half-time. When Titus Bramble, on loan from Ipswich Town, fouled David Pritchard, this injury effectively ending the pugnacious full-back's career, Cureton's fifty-seventh-minute penalty put Rovers 3-1 up. Seven minutes later, Cureton could have sent Rovers into a 4-2 lead, but missed from a second penalty. Instead, Karl Duguid scored twice in three minutes, only for substitute Nathan Ellington to equalise for Rovers when Robbie Pethick's cross rebounded off the crossbar with four minutes remaining. In the dying moments, home substitute Lomana Trésor Lua-Lua burst through the Rovers defence for a dramatic winning goal.

In the League, Rovers played just twice away from home during January, but both games produced great excitement. The 5-4 defeat at Layer Road was followed by a 5-0 win at Oxford United as Rovers echoed the Madejski Stadium performance of twelve months earlier. Cureton scored either side of half-time and, after Pethick and Ellington had scored in the space of sixty seconds, he completed another away hat-trick ten minutes from time. Pethick's first goal for the club matched the achievement of Challis against Wigan Athletic and that of Rob Trees when Rovers defeated Wrexham in January to return to the top of Division Two.

Perhaps more unexpected was David Pritchard's winning goal at Chesterfield in November, where he became bizarrely the first Rovers midfielder to score all season. The unlikely sight of this first Football League goal from Pritchard led nineteen-year-old Ben Davies to honour a promise to walk home from Saltergate, being accompanied on his 154-mile walk by Ralph and Sue Ellis, Mike Bullock, Paul Thomas and John Spilsbury. This charity walk, which raised £3,255.70 for MacMillan Cancer Research and the supporters' club's 'Raise the Roof' fund, reached the Memorial Stadium in time for the return fixture in which Chesterfield, with Steve Blatherwick sent off, were comfortably defeated to leave Rovers in late March seven points inside the promotion places and fourteen points inside the play-off places.

Rovers were playing devastatingly well. Consecutive 4-1 victories at Luton Town and Oldham Athletic merely illustrated the power of the side, Cureton and Roberts scoring twice each after Luton had scored inside a quarter of an hour. Rovers' first win at Boundary Park since December 1974 was a foregone conclusion once two Cureton goals and one for Astafjevs had put the side 3-0 up after only eleven minutes, although the Latvian was stretchered off before half-time. Later, Rovers were to record a highly committed and hugely impressive first derby win at the Memorial Stadium. This followed a goalless draw in October at Ashton Gate, where Bristol City fielded the Hungarian Vilmos Sebők as substitute, just twenty-four hours after the death of Bill Dodgin, a pre-war Rovers player and successful club manager from December 1969 to July 1972.

From being so ensconced in the promotion places, Rovers' fall from grace was dramatic. Even the final home programme of the season contained messages of hope that Rovers could avoid the play-offs by gaining automatic promotion, but few thought they could do so by slipping up so severely. Lowly Reading achieved a league double over Rovers, who also lost at relegated Blackpool and Cardiff City. John Macken's forty-first-minute goal, after Paul McKenna had hit a post, enabled Preston to win at the Memorial Stadium. Had Rovers defeated the champions-elect, they would have retained their fate in their own hands with just four games to play. With only already relegated Cardiff City to play, Rovers still stood in a play-off position, requiring just a victory. A win at Reading on 22 March would have put Rovers top of Division Two; defeat to Scott Young's twenty-seventh-minute header from Mark Bonner's right-wing corner at Ninian Park left them two points adrift of the play-off places. Cureton, the club's only ever-present, had scored twenty-two League goals, to finish the season as joint top-scorer with Roberts.

While there had been injuries, with Shore out all season and Maugé and Pritchard missing the run-in, Rovers' sharp decline was inexplicable. Half of the twelve League defeats all season came in those fateful final ten games, in which Rovers won just once – a morale-boosting Easter Saturday victory over a Bristol City side that included the Moldovan international Ivan Testimetanu. Only eleven games were drawn in Division Two all season, the most exciting being the home fixture with Stoke City in April. A goal down after ten minutes, Rovers twice led only to draw 3-3, with the visitors' Peter Thorne completing a well-taken hat-trick. It was the first hat-trick conceded in the League by Rovers since February 1994, and the sixth occasion an opponent had scored three times and not ended up on the winning side. Sadly, two spectators raced onto the pitch in an attempt to attack the visiting goalkeeper Gavin Ward and were rightly arrested and subsequently banned by the club. This incident led to an FA enquiry, held on 30 June, at which Rovers were found guilty of failing to control their supporters and given a suspended sentence of one docked league point and a £10,000 fine. This punishment would only be imposed if a similar offence were to occur within twelve months.

After Roberts had seen off Luton Town, Rovers were knocked out of the Worthington Cup by Birmingham City. Likewise a slick Preston North End side put paid to hopes of a repeat of the 1998/99 FA Cup success. On-loan midfielder Shaun Byrne scored the winning penalty, after Brian Parkin, in his first start for almost four years, had saved one in a penalty shoot-out following a goalless draw at Northampton Town in the Auto Windscreens Shield. Rovers went out tamely at home to Reading in the next round. In the Gloucestershire Senior Challenge Cup, a Rovers reserves side lost to Bristol City reserves, Simon Clist scoring ten minutes from the end of extra time. Meanwhile, Rovers' match-day magazine was voted Division Two programme of the year by the National Programme Directory for the second time in three years. Despite turnover at the stadium rising from £1.79 million to £2.32 million, Rovers reported an overall loss of £885,531 in the year to 30 June 2000, largely through spiralling operating costs and wages.

The Memorial Stadium hosted an England under-15 international against Holland in March. Before a crowd of 5,344, Blackburn Rovers' Andy Bell headed the winning goal shortly before half-time for an England side boasting Bristol Rovers' full-back Neil Arndale. In May, Sue Smith of Tranmere Rovers scored ten minutes after half-time to give England a 1-0 victory over Switzerland at the Memorial Stadium, before a crowd of 2,587, in a qualifying game for the women's Euro 2001 tournament. Twenty-four hours later, on the same ground, 7,775 spectators watched Leicester defeat Bristol 30-23 to secure rugby union's Allied Dunbar League championship.

11

The Noughties

2000/01

A season that opened with great optimism ended in tears on a Wednesday night in May, as Rovers slipped into the basement division for the first time. Relegation ended Rovers' proud record of being the only club never to have played in either the top or the bottom division of the Football League. Requiring at least a point at home to Wycombe Wanderers, Rovers conceded a seventy-third-minute deflected shot from the future Rovers defender Danny Senda and a spectacular volley from Dannie Bulman five minutes later. A spirited revival, kick-started by a goal from substitute Kevin Gall, did not produce the late equaliser Rovers needed to keep their hopes alive.

Only six minutes into the season, at a warm, sunny Memorial Stadium, Jamie Cureton was fouled by Bournemouth's Stevland Angus and stroked home the resultant penalty past French goalkeeper Mickaël Ménétrier to give Rovers an early lead. Rovers were unbeaten in their opening twelve League and Cup games, and recorded comprehensive victories at Brentford and at second-placed Cambridge United. However, the warning signs were already there and Rovers, in particular, had not yet won at home. Jason Roberts had commanded a club record fee of £2 million to move to West Bromwich Albion. The sales of influential defender Andy Tillson for just £10,000 to early leaders Walsall, whom he captained to promotion via the play-offs, and, after the opening game, of Cureton to Reading were regarded by supporters with disbelief. Rovers had sold three strikers, in Roberts, Cureton and Bobby Zamora for a profit of just over £2 million. Zamora was to be the top scorer in all four divisions, as Brighton were Third Division champions, while Cureton and Roberts scored thirty and sixteen times respectively. In their place, Nathan Ellington was top scorer but was never able to count on a reliable attacking partner, Vitalijs Astafjevs' five goals rendering him an unlikely second-highest scorer for the season. Rovers failed to score in nineteen of their forty-six league fixtures.

Moreover, new signing Martin Cameron was ruled out for much of the season following an ankle injury sustained in the closing minutes of the large victory at Griffin Park, while new club captain Andy Thomson broke his foot in September. Nick Culkin, a season-long loan signing, one of seven loan players, was an inspirational goalkeeper, his fifty-sixth-minute penalty save from Richard Hughes being a pivotal moment in paving the way to a morale-boosting victory at Bournemouth in February, while Player of the Year Steve Foster also missed few games. Beyond these two, however, few players could lay claim to a regular place in the side, although Astafjevs and Ellington appeared often alongside the new generation of Rovers players in Simon Bryant and Lewis Hogg, the club's Young Player of the Year. Hogg made his League debut as an opening-day substitute and scored his first two goals at Brentford. New signings Che Wilson and Scott Jones, alongside Marcus Bignot early in the season, were also pivotal figures, but Rovers used a seasonal total of thirty-five players.

The long unbeaten run ended at second-placed Bury in October, where the home side recorded their 1,500th league win. Bury's goalkeeper Paddy Kenny was booked after hauling down Ellington, as was Jason Jarrett for a foul that forced Culkin to leave the field, but Rovers lost Foster to a red card for retaliation. The substitute goalkeeper was Brian Parkin, who thus set a post-war club appearance record for a goalkeeper. Culkin was also unable to finish the game at Wycombe, following a foul that earned Andy Rammell a sending-off and caused Rovers to be fined £10,000 after alleged comments from the bench were reported by the fourth official, Mike Tingey. There was also controversy at Meadow Lane where, after Ellington had missed a penalty, Notts County equalised in the last minute in bizarre circumstances. With Foster injured, Culkin kicked the ball out of play, but rather than returning the throw to Rovers as is customary, Craig Ramage threw to Richard Liburd, whose cross was turned in by Mark Stallard. In the ensuing confusion, Ramage was sent off for threatening Bignot. All in all, eight Rovers players and eight opponents were sent off during the 2000/01 season. Controversial events were also seen at Wigan, after which referee Bill Burns rang Rovers to apologise for not awarding a penalty following a blatant second-half foul on Ansah Owusu by goalkeeper Derek Stillie. The attendance at Wrexham, some 2,575 people, was the lowest to watch a Rovers League game since the journey to Shrewsbury Town in November 1996.

Early in the season, Rovers could rely on goals from a variety of sources. Marcus Andreasson fired home from 10 yards for his first goal for the club, one of three goals in twenty-three first-half minutes at Swindon Town in October, where 2,400 Rovers supporters saw Mark Walters star against his former club. Bignot scored with his left knee after just twenty-seven seconds on the Friday before Christmas, but Rovers lost to three second-half goals at Ashton Gate, including one headed home by the former Rovers player Peter Beadle, four minutes after coming on as a substitute. Then, following a dramatic Boxing Day draw with

Reading, in which Hogg was sent off for a foul on goalscorer Neil Smith and Trevor Challis for retaliation, Rovers went an astonishing 576 minutes without a goal in League or Cup football. This run, which included defeat to Cureton's right-foot drive three minutes before half-time at Reading, and celebrations that led to repercussions, was to end when Astafjevs scrambled the ball past French goalkeeper Lionel Pérez to give Rovers a thirty-third-minute lead over Cambridge United. This goal, coupled with substitute Ellington's header a minute after half-time, finally gave Rovers their long-awaited first home League win of the season. They were the last League side to do so, and the winless run since Easter Saturday had finally stretched to thirteen home League matches.

Ultimately, Rovers' six home League wins equalled the total of away League victories, and matched the six home wins of the 2010/11 relegation campaign. Success at Dean Court for a second consecutive season was the only victory away from home after the first week in November, and Rovers lost their final six away matches. Only on one occasion in the season were consecutive league fixtures won, and Rovers recorded ten draws at home and fifteen in all, eight of them goalless. Three points from any one of these – for instance the local derby where a seasonal highest home crowd of 9,361 saw Bristol City earn a point when Steve Phillips saved Scott Jones' penalty deep into injury time, one of four penalties Rovers squandered all season – would, in hindsight, have prevented relegation. A run through the winter of twelve league games without a win cost manager Ian Holloway his job on 29 January. He subsequently succeeded the former Rovers manager Gerry Francis at Queen's Park Rangers, taking Bignot with him, but was unable to prevent the West London side's eventual relegation from Division One. Promotion from within saw Garry Thompson, a former Coventry City striker who had served Rovers in a coaching capacity since 1997, appointed as caretaker manager.

Rovers crashed to a 4-1 defeat at Stoke City, for whom full-back Mikael Hansson scored with two shots in the opening fifteen minutes, and suffered three-goal defeats at both promoted sides Millwall, where Dwayne Plummer and goalscorer Tim Cahill were both sent off, and Rotherham United, as well as at home to both Potteries sides. Stoke City's visit in December featured the first occasion since Bob Hatton in 1979 that Rovers had conceded a first-half hat-trick. Peter Thorne, in scoring after two, twenty and forty minutes from two side-foots and a header from Bjarni Gudjohnsen's cross, became only the fifth opponent to have scored hat-tricks against Rovers in two separate league matches, and the first to do so twice on Rovers' home ground. Scott Jones and Stoke substitute Ben Petty were both sent off in the second half.

On three occasions, Rovers recorded League victories by four clear goals, a margin never suffered in defeat in the League. A comfortable 6-2 win at Brentford was only the second time the club had won by this score in the Football League, a third such occasion duly arriving when already relegated Oxford United visited in

April. From a goal behind, Rovers scored five second-half goals, including three in the final ten minutes, and Mark Walters contributed two in the last four minutes to equal Graham Withey's feat, accomplished in October 1982, of scoring twice as a substitute. Oxford goalkeeper Richard Knight was sent off eleven minutes from the end, with Phil Wilson saving the resultant Plummer penalty with his first touch in senior football. Wilson was himself booked in conceding a second penalty in the last minute, which Walters, who had also set up the third goal for the impressive Astafjevs, successfully converted. It was the first time since Alex Munro and Tony Ford against Luton Town in February 1970 that Rovers had used two penalty-takers in one game and, following Peter Beadle in November 1997, Walters was only the second Rovers substitute to score from the penalty spot in League football.

A goalless draw with Notts County in February sent Rovers into the relegation zone, from which, as games in hand were frittered away, escape was only sporadic. Dave Savage, later a Rovers player, scored a penalty for Northampton Town as Rovers lost 2-1 in March. In April, defeats came thick and fast, with two Monday evening losses at the hands of a rejuvenated Port Vale side especially damaging. Tony Carss of Oldham Athletic, Port Vale's Marc Bridge-Wilkinson and Wycombe Wanderers' Dannie Bulman all scored spectacular long-range goals to consign Rovers to defeat. Three straight losses led to relegation on 2 May, eleven years to the day since promotion had been achieved from the same division. With hindsight, only a point had been required from consecutive home fixtures, and a seventh home League defeat sent Rovers through the trapdoor, just a point below Swindon Town. Final-day victory over Wrexham, where Walters doubled his seasonal goal tally after two first-half mistakes by Lee Roche against opponents who had Danny Williams and Lee Trundle sent off, left Rovers with a minus-four goal difference. The match-day programme once again won the divisional Programme of the Year award.

Once Cameron and Bignot had registered their first goals for the club to see off Plymouth Argyle, Rovers enjoyed a hugely successful Worthington Cup run. A crowd of over 25,000 at Goodison Park, which included over 3,000 from Bristol, saw Premier Division Everton, who fielded the veteran England midfielder Paul Gascoigne as a substitute, stunned by Hogg's volleyed equaliser three minutes from time. Then, on an emotional night at the Memorial Stadium, Bignot's fifty-eighth-minute goal, after Ellington's initial shot had been saved, took Rovers into a penalty shoot-out where Plummer despatched the decisive kick to give the home side a memorable scalp. Sunderland then attracted a new record attendance of 11,433 to the ground, only for Don Hutchison's second goal of the game, off a post three minutes from time, to earn the Black Cats a 2-1 victory. Rovers lost at Cirencester Town in the Gloucestershire Senior Challenge Cup and, after two victories over Devon opposition, at Southend United in the LDV Vans Trophy. The first round of the FA Cup saw Rovers revisit the theatre of the previous

May's end-of-season disappointment. Following a Sunday lunchtime kick-off to suit live coverage on the satellite television channel, Sky Two, Rovers took an eighth-minute lead through an own goal by Cardiff City's debutant defender, Andrew Jordan, a former Bristol City player, before being destroyed by four second-half goals, with the Zambian-born striker Rob Earnshaw scoring a thirty-one-minute hat-trick for the Third Division side.

2001/02

Any promotion hopes that Rovers supporters may have entertained prior to the club's first-ever season in the League's lowest division were dashed as Rovers struggled through an unrewarding and at times difficult campaign. A season that began with great optimism turned into one of the low points of the Pirates' long history. Ultimately, a final Division Three placing of twenty-third was only achieved thanks to the forlorn struggle of Halifax Town, whose second direct relegation from the Football League was confirmed by Sergio Ommel's late, scrambled winning goal for Rovers against Kidderminster Harriers in April. Nathan Ellington's fifteen league goals clearly made him the club's top scorer in League football, despite his March move to Wigan Athletic, and goalkeeper Scott Howie was the only ever-present in the side.

The new manager was unveiled as Gerald Charles James Francis, the very man who had led Rovers to the Third Division championship in 1989/90, and had rebuilt the side in preparation for the long-awaited return to Bristol. On this occasion, however, he was not able to make many changes in personnel, though the experienced goalkeeper Howie signed on a free transfer. Rovers also acquired three of Francis' former protégés at Queen's Park Rangers in Alvin Bubb, Ross Weare and Rik Lopez. Mark Smith made a welcome return to first team action at Carlisle United in October, his first start for the side since December 1998. Robbie Pethick moved to Brighton, where he won a Second Division championship medal alongside former Rovers teammates Michel Kuipers and Bobby Zamora, while Marcus Andreasson returned to Sweden to join Bryne FK.

The firework display that greeted the Rovers side and its returning manager for the opening day encounter at home to Torquay United proved a false dawn. An enthusiastic and patient crowd of over 10,000 saw the Gulls' Tony Bedeau hit the post after only two minutes from Eifion Williams' right-wing cross before the first of four consecutive League and Cup victories was earned. On the evening of 25 August, Rovers sat proudly on the top of the table. However Gerry Francis, reappointed to much acclaim in the close season, was never able to recapture the glory years of a decade earlier and stood down for personal reasons on Christmas Eve.

The second Francis era was marked by a goal drought of worrying proportions. Martin Cameron's crisp downward header five minutes from the end of a televised defeat at home to runaway League leaders Plymouth Argyle in October – the first Rovers game for over a decade shown live on terrestrial television – was the club's first for 491 minutes since the same player's 14-yard shot a minute before half-time at home to Oxford United. The next goal was 509 minutes away, Cameron's fifty-fourth-minute penalty being Rovers' first away goal for 646 minutes, shattering a previous worst run of 580 minutes set in the spring of 1986.

Defeat at Darlington was down partly to a spectacular last-minute save by the former Rovers goalkeeper Andy Collett from substitute Bubb's header. Other former Rovers players were to score decisive goals, Julian Alsop providing Cheltenham Town's seventieth-minute winning goal on their first League visit to Bristol, and Martin Phillips sweeping the ball home from a second-minute left-wing corner when eventual champions Plymouth Argyle were the visitors. The Pilgrims scored after only twenty-nine seconds in the return fixture, Marino Keith shooting home right-footed after Steve Adams' shot had rebounded off the post. Scott Partridge, a former Bristol City striker, scored in the first minute of each half of Rovers' first-ever League encounter with Rushden and Diamonds, for whom the Jamaican international Onandi Lowe scored in both one-sided meetings. The former Rovers club captain Andy Tillson was outstanding in the Northamptonshire side's decisive 3-0 win at the Memorial Stadium in March. Drewe Broughton scored in both Rovers' first Football League encounters with Kidderminster, for whom midfielder Sam Shilton hit the crossbar in the fixture at Aggborough with a lob in the closing stages.

On 6 October, Rovers played at Brunton Park in the only 3 p.m. kick-off in the Nationwide League. The game was lost to Steve Halliday's eleventh-minute goal from Mark Winstanley's left-wing cross before an understandably paltry crowd of 1,849, the lowest at a Rovers game since the fixture at York City in April 1988. There were six red cards accumulated by Rovers players during the season, five of them in Division Three, with Mark Walters, dismissed ten minutes from time at Exeter City in October, becoming the oldest-ever Rovers recipient. When Rovers lost after leading at Swansea, both Astafjevs and Mike Trought were sent off in the closing four minutes. Nottingham referee Frazer Stretton dismissed three Kidderminster players at the Memorial Stadium on April Fool's Day. Abdou Sall was sent off after only four minutes for the foul that led to James Quinn's penalty, Rovers' first goal for 301 minutes. This was followed by goalkeeper Gary Montgomery and Ian Foster, with Rovers' substitute Sergio Ommel, who had earlier hit the crossbar, scoring the winning goal two minutes from time. Equally bizarrely, York City's Graham Potter became only the fourth opponent to score for both sides in a League encounter, his quickly taken seventy-fourth-minute free-kick from the edge of the penalty area being cancelled out ten minutes later when he steered Ellington's cross past his own goalkeeper to give Rovers a late lead.

The new manager was Garry Thompson, who had worked as Rovers' coach since 1997, but whose temporary tenure of the post twelve months earlier had seen Rovers relegated. He had enjoyed a long career with many clubs and had won six England under-21 caps while appearing as centre-forward for Coventry City. Thompson's time as manager opened with an impressive series of performances and some high-scoring and high-profile victories. Responding to a change in leadership, Rovers crushed Leyton Orient in a highly entertaining Boxing Day fixture at the Memorial Stadium. Ellington's first hat-trick for the club, one of three in less than a month, all came from low drives, two in three first-half minutes, and a third after seventy-three minutes to register Rovers' 3,000th home League goal. With the former Rovers defender Matt Lockwood on as a half-time substitute, Orient rallied with three second-half goals of their own, and Rovers ran out 5-3 winners. After the phenomenal result in the third round of the FA Cup, Ellington also grabbed three goals in a deceptively easy 4-1 victory at home to Swansea City in January, before Rovers endured a dismal run of results through the spring.

After the initial honeymoon period, Rovers lapsed into their losing ways. One particularly poor run in the spring of six consecutive defeats (just one short of the club record set in 1961) was halted by Ellington's right-footed sixty-fourth-minute equaliser at Hartlepool United, his final goal for the club. One cause for optimism was the goalscoring form of Dutch-born Ommel, a foil for Ellington signed on a free transfer from Icelandic football, where he had played alongside Moussa Dagnogo at KR Reykjavik, and was to end the season as Rovers' second highest goalscorer. Another overseas-born player was Carlos López Sánchez, who joined Rovers in February from the Madrid side Getafe. Thompson left the club after a run of one win in thirteen games and, with Phil Bater temporarily guiding Rovers through the final three defeats, Rovers appointed their former winger Ray Graydon to the post of manager on 26 April 2002.

Away from the pitch, too, there were rumblings of discontent. On the last Friday in October, the club was temporarily put up for sale by the majority shareholders, Ron Craig and Geoff Dunford. The latter succeeded his father as club chairman, and there were further additions to the board of directors in the spring. New floodlights to an American design were installed at a cost of some £150,000 and first used for the convincing victory over Swansea City in January. The older floodlights were dismantled on 28 June 2002 and transported by a Bridgwater firm to their new home at Aldershot Town's training ground. Yet it was the frozen pitch that caused the abandonment, after only twelve minutes, of the home game with Hartlepool United in mid-December, the first Rovers home game to be abandoned since March 1982.

The oasis in the desert that was the 2001/02 season was Rovers' FA Cup run. A hesitant pair of games with Ryman Premier Division side Aldershot Town was decided only when Astafjevs' eighty-fourth-minute deflected shot brought a replay victory, with the visitors' Richard Gell later sent off. Visibly growing in confidence, Rovers then earned a deserved draw at high-flying Plymouth Argyle, where Mark Walters' fifty-ninth-minute equaliser made him the second-oldest scorer in the club's FA Cup history. An enthralling replay saw Rovers' 2-0 lead clawed back by a powerful visiting side, before Ellington struck the winner with a rasping drive three minutes from time to set up a third round tie away to Premier Division Derby County.

Since the establishment of the Premier Division in 1992, no top division side had lost to one from below Division Two. The achievement of Bristol Rovers in winning away to Derby County ranks alongside the greatest of the club's successes. It was the seventh occasion that Rovers had won an FA Cup tie against top division opponents but, given Rovers' League status, it was most memorable. Moreover, the only other away victory over a club of this stature had been at Burnley in 1958, when Rovers were in the old Division Two. A ground record of 6,602 away supporters were among the 18,000 crowd at Pride Park on the first Sunday in January to witness the biggest shock of round three. Mart Poom, with seventy-seven full international caps for Estonia, played in goal for Derby, with Argentinians Horacio Carbonari and Luciano Zavagno in front of him, and two highly experienced Italians in the side in the shape of Fabrizio Ravanelli and Benito Carbone. After just fourteen minutes, Rovers took the lead when Howie's long kick was headed over the advancing goalkeeper by Ellington. The same player added a second five minutes before half-time with a right-foot shot after a mazy run had taken him past François Grenet and the former Lens defender Youl Mawéné. Astonishingly, with a goal that would have graced any occasion, Ellington completed his hat-trick after sixty-two minutes with a cracking right-foot volley, and there was even time for Mark Walters to hit a post late in the game. Even a scrambled consolation goal, two minutes from time from the White Feather himself, Ravanelli, could not mar the occasion for the Rovers players and supporters. Incredibly, it was the first time that a Rovers player had scored three goals in an away FA Cup tie. Then, armed with the knowledge that a trip to play the eventual FA Cup winners at Highbury awaited the victors, Rovers were outplayed at Gillingham in round four, losing to a side that included former Rovers players Marcus Browning and Guy Ipoua; Ty Gooden's right-footed free-kick after thirty-two minutes was headed into his own net by the unfortunate Ronnie Maugé.

Meanwhile, the Worthington Cup brought a degree of revenge. Rovers, in orange shirts and socks after their black-and-grey quarters were deemed to constitute a colour clash, were able to win at Wycombe Wanderers, the club whose victory in May had condemned Rovers to Division Three. The single goal came from an unlikely source, as experienced midfielder David Hillier struck his first goal for the club, left-footed after sixty-five minutes. His second goal came at home to Luton Town four days later. Andy Johnson and Michael Johnson were both on the scoresheet as the 2001 beaten finalists Birmingham City were comfortable winners at the Memorial Stadium in the second round. The LDV Vans Trophy also ended in a 3-0 defeat, this time at Ashton Gate, but only after victories over non-League opposition. Michael McIndoe's cross-shot from the right had given Tom White's Yeovil Town the lead, but he was to miss the decisive kick as Rovers won the penalty shoot-out 5-4 and Ellington's first two goals for over three months paved the way to a comfortable victory over Dagenham & Redbridge.

2002/03

With fifteen minutes to go in the penultimate game of the season, Wayne Carlisle curled his right-footed 20-metre free-kick past Darlington's former Rovers goalkeeper Andy Collett to secure Rovers' third consecutive victory and ensure the Pirates' continued status as a Football League club. Such a nail-biting conclusion to the season had tried the patience of even the most confident supporter, and had seemed implausible at the start of the campaign. Newly appointed as manager, the former Rovers outside-right Ray Graydon and his assistant John Still, a former manager at both Barnet and Peterborough United, had recruited a number of players for the 2002/03 season, which the club approached in a positive frame of mind. Graydon instilled in his players a greater sense of discipline, and this certainly had a bearing on the eleventh-hour escape from the clutches of relegation. However, twenty-one debutants were among the thirty-three players used as the manager's first season at his home town club proved tougher than he had envisaged.

The Mansfield Town defender Adam Barrett, who had experienced promotion from the basement division in 2001/02, was joined in the centre of defence by the untried former Sheffield Wednesday and West Ham United youngster Anwar Uddin, while Brentford's former Eire under-21 international Danny Boxall accompanied them at full-back. A decade of Football League experience had hinted that Kevin Austin could become a pivotal figure in the Rovers story, though the powerful former Cambridge United defender's Rovers debut was delayed through injury until late September. Oxford United's Rob Quinn, another former Eire under-21 international and erstwhile colleague at Crystal Palace of Danny Boxall, joined Wayne Carlisle, now signing for Rovers on a permanent basis, in midfield. Two new strikers, in the form of Paul Tait, who had fallen out of favour at Crewe Alexandra, and the influential Swindon Town player Giuliano Grazioli, gave early promise of their goalscoring potential. Grazioli had been given his first break in the professional game by John Still at Peterborough and, once Still had moved to Barnet, had scored five times against his former manager's side when the two clubs met in a Third Division game at Underhill in September 1998, Peterborough winning 9-1.

With six debutants in the side, Rovers took a fifth-minute lead at Plainmoor on the opening day of the 2002/03 season, Grazioli scoring the first goal recorded in the Third Division that season. However, succumbing to a Torquay United comeback, Rovers discovered that further struggles lay ahead. Tait, who had not scored a league goal for two-and-a-half years, missed a forty-first-minute penalty at Carlisle and was sent off on the stroke of half-time at Darlington in October. Grazioli missed a second-half penalty at home to Exeter City. Rovers were two goals behind at both Scunthorpe, where a point was rescued by Wayne Carlisle's successful last-minute penalty kick, and before the Sky television cameras at Macclesfield. Rochdale, who arrived without their kit, borrowed Rovers' third choice of black-and-stone quartered shirts, and proceeded to hit the bar twice before half-time en route to a victory at the Memorial Stadium, confirming Rovers' worst start to a season since 1985/86. The future Rovers midfielder Bo Henriksen scored Kidderminster Harriers' seventy-fifth-minute winner at The Mem that September. By this stage, Rovers were also out of the Worthington Cup, defeated at home by Boston United, who were to find themselves four goals behind to Cardiff City by half-time in the next round. By dint of their poor league placing in 2001/02, and the fact that Ipswich Town had been given a bye thanks to their UEFA Cup success, Rovers were obliged to play off for a once-automatic place in the first-round draw. Having staged the first-ever League Cup tie in 1960, Rovers had now also hosted (and lost) the first preliminary round tie in the history of the competition.

Yet, good times lay around the corner. Tait's long-awaited first goal, a fifty-second-minute header in the home win over Swansea City, after which he hit the crossbar with an audacious 40-yard lob, proved the break he needed. The former Everton trainee was to score in four consecutive home games in the autumn. His striking partner, Grazioli, scored in each of his first two games in a Rovers shirt, and added a hat-trick in the space of thirty minutes at Shrewsbury Town in September, when Rovers hit a purple patch. The 5-2 victory at Gay Meadow, coming as it did on the back of a hard-fought home win over Bury, helped propel Rovers away from the now-customary penultimate position towards mid-table safety. A settled side and the promise of better days to come was bolstered in the autumn with renewed talk of converting the Memorial Stadium into an all-seater complex capable of holding 20,000 spectators. Furthermore, plans for a multi-million-pound sports development project, backed by South Gloucestershire Council, were drawn up to include a 10,000-square-metre purpose-built sports complex, floodlit all-weather pitches, laboratories, a gymnasium, indoor theatres and studios and the promise of vocational and educational courses being on offer.

As Christmas approached, Rovers hit the bottom of Division Three for the first time after a club record run of eight consecutive League defeats. During this disastrous run, there was a four-game spell in which Rovers failed to score, the worst result coming at home to Wrexham, who managed nineteen shots on target to Rovers' two. The record-breaking eighth defeat in a row was a 3-1 loss at Cambridge in December, in which Sonny Parker conceded a debut own goal after seventeen minutes. Combined with Boston United's emphatic 6-0 win at home to Shrewsbury Town, this result left Rovers at an all-time low.

However, the process of rebuilding had already started. Graydon's ability to search far and wide for extra players began to reap its rewards as seven players arrived on loan. Of these, Adrian Coote and Chris Llewellyn, whose two goals at Wrexham brought Rovers back from 2-0 down only for the side to lose to a Carlos Edwards goal two minutes from time, both offered international experience, while David Lee had played for Hull City against Rovers in November 2001. Six highly experienced players were signed as the season progressed, and they had major roles to play as the relegation battle developed. Bradley Allen was a brother of the England international Clive and the son of Les, a League and FA Cup double winner with Spurs in 1960/61; Graham Hyde, sent off at Cambridge, had appeared in FA Cup and League Cup finals while on the books of Sheffield Wednesday; Ijah Anderson, Kevin Street and Lee Hodges possessed vast experience of life in the lower divisions; while the former Manchester United youngster Andy Rammell had scored Barnsley's opening goal when Rovers were defeated 5-1 at Twerton Park in November 1992, as well as being sent off when Rovers defeated Wycombe Wanderers at Adams Park in September 2000. The loosening of the club's purse strings by chairman Geoff Dunford and his supportive board proved to be highly significant in Rovers' ultimately successful battle against relegation to the Conference.

Nevertheless, Rovers had an intense battle on their hands to retain their eighty-three-year-old Football League status. In three consecutive home games around New Year, Rovers trailed, Wayne Carlisle scored and defeat was averted. Moreover, in the third of these, Rovers' first home win in three months, Scunthorpe actually led 1-0 after eighty-six minutes. Ben Futcher deflected a Mark McKeever shot into his own net after seventeen minutes of the game at home to Lincoln City, and then scored his side's winning goal at Sincil Bank. After four straight draws, an unexpected but thoroughly deserved win at Bury, Rovers' first at Gigg Lane since March 1956, was earned when Rob Quinn waltzed through the home side's defence after sixty-five minutes. A revitalising run of seven games without defeat offered hope but was shattered abruptly by a spectacular long-range goal from York City's Darren Edmondson, after the former Rovers trialist Jon Parkin had struck a first-half penalty against a post. Rovers also took early leads against the top two sides in successive home games in the run-up to Easter: Hartlepool United, who featured the former Rovers goalkeeper Anthony Williams, and Marcus Bignot's latest side, Rushden and Diamonds. Vitalijs Astafjevs returned to the side to score crucial goals in three consecutive matches in the spring and leave the veteran Latvian international captain as an unlikely second-highest scorer at the club, behind eleven-goal Grazioli. Beneath Rovers, the maelstrom gathered momentum; for the first time, two clubs would be automatically relegated to the Conference, and there was so little to choose between a multitude of sides. Rovers were bottom of the table again after the draw at Southend United in February, and were only out of the drop zone on goal difference as late as 19 April. At home to the other struggling sides, Rovers gained few points, losing disappointingly to Carlisle United and drawing with Boston United, Exeter City, Macclesfield Town and Shrewsbury Town.

The final season before the Second World War notwithstanding, Rovers were now in the most perilous position in the club's Football League history. Back in 1939, re-election was secured without any great worries. Between 1931 and 1951, only one club (Gillingham in 1938) had failed to be re-elected, and they swiftly returned to the league after the war. The trapdoor to Conference football was, by 2003, proving to be something of a chasm. For six consecutive seasons, from 1996/97, the relegated side had never yet returned to league action, and the Conference contained eight former league sides in 2002/03. As Bristol Rugby Club teetered on the brink of financial ruin and faced being swallowed up by their arch-rivals Bath, dropping a division, both in footballing and in financial terms, was not a viable option for Rovers. As it was, figures released for the year to June 2002 showed that Rovers had made an overall loss of £608,402, compared with a deficit of £174,000 over the previous twelve months. Yet Rovers could count on considerable support, taking some 2,876 away fans to Oxford, 1,711 to Torquay, 1,582 to Exeter and 1,286 to Bournemouth. On the final day of the season, Kidderminster's highest home crowd of the season was partly explained by the presence of 1,591 away supporters who were able to cheer Tait's seventy-first-minute header from Llewellyn's right-wing corner on a ground where Rovers have still not won since Easter Monday 1898. Rovers' average home League attendance for 2002/03 was 6,934, greater than fifteen Division Two clubs and three sides in Division One. Consequently, the directors gave their full backing to December's launch of the Share Issue Scheme, the long-term aim of which was to bring some £3 million to the club. This involved establishing a holding company that would include all shareholders, the largest of which would be the supporters' club, whose 700,000 shares effectively gave them the casting vote in any major future decision-making process. Celebrities such as the boxer Jane Couch soon signed up, and the club was already assured of over £10,000 per month by the season's end. Moreover, this scheme funded the signing of Andy Rammell, whose four goals in three games over Easter secured Rovers' immediate Football League future.

A distinct lack of success in the LD Vans Trophy and League Cup was barely bettered in the FA Cup. Rovers required extra time in a replay at Runcorn and, after Barrett had conceded an own goal, only won through after the home side's Lee Parle had been sent off for a second bookable offence. Following a home draw with Rochdale, an exciting replay was lost by the odd goal in five at Spotland. Premier Division side Leicester City were the visitors in May for a testimonial game for Roy Dolling, whose thirty-eight years with the club in many capacities had ended upon his retirement in 2001. An all-conquering Rovers women's side, managed by Tony Ricketts, won its first eight Premier League Southern Division games of 2002/03, the seventh being a comprehensive 13-0 victory over Barking, Trudy Williams scoring six times and Stef Curtis five. Williams scored seven times in the Gloucestershire County Cup final in May in which Rovers, courtesy of a 10-1 victory over Forest Green Rovers, secured the trophy for a fifth consecutive year. The 'Gas Girls' were promoted to the Premier League in the spring and reached the semi-finals of the FA Cup, where they lost 7-2 to a powerful Fulham side that included Rachel McArthur, whose paternal grandfather Wally had served Rovers so loyally either side of the Second World War.

2003/04

For a third season in succession, Rovers flirted with the trapdoor to Conference football, playing under five managers and using thirty-three players in the process. Loyal supporters had hoped for better, but Ray Graydon's side found the going difficult. Only thirty-seven goals had been scored by mid-March and the side had lost as many as seven League matches at the Memorial Stadium by early April. Ultimately, as York City and Carlisle United lost the battle for survival, Rovers completed the season in fifteenth place in Division Three. Remarkably, after all the scares as the season progressed, victory over Lincoln City in May took Rovers temporarily into the top half of the Third Division table. Adam Barrett, an inspirational captain, missed just one League game, and reliable goalkeeper Kevin Miller two, while Paul Tait was top scorer, seven of his twelve goals being scored from within the 6-yard box.

Rovers' third season in the basement division began in sweltering heat. An opening-day victory at Scunthorpe, where Lee Hodges scored the winning goal two minutes from time against his former club, was played out in 90°F. Six new faces appeared in this game, four permanent signings and Calum Willock, who joined on loan from Fulham. Goalkeeper Kevin Miller could claim well over 500 appearances in the Football League, and had played against Rovers for Watford in 1996/97 and for Exeter City in 2002/03. Christian Edwards, from Nottingham Forest, had won a Welsh cap in the centre of defence, while Oxford United's midfielder Dave Savage, the winner of five caps with Eire, had scored a penalty for Northampton Town against Rovers in March 2001. The loss of top scorer Giuliano Grazioli to Barnet was part of a swap deal that brought the exciting striker Manuel 'Junior' Agogo to the Memorial Stadium. Ghanaian by birth and fluent in two African dialects, Agogo had enjoyed spells with six separate League clubs, as well as two top North American sides. Into April, he still had just three goals to his name, but a change in management appeared to bring out the real Agogo as the season drew to a close. The new squad also included veteran

Andy Rammell who, after scoring four important goals to secure Rovers status as a league club, had to miss the start of the season due to two knee operations and, subsequently, his headers at Darlington proving to be his only goals of an injury-ridden season, was forced to retire from the game.

Two first-half goals in five minutes from Wayne Carlisle, appropriately at Carlisle's Brunton Park, and an excellent right-foot winner from Hodges after seventy minutes against Kidderminster brought early season success. Rovers even recovered to draw after trailing 2-0 inside fourteen minutes, Ijah Anderson conceding an own goal, at home to Macclesfield Town. Carlisle's goals included a calmly accepted, twice-taken penalty to defeat Scunthorpe United, and he was to score all three of Rovers' goals as they completed the double over his Cumbrian namesakes. John Ward's Cheltenham Town side was also defeated at home and away. Promoted Hull City were defeated in Horfield at the end of November, the winning goal coming from Ryan Williams, who was on loan to Rovers from the Humberside team. Sonny Parker's excellent fifty-second-minute header to equalise at home to Torquay, as Rovers recovered from conceding two goals in the opening seventeen minutes to their future striker Jo Kuffour, was one highlight of the season, as was the accomplished start to eighteen-year-old Lewis Haldane's professional career, his five goals being exemplified by an astonishingly good second-half volley to give Rovers the lead in the home game against Bury. Yet Rovers were only to achieve two consecutive wins in Division Three on two occasions in 2003/04.

In September, Simon Bryant was shown a red card only seven minutes after taking to the field at York as a substitute, the first Rovers player to be sent off as a replacement. Both games against Orient featured goals from the East London side's substitute Jabo Ibehre, the first time this feat had been achieved by a substitute in Rovers' history, and both games also included a red card for Ijah Anderson. Kevin Austin and Graham Hyde each received two red cards as well during the course of the season, Rovers players being shown nine red cards in League and Cup action. Hugo Rodrigues, who played in both Rovers' games against Yeovil Town became, at 6 feet 8 inches, the tallest opponent to face Rovers, while 6-foot 7-inch Ben Futcher scored for Lincoln City in both their fixtures against Rovers. Richard Walker, whose goals at Wembley in 2007 were to see Rovers promoted, scored an eighty-sixth-minute winner for Northampton Town in Horfield on Boxing Day. Andy White appeared against Rovers in the colours of Boston United and Mansfield Town, as well as being an unused substitute for Kidderminster Harriers when Rovers visited Aggborough three days after Christmas Day. Southend United contrived to miss two penalties in December, the first time since 1935 that any side had missed two in a game featuring Rovers. Mark Gower, after twenty-four minutes, and substitute Drewe Broughton, eight minutes from time, were the culprits.

Enjoying a season free from concerns would not, however, have been Rovers' style. In the autumn, five matches were lost out of seven at one stage. A further run of ten games without a win over the New Year helped enable Cambridge, Northampton and the two newly promoted sides, Doncaster and Yeovil, to complete League doubles over Rovers. Five separate players scored against Rovers for both Yeovil and Doncaster. Relegated York City defeated Rovers at Bootham Crescent, while lowly Darlington recorded a morale-destroying 3-0 victory at the Memorial Stadium. For the first time in the club's long Football League history, three first-half goals were conceded in consecutive games as Mansfield Town and Doncaster Rovers imposed heavy autumnal defeats on Graydon's side. At Belle Vue, Michael McIndoe's hat-trick helped consign Rovers to their first four-goal defeat since 1997. Worse still was the debacle at Yeovil Town's Huish Park in February. Having lost the first-ever League meeting with the newcomers, Rovers were lucky to escape from Somerset with only a four-goal defeat and, within days, a rescue package was being formulated to prevent the club from sinking into the mire at the foot of the division.

Ray Graydon's mid-season departure had appeared increasingly inevitable and, after his assistant John Still had departed on 13 December, the former Rovers winger left the club on 19 January. The popular youth team coach Phil Bater had been promoted from within at the start of the season to the post of first team coach, and he at first took temporary control of a struggling team. Tony Ricketts, a highly qualified coach and manager of Rovers' women's team, was given the role of assisting Bater but, despite their best efforts, Rovers were not to achieve better results on the pitch. As relegation to the Conference became a distinct possibility, two experienced football practitioners were drafted in on 22 March to steady a sinking ship. The former England centre-back Russell Osman had played in the Leicester City side that Rovers knocked out of the FA Cup in January 1986 before later managing Bristol City, while Kevan Broadhurst had appeared against Rovers in January 1980 in the all-yellow away kit of Birmingham City. Their brief, as joint managers, was to preserve Rovers' Football League status. A flurry of transfer activity led to the arrival of Gary Twigg, Lee Thorpe, who renewed a striking partnership he had earlier forged with Agogo at Lincoln City, and five further debutants in the crucial home fixture with York City at the end of March. With survival assured, Ian Leslie Atkins, the scorer of the first of Shrewsbury Town's three goals against Rovers in November 1980, took the reins at the Memorial Stadium on Monday 26 April. His initial appointment on 19 March, though, had caused upheavals at his previous club, Oxford United, whose chairman Firoz Kassam's claims of an illegal approach in March were rejected by Rovers. At that stage, on 21 March, Geoff Dunford had reportedly offered to resign as Rovers' chairman. As Oxford fell dramatically from an automatic promotion place to missing out on the play-offs, Atkins had been released and replaced by caretaker manager Graham Rix. He was therefore in place at Rovers for the final two matches of an anxious season.

The five new faces on transfer deadline day were not unknown to Rovers supporters. Two signings from Kidderminster Harriers were Bo Henriksen, who had scored against Rovers in September 2002 and remains the only Harrier to score twenty goals in a Football League season, while Danny Williams, a former Welsh under-21 midfielder who had been a Liverpool apprentice with Michael Owen and Steven Gerrard, had been sent off at the Memorial Stadium while on Wrexham's books in May 2001 and had hit the bar when Rovers travelled to Aggborough in April 2003. A pair of Stockport County midfielders arrived in Aaron Lescott, the recipient of a red card at Ashton Gate in January 2003, and Ali Gibb, who had played against Rovers on four occasions in the Football League for Northampton Town. 'It would be nice to look back after my career has finished,' Gibb remarked, 'and be able to say I kept Bristol Rovers up.' John Anderson, a tough Scottish-born central defender with eight years' experience north of the border, arrived from Hull City, for whom he had played twice against Rovers during the 2002/03 season. On the morning of 27 March, Rovers were three points above the bottom two clubs and had played one game more. The key fixture at home to York was won by three clear goals, Danny Williams opening the scoring on his debut with a low shot after just seventeen minutes. Rovers then won two games through Agogo winners after the side had trailed to a first-half goal and League survival was at last assured.

An early exit from each of the three cup competitions merely served to underline Rovers' precarious position. It did take some spectacular goals to knock Rovers out, though, with ten-man Brighton securing League Cup success at the Memorial Stadium through Chris McPhee's overhead kick, and Mark Gower's excellent extra-time shot sealing Rovers' fate in the LDV Vans clash at Southend. A potentially lucrative end-of-season game against the Iraqi national side in May, designed to commemorate fifty years since Youri Eshaya had appeared for Rovers reserves, the only Iraqi national to perform to this level in Great Britain, had to be cancelled at short notice amid fears for security. On the other hand, Rovers' women's team not only preserved their hard-won Premier League status, but also reached the semi-finals of the FA Cup before losing to two second-half goals in a minute from a highly talented Arsenal team, the first from Julie Fleeting, whose hat-trick helped Arsenal defeat Charlton Athletic 3-0 in the final.

No summary of a Rovers season could be complete without a further twist to the question of their home ground. In September 2003, South Gloucestershire Arenas proposed a 30,000-seater sports complex on a 220-hectare site near the A49 at Easter Compton, some 6 miles from the Memorial Stadium, to include a stadium for football, rugby and greyhound racing with provision for 10,000 spectators. By 2008, Geoff Dunford concurred, both Bristol's professional football clubs could be sharing these facilities. On 6 January 2004, with 85 per cent of local residents reported to be opposed to the proposal to build on that site, the Severnside Stadium plan was scrapped. Support, though, did not dwindle, and Rovers took 1,600 spectators to both Yeovil and Cheltenham, almost 1,500 to Hull and over 1,200 to Torquay and Oxford, while the highest home crowd was that of 9,812 for the visit of Yeovil in December. An average home crowd of 7,141 put Rovers in third place in their division and ahead of seventeen sides in Division Two as well as two in Division One.

2004/05

Armed with a new manager and his hand-picked side, Bristol Rovers shot out of the starting blocks and were top of the newly renamed League Two by the end of August. Thereafter, a deluge of draws ensured that the club completed the season in twelfth place, thankfully well clear of the dreaded trapdoor that saw Cambridge United and Kidderminster Harriers plunge into Conference football, but also well short of the anticipated play-off berth. In losing just once in the League at home, a record only bettered in the 1989/90 championship season, Rovers also scored thirty-nine times at the Memorial Stadium, more than in any season since 1997/98; only Orient, Yeovil and Scunthorpe, who each put four goals past Rovers, registered more home goals in League Two.

Having seen first hand, at the tail end of 2003/04, what was required, new manager Ian Atkins set about building a side he felt could challenge for promotion to League One. Having enjoyed a modicum of success elsewhere, Atkins brought in a plethora of players who had played under him at Northampton Town and Oxford United. Of these, James Hunt, Richard Walker, Jamie Forrester and Paul Trollope, the winner of nine full Welsh caps, figured strongly in the first team. Midfielder Craig Disley was an inspired signing from Mansfield Town, while Robbie Ryan, an Eire international at under-21 level, had just appeared for Millwall in the 2004 FA Cup final, where he had marked Cristiano Ronaldo. Grimsby Town's former Scotland under-21 international Stuart Campbell strengthened the midfield further, while Kidderminster's Craig Hinton, and Steve Elliott, a former England under-21 international previously with Derby County and Blackpool, played key roles in defence. Having, for the third successive year, sold their leading scorer, Rovers depended on the early season form of Junior Agogo and on the strike rate of Walker, a signing from Oxford, as the season progressed. Agogo finished the season with twenty League Two goals and Walker, who did not score in the League until the end of January, with eleven. No one appeared in every game. Hunt and Elliott were both sent off twice as Rovers accumulated nine red cards in League and Cup action. Rovers also offered trials to a series of players, from the former Real Madrid midfielder Pedro Matias, to goalkeeper Keita Karamoko, former Viktoria Aschaffenburg midfielder Thorsten Dinkel, striker Blair Sturrock and the exotically named central defender Exodus Geohaghon.

In shattering the club's long-standing highest total of draws in a season, Rovers also lost significantly on the points that might have secured a promotion or play-off place. Indeed, champions Yeovil Town lost more League matches than

Rovers during the season. Twenty-one League draws bettered the previous highest total of seventeen, while twelve home draws constituted one more than in the record 1988/89 season. There were goalless draws, 1-1 draws and scores of 2-2, 3-3 and even 4-4. On four occasions, Rovers clawed back a two-goal deficit to claim a point, and a two-goal half-time lead was lost at Chester City in a match broadcast live by a cable television company in Thailand. Rovers won three consecutive League matches in August and lost all three League Two matches they played in November, but, most remarkably, never won or lost two games in a row. Darlington scored after just fifty-four seconds through Craig Russell when they claimed a point at the Memorial Stadium on Easter Monday. Mansfield Town led 4-2 in March before being held to what was the eighth 4-4 draw in Rovers' League history, both Walker and Agogo converting controversial penalties. If this was the second time, following the victory over Luton Town in February 1970, that two Rovers players had converted penalties in a League game, it must be added that the club had been awarded two more in the home draw with Bury, Forrester converting one and spurning the other on his home debut.

However, the most unlikely of draws was the product of a tempestuous home local derby with Yeovil Town in October. After dominating early play, Rovers had fallen behind to a deflected Paul Terry goal. In injury time at the end of the first half, the visitors' Gavin Williams, later a Rovers midfielder, crashed to the floor and Rovers' Dave Savage, who had clearly lashed out, though without making contact, was sent off by referee Phil Crossley. Within a minute, Steve Elliott became the second Rovers player to be dismissed as the atmosphere turned sour. Swiftly 2-0 down, nine-man Rovers then staged a comeback of epic proportions, as first Hunt and then, with four minutes remaining, man of the match Agogo completed Rovers' unexpected yet, on the basis of their second-half display, well-merited recovery.

Seven captains were employed during the season. Kevin Miller, the experienced goalkeeper, whose 600th League appearance had come in that Yeovil clash, opened the season by shaking hands with another goalkeeper called Kevin, Mansfield's captain Kevin Pilkington. Lescott, Forrester, Hunt, Lee Thorpe, John Anderson and Elliott all captained the side at some stage. The referee at Mansfield had been Clive Oliver, and it was his son Mike Oliver who took charge when Rovers visited Darlington. Jarnail Singh, who awarded Rovers two penalties in the home fixture with Bury, was the first turbaned referee to officiate a Rovers game.

When Southend United visited at the tail end of August, an eighty-sixth-minute goal from player-of-the-season Hunt earned Rovers victory and put the club, for twenty-four hours at least, on top of the table. A crowd of 9,287 observed an impeccable one-minute's silence that evening to the memory of Jackie Pitt, the stalwart Rovers wing-half of the immediate post-war period, who had passed away earlier that month. In a bizarre symmetrical twist, Rovers' 2-0 defeat at Southend, again on a Friday night, put the Essex side top. Adam Barrett, returning to old pastures, was one of several former Rovers players to play well against their old club. Wayne Carlisle masterminded Orient's three goals in eight minutes at Brisbane Road. Andy Gurney, Lee Thorpe and Kevin Austin all played for Swansea against their former club. When Rovers' line-up was unexpectedly and by chance numbered one to eleven for the visit of Shrewsbury Town, the opposition fielded Scott Howie, Trevor Challis and Kevin Street. On the other hand, the Rovers party that travelled to Northampton included two of the Cobblers' former managers and six of their former players, while the future Rovers striker Scott McGleish scored a brace for the Cobblers. In that game, Hunt, a former Northampton midfielder, was sent off for a foul on Josh Low, a former Rovers midfielder. When the sides met in Horfield, Agogo's appearance as a seventh-minute substitute for the injured Savage rendered him the fourth earliest substitute in Rovers' League history. Ryan Williams, at home to Grimsby Town, became the first Rovers substitute to score before half-time.

Richard Walker's late-season goalscoring form was sparked by a last-minute goal at Oxford, his former club; coming in the final days of January, this was his first League goal for Rovers. Oxford included two South Americans in their side in Uruguayan Mateo Corbo and Argentinian Lucas Cominelli. Grimsby's Stacy Coldicott, bleeding from an early injury, wore three differently numbered shirts in the first nine minutes of the game in February, chronologically 9, 27 and 20. Bury became the first opposition to field two players with double-barrelled names, Brian Barry-Murphy and Colin Kazim-Richards both appearing as second-half substitutes. Kidderminster Harriers were fined £6,000 after they had fielded the ineligible James Keane, a loan signing from Portsmouth who enjoyed many years of football in Sweden, in their game at the Memorial Stadium. On the final day of the season, Rovers defeated a Wycombe Wanderers side for whom the future Rovers goalkeeper Lance Cronin was making his sole appearance in goal. As the Cambridge United website 'Moosenet' reported in January 2005, 'Atkins' talk of a promotion push resembled a Pukka-Pie in the sky on this mediocre evidence.'

Heavy defeats were few and far between. More frustratingly, Rovers twice lost to twice-taken disputed penalties, converted eventually by Swansea's Lee Trundle and Oxford's Lee Duxbury. Yeovil Town inflicted a comprehensive defeat on Rovers for the second year in succession. A staunch away following of 1,508, bettered only by the 1,686 who travelled to Cheltenham at Christmas, helped ensure that a new ground attendance record for a League fixture at Huish Park would be set, 9,153 spectators watching Craig Disley's excellent early goal give Rovers the lead. Inspired by Phil Jevons, whose hat-trick after twenty-six, fifty-three and sixty-three minutes was the first conceded by Rovers for sixteen months, Yeovil ran up four goals for the second consecutive year in this fixture. Scunthorpe, promoted alongside Yeovil at the season's end, scored seven times in the two fixtures against the Pirates, running in two in each half late in April in a game that saw Disley sent off for a challenge that broke Richard Kell's leg.

Hope for the future was high, especially in the success experienced by Rovers at junior level, the under-18s finishing in second place in the Merit Division. The most tangible reward was the arrival on the scene of Bath-born striker Scott Sinclair, who became Rovers' youngest post-war League player, and the youngest at the club since Ronnie Dix's prodigious start in 1928. Aged fifteen years and 276 days, Sinclair made his debut on Boxing Day, when Rovers played with ten men for eighty-five minutes, Ryan's fifth-minute red card for handball being the second fastest in the club's history, behind Carl Saunders' third-minute dismissal against West Bromwich Albion at Twerton Park in May 1991. A reserve side lost 2-0 to Yate Town in the Gloucestershire FA Cup final. Rovers' women's team finished another highly successful season in fifth place, their highest-ever showing in the Premier League. Fielding players from Canada, USA, Guam, the Netherlands, Wales and Ireland, Rovers could also call on England under-19 international Louise Hutton. Trudi Williams scored a hat-trick when Doncaster Belles were defeated 5-0, and she added the opening goal of a 12-0 drubbing, through eight separate scorers, of Cirencester Town in the Gloucestershire FA Women's Challenge Cup, setting up a 2-0 final victory against Bristol City, Williams and Stef Curtis both scoring in the opening twenty-three minutes. Both the women's and men's sides were able to benefit from extensive links with Filton College. The establishment of Club Rovers, a unique initiative that would combine supporters, local companies and the local community, offered much hope. With an average seasonal home gate of 7,077, plans for a new 5,500 all-seated stand to replace the Blackthorn End represented the first of three steps towards creating a 17,000 all-seated arena. The club's match-day programme once again won the top honours nationally, winning the three categories of Best Read, Best Value and Best Programme for the division. An April Fool's Day hoax on the club website was swiftly taken on board, and Rovers agreed to issue a limited edition pink club shirt. Over Easter 2005, Rovers announced an ambitious four-year sponsorship deal with the Italian sports giants Errea from Parma.

Cup tournaments brought a mixture of success and disappointment. An improbable win at Brighton, two divisions higher, was followed by League Cup exit, in honourable circumstances, at Premier League Norwich City, where Rovers, down to ten men after Elliott's dismissal, lost by just one goal, scored in first-half stoppage time from a low 30-yard drive by Moroccan midfielder Youssef Safri. As they had done for games at Cardiff in February 1934 and at Newcastle in April 1991, Rovers chartered a flight to transport players and supporters to Carrow Road. In the FA Cup, Brazilian Magno Vieira's headed goal from a Chris Lumsdon cross after 109 minutes of the replay saw Rovers crash out of the tournament at Conference side Carlisle United. Four straight wins in the LDV Vans Trophy, the last through a ninetieth-minute Lewis Haldane shot after the side had trailed at Orient, left Rovers just a two-legged tie away from a final at the Millennium Stadium. Succumbing to defeat with a makeshift side in the home leg,

Rovers drew 2-2 at Southend to be eliminated by just one goal, despite a stunning volleyed goal from Agogo, described by many as his best ever for the Pirates. Chris Llewellyn and Danny Williams, the latter as substitute, played for the Wrexham side that defeated Adam Barrett and Che Wilson in the Southend side in the final. England lost 2-1 to Russia in a women's international match staged at the Memorial Stadium in August. On Monday 2 May, as the season drew to a close, Rovers played National Division One champions Bristol Shoguns at the Memorial Stadium in a thirty-minute football, thirty-minute tag rugby encounter, refereed respectively by former player Geoff Twentyman and rugby World Cup final referee Ed Morrison. A goalless draw at football preceded a 17-7 defeat at the oval-ball game, Edwards' late try being converted by Williams.

2005/06

Amid the ashes of the 2005/06 season lay the hope that Rovers could have pulled out of the basement division at the fifth time of asking. Early season hopes and the eternal optimism of ardent supporters were not ultimately rewarded, and a final placing of twelfth was a fair reflection on what proved to be an average campaign in terms of performance and results.

Rovers took to the field for the new season with just one new face in Scott Shearer. He arrived a fortnight before the new season, as Ryan Clarke had been allowed to join Conference side Forest Green Rovers on a year-long loan to gain first-team experience. Shearer, a former Coventry goalkeeper, had been credited in some quarters with a goal for Albion Rovers against Queen's Park in February 2003, and had been debited with an own goal when he played at the Memorial Stadium in Rushden's colours in April 2005. Despite criticism in some circles, Shearer was a regular and dependable 'keeper, and only sixty-seven goals were conceded in the League. He almost scored, too, sending a last-minute header from a corner wide of the post in an eventful 3-2 defeat at home to Peterborough in August, after Rovers had clawed back a 2-0 deficit against ten men. Loan arrival Michael Leary's first two games of 2005/06 were away wins at Brisbane Road, first with Luton Town and subsequently with Rovers, for whom he was booked in three of his first four appearances. Alongside loan signings, two young local players emerged, in the shape of Darren Mullings and Chris Lines, whose presence offered significant hope for Rovers' future. Despite the loss to Chelsea of the prodigious talent of sixteen-year-old Scott Sinclair, Rovers' youth policy appeared to be bearing fruit. Goalkeeping coach and sometime reserve goalkeeper Steve Book played just once, when the otherwise ever-present Shearer missed the Notts County game, Book becoming in the process, at thirty-six years 247 days, the seventh-oldest man to make his club debut. Shearer, Steve Elliott, a strong figure in defence, and Richard Walker missed only occasional games, while Walker and Junior Agogo spent much of the season bracketed among the division's top scorers. Craig Disley was an able contributor of goals from midfield, his seasonal tally of eight being a personal best. Walker was the first Rovers player since Jamie Cureton in 1999/2000 to score twenty League goals in a season, finishing ahead of Agogo's fifteen.

Mid-season reports highlighted the issue of crowd control at the Memorial Stadium. In 2004/05, Rovers had registered the highest number of arrests at a League Two club, some thirty-four in total, fifteen at home games and nineteen away, of which twenty-six had been for 'public disorder' offences. Although up from the thirty recorded in 2004/05, this figure still fell below the total at Bristol City, where there had been sixty-eight arrests in 2004/05 and forty-three in 2005/06. A figure of 2,725 arrests at all Football League matches in 2004/05, from a total attendance of 29.2 million, indicated the lowest ratio per spectator since 1980, and there had been no arrests whatsoever at 67 per cent of all fixtures. Rovers, meanwhile, continued to initiate plans to develop the Memorial Stadium further. Proposals put forward in June 2005 had provoked 600 letters of complaint from local residents, yet October saw the club come forward with a £16 million plan to create a 18,000 all-seater stadium, funded by 114 student apartments within the ground.

Bizarrely, Rovers found themselves 2-0 down in five consecutive games in August. This included the League Cup exit at Millwall, for whom the former Rovers striker Barry Hayles opened the scoring ten minutes after half-time and Sammy Igoe, on loan at the club later in the season, played in midfield. This run also encompassed an exciting comeback at Torquay, where Rovers scored three times in the final sixteen minutes, including a potential 'Goal of the Season' from Agogo, to record a memorable victory. Indeed, two goals in the last three minutes led to victories over both Torquay and Wrexham, and Richard Walker's penchant for ninetieth-minute goals kept Rovers in the play-off hunt until the end of April. One last-minute goal was accounted in January for Rushden, who included in their side sixteen-year-old Lee Tomlin, while another completed a comeback from 2-0 down in a 3-3 draw with Mansfield, for whom seventeen-year-old Nathan Arnold got on the scoresheet. When Rovers visited promotion hopefuls Cheltenham Town in January, the home side took an eighty-seventh-minute lead, only for Rovers to snatch a late victory, substitute John Anderson recording his only goal of the season in the dying seconds to secure victory.

As the season drew to a close, Rochdale's Rickie Lambert, later a celebrated Rovers striker, missed the opportunity to become only the seventh opponent to score two penalties against Rovers in a League game, Shearer saving his second spot-kick of the game. Rovers had also been awarded two penalties in the home game with Orient, Agogo missing and Walker scoring, in a match in which the London club were indebted to two goals from substitute Jabo Ibehre. Indeed, nine substitutes scored against Rovers in a demoralising fourteen-match spell through the spring. The ability of other clubs to alter their play through tactical substitutions may have been a factor in Rovers' failure to reach the play-offs. Only twice in forty-six League matches did a Rovers substitute score. Glynn Hurst, who scored a winner against Rovers for Shrewsbury, scored after only fifty-two seconds when Rovers visited Notts County; Aaron Lescott was sent off in that game, as were captain James Hunt at Rushden, Junior Agogo at Peterborough and Craig Hinton at Rochdale.

On the positive side, Rovers contrived to win away to five of the top six sides in the division. Carlisle, deserved champions at the season's close, were comprehensively defeated 3-1 at Brunton Park in October. On that occasion, two own goals helped Rovers on their way. Danny Livesey diverted an Ali Gibb cross into his own net after fifty-seven minutes to score the 5,000th goal recorded by Rovers since entry to the Football League in 1920. Zigor Aranalde added a second own goal twenty-five minutes later before Agogo completed the scoring late on with a delightful lob. Long-time divisional leaders Wycombe Wanderers were also crushed 3-1 at home in a strong Rovers performance over Easter; they fielded the former England midfielder Rob Lee in their side, one of only twenty-two players who have appeared against Rovers in League action after their fortieth birthday. Chris Carruthers' first goal for Rovers defeated high-flying Grimsby Town away from home. *The Pirate*, Rovers' match-day programme, was named divisional Programme of the Year for the third consecutive season.

Why, then, did Rovers not secure a play-off berth as the season drew to a close? Initially under Ian Atkins' management, Rovers slipped steadily down the table, reaching nineteenth spot on two occasions, both coincidentally after crushing 4-0 defeats. The first came at Chester in September, when Rovers took just 163 away supporters, two of whom famously spent the second half with their backs to the action in protest, facing a brick wall at the back of the stand, and which precipitated Atkins' departure. The second was a demoralising loss at Northampton, who were to be promoted at the season's end. Despite a steady improvement after that point, consistency was clearly lacking, and a mid-January run proved the only occasion that the side won three League games in succession. Not once all season could the team score four goals in a game, and no League doubles were completed, though Macclesfield Town, Rochdale and Notts County, by no means high fliers, all beat Rovers both home and away. Rovers also lost at home to relegated Rushden as well as strugglers Torquay; indeed, on four occasions Rovers lost at home to the side currently at the foot of the table. Defeat at home to Torquay represented the Gulls' first away victory over Rovers since Boxing Day 1947. After mid-March there were four fairly tepid 1-0 defeats, and these cost Rovers dearly. Just when the play-offs were in sight, the controversial red card received by Agogo at Peterborough led to a three-match ban; Rovers lost all three games and hopes of success were effectively dashed. Rovers came close, but no League table ever showed the club in the play-off zone, eighth place being the highest recorded all season.

Ian Atkins' tactics and player management attracted increased criticism as the season progressed, and he was relieved of his duties on 22 September. He had already used twenty players in an ever-changing side, with Jefferson Louis, Michael Husbands and Matt Somner appearing on a non-contract or temporary basis, as the manager appeared uncertain of his line-up. In Atkins' place, the club appointed Paul Trollope from within as first team coach, with John Anderson to support him for nine games. After that, the directors created the role of director of football for Lennie Lawrence, an experienced manager with Charlton Athletic, Middlesbrough, Bradford City, Luton Town, Grimsby Town, Plymouth Argyle and Cardiff City. 'What he has got is legs,' Lawrence had once been quoted as saying about a player, 'which none of the other midfielders have.' He also bemoaned Rovers' ill-fortune, '[the] last time we got a penalty away from home, Christ was still a carpenter.' After an impressive honeymoon period, in which Rovers won four out of five League and Cup games, the momentum could not be maintained. The three straight victories accumulated at this point represented, in many ways, the high point of the season. Optimism was high, following the arrival of the new management team, and exciting victories at Rushden and Cheltenham were followed by a tough win at home to Chester. Yet, frustratingly, excellent form was shown by Ryan Williams when on loan at Aldershot, and Jamie Forrester when on loan at Lincoln, as Rovers missed out on the play-offs. Continued support was illustrated by a seasonal best away following of 1,999 at Oxford and an average home crowd of 5,989, the second highest in the division; the highest home crowd was the 7,551 who witnessed the Boxing Day victory over Shrewsbury Town.

One severe mid-season loss to the club was the death on Christmas Eve 2005 of Ray Kendall. His fifty years' service to the club had seen him undertake a plethora of jobs, from kit man to PA announcer, from steward to working in the club shop, and he was viewed by many as 'Mr Bristol Rovers'. He was always a true gentleman, and his memoirs *An Away Game Every Week*, published in 2001, have proved an indication of the dedication he showed to the club. His funeral, at St John's, Keynsham, on 5 January, was attended by many former players from across the fifty years he had been involved with the club.

A speedy exit from the League Cup was mirrored by the early defeat, albeit after extra time, at Peterborough in the LDV Vans Trophy, Richard Logan coming on as substitute to score the winner, just as he had in the earlier League meeting between the sides. The FA Cup saw victory at Grimsby, though the encounter was like 'two bald men fighting over a comb' (Richard Butcher), and a late lead held at Vale Park through Ali Gibb's rare goal. Port Vale then won the second round replay at the Memorial Stadium through a goal from Trinidadian World Cup midfielder Chris Birchall. Agogo's positive end-of-season form earned a call-up to the full Ghanaian international side in May, while Bo Henriksen, a Rovers player in the spring of 2004, played in the Icelandic Cup final in September 2005, his blue-shirted Fram side losing 1-0 to his former club

Valur, and the former Rovers striker Bobby Zamora played for West Ham in the 2006 FA Cup final.

2006/07

Just before five o'clock on the last Saturday in May 2007, Sammy Igoe collected the ball on the edge of his own penalty area at the newly reopened Wembley and made the most significant run of his footballing career.

> Sixty yards, two look-ups and a slight swerve to the right later, he let go a shot that, by the time it rolled in, had secured the fourth promotion of Rovers' 87 years in the Football League.
>
> Jamie Jackson, *The Observer*

There was a brief moment, as the ball trickled accurately and gently towards the goal line, during which the largest-ever assembly of 'Gasheads', some 40,000 or more contributing to a Wembley crowd of 61,589, held its collective breath – would it or wouldn't it? Then came the most explosive eruption of sound. Igoe disappeared beneath a mound of players, the crowd became ecstatic, 'Goodnight Irene' was sung by the collected masses and Rovers had returned to League One, so ending a dismal six seasons entrenched in the basement division. Steve Phillips, whose penalty save as a Bristol City player from Scott Jones in 2001 had gone some way to relegating Rovers, ended his season as Player of the Year by making a breathtaking save from Derek Asamoah with fourteen minutes left to play. Earlier in this play-off final, Shrewsbury Town had taken a third-minute lead through Stewart Drummond, only for two left-foot strikes from top scorer Richard Walker to give Rovers an interval lead. Just as Rovers and Chelsea were the two sides to appear at the Millennium Stadium and Wembley in the same season, so were Didier Drogba, Walker and Igoe the only three players to score at both. Reduced to ten men following Marc Tierney's late dismissal, the Shrews had thrown goalkeeper Chris MacKenzie forward for an injury-time corner in search of an equaliser and left the way clear for Igoe's breakaway goal that sealed promotion. Rovers' success came courtesy of 'two picture-book goals by the much-travelled Richard Walker and a late curiosity by Sammy Igoe' (Colin Malam, *Sunday Telegraph*).

Thirty-four-year-old first team coach Paul Trollope and experienced director of football Lennie Lawrence earned just reward for their work this season, as their side progressed from seventeenth place on the morning of 17 March to secure an unlikely play-off berth on the final pulsating day of the regular season. An enthralling run of six wins and two draws in the final eight games propelled Rovers into the play-off mix, as the campaign drew to an exciting close. Substitute

Sean Rigg's first senior goal earned a 1-0 win at lowly Macclesfield, a ground on which Rovers had experienced a poor return down the years, before a stunning 30-yard volley from Rickie Lambert, which was voted goal of the season by the fans, defeated Swindon Town at home to push Rovers, for the first time all season, into the play-offs with one game remaining. Rovers had to visit Hartlepool United, who required a win to become divisional champions, and equal or better the score achieved by Stockport County at Darlington. While County ran up a 5-0 win, their largest away from home since September 1965, Rovers trailed to Joel Porter's low shot after thirty-two minutes at Hartlepool. Nine minutes after half-time, man of the match Craig Disley was fouled by Willie Boland, and Walker kept his head to equalise from the penalty spot. With just four minutes remaining and Rovers outside the play-offs by a point, Ryan Green's cross from the right was met by a nonchalant header from Lambert. Rovers had secured an improbable victory and their place in the play-offs at the expense of Stockport County.

The first leg of the play-off semi-final attracted an enthusiastic crowd of 10,654 as Rovers took on Lincoln City, who were in the play-offs for a fifth consecutive season. Indeed, Rovers got off to a wonderful start, as they took the lead through a powerful downward header from Disley after nine minutes. Walker's calm finish from Steve Elliott's swiftly taken free-kick early in the second half then secured a first-leg victory after The Imps had equalised through a direct free-kick from the Northern Irish international Jeff Hughes, a future Rovers player. At Sincil Bank, Stuart Campbell's astonishing 30-yard strike saw Rovers ahead after just two minutes and, with Lambert putting the side 2-0 up with only ten minutes on the clock, the team coasted to a 5-3 victory, Walker, Igoe and Rigg scoring. It was the first time since September 2002 that Rovers had scored five times in a match and, ironically, the goals had come when a goalless draw would have sufficed to take the club to Wembley for the third time in its 124-year history. 'This has happened before,' Spencer Vignes reported in *The Observer*, 'the side who make it into the play-off positions at the last minute end up being the ones who make the jump, fuelled by a winning streak and positive vibes'.

On 1 April 2007, Bristol Rovers played at the Millennium Stadium for the first and quite possibly only time in the club's history. Amid the rebuilding of Wembley Stadium, the smart stadium in the Welsh capital was being used to host domestic finals and, having progressed through the rounds of the Football League Trophy, now known as the Johnstone's Paint Trophy, Rovers faced Doncaster Rovers in the final. The road there had been smooth – five games and five clean sheets. If Byron Anthony's last-minute header to defeat Torquay United had been crucial, one of the defining moments in Rovers' recent history had been the semi-final against local rivals Bristol City. A hard-earned goalless draw at Ashton Gate ignited belief that was justified when Lambert crashed home a 12-yard volley twenty-five minutes from time at the Memorial Stadium to earn Rovers a place in the final and, more importantly in the eyes of many, secure local bragging rights.

Victory over City is always sweet, yet it tastes better still when the stakes are so high.

Having not conceded a goal in 450 minutes in the tournament, Rovers took more than 37,000 supporters to Cardiff. The total crowd of 59,025 represented the fourth-highest ever to watch a game featuring Rovers, but this was the highest number of 'Gasheads' ever to assemble in a ground and watch their side play. The game was billed by the Doncaster Rovers side as 'the friendly final' and so it was, a game brimming with excitement and epitomising all that is good in lower League football. A goal behind to Jonathan Forte's shot inside forty-five seconds, Rovers were 2-0 down inside five minutes, as Paul Heffernan, a Rovers player in the 2009/10 season, capitalised on another uncharacteristic error. As The Kaiser Chiefs' 'Ruby' blasted across the stadium at half-time, the Pirates found themselves two goals in arrears on arguably their biggest day out for many years. Rovers were spurred into action and, roared on by their vociferous support, pulled a goal back four minutes after half-time when Walker converted a penalty following a foul on Igoe. Then Igoe himself equalised after sixty-two minutes, after good work from Lambert, and the strains of 'Goodnight Irene' reverberated around the stadium. Efforts from Lambert and Igoe went close but, unable to make their increased pressure tell, Rovers were forced into extra time, where the game was lost to a powerful header from the Doncaster captain Graeme Lee from Sean Thornton's left-wing corner. Nonetheless, Rovers and their huge support had done themselves proud.

Such end-of-season excitement appeared a million miles away as Rovers trailed by three clear goals after thirty-five minutes on the opening day of the season. This 4-1 defeat to Peterborough United was to be the heaviest suffered by a side that improved exponentially as the campaign progressed. Sure, four goals were conceded at Grimsby, but the 4-3 defeat there came after Rovers had led 2-0 inside twenty minutes, with the former Pirate Ciarán Toner contributing the home side's fourth before Disley's second goal of the game arrived in injury time. Rovers also trailed 2-0 inside five minutes at the Millennium Stadium, and inside seven minutes at Boston in March, where Albert Jarrett converted a second-minute penalty awarded for handball against Rovers' on-loan defender Samuel Oji.

It was certainly an inauspicious start for what had appeared to be a strong Rovers side. The two major new signings had seemed to be that of goalkeeper Steve Phillips from Bristol City, where he had played in over 250 League games, and future England striker Rickie Lambert, a £200,000 arrival who had previously scored against Rovers for both Macclesfield Town and Rochdale. They were joined by left-winger Andy Sandell from Bath City, central defender Byron Anthony, a former Cardiff City player, and full-back Ryan Green, the holder of two full caps for Wales, whose goal in May 2006 had elevated Hereford United back to the Football League after an absence of nine years. Stuart Nicholson, a Geordie supporter of Rovers, arrived on loan from West Bromwich Albion and impressed with his speed of movement up front, while Joe Jacobson, a left-sided player, had scored for Wales under-21 against Northern Ireland just weeks prior to his arrival on loan. Briefly in the autumn, Rovers had two Walkers in attack, while Sean Rigg and Chris Lines were the two young players pushed through the ranks, with Tom Parrinello and Darren Mullings being unused substitutes. Junior Agogo played in just the first three games, before leaving for Nottingham Forest in a deal worth £150,000.

Without doubt, much of the success of the 2006/07 season was a result of the dependable form of goalkeeper Phillips, who bridged the divide between the two Bristol clubs and was deservedly named Rovers' Player of the Season. From his debut in July, when six separate scorers enabled Rovers to defeat Clevedon Town 6-0, he impressed with his fine saves and excellent positional play. He appeared in fifty-seven of Rovers' sixty-two games in all competitions. Igoe, Disley and Walker were also regular players in the side all season, the last named finishing as the club's top scorer with twenty-three goals, twelve of them in League Two proper. With Aaron Lescott and Steve Elliott regulars in the defence in front of him, Phillips conceded only forty-one goals in forty-four League matches, a total that included twenty-two clean sheets, equalling a club League record set in the 1973/74 promotion season. Indeed, in all tournaments, Rovers did not concede a goal in thirty fixtures, better than the previous club record of twenty-seven in the Third Division championship and Leyland Daf final season of 1989/90. That apart, the campaign barely resembled previous promotion seasons. In 1952/53 and 1989/90, Rovers had won twenty-six League fixtures; this time the side won twenty. Ninety-two League goals in 1952/53 contrasts with forty-nine in 2006/07, while ninety-three points accumulated in 1989/90 exceeded significantly the seventy-two this time round. The 1952/53 and 1973/74 seasons included twenty-seven-match unbeaten runs, and the latter run of conceding no goals in 707 minutes; the 2006/07 campaign was not like that at all.

Having won just two of their opening ten League games, Rovers gradually moved up the table. Two goals in a minute, midway through the second half, brought about a hard-fought home win over newly promoted Hereford United. New captain Stuart Campbell, who took over from James Hunt, a long-term loanee to Grimsby Town, struck a glorious last-minute winner from a free-kick to secure a 3-2 win at home to Peterborough United, after a two-goal lead had been squandered. The 2-0 win at Gigg Lane in November ended Bury's run of six consecutive wins. A 4-0 win in the first-ever home League game against Accrington Stanley proved the largest of the season, with Rovers scoring three times in the opening twenty-six minutes. Yet given that Torquay United lost their eighty-year League status in the spring, the goalless draw at Plainmoor must be seen as two points dropped, especially since television replays were to show that Walker's speculative lob in the second half had crossed the line before being spectacularly cleared by the former Rovers player Lee Thorpe. Walker himself missed a penalty at Rochdale, while Rovers also conceded last-minute equalisers against both Darlington and Accrington Stanley. The home game against struggling Macclesfield Town remained goalless, even though Rovers recorded fifteen shots to their visitors' four, while struggling Wrexham completed a League double over Rovers, Jeff Whitley's very late winner in Horfield over Easter leading to Rovers' only defeat in their final eleven League fixtures.

Representative honours came the way of Lewis Haldane in September, who won his solitary cap for the Welsh under-21 side as a second-half substitute against Turkey at Ninian Park. While the former Rovers prodigy Scott Sinclair furthered his future international claims at Chelsea and on loan to Plymouth Argyle, others gained international honours. Calum Willock won his first caps for St Kitts and Nevis, while Louie Soares (Barbados), James Quinn (Northern Ireland), Junior Agogo (Ghana) and Chris Llewellyn (Wales) all represented their countries. Vitalijs Astafjevs played his 131st full international game for Latvia in their defeat at the hands of Hungary in February.

Off the field, chairman Geoff Dunford stepped down on the day of the JPT final after years at the helm of the club he has always supported; his years in charge had seen the club survive relegation and begin to rebuild at their new home. His input into the club, both in terms of finance and in terms of time, should not be underestimated. Under new chairman Ron Craig, Rovers faced a period of time away from the Memorial Stadium as redevelopment work got underway from Christmas 2007. The club received a major boost with the approval of plans to increase the capacity of the ground from 11,724 to become an all-seater stadium for 18,500 spectators. These plans, to include 120 accommodation units to house 674 people, shops, offices and parking facilities, were given the green light on 17 January 2007 through a vote of 8-3 after a three-and-a-half hour council meeting. Geoff Dunford described it as 'a proud and historic moment' and 'the start of a new era for Bristol Rovers'. With the all-seater requirements stipulated in the 1989 Taylor report now becoming legally binding for League Two clubs, and the government's 1991 all-seater policy becoming more stringently implemented, Rovers were to redevelop their new home with the full support of Sport England, the Football Association and Lord Brian Mawhinney, the chairman of the Football League.

The season also saw the tragically early deaths of Angela Mann, aged only fifty-six, a long-serving employee of the club in a variety of roles, and of Alan Ball, a World Cup winner with England in 1966 and a Rovers player in 1983, who was accorded a one minute round of applause prior to the final regular home game of the season. The award-winning match-day programme was named Programme of the Year for the division for the eighth time in ten years. Rovers drew a crowd of 11,530 for the home tie against Bristol City in the Johnstone's Paint Trophy, while the League Two game at home to Swindon Town drew an attendance of 9,902; the average home gate for Rovers' home Division Two fixtures was 5,475.

Through the cup competitions, Paul Trollope's side was able to offer great excitement for its supporters. The early exit in the League Cup came only through a penalty shoot-out after Rovers had held Luton Town, from two divisions above them, to a draw. The excitement of the Johnstone's Paint Trophy run, as previously highlighted, was almost matched by an enthralling run to the fourth round of the FA Cup. The drama began at Barrow's Holker Street ground in November, when Rovers almost let slip a 3-0 lead, conceding twice in the final twenty minutes in a gale. This match, though, will be remembered longer for the unprovoked left hook from Barrow's James Cotterill that broke eighteen-year-old Sean Rigg's jaw – the punch was captured by BBC *Match of the Day* cameras and Cotterill, immediately released from his contract by his club, was given a four-month prison sentence for grievous bodily harm. Richard Walker scored in each of Rovers' first four FA Cup ties, as Bournemouth, fielding three seventeen-year-olds over the two games as well as the experienced former England midfielder Darren Anderton, were defeated at Dean Court and Hereford were beaten in Horfield. This victory set up a trip to Derby County's Pride Park for a repeat of the famous game in January 2002, when Nathan Ellington's hat-trick had secured victory on one of Rovers' glory days.

With Paul Trollope and Steve Elliott both being former Derby players, and the memories of 2002 playing on the minds of their hosts, Rovers visited the Championship leaders for this fourth-round FA Cup tie with good reason for optimism. The club's approach was sensed by independent reporters: '[these] passions ... reflected throughout [the] side, who were backed by a vociferous following,' noted Arindam Rej in *The Observer*. Rovers took 5,808 supporters to Derby; though not the 6,602 of five years earlier, this represented a significant segment of the crowd of 25,033. Support all season was high, with Rovers taking 2,872 to Ashton Gate for the Johnstone's Paint Trophy semi-final and 2,134 to Swindon Town in League Two. Rovers certainly gave a good account of themselves and were unfortunate to see Andy Sandell's headed strike disallowed on the stroke of half-time. The perhaps harsh sending-off of Aaron Lescott after sixty-nine minutes left the side short in defence, and Canadian substitute Paul Peschisolido scored a well-taken goal eight minutes from time to knock Rovers out of the tournament. However, Rovers 'embraced the grand old lady of football competitions and their 6,000 supporters joyously serenaded them,' as Derick Allsop reported in the *Sunday Telegraph*.

2007/08

Amid the excitement of Wembley and Rovers' last-gasp dash to promotion from League Two in 2006/07 was the realisation that avoiding immediate relegation had to be the priority for Bristol Rovers in 2007/08. This was achieved relatively comfortably, though not without a late glance over the proverbial shoulder, while a hugely impressive FA Cup run to the club's first quarter-final in half a century added a touch of gloss to the season. The management team of Paul Trollope and Lennie Lawrence had achieved their aims, and the process of consolidation in League Two had begun.

Prior to the side's first season in the third tier of English football since 2000/01, there was the small matter of building up a side capable of holding its own at this level. Trollope and Lawrence held onto the shape and personnel that had taken the club to this point, adding in a few players in key positions. First, the signing of left-back Joe Jacobson was made permanent and the young Welshman continued to impress, captaining his country at under-21 level during the season. Midfielder David Pipe, striker Andy Williams and strong central defender Danny Coles were added to the squad and all had significant roles to play as the season progressed. A brief Scottish tour that followed a 5-2 victory over Bath City saw the team remain undefeated against Dunfermline Athletic, Cowdenbeath and Airdrie United, Richard Walker scoring in all three games north of the border. Though he and Sammy Igoe had both scored at the Millennium Stadium and again at Wembley, neither was to score from open play in 2007/08, and Igoe left on loan to Hereford United in the spring.

If survival was the primary concern during the season, it is one that Rovers achieved with the minimum of fuss. Though three Yorkshire sides completed a League double over Rovers (Leeds United, Huddersfield Town and Doncaster Rovers), as did Swindon Town, Leyton Orient and relegated Bournemouth, this was achieved in turn over both Oldham Athletic and Millwall, who were both defeated by last-minute goals at the Memorial Stadium. Rovers took four points off promotion favourites Carlisle United, for whom the future Rovers player Joe Anyinsah appeared in the Brunton Park fixture, and drew both games with the former European champions Nottingham Forest, who were promoted on the final day. The side rode its luck on occasions, securing victory over Millwall twice through injury time goals and scoring five minutes into stoppage time to earn a point at home to Yeovil Town. However, Rovers were unbeaten in their first five League games of the season, a run that stretched to sixteen matches undefeated if the tail end of 2006/07 and the play-offs were taken into consideration, and there was another run of eleven matches unbeaten in all competitions from Boxing Day until the trip to Doncaster in mid-February. With club captain Stuart Campbell controlling midfield and Aaron Lescott playing with renewed vigour at full-back, the side had greater shape. The two Craigs contributed greatly to the goals for column, Disley achieving a personal highest seasonal goals tally of six League goals, and Hinton, who had not scored at all in over 100 games for the club, hitting a purple patch with two League goals and, astonishingly, three more in the FA Cup.

However, there were tell-tale signs that League One was to be a tougher proposition than all that the club had experienced in recent years. Luton Town equalised and held on for a point at the Memorial Stadium, even though they were playing with only eight men. At relegation-threatened Gillingham, Rovers led 2-1 with five minutes remaining, only to snatch defeat from the jaws of victory, with the future Rovers striker Chris Dickson scoring the Gills' winning goal. Southend United scored an injury time equaliser for a point in Horfield, and Forest recovered a 2-0 deficit to escape from the Memorial Stadium with a point. Three of the four relegated sides escaped from the Mem with at least a point, Bournemouth defeating Rovers three times during the campaign, with their striker Jo Kuffour, later a Rovers player, scoring against Rovers in both the League and the Johnstone Paint Trophy. Indeed, in an alarming run that hinted at the 2000/01 relegation season, Rovers did not won at home in the League until mid-November, their eleventh home match in all competitions, and there was a slump either side of the FA Cup quarter-final, when Rovers secured one point in five League encounters and did not win in ten League matches. Indeed, there was just one League win in the final fifteen games of the campaign. At this point, Trollope and Lawrence acted in the loan market and brought in two experienced campaigners, striker Wayne Andrews and midfielder Jeff Hughes. Andrews lasted just seventeen minutes at Yeovil before injury brought his Rovers career to a premature end and Hughes did not even make the team, receiving an injury in a reserve game that prevented him from getting onto the pitch at all, though he was to give Rovers sterling service in seasons to come.

One highlight of the League season was Rickie Lambert's astonishing goal at Luton that was voted second best in the division by an independent panel. Just sixty-seven seconds into Rovers' 2-1 victory at Kenilworth Road in September, he volleyed home from a full 35 yards past goalkeeper David Forde for a spectacular goal. The same game also featured a thrice-taken penalty, as the referee continued to spot infringements as the kick was taken – to his credit, Luton's Matt Spring scored on all three occasions and the goal eventually stood. When the sides later met at The Mem, Luton became only the second side ever to have three men sent off against Rovers, with Chris Coyne, Steve Robinson and Tony Grant all seeing red; Grant's unorthodox form against Rovers continued when he scored own goals in the Pirates' favour in both fixtures against Southend United in the 2009/10 season. Rovers themselves received only two red cards all season, yet these were both in a controversial close to the single-goal defeat at Swindon, when Richard Walker and Steve Elliott were both dismissed in mystifying circumstances along with Swindon's future Rovers defender Jerel Ifil; their substitute Sofiane Zaaboub was also sent off, just two minutes after coming on the pitch. The red card to Swansea's Febian Brandy at The Mem took the number of opposition substitutes sent off in League action against Rovers to six. Walker became only the seventh player to score twice from the penalty spot in a League fixture, giving Rovers a 2-0 lead at home to Orient in September, a lead that was squandered as the East London side came away with all three points. Doncaster Rovers also scored from two penalties when Rovers lost 2-0 at The Keepmoat, Brian Stock and substitute Paul Heffernan, later a Rovers player, converting the spot-kicks. That match included the entire, yet brief Rovers career of Anthony Pulis, the son of a former Rovers stalwart, who appeared as a late substitute, picked up a yellow card and conceded the second penalty. Byron Anthony's first League goal for Rovers was followed three minutes later by an own goal, inadvertently diverting a free-kick into the net off his head at home to Nottingham Forest in September as he became the fifth Rovers player to score for both sides in a League match.

This first season back in League One had enabled Rovers to attract an average home attendance in the League of 6,937, almost 1,500 more than in the promotion campaign twelve months earlier. Rovers finished the season in sixteenth place in League One, having scored just forty-five goals in forty-six League encounters, and secured just five home victories in the League. Goalkeeper Steve Phillips and captain Stuart Campbell were both ever-presents, while Rickie Lambert, though substitute on four occasions, featured in every League fixture as well as top-scoring with thirteen League goals in addition to his six Cup strikes. Rovers also supplied the opposition when Cheltenham Town fielded their oldest-ever League player, Jerry Gill being thirty-seven years 190 days, while Alan Wright, who played alongside him, had also been in the Blackpool side that opposed Rovers in April 1989. Millwall's Ali Fuseini came on as a fourth-minute substitute at The Mem and his goal, timed at seven minutes forty-nine seconds, is the earliest in a Rovers game from a substitute.

Cup competitions were of critical importance to Bristol Rovers in 2007/08. While the Johnstone Paint Trophy did not bring the success of the previous campaign, Rovers bowing out meekly at home to a Bournemouth side that included the former Bristol City player Rob Newman, success lay elsewhere. First, victory over Championship side Crystal Palace in a dramatic League Cup penalty shoot-out set up a home tie with Premier League West Ham United. A narrow 2-1 defeat was marred by the broken leg suffered by England winger Kieran Dyer in a tackle from Joe Jacobson. Then the FA Cup took over Rovers' season, though the side had almost been eliminated in the first round at Orient. As the cup run gained momentum, Rovers began to draw the attention of the national press and, by the beginning of March, Rovers were 'unquestionably the Cinderella team of the FA Cup' (Dave Rogers). They had defeated teams from each of the top five tiers of English football. For only the third time in the club's 125-year history and the first time since 1958, Rovers found themselves in the quarter-finals of this famous old competition.

Struggling through to defeat nine-man Orient in a penalty shoot-out at the Memorial Stadium (Wayne Corden and Jabo Ibehre having been sent off) Rovers recovered from trailing to an early, wind-assisted, long-range goal from Rushden's Marcus Kelly to defeat their Conference opponents 5-1 in atrocious conditions in round two. This victory earned them a trip to Craven Cottage where 'it was sometimes hard to tell who were the Premier League team' (Simon Burnton, *The Guardian*, 7/1/08). With 'the euphoria … [and] pride of Rovers' travelling band' (Oliver Brown, *The Telegraph*, 7/1/08) behind them, Rovers twice took the lead through central defenders, Craig Hinton and Danny Coles both seeing their goals cancelled out by Fulham equalisers. Tenacious and determined, and cheered on by a partisan crowd, Rovers were 'vastly superior in terms of both adventure and endeavour [on] a famous night for Rovers' in the Horfield replay (James Corrigan, *The Independent*, 23/1/08). Rovers triumphed 5-3 on penalties, with Disley converting the decisive spot-kick. A single Lambert goal at Barnet set up a fifth-round tie at home to Southampton, who were the 2003 finalists but at time uncharacteristically vulnerable near the foot of their division. Live on the BBC, Rovers ground out a barely pretty but wholly effective 1-0 victory, Lambert having one headed 'goal' disallowed before marking his twenty-sixth birthday with a famous goal from a free-kick with six minutes remaining, his shot deflecting in off Jermaine Wright. 'If anyone questions the magic of the FA Cup,' wrote Andrew Warshaw, 'they should have been down in this part of the West Country' (*The Sunday Telegraph*, 17/2/08). Rovers were through to their first FA Cup quarter-final in half a century, and having been given a home tie against non-Premier League opponents, there was a very real hope that the side could reach its first-ever semi-final.

Alas, further FA Cup success was not to be. Before a fiercely vocal record attendance of 12,011, Rovers were undone by a slick and effective West Bromwich Albion side that played with great skill and showed clinical finishing. The margin of defeat (5-1) was harsh on a Rovers side that competed well, but reflected the power of an Albion side who were top scorers in the four divisions of English football. Ishmael Miller, a cut above everyone else on the day, scored a hat-trick, only the second opponent ever to do so at the Memorial Stadium. For some time, after Coles' scrambled goal on thirty-one minutes from Campbell's right-wing corner had cut the score to 2-1, Rovers were in the tie, but 'Miller, retreating from an offside position' (Russell Kempson, *The Times*, 10/3/08) put the Baggies 3-1 ahead with twenty minutes remaining, and the efficiency of Tony Mowbray's side ultimately proved too strong for the Pirates. Nonetheless, a quarter-final had been beyond Rovers' preseason aspirations and Coles could lay claim to being only the second Rovers player, following the late Geoff Bradford, to have scored for the club at this stage in the competition.

A good deal of positives could be taken out of the 2007/08 season. The management team continued to add stability to a side that had chopped and changed through the roughest years of the basement division. A regular line-up now played with greater consistency and only three games were lost by more than a single goal in the League. Youth was allowed to flourish, with Chris Lines given an extended run in midfield and both Sean Rigg and Josh Klein-Davies playing and scoring in attack. Charlie Reece, Tom Parrinello, Matt Groves and seventeen-year-old Charlie Clough, the first 1990s-born Rovers player, were given brief cameo roles. The club continued to attract positive support, taking 2,781 fans to Leeds, and a total of 6,976 to the FA Cup game at Fulham, this figure representing more than half of the 13,634 crowd. It was said that no top division side had ever been so outnumbered by a lower League side in its own ground. *The Pirate* was voted Programme of the Year for League One by *Programme Monthly*, who said it offered 'unbeatable value for money and a tremendous service for supporters'. Finally, the redevelopment of the Memorial Stadium was given the green light on 2 April, when Bristol City Council, heeding the persuasive argument of community liaison officer Carl Saunders, a former Rovers striker, voted 7-1, with one abstention, to agree to the original plans. The number of student flats was to be reduced from 105 to 97, hotel bedrooms from 112 to 97, and hospitality boxes from 28 to 20, but this plan would otherwise follow closely that already agreed, with the result that the pitch would be enlarged from 100 by 64m to 100 by 66m. A long-anticipated announcement of Rovers' temporary move to play home fixtures at Cheltenham Town's Whaddon Road was made public as the season drew to a close, the curtain apparently coming down on the Old Mem in a disappointing 2-0 defeat at the hands of Brighton in a meaningless end-of-season anticlimax.

2008/09

Doom-mongers in certain quarters had predicted a season of struggle and that the spectre of relegation would hang over the Memorial Stadium in the spring of 2009. Indeed, some speculated that a West Country quartet could be relegated back to the basement division. However, while Hereford United, a side Rovers dismantled twice in the season, and Cheltenham Town, who might have been Rovers' host club had the financial situation internationally been different, suffered relegation, both Yeovil Town and Rovers survived. Indeed, it was more than survival for Paul Trollope and Lennie Lawrence's side, who finished the season in a highly commendable eleventh place in the table, having secured sixty-three League points.

Prior to the start of the campaign, Rovers had signed two new senior professionals in the shape of Darryl Duffy, a former Swansea City striker who had briefly experienced Champions League football while with Rangers, and the Northern Ireland international midfielder Jeff Hughes, who had scored three times for Lincoln City against Rovers in the 2007 play-offs, as well as taking on the promising West Ham United youngster Ben Hunt. Sammy Igoe joined Bournemouth, Richard Walker moved to Shrewsbury Town on loan, and the young pairing of Lewis Haldane and Andy Williams spent season-long loans at Oxford United and Hereford United respectively. A string of preseason games around the country sandwiched a four-day tour to Sweden, in which Rovers lost 3-2 to FC Copenhagen before beating both Malmö Anadolu 4-0, with Josh Klein-Davies scoring all the goals in the nineteenth, fifty-ninth, eightieth and eighty-third minutes, and Limhamn Bunkeflo through Duffy's curling shot after half an hour. The only home game before the start of the season resulted in a 3-2 defeat to a strong Dutch side, ADO Den Haag. Three weeks into the new campaign, Jo Kuffour was signed from Bournemouth to add extra emphasis to the Rovers attack. Much touted, he had scored for both Torquay United and Bournemouth against Rovers in previous years.

Led by captain Stuart Campbell, Rovers' midfield was more creative than in recent years, with Hughes, Chris Lines, David Pipe and Craig Disley playing regularly. Behind them, Aaron Lescott was superb at full-back, supported by Ryan Green or Joe Jacobson on the other flank, and with a central defensive pairing comprising Steve Elliott, Byron Anthony, Craig Hinton or, until his season was prematurely ended by a knee injury, Danny Coles. Behind them, Steve Phillips in goal was the only player to start every game all season. All this took place at the Memorial Stadium, as talks of refurbishment and a spell away at Cheltenham had fallen through.

Goalscoring might have been a failing of the Rovers side over the past few seasons, but there were precious few signs of it this time round. With Kuffour and Duffy supporting the prolific Lambert, the side ran in seventy-nine goals in League action, thirty more than in the 2006/07 promotion season. For the first time since 1997/98, three separate Rovers players reached double figures in their individual tally of League goals. Five goals at Walsall in March and six at home to Hereford showed that the team could score at will when the opportunity arose. Thirteen players scored in the League, which represented a fair sharing around of the goals, though in fairness the lion's share fell to the prolific Rickie Lambert. To start with, the free-scoring striker scored in each of Rovers' first five League matches of the season. When Geoff Bradford set the club seasonal record of thirty-three League goals in the 1952/53 season, twenty-four of his strikes had come in home matches; though Rovers scored forty times at home in the League in 2008/09, Lambert himself contributed seventeen at home and a further eleven in away games. In scoring twenty-nine times in the League, Lambert ended as the equal highest goalscorer in all four divisions of English League football with Swindon Town's Simon Cox. In fact, Lambert had led the Golden Boot list for much of the season and his form earned him a place in the prestigious Professional Football Association League One XI for 2008/09. Almost inevitably, he was voted Rovers' Player of the Year. It was the first time that any Rovers player had scored so many times in one League season since Alfie Biggs had hit thirty in the 1963/64 season.

It is difficult to put a finger on any moment that in itself could define Lambert's free-scoring grip on Rovers' on-field success. The 7,055 crowd for the home game with Southend United in October, however, was treated to a vintage display from the striker, who scored all Rovers' goals in a 4-2 victory. Three goals ahead at the break, with two headers and a shot after ten, sixteen and thirty-three minutes, Lambert headed home Stuart Campbell's free-kick after fifty-five minutes to put Rovers four goals up, a lead that was reduced late on by the visitors' Peter Clarke and substitute Francis Laurent. A further hat-trick followed in March, with two first-half shots and a fifty-ninth-minute penalty at Edgar Street, as Lambert single-handedly saw off a Hereford side staring relegation in the face. He also scored one of the three goals, a powerful 25-yard free-kick, through which local rivals Yeovil Town were comfortably despatched 3-0 in February. Two more Lambert goals also helped Rovers to four first-half goals against Millwall in April, a game that was eventually won 4-2 after Rovers had scored three times in the final thirteen minutes of a glorious first period.

Early season form certainly converted sceptical fans, and Rovers were fortunate to have the good fortune to play at home to Hereford United in the third game of the campaign. A 6-1 victory before a crowd of 6,735 showed what could be achieved. Duffy and Lambert both scored in the opening six minutes and registered two apiece, with Hughes crashing home an unstoppable shot from the edge of the area just seconds into the second half and Lines scoring the sixth with a 30-yard free-kick in off the crossbar two minutes from time. 'You'd be hard pressed to see a better collection of goals anywhere in the country,' first team coach Paul Trollope said at the time.

Rovers' inauspicious start of one point in their opening two games heralded a consistent run of form through the campaign. Only the three top sides in the division (champions Leicester City, Peterborough United and MK Dons) were able to complete a League double, while Rovers achieved this feat over three sides themselves (Hereford United, Orient and play-off hopefuls Oldham Athletic). Rovers also won 2-0 away to high-flying Scunthorpe United, after Phillips had saved Paul Hayes' second-half penalty. There was one September run of three consecutive defeats, which temporarily took Rovers into the bottom four, but otherwise Rovers retained a balanced and unchanging side that played with great consistency. Incredibly, prior to Charlie Reece's inclusion for the 4-1 demolition of Hartlepool United in a meaningless final game of the season, only sixteen different players had started a League match for Rovers. Trollope instilled a sense of fair play in his charges that resulted in a low number of cards being shown, as had also been an element of Rovers' play in previous seasons. In League football, Lines was sent off for an over-exuberant goal celebration after his last-minute equaliser at home to Swindon, and defenders Anthony and Elliott also saw red against Walsall and Millwall respectively. Three red cards and forty-five yellows, fewer than one booking every League game all season, represents a degree of self-control that epitomised Rovers' mid-table display.

Although champions Leicester City completed a League double, Rovers could consider themselves unlucky, particularly on their visit to the Walkers Stadium.

On the back of a seven-game unbeaten run, Rovers led through Kuffour's superbly executed volley from Lambert's flick after sixty-one minutes, only to concede two in the final couple of minutes and lose 2-1. Rovers performed well against other high-flying sides, drawing twice with Leeds United, these 2-2 draws attracting both the highest crowd at the Memorial Stadium all season (10,293 to see Kuffour claim a last-gasp equaliser for Rovers) and the highest on Rovers' travels (21,046 at Elland Road in the autumn). A stunning long-range strike from Lambert helped defeat promotion hopefuls Oldham, who fielded the future Rovers left-back Daniel Jones in their side, in an enthralling home game in October that, along with another 2-0 home win, this time over Tranmere Rovers, represented perhaps the most professional display of the season.

Even more exciting, though, was the televised game at Peterborough United's London Road the previous month. Craig Mackail-Smith scored a hat-trick for the home side, who led by two clear goals on four occasions. Much as Rovers could not be finished off, the Pirates were also unable to conjure an equaliser, let alone a winning goal, in an extraordinary match that was lost 5-4. Aaron McLean and substitute Scott Rendell, a future Rovers striker, also scored for the Posh, while Elliott, Hughes, Lambert and a Shane Blackett own goal proved all in vain for the visitors. Craig Davies was the only other opponent to register a hat-trick against Rovers during the season. The Stockport County striker scored after twenty-seven minutes, and then again in the final seconds of each half, as Rovers were defeated 3-1 at Edgeley Park a week before Christmas.

Having lost at home to Walsall, Rovers exceeded expectations by recording a 5-0 victory at the Banks Stadium in March on the occasion of Paul Trollope's 200th match as Rovers' first team coach. Pipe set up Duffy for the first goal after only three minutes, and Disley doubled the lead three minutes later. Just nineteen minutes in, Rovers were three goals ahead as Lescott hit a low left-foot shot home for his first goal in 174 League matches for Rovers. After Duffy had added his second of the game and Lambert had hit the bar, Lescott astonished all those present by doubling his own tally eleven minutes from time, to leave Rovers supporters puzzled as to why it had taken him so long to score at all. Remarkably, Lescott scored again on the final day of the season, when Rovers led 2-0 after just four minutes and defeated Hartlepool United 4-1 at the Memorial Stadium.

Many supporters believed that although there had been wealth of astonishing goals from Lambert's boot, the best goal seen at the Memorial Stadium in the 2008/09 season was Anthony Pilkington's seventieth-minute equaliser at the end of March, as Huddersfield Town came from a goal down to defeat Rovers 2-1. When Colchester United drew in Horfield in January, their substitute Anthony Wordsworth was booked for putting off Campbell as he shaped to take a corner at the Blackthorn End just before half-time; Wordsworth never did get on the pitch. In addition, *The Pirate*, the match-day publication, won *Programme Monthly*'s coveted Programme of the Year award for the division for the sixth consecutive season. The average home crowd for 2008/09 was 7,171, a 4.7 per cent increase on the previous campaign. As Rovers' season drew to a close, Ryan Green, Craig Disley, Craig Hinton, Richard Walker and Joe Jacobson were all out of contract. The popular former Rovers manager Bobby Campbell died on 3 May 2009, at the age of eighty-six.

Following the astonishing run to the FA Cup quarter-finals in 2007/08, Rovers were unable to live up to their new billing as a successful Cup side. Early exits from all three competitions was a disappointment, Rovers losing to their future striker Will Hoskins' goal two minutes from time at Watford in the League Cup and then crashing out of both the Johnstone's Paint Trophy and the FA Cup, after Anthony had been dismissed, at Bournemouth's Dean Court. Sammy Igoe, so recently a Rovers hero when he scored at both the Millennium Stadium and Wembley in the spring of 2007, tucked home Josh McQuoid's low cross after sixty-seven minutes of the 3-0 JPT defeat to help knock Rovers out of a tournament they had come so close to winning just eighteen months earlier.

2009/10

The third season back in League One under the management team of Paul Trollope and Lennie Lawrence proved as successful in terms of the League position. It was, however, frustrating at times for the club's supporters, as they were expectant of ever-increasing success. Rovers were to register a four-goal away victory as well as suffer a four-goal defeat at home, a feat previously only encountered by the club in the League during the 1948/49 season. Such inconsistency was reflected in defeats against several struggling sides and a run of victories over play-off hopefuls. However, the reality was that, under this management duo, the team had consolidated its position in the upper middle reaches of the third tier of English football, while several contemporaries from the early years of the twenty-first century had slipped out of League football.

From the old guard, Rovers were bereft of the 2008/09 top scorer Rickie Lambert who, after adding his fifty-second League goal for the Pirates on the opening day of the season, left for fellow League Two side Southampton, where he scored a further thirty League goals in 2009/10, and of goalkeeper Steve Phillips who played on loan at Shrewsbury Town and Crewe Alexandra. Sean Rigg, Lewis Haldane and, later in the season, Darryl Duffy, also left the club in long-term loan deals. In their place, Rovers signed three former Milton Keynes Dons players in Carl Regan and Mark Wright, teammates in the Dons' League Two championship season, and midfielder Dominic Blizzard. Appropriately named for a player in a season dominated by weeks of midwinter snow, Blizzard was the scorer of Stockport County's earliest ever goal in a League match, having scored against Hereford United after just fourteen seconds in January 2009, but had to wait until February to notch his first goal in a Rovers shirt. Rhys Evans returned from Bradford City, his game at Wycombe in September, when the future Rovers striker Chris Zebroski was in the opposition, being his first for the club in nine years and six months, a club record gap. Following a disciplinary discretion, David Pipe's Rovers career drew to a close, initially by being sent on a loan spell to Cheltenham Town. Trollope also gave several younger members of the squad a first taste of League football, notably left-sided midfielder Ben Swallow, who appeared sporadically throughout the campaign, and promising striker Elliot Richards. Charlie Reece was given more time to begin to emulate the career of local boy Chris Lines, on whom Rovers became increasingly dependent in the engine-room of the team as the season wore on.

The side was supplemented by three loan signings of international footballers: Geordie goalkeeper Fraser Forster, at 6 feet 7 inches the club's tallest ever player and a future England cap, the replacement in goal; the reliable Denmark under-21 international Mikkel Andersen; and Ghanaian international striker Chris Dickson, who scored twice before half-time on his debut at Brentford. Pat Baldwin, whose almost 200 League appearances for Colchester United had helped propel the Essex club into the Championship, was also at The Mem on loan, conceding an own goal off his shin at Millwall with his final touch in a Rovers shirt. Later in the campaign, Fulham's Wayne Brown, the Wolves full-back Daniel Jones, and Doncaster Rovers' record signing Paul Heffernan, who had scored their second goal against Rovers in the Johnstone's Paint Trophy Final at the Millennium Stadium in April 2007, also arrived on loan.

Once again, the midfield pairing of Lines and ever-present captain Stuart Campbell proved critical in Rovers' on-field success. Aaron Lescott was a reliable figure in defence, adding to his uncharacteristic goal flurry at the end of 2008/09 with early season strikes at Hartlepool and Brentford, before a hip injury led to a loan spell at Cheltenham Town, while Steve Elliott, Danny Coles and Byron Anthony vied for places at centre-back. Anthony's confidence was boosted in the preseason when he was able to score twice as Rovers defeated a Liverpool XI 4-3 in an inspiring game at the Memorial Stadium, and he came close to a sensational goal at Exeter in March, when his dipping 40-yard strike rebounded back off the underside of the bar. Jeff Hughes, aided by a reliable spot-kick record that was to equal Ray Warren's club seasonal record, set in the 1948/49 season, of seven in the League, was a consistent goalscorer and finished the season with twelve League goals, just two short of top scorer Jo Kuffour. Hughes took over as the regular penalty taker after Duffy had missed from the spot against Aldershot Town in the League Cup and in the home League game against Huddersfield Town. Kuffour's pace up front produced many openings, though his partner was to vary considerably, from Lambert to Heffernan, Duffy to Andy Williams.

One highlight of the season was a stirring 3-2 win away to Southampton achieved, after the Saints' Lambert had hit the bar against his former club, by a stunning individual goal from Williams five minutes into added time. This result, coming as it did in 'a quality game' (Paul Trollope) after a run of seven wins in nine League matches through the autumn, temporarily sent Rovers into second place in the table, a position they were unable to match later on. Rovers were also 2-0 up inside eight minutes at Stockport in August – 'that was a pretty disastrous start,' commented County's manager Gary Ablett – and three goals ahead in thirty-four minutes at home to Swindon, inside forty-five minutes at both Yeovil and Swindon and in forty-one minutes at Brentford. Last-minute goals helped defeat Oldham Athletic in September, Kuffour slotting home from Coles' through ball, and Carlisle United in November, when Rovers had trailed 2-1 after eighty-two minutes to a side featuring the future Rovers player Joe Anyinsah. Another encouraging display, including Heffernan's first goal for his new club, had helped defeat promotion hopefuls Charlton Athletic 2-1 at the Memorial Stadium in a Monday night game in front of television cameras in February; this game was marred by a serious injury endured by the Addicks' Grant Basey after just twenty-six seconds, in a challenge as a result of which Blizzard could consider himself fortunate to receive only a yellow card.

On the other hand, sceptics would point to a disastrous run of away games, in particular away scoring, from Lines' goal after fifty-four minutes at Charlton in November. The next away goal did not arrive until twenty-five minutes into the match at Swindon in March, after a club record gap of 689 minutes, though Kuffour's strike proved to be the first of four in a thirty-six-minute purple patch as Rovers demolished play-off-finalists Swindon 4-0 on their own patch before winning the next away game 3-0 at Yeovil. During this goalless run, Rovers had come close to scoring on many occasions, in particular when Lines hit the bar at Tranmere. The run began after a 4-2 defeat at Charlton, when Rovers had fought back after trailing by two goals inside sixteen minutes. The Latics' second goal was a Deon Burton penalty – 'I thought the decision was a bit harsh,' said an aggrieved Pat Baldwin. Rovers also conceded four goals at home to League leaders Leeds United, though Campbell had hit the bar when Rovers were just one goal down. Jermaine Beckford scored after nine and sixty-five minutes, Sam Vokes after fifty-five and substitute Trésor Kandol with three minutes left on the clock. Heavier defeats still came at Norwich City and Orient and at home to Southampton, for whom Lambert scored twice. At Carrow Road, Jamie Cureton was on the scoresheet for Norwich, who led 4-1 after forty minutes; Rovers have still not conceded as many as five first-half goals since the visit to Swansea over Easter 1922. Rovers fell apart at Brisbane Road, though Andersen was unlucky to concede an own goal, when the future Rovers striker Scott McGleish's penalty after sixty-two minutes came back off the post, hit the goalkeeper's head and rebounded into the net. Rovers were 'woefully inept' (*Waltham Forest Guardian*) as Orient recorded their largest League victory for almost a decade. The goalless draw at home to Walsall in February was described as 'an instantly forgettable first half followed by an equally turgid second' (*Wolverhampton Express & Star*). In the games at both Norwich and Charlton, both sides scored from the penalty spot. Over 180 minutes, Rovers failed to score against struggling Tranmere Rovers. In addition, Rovers conceded last-minute goals at home to Colchester United and away to Millwall, Brighton and Exeter City, as well as losing at home to several sides they might have expected to beat, among them Walsall, after missing a penalty, Yeovil Town, for whom Jonathan Chiedozie Obika scored just seconds after coming on as a substitute, and Wycombe Wanderers. Brighton's game in Horfield in September, in which the future Rovers defender Adam Virgo was sent off, also featured a first-ever League goal for James Tunnicliffe, who was to become a Rovers player on loan at the end of the campaign.

That home fixture against Wycombe was an unexpected result, coming as it did in the midst of a spectacularly good run of home results through the winter and spring. It also featured two penalties to the visitors, duly converted by Matt Harrold, Rovers' top scorer in 2011/12, and Alex Revell. Rovers themselves were awarded two penalties in the League Cup tie at home to Aldershot Town and the League fixture against Huddersfield Town. Ian Harte then despatched a brace of penalties as Rovers lost 3-1 at Carlisle in April. Wycombe's winning goal was scored by Stuart Beavon. Promoted Norwich City and Leeds United, relegated Wycombe and mid-table Orient and Southampton thus completed League doubles over Rovers, while Rovers themselves defeated Stockport County, Hartlepool United and Swindon Town at home and away. Promotion hopefuls Swindon Town were despatched 4-0 on their own ground, but Rovers gained only one of a possible twelve points against relegated Wycombe Wanderers and Tranmere Rovers.

Astonishingly, Southend United's Anthony Grant scored twice for Rovers. Sandy Pate had twice conceded own goals while playing for Mansfield Town against Rovers in the 1970s, but these had not been in the same season. Having scored against his own club in the Roots Hall fixture, Grant conceded an injury time own goal in Horfield at the end of March as Rovers completed a remarkable 4-3 victory over the Shrimpers, having trailed 2-0 after just twelve minutes. Grant had been one of three Luton Town players sent off at the Memorial Stadium on Boxing Day 2007.

Overall, Rovers were to use a total of twenty-eight players during the League campaign. Support was consistent, with an average home crowd in the League of 7,043, which featured a highest attendance of 11,448 for the demoralising home defeat against Leeds United. The final home fixture, against champions Norwich City in May, was preceded by a foiled attempt to break the world record number of 'pirates' in one place, an event controlled by representatives from *The Guinness Book of Records*. There were 38,234 spectators at Elland Road in May, when Rovers, despite taking the lead against ten men, could not secure the point that would have denied the Yorkshire outfit promotion; this attendance represented the second-highest ever to watch Rovers play in a third-tier League match. Rovers took 2,872 to Southampton for the fixture there in September, but only 126 to the goalless draw at Huddersfield Town in January. In addition, there were only 970 hardy souls at Hereford United, where Rovers' early exit from the JPT mirrored their inability to progress in the League Cup and FA Cup, where the home tie with Southampton had promised a re-run of the fifth round-tie of 2008. Ultimately, Rovers finished in eleventh place, as in 2008/09, level on points with the ninth-placed club but with a relatively poor goal difference of minus eleven. One oddity about the 2009/10 season was the severe paucity of draws. A fifth draw, in the penultimate home fixture, finally banished the spectre of equalling the tally of just four League draws achieved in the 1927/28 season, yet Rovers were to start the 2010/11 season on the back of an astonishing thirty-seven-game run without a draw.

A large number of former Rovers players appeared against the club, one who received a particularly warm welcome being Marcus Stewart, who came on as substitute for Exeter City in December against the club for whom he had made his League debut in August 1991. When Stockport County visited in March, referee Dean Whitehouse was injured during the game and replaced at half-time by Andy Bennett. In addition, there was a real dearth of red cards in matches featuring Rovers in 2009/10: only five opponents were sent off at The Mem, three of them in the ninetieth minute, and no one, for Rovers or for the opposition, saw red in any League or Cup game away from home until Hughes' dismissal after fifty-five minutes at Carlisle in April – later that month, Rovers' Coles and Brighton's substitute Glenn Murray were both sent off at The Withdean and Leeds United's Max Gradel at Elland Road. Indeed, prior to Hughes, no player had been sent off in a Rovers match away from Horfield over an eighteen-month period since November 2007. Rovers' players picked up a total of just sixty-one yellow cards, Anthony leading the way with ten. Early in December 2009, the club was saddened by the news of the death of Ron Craig, a long-term director of Rovers and club chairman for the promotion period from April 2007. Gordon Pearce, a long-term supporter and founder member of the 92 Club, a group that aims to watch League fixtures on every host ground, died on 29 April 2010 at the age of sixty-six.

While football violence was no longer a hot potato in political circles, a comment can be made here about the contemporary state of affairs within Football League stadia. From overall attendances exceeding 30 million at all Football League matches in 2009/10, there were 2,507 arrests, the figure for League One falling from 458 in 2008/09 to 393 in 2009/10. Twenty Rovers 'supporters' were arrested, mainly outside the ground and predominantly for public order or alcohol-related offences. Of four arrests in the division all season for racist chanting, one was at the Memorial Stadium and Rovers had imposed nine banning orders during the season, taking the tally of those excluded from home matches to twenty-three.

Continued talk of redeveloping the stadium moved no further forward during the campaign, though it was prudent to stem financial outlay in the ongoing economic climate. Money from the sale of Rickie Lambert was used to offset accumulated debts of an estimated £4 million as Rovers kept their head above water, unlike other clubs around the country. Portsmouth's move into administration helped relegate them from the Premiership, Southampton would in all likelihood have been promoted from League One were it not for their preseason handicap of ten points for financial issues and Chester City, who had played Rovers as recently as 2007, disappeared altogether from the English footballing map.

12

The Recent Years

2010/11

Despite a late-season flurry that offered Rovers supporters a faint glimmer of hope, the Gas lost their League One status, secured on a warm May afternoon at Wembley in 2007, and tumbled into the basement division of the Football League for only the second time in the club's long history. Ultimately, too many important mid-season games had been lost and even the commitment of the fourth manager of a tumultuous season was insufficient to prevent relegation. The visit of Sheffield Wednesday for the final home fixture drew a seasonal highest home crowd of 8,340, surpassing the 8,226 for the August visit of Southampton. A penalty apiece in the opening twelve minutes was not enough to prevent Rovers' relegation, all but certain as rivals Walsall and Dagenham both recorded crucial victories, to the fourth tier of English football; final-day defeat at Colchester United left Rovers in twenty-second place in the table. Will Hoskins top scored for the club with seventeen League goals and the average home attendance in the League was 6,253, down almost a thousand from the previous campaign.

Even the most optimistic of Rovers fans had afforded an uneasy glance over his shoulder as the team finished the 2009/10 season with an unhealthy run of one point in their final six League games. It was critical that the side should come out of the starting blocks in a positive manner. Instead, Rovers conceded three second-half goals at London Road on the opening day of the new campaign, though Peterborough's home record was to prove excellent all season. Rovers followed this up with an embarrassing 6-1 defeat at League Two Oxford United in the League Cup, where debutant goalkeeper Mike Green conceded four goals in an eleven minute spell before half-time on 'an embarrassing and very poor night' (Paul Trollope), which proved a precursor to a dismal season in Cup football. The FA Cup ended before it began, as Rovers were defeated 2-1 at non-League Darlington. There was an encouraging start to their cup run in the Johnstone's Paint Trophy, where Jo Kuffour, getting 'his reward for playing with real energy and drive' (Paul Trollope), and Wycombe's future Rovers striker Scott Rendell both scored hat-tricks in Rovers' 6-3 win at Adams Park. But Rovers bowed out in the southern semi-final against Exeter City in December, with Byron Anthony conceding an own goal and missing a penalty in the subsequent shoot-out. This result, following on from conceding six goals at Hillsborough and Rovers' consequent drop into the relegation zone, precipitated Paul Trollope's departure after over five years in charge of the club, a period that included promotion, a JPT final and an FA Cup quarter-final. Trollope had overseen 106 wins and 107 defeats in his 284 League matches as the second longest serving Rovers manager.

It was Rovers' League form rather than their cup exits that were brought sharply into focus as the season progressed. Having released Andy Williams to Yeovil Town and Aaron Lescott to Walsall, Rovers loaned out Mark Wright to Shrewsbury Town and Darryl Duffy to Hibernian, while Steve Elliott joined Cheltenham Town and Ben Hunt left to sign for Dover Athletic. Rovers suffered poor goalkeeping luck, as loan signing from West Brom Luke Daniels was injured in the warm-up to a preseason friendly and returned to his parent club. Mikkel Andersen returned on loan from Reading, later followed by both Daniels and Leicester City's Conrad Logan on loan. Tall defender James Tunnicliffe, who had scored for Brighton at The Mem in September 2009, and Plymouth Argyle's Gary Sawyer joined the club, as did striker Will Hoskins, whose goal for Watford in August 2008 had knocked Rovers out of the League Cup, and inexperienced midfielder Harry Pell from Charlton Athletic. At the heartbeat of the side were old hands in captain Stuart Campbell, Jeff Hughes and Chris Lines. The new-look side, though, lost 3-0 at Peterborough on the opening day of the season and followed this up with a 4-0 home defeat against Southampton and a 3-0 loss at home to Orient. Bizarrely, the Saints sacked their manager Alan Pardew after their four-goal victory, though 'we didn't play well enough and Southampton tore us apart' (Byron Anthony).

As the campaign progressed, there were positive moments. Anthony, ably supported in defence by Tunnicliffe and Danny Coles, came to the fore with a last-minute winning goal at home to Yeovil Town – a rising shot from the edge of the area into the top left corner of the goal – as well as a ninetieth-minute equaliser at Hartlepool as Rovers rallied from two-down. Another last-minute goal, this time a rising volley from the indomitable Hoskins, forging a partnership with Kuffour, earned a 1-0 win at promotion hopefuls Huddersfield Town. A first-ever League fixture against Dagenham & Redbridge resulted in a 3-0 away win for Rovers, Jeff Hughes registering all three goals past forty-one-year-old goalkeeper Tony Roberts. In November, Rovers drew successive matches away from home against the top two sides in the division. First, a last-minute Elliott Bennett own goal from Stuart Campbell's corner earned Rovers a 2-2 draw at champions Brighton, a well-merited result in a game when Hughes scored an own goal and Rovers target Chris Wood converted a penalty on his debut – it was the first time ever that both sides had benefitted from an own goal in a League fixture involving Rovers. Three days later, second-placed Charlton Athletic were held to a 1-1 draw, when Wayne Brown scored his first goal for the club, cashing in on a through-ball from Swallow, even though Charlton registered twelve shots to Rovers' three.

However, the tide was turning against Rovers, and there had been a series of disappointing performances and results. Although Rovers dominated early on, defeat to two headed goals followed at relegated Swindon Town. After dominating for eighty-seven minutes at home to Carlisle United, Rovers conceded a late equaliser and were dependent on Andersen saving Gary Madine's injury-time penalty to preserve a point. Orient's first away win of the season came at The Mem, as Rovers' poor performance was compounded by Carl Regan's first-half red card for a shocking foul on Orient captain Stephen Dawson. Seventeen-year-old Dale Jennings scored lowly Tranmere Rovers' winning goal at The Mem in first-half stoppage time, and though sixteen-year-old Jack Stephens was in their side alongside a future Rovers favourite in Jim Paterson, struggling Plymouth Argyle also won in Horfield, their late winner proving to be the last goal conceded by on-loan Danish under-21 international goalkeeper Andersen. In December, as Britain was covered with snow, Rovers crashed 6-2 at Sheffield Wednesday and Paul Trollope's managerial career at Rovers was over. This result saw Rovers drop, for the first time that campaign, into the bottom four, and it was also the first time that six separate opponents had scored in the same fixture, a tally that could have been higher had Clinton Morrison and Daniel Jones not missed decent chances. To rub salt into the wounds, the sixth goal was scored by the former Rovers striker Paul Heffernan. Under Trollope, Rovers had won five and lost seven of their opening nineteen League fixtures, but had a minus eleven goal difference.

Initially, Darren Patterson was promoted from within but, after two uninspiring defeats, the latter when Rovers let slip a 2-0 lead inside eleven minutes to lose at home to Plymouth Argyle, Patterson was replaced by the former Doncaster Rovers, Darlington and Oldham Athletic manager Dave Penney, with the experienced Martin Foyle joining later as his assistant. In Penney's first game in charge, Rovers conceded a late equaliser at home to relegation rivals Walsall, with Aaron Lescott returning to haunt his former employers. Through the winter months, Rovers won just two and lost nine of Penney's thirteen League games in charge, scoring just twelve and conceding a horrific thirty goals – Rovers were only not propping up the table because of the lifeline thrown to all relegation candidates when Plymouth Argyle were docked ten points as a result of going into administration. Despite several loan signings, the new manager was unable to prevent the long, unsuccessful run from continuing. Dave McCracken, who had played for MK Dons against Rovers, and young, talented Cian Bolger bolstered the defence, while the Yeovil pair of Jean-Paul Kalala, who had been sent off against Rovers in August, and Gavin Williams, as well as Reading's Scott Davies, strengthened the midfield. René Howe was an experienced striker who had partnered the former Rovers forward Lee Thorpe at Rochdale, but he managed just one League goal, a critical close-range winner at home to Oldham Athletic. Conrad Logan ultimately proved an excellent goalkeeper, adept at saving crucial penalty kicks, while Danny Senda was an able full-back, being paid on a match-by-match basis after eighteen months out injured, whose goal for Wycombe Wanderers in May 2001 had relegated Rovers to League Two.

Sadly for the new manager, all these signings made only minimal impact at first, as Rovers stumbled from heavy defeat to embarrassing debacle. Loan signing striker John Akinde from Bristol City did not score in his fourteen League appearances in a Rovers shirt. Carlisle United defeated the Gas comfortably 4-0, with James Berrett becoming the eighth opponent in Rovers' League history to convert two penalties in a game, both for fouls committed by Sawyer. Rovers crashed to an embarrassing 6-1 defeat at bottom-placed Walsall, the Saddlers' largest League win since defeating Rovers 6-0 in 1986; the future Rovers midfielder Matt Gill scored one of the goals. Rovers conceded nineteen goals in five matches at this stage and hit twenty-fourth place in the table on 12 February. Despite being reduced to ten men, MK Dons then won 2-1 in Horfield, with the future Rovers defender Dan Woodards in their side, having taken the lead after just forty-five seconds. Rovers took a second-minute lead before conceding four goals at home to Brighton in a match that featured three disallowed goals. They then crashed 3-1 before a seasonal lowest crowd of 2,372 at Rochdale to two goals in stoppage time, and lost at home to both Colchester United and Dagenham & Redbridge, games they should have been expected to have won. Having conceded an own goal against Brighton off his back, Bolger was then sent off at Rochdale and his loan spell came to a close. Orient's Harry Kane scored twice as substitute, only the third opponent to achieve this feat against Rovers. Jerel Ifil joined the club from Aberdeen and was promptly sent off against Dagenham, for whom his brother was playing; it was the player's tenth red card of a combative career and he became the first player to have been sent off while playing both against (for Swindon Town in November 2007) and for Rovers in the League. Losing this six-pointer left Rovers six points inside the relegation zone and, with most of their rivals having at least a game in hand, relegation looked inevitable.

One final throw of the dice saw the removal of Dave Penney, with captain Stuart Campbell taking on the challenging job, on 7 March 2011 as the manager entrusted with the job of rescuing Rovers' League One status. Under Campbell, Rovers began to string together not only a few victories but also, with Logan in fine form in goal, a few clean sheets. The club seasonal record of ninety-five League goals conceded in 1935/36, which had looked under threat at one stage, was never again challenged. Within twenty-four hours of Campbell's appointment, Chris Lines' goal had earned an invaluable win at Tranmere, the club's first win in midweek for over twelve months. Rovers then won 1-0 at fellow strugglers Notts County where, for the first time in Football League history, all four match officials were from the Army. After Anthony had conceded another own goal, Rovers held free-scoring Peterborough to a 2-2 draw, in a match where Reginald Thompson-Lambe, who had scored four times in one game for Bermuda against St Martin when only sixteen, was given his League debut. Two more victories and clean sheets followed, Gavin Williams' first goal for his new club defeating his former employers Yeovil Town at Huish Park, after Rovers had withstood a concerted onslaught on their goal and Jeff Hughes' thirty-third-minute penalty seeing off a Bournemouth side who had twenty-one shots as compared to Rovers' six. Rovers had won four games out of six and, on the morning of 9 April, sat in nineteenth place in the table.

As Rovers temporarily eased out of the bottom four, there was light at the end of the tunnel, a glimmer of hope snuffed quickly by a run of one point in three games at the end of April. First, a seasonal highest attendance of 23,647 at Southampton saw Rovers lose to a goal six minutes from time from the Brazilian Guilherme do Prado Raymundo, after Campbell had bravely flung on two seventeen-year-old substitutes in the highly promising Lamar Powell and Ellis Harrison. Then, visitors Charlton Athletic had two men sent off at The Mem (Kyel Reid and José Semedo) before Rovers, for the second time in the campaign, clawed back a two-goal deficit to claim a dramatic draw. Two days later, the Easter Monday trip to Bournemouth saw Rovers lead for eighty minutes, Wayne Brown scoring for the second match in succession, before conceding two late goals in heart-breaking circumstances to the home side's substitutes. The winning goal was scored by Steve Fletcher whose first goal against Rovers had come in August 1993.

So why was the club relegated back to League Two? Changing managers is always a risky business and the experiment of using Dave Penney, especially with such a high influx of new players, did not work. Under his tutelage, Rovers gained just eight League points from a potential thirty-nine. Rovers lost ten League matches at home and only at the very start and finish of the campaign were able to string together successive League victories. The goals against column was of concern all season, save perhaps the first matches under Stuart Campbell, and a goal difference of minus thirty-four was effectively a one-point difference compared to the other relegation candidates; Rovers were the only side to concede six goals in two separate League One fixtures. Significantly, the side also conceded sixteen goals in the final ten minutes of fixtures. Rovers managed just eleven League wins all season, though this was significantly more than the nine achieved by Swindon Town. The club used thirty-five players in League action, exactly the figure used in the 2000/01 relegation campaign, but only eight of these had scored a League goal prior to Elliot Richards' final-day consolation goal. Only Lines, Hughes and Hoskins started forty of the forty-six League fixtures, though

Kuffour played some part in most games; the only player in every match-day squad was reserve goalkeeper Green, who spent the majority of the campaign on the bench. Lines hit the woodwork six times, yet scored only three League goals. Significantly, though Rovers drew at champions Brighton and won away to play-off side Huddersfield Town, the side also lost at home to three relegation rivals in Tranmere, Dagenham and Plymouth. The very late Walsall equaliser at The Mem proved highly costly at the end of the season. Doubles were competed over Notts County and Yeovil Town, but five sides, most crucially fellow relegated side Plymouth Argyle, defeated Rovers both at home and away. Rovers lost several key defenders through suspension, all seven of the club's red cards (Coles receiving two) being defensive players. Rovers picked up only seventy-two yellow cards in the League all season, Sawyer and Lines receiving eleven each. Nine opponents received their marching orders, including Graeme Lee of Notts County, who had scored Doncaster Rovers' winning goal against Rovers at the Millennium Stadium in April 2007. While Rovers lost twenty-two games in the 1961/62 season, the club lost twenty-three League fixtures in 2010/11. Only twenty-four goals were scored at home, as compared to the twenty-one when relegation followed in 1980/81. There were six home wins, exactly as in the relegation campaign of 2000/01. The club's paucity of draws continued, and to the summer of 2011, Rovers had drawn just seventeen of their last 112 League fixtures.

As the season ended in the disappointment of relegation, several former Rovers players enjoyed football-based success elsewhere. Tony Pulis, a fine midfielder during the Eastville era, led his unfashionable Stoke City side to the FA Cup final, Bobby Zamora earned an England call-up late in his career and Vitalijs Astafjevs concluded his long career with a European record 167th cap in Latvia's single-goal defeat to China in November 2010. Marcus Stewart, a Rovers legend in his day, ended his career at The Mem as his Exeter City side recorded a 2-0 victory, while the former Rovers manager Malcolm Allison, 'the flawed genius in a lucky fedora' (*The Week*, 23/10/10), passed away on 15 October 2010 at the age of eighty-three. The Rovers match-day programme was once again named Programme of the Year in its category.

2011/12

Preseason favourites to return immediately to League One football, Rovers endured an interesting season in two instalments. First, Paul Buckle was installed as the new manager, bringing with him a raft of new faces but minimal on-field success. Then, the vastly experienced Mark McGhee succeeded him in this post and guided Rovers to a series of better performances, including no home defeats in 2012 and a more acceptable mid-table final position in League Two. Thirteenth place in the table with fifty-seven League points was explained by the season of two halves and aided by twelve goals scored in the final two home League fixtures of the campaign. There was no great success in cup football either, though Rovers reached the third round of the FA Cup and entertained Aston Villa before live television cameras at the Memorial Stadium.

Rovers took to the field at Kingsmeadow for the televised early kick-off on the opening day, fresh from an encouraging 2-0 friendly victory over Championship side Burnley and with ten new faces in their starting line-up. The cameras were present for AFC Wimbledon's first Football League fixture, yet recorded a memorable Rovers performance as the Pirates sped to a two-goal half-time lead and won 3-2 through an eighty-fifth-minute penalty converted by Adam Virgo. The ten new faces were but part of the sixteen signings prior to the end of September, as new manager Paul Buckle attempted to stamp his mark on the club. Buckle, who had played in League action against Rovers for both Colchester United and Exeter City, had led Torquay United to the play-offs in League Two in three of the previous four seasons, so his acquisition as manager was seen as a positive step towards lifting Rovers out of the basement division at the first attempt. He brought with him from Plainmoor goalkeeper Scott Bevan, the only player in the League with only one kidney, the legacy of an accident sustained while playing for Tamworth against Forest Green Rovers in January 2006, and Chris Zebroski who, like Matt Harrold from Shrewsbury Town, had played against Rovers while at Wycombe Wanderers. Gambian-born Mustapha Carayol joined from Lincoln City, who had just surrendered their Football League status, while Joe Anyinsah, a former Bristol City trainee who had played for Carlisle United against Rovers, joined from Charlton Athletic, and Danny Woodards, who had played three times each for MK Dons and Crewe Alexandra against Rovers, strengthened the defensive line. He was supported there, until his season was curtailed by injury, by Adam Virgo from Yeovil Town, who had been sold by McGhee when at Brighton and had joined Celtic for £1.5 million; he had been sent off against Rovers while with Brighton in September 2009, as well as scoring at The Mem with Yeovil in August 2010.

Buckle's emphasis on experience was epitomised by the signing of Orient's Scott McGleish. A veteran of 551 (plus 112 as substitute) League matches and 202 goals with eight clubs prior to his arrival, McGleish had played for five separate clubs against Rovers in the League and sat on the committee of the Professional Footballers' Association. Only five players in Rovers' history had appeared in a greater number of League matches, Alan Ball topping the pile with 743 games. A goal on his debut, as Rovers' seventh-oldest debutant, prefaced a season in which he became Rovers' seventh-oldest player ever and the third-oldest goalscorer. Alongside McGleish was new Rovers captain Matt Gill, a signing from Norwich City who had scored for Walsall when they defeated Rovers 6-1 in January 2011, and had, as an Exeter City player, become the first player sent off at the renovated Wembley in 2007 for a headbutt on Morecambe's Craig Stanley, who now joined him in Rovers' combative midfield. Scott Rendell, who had scored Peterborough's winner in a nine-goal thriller against Rovers at London Road in September 2008, and a hat-trick for Wycombe Wanderers against Rovers in the Johnstone's Paint Trophy in November 2010, joined on a brief loan deal.

Early season form, though, did not go exactly to plan. True, victories at Wimbledon and Morecambe, where Rovers came back from a 2-1 deficit in a game that featured four goals in fifteen second-half minutes, as well as a point gained at Bradford City, who relied on Michael Flynn for two equalisers from the penalty spot, indicated success. On the other hand, Rovers drew at home to struggling Hereford United and Macclesfield Town, and lost at home to Torquay United, Aldershot Town, Barnet and Cheltenham Town, all fixtures the side would have realistically expected to win. After the defeat at Underhill, Eric Hitchmo wrote on a Barnet website, 'Monday's laborious victory over Bristol Rovers, as two dreadful teams took to the field in an attempt to be worse than each other. Goodness me, it was a chore.' Rovers were two goals down inside half an hour at Accrington Stanley. In addition, a calamitous 4-1 defeat at League newcomers Crawley Town followed by a three-goal defeat at Oxford United was the proof many Rovers supporters feared that success in League Two was to be no walkover. One moment when Rovers' fortunes appeared to be turning came on a Friday night in October, when Rovers scored five times against Rotherham United at the Memorial Stadium. Two early McGleish goals paved the way towards a 3-0 lead, after which, though pegged back twice, Rovers progressed to a 5-2 win, Anyinsah's 30-yard strike two minutes from time securing a memorable victory. This, though, proved to be a false dawn.

Disastrously, Rovers crumbled to a 3-2 defeat at home to bottom club Plymouth Argyle on Boxing Day, having led by two clear goals after only half an hour. This stoppage-time defeat was the second successive season in which the Pilgrims had won in this way at The Mem; it was followed by a demoralising 5-2 drubbing at home to Crewe Alexandra, where Jay Leitch-Smith gave the visitors the lead after sixty-nine seconds (the same player scored after seventy-two seconds in the return fixture) and Rovers, trailing 4-1 at the interval, brought on three half-time substitutes, including replacement goalkeeper Lance Cronin, and signed two further loan players within hours. When relegation rivals Barnet completed a League double in front of just 2,537 hardy supporters at Underhill, Buckle was dismissed as Rovers' manager and the side faced an FA Cup third-round fixture against Premier League Aston Villa with caretaker manager Shaun North at the helm, loan signing Michael Poke in goal and Australian defender Aaron Downes due to make their home debuts against the Premier League side. Four goalkeepers used in the League nonetheless constituted a lower figure than that for 1998/99. However, tellingly, Rovers had won just six League games under Buckle's tutelage.

Having recorded the first victory in almost three months (a 2-1 win at Hereford United) and kept the first clean sheet in that period (at home to table-toppers

Crawley Town) caretaker North's brief tenure came to an end and the highly experienced Mark McGhee was unveiled on 18 January as Rovers' sixth manager in thirteen months. McGhee, a former Scottish international forward who had helped Aberdeen win the European Cup Winners' Cup in 1983, had previously managed five League clubs south of the border and two in Scotland. Prior to McGhee's first game in charge, a fixture at Cheltenham Town who had not lost in ten matches, his opposite number Mark Yates stated, 'I am not bothered about Bristol Rovers in the slightest.' Rovers won 2-0 through goals from Zebroski and Elliot Richards as the new manager fielded the same side as in the previous fixture. Having played for Plymouth Argyle against Rovers in January 2011, Jim Paterson signed on as a Rovers player after experiencing Europa League football with Shamrock Rovers, and was joined by loan signings Matt Lund from Stoke City and another tall, young defender from Leicester City in Tom Parkes – 'we believe he is a great option for us,' said his manager. McGhee's honeymoon period continued as the side pulled clear of relegation worries with a string of strong performances and encouraging results, epitomised by the last-minute winning goal at Rotherham United as well as victories over Morecambe and Bradford City.

For a brief moment, the unrealistic thought that the side could emulate that of the 2006/07 season flashed across the minds of the ever-optimistic Rovers supporters. However, the possibility of winning ten of the final twelve League fixtures predictably proved too great a challenge, Rovers never quite showing the consistency to accumulate the required points. Symptomatic of this was the way the side fell three goals behind inside twenty minutes at bottom-of-the-table Northampton Town, before almost reclaiming a point. They also trailed 2-0 after five minutes at Crewe's Gresty Road and conceded ninetieth-minute equalisers at home to Gillingham and at Plainmoor, where Torquay United recovered from a two-goal deficit to claim an unlikely, though probably well-merited point. Indeed, fixtures against Torquay proved of great interest, not just because of Paul Buckle's recent history, but also with Rovers fielding a bevy of former Plainmoor heroes, among them Zebroski who scored perhaps the club's goal of the season on his own former ground, while René Howe scored for the Gulls against his former side. Gradually, the season fizzled out, with Rovers content to settle for a mid-table position, initially disdained but later to be viewed as probable success after the start to the campaign the club had endured.

However, supporters' burgeoning faith in manager McGhee was rewarded in mid-April as Rovers, unbeaten at home under his tutelage, scored seven times in a League game for the first time since December 1973. A goal shortly before half-time from Carayol heralded six more after the interval as Burton Albion, on their first visit to The Mem, were swamped 7-1. Twenty-year-old Richards scored three times, the fourth-youngest hat-trick scorer in Rovers' League history, and Paterson added his first for the club, as Rovers scored a club-record five times in a twenty-minute spell and seven times in thirty-eight minutes. Following the game at home to Brighton in November 1952 and the win at Reading in January 1999, it was only the third occasion that the side had scored six goals in one half of League football. In inflicting the heaviest defeat of the Staffordshire club's brief League history, Rovers also compiled the highest score in the Football League that day. Rovers followed this up with a 5-1 home win over Accrington Stanley, Lund becoming the fourth substitute to score twice for the club in a League fixture, to complete the season unbeaten at home since December and having scored an incredible twelve goals in the final 138 minutes of home League action.

During the course of the League campaign, Rovers completed doubles over Morecambe, Rotherham United and AFC Wimbledon; both games against divisional champions Swindon Town were drawn. On the other hand, Barnet, Aldershot, Port Vale and Crewe Alexandra, the last-named side scoring eight times against Rovers, all completed a League double over the Pirates. With eighteen goals to his name in all competitions, sixteen of them in League Two, Harrold was a popular top scorer for the club in 2011/12, Gill being credited with eight assists. Woodards started the highest number of League fixtures, thirty-nine in all, though Lee Brown played a role in forty-two and Harrold in two fewer. Red cards were at a premium in Rovers' fixtures, with Bolger and Downes the only Pirates sent off in the League, Zebroski receiving twelve yellow cards, while Rotherham United's future Rovers defender Guy Branston, Peter Murphy of Accrington Stanley, Hereford United's Benoît Dalibord and Bradford City's Rob Kozluk were all also dismissed. The 2011/12 season represented the first occasion in Rovers' history that four separate players had scored from the penalty spot in the Football League, Virgo, Harrold, McGleish and Lee Brown all being successful. Nine successful spot-kicks in the League equated to a club seasonal record, while the six conceded included two each in a game from Bradford City's Michael Flynn and Gillingham's Danny Kedwell, the striker then missing a first-half penalty in Horfield on Good Friday, thereby eschewing the chance to equal Swansea's Len Emmanuel's long-standing record from 1947/48 of three League penalties against Rovers in one season. No fewer that twenty-four players made their first League appearance for Rovers during the 2011/12 League season, with others appearing on the bench and in Cup ties; Rovers used thirty-two players in the League in all, fewer than the thirty-five used in 2010/11. Young players coming through the ranks included Shaquille Hunter, a regular on the bench as winter approached, young Jordan Goddard, who featured as a very late substitute in the FA Cup victory over Corby Town in November and under-18 Player of the Year Mitch Harding, whose debut on the final day of the season was overshadowed by Brian Woodall's hat-trick as Rovers crashed 4-0 at Dagenham & Redbridge. Darren Jefferies appeared briefly in the FA Cup against Totton, while goalkeeper Matt Macey made it onto the substitutes' bench in March.

One indication as to how the season progressed is that the 8,427 crowd for the opening home fixture remained the highest of the campaign in League games,

Rovers' average home crowd in the League being 6,035; there were crowds of 10,023, 9,645 and 9,291 for the matches at Bradford City, Swindon Town and Oxford United respectively. Dagenham & Redbridge brought just seventy away supporters for the game in Horfield at the end of October, a very low tally partly explained by their neighbours Redbridge FC's heroics in the FA Cup on the same afternoon. There were only 1,643 hardy souls at the Fraser Eagle Stadium when Rovers lost to Accrington Stanley on Guy Fawkes' Day, and 1,865 at Macclesfield; only 771 witnessed the Johnstone's Paint Trophy defeat at Wycombe Wanderers. One of a series of fundraising events around the Bristol area on behalf of the Wow! Gorilla campaign to celebrate 150 years of Bristol Zoo was the appearance of the monkey Irene, who sported Rovers' colours; her stint at the foot of Zetland Road ended in September as Bristol Zoo auctioned off all their monkeys for a combined figure of £427,300 for charity, Irene raising £6,000. On a more serious note, the former club chairman Denis Dunford, who had helped save Bristol Rovers from extinction during his tenure and who had been club president since 5 January 2005, died on 4 January 2012 at the age of eighty-nine, and a minute's applause was held prior to the FA Cup game at home to Aston Villa later that week. Another one-minute memorial was held prior to the home game against Barnet to the memory of Alan Lacock, who had died the previous morning, a supporter of long standing who had not missed a home fixture in over fifty years. A similar show of respect was held, prior to the final home game of the season, for Alfie Biggs, Rovers' second highest goalscorer of all time, who died in Poole on 20 April.

At the club's annual meeting on 13 February, the shareholders were presented with the news that Rovers had suffered operating losses of over £3.4 million for the previous year, this figure including a £2.1 million build-up for the proposed redevelopment of the Memorial Stadium. With directors' loans to the club rising from £1.94 million in 2010 to £3.2 million, Rovers had an underlying operating loss for 2011 of £1,939,141. Further to this, developments continued apace towards the creation of a new stadium in Bristol, with the proposed UWE stadium said to be ready for 2014 at a cost of £40 million.

Cup competitions brought minimal success, least of all the Johnstone's Paint Trophy, in which Rovers lost to Stuart Beavon's hat-trick in an opening tie at Wycombe. The League Cup brought victory in a penalty shoot-out at home to Watford, before Rovers lost to Jamie Cureton's Orient side in the next round. In the FA Cup, Rovers just about saw off plucky non-Leaguers Corby Town, who featured a thirty-nine-year-old goalkeeper Chris MacKenzie, who had last played against Rovers for Shrewsbury Town at Wembley in 2007; two late goals before a disappointing home crowd of 3,787 sealed a 3-1 win that was not as straightforward as it sounded, despite Rovers' tally of twenty shots to the visitors' four. Rovers' reward was a second round trip to Evo-Stik Premier League side AFC Totton, who had put eight goals past Bradford Park Avenue in round one, the first occasion since the Second World War that a non-League side had scored as many goals in a tie in the competition proper. Live on ITV, Rovers scored three excellently created goals in a five-minute purple patch early on and despite a red card for Ben Swallow, just five minutes after entering the field as a late substitute – cruised to a 6-1 victory, with substitute Richards notching a brace, to set up a home tie against Premier League Aston Villa. Despite live television coverage, a bumper crowd of 10,883 turned out for this game, and Howard Webb, who had refereed the 2010 World Cup final between Spain and Holland, took charge. Rovers, however, never threatened a Villa side that included international names such as Darren Bent, Emile Heskey and Gabriel Agbonlahor, as well as Stilyian Petrov, holder of over 100 full caps for Bulgaria. The visitors treated the game like a training ground exercise, though substitute McGleish's ninetieth-minute goal, and even later penalty miss, threatened to spark the 3-1 defeat into life. Rovers were left with a serious fight on their hands to avoid relegation out of the Football League ninety-two years after their election to Division Three, a battle that, to the relief of all Bristol Rovers supporters, was comfortably secured.

2012/13

As with Rovers' first post-war Football League campaign, the 2012/13 season can be neatly summarised in two halves. Under manager Mark McGhee, Rovers struggled to find success though the autumn of 2012, crushing defeats at Gillingham, Port Vale and York City leaving the club rooted to the foot of the Football League at Christmas, before returning manager John Ward, 'a stickler for shape, discipline and defensive resilience' (James McNamara), made a number of astute signings and restored the players' self-belief. An astonishing run then took the club within shouting distance of an unexpected play-off berth. Spring success enabled Rovers, despite not winning any of their final four fixtures, to complete their second campaign back in the basement division in fourteenth place.

Undefeated at home in 2012, Rovers approached the new season with realistic optimism. Mark McGhee had signed new playing staff, and Seanan Clucas, FA Youth Cup winning goalkeeper Sam Walker and former Bristol City player David Clarkson all made their club debuts at Ipswich in the League Cup. Rogvi Baldvinsson, a Faroe Islands international, played in the preseason fixtures before returning to Norway for personal reasons, but several other players were soon to appear in the side. Garry Kenneth, a rock at the heart of the defence and a veteran of two Scottish Cup finals at Dundee United, was ruled out initially following a calf injury sustained while warming up for his debut at Barnet. Neil Etheridge, a Filipino international, was a useful and efficient goalkeeper; Derek Riordan, the third-highest scorer in the Scottish Premier League, played for the club before returning goalless to Scotland. Tom Eaves proved a useful loan signing in a struggling side; and squad member Fabian Broghammer, a German midfielder, soon accrued popular status among the Rovers following.

However, illusions were swiftly shattered as the club's unbeaten home record under McGhee crumbled 2-0 against Oxford, the visitors bringing 1,019 supporters for the opening day fixture, a seasonal highest; Morecambe brought just forty-seven. A fortnight later, Rovers dropped into the relegation zone when the second home fixture was lost 3-0 to Morecambe. Suddenly, from the jaws of a potential promotion campaign, Rovers were clutching at the ashes of a proposed relegation dogfight. Three goals behind by half-time at champions Gillingham, 'toothless Rovers' (*Football League Paper*) crumbled 4-0. Defeat at Vale Park by the same score, Rovers taking just 132 hardy supporters, included a hat-trick by Tom Pope and young hopeful Tom Parkes departing early from that game with what appeared to be a serious leg injury. Three goals were conceded in fourteen first-half minutes at Wimbledon, three in fifteen minutes before the interval at Port Vale, and four in a disastrous twenty minutes before half-time at York. In December, Rovers were the only side in the division to have received six red cards, both Elliot Richards and Kenneth being dismissed in the defeat at Rochdale. The side only managed a point after three times taking the lead at home to Bradford City, and only 1,794 spectators turned up when Rovers visited Barnet. When the first victory appeared on the cards, Rovers' game at Wycombe was controversially abandoned after sixty-three minutes; leading 3-1 in a storm with Richards having registered a brace, Rovers found the game called off not by the referee or the police, but by the home side's Health and Safety Officer. When the fixture was replayed, they crashed to a 2-0 defeat with Matt Lund being sent off. The subsequent irony of Rovers' victory at Wycombe in April 2014, which ensured Rovers' League safety and all but relegated Wanderers to Conference football, was not lost on Rovers' supporters.

More than this, Rovers appeared to be having a very poor run with injuries. Top scorer from 2011/12 Matt Harrold had contributed just one goal when he suffered a cruciate ligament injury at Gillingham, and Kenneth also underwent knee surgery. In addition to this, Matt Gill, Scott Bevan and Adam Virgo were long-term absentees with injury, even before Clucas suffered a serious knee injury at Morecambe in February. Dan Woodards also suffered a cruciate knee injury in April that threatened to keep him out of football for nine months. Encouragingly, Harrold returned to the side on the final day, his late substitute cameo appearance including a headed equaliser three minutes into injury-time.

Yet amid the gloom there were a few burgeoning positive signs. Despite the early season poor results, Rovers contrived to pick up four points from their two September trips to Devon, victory at Exeter paving the way to a League double. Before injury took its toll, new signing Clarkson proved he had an eye for goal, and Lee Brown also indicated he was reliable from the penalty spot; his tally included a twice-taken effort at Oxford, though former Rovers 'keeper Michael Poke saved his spot-kick at Torquay on the final day of the season. A morale-boosting 3-1 home victory over Northampton in October featured first goals for the club for Eaves, man of the match Kenneth and young Ollie Norburn. Eaves, impressively scoring seven times to become the club's seasonal highest scorer despite the side's failings around him, added two goals as ten-man Torquay United were defeated 3-2. Two former Rovers men, René Howe and Aaron Downes, both scored for the Gulls in that game, the former thereby equalling a club record by scoring in his seventh consecutive League outing. When Rovers staged a November book signing of Geoff Bradford's long-awaited biography, pleasingly against his namesake club Bradford City, loanee central defender Guy Branston scored after seventy-nine seconds with his first touch in a quartered shirt. As Christmas approached, Rovers had won just four of their twenty-two League fixtures and relegation from the Football League appeared a distinct possibility.

Shortly before Christmas, Rovers trailed 4-1 before half-time at York and McGhee was removed from his managerial duties; the inspirational Scot took on the role of assistant manager of the Scottish national side. Rovers, for their part, moved swiftly to reappoint John Ward, whose previous spell at the helm had seen Rovers reach a Wembley play-off final in 1995. Within days, the club's fortunes appeared to change for the better. Christmas Day saw Rovers propping up all four divisions of the Football League, but Ward reinstilled the self-confidence to succeed. Swift work on the transfer front saw the arrival of experienced goalkeeper Steve Mildenhall, effectively strong defender Mark McChrystal, tough midfielder John-Joe O'Toole, efficient striker Ryan Brunt, giant central defender Clayton McDonald and youthful frontman Tom Hitchcock. On New Year's Day, a hard-fought 2-1 home victory over relegation rivals Plymouth set the tone and was swiftly followed by two excellent away performances. First, play-off hopefuls Fleetwood were brushed aside 3-0 on their own pitch, Ellis Harrison starting for the first time and Tom Lockyer making his debut from the bench – 'Fleetwood put up little fight as they were rolled over at home by strugglers Bristol Rovers', reported the *Blackpool Gazette*. Then, with Claud Davies sent off before half-time on his Rotherham debut, Rovers won 3-1 at another play-off side, Harrison chipping in with his first League goal, a long, mazy run seven minutes after the interval ending with a fierce right-footed shot. Still bottom of the table on 26 January, Rovers appeared in the top half of the division on 6 April, when Hitchcock's late winner defeated AFC Wimbledon. Even when Rovers did not win, play-off hopefuls Cheltenham were stung by an astonishing 35 yard goal in stoppage time from the ever-improving Norburn, the best goal scored by the club all season, which earned Rovers a welcome if unexpected point away from home. Rovers had regained their self-belief.

As supporters began to understand the club had been transformed, the crowds gradually flocked back. The opening day attendance of 7,451, which had looked like being a seasonal best, was almost broken by the 7,332 for Ward's first game in charge and fell when 8,527 came to see a third consecutive League victory, as Brunt's ninety-third-minute goal defeated Barnet at The Mem on a freezing Friday evening, the visitors including their veteran player-manager Edgar Davids, once of Barcelona and both Milan clubs, in their midfield. Under McGhee, Rovers had averaged 5,479 spectators at home fixtures; under Ward the figure was 7,069, rendering a seasonal average home League crowd of 6,309. The impressive spring run had included, at one stage, ten consecutive League goals scored by different players, yet Brunt soon emerged as the goalscoring star of the side. His winning goal at home to Wycombe was followed by a first-half brace as Rovers outplayed second-placed Port Vale at home in mid-March. An official count of 1,932 Gasheads supported the side at Oxford, a game that was won 2-0, 1,416 travelled to the fixture at Cheltenham, 1,147 to Exeter, and 1,534 were at Plainmoor on the final day of the campaign. By the middle of April, Rovers had lost just four League fixtures out of the twenty played with Ward in charge; this run included four consecutive home victories against strong opposition in the spring and encompassed eight clean sheets. Rovers won consecutive League fixtures on five separate occasions during the second half of the season. Defeat at Bradford in mid-April brought the unbelievable outside chance of a play-off appearance to a close, indicating as it did the gulf between those who could press for promotion and those clubs still a step away. It did, however, underline how far Rovers had come since the start of the calendar year.

As the season drew to an ultimately satisfying close, Rovers' supporters could sense that the future held a degree of promise. Winning 3-1 at Carlisle to secure the League and Cup double, the under-18 side offered hope of positive things to come; from this side, Alefe Santos and Tom Lockyer both featured in the League squad. Richards, a product of the system, enjoyed good runs in Rovers' side, was called up to the Welsh under-21 squad and finished the season with six goals, the joint second-highest scorer in Rovers' League campaign; with forty-one League appearances to his name, he also played in more fixtures than any other player, narrowly ahead of Young Player of the Year Parkes, a captain at twenty-one, Lee Brown and Michael Smith. Ollie Clarke, who had also worked his way up the ranks, enjoyed a first start when Rovers lost to Accrington's Lee Molyneux's sixty-nine-second 30-yard free-kick in the final home fixture of the season. Goalkeeper Conor Gough had now appeared in two League fixtures for Rovers, both times playing away to Dagenham & Redbridge. Exciting full-back Michael Smith was deservedly voted the club's Player of the Year, while Brunt gave clear indication that goals could follow later in his career.

During the autumn, nine players were dismissed in League fixtures involving Rovers, just one being sent off after Christmas. While Rovers had accumulated six red cards under McGhee's management, there were no Rovers players sent off at all that campaign under Ward's tutelage. This greater sense of discipline served to help the side surge up the divisional table. Rovers used thirty-five players in the League, exactly the same figure as in the relegation campaigns of 2000/01 and 2010/11, while sixteen former Rovers players reappeared against the side, among them Chris Zebroski, who struck Cheltenham's winning goal at The Mem, and Justin Richards, who played against his former club with both Burton Albion and Oxford United. Phil Taylor, the last surviving player from Rovers' campaigns before the Second World War, died in December 2012 at the age of ninety-five, and two club favourites from the halcyon days of the 1950s, Bill Roost and the mercurial George Petherbridge, both passed away in the spring. Ever popular club kit-man Roger Harding passed away on 19 June 2013, and journalists Robin Perry and Colin Howlett, who had reported Rovers' fixtures for many years, both died over the summer.

As all too often in the Rovers story, cup campaigns were perhaps better forgotten. A 3-1 defeat at Ipswich Town in the League Cup, after Smith had given the Pirates a first-half lead, was followed by a 2-1 home defeat against Sheffield United before an FA Cup crowd of just 4,712. Possibly more worryingly, the side crumbled to a 3-0 defeat in the Johnstone's Paint Trophy, even though visitors Yeovil Town had their captain Jamie McAllister sent off. As the season ended, a Rovers Legends side lost on penalties after drawing 5-5 with Bristol City Legends, and was then defeated 3-0 by Rovers' under-18 side in Lewis Haldane's testimonial game.

Alongside John Ward's on-field success, Rovers enjoyed spring cheer in the hunt for a new ground. On 19 July 2012, South Gloucestershire Council had approved plans, by a 12-1 vote, for a proposed 21,700-seater stadium next to the University of the West of England at Stoke Gifford, with building work commencing in the summer of 2013. On 16 January 2013, Bristol City councillors approved the plan to build a Sainsbury's supermarket on the site of the Memorial Stadium, the suggestion being accepted 6-3; this would fund Rovers' move but result in the demolition of the old stadium and the construction of sixty-five houses and apartments as well as the superstore. Secretary of State for Communities and Local Government Eric Pickles approved the plans on 12 March, and Rovers appeared on course for their latest new home.

2013/14

Shortly before five o'clock on the first Saturday of May 2014, Rovers' ninety-four year tenure of Football League status came to a dismal and sudden close. Needing simply a draw at home to mid-table Mansfield Town, Rovers fell behind to Colin Daniel's low volley off a post nine minutes before half-time, and despite producing eighteen shots to the Stags' four, disappeared off the League radar.

Just a week earlier, there had been jubilation as, with sixteen minutes left on the clock at Adams Park in the penultimate match of a turbulent season, David

Clarkson had swept a loose ball home from close range. As the weeks had gone by, Rovers had slipped from a poor position into a precarious one but had not quite slipped into the two relegation places. Lee Brown's eleventh-minute free-kick had put the Pirates ahead away to Wycombe Wanderers, who were just above Rovers on goal difference, only for the Chairboys to equalise nine minutes later through Matt McClure's back-flicked volley. Results elsewhere indicated that the other five clubs in the bottom seven places were all winning; the Gas had temporarily dropped to second from bottom and, ultimately, Football League survival appeared to hinge on securing victory in Buckinghamshire. With time ticking away, Clarkson, the villain of the piece when the sides had met in Horfield earlier in the season, was on the spot with the goal that rescued Rovers' spirit and relegated Torquay United to Conference football. Just a week later, Rovers joined the Gulls in fifth-tier football, finishing in twenty-third place with fifty points and just forty-three League goals to their collective name.

Manager John Ward had made just two summer signings, but what signings they were! Reinforcing the spine of the side, he acquired on a permanent basis goalkeeper Steve Mildenhall and influential midfielder and top scorer John-Joe O'Toole, who had both featured in the side the previous campaign. In addition, Mark McChrystal's contract was extended and he was to play a key role in Rovers' defensive formation.

In stark contrast to August 2011, when Rovers had fielded ten debutants on the opening day at Wimbledon, the only player making his first appearance in the side at Exeter in August 2013 was young substitute Shaquille Hunter. He was one of a handful from Rovers' successful youth side to break into League reckoning. Mitch Harding started on the opening day, Rovers' squad opening the new campaign with twelve players out of action through injury, and Alefe Santos and Young Player of the Year Tom Lockyer very quickly established themselves as integral cogs in the Rovers machine, while Pat Keary and Jamie Lucas also broke into the side. Salisbury City manager Darrell Clarke, a former Hartlepool United midfielder, joined the club, working alongside development coach Marcus Stewart as Ward's assistant manager.

A youthful Rovers side picked up just one point from the opening three League fixtures, perhaps an ominous sign of the struggles ahead through the campaign, before kick-starting the season with back-to-back wins at home to York City and Northampton Town. Clarkson scored twice in the opening thirty-two minutes in the former, Lockyer after just ninety-six seconds from Lee Brown's cross in the latter. Both York and Northampton had a man dismissed; York's Ryan Bowman was sent off only five minutes after his arrival, becoming the first substitute ever in a Rovers match to receive a red card before half-time. An early season addition to the side was the arrival of midfielder Andy Bond, who had previously opposed Rovers in the FA Cup with Barrow and in League fixtures with Colchester United.

In September, Rovers avoided a home defeat against hapless Hartlepool, thanks to John-Joe O'Toole's last-gasp equaliser, after eighteen-year-old Luke James had scored twice for the visitors in nine first-half minutes. Keary's first League appearance, as a substitute at Mansfield Town in October, saw Rovers field their youngest back four since the 1967/68 season, with a combined age of eighty-five years 216 days, including club captain Tom Parkes. This could not compete with the eighty-four years 164 days of Rovers' back four against Shrewsbury Town at Gay Meadow in October 1968 or the eighty-four years 291 days at Wrexham in May 1979.

As the anticipated victories failed to materialise, Ward dipped into the loan market and signed Will Packwood from Birmingham City, the first United States-born player to don a Rovers shirt, and Manchester City's left-sided midfielder Alex Henshall. The pair made their Rovers bow in the depressing home defeat against Wycombe Wanderers, Rovers playing the final sixty-five minutes a man short after Clarkson received a straight red card for a foul on the Chairboys' Josh Scowen. Much appeared to hinge on the Tuesday night trip to winless, bottom-placed Accrington Stanley. After going a goal up in four minutes, Rovers lost 2-1 to be drawn apparently inextricably into a relegation struggle.

As the season progressed, Rovers never quite stumbled into the relegation zone, yet also never appeared immune from the dangers posed by the drop zone yawning cavernously beneath them. A revival of sorts was kick-started when O'Toole's penalty nineteen minutes from time earned Rovers an unexpected 1-0 victory at top-of-the-table Oxford United. However, both on-loan Chris Beardsley and O'Toole were then sent off as Rovers crashed to defeat at Burton Albion and moved to within a point of the relegation zone; the Brewers' Jimmy Phillips was also sent off in a game Albion won through Robbie Weir's fifty-eighth-minute strike. With these two key figures missing, Rovers conjured up their largest victory of the season, defeating Wimbledon 3-0 before a Memorial Stadium crowd of 5,860, the visitors having Sammy Moore dismissed eight minutes from time. Suddenly, late winners abounded, a last-minute FA Cup winner at Crawley being followed by O'Toole's last-gasp goal to secure a 2-1 home victory at home to Exeter City in January, the first time since 2011 that Rovers had come from behind to win in the League. In the next home fixture, loan debutant Kaid Mohamed scored against his former club, Newport County, as Rovers ran up a 3-1 victory. This precipitated a series of home wins and clean sheets in spring, with new signings Alan Gow and Steven Gillespie briefly able to contribute. It was a stark contrast to a run of nine League fixture without a win in the autumn, Rovers were unbeaten in six League matches through February and March.

However, there were too many lacklustre performances and goals were sparse, Rovers hitting April with only ten away League goals to their name. On 28 March, with Rovers languishing just three points clear of the relegation zone, manager John Ward was moved upstairs to a director of football role, with Darrell

Clarke taking control of the day-to-day running of the side. Just the following day, a Mohamed goal four minutes into stoppage-time defeated Morecambe and paved the way for Rovers, with McChrystal captaining the side in Clarke's first game in charge, to attempt to effect an end-of-season escape from the potential perils of relegation to the Conference. The venture was not without its twists and turns, though, as Rovers lost three successive fixtures over a frenetic and nerve-tingling Easter period. Inexplicably, this run started with a 2-1 loss at home to a Torquay side already staring relegation to the Conference in the face. As a disappointing season moved towards a nerve-wracking climax, Rovers scored twice away from home for first time all campaign in an astonishing game at Portsmouth over Easter, when Harrold's brace twice brought the Pirates level in a frenetic first half. Despite taking an early lead, Rovers lost at home to Rochdale on Easter Monday, substitute Joe Bunney scoring just fifty-four seconds into the second half before the former Rovers player Matt Lund popped up with a winning goal that left Rovers' Football League status hanging by a thread. That thread snapped on the final day of the season, when only a home draw was required in front of The Mem's highest crowd of the campaign. Tellingly, Rovers lost their final three home fixtures when a draw in just one of them would have sufficed.

Perilously close under Rovers' feet, the gaping exit to Conference football was proving something of a one-way door. Fourteen former League sides plied their trade in fifth-tier football in 2013/14, including former opponents such as Grimsby Town and Wrexham. Twenty-one former Football League clubs, during their present or previous incarnations, were in the three Conference divisions during 2013/14, including recent rivals Stockport County, one of five former Football League sides plying their trade in the Conference North. Since 2004/05, of eighteen teams to lose their League status, only Oxford United, Torquay United and Mansfield Town had returned to the League fold. A fourth side, Luton Town, supported by greater financial backing than Rovers were likely to attract, were Conference champions in 2014, though Torquay again dropped out of League Two. It had become evident that as Rovers dropped out of the Football League, the return journey would prove long, dangerous and quite possibly unattainable. Clarkson's late winning goal at Wycombe appeared to pave the way for Rovers' ultimate escape from the jaws of non-League football, only for the final day of the season to prove a slap in the face.

In a frustrating season, Rovers could not complete a League double over any opponents; unfashionable Fleetwood, Accrington, Rochdale and Dagenham all defeated the Pirates both home and away. The lowest home crowd was the 5,303 who witnessed the defeat against Fleetwood, and twelve of the home League attendances had been under 6,000, though a final day crowd of 10,594 brought the seasonal home League average up to 6,412. John-Joe O'Toole was top scorer in League action, with thirteen of Rovers' forty-three League goals, Lee Brown supplying seven assists. Of thirty players used, stalwart goalkeeper Mildenhall started every match, with Parkes, Player of the Year Michael Smith, Brown and O'Toole missing just the occasional fixture. O'Toole picked up eleven yellow cards and one red, having apparently committed sixty-six fouls in the League; he also had more shots on target than any other player, his twenty-four exceeding Clarkson's tally by one. Meanwhile, former Pirates Fraser Forster and Rickie Lambert won international recognition ahead of England's 2014 World Cup final campaign in Brazil.

Rovers faced nineteen former players as the season progressed, among them René Howe, who played for both Burton Albion and Newport County, scoring for the Ambers, as Matt Lund did for Rochdale. Oxford fielded three former Rovers players, the Pirates taking 862 supporters to boost a crowd of 6,374 in November for Rovers' solitary away victory prior to the dramatic events on the penultimate Saturday at Wycombe, where there were 1,953 Gasheads amongst the crowd of 6,752. There were 2,009 Gasheads among a 17,998 crowd for the relegation six-pointer at Fratton Park on Easter Saturday; amid a crowd of 8,631 at Plymouth were 1,273 Rovers supporters. Only 1,423 in all attended the defeat at Dagenham in September, when Matt Harrold missed a penalty, 1,514 were at Morecambe and 2,302 were at Burton. The 1,101 at Accrington was the lowest to watch a Rovers Football League encounter since 1933. At £500 a head, Rovers' adult season tickets for 2013/14 were the highest-priced in League Two. One notable supporter, Malcolm Norman, has not missed a home Rovers fixture since February 1966. An impressive attendance of 8,158 experienced the Easter Monday collapse at home to promotion-chasing Rochdale. Previously, 7,537 had watched the encouraging 2-0 victory over Portsmouth in December, the opposition featuring Johnny Ertl in their side, the only Austrian international to face Rovers in League football, while 7,288 witnessed the exciting 3-1 home victory over Newport the following month.

Once again, cup competitions brought minimal joy for Rovers. A predominantly Italian Watford side saw off Rovers with three well-taken goals in sixteen first-half minutes, their team containing players who had represented Italy, Switzerland, the Czech Republic, Jamaica and Sweden at international level. An enthralling draw saw Rovers travel to Ashton Gate in the opening round of the Johnstone's Paint Trophy, where, in front of a crowd of 17,888, containing an official figure of 2,429 Gasheads, the only cheer was McChrystal's first goal for the club, a headed effort after half-time, as Bristol City emerged 2-1 victors. Wes Fletcher scored a last-minute equaliser as York City drew 3-3 at The Mem in the FA Cup and then hit two goals in sixty seconds as Rovers, 3-0 up in fifty minutes, held on for a 3-2 victory in the first-round replay, Beardsley scoring for the Pirates in both fixtures. York featured in their side Sander Puri, the second Estonian, after Derby County's Mart Poom in January 2002, to oppose Rovers in a competitive fixture. In the following round, the replay at Crawley was abandoned after seventy-four minutes in a deluge by referee Stuart Attwell; for a few hours Rovers held out hope of a potential fourth-round tie at home to beleaguered reigning champions Manchester United, only for the Red Devils to be knocked out by Swansea. Two goals in the final seven minutes of the rearranged fixture at Crawley enabled Rovers to win their second-round replay and progress to a third-round tie at Birmingham City. Supported by an official figure of 2,900 travelling Gasheads, Rovers conceded two very late goals to Chris Burke, which embellished the Championship side's ultimately comfortable 3-0 victory.

After many years of effort, and despite the disappointment of relegation, it appeared as the season drew to a close that Rovers could face an imminent move to a new home. The construction of a 21,700-capacity stadium on 3.3 hectares of land at the University of the West of England at Stoke Gifford had been delayed by a local campaign, opposing the erection of a Sainsbury's supermarket on the Memorial Stadium site. Rovers required the sale of the land in order to fund their new ground. Sainsbury's had been given permission on 4 May 2012, this being approved by Bristol City Council on 16 January 2013, to build a superstore on the site, where the 9,000-square-metre supermarket would be joined by sixty-five dwellings and a public open space, to be poignantly named Memorial Square. The whole enterprise was intended to create 350 potential jobs amid an investment of some £200 million in all. Building Rovers' new ground would also lead to the construction of 500 new houses and 100 extra-care units, and the £100 million raised by the sale of the UWE land would be invested in university business and media centres as well as teaching and accommodation blocks. At the hearing of 13 March 2014, Mr Justice Hickingbottom overruled the objections raised on 4 September 2013 by the local group TRASHorfield, who had gathered over 1,000 signatures, and the diggers soon moved in to the proposed site. Ominously, though, in January 2014, Rovers announced pre-tax losses of £781,911 for the year to June 2013, a significant increase from the losses of £353,219 in the year to June 2012; turnover had dropped by 17 per cent to £3.8 million.

This is the Bristol Rovers story. It is one of triumphs and disasters, of brushes with glory and of eternal years of optimism. The phoenix will rise once again from the ashes. The Pirates have sailed all too often into troubled waters and the choppy seas of the basement division are no exception, but all must hope that calmer straits lie ahead and that the good ship Bristol Rovers can steer an even course through the oceans of time to come.

Bibliography

Research for this book has necessitated a thorough investigation of local newspapers, primarily the *Bristol Evening News*, *Bristol Times*, *Bristol Herald*, *Western Daily Press* and, in comparatively recent years, the *Bristol Evening Post*. Researching details relating to other clubs has taken the authors to a wide range of libraries to consult all manner of newspapers and journals, and our thanks is due to the staff at each of these. It has also involved comparing facts and figures against numerous excellent histories of other clubs, far too many to mention here, *Rothmans Football Yearbooks*, as well as similar if less detailed equivalents in years gone by and various editions of *Burke's Peerage*, *Burke's Landed Gentry*, *Kelly's Directory* and *Crockford's Clerical Directory*. Other books that have provided valuable information and may be of further interest to the reader include:

Armstrong, Gary, *Football Hooligans: Knowing the Score* (Berg, 1998).

Bailey, John, *Not Just on Christmas Day: An Overview of Association Football in the First World War* (3-2 Books, 1999).

Bailey, Philip, Philip Thorne and Peter Wynne Thomas, *Who's Who of Cricketers* (Hamlyn, 1993).

Birley, Derek, *Sport and the Making of Britain* (Manchester University Press, 1993).

Board of Trade, *Inspection of Bristol Rovers Football Club Limited* (Board of Trade, HMSO, 1951).

Braine, A., *The History of Kingswood Forest* (First published 1891, Kingsmead, 1961).

Census, *Gloucestershire Population Figures, 1801–1921* (Census returns).

Columbus, Lesser, *Greater Bristol* (Pelham, 1893).

Dahl, Louis Harald, *Stapleton, Past and Present* (1934).

Ekwal, Eilert, *Concise Oxford Dictionary of English Place-Names* (Clarendon, 1936 and 1960).

Eveleigh, David J., *Bristol, 1850–1919* (Britain in Old Photographs series, Budding Books, 1996).

Eveleigh, David J., *Old Cooking Utensils* (Shire, 1986).
Freddi, Cris, *England Football Fact Book* (Guinness, 1991).
Harding, J. A., *The Diocese of Clifton, 1850–2000* (Clifton Catholic Diocesan Trustees, 1999).
Headley, Gwyn, Wim Meulenkamp, *Follies: A Guide to Rogue Architecture in England, Scotland and Wales* (Jonathan Cape, 1986).
Hitchings, Henry, *The Language Wars* (John Murray, 2011).
Hollinsworth, Brian, Arthur Cook, *The Great Book of Trains* (Salamander, 1996).
Holt, Richard, *Sport and the British: A Modern History* (Oxford University Press, 1989).
Hoppen, K. Theodore, *The Mid-Victorian Generation, 1846–1886* (Clarendon Press, 1998).
Hughman, Barry J. (ed.), *Football League Players' Records* (Tony Williams, 1992).
Inglis, Simon, *The Football Grounds of Great Britain* (Collins Willow, 1985).
Jones, Frederick Creech and William Gordon Chown, *History of Bristol's Suburbs* (Reece Winstone, 1977).
Large, David, *The Municipal Government of Bristol, 1850–1901* (Bristol Record Society, 1999).
Latimer, John, *Annals of Bristol* (J. Latimer, 1893).
Leach, Joseph, *The Church Goer, Rural Rides or Calls at Country Churches* (Ridler, 1847).
Living Easton, *Easton in the Twentieth Century* (Living Easton, 2001).
Living Easton, *Walk the Historic River Frome* (Living Easton, 2000).
McIntosh, Peter, *Sport in Society* (West London Press, 1987).
Minute Book of the Kingswood Enclosure Commissioners, 1779–1784.
Morris, Jan, *The Matter of Wales* (Penguin, 1984).
Nicholls, J. F., John Taylor, *Bristol Past and Present, Vol. 1* (Arrowsmith, 1881).
Owen, Gale R., *Rites and Religions of the Anglo-Saxons* (Barnes & Noble, 1996).
Parry-Jones, William, *The Trade in Lunacy* (Routledge and Kegan Paul, 1972).
Pierson, Arthur T., *George Müller of Bristol* (James Nisbet, 1899).
Potter, K. R. (ed), *Oxford Medieval Texts* (Oxford, 1976).
Reid, Helen, *Life in Victorian Bristol* (Redcliffe, 2005).
Rollin, Jack, *Soccer at War, 1939–45* (Collins Willow, 1985).
Sandbrook, Dominic, *Seasons in the Sun: The Battle for Britain, 1974–79* (Allen Lane, 2012).
Schama, Simon, *A History of Britain: At the Edge of the World?* (BBC, 2000).
Smailes, Breedon, *The Breedon Book of Football League Records* (Breedon, 1991).
Smith, Veronica, *The Street Names of Bristol* (Broadcast Books, 2001).
Stubbs, W. (ed) *Willelmi Malmesbiriensis Monachi de Gestis Regum Anglorum,*

Rolls Series I, 1885/86.
Tabner, Brian, *Through the Turnstiles* (Yore Publications, 1992).
Timbs, John, *Things Not Generally Known* (Lockwood, 1861).
Walker, Frank, *The Bristol Region* (Nelson, 1972).
Webb, Sandie and Doug, *A View From the Terraces: One Hundred Years of Western League Football* (Addkey Print Limited, 1992).
Wright, J. and Co., *Bristol and Clifton Directory* (1890).

Of seeing Wally Hammond, and that peerless cover drive,
Memories of my school chums, football grounds that I've played on,
How I idolised Jesse Whatley, Tot Walsh, and Jim Haydon.
So – there 'tis, and though time goes,
Still the muddy Avon flows,
And my God I – my biggest frown ...
WHO KNOCKED THE THIRTEEN ARCHES DOWN ?

Jack Harcombe

Acknowledgements

The greatest thanks of all are of course due to the authors' wives, Stitch Byrne and Julie Jay, without whose love, care and support this book would never have been possible. Our growing families are also due our grateful thanks: Kelly Sessions and Ian Jay as well as Toseland, Ophelia, Horatio and Harriet Byrne.

No book containing this degree of information could be a feasible proposition without recourse to considerable help from a number of sources: Mervyn Baker, Michael Joyce, Jim Creasy, Mike Davage, Keith Brookman, Ian Haddrell, Alan Lacock, Alan Marshall, Jeff Davis, Neil Brookman, David Woods, Ray Spiller, David Foot, Don Veale, Gerry Prewett, Julie 'Mole' Osman, Martin O'Connor, Darren Stobbs, Andy Wildgoose, Susan Gardiner, Ian King, Judith Upton, Martin Gallier, John Taylor, Nichol Forbes, Andrew Williams, Clifford Whitehead, Pat James, Darren Flowers, June Pritchard, Steve Palmer, Pauline Panter, John Hansford, Richard Laurence, David Eveleigh, Iain McColl, Jim McNeill, John Penny, Peter Fleming, Alex Young, Ivor Cornish, Pam Bishop, Margaret McGregor, Margaret Ferre, Colin Timbrell, John Jurica, Kevin Byrne, Garth Dykes, Tony Matthews, Mike Jones, Trefor Jones, Richard Harnwell, Michael Braham, David Downs, Paul Taylor, Tony Brown, David Bull, Gary Chalk, Ron Parrott, Brian McColl, David Potter, Douglas Gorman, Derek Hyde, Fraser Clyne, Tony Ambrosen, Gordon Baird, Paul Plowman, Neilson Kaufman, Donald and Ian Nannestad, Duncan Carmichael, Gordon Sydney and Drummond Calder.

Tom Furby at Amberley Books has been a supportive and enthusiastic ally, as eager to see the club's history meticulously documented as we are.

While every effort has, of course, been made to ensure that the details included in this book are as accurate as possible, typographical errors are inevitable in a work of this magnitude, and the authors apologise for these in advance. We are also keen to point out that any opinions stated are the views of the authors, reflecting on the statistics to hand, and not necessarily those of Bristol Rovers Football Club.

Authors' Note

Due to the sheer amount of narrative in this Bristol Rovers history, it was unfortunately not possible to include the full seasonal statistics from the club's earliest days from 1883 to 1945 and the players' indexes (both Southern League and Football League 1899–2014), which we had intended. Much of this was researched and compiled, but space restrictions precluded them being published. However, readers can contact the authors directly to receive further information and statistics by emailing them: eastvillegas@live.co.uk or skbyrne17@hotmail.com.

BRISTOL ROVERS SEASON STATISTICS 1946–2014

1946/47

Date	Opponent	H/A	F	A	Att	WEARE John	SMITH Wilfred V	WATKINS Barry	PITT John	WARREN Raymond	WHITFIELD Wilfred	LEWIS Idris	BAMFORD Henry	LAMBDEN Victor	CURRAN Frank	CARR Lance	HODGES Leonard	BALDIE Douglas	PEACOCK George	PETHERBRIDGE George	LILEY Henry	WINTER-ALSOP Herbert	HAYWARD Douglas	ALLAWAY James	GILES Albert	SMITH Henry	MORGAN James	McARTHUR Walter	MORGAN Wynffrwd	COOK John	LEAMON Frederick	WINDLE Charles	WOOKEY Kenneth	BAKER Clifford	Scorers			
	DIVISION 3 SOUTH																																						
31/08/1946	READING	H	2	2	11000	1	2	3	4	5	6	7	8	9	10	11																			LAMBDEN	CURRAN		
04/09/1946	IPSWICH TOWN	A	2	0	12012	1	2	3	4	5	6	7	8	9	10	11																			LAMBDEN 2			
07/09/1946	CRYSTAL PALACE	A	1	2	18141	1	2	3	4	5	6	7	8	9	10	11																			LAMBDEN			
09/09/1946	WATFORD	H	3	4	11838	1	2	3	4	5	6	7	8	9	10	11																			LAMBDEN	BAMFORD	LEWIS	
14/09/1946	TORQUAY UNITED	H	3	0	14076	1	2	3	4	5	6	7	8		10	11	9																		CURRAN	CARR	HODGES	
18/09/1946	WATFORD	A	0	1	4858	1	2	3	4	5	6	7	8		10	11	9																					
21/09/1946	MANSFIELD TOWN	A	1	3	9183	1	2	3	4	5	6	7	8	9	10	11																			CURRAN			
28/09/1946	BRISTOL CITY	H	0	3	25900	1	2	3	4	5	6	7		9	10	11		8																				
05/10/1946	SOUTHEND UNITED	H	1	3	9812	1		3	8	5	6	11	4	9		10			2	7															LEWIS			
12/10/1946	QUEENS PARK RANGERS	A	2	0	20300			3	8	2	6	7	4	9		10				11	1	5													PETHERBRIDGE	WARREN pen		
19/10/1946	SWINDON TOWN	A	0	1	16015	1		3	8	2	6	7	4	9		10				11		5																
26/10/1946	BOURNEMOUTH	H	0	2	11500	1		3	8	2	6	7	4		9	10				11		5																
02/11/1946	CARDIFF CITY	A	0	4	35000	1		3		2	6	7	4	9		10				11		5	8															
09/11/1946	NORWICH CITY	H	1	2	8963	1		3		2	6		4	8	9	11				7		5		10											FLACK og			
16/11/1946	NOTTS COUNTY	A	0	6	14390	1		3		2	6		9	8		11				7		5		10	4													
23/11/1946	NORTHAMPTON TOWN	H	0	3	7886			3	6	4			8	9		11				7	1	5				2	10											
07/12/1946	BRIGHTON & HOVE ALBION	H	0	0	6097	1	2	3	4	5				10		11												6	7	8	9							
14/12/1946	EXETER CITY	A	2	3	7528	1		3	4	5				8		11								10		2		6	7		9				LEAMON	CARR		
21/12/1946	PORT VALE	H	0	0	5734	1		3		5				8		11			2					10		4		6			9	7						
25/12/1946	WALSALL	H	2	2	6624	1		3	4	5				10		11										2		6		8	9	7			WINDLE	LEAMON		
26/12/1946	WALSALL	A	0	2	14564	1		3	4	5	11			8		10			2									6			9	7						
28/12/1946	READING	A	1	1	14128	1		3	4	5						11			2									6			9	7	8	10	LEAMON			
04/01/1947	CRYSTAL PALACE	H	2	1	13341	1		3	4	5						11			2									6			9	7	8	10	LEAMON	BAKER		
11/01/1947	ALDERSHOT	A	2	0	4000	1		3	4	5						11			2									6			9	7	8	10	LEAMON	BAKER		
18/01/1947	TORQUAY UNITED	A	0	3	6386	1		3	4	5						11			2									6			9	7	8	10				
25/01/1947	MANSFIELD TOWN	H	1	0	9448	1		3	4	5			2			11	8											6			9		7	10	CARR			
01/02/1947	BRISTOL CITY	A	0	4	17119	1		3	4	5			2			11	8										10	6			9		7					
08/02/1947	SOUTHEND UNITED	A	3	2	5986	1		3	4	5			2			11	8										10	6			9		7		CARR	HODGES	HANKEY og	
15/02/1947	QUEENS PARK RANGERS	H	3	1	18781	1		3	4	5			2			11	8										10	6			9		7		LEAMON	WARREN pen	CARR	
22/02/1947	SWINDON TOWN	H	3	0	9000	1		3	4	5			2			11	8										10	6			9		7		WOOKEY	LEAMON	J MORGAN	
01/03/1947	BOURNEMOUTH	A	3	1	11000	1		3	4	5			2			11	8										10	6			9		7		LEAMON 2	J MORGAN		
08/03/1947	CARDIFF CITY	H	1	0	30417	1		3	4	5			2			11	8										10	6			9		7		CARR			
15/03/1947	NORWICH CITY	A	3	3	18051	1		3	4	5			2			11	8										10	6			9		7		WOOKEY	HODGES	CARR	
22/03/1947	NOTTS COUNTY	H	4	1	12087	1		3	4	5			2			11	8										10	6			9		7		LEAMON 2	WOOKEY	WARREN pen	
29/03/1947	NORTHAMPTON TOWN	A	2	1	6846	1		3	4	5			2			11	8										10	6			9		7		J MORGAN	LEAMON		
04/04/1947	LEYTON ORIENT	A	0	3	13602	1		3	4	5			2			11	8										10	6			9		7					
05/04/1947	ALDERSHOT	H	0	0	13717	1		3	4	5			2			11	8										10	6			9		7					
07/04/1947	LEYTON ORIENT	H	6	1	14045	1		3	4	5			2			11	8										10	6			9		7		HODGES 2	J MORGAN 2	CARR	PITT pen
12/04/1947	BRIGHTON & HOVE ALBION	A	2	1	7685	1		3	4	5			2			11	8	10										6			9		7		BALDIE 2			
19/04/1947	EXETER CITY	H	1	0	13775	1		3	4	5			2			11	8	10										6			9		7		BALDIE			
26/04/1947	PORT VALE	A	1	2	8323	1		3	4	5			2			11	8										10	6			9		7		McARTHUR			
10/05/1947	IPSWICH TOWN	H	1	1	10459	1		3	4	5			2			11	8										10	6			9		7		LEAMON			
	APPEARANCES					40	9	42	38	42	16	13	32	18	10	42	19	3	7	8	2	7	1	4	1	4	15	26	2	2	26	7	21	5				
	GOALS					0	0	0	1	3	0	2	1	5	3	8	5	3	0	1	0	0	0	0	0	0	5	1	0	0	13	1	3	2	OWN GOAL 2			
	FA CUP																																					
30/11/1946	MERTHYR TOWN	A	1	3	14000			3		5			2	9		11				7	1					4	10	6		8					LAMBDEN			
	GLOUCESTERSHIRE CUP																																					
26/05/1947	BRISTOL CITY	H	2	2	17151	1		3	4	5			2			11	8	7									10	6			9				LEAMON	HODGES		
07/06/1947	BRISTOL CITY	A	0	2	11434	1		3	4	5			2			11	8										10	6			9		7					

1947/48

Date						WEARE John	BAMFORD Henry	WATKINS Barry	PITT John	WARREN Raymond	McARTHUR Walter	WOOKEY Kenneth	HODGES Leonard	LEAMON Frederick	MORGAN James	CRANFIELD Harold	CHADWICK Frederick	FOX Geoffrey	WINTER-ALSOP Herbert	PETHERBRIDGE George	BALDIE Douglas	LAMBDEN Victor	JONES Ralph	WATLING John	LILEY Henry	BUSH Bryan				
	DIVISION 3 SOUTH																													
23/08/1947	PORT VALE	A	1	1	15714	1	2	3	4	5	6	7	8	9	10	11											CRANFIELD			
25/08/1947	SWINDON TOWN	H	3	1	19372	1	2	3	4	5	6	7	8	9	10	11											PITT 2	LEAMON		
30/08/1947	QUEENS PARK RANGERS	H	0	1	19632	1	2	3	4	5	6	7	8	9	10	11														
03/09/1947	SWINDON TOWN	A	1	1	18000	1	2	3	4	5	6	7	8	9	10	11											WOOKEY			
06/09/1947	WATFORD	A	2	3	10315	1	2	3	4	5	6	7	8	9	10	11											LEAMON	WOOKEY		
08/09/1947	CRYSTAL PALACE	H	1	1	12430	1	2	3	4	5	6	7	8	9	10	11											CRANFIELD			
13/09/1947	BRIGHTON & HOVE ALBION	H	4	1	13833	1	2	3	4	5	6	7	8	9		11	10										LEAMON	WOOKEY	CHADWICK	WARREN pen
17/09/1947	CRYSTAL PALACE	A	0	0	12172	1	2	3	4	5	6	7	8	9		11	10													
20/09/1947	NORWICH CITY	A	5	1	15209	1	2	3	4	5	6	7	8	9		11	10										LEAMON 2	HODGES 2	WOOKEY	
22/09/1947	SWANSEA CITY	H	2	2	15281	1	2	3	4	5	6	7	8	9		11	10										LEAMON	McARTHUR		
27/09/1947	BRISTOL CITY	H	0	2	34188	1	2		4	5	3	7	8	9		11	10	6												
04/10/1947	NORTHAMPTON TOWN	H	1	2	15098	1	2	3	4		6	7	8	9		11	10		5								LEAMON			
11/10/1947	READING	A	0	0	13000	1	2	3	4	5	6		8	9		11				7	10									
18/10/1947	WALSALL	H	2	3	17573	1	2	3	4	5	6	7	8			11					10	9					McARTHUR	HODGES		
25/10/1947	LEYTON ORIENT	A	4	2	11164	1	2	3	4	5	6	7	8		10	11						9					LAMBDEN 2	HODGES	WARREN pen	
01/11/1947	EXETER CITY	H	2	2	14399	1	2	3	4	5	6	7	8		10	11						9					MORGAN	WOOKEY		
08/11/1947	NEWPORT COUNTY	A	2	2	12000	1	2	3	4	5	6	7	8		10	11						9					WOOKEY	MORGAN		
15/11/1947	SOUTHEND UNITED	H	1	2	12613	1	2	3	4	5	6	7			10	11					8	9					BALDIE			
22/11/1947	NOTTS COUNTY	A	2	4	29437	1	2	3	4	5	6	7	8		10	11						9					LAMBDEN 2			
06/12/1947	BOURNEMOUTH	A	0	3	13000	1	2		4	5		7			10	11		6			8	9	3							
20/12/1947	PORT VALE	H	2	1	11651	1	2		4	5	6		8	9	10	11				7			3				LEAMON	McGARRY og		
26/12/1947	TORQUAY UNITED	H	0	2	16554	1	2	3	4		6		8		10	11			5	7		9								
27/12/1947	TORQUAY UNITED	A	2	1	7148	1	2	3	4		6		8		10	11			5	7		9					PETHERBRIDGE	LAMBDEN		
03/01/1948	QUEENS PARK RANGERS	A	2	5	22000	1	2		4		6		8		10	11		3	5	7		9					MORGAN	PETHERBRIDGE		
17/01/1948	WATFORD	H	3	0	12864	1	2	3	4	5	6	7	8		10					11		9					McARTHUR	WATKINS	LAMBDEN	
31/01/1948	BRIGHTON & HOVE ALBION	A	1	3	14081	1	2	3	4	5	6	7	8		10					11		9					PETHERBRIDGE			
07/02/1948	NORWICH CITY	H	2	3	11226	1	2	3	4	5	6	7	8		10					11		9					MORGAN	PETHERBRIDGE		
14/02/1948	BRISTOL CITY	A	2	5	25908	1	2	3	4	5	6	8			10					7		9		11			McARTHUR	MORGAN		
21/02/1948	NORTHAMPTON TOWN	A	3	1	5149	1		3	4		6		8		10				5	7		9	2	11			MORGAN	LAMBDEN	PITT pen	
28/02/1948	READING	H	2	3	14356	1		3	4		6		8		10				5	7		9	2	11			PETHERBRIDGE	HODGES		
06/03/1948	WALSALL	A	0	2	13442	1	5		4	2	6		8		10					7		9	3	11						
13/03/1948	LEYTON ORIENT	H	0	2	11987	1	8	3	4	5	6									7	10	9	2	11						
20/03/1948	EXETER CITY	A	0	4	8000		2		4	5	6	7	8	9	10					11			3		1					
26/03/1948	ALDERSHOT	A	0	2	6980		2		4	5	6	7	8	9	10			3		11					1					
27/03/1948	NEWPORT COUNTY	H	2	3	13292		2		4	5	6	7	10	9	11			3				8			1		PITT 2-2pens			
29/03/1948	ALDERSHOT	H	7	1	10996		2	10	4	5	6	7	8					3				9		11	1		LAMBDEN 4	PITT 2	WATKINS	
03/04/1948	SOUTHEND UNITED	A	0	1	8410		2	10	4	5	6	7	8					3				9		11	1					
10/04/1948	NOTTS COUNTY	H	2	0	12094		2	10	4	5	6	7	8					3				9		11	1		WATKINS	PITT		
17/04/1948	SWANSEA CITY	A	1	0	15320		2	10	4	5	6	7	8					3				9		11	1		WARREN			
24/04/1948	BOURNEMOUTH	H	1	2	14827		2	10	4	5	6	7	8					3				9		11	1		WATKINS			
28/04/1948	IPSWICH TOWN	H	2	0	8722		2	10	4	5	6		8					3				9		11	1	7	WATKINS	GREEN og		
01/05/1948	IPSWICH TOWN	A	4	0	10605		2	8	4	5	6				10			3		11		9			1	7	BUSH	MORGAN	PETHERBRIDGE 2	
	APPEARANCES					32	40	34	42	36	41	31	37	17	27	24	6	12	6	16	5	26	7	11	10	2				
	GOALS					0	0	5	8	3	4	6	5	8	7	2	1	0	0	7	1	11	0	0	0	1	OWN GOAL 2			
	FA CUP																													
29/11/1947	LEYTONSTONE	H	3	2	16000	1	2	3	4	5	6	7			10	11					8	9					BALDIE	LAMBDEN	MORGAN	
13/12/1947	NEW BRIGHTON	H	4	0	10732	1	2	3	4	5	6	7	8		10	11						9					MORGAN 2	McARTHUR	LAMBDEN	
10/01/1948	SWANSEA TOWN	H	3	0	23596	1	2	3	4	5	6	7	8		10					11		9					WOOKEY	LAMBDEN	MORGAN	
24/01/1948	FULHAM	A	2	5	20000	1	2	3	4	5	6	7	8		10					11		9					McARTHUR	PETHERBRIDGE		
	GLOUCESTERSHIRE CUP																													
08/05/1948	BRISTOL CITY	A	2	1	16000		2	8	4	5	6		7		10			3		11		9			1		MORGAN	WATKINS		

1948/49

Date	Opponent	H/A	F	A	Att	LILEY Henry	BAMFORD Henry	FOX Geoffrey	SAMPSON Peter	WARREN Raymond	McARTHUR Walter	WOOKEY Kenneth	HODGES Leonard	LAMBDEN Victor	WATKINS Barry	PETHERBRIDGE George	WEARE John	PITT John	BUSH Bryan	LAING Frederick	MORGAN James	WATLING John	HADDON Harold	ROOST William	Scorers			
	DIVISION 3 SOUTH																											
21/08/1948	IPSWICH TOWN	H	1	6	16314	1	2	3	4	5	6	7	8	9	10	11									LAMBDEN			
26/08/1948	BOURNEMOUTH	A	0	1	16067		2	3		5	6		8	9	10	11	1	4	7									
28/08/1948	NOTTS COUNTY	A	1	4	33747		2	3		5	6			9		11	1	4	7	8	10				PETHERBRIDGE			
30/08/1948	BOURNEMOUTH	H	4	0	14121		2	3		5	6		8	9		11	1	4	7		10				PETHERBRIDGE	MORGAN 2	HODGES	
04/09/1948	WALSALL	H	3	0	17244		2	3		5	6		8	9		11	1	4	7		10				WARREN pen	BUSH	FOULKES og	
08/09/1948	CRYSTAL PALACE	A	0	1	10827		2	3		5	6		8	9		11	1	4	7		10							
11/09/1948	TORQUAY UNITED	A	2	0	8360		2	3		5	6		8	9		11	1	4	7		10				LAMBDEN	BUSH		
13/09/1948	CRYSTAL PALACE	H	1	0	14509		2	3		5	6		8	9		11	1	4	7		10				LAMBDEN			
18/09/1948	BRISTOL CITY	H	3	1	29740		2	3		5	6		8	9		7	1	4			10	11			PETHERBRIDGE	LAMBDEN	BUSH	
20/09/1948	MILLWALL	H	2	0	16260		2	3		5	6		8	9		7	1	4			10	11			HODGES	MORTON og		
25/09/1948	NEWPORT COUNTY	H	3	1	21542		2	3		5	6		8	9		7	1	4			10	11			HODGES	MORGAN	WATLING	
02/10/1948	SWANSEA TOWN	A	0	5	28350		2	3		5	6		8	9		7	1	4			10	11						
09/10/1948	SWINDON TOWN	A	1	1	20720		2	3		5	6		8	9		7	1	4			10	11			LAMBDEN			
16/10/1948	LEYTON ORIENT	H	2	3	13719		2	3		5	6		8	9		7	1	4			10	11			LAMBDEN 2			
23/10/1948	SOUTHEND UNITED	A	1	0	12211		2	3		5	6		8	9		7	1	4			10	11			LAMBDEN			
30/10/1948	NORTHAMPTON TOWN	H	1	0	14641		2	3		5	6		8	9		7	1	4			10	11			MORGAN			
06/11/1948	ALDERSHOT	A	5	1	9000		2	3		5	6		8	9		7	1	4			10	11			PETHERBRIDGE 2	LAMBDEN	WARREN pen	WATLING
13/11/1948	BRIGHTON & HOVE ALBION	H	0	0	21879		2	3		5	6		8	9		7	1	4			10	11						
20/11/1948	PORT VALE	A	0	2	10342		2	3		5	6			9		7	1	4		8	10	11						
04/12/1948	NORWICH CITY	A	0	3	20246		2	3		5	6		8	9		7	1	4			10	11						
18/12/1948	IPSWICH TOWN	A	1	0	8751		2	3		5	6		8	9		7	1	4			10	11			MORGAN			
25/12/1948	WATFORD	H	3	1	13853		2	3		5	6		8	9		7	1	4			10	11			PETHERBRIDGE 2	LAMBDEN		
27/12/1948	WATFORD	A	0	0	11949		2	3		5	6		8	9		7	1	4			10	11						
01/01/1949	NOTTS COUNTY	H	3	2	11981		2	3		5	6		8	9		7	1	4			10	11			WARREN 2	MORGAN		
15/01/1949	WALSALL	A	1	0	13000		2	3		5	6		8	9		7	1	4			10	11			LAMBDEN			
22/01/1949	TORQUAY UNITED	H	1	0	18489		2	3		5	6		8	9		7	1	4			10	11			PETHERBRIDGE			
05/02/1949	BRISTOL CITY	A	1	1	27006		2	3		5	6		8	9		7	1	4			10	11			HODGES			
12/02/1949	EXETER CITY	H	3	1	16802		2	3		5	6		8	9		7	1	4			10	11			PETHERBRIDGE	LAMBDEN	HODGES	
19/02/1949	NEWPORT COUNTY	A	1	2	21000		2	3		5	6		8	9		7	1	4			10	11			MORGAN			
26/02/1949	SWANSEA TOWN	H	1	1	30216		2	3		5	6		8	9		7	1	4			10	11			WARREN pen			
05/03/1949	SWINDON TOWN	H	1	1	12688		2	3		5	6		8	9		7	1	4			10	11			WARREN pen			
12/03/1949	LEYTON ORIENT	A	1	1	10154		2	3		5	6		8	9		11	1	4	7				10		PETHERBRIDGE			
19/03/1949	SOUTHEND UNITED	H	0	0	12500		2	3		5	6		8	9		11	1	4	7				10					
26/03/1949	NORTHAMPTON TOWN	A	1	0	7425		2	3		5	6		8	9		7	1	4			10	11			LAMBDEN			
02/04/1949	ALDERSHOT	H	0	2	11147		2	3		5	6		8	9		7	1	4			10	11						
09/04/1949	BRIGHTON & HOVE ALBION	A	1	2	14828		2	3		5	6		8	9		7	1	4			10	11			WARREN pen			
15/04/1949	READING	H	4	1	20836		2	3		5	6		8			7	1	4			10	11		9	WARREN	PETHERBRIDGE	ROOST 2	
16/04/1949	PORT VALE	H	4	1	15268		2	3		5	6		8	7			1	4			10	11		9	WATLING 2	MORGAN	WARREN	
18/04/1949	READING	A	0	1	18975		2	3		5	6		8	7	10		1	4			11			9				
23/04/1949	MILLWALL	A	1	1	20648		2	3		5	6		8	7	10		1	4			11			9	WATKINS			
30/04/1949	NORWICH CITY	H	2	2	12755		2	3		5	6		8	7		11	1	4			10			9	ROOST	WARREN pen		
07/05/1949	EXETER CITY	A	1	2	7000		2	3		5	6			7	8	11	1	4			10			9	WARREN pen			
	APPEARANCES					1	42	42	1	42	42	1	39	41	4	39	41	41	9	2	38	29	2	6				
	GOALS					0	0	0	0	11	0	0	5	13	1	11	0	0	3	0	8	4	0	3	OWN GOAL 2			
	FA CUP																											
27/11/1948	WALSALL	A	1	2	16000		2	3		5	6			9		7	1	4		8	10	11			LAMBDEN			
	GLOUCESTERSHIRE CUP																											
14/05/1949	BRISTOL CITY	H	2	0	15111	1	2	3		5	6		8	9	7			4		10	11				LAMBDEN	MORGAN		

1949/50

						WEARE John	BAMFORD Henry	FOX Geoffrey	PITT John	WARREN Raymond	McARTHUR Walter	PETHERBRIDGE George	HODGES Leonard	ROOST William	MORGAN James	WATLING John	BUSH Bryan	McCOURT Francis	JAMES Anthony	LAMBDEN Victor	BRADFORD Geoffrey	LILEY Harold	SAMPSON Peter	JONES Ralph	WATKINS Barry	TIPPETT Michael	PARSONS Edward	LOCKIER Maurice					
	DIVISION 3 SOUTH																																
20/08/1949	PORT VALE	A	0	1	15097	1	2	3	4	5	6	7	8	9	10	11																	
22/08/1949	IPSWICH TOWN	H	2	0	17508	1	2	3	4	5	6		8	9	10	11	7												ROOST 2				
27/08/1949	NOTTS COUNTY	H	0	3	24794	1	2	3	4	5	6	7	8	9	10	11																	
30/08/1949	IPSWICH TOWN	A	1	3	12708	1	2	3	4	5	6		8	9	10	11	7												WATLING				
03/09/1949	SOUTHEND UNITED	A	1	3	13000	1	2	3	4	5		7	8	9	10	11		6											ROOST				
05/09/1949	READING	H	2	1	12969	1	2	3	4	5			8	9		11	7	6	10										JAMES	WATLING			
10/09/1949	BRISTOL CITY	H	2	3	34463	1	2	3	4	5			8	9		11	7	6	10										ROOST	HODGES			
17/09/1949	BOURNEMOUTH	H	0	0	18548	1	2	3	4	5			8	9		11	7	6	10														
24/09/1949	CRYSTAL PALACE	A	0	1	15466	1	2	3	4	5			8			11	7	6		9	10												
01/10/1949	WATFORD	H	0	2	14906	1	2	3	4	5			8			11	7	6		9	10												
08/10/1949	BRIGHTON & HOVE ALBION	A	2	1	16031	1	2	3	4	5			8			11	7	6	10	9									JAMES	BUSH			
15/10/1949	WALSALL	H	1	1	14185	1	2	3	4	5			8			11	7	6	10	9									JAMES				
22/10/1949	MILLWALL	A	1	0	19066	1	2	3	4	5			8			11	7	6	10	9									WATLING				
29/10/1949	SWINDON TOWN	H	2	0	17259	1	2	3	4	5			8			11	7	6	10	9									LAMBDEN	JAMES			
05/11/1949	TORQUAY UNITED	A	0	1	7567	1	2	3	4	5			8			11	7	6	10	9													
12/11/1949	ALDERSHOT	H	2	1	12800	1	2	3	4	5		7	8			11		6	10	9									PETHERBRIDGE	HODGES			
19/11/1949	NOTTINGHAM FOREST	A	0	2	22540	1	2	3	4	5		7	8			11		6	10	9													
03/12/1949	NORWICH CITY	A	0	4	19207	1	2	3	4	5		11	8	9			7	6	10														
17/12/1949	PORT VALE	H	2	1	9890	1	2	3	4	5		7		9	10	11		6		8									PETHERBRIDGE	WATLING			
24/12/1949	NOTTS COUNTY	A	0	2	31995	1	2	3	4	5		7		9	10	11		6		8													
26/12/1949	LEYTON ORIENT	A	0	1	11761	1	2	3	4	5		7		9	10	11		6		8													
27/12/1949	LEYTON ORIENT	H	3	0	19566	1	2	3	4	5		7	8	9	10	11		6											HODGES	ROOST 2			
31/12/1949	SOUTHEND UNITED	H	1	1	15406	1	2	3	4	5		7	8	9	10	11		6											ROOST				
14/01/1950	BRISTOL CITY	A	2	1	33697	1	2	3	4	5		7		9	10	11		6	8										ROOST	JAMES			
21/01/1950	BOURNEMOUTH	A	2	0	12211	1	2	3	4	5		7		9	10	11		6	8										MORGAN	WATLING			
04/02/1950	CRYSTAL PALACE	H	0	0	17259	1	2	3	4	5		7		10			11	6	8	9													
20/02/1950	WATFORD	A	2	0	14591		2	3	4	5				10		11	7	6		9	8	1							BRADFORD	LAMBDEN			
27/02/1950	BRIGHTON & HOVE ALBION	H	3	0	13149		2	3	4	5				10		11	7	6		9	8	1							McCOURT	LAMBDEN 2			
04/03/1950	WALSALL	A	1	3	9179		2	3	4	5		7		10			11	6		9	8	1							LAMBDEN				
11/03/1950	MILLWALL	H	3	1	14719		2	3		5		7		10			11	6		9	8	1	4						LAMBDEN	ROOST	WARREN pen		
18/03/1950	SWINDON TOWN	A	0	1	11955		2	3		5		7		10			11			9	8	1	4	6									
25/03/1950	TORQUAY UNITED	H	2	0	18064		2	3	4	5		7		10			11			9	8	1		6					PETHERBRIDGE	JONES			
01/04/1950	ALDERSHOT	A	1	3	7500		2	3	4	5		7		9			11		10		8	1		6					ROOST				
07/04/1950	EXETER CITY	A	0	2	12121	1		3	8	5		11	7	10							9		4	6	2								
08/04/1950	NOTTINGHAM FOREST	H	0	3	16732	1		3	6	5		7		10			11			9	8		4		2								
10/04/1950	EXETER CITY	H	1	0	9698			3	4	5		11							10		8	1		6	2	7	9		BRADFORD				
17/04/1950	NORTHAMPTON TOWN	A	0	2	9622		2	3	4	5		11						6			8	1			10	7	9						
22/04/1950	NORWICH CITY	H	5	1	12631		2	3	4	5		11		9				6			8	1			10	7			PETHERBRIDGE	BRADFORD	ROOST	WATKINS	TIPPETT
24/04/1950	NEWPORT COUNTY	H	3	0	10631		2	3	4	5		11		9				6			8	1			10	7			ROOST 2	TIPPETT			
29/04/1950	NEWPORT COUNTY	A	3	2	8173		2	3	4	5		11	10					6			8	1				7	9		HODGES 2	PARSONS			
01/05/1950	NORTHAMPTON TOWN	H	0	0	11780		2	3	4	5			10					6			8	1				7	9	11					
06/05/1950	READING	A	1	0	9252		2	3	4	5								6			8	1			10	7	9	11	PARSONS				
	APPEARANCES					28	39	42	40	42	4	26	23	28	12	26	22	32	16	20	18	14	4	5	7	7	5	2					
	GOALS					0	0	0	0	1	0	4	5	13	1	5	1	1	5	6	3	0	0	1	1	2	2	0					
	FA CUP																																
26/11/1949	SWINDON TOWN	A	0	1	19640	1	2	3	4	5	6	7	8			11			10	9													
	GLOUCESTERSHIRE CUP																																
13/05/1950	BRISTOL CITY	A	0	2	16560		2	3	4	5						11		6		9	8	1			10	7							

1950/51

Date	Opponent	Venue	F	A	Att.	HOYLE Herbert	BAMFORD Henry	FOX Geoffrey	PITT John	WARREN Raymond	SAMPSON Peter	PETHERBRIDGE George	JAMES Anthony	LAMBDEN Victor	ROOST William	BUSH Bryan	BRADFORD Geoffrey	MURPHY William	MEYER Barrie	MORGAN James	WATLING John	EDWARDS Leslie	WATKINS Barry	GOUGH Claude	Scorers		
	DIVISION 3 SOUTH																										
19/08/1950	SWINDON TOWN	H	1	0	19057	1	2	3	4	5	6	7	8	9	10	11									LAMBDEN		
23/08/1950	ALDERSHOT	A	1	1	8812	1	2	3	4	5	6	7	8	9	10	11									BILLINGTON og		
26/08/1950	COLCHESTER UNITED	A	0	0	13687	1	2	3	4	5	6	7		9	10	11	8										
28/08/1950	ALDERSHOT	H	3	0	10282	1	2	3	4	5	6	7		9	10		8	11							BRADFORD	LAMBDEN	ROOST
02/09/1950	BRISTOL CITY	A	0	1	28168	1	2	3	4	5	6	7		9	10	11	8										
04/09/1950	GILLINGHAM	H	3	0	14414	1	2	3	4	5	6	7		9	10	11	8								LAMBDEN	ROOST	BRADFORD
09/09/1950	CRYSTAL PALACE	H	1	1	16804	1	2	3	4	5	6	7		9	10		8	11							BRADFORD		
13/09/1950	GILLINGHAM	A	0	1	12293	1	2	3	4	5	6	7	8	9	10			11									
16/09/1950	BRIGHTON & HOVE ALBION	A	2	2	11716	1	2	3	4	5	6	7	8	9	10	11									LAMBDEN 2		
23/09/1950	NEWPORT COUNTY	H	1	0	19518	1	2	3	4	5	6	7	8	9	10	11									LAMBDEN		
30/09/1950	NORWICH CITY	A	0	2	22944	1	2	3	4	5	6	7		9	10	11	8										
07/10/1950	BOURNEMOUTH	H	2	0	18074	1	2	3	4	5	6	7		9	10	11			8						MEYER	LAMBDEN	
14/10/1950	EXETER CITY	A	2	0	11000	1	2	3	4	5	6	7		9	10	11			8						LAMBDEN	ROOST	
21/10/1950	SOUTHEND UNITED	H	4	1	19614	1	2	3	4	5	6	7		9	10	11	8								PETHERBRIDGE	LAMBDEN	ROOST 2
28/10/1950	READING	A	0	0	16092	1	2	3	4	5	6	7		9	10	11	8										
04/11/1950	PLYMOUTH ARGYLE	H	3	1	29654	1	2	3	4	5	6	7		9	10	11	8								PETHERBRIDGE	BRADFORD	LAMBDEN
11/11/1950	IPSWICH TOWN	A	3	2	15000	1	2	3	4	5	6	7		9	10	11	8								PETHERBRIDGE 2	BRADFORD	
18/11/1950	LEYTON ORIENT	H	2	1	15003	1	2	3	4	5	6	7		9	10	11	8								PETHERBRIDGE	BRADFORD	
16/12/1950	SWINDON TOWN	A	2	1	7030	1	2	3	4	5	6	7		9			8			10	11				MORGAN	PITT	
23/12/1950	COLCHESTER UNITED	H	1	1	14341	1	2	3	4	5	6	7		9	10		8				11				PETHERBRIDGE		
25/12/1950	PORT VALE	A	0	0	13250	1	2	3	4	5	6			7	9		8			10	11						
26/12/1950	PORT VALE	H	2	0	22409	1	2	3	4	5	6	7		9	10		8				11				BRADFORD	ROOST	
30/12/1950	BRISTOL CITY	H	2	1	31518	1	2	3	4	5	6	7		9	10		8				11				LAMBDEN 2		
13/01/1951	CRYSTAL PALACE	A	0	1	10632	1	2	3	4	5	6	7		9	10		8				11						
17/01/1951	TORQUAY UNITED	A	2	1	3918	1	2	3	4	5	6	7		9	10		8				11				ROOST	McGUINNESS og	
20/01/1951	BRIGHTON & HOVE ALBION	H	3	2	17121	1	2	3	4	5	6	7		9	10		8				11				LAMBDEN	WATLING	WARREN
31/01/1951	TORQUAY UNITED	H	1	1	10662	1	2	3	4	5	6	7		9	10		8				11				BRADFORD		
03/02/1951	NEWPORT COUNTY	A	1	2	15000	1	2	3	4	5	6	7		9	10		8				11				BAMFORD		
17/02/1951	WALSALL	A	2	1	4000	1	2	3		5	6			9		7	8			10	11	4			MORGAN	BRADFORD	
03/03/1951	EXETER CITY	H	3	1	25294	1	2	3	4	5	6			9	10	7	8				11				BRADFORD	LAMBDEN	WARREN pen
10/03/1951	SOUTHEND UNITED	A	1	1	12000	1	2	3	4	5	6			9	10	7	8				11				BRADFORD		
14/03/1951	BOURNEMOUTH	A	0	2	9177	1	2	3	4	5	6			9	10	7	8				11						
17/03/1951	READING	H	4	0	20803	1	2	3	4	5	6			9	10	7	8				11				BUSH	BRADFORD	LAMBDEN 2
24/03/1951	PLYMOUTH ARGYLE	A	0	0	21066	1	2	3	4	5	6	7		9	10		8				11						
26/03/1951	NOTTINGHAM FOREST	A	1	2	27157	1	2	3	4	5	6	7		9	10		8				11				LAMBDEN		
31/03/1951	IPSWICH TOWN	H	1	1	16885	1	2	3	4	5	6	7		9	10		8				11				SAMPSON		
07/04/1951	LEYTON ORIENT	A	0	1	8000	1	2	3	4	5	6	11		9		7	8			10							
11/04/1951	MILLWALL	A	0	1	10485	1	2	3	4	5	6			9	10	7	8				11						
14/04/1951	WALSALL	H	1	1	13806	1	2	3	4	5	6	7		9	10		8				11				WATLING		
19/04/1951	NORTHAMPTON TOWN	A	1	1	6796	1	2		4	5	6	7		9	10		8				11		3		WATLING		
21/04/1951	WATFORD	A	0	1	6000	1	2		4	5	6	7		9	10	8					11		3				
23/04/1951	WATFORD	H	3	0	10700	1	2		4	5	6			9	10	7	8				11		3		BRADFORD 2	WARREN	
28/04/1951	MILLWALL	H	1	0	11782	1	2		4	5	6			9	10	7	8				11		3		LAMBDEN		
30/04/1951	NORWICH CITY	H	3	3	12957	1	2			5	6	11		9	10	7	8					4	3		WARREN pen	LAMBDEN	BRADFORD
03/05/1951	NOTTINGHAM FOREST	H	0	2	28355	1	2		4	5	6	11		9	10	7	8						3				
05/05/1951	NORTHAMPTON TOWN	H	1	1	10832	1		3	8	5	6			9	10	7					11	4	2		LAMBDEN		
	APPEARANCES					46	45	40	44	46	46	36	5	46	43	28	37	3	2	4	25	3	7				
	GOALS					0	1	0	1	4	1	6	0	20	7	1	15	0	1	2	3	0	0		OWN GOAL 2		
	FA CUP																										
25/11/1950	LLANELLI	H	1	1	16594	1	2	3	4	5	6	7		9	10	11	8								PETHERBRIDGE		
28/11/1950	LLANELLI	A	1	1	12943	1	2	3	4	5	6	7		9	10	11	8								BUSH		
05/12/1950	LLANELLI	N	3	1	9044	1	2	3	4	5	6	7		9	10	11	8								PITT	PETHERBRIDGE	BRADFORD
09/12/1950	GILLINGHAM	H	2	2	14420	1	2	3	4	5	6	7		9	10	11	8								BUSH	LAMBDEN	
13/12/1950	GILLINGHAM	A	1	1	10642	1	2	3	4	5	6	7		9		11	8							10	GOUGH		
18/12/1950	GILLINGHAM	N	2	1	3924	1	2	3	4	5	6	7		9	10		8				11				BRADFORD	WARREN pen	
10/01/1951	ALDERSHOT	H	5	1	13429	1	2	3	4	5	6	7		9	10		8				11				LAMBDEN 3	ROOST	PETHERBRIDGE
27/01/1951	LUTON TOWN	A	2	1	25586	1	2	3	4	5	6	7		9	10		8				11				LAMBDEN 3	PETHERBRIDGE	
10/02/1951	HULL CITY	H	3	0	31660	1	2	3	4	5	6			9	10	7	8				11				LAMBDEN 3	WATLING 2	
24/02/1951	NEWCASTLE UNITED	A	0	0	62787	1	2	3	4	5	6	7		9	10		8				11						
28/02/1951	NEWCASTLE UNITED	H	1	3	30074	1	2	3	4	5	6			9	10	7	8				11				BRADFORD		
	GLOUCESTERSHIRE CUP FINAL																										
12/05/1951	BRISTOL CITY	H	1	1	16673	1		3	4	5	6	7		9	10	11	8						2		LAMBDEN		

1951/52

Date	Opponent				Att	HOYLE Herbert	WATKINS Barry	FOX Geoffrey	PITT John	WARREN Raymond	SAMPSON Peter	PETHERBRIDGE George	BRADFORD Geoffrey	LAMBDEN Victor	MEYER Barrie	WATLING John	PICKARD Leonard	ROOST William	BUSH Bryan	BAMFORD Henry	MORGAN James	RADFORD Howard	TIPPETT Michael	MICKLEWRIGHT Andrew	TAYLOR Geoffrey	POWELL Kenneth	GREEN Stanley	Scorers			
	DIVISION 3 SOUTH																														
18/08/1951	WALSALL	A	0	1	10798	1	2	3	4	5	6	7	8	9	10	11															
20/08/1951	SWINDON TOWN	H	1	0	24275	1	2	3	4	5	6	7	8	9	10	11												LAMBDEN			
25/08/1951	SHREWSBURY TOWN	H	3	3	20691	1	2	3	4	5	6	7	8	9		11	10											PICKARD	WARREN	LAMBDEN	
29/08/1951	SWINDON TOWN	A	0	0	12425	1	2	3	4	5	6	7	8	9				10	11												
01/09/1951	ALDERSHOT	H	5	1	17510	1	2	3	4	5	6	7	8	9				10	11									LAMBDEN 2	ROOST 2	BRADFORD	
03/09/1951	CRYSTAL PALACE	H	4	0	14467	1	2	3	4	5	6	7	8	9	10				11									LAMBDEN 2	MEYER	BUSH	
08/09/1951	WATFORD	H	0	1	20540	1	2	3	4	5	6	7	8	9	10				11												
12/09/1951	CRYSTAL PALACE	A	1	0	10289	1		3	4	5	6	7	8	9			10		11	2								PETHERBRIDGE			
15/09/1951	BRISTOL CITY	A	1	1	29782	1		3	4	5	6	7	8	9		11		10		2								LAMBDEN			
22/09/1951	PLYMOUTH ARGYLE	A	2	1	25893	1		3	4	5	6	7	8	9		11				2	10							LAMBDEN	WARREN		
29/09/1951	NORWICH CITY	H	1	1	26022	1		3	4	5	6	7	8	9		11		10		2								BRADFORD			
06/10/1951	NORTHAMPTON TOWN	H	2	2	20905	1		3	4	5	6	7	8	9		11		10		2								BRADFORD 2			
13/10/1951	READING	A	2	4	15175	1		3	4	5	6	7	8	9		11		10		2								PETHERBRIDGE	LAMBDEN		
20/10/1951	NEWPORT COUNTY	H	1	1	17493	1		3	4	5	6	7	8	9					11	2	10							LAMBDEN			
27/10/1951	SOUTHEND UNITED	A	1	2	12000		2	3	4	5	6	11	8	9							10	1	7					BRADFORD			
03/11/1951	BOURNEMOUTH	H	1	2	17241		2	3	4	5	6	7		9		11		8			10	1						ROOST			
10/11/1951	MILLWALL	A	1	1	23988	1		3	4	5	6	7	10	9		11		8		2								BRADFORD			
17/11/1951	BRIGHTON & HOVE ALBION	H	5	0	18002	1		3	4	5	6	7	10	9		11		8		2								LAMBDEN 2	BRADFORD	WARREN pen	ROOST
01/12/1951	TORQUAY UNITED	H	5	0	19338	1		3	4	5	6	7	10	9		11		8		2								PETHERBRIDGE 4	LAMBDEN		
08/12/1951	IPSWICH TOWN	A	2	1	9546	1		3	4	5	6	7	10	9		11		8		2								PETHERBRIDGE	ROOST		
22/12/1951	SHREWSBURY TOWN	A	1	2	7408	1		3	4	5	6	7	10	9		11		8		2								LAMBDEN			
25/12/1951	PORT VALE	H	4	1	16691	1		3	4	5	6	7	10	9		11		8		2								LAMBDEN 2	PETHERBRIDGE	BRADFORD	
26/12/1951	PORT VALE	A	1	1	16734	1		3	4	5	6	7	8	9					11	2	10							MORGAN			
29/12/1951	ALDERSHOT	A	3	1	6019	1		3	4	5	6	7	8	9					11	2	10							PITT	BRADFORD	LAMBDEN	
05/01/1952	WATFORD	A	3	0	10664	1		3	4	5	6	7	10	9				8		2	11							LAMBDEN	BRADFORD	MORGAN	
12/01/1952	EXETER CITY	A	1	0	7088	1		3	4	5	6	7	10	9				8	11	2								SAMPSON			
19/01/1952	BRISTOL CITY	H	2	0	34612	1		3	4	5	6	7	10	9				8	11	2								BRADFORD	PETHERBRIDGE		
26/01/1952	PLYMOUTH ARGYLE	H	1	2	28937	1		3	4	5	6	7	10	9				8		2	11							BRADFORD			
07/02/1952	LEYTON ORIENT	A	3	3	10000		8	3	4	5	6	7	10			11	9			2		1						BRADFORD 2	DEVERALL og		
09/02/1952	NORWICH CITY	A	0	1	16420	1		3	4	5	6	7	10		8	11	9			2											
16/02/1952	NORTHAMPTON TOWN	A	0	2	11704	1		3	4	5	6	7	10	9		11				2				8							
27/02/1952	LEYTON ORIENT	H	1	0	7663			3	4	5	6	7	10	9		11		8		2		1						BRADFORD			
01/03/1952	READING	H	1	2	21915	1		3	4	5	6	7	10	9		11		8		2								LAMBDEN			
08/03/1952	NEWPORT COUNTY	A	2	2	18000			3	4	5	6	7	10	9		11				2		1		8				WATLING	PETHERBRIDGE		
15/03/1952	SOUTHEND UNITED	H	2	0	14496			3	4	5	6	7	10	9		11				2		1		8				PETHERBRIDGE	LAMBDEN		
22/03/1952	BOURNEMOUTH	A	0	1	10239			3	4	5	6	7	10	9				8		2		1			11						
29/03/1952	MILLWALL	H	2	1	4666			3	4	5	6	7	10	9				8		2		1			11			BRADFORD	PETHERBRIDGE		
05/04/1952	BRIGHTON & HOVE ALBION	A	1	1	14268			3	4	5	6	7	10	9				8		2		1			11			LAMBDEN			
11/04/1952	COLCHESTER UNITED	A	1	2	12440			3	4		6	7	10	9		11		8		2		1				5		BRADFORD			
12/04/1952	GILLINGHAM	H	5	0	12877			3	4		6	7	10	9		11		8		2		1				5		PETHERBRIDGE	LAMBDEN	BRADFORD	ROOST 2
14/04/1952	COLCHESTER UNITED	H	6	0	10594			3	4		6	7	10	9		11		8		2		1				5		LAMBDEN 4	BRADFORD 2		
19/04/1952	TORQUAY UNITED	A	2	4	8259			3	4		6	7	10	9		11		8		2		1					5	BRADFORD 2			
23/04/1952	GILLINGHAM	A	1	2	9000			3	4		6	7	10	9		11		8		2		1				5		BRADFORD			
26/04/1952	IPSWICH TOWN	H	1	0	12089			3	4	5	6	7	10	9		11				2		1		8				LAMBDEN			
28/04/1952	WALSALL	H	5	1	9213		2	3	4	5	6	7	10	9		11						1		8				BRADFORD 2	PETHERBRIDGE	MICKLEWRIGHT	LAMBDEN
01/05/1952	EXETER CITY	H	2	2	9023			3	4	5	6	7	10	9		11				2		1		8				LAMBDEN	BRADFORD		
	APPEARANCES					29	11	46	46	41	46	46	45	44	5	30	4	27	10	36	8	17	1	6	3	4	1				
	GOALS					0	0	0	1	3	1	14	26	29	1	1	1	7	1	0	2	0	0	1	0	0	0	OWN GOAL 1			
	FA CUP																														
24/11/1951	KETTERING TOWN	H	3	1	18062	1		3	4	5	6	7	10	9		11		8		2								LAMBDEN 2	BRADFORD		
15/12/1951	WEYMOUTH	H	2	0	27808	1		3	4	5	6	7	10	9		11		8		2								LAMBDEN	PETHERBRIDGE		
12/01/1952	PRESTON NORTH END	H	2	0	30681	1		3	4	5	6	7	10	9				8	11	2								LAMBDEN	BRADFORD		
02/02/1952	SOUTHEND UNITED	A	1	2	22424	1		3	4	5	6	7	10	9		11		8		2								BRADFORD			
	GLOUCESTERSHIRE CUP																														
10/05/1951	BRISTOL CITY	A	1	2	16214		2	3	4	5	6	7	10	9		11		8				1						PETHERBRIDGE			

1952/53

Date	Opponent	H/A	F	A	Att	HOYLE Herbert	BAMFORD Henry	FOX Geoffrey	PITT John	WARREN Raymond	SAMPSON Peter	McILVENNY John	LEONARD Patrick	LAMBDEN Victor	BRADFORD Geoffrey	PETHERBRIDGE George	JONES Desmond	MICKLEWRIGHT Andrew	BUSH Bryan	WATLING John	ROOST William	RADFORD Howard	ANDERSON Robert	ALLCOCK Frank	Scorers				
	DIVISION 3 SOUTH																												
23/08/1952	SHREWSBURY TOWN	H	2	1	24139	1	2	3	4	5	6	7	8	9	10	11									LAMBDEN	WARREN			
27/08/1952	TORQUAY UNITED	A	0	1	10179	1	2	3	4	5	6			9	10	11	7	8											
30/08/1952	WALSALL	A	5	3	8023	1	2	3	4	5	6			9	10	11	7		8						BRADFORD	LAMBDEN 2	BUSH 2		
01/09/1952	TORQUAY UNITED	H	3	0	19248	1	2	3	4	5	6			9	10	11	7		8						BRADFORD 3				
06/09/1952	GILLINGHAM	H	3	1	20254	1	2	3	4	5	6			9	10	11	7		8						BRADFORD	PETHERBRIDGE	LAMBDEN		
11/09/1952	COLCHESTER UNITED	A	3	0	8960	1	2	3	4	5	6			9	10	11	7		8						BUSH	LAMBDEN	PETHERBRIDGE		
13/09/1952	MILLWALL	A	0	3	22622	1	2	3	4	5	6			9	10	11	7		8										
15/09/1952	COLCHESTER UNITED	H	3	1	17536	1	2	3	4	5	6	7		9	10	11			8						LAMBDEN	PETHERBRIDGE	BRADFORD		
20/09/1952	BRISTOL CITY	H	0	0	29880	1	2	3	4	5	6	7		9	10	11			8										
25/09/1952	WATFORD	A	3	2	13178	1	2	3	4	5	6	7		9	10	11			8						LAMBDEN	BUSH	PETHERBRIDGE		
27/09/1952	EXETER CITY	H	0	0	23373	1	2	3	4	5	6	7		9	10	11			8										
29/09/1952	NORWICH CITY	H	3	1	22847	1	2	3	4	5	6	7	8	9	10	11									LAMBDEN	BRADFORD 2			
04/10/1952	COVENTRY CITY	A	1	1	19052	1	2	3	4	5	6	7		9	10	11			8						BUSH				
11/10/1952	NORTHAMPTON TOWN	A	2	2	19043	1	2	3	4	5	6	7		9	10	11			8						BUSH	BRADFORD			
18/10/1952	LEYTON ORIENT	H	2	1	24194	1	2	3	4	5	6	7		9	10	11			8						McILVENNY	LAMBDEN			
25/10/1952	IPSWICH TOWN	A	5	1	14839	1	2	3	4	5	6	7		9	10	11			8						BUSH	LAMBDEN	BRADFORD 2	PETHERBRIDGE	
01/11/1952	READING	H	4	0	26858	1	2	3	4	5	6	7		9	10				8	11					McILVENNY	BRADFORD	LAMBDEN	WARREN	
08/11/1952	BOURNEMOUTH	A	2	1	18632	1	2	3	4	5	6	7		9	10	11			8						PETHERBRIDGE	BUSH			
15/11/1952	SOUTHEND UNITED	H	2	1	20227	1	2	3	4	5	6	7		9	10	11			8						LAMBDEN	BRADFORD			
29/11/1952	BRIGHTON & HOVE ALBION	H	7	0	11647	1	2	3	4	5	6	7		9	10	11					8				PETHERBRIDGE 2	ROOST 2	LAMBDEN	BRADFORD	FOX og
13/12/1952	CRYSTAL PALACE	H	2	0	20042	1	2	3	4	5	6	7		9	10				11		8				BRADFORD	LAMBDEN			
20/12/1952	SHREWSBURY TOWN	A	1	0	8810	1	2	3	4	5	6	7		9	10				11		8				BUSH				
26/12/1952	QUEENS PARK RANGERS	A	1	0	13866	1	2	3	4	5	6	7		9	10				8		11				BRADFORD				
27/12/1952	QUEENS PARK RANGERS	H	2	1	30995	1	2	3	4	5	6	7		9	10				8		11				LAMBDEN 2				
03/01/1953	WALSALL	H	2	0	24171	1	2	3	4	5	6	7	8	9	10				11						BRADFORD	BUSH			
17/01/1953	GILLINGHAM	A	4	0	16600	1	2	3	4	5	6	7		9	10				11		8				BRADFORD	BUSH	FOX	LEWIN og	
24/01/1953	MILLWALL	H	1	1	31035	1	2	3	4	5	6	7		9	10	11					8				BRADFORD				
31/01/1953	ALDERSHOT	H	4	1	18263	1	2	3	4	5	6	7		9	10	11			8						LAMBDEN 2	BRADFORD 2			
07/02/1953	BRISTOL CITY	A	0	0	35372	1	2	3	4	5	6	7		9	10	11			8										
14/02/1953	EXETER CITY	A	0	0	13113		2	3	4	5	6	7		9	10	11			8			1							
21/02/1953	COVENTRY CITY	H	5	2	28614		2	3	4	5	6	7		9	10	11			8			1			LAMBDEN 2	PETHERBRIDGE	BRADFORD 2		
28/02/1953	NORTHAMPTON TOWN	H	1	1	31115		2	3	4	5	6	7		9	10	11			8			1			BRADFORD				
07/03/1953	LEYTON ORIENT	A	3	3	16136		2	3	4	5	6	7		9	10	11			8			1			McILVENNY	LAMBDEN 2			
14/03/1953	IPSWICH TOWN	H	3	0	21244		2	3	4	5	6	7	8	9	10	11						1			PETHERBRIDGE	BRADFORD	BAMFORD		
21/03/1953	READING	A	0	2	17789		2	3	4	5	6	7		9	10	11			8			1							
28/03/1953	BOURNEMOUTH	H	2	1	16065		2	3	4	5	6	7		9	10	11			8			1			LAMBDEN	BUSH			
03/04/1953	SWINDON TOWN	A	3	1	24559		2	3	4	5	6			9	10	7			11		8	1			BATCHELOR og	BRADFORD 2			
04/04/1953	SOUTHEND UNITED	A	1	2	16010		2	3	4	5	6			9	10	7			11		8	1			BRADFORD				
06/04/1953	SWINDON TOWN	H	1	2	24406		2	3	4	5	6	7		9	10	11			8			1			BRADFORD				
11/04/1953	WATFORD	H	0	3	22614		2	3	4	5	6	7		9	10	11			8				1						
13/04/1953	NEWPORT COUNTY	A	2	2	16007		2	3	4	5	6	7	8	9	10	11							1		LAMBDEN	BRADFORD			
18/04/1953	BRIGHTON & HOVE ALBION	A	1	2	22800		2	3	4	5	6	7	8	9	10	11							1		LEONARD				
22/04/1953	NORWICH CITY	A	0	0	30548		2	3	4	5	6			9	10	7				11	8		1						
25/04/1953	NEWPORT COUNTY	H	3	1	29451		2	3	4	5	6			9	10	7				11	8		1		BRADFORD 3				
29/04/1953	ALDERSHOT	A	0	0	7593		2	3	4	5	6			9	10	7				11	8		1						
01/05/1953	CRYSTAL PALACE	A	0	1	5712		2	3	4	5	6			9		7			8	11	10		1						
	APPEARANCES					29	46	46	46	46	46	34	6	46	45	39	6	1	35	5	13	10	7						
	GOALS					0	1	1	0	2	0	3	1	24	33	10	0	0	12	0	2	0	0		OWN GOAL 3				
	FA CUP																												
22/11/1952	LEYTON ORIENT	A	1	1	10700	1	2	3	4	5	6			9	10	7				11	8				BRADFORD				
24/11/1952	LEYTON ORIENT	H	1	0	15032	1	2	3	4	5	6			9	10	7				11	8				ROOST				
06/12/1952	PETERBOROUGH UNITED	A	1	0	15280	1	2	3	4	5	6	7		9	10	11					8				LAMBDEN				
10/01/1953	HUDDERSFIELD TOWN	A	0	2	34967	1	2	3	4	5	6		8	9	10				7	11									
	GLOUCESTERSHIRE CUP																												
08/05/1953	BRISTOL CITY	H	0	2	19214	1		3	4	5	6			9	10	7			8	11				2					

1953/54

Date	Opponent				Att	ANDERSON Robert	BAMFORD Henry	FOX Geoffrey	PITT John	WARREN Raymond	SAMPSON Peter	PETHERBRIDGE George	BRADFORD Geoffrey	LAMBDEN Victor	MEYER Barrie	WATLING John	RADFORD Howard	CAIRNEY Charles	ROOST William	BUSH Bryan	LEONARD Patrick	WATKINS Barry	LYONS Michael	McILVENNY John	HALE Denzil	BIGGS Alfred	WILSHIRE Peter	HOOPER Peter	MUIR Ian	CHANDLER Raymond	ALLCOCK Frank	STEEDS Cecil			
	DIVISION 2																																		
20/08/1953	FULHAM	A	4	4	25000	1	2	3	4	5	6	7	8	9	10	11																	BRADFORD 3	FOX	
22/08/1953	BLACKBURN ROVERS	A	1	1	26145		2	3	4	5	6	7	8	9	10	11	1																MEYER		
24/08/1953	DONCASTER ROVERS	H	0	1	28173		2	3	4	5	6	7	8	9	10	11	1																		
29/08/1953	DERBY COUNTY	H	3	0	20046		2	3	4	5	6	7	8	9	10	11	1																PETHERBRIDGE	LAMBDEN	MEYER
02/09/1953	DONCASTER ROVERS	A	0	1	20734		2	3	4	5	6	7	8	9	10	11	1																		
05/09/1953	BRENTFORD	A	3	0	21600		2	3	4	5		7	8	9	10	11	1	6															BRADFORD 3		
07/09/1953	BURY	H	2	0	29002		2	3	4	5		7	8	9	10	11	1	6															PETHERBRIDGE	MASSEY og	
12/09/1953	WEST HAM UNITED	H	2	2	28736		2	3	4	5		7	8	9	10	11	1	6															CAIRNEY	MEYER	
16/09/1953	BURY	A	1	3	11462		2	3	4	5		7	8	9	10	11	1	6															BRADFORD		
19/09/1953	LINCOLN CITY	H	0	1	24650		2	3	4	5	6	7	8	9	10	11	1																		
26/09/1953	NOTTS COUNTY	A	5	1	16318		2	3	4	5	6	7	9			11	1		8	10													BRADFORD 3	ROOST	WATLING
03/10/1953	HULL CITY	H	4	2	25224		2	3	4	5	6	7	9			11	1		8	10													ROOST 2	BRADFORD	WATLING
10/10/1953	LEEDS UNITED	A	3	3	19000		2	3	4	5	6	7	9			11	1		8	10													BRADFORD 2	ROOST	
17/10/1953	BIRMINGHAM CITY	H	1	1	35614		2	3	4	5	6	7	9			11	1			10	8												BRADFORD		
24/10/1953	NOTTINGHAM FOREST	A	1	3	22987		2	3	4	5	6	7	9			11	1			10	8												BUSH pen		
31/10/1953	LUTON TOWN	H	3	3	20002	1	2		4	5	6	7	9			11				10	8	3											BRADFORD 3		
07/11/1953	PLYMOUTH ARGYLE	A	3	3	23784		2		4	5	6	7	9		10	11	1		8			3											PETHERBRIDGE	BRADFORD	MEYER
14/11/1953	SWANSEA TOWN	H	0	1	25692		2	3	4	5	6	7			10	11	1		8				9												
21/11/1953	ROTHERHAM UNITED	A	1	1	13210		2	3	4	5	6				10	11	1		8				9	7									MEYER		
28/11/1953	LEICESTER CITY	H	3	0	26250		2	3	4	5	6				10	11	1		8					7	9								McILVENNY	HALE	MEYER
05/12/1953	STOKE CITY	A	2	3	13177		2	3	4	5	6				10	11	1		8					7	9								McILVENNY	MEYER	
12/12/1953	FULHAM	H	2	1	22885		2	3	4	5	6				10	11	1		8					7	9								HALE	PITT pen	
19/12/1953	BLACKBURN ROVERS	H	1	2	22398		2	3	4	5	6	8				11	1		10					7	9								PITT		
25/12/1953	EVERTON	A	0	4	27484		2	3	4	5	6	7			10	11	1		9		8														
28/12/1953	EVERTON	H	0	0	34015	1	2	3	4	5	6	7			10	11		8	9																
02/01/1954	DERBY COUNTY	A	1	0	16506		2	3	4	5	6	7			10	11	1	8							9								HALE		
16/01/1954	BRENTFORD	H	0	0	20500		2	3	4	5	6	7			8	11	1		10						9										
23/01/1954	WEST HAM UNITED	A	1	1	27250		2	3	4	5	6	7				11	1		10		8				9								HALE		
06/02/1954	LINCOLN CITY	A	2	1	11914		2	3		5	6	7		9		11	1	4							10	8							HALE	LAMBDEN	
13/02/1954	NOTTS COUNTY	H	1	1	20767		2	3	4	5	6	7		9		11	1								10	8							HALE		
27/02/1954	LEEDS UNITED	H	1	1	26772		2	3	4	5	6	7				11	1								10	8	9						HALE		
06/03/1954	BIRMINGHAM CITY	A	1	1	25300		2	3	4	5	6					11	1				10			7	9	8							LEONARD		
13/03/1954	NOTTINGHAM FOREST	H	1	0	21753		2	3	4	5	6					11	1				10			7	9	8							HALE		
20/03/1954	LUTON TOWN	A	1	1	12915		2	3	4	5	6					11	1				10			7	9	8							PITT pen		
27/03/1954	ROTHERHAM UNITED	H	1	0	19668		2	3	4	5	6	7			10		1								9	8		11					HALE		
03/04/1954	LEICESTER CITY	A	0	1	27368		2	3	4	5	6	7		9		11	1		8						10										
10/04/1954	PLYMOUTH ARGYLE	H	3	1	23799		2	3	4	5	6	11			10		1							7	9	8							BIGGS	HALE	MEYER
12/04/1954	HULL CITY	A	1	4	11541		2	3	4		6	11			10		1							7	9	8			5				HALE		
16/04/1954	OLDHAM ATHLETIC	H	1	0	21139		2	3		5	6	7			10			4							9	8		11		1			PETHERBRIDGE		
17/04/1954	SWANSEA TOWN	A	1	3	21753		2	3	4	5	6	7			10										9	8		11		1			HALE		
19/04/1954	OLDHAM ATHLETIC	A	0	0	11961			3	4	5	6	11		9	8			10								7				1	2				
24/04/1954	STOKE CITY	H	3	2	22687			3	4	5	6	7	8	9	10													11		1	2		BRADFORD 3		
	APPEARANCES					3	40	40	40	41	38	35	18	15	27	35	35	9	15	6	8	2	2	10	19	12	1	4	1	4	2				
	GOALS					0	0	1	3	0	0	4	21	2	8	2	0	1	4	1	1	0	0	2	12	1	0	0	0	0	0		OWN GOAL 1		
	FA CUP																																		
09/01/1954	BLACKBURN ROVERS	H	0	1	25017		2	3	4	5	6	7				11	1	8							9							10			
	GLOUCESTERSHIRE CUP																																		
03/05/1954	BRISTOL CITY	A	2	2	13668	1		3		5	6	11			8			4	10					7	9						2		WARREN	MEYER	

1954/55

						RADFORD Howard	BAMFORD Henry	FOX Geoffrey	PITT John	WARREN Raymond	SAMPSON Peter	PETHERBRIDGE George	BIGGS Alfred	BRADFORD Geoffrey	MEYER Barrie	HOOPER Peter	HALE Denzil	ROOST William	EDWARDS Leslie	ANDERSON James	MUIR Ian	WATKINS Barry	ALLCOCK Frank	CAIRNEY Charles	WATLING John	McILVENNY John	LAMBDEN Victor	BUSH Bryan	CHANDLER Raymond	WARD David					
	DIVISION 2																																		
21/08/1954	PORT VALE	H	1	0	32367	1	2	3	4	5	6	7	8	9	10	11															BRADFORD				
25/08/1954	BIRMINGHAM CITY	A	1	2	26000	1	2	3	4	5	6	7		9	10	11	8														BRADFORD				
28/08/1954	DONCASTER ROVERS	A	2	2	16399	1	2	3	4	5	6	7		8	10	11	9														BRADFORD	PITT			
30/08/1954	BIRMINGHAM CITY	H	1	1	26191	1	2	3	4	5	6	7		8		11	10	9													BRADFORD				
04/09/1954	DERBY COUNTY	H	4	1	23500	1	2		4	5	6	7		9		11	8	10	3												BRADFORD 3	HOOPER			
06/09/1954	LIVERPOOL	H	3	0	25574	1	2		4	5	6	7		9		11	8	10	3												BRADFORD 3				
11/09/1954	WEST HAM UNITED	A	2	5	22500	1	2		4	5	6	7		9		11	8	10	3												ROOST 2				
15/09/1954	LIVERPOOL	A	3	5	31100	1	2		4	5		7		9		11	8	10	3	6											HOOPER 2	BAMFORD			
18/09/1954	BLACKBURN ROVERS	H	2	1	26690	1	2		4			7		9		11	8	10	3	6	5										ROOST 2				
25/09/1954	FULHAM	A	3	2	31648	1	2		4			7		9	8	11		10		6	5	3									MEYER 2	BRADFORD			
02/10/1954	SWANSEA TOWN	H	7	0	28731	1	2		4			7		8	9	11		10		6	5	3									BRADFORD 2	HOOPER 2	ROOST	CHARLES og	BURGESS og
09/10/1954	LUTON TOWN	H	3	2	30654	1	2		4			7		8	9	11		10		6	5	3									BRADFORD 2	MEYER			
16/10/1954	ROTHERHAM UNITED	A	2	6	17478	1	2		4			7		8	9	11		10		6	5	3									BRADFORD 2				
23/10/1954	LEEDS UNITED	H	5	1	24568	1	2		4	5		7		8	9	11		10		6		3									MEYER 2	BRADFORD 2	HOOPER		
30/10/1954	BURY	A	1	3	15373	1	2		4	5		7		8	9	11		10		6		3									MEYER				
06/11/1954	LINCOLN CITY	H	2	2	22102	1	2		4	5		7		8		11	9	10		6		3									PETHERBRIDGE	HOOPER			
13/11/1954	HULL CITY	A	1	0	19023	1	2		4	5		7		8	9			10					3	6	11						BRADFORD				
20/11/1954	IPSWICH TOWN	H	4	0	20012	1	2		4	5		7		8	9			10					3	6	11						PETHERBRIDGE 2	BRADFORD	MEYER		
27/11/1954	NOTTINGHAM FOREST	A	0	1	13623	1	2		4	5		7		8		11	9	10		6			3												
04/12/1954	STOKE CITY	H	1	1	21240	1	2		4	5		7	8	10	9	11				6			3								BIGGS				
11/12/1954	MIDDLESBROUGH	A	0	1	21051	1	2		4	5		11		10				8		6			3			7	9								
18/12/1954	PORT VALE	A	0	1	16434	1	2		4	5				10				8		6			3		11	7	9								
25/12/1954	NOTTS COUNTY	A	0	2	19647	1	2		4	5		7		10	9	11		8			6		3												
27/12/1954	NOTTS COUNTY	H	1	4	28855	1	2		4			7		10		11		8		6	5		3				9				LAMBDEN				
01/01/1955	DONCASTER ROVERS	H	1	0	19153	1	2	3	4	5		7		10				8						6	11		9				BRADFORD				
22/01/1955	WEST HAM UNITED	H	2	4	27552	1	2	3	4	5		7		10				8						6	11		9				BRADFORD	LAMBDEN			
05/02/1955	BLACKBURN ROVERS	A	3	8	24600	1		3	4	5		7						10					2	6	11		9	8			LAMBDEN 2	ROOST			
12/02/1955	FULHAM	H	4	1	19311	1	2		4	5	6	7		8		11		10					3				9				LAMBDEN 2	PETHERBRIDGE	ROOST		
19/02/1955	DERBY COUNTY	A	1	1	11000	1	2		4	5	6	7		8		11		10					3				9				PETHERBRIDGE				
05/03/1955	ROTHERHAM UNITED	H	1	0	19739	1	2		4	5	6	7		8		11		10					3				9				HOOPER				
12/03/1955	LEEDS UNITED	A	0	2	16922	1	2		4	5	6	7	11	8				10					3				9								
19/03/1955	BURY	H	2	1	17675	1	2		4	5	6	11		8	9			10					3			7					BRADFORD	MEYER			
26/03/1955	LINCOLN CITY	A	2	0	6456	1	2		4	5	6		8	9				10					3		11	7					BRADFORD	BAMFORD			
31/03/1955	SWANSEA TOWN	A	1	1	17804	1	2		4	5	6		8	9				10					3		11	7					WATLING				
02/04/1955	HULL CITY	H	1	0	17168		2		4	5	6		8	9	10								3		11	7			1		WATLING				
08/04/1955	PLYMOUTH ARGYLE	H	3	1	26010		2		4		6	7	8	9	10						5		3		11				1		BIGGS 2	BRADFORD			
09/04/1955	IPSWICH TOWN	A	0	1	16186		2		4	5	6	7	8	10									3		11		9		1						
11/04/1955	PLYMOUTH ARGYLE	A	1	0	26134		2		4	5	6	7	8	10									3		11		9		1		LAMBDEN				
16/04/1955	NOTTINGHAM FOREST	H	2	1	3E+05			3	4		6	7	8		9	11					5		2						1	10	BIGGS	MEYER			
23/04/1955	STOKE CITY	A	0	2	16694		2		4	5	6	7	8	9	10								3		11				1						
27/04/1955	LUTON TOWN	A	0	2	20097		2		4	5	6	7	8		10			9					3		11				1						
30/04/1955	MIDDLESBROUGH	H	2	2	14707		2		4	5	6		7	9	10	11		8					3						1		MEYER	HOOPER			
	APPEARANCES					34	40	8	42	34	22	37	13	39	20	25	10	32	5	14	9	7	24	5	14	6	12	1	8	1					
	GOALS					0	2	0	1	0	0	5	4	26	10	9	0	7	0	0	0	0	0	0	2	0	7	0	0	0	OWN GOAL 2				
	FA CUP																																		
08/01/1955	PORTSMOUTH	H	2	1	35921	1	2	3	4	5		7		10				8						6	11		9				BRADFORD	ROOST			
29/01/1955	CHELSEA	H	1	3	35972	1	2	3	4	5		7		10				8						6	11		9				PITT pen				
	GLOUCESTERSHIRE CUP																																		
02/05/1955	BRISTOL CITY	H	2	1	20097	1	2	3	4	5	6	7	8	9				10							11						WARREN	PEACOCK og			

1955/56

Date					Att	RADFORD Howard	BAMFORD Henry	ALLCOCK Frank	PITT John	WARREN Raymond	SAMPSON Peter	PETHERBRIDGE George	BIGGS Alfred	MEYER Barrie	BRADFORD Geoffrey	WATLING John	MUIR Ian	ROOST William	WARD David	HOOPER Peter	HALE Denzil	McILVENNY John	NICHOLLS Ronald	ANDERSON James	SEATHERTON Raymond	EDWARDS Leslie	SYKES Norman				
	DIVISION 2																														
20/08/1955	PORT VALE	A	1	1	21270	1	2	3	4	5	6	7	8	9	10	11												MEYER			
22/08/1955	STOKE CITY	H	4	2	21103	1	2	3	4	5	6	7	8	9	10	11												BRADFORD	PETHERBRIDGE	PITT	MEYER
27/08/1955	DONCASTER ROVERS	H	4	2	23000	1	2	3	4	5	6	7	8	9	10	11												BRADFORD 2	PETHERBRIDGE	MEYER	
29/08/1955	STOKE CITY	A	2	1	18875	1	2	3	4	5	6	7	8	9	10	11												BRADFORD 2			
03/09/1955	SHEFFIELD WEDNESDAY	A	2	4	30526	1	2	3	4	5	6	7	8	9	10	11												BRADFORD	WATLING		
07/09/1955	LIVERPOOL	A	2	0	38320	1	2	3	4		6	7	8	9	10	11	5											BIGGS	BRADFORD		
10/09/1955	NOTTINGHAM FOREST	H	4	1	25875	1	2	3	4		6	7	8	9	10	11	5											BRADFORD 2	BIGGS 2		
17/09/1955	HULL CITY	A	2	1	14014	1	2	3	4		6	7	8	9	10	11	5											BRADFORD 2			
24/09/1955	BLACKBURN ROVERS	H	1	0	29489	1	2	3	4	5	6	7	8	9	10	11												SAMPSON			
01/10/1955	LINCOLN CITY	A	0	2	15076	1	2	3	4	5	6	7	8	9		11		10													
08/10/1955	ROTHERHAM UNITED	A	0	1	12221	1	2	3	4	5	6	7		9	10				8	11											
15/10/1955	SWANSEA TOWN	H	1	2	30122	1	2	3	4	5	6	7		9	10				8	11								BRADFORD			
22/10/1955	BRISTOL CITY	A	1	1	37797	1	2	3	4	5	6	7		9	10				8	11								MEYER			
29/10/1955	LEEDS UNITED	H	4	1	25574	1	2	3	4		6	7		9	10		5		8	11								BRADFORD 2	MEYER	WARD	
05/11/1955	FULHAM	A	5	3	29574	1	2	3	4		6	7		9	10		5		8	11								MEYER 3	BRADFORD	WARD	
12/11/1955	BURY	H	4	2	23145	1	2	3	4		6	7		9	10		5		8	11								MEYER 2	BRADFORD	WARD	
19/11/1955	BARNSLEY	A	3	4	11625	1	2	3	4		6	7		9	10		5		8	11								BRADFORD 2	MEYER		
26/11/1955	MIDDLESBROUGH	H	7	2	23728	1	2	3	4		6	7		9	10		5		8	11								PETHERBRIDGE	BRADFORD 2	HOOPER 2	WARD
03/12/1955	NOTTS COUNTY	A	2	5	15525	1	2	3	4		6	7		9	10		5		8	11								WARD	HOOPER pen		
10/12/1955	WEST HAM UNITED	H	1	1	20708	1	2	3	4		6	7		9	10		5		8	11								WARD			
17/12/1955	PORT VALE	H	1	2	19129	1	2	3	4	5	6	7		9	10				8	11								PETHERBRIDGE			
24/12/1955	DONCASTER ROVERS	A	1	2	12083	1	2	3	4		6		8		9				10	11	5	7						BIGGS			
26/12/1955	LEICESTER CITY	H	2	1	21652	1	2	3	4		6	7	8	10	9	11					5							BIGGS	MEYER		
27/12/1955	LEICESTER CITY	A	2	4	35000	1	2	3	4		6	7	11	10	9				8		5							BRADFORD	MEYER		
31/12/1955	SHEFFIELD WEDNESDAY	H	4	2	30887		2	3	4		6	7	8	10	9					11	5		1					BIGGS 2	BRADFORD	MEYER	
14/01/1956	NOTTINGHAM FOREST	A	1	1	12291		2	3			6	7	8	10	9					11	5		1	4				MEYER			
21/01/1956	HULL CITY	H	4	2	23854		2	3	4		6	7	8	10	9					11	5		1					BRADFORD 3	HOOPER		
04/02/1956	BLACKBURN ROVERS	A	0	2	19099		2	3	4		6	7	8	9		11		10			5		1								
11/02/1956	LINCOLN CITY	H	3	0	17649		2	3	4		6	7		10					8	11	5		1		9			SEATHERTON	MEYER	HOOPER pen	
18/02/1956	BARNSLEY	H	1	1	20995		2	3	4		6	11	7	10					8		5		1		9			SEATHERTON			
25/02/1956	SWANSEA TOWN	A	2	1	23528		2	3	4		6	7	8	9		11			10		5		1					MEYER 2			
03/03/1956	BRISTOL CITY	H	0	3	35324		2	3	4		6	7	8	9		11			10		5		1								
10/03/1956	WEST HAM UNITED	A	1	2	20000	1	2	3			4	7	8	9					10	11	5			6				BIGGS			
17/03/1956	FULHAM	H	2	2	21836	1	2				4	7	8	9					10	11	5			6		3		MEYER	WARD		
24/03/1956	BURY	A	1	0	11569	1	2					7	8	9			4		10	11	5			6		3		WARD			
30/03/1956	PLYMOUTH ARGYLE	H	2	1	27814	1	2		4			7	8	9					10	11	5			6		3		WARD 2			
31/03/1956	ROTHERHAM UNITED	H	1	4	23367	1	2		4			7	8	9					10	11	5			6		3		WARD			
02/04/1956	PLYMOUTH ARGYLE	A	1	0	19181	1	2				4	7				11	5	8	10		9			6		3		WARD			
07/04/1956	MIDDLESBROUGH	A	1	0	12536	1	2				4	7		8			5		10	11	9			6		3		WARD			
14/04/1956	NOTTS COUNTY	H	2	0	15505	1	2				4	7	8	9					10	11	5			6		3		MEYER	WARD		
21/04/1956	LEEDS UNITED	A	1	2	49274	1	2		4		6	7	8	9					10	11	5					3		WARD			
28/04/1956	LIVERPOOL	H	1	2	24106	1	2				6	7		8			4	9	10	11	5					3		HOOPER			
	APPEARANCES					34	42	33	34	11	39	41	27	40	26	15	14	4	27	25	21	1	8	9	2	9					
	GOALS					0	0	0	1	0	1	4	8	20	25	1	0	0	16	6	0	0	0	0	2	0					
	FA CUP																														
07/01/1956	MANCHESTER UNITED	H	4	0	35872		2	3	4		6	7	8	10	9					11	5		1					BIGGS 2	MEYER	BRADFORD pen	
28/01/1956	DONCASTER ROVERS	H	1	1	35420		2	3	4		6	7	8	10	9					11	5		1					HOOPER pen			
31/01/1956	DONCASTER ROVERS	A	0	1	22093		2	3	4		6	7	8		9		11		10		5		1								
	GLOUCESTERSHIRE CUP																														
30/04/1956	BRISTOL CITY	A	1	0	11952	1	2				6	7	8	10				9		11	5					3	4	MEYER			

1956/57

Date						RADFORD Howard	BAMFORD Henry	EDWARDS Leslie	PITT John	HALE Denzil	SAMPSON Peter	PETHERBRIDGE George	BIGGS Alfred	BRADFORD Geoffrey	WARD David	HOOPER Peter	LAWRENCE David	MEYER Barrie	NICHOLLS Ronald	ROOST William	WATLING John	McILVENNY John	MUIR Ian	SYKES Norman	ANDERSON James	STEEDS Cecil	RICKETTS Graham	PYLE David				
	DIVISION 2																															
18/08/1956	GRIMSBY TOWN	H	1	0	27818	1	2	3	4	5	6	7	8	9	10	11													WARD			
23/08/1956	LEYTON ORIENT	A	1	1	20173	1	2	3	4	5	6	7	8	9	10	11													BIGGS			
25/08/1956	DONCASTER ROVERS	A	4	2	9314	1	2	3	4	5	6	7	8	9	10	11													BRADFORD 2	WARD	HOOPER	
27/08/1956	LEYTON ORIENT	H	3	2	24776	1	2	3	4	5	6	7	8	9	10	11													BRADFORD 2	WARD		
01/09/1956	STOKE CITY	H	4	0	25430	1	2	3	4	5	6	7	8	9	10	11													HOOPER	BIGGS	BRADFORD	WARD
03/09/1956	HUDDERSFIELD TOWN	A	1	2	14560	1	2	3	4	5	6	7	8	9	10	11													BIGGS			
08/09/1956	MIDDLESBROUGH	A	2	3	19149	1	2		4	5	6	7	8		10	11	3	9											HOOPER	BIGGS		
10/09/1956	HUDDERSFIELD TOWN	H	4	0	27553	1	2		4	5	6	7	8		10	11	3	9											WARD 2	MEYER	BIGGS	
15/09/1956	LEICESTER CITY	H	1	2	28500	1	2		4	5	6	7	8		10	11	3	9											MEYER			
22/09/1956	BRISTOL CITY	A	3	5	36951	1	2		4	5	6	7	8		10	11	3	9											WARD 2	BIGGS		
29/09/1956	NOTTS COUNTY	A	2	0	12720		2	3	4	5	6	7	8		10	11			1	9									WARD	BIGGS		
06/10/1956	SHEFFIELD UNITED	H	3	1	28393		2	3	4	5	6	7	8	9	10	11			1										BRADFORD 2	BIGGS		
13/10/1956	BARNSLEY	A	2	0	15052		2	3	4	5	6	7	8	9	10	11			1										HOOPER	WARD		
20/10/1956	WEST HAM UNITED	H	1	1	24402		2	3	4	5	6	7	8	9		11		10	1										BIGGS			
27/10/1956	ROTHERHAM UNITED	A	0	0	11824		2	3	4	5	6	7	8	9		11		10	1													
03/11/1956	LINCOLN CITY	H	0	1	22322		2	3	4	5	6	7	8	10		11		9	1													
10/11/1956	SWANSEA TOWN	A	3	2	16833		2		4	5	6		8			11		10	1	9	3	7							BIGGS 2	MEYER		
17/11/1956	FULHAM	H	4	0	24658		2		4	5	6		8			11		10	1	9	3	7							BIGGS	ROOST	MEYER	HOOPER
24/11/1956	NOTTINGHAM FOREST	A	1	1	17996		2	3	4	5	6		8			11		10	1	9		7							BIGGS			
01/12/1956	PORT VALE	H	2	1	21308		2	3	4	5	6		8			11		10	1	9		7							ROOST	HOOPER pen		
08/12/1956	BLACKBURN ROVERS	A	0	2	20400		2	3	4	5	6		8			11		10	1	9		7										
15/12/1956	GRIMSBY TOWN	A	2	3	10460		2		4	5	6	7	8	10		11		9	1				3						MEYER 2			
22/12/1956	DONCASTER ROVERS	H	6	1	12186		2		4	5	6	11	7	10	8			9	1		3								MEYER 2	WARD 3	BRADFORD	
25/12/1956	BURY	A	2	7	8962		2	3	4	5	6	7	8		10	11		9	1										PETHERBRIDGE	BIGGS		
26/12/1956	BURY	H	6	1	19672		2	3	4	5	6	7	8			11		9	1					10					HOOPER 3	MEYER 2	BIGGS	
29/12/1956	STOKE CITY	A	1	2	31000		2	3	4	5	6	7	8			11		9	1					10					HOOPER			
12/01/1957	MIDDLESBROUGH	H	0	2	24069				4	5		7	8	9	10	11	3		1				2		6							
19/01/1957	LEICESTER CITY	A	2	7	32288		2		4	5	6	7	8	9	10	11			1							3			HOOPER 2			
02/02/1957	BRISTOL CITY	H	0	0	32055		2	3	4	5	6	7	9		10	11			1					8								
09/02/1957	NOTTS COUNTY	H	3	0	17137		2	3		5	6	7	9		8	11			1					10			4		WARD	SYKES	HOOPER	
16/02/1957	SHEFFIELD UNITED	A	0	0	18019		2	3	4	5	6	7	8			11		9	1					10								
23/02/1957	BARNSLEY	H	1	1	14004		2	3	4		6		8	5		11		9	1			7		10					MEYER			
02/03/1957	WEST HAM UNITED	A	2	1	22500			3	2		6	7	8	5	10	11			1	9				4					WARD	HOOPER		
09/03/1957	ROTHERHAM UNITED	H	4	2	15011			3				7	8	2	10	11			1	9				6			4	5	ROOST 2	WARD	HOOPER	
16/03/1957	LINCOLN CITY	A	0	1	8907		2	3	4	5			8		10	11			1	9		7		6								
23/03/1957	SWANSEA TOWN	H	1	1	21270		2	3		5	6		8	10		11			1	9		7		4					ROOST			
30/03/1957	FULHAM	A	2	3	22000		2	3	4	5			8	9	10	11			1			7		6					WARD	BIGGS		
06/04/1957	NOTTINGHAM FOREST	H	3	2	21087		2	3	4	5		7	8	9	10	11			1					6					HOOPER	BIGGS	WARD	
13/04/1957	PORT VALE	A	3	2	9006	1	2		4	5		7	8	9	10	11					3			6					BRADFORD 2	WARD		
19/04/1957	LIVERPOOL	A	1	4	40776	1	2		4	5		7	8	9	10	11					3			6					BRADFORD			
20/04/1957	BLACKBURN ROVERS	H	0	1	20794	1	2	3	4	5			8	7	10	11		9						6								
22/04/1957	LIVERPOOL	H	0	0	14794	1	2	3	4	5		11	8	9				10				7		6								
	APPEARANCES					14	39	30	39	39	33	32	42	25	27	40	5	21	28	10	5	10	2	16	1	1	2	1				
	GOALS					0	0	0	0	0	0	1	17	11	19	16	0	11	0	5	0	0	0	1	0	0	0	0				
	FA CUP																															
20825	HULL CITY	A	4	3	22752		2	3	4	5	6	7	8	9	10	11			1										BRADFORD 2	WARD	BIGGS	
26/01/1957	PRESTON NORTH END	H	1	4	32000		2	3	4	5	6	7	8	9		11			1	10									HOOPER pen			
	GLOUCESTERSHIRE CUP FINAL																															
29/04/1957	BRISTOL CITY	H	1	2	14608	1	2	3	4	5		7	8	9		11		10						6					BRADFORD			

1957/58

Date	Opponent				Att	RADFORD Howard	BAMFORD Henry	WATLING John	PITT John	HALE Denzil	SYKES Norman	PETHERBRIDGE George	BRADFORD Geoffrey	MEYER Barrie	WARD David	HOOPER Peter	BIGGS Alfred	RICKETTS Graham	MABBUTT Raymond	NICHOLLS Ronald	SAMPSON Peter	PYLE David	JONES Robert	DOYLE Brian	McILVENNY John	Scorers			
	DIVISION 2																												
24/08/1957	BARNSLEY	A	2	2	12673	1	2	3	4	5	6	7	8	9	10	11										WARD	BRADFORD		
26/08/1957	DERBY COUNTY	H	5	2	25371	1	2	3	4	5	6		8	9	10	11	7									MEYER 3	HOOPER	BIGGS	
31/08/1957	WEST HAM UNITED	H	2	3	25910	1	2	3	4	5	6		8	9	10	11	7									WARD 2			
04/09/1957	DERBY COUNTY	A	1	2	20529	1	2	3		5	6			9	10	11	8	4	7							WARD			
07/09/1957	SHEFFIELD UNITED	A	0	2	15796		2	3		5	6		9		10	11	8	4	7	1									
09/09/1957	STOKE CITY	A	5	3	23090		2	3	4	5		7	9		10	11	8			1	6					WARD	BIGGS 3	BRADFORD	
14/09/1957	BLACKBURN ROVERS	H	4	0	22822		2	3	4	5		11	9		10		8		7	1	6					BRADFORD 2	BIGGS	MABBUTT	
16/09/1957	STOKE CITY	H	2	0	20022		2	3	4	5		11	9		10		8		7	1	6					BRADFORD	BIGGS		
21/09/1957	IPSWICH TOWN	A	2	3	20433		2	3	4	5		11	9		10		8		7	1	6					BRADFORD	BIGGS		
28/09/1957	NOTTS COUNTY	H	5	2	20388		2	3	4			7	9		10	11	8			1	6	5				BRADFORD 2	HOOPER	CRUICKSHANK og	McGRATH og
05/10/1957	LINCOLN CITY	A	1	0	9147		2	3	4				9	10		11	8		7	1	6	5				BRADFORD			
12/10/1957	BRISTOL CITY	A	2	3	33465		2	3					9	8	10	11	5	4	7	1	6					WARD	HOOPER		
19/10/1957	CARDIFF CITY	H	0	2	23292		2	3	4	5			9		10	11	8		7	1	6								
26/10/1957	LIVERPOOL	A	0	2	36686		2	3	4	5		7	9		10	11	8			1	6								
02/11/1957	MIDDLESBROUGH	H	5	0	20153		2	3		5	4	7	9			11	10			1	6		8			PETHERBRIDGE 2	JONES 2	BRADFORD	
09/11/1957	LEYTON ORIENT	A	3	1	14826		2	3		5	4	7	9			11	10			1	6		8			BRADFORD 2	PETHERBRIDGE		
16/11/1957	CHARLTON ATHLETIC	H	1	0	24217		2	3		5	4	7	9			11	10			1	6		8			BIGGS			
23/11/1957	DONCASTER ROVERS	A	2	3	9158		2	3		5	4	7		9		11	10			1	6		8			PETHERBRIDGE	HOOPER		
30/11/1957	ROTHERHAM UNITED	H	1	3	17606		2	3		5	4	7		9		11	10			1	6		8			WILLIAMS og			
07/12/1957	HUDDERSFIELD TOWN	A	0	0	11028		2	3	4	5	9	7			10	11	8			1	6								
14/12/1957	GRIMSBY TOWN	H	0	7	14577		2	3	4	5	9	7			10	11	8			1	6								
21/12/1957	BARNSLEY	H	1	1	13355		2	3		5	4	7			10	11	9			1	6		8			JONES			
25/12/1957	SWANSEA TOWN	A	4	6	11340		2	3		5	4	7		9	10	11	8			1	6					SAMPSON	BIGGS	MEYER	WARD
26/12/1957	SWANSEA TOWN	H	3	0	22640		2			3	4	7		9	10	11	8			1	6	5				PETHERBRIDGE 2	MEYER		
28/12/1957	WEST HAM UNITED	A	1	6	28000		2			3	4	7		9	10	11	8			1	6	5				HOOPER			
11/01/1958	SHEFFIELD UNITED	H	2	2	19892		2				4	7	9	8	10	11				1	6	5		3		WARD 2			
18/01/1958	BLACKBURN ROVERS	A	0	2	16800		2	3			4	7	9	8	10	11				1	6	5							
01/02/1958	IPSWICH TOWN	H	3	1	21554		2	3	4		8	7	9		10	11				1	6	5				HOOPER 2	BRADFORD		
19/02/1958	LINCOLN CITY	H	3	0	13305		2	3			4	7	9	8	10	11				1	6	5				WARD	HOOPER 2		
22/02/1958	DONCASTER ROVERS	H	2	1	17821		2	3			4		9		10	11	8			1	6	5			7	BRADFORD	GRAHAM og		
08/03/1958	LIVERPOOL	H	3	1	19299		2				4		9	8	10	11				1	6	5		3	7	McILVENNY	HOOPER	WARD	
15/03/1958	MIDDLESBROUGH	A	3	4	20000		2	3			4		9	8	10	11				1	6	5			7	WARD 2	BRADFORD		
22/03/1958	LEYTON ORIENT	H	4	0	15533		2				4		9	8	10	11				1	6	5		3	7	MEYER 2	McILVENNY	HOOPER	
26/03/1958	CARDIFF CITY	A	2	0	6000		2				4		9	8	10	11				1	6	5		3	7	BRADFORD	HOOPER		
29/03/1958	CHARLTON ATHLETIC	A	3	2	20064		2				4		9	8	10	11				1	6	5		3	7	BRADFORD	MEYER	McILVENNY	
04/04/1958	FULHAM	H	2	2	31109		2				4		9	8	10	11				1	6	5		3	7	WARD	HOOPER		
05/04/1958	BRISTOL CITY	H	3	3	24782		2				4		9	8	10	11				1	6	5		3	7	BRADFORD 2	HOOPER		
07/04/1958	FULHAM	A	0	3	31300	1	2				4		9		10	11	8				6	5		3	7				
12/04/1958	ROTHERHAM UNITED	A	0	2	6942		2				4		9		10	11	8			1	6	5		3	7				
19/04/1958	HUDDERSFIELD TOWN	H	1	1	16185		2	3		5			9	8	10	11		4	7	1	6					BRADFORD			
23/04/1958	NOTTS COUNTY	A	0	0	13467	1	2	3		5			9	8	10	11		4	7		6								
26/04/1958	GRIMSBY TOWN	A	2	3	10030	1	2	3			8		5	9	10	11		4	7		6					MABBUTT	MEYER		
	APPEARANCES					7	42	31	14	24	31	22	33	24	36	39	27	6	11	35	37	18	6	9	10				
	GOALS					0	0	0	0	0	0	6	20	9	14	14	9	0	2	0	1	0	3	0	3	OWN GOAL 4			
	FA CUP																												
04/01/1958	MANSFIELD TOWN	H	5	0	20446		2	3			4	7	9		10	11	8			1	6	5				HOOPER 2	BIGGS	WARD	PETHERBRIDGE
25/01/1958	BURNLEY	H	2	2	34229		2	3		8	4	7	9		10	11				1	6	5				HALE	SHANNON og		
28/01/1958	BURNLEY	A	3	2	40813		2	3	4		8	7	9		10	11				1	6	5				SYKES	WARD 2		
15/02/1958	BRISTOL CITY	A	4	3	39126		2	3			4	7		8	10	11				1	6	5				MEYER	SYKES	WARD	BRADFORD
01/03/1958	FULHAM	A	1	3	42000		2	3			4			8	10	11	7			1	6	5				BRADFORD			
	GLOUCESTERSHIRE CUP FINAL																												
29/04/1958	BRISTOL CITY	A	1	4	10590	1	2	3	5		4		9		10	11	8		7		6					BRADFORD			

1958/59

Date						RADFORD Howard	BAMFORD Henry	WATLING John	SYKES Norman	PYLE David	SAMPSON Peter	PETHERBRIDGE George	BIGGS Alfred	BRADFORD Geoffrey	WARD David	HOOPER Peter	SINCLAIR Harvey	DOYLE Brian	McILVENNY John	JONES Robert	RICKETTS Graham	HALE Denzil	HAMILTON Ian	HILLARD Douglas	NORMAN Malcolm	MABBUTT Raymond	SMITH Granville	FROWEN John	DRAKE Leonard	TIMMINS John	GOUGH Anthony				
	DIVISION 2																																		
23/08/1958	LEYTON ORIENT	A	3	1	17304	1	2	3	4	5	6	7	8	9	10	11																PETHERBRIDGE	WARD	WRIGHT og	
30/08/1958	SCUNTHORPE UNITED	H	4	0	24273	1	2	3	4	5	6	7	8	9	10	11																HOOPER pen	PETHERBRIDGE	BRADFORD	WARD
03/09/1958	DERBY COUNTY	A	2	3	20130		2	3	4	5	6	7	8	9	10	11	1															BRADFORD	HOOPER pen		
06/09/1958	SHEFFIELD WEDNESDAY	A	1	3	28968	1		3	4	5	6	7	8	9	10	11		2														WARD			
08/09/1958	CARDIFF CITY	H	2	0	20604	1		3	4	5	6	7	8	9	10	11		2														BRADFORD	WARD		
13/09/1958	FULHAM	H	0	0	30076	1		3	4	5	6	7	8	9	10	11		2																	
17/09/1958	CARDIFF CITY	A	4	2	15000	1		3	4	5	6	7	8	9	10	11		2														BRADFORD	WARD	BIGGS	HOOPER pen
20/09/1958	LINCOLN CITY	A	1	4	9223	1		3	4	5	6		8	9	10	11		2	7													BRADFORD			
22/09/1958	DERBY COUNTY	H	2	1	14317	1		3	4	5	6		8	9	10	11		2	7													WARD 2			
27/09/1958	SUNDERLAND	H	2	1	24602	1		3	4	5	6			9	10	11		2	7	8												WARD	McILVENNY		
04/10/1958	STOKE CITY	A	2	2	19763	1		3	4	5	6			9	10	11		2	7	8												JONES	WARD		
11/10/1958	HUDDERSFIELD TOWN	A	2	1	16773	1		3	4	5	6			9	10	11		2	7	8												McILVENNY	WARD		
18/10/1958	BARNSLEY	H	0	2	20249	1		3	4	5	6		9		10	11		2	7	8															
25/10/1958	ROTHERHAM UNITED	A	3	3	7928	1		3		5	6		9		10	11		2	7	8	4											BIGGS 2	McILVENNY		
01/11/1958	BRISTOL CITY	H	1	2	32104	1		3	4	5	6		8	9	10	11		2	7													SYKES			
08/11/1958	BRIGHTON & HOVE ALBION	A	1	1	22155	1		3	4	5	6	7	8	9	10	11		2														WARD			
15/11/1958	GRIMSBY TOWN	H	7	3	15733	1		3	4	5		7		9	10	11		2		8	6											BRADFORD 2	WARD 2	HOOPER 3	
22/11/1958	LIVERPOOL	A	1	2	39365	1		3	4	5	6	7			10	11		2		8		9										PETHERBRIDGE			
29/11/1958	MIDDLESBROUGH	H	3	1	15803	1		3	4	5		7		9	10	11		2		8	6											BRADFORD 2	HOOPER		
06/12/1958	CHARLTON ATHLETIC	A	3	4	13879	1		3	4	5		7		9	10	11		2			6		8									WARD 2	BRADFORD		
13/12/1958	SHEFFIELD UNITED	H	1	1	16136	1		3	4			7		9	10	11				8	6	5		2								WARD			
20/12/1958	LEYTON ORIENT	H	1	3	10004			3	4			7	9		10	11				8	6	5		2	1							PETHERBRIDGE			
26/12/1958	IPSWICH TOWN	A	2	0	15808			3	4			7		9	10	11		2		8	6	5			1							BRADFORD	HOOPER pen		
27/12/1958	IPSWICH TOWN	H	1	1	20615			3	4			7		9	10	11				8	6	5		2	1							WARD			
03/01/1959	SCUNTHORPE UNITED	A	0	0	11130			3	4		6	7		9	10	11		2		8		5			1										
31/01/1959	FULHAM	A	0	1	23203			3	4				8		9	11		2		10		5			1	6	7								
07/02/1959	LINCOLN CITY	H	3	0	15279			3	4	5			8		9	11		2		10					1	6	7					WARD	BIGGS 2		
14/02/1959	SUNDERLAND	A	1	3	24188			3	4				8		9	11		2		10					1	6	7	5				WARD			
21/02/1959	STOKE CITY	H	1	0	16341			3	4	5			10		9	11		2							1	6	7		8			BIGGS			
28/02/1959	BRIGHTON & HOVE ALBION	H	2	0	15785			3	4	5			10		9	11								2	1	6	7		8			SMITH	WARD		
07/03/1959	BARNSLEY	A	0	0	5503			3	4	5			10	9		11		2							1	6	7		8						
14/03/1959	ROTHERHAM UNITED	H	4	1	10810			3	4	5			10	9		11		2							1	6	7		8			BRADFORD 4			
21/03/1959	BRISTOL CITY	A	1	1	26868			3	4	5			10	9	8	11		2							1	6	7					WARD			
27/03/1959	SWANSEA TOWN	A	1	2	14921				4	5			10	9	8	11		2							1	6	7			3		BIGGS			
28/03/1959	HUDDERSFIELD TOWN	H	1	1	16029				4	5				9	8	11		2							1	6	7		10	3		BRADFORD			
30/03/1959	SWANSEA TOWN	H	4	4	15151				4	5		7	8	9	10	11		2							1	6				3		WARD 2	HOOPER	BRADFORD	
04/04/1959	GRIMSBY TOWN	A	2	1	9200			3	4				8	9	10	11								2	1	6	7	5				SMITH	WARD		
11/04/1959	LIVERPOOL	H	3	0	14810			3	4				8	9	10	11								2	1	6	7	5				WARD	HOOPER 2-1pen		
18/04/1959	MIDDLESBROUGH	A	2	2	17262			3	4				10	9	8	11								2	1	6	7	5				WARD	STONEHOUSE og		
20/04/1959	SHEFFIELD UNITED	A	2	5	11310			3	4				10	9		11				8				2	1	6		5	7			BRADFORD	JONES		
25/04/1959	CHARLTON ATHLETIC	H	2	1	11166			3	10	5				9		11					4			2	1	6	7		8			BRADFORD	TOWNSEND og		
30/04/1959	SHEFFIELD WEDNESDAY	H	2	1	16653			3	4	5			8	9		11								2	1	6	7				10	BIGGS	BRADFORD		
	APPEARANCES					20	3	39	41	31	18	18	29	33	37	42	1	29	8	17	9	7	1	10	21	17	15	5	7	3	1				
	GOALS					0	0	0	1	0	0	4	8	20	26	11	0	0	3	2	0	0	0	0	0	0	2	0	0	0	0	OWN GOAL 3			
	FA CUP																																		
10/01/1959	CHARLTON ATHLETIC	H	0	4	23203	1		3	4		6	7		9	10	11		2		8		5													
	GLOUCESTERSHIRE CUP FINAL																																		
04/05/1959	BRISTOL CITY	H	1	1	11022			3	4	5			10	9	8	11								2	1	6	7					WARD			

1959/60

Date	Opponent				Att	NORMAN Malcolm	HILLARD Douglas	WATLING John	SAMPSON Peter	PYLE David	MABBUTT Raymond	SMITH Granville	BIGGS Alfred	BRADFORD Geoffrey	WARD David	HOOPER Peter	SYKES Norman	DRAKE Leonard	JONES Robert	DOYLE Brian	TIMMINS John	PETHERBRIDGE George	RICKETTS Graham	HAMILTON Ian	EDGE Anthony	JARMAN Harold	FROWEN John	RADFORD Howard			
	DIVISION 2																														
22/08/1959	LEYTON ORIENT	H	2	2	20003	1	2	3	4	5	6	7	8	9	10	11													HOOPER	BRADFORD	
26/08/1959	CHARLTON ATHLETIC	A	2	2	13828	1	2	3		5	6		8	9	10	11	4	7											WARD	HOOPER pen	
29/08/1959	LINCOLN CITY	A	1	0	9284	1	2	3		5	6		8	9	10	11	4		7										BRADFORD		
05/09/1959	ASTON VILLA	H	1	1	26162	1	2	3		5	6	7	8	9	10	11	4												WARD		
07/09/1959	IPSWICH TOWN	H	2	1	24093	1	2	3		5	6	7	8	9	10	11	4												HOOPER 2		
12/09/1959	SUNDERLAND	A	2	2	29968	1	2	3		5	6		8	9	10	11	4			7									DOYLE	BRADFORD	
16/09/1959	IPSWICH TOWN	A	0	3	10868	1	2	3		5	6		8	9	10		4			7	11										
19/09/1959	PORTSMOUTH	H	2	0	20634	1	2	3		5	6		8		10	11	4					7	9						BIGGS	WARD	
21/09/1959	CHARLTON ATHLETIC	H	2	2	24345	1	2			5	6		8		10	11	4			3		7	9						HOOPER	BIGGS	
26/09/1959	STOKE CITY	A	1	0	17990	1	2			5	6		8			11	4			3		7	9	10					BIGGS		
03/10/1959	BRIGHTON & HOVE ALBION	H	4	5	20058	1	2			5	6		8		10	11	4			3		7	9						PETHERBRIDGE	HOOPER 2	BIGGS
10/10/1959	BRISTOL CITY	A	1	2	27548	1	2	3		5	6	7	8	9		11	4		10										BIGGS		
17/10/1959	SCUNTHORPE UNITED	H	1	1	15314	1	2	3		5	6	7	8	9		11	4		10										HILLARD		
24/10/1959	ROTHERHAM UNITED	A	0	3	10150	1	2	3		5	6	7	8	9	10	11	4														
31/10/1959	CARDIFF CITY	H	1	1	27549	1	2	3		5	6		8	7	10	11	4								9				BIGGS		
07/11/1959	HULL CITY	A	1	3	16972	1	2	3		5	6			7	10	11	4		8						9				EDGE		
14/11/1959	SHEFFIELD UNITED	H	3	2	14649	1	2	3		5	6		8		10	11						7	4		9				WARD	EDGE	BIGGS
21/11/1959	MIDDLESBROUGH	A	1	5	24116	1	2	3		5	6		8		10	11						7	4		9				BIGGS		
28/11/1959	DERBY COUNTY	H	2	1	15018	1	2	3		5	6		10			11	8					7	4		9				EDGE	HOOPER	
05/12/1959	PLYMOUTH ARGYLE	A	3	5	16675	1	2	3		5	6		8		10	11						7	4		9				BIGGS	WARD	HOOPER pen
12/12/1959	LIVERPOOL	H	0	2	15615	1	2	3		5	6		8		10	11	4					7			9						
19/12/1959	LEYTON ORIENT	A	2	1	6914	1	2	3		5	6		8	9	10	11	4					7							PETHERBRIDGE	BIGGS	
26/12/1959	SWANSEA TOWN	H	3	1	16501	1	2	3		5	6		8	9	10	11	4									7			BRADFORD	BIGGS 2	
28/12/1959	SWANSEA TOWN	A	0	3	15270	1	2	3		5	6		8		10	11	4								9	7					
02/01/1960	LINCOLN CITY	H	3	3	14148	1	2	3			6		8	9		11	4		10			7					5		BIGGS 2	BRADFORD	
15/01/1960	ASTON VILLA	A	1	4	29726	1	2	3			6		8	9	10	11	4					7					5		BRADFORD		
23/01/1960	SUNDERLAND	H	3	1	17883	1	2	3			6		8	9	10	11	4					7					5		BRADFORD	BIGGS	WARD
06/02/1960	PORTSMOUTH	A	5	4	14136	1	2	3			6		8	9	10	11	4					7					5		WARD 2	HOOPER 2	HOWELLS og
13/02/1960	STOKE CITY	H	3	1	11421		2	3		5	6		8	9	10	11	4					7						1	BRADFORD 2	WARD	
27/02/1960	BRISTOL CITY	H	2	1	27048		2	3		5	6		8	9	10	11	4					7						1	HOOPER	BIGGS	
02/03/1960	BRIGHTON & HOVE ALBION	A	2	2	10451		2	3		5	6		8	9		11	4					7		10				1	BIGGS	BRADFORD	
05/03/1960	SCUNTHORPE UNITED	A	4	3	9227		2	3		5	6		8	9		11	4					7		10				1	HAMILTON 2	BRADFORD	MABBUTT
12/03/1960	ROTHERHAM UNITED	H	3	1	15126		2	3		5	6		8	9		11	4					7		10				1	HAMILTON 2	BIGGS	
19/03/1960	DERBY COUNTY	A	0	1	13539		2	3		5	6		8		9	11							4	10		7		1			
26/03/1960	HULL CITY	H	1	0	12268		2	3		5	6		8	9	10	11						7	4					1	BIGGS		
02/04/1960	SHEFFIELD UNITED	A	1	1	14521		2	3		5	6		8	9	10	11	4					7						1	WARD		
09/04/1960	MIDDLESBROUGH	H	0	2	15837		2	3		5	6		8		10	11	4					7			9			1			
15/04/1960	HUDDERSFIELD TOWN	H	2	0	16069		2	3		5	6		8	9	10	11	4					7						1	BRADFORD	BIGGS	
16/04/1960	LIVERPOOL	A	0	4	27317		2	3		5	6		8	9	10	11						7					4	1			
18/04/1960	HUDDERSFIELD TOWN	A	1	0	13820		2	3		5	6		8	9	10	11	4					7						1	HOOPER		
23/04/1960	PLYMOUTH ARGYLE	H	2	0	17073			3		5	6		8	9	10	11	4					7					2	1	BIGGS 2		
30/04/1960	CARDIFF CITY	A	2	2	25000			3		5	6		8	9	10	11	4					7					2	1	WARD 2		
	APPEARANCES					28	40	39	1	38	42	6	41	30	34	41	35	1	5	5	1	27	10	5	9	3	7	14			
	GOALS					0	1	0	0	0	1	0	22	12	12	13	0	0	0	1	0	2	0	4	3	0	0	0	OWN GOAL 1		
	FA CUP																														
09/01/1960	DONCASTER ROVERS	H	0	0	15522	1	2	3			6		8		10	11	4		9			7					5				
12/01/1960	DONCASTER ROVERS	A	2	1	15217	1	2	3			6		8		10	11	4		9			7					5		BIGGS	WARD	
30/01/1960	PRESTON NORTH END	H	3	3	38472	1	2	3			6		8		10	11	4		9			7					5		BIGGS 2	SMITH og	
02/02/1960	PRESTON NORTH END	A	1	5	33164	1	2	3			6		8		10	11	4		9			7					5		HOOPER		
	GLOUCESTERSHIRE CUP FINAL																														
02/05/1960	BRISTOL CITY	A	2	3	7195		2	3			6		8	9	10	11	4					7					5	1	BIGGS2		

1960/61

Date	Opponent	H/A	F	A	Att	RADFORD Howard	HILLARD Douglas	WATLING John	SYKES Norman	PYLE David	MABBUTT Raymond	PETHERBRIDGE George	BIGGS Alfred	BRADFORD Geoffrey	WARD David	HOOPER Peter	RICKETTS Graham	NORMAN Malcolm	EDGE Anthony	HAMILTON Ian	FROWEN John	COGGINS Philip	BEARPARK Ian	SAMPSON Peter	JONES Robert	JARMAN Harold	PURDON Edward	RIDEOUT Brian	COLLINS George	OLDFIELD Terence	DAVIS Joseph	WATKINS John	JAMES Royston	HALL Arthur	STONE David	Scorers			
	DIVISION 2																																						
20/08/1960	MIDDLESBROUGH	H	2	3	20302	1	2	3	4	5	6	7	8	9	10	11																				HOOPER	HILLARD		
24/08/1960	LEEDS UNITED	A	1	1	11330	1	2	3		5	6	7	8	9	10	11	4																			HOOPER			
27/08/1960	BRIGHTON & HOVE ALBION	A	1	6	15437	1	2	3		5	6	7	8	9	10	11	4																			BRADFORD			
29/08/1960	LEEDS UNITED	H	4	4	19028		2	3		5	6	7	8			11	4	1	9	10																HOOPER 2	PETHERBRIDGE	HAMILTON	
03/09/1960	IPSWICH TOWN	H	1	1	15467		2	3	4	5	6	7	8			11		1	9	10																BIGGS			
07/09/1960	ROTHERHAM UNITED	A	0	4	8219		2	3	8		6	7	10	9		11	4	1			5																		
10/09/1960	SCUNTHORPE UNITED	A	1	2	10262		2	3		5	6		8		10	11	4	1	9			7														BIGGS			
12/09/1960	ROTHERHAM UNITED	H	2	1	13088		2	3		5	6		9		10	11						7	1	4	8											WARD	HOOPER pen		
17/09/1960	LEYTON ORIENT	H	4	2	15337		2	3		5	6		8			11			9			7	1	4	10											BIGGS 2	HOOPER	EDGE	
24/09/1960	DERBY COUNTY	A	1	1	12826	1	2	3		5	6		8	9		11						7		4	10											HOOPER pen			
01/10/1960	SWANSEA TOWN	H	4	2	15177	1	2	3		5	6		8	9		11								4		7	10									BRADFORD	HOOPER	HILLARD	NURSE og
08/10/1960	LUTON TOWN	A	2	4	9373	1	2	3	4	5	8			9		11								6		7	10									BRADFORD	PURDON		
15/10/1960	LINCOLN CITY	H	3	1	16853	1	2		4	5	6		8			11				10						7		3	9							HAMILTON	COLLINS	JARMAN	
29/10/1960	HUDDERSFIELD TOWN	H	1	2	15381	1	2	3		5	6			8		11				10				4		7			9							HAMILTON			
05/11/1960	SUNDERLAND	A	0	2	17942	1	2			5	6	7				11					3			4	8		10			9									
12/11/1960	PLYMOUTH ARGYLE	H	2	5	17005	1	2		4	5		7	8		10	11					3						6			9						PETHERBRIDGE	HOOPER		
19/11/1960	NORWICH CITY	A	1	2	22581	1	2	3	4	5	6	7	8	9	10	11																				BRADFORD			
26/11/1960	CHARLTON ATHLETIC	H	3	1	10186	1	2	3	4	5	6	7	8	9	10	11																				BIGGS	BRADFORD	WARD	
03/12/1960	SHEFFIELD UNITED	A	3	2	12877	1	2		4	5	6		8	9	10	11					3					7										BIGGS	WARD	HOOPER	
10/12/1960	STOKE CITY	H	1	0	13407	1	2		4	5	6		8	9	10	11					3					7										BRADFORD			
17/12/1960	MIDDLESBROUGH	A	1	1	11594	1	2		4	5	6		8	9	10	11					3					7										HOOPER			
26/12/1960	SOUTHAMPTON	A	2	4	21901	1	2		4	5	6			9	10	11					3				8	7										JONES	JARMAN		
31/12/1960	BRIGHTON & HOVE ALBION	H	0	1	12823	1	2		4	5	6		8	9	10	11					3					7													
14/01/1961	IPSWICH TOWN	A	2	3	11939	1	2		9	5	6	11	8			10					3			4		7										BIGGS 2			
21/01/1961	SCUNTHORPE UNITED	H	3	3	11316	1		3	9	5	6	11	8			10					2			4		7										PETHERBRIDGE	SYKES	HORSTEAD og	
04/02/1961	LEYTON ORIENT	A	2	3	12334	1	2		4	5	6	7	8	9		10					3				11											BRADFORD	JONES		
11/02/1961	DERBY COUNTY	H	1	1	11164	1	2		4	5	6	7	8	9		10					3				11											PETHERBRIDGE			
25/02/1961	LUTON TOWN	H	4	1	13102	1	2		4		6	7		9		10					3				8						5	11				BRADFORD 2	PETHERBRIDGE	HOOPER	
28/02/1961	SWANSEA TOWN	A	1	2	12562	1	2		4		6	7		9		10					3				8						5	11				HOOPER			
04/03/1961	LINCOLN CITY	A	2	1	15006		2		4		6	7		9		10		1			3				8						5	11				HOOPER 2			
11/03/1961	PORTSMOUTH	H	2	0	5623		2		4		6	7		9		10		1			3				8						5	11				BRADFORD	HOOPER		
18/03/1961	STOKE CITY	A	0	2	7826		2		4		6	7		9		10		1			3				8						5	11							
20/03/1961	SOUTHAMPTON	H	4	2	15699		2		4		6			9		10		1			3				8	7					5	11				HOOPER	BRADFORD	JONES	HILLARD
25/03/1961	SUNDERLAND	H	1	0	15261		2		4		6			9		10		1			3				8	7					5	11				HOOPER			
31/03/1961	LIVERPOOL	A	0	3	36538		2		4		6			9		10		1			3				8	7					5	11							
01/04/1961	CHARLTON ATHLETIC	A	1	2	9139		2		4		6			9		10		1			3				8	7					5	11				JONES			
04/04/1961	LIVERPOOL	H	4	3	16522		2		4		6			9		10		1			3				8	7					5	11				JONES 2	JARMAN	HOOPER	
08/04/1961	NORWICH CITY	H	3	1	18234		2		4		6			9		10		1			3				8	7					5	11				JONES 2	HOOPER		
15/04/1961	PLYMOUTH ARGYLE	A	0	5	14026		2		4		6			9		10		1			3				8	7					5	11							
19/04/1961	PORTSMOUTH	A	0	3	10793		2		4					6		10		1			3				8	7					5	11	9						
22/04/1961	SHEFFIELD UNITED	H	3	1	13052		2		4		6			9		10		1			3				8	7					5	11				BRADFORD	JONES	JARMAN	
29/04/1961	HUDDERSFIELD TOWN	A	0	4	10322				4		6			9		11		1		10	3				8	7					5			2					
	APPEARANCES					23	40	16	32	26	40	19	23	32	13	42	5	17	4	5	27	4	2	9	22	21	4	1	2	2	15	14	1	1					
	GOALS					0	3	0	1	0	0	5	8	12	3	20	0	0	1	3	0	0	0	0	9	4	1	0	1	0	0	0	0	0		OWN GOAL 2			
	LEAGUE CUP																																						
26/09/1960	FULHAM	H	2	1	20022	1	2	3		5	6		8	9		11								4		7	10									JARMAN	BRADFORD		
12/10/1960	READING	A	5	3	8323	1	2		4	5	6		8			11				10						7		3	9							HAMILTON 2	BIGGS	JARMAN	SYKES
23/11/1960	ROTHERHAM UNITED	A	0	2	10912	1	2	3	4	5	6	7	8	9	10	11																							
	FA CUP																																						
07/01/1961	ASTON VILLA	H	1	1	34061	1	2	3	4	5	6	7	8		10	11									9											BIGGS			
09/01/1961	ASTON VILLA	A	0	4	26998	1	2			5	6	7	8		10	11					3			4			9												
	GLOUCESTERSHIRE CUP FINAL																																						
01/05/1961	BRISTOL CITY	H	1	3	12109		2				6			9		10		1			3				8	7					5	11			4	JARMAN			

1961/62

Date	Opponent	H/A	F	A	Att	NORMAN Malcolm	HILLS John	FROWEN John	MABBUTT Raymond	DAVIS Joseph	CARTER Brian	JARMAN Harold	JONES Robert	BRADFORD Geoffrey	HAMILTON Ian	HOOPER Peter	WATKINS John	SYKES Norman	RADFORD Howard	HILLARD Douglas	SLOCOMBE Michael	OLDFIELD Terence	HALL Arthur	PETHERBRIDGE George	WATLING John	PYLE David	BUMPSTEAD David	WILLIAMS Keith	HALL Bernard	HALL Bernard	Scorers		
	DIVISION 2																																
19/08/1961	LIVERPOOL	H	0	2	19438	1	2	3	4	5	6	7	8	9	10	11																	
22/08/1961	BURY	A	0	2	12785	1	2	3	4	5	6	7	8	9		11	10																
26/08/1961	ROTHERHAM UNITED	A	0	4	7921	1	2	3		5	6	7	8	9		10	11	4															
28/08/1961	BURY	H	0	1	13943			3		5			10	9		7		4	1	2	6	8	11										
02/09/1961	SUNDERLAND	H	2	3	12209			3		5		7	10	9			11	4	1	2	6	8									BRADFORD 2		
05/09/1961	SCUNTHORPE UNITED	A	1	2	9558		2	3		5			10	9				4	1	8	6			7	11						JONES		
09/09/1961	STOKE CITY	A	1	2	9075		2	3		5			8	9		10		4	1		6			7	11						BRADFORD		
16/09/1961	LEYTON ORIENT	H	2	1	11824		2	3	4				10	9		11		8	1		6			7		5					HOOPER	JONES	
18/09/1961	SCUNTHORPE UNITED	H	2	1	14100			3	4	2			10	9		11		8	1		6			7		5					SYKES	HOOPER	
23/09/1961	LEEDS UNITED	H	4	0	13653			3	4	2		8	10	9		11			1		6			7		5					HOOPER 2	JONES	BRADFORD
30/09/1961	NORWICH CITY	A	2	2	18869			3	4	2			10	9		11		8	1		6			7		5					JONES	HOOPER pen	
07/10/1961	PRESTON NORTH END	A	0	1	11331			3	4	2			10	9		11		8	1		6			7		5							
14/10/1961	PLYMOUTH ARGYLE	H	4	3	14435			3	4	2			10	9		11		8	1		6			7		5					JONES 2	HOOPER	SYKES
21/10/1961	HUDDERSFIELD TOWN	A	1	4	11845			3	4	2	8			9	10	11		5	1		6			7							BRADFORD		
28/10/1961	SWANSEA TOWN	H	4	1	12768			3	4	2		7	8	9		10			1		6			11		5					JONES 3	BRADFORD	
04/11/1961	SOUTHAMPTON	A	2	0	14840			3	4	2		7	8	9		10			1		6			11		5					BRADFORD 2		
11/11/1961	DERBY COUNTY	H	1	4	10622			3	4	2		7	8	9		10			1		6			11		5					PETHERBRIDGE		
18/11/1961	NEWCASTLE UNITED	A	2	5	23180			3	4	2		7	8	9		10			1		6			11		5					JARMAN	HOOPER	
25/11/1961	MIDDLESBROUGH	H	0	2	9504			3	4	2		7	8	9			10		1		6			11		5							
02/12/1961	WALSALL	A	0	0	9429		2	3				7		9	8	11	10		1		6					5	4						
09/12/1961	LUTON TOWN	H	1	0	9688			3		2		7		9	8	11	10		1		6					5	4				HAMILTON		
16/12/1961	LIVERPOOL	A	0	2	29957			3	6	2		7	9		8	11	10		1							5	4						
22/12/1961	ROTHERHAM UNITED	H	4	2	8876			3	6	5			9	2	10	11		4	1					7			8				HAMILTON 2	JONES	HOOPER
26/12/1961	BRIGHTON & HOVE ALBION	H	0	1	13102			3				8	9	2	10	11		4	1					7		5	6						
30/12/1961	BRIGHTON & HOVE ALBION	A	0	1	8951			3	6			7	9	2	10			4	1					11		5	8						
13/01/1962	SUNDERLAND	A	1	6	32650			3		2		7	9		8	11	10	6	1							5	4				JARMAN		
20/01/1962	STOKE CITY	H	0	2	8852			3		2		7	8	9		11	10	6	1							5	4						
03/02/1962	LEYTON ORIENT	A	3	2	14737			3	9			7	10	2		11		6	1							5	4	8			WILLIAMS	MABBUTT	JARMAN
10/02/1962	LEEDS UNITED	A	0	0	9108			3	9			7	10	2		11		6	1							5	4	8					
24/02/1962	PRESTON NORTH END	H	2	1	10601			3	9			7	10	2		11			1		6					5	4	8			JONES	HOOPER	
27/02/1962	NORWICH CITY	H	2	1	9209			3	9			7	10	2		11			1		6					5	4	8			MABBUTT	JARMAN	
03/03/1962	PLYMOUTH ARGYLE	A	1	3	15350			3	9			7	10	2		11			1		6					5	4	8			JONES		
10/03/1962	HUDDERSFIELD TOWN	H	1	1	10712			3	9			7	10	2		11			1		6					5	4	8			HOOPER		
17/03/1962	SWANSEA TOWN	A	1	1	5000			3	9			7	10	2		11			1		6					5	4	8			BRADFORD		
24/03/1962	SOUTHAMPTON	H	1	0	12336			3	9	5		7	10	2		11		6	1								4	8			HOOPER		
31/03/1962	DERBY COUNTY	A	1	4	8269			3	9	5		7		2	10	11		6	1								4	8			HAMILTON		
07/04/1962	NEWCASTLE UNITED	H	2	1	10770			3	9	5		7	10	2		11			1		6						4	8			JARMAN 2		
14/04/1962	MIDDLESBROUGH	A	0	5	10416			3	9	5		7	10	2		11		6	1								4	8					
20/04/1962	CHARLTON ATHLETIC	H	2	2	17606			3		5		7	10	9		11		6		2							4	8	1		JONES	HOOPER	
21/04/1962	WALSALL	H	2	2	10455			3	6	5		7	10	9		11		4		2								8	1		BRADFORD 2		
23/04/1962	CHARLTON ATHLETIC	A	1	2	16639			3	6	5		7	10			11		8	1	2		9					4				SYKES		
28/04/1962	LUTON TOWN	A	0	2	6555			3	6	5		7	10	9		11		8	1	2							4						
	APPEARANCES					3	7	42	31	31	4	32	38	39	10	38	9	25	37	7	24	3	1	17	2	25	22	13	2				
	GOALS					0	0	0	2	0	0	6	13	11	4	12	0	3	0	0	0	0	0	1	0	0	0	1	0				
	LEAGUE CUP																																
11/09/1961	HARTLEPOOL UNITED	H	2	1	8469		2	3	4				10	9		11		8	1		6			7		5					HOOPER	BRADFORD	
02/10/1961	BLACKBURN ROVERS	H	1	1	15711			3	4	2			10	9		11		8	1		6			7		5					BRADFORD		
16/10/1961	BLACKBURN ROVERS	A	0	4	5157			3	4	2			10	9		11		8	1		6			7		5							
	FA CUP																																
22654	OLDHAM ATHLETIC	H	1	1	14610			3	6	2		7		9	10	11		8	1							5	4				SYKES		
22656	OLDHAM ATHLETIC	A	0	2	27045			3		2		7	8	9	10	11		6	1							5	4						
	GLOUCESTERSHIRE CUP FINAL																																
01/05/1962	BRISTOL CITY	A	1	3	9201			5				7	10	3	8	11		4		2							6	9		1	WILLIAMS		

1962/63

Date	DIVISION 2				Att	MILLION Esmond	HILLARD Douglas	JONES Gwynfor	SLOCOMBE Michael	SYKES Norman	MABBUTT Raymond	JARMAN Harold	WILLIAMS Keith	BRADFORD Geoffrey	HAMILTON Ian	JONES Robert	DAVIS Joseph	OLDFIELD Terence	WOOD Allan	STONE David	RYDEN Hugh	BAKER Thomas	HUMES James	BUMPSTEAD David	BIGGS Alfred	FROWEN John	MUNRO Alexander	HALL Bernard	HURFORD David	MUXWORTHY Graham				
18/08/1962	HULL CITY	A	0	3	8261	1	2	3	4	5	6	7	8	9	10	11																		
21/08/1962	NORTHAMPTON TOWN	H	2	2	11649	1	2	3		5	4	7	8	9		11	6	10													WILLIAMS	OLDFIELD		
25/08/1962	CRYSTAL PALACE	H	2	0	10889	1	2	3		5	6	7	8	9		11		10	4												JARMAN	WILLIAMS		
28/08/1962	NORTHAMPTON TOWN	A	0	2	15661	1	2	3		5	6	7	8			11		9		4	10													
01/09/1962	WREXHAM	A	2	5	11519	1		3		5	6	7	8	2		11		9		4		10									R JONES	OLDFIELD		
04/09/1962	PETERBOROUGH UNITED	H	3	1	11860	1		3		5	6	7	8	2	10	11		9		4											WILLIAMS	HAMILTON	R JONES pen	
08/09/1962	HALIFAX TOWN	H	5	2	9578	1		3		5	6	7	8	2	10	11		9		4											OLDFIELD 2	JARMAN	HAMILTON	SOUTH og
10/09/1962	PETERBOROUGH UNITED	A	0	1	13180	1		3		5	6	7	8	2	10	11		9		4														
15/09/1962	BRISTOL CITY	H	1	2	20708	1		3		5	6	7	8	2	10	11		9		4											WILLIAMS			
18/09/1962	BARNSLEY	H	3	2	10256	1		3		5	6	7	8	2	10	11		9		4											JARMAN	HAMILTON	LEIGHTON og	
22/09/1962	BRIGHTON & HOVE ALBION	A	1	1	7943	1		3		5	6		8	2	10	11		9		4			7								WILLIAMS			
29/09/1962	CARLISLE UNITED	H	1	1	9104	1		3	4	5	6	9	8	2	10	11							7								R JONES			
02/10/1962	SWINDON TOWN	A	0	3	15028	1		3		5	6	7	8	2	10	11		9						4										
06/10/1962	PORT VALE	H	1	1	12416	1		3		5	6	7	8	2	10	11								4	9						BIGGS			
09/10/1962	SWINDON TOWN	H	2	0	17702	1		3	6	5		7	8	2	10	11								4	9						BIGGS	WILLIAMS		
13/10/1962	SHREWSBURY TOWN	A	2	7	6291	1		3		5	6	7	8	2	10	11								4	9						WILLIAMS	JARMAN		
20/10/1962	MILLWALL	H	2	0	11000	1		3		5	6	7	8	2	10	11								4	9						MABBUTT	R JONES pen		
27/10/1962	SOUTHEND UNITED	A	2	3	9180	1			3	5	6	7	8	2	10	11								4	9						HAMILTON	BRADFORD pen		
10/11/1962	NOTTS COUNTY	A	3	1	5950	1	2	3		5	6	7	10		11			9						4	8						JARMAN	OLDFIELD	WILLIAMS	
17/11/1962	AFC BOURNEMOUTH	H	1	2	8025	1		3		5	6	7	10		11			9						4	8	2					OLDFIELD			
27/11/1962	BARNSLEY	A	0	4	8667	1		3		5	6	7	8		10	11								4	9	2								
01/12/1962	BRADFORD	H	3	3	6593	1		3	4	5	11	7	8		10										9	2	6				MABBUTT	WILLIAMS	HAMILTON	
08/12/1962	WATFORD	A	1	0	7955	1	2	3	4	5	11	7	8		10										9		6				WILLIAMS			
15/12/1962	HULL CITY	H	2	5	6059	1	2	3	4	5	11	7	8		10										9		6				WILLIAMS	BIGGS		
09/02/1963	BRIGHTON & HOVE ALBION	H	4	1	7816	1	2	3		5	6	7	8		10	11		4							9						BIGGS 2	WILLIAMS	R JONES	
26/02/1963	READING	H	1	0	6456	1	2	3		5	6	7	8		10	11		4							9						WILLIAMS			
02/03/1963	SHREWSBURY TOWN	H	2	0	7575	1	2	3		5	6	7	8		10	11		4							9						BIGGS	OLDFIELD		
09/03/1963	MILLWALL	A	1	2	5260	1	2	3		5	6	7	8		10	11		4							9						HAMILTON			
16/03/1963	SOUTHEND UNITED	H	1	2	7215		2	3			6		10			11		4		5	9				8			1	7		RYDEN			
20/03/1963	CRYSTAL PALACE	A	1	2	15451	1	2	3							10	11		4		5	9				8		6		7		HAMILTON			
22/03/1963	COLCHESTER UNITED	A	0	1	4560	1	2	3							10	11		4		5	9				8		6		7					
30/03/1963	NOTTS COUNTY	H	1	1	5960	1	2	3		5	6		8		10	11		4							9				7		HAMILTON			
02/04/1963	CARLISLE UNITED	A	0	4	5354	1	2	3		6					10	11		8		5				4	9				7					
06/04/1963	AFC BOURNEMOUTH	A	1	1	9087	1	2	3				7	8			10	5	6						4	9					11	BIGGS			
12/04/1963	QUEENS PARK RANGERS	A	5	3	10165	1	2	3				7	8			10	5	6						4	9					11	BIGGS	WILLIAMS 2	R JONES 2	
13/04/1963	COVENTRY CITY	H	2	2	13145	1	2	3				7	8			10	5	6						4	9					11	R JONES	WILLIAMS		
15/04/1963	QUEENS PARK RANGERS	H	0	0	11028	1	2	3				7	8			10	5	6						4	9					11				
20/04/1963	BRADFORD	A	2	2	6794	1	2	3			4	7	8			10	5	6			9									11	R JONES	RYDEN		
23/04/1963	BRISTOL CITY	A	1	4	22739	1	2	3			4	7	8			10	5	6							9					11	WILLIAMS			
27/04/1963	WATFORD	H	3	1	7800		2	3			4	7				10	5	6			9				8			1		11	RYDEN 2	HILLARD		
29/04/1963	COVENTRY CITY	A	0	5	20412		2	3	4			7		5		10		6			9				8			1		11				
08/05/1963	READING	A	0	1	7878		2			5	11	7			10	8	3	6		4					9			1						
11/05/1963	WREXHAM	H	1	1	7889		2	3			6	7		11		10	5	4			9				8			1			JARMAN			
14/05/1963	COLCHESTER UNITED	H	2	0	9004		2	3			6	7		11	10	8	5	4							9			1			BIGGS pen	BRADFORD		
18/05/1963	HALIFAX TOWN	A	3	2	2126		2	3			6	7		11	10	8	5	4							9			1			R JONES	HAMILTON 2		
20/05/1963	PORT VALE	A	0	2	5015		2	3			11	7				10	5	9		6				4	8			1						
	APPEARANCES					38	29	44	8	31	37	40	36	21	31	41	13	35	1	14	8	1	2	15	32	3	5	8	5	8				
	GOALS					0	1	0	0	0	2	6	17	2	10	10	0	7	0	0	4	0	0	0	9	0	0	0	0	0	OWN GOAL 2			
	LEAGUE CUP																																	
27/09/1962	PORT VALE	H	2	0	6126	1		3	4	5	6	9	8	2	10	11							7								WILLIAMS	R JONES		
23/10/1962	CARDIFF CITY	H	2	0	12142	1		3		5	6	7	8	2	10	11		9						4							WILLIAMS	JARMAN		
13/11/1962	BURY	A	1	3	7194	1	2	3		5	6	7	10		11	8		9						4							ROBERTSON og			
	FA CUP																																	
03/11/1962	PORT VALE	H	0	2	8180	1	2			4	6	7	8	3	10	11	5								9									
	GLOUCESTERSHIRE CUP FINAL																																	
23/05/1963	BRISTOL CITY	H	2	1	8018		2	3			6	7		11	10	8	5	4							9			1			HAMILTON	R JONES		

1963/64

						HALL Bernard	HILLARD Douglas	JONES Gwynfor	BUMPSTEAD David	DAVIS Joseph	SYKES Norman	JARMAN Harold	BIGGS Alfred	JONES Robert	HAMILTON Ian	JENKINS Brian	OLDFIELD Terence	MABBUTT Raymond	BROWN John	BRADFORD Geoffrey	STONE David	MUNRO Alexander	FRUDE Roger	PARSONS Lindsay					
	DIVISION 3																												
24/08/1963	BRISTOL CITY	A	0	3	20697	1	2	3	4	5	6	7	8	9	10	11													
27/08/1963	WREXHAM	H	1	1	9129	1	2	3	4	5	6	7	8	9	10	11									BIGGS				
31/08/1963	OLDHAM ATHLETIC	H	0	1	8787	1	2	3	4	5	6	7	8	9	10	11													
07/09/1963	PETERBOROUGH UNITED	A	2	2	12256	1	2	3		5		7	9	8			4	6	10	11					BROWN 2				
11/09/1963	WREXHAM	A	2	1	6780	1	2	3		5		7	9	8			4	6	10	11					BIGGS	BROWN			
14/09/1963	SOUTHEND UNITED	H	3	1	8603	1	2	3		5		7	9	8			4	6	10	11					BIGGS 2	JARMAN			
17/09/1963	QUEENS PARK RANGERS	H	0	0	12299	1	2	3		5		7	9	8	10		4	6		11									
21/09/1963	WATFORD	A	2	3	9782	1	2	3		5		7	9	8	10		4	6		11					JARMAN	BIGGS			
28/09/1963	COLCHESTER UNITED	H	3	1	10724	1	2	3		5		7	9	8	10		4	6		11					R JONES	JARMAN	BIGGS		
30/09/1963	QUEENS PARK RANGERS	A	0	1	8713	1	2	3		5		7	9	11	10		4	6	8										
05/10/1963	MILLWALL	A	1	0	6319	1	2	3		5		7	9		10		4	6	8	11					JARMAN				
08/10/1963	HULL CITY	H	4	0	10681	1	2	3		5		7	9		10		4	6	8	11					BIGGS	HAMILTON	BROWN	BRADFORD	
12/10/1963	BRENTFORD	A	5	2	13409	1	2	3		5		7	9		10		4	6	8	11					HAMILTON 3	BIGGS	BROWN		
19/10/1963	CREWE ALEXANDRA	H	1	2	12854	1	2	3		5		7	9		10		4	6	8	11					BIGGS				
22/10/1963	BARNSLEY	H	1	1	13579	1	2	3		5		7	9	11	10		4	6	8						BIGGS				
26/10/1963	CRYSTAL PALACE	A	0	1	18389	1	2	3		5		7	9	11	10		4	6	8										
29/10/1963	BARNSLEY	A	2	1	6338	1	2	3		5		7	9		10		4	6	8	11					HILLARD	BIGGS			
02/11/1963	WALSALL	H	3	0	10840	1	2	3		5		7	9		10		4	6	8	11					JARMAN	BROWN	BRADFORD		
09/11/1963	READING	A	1	3	7976	1	2	3		5		7	9		10			6	8	11	4				HAMILTON				
23/11/1963	COVENTRY CITY	A	2	4	21901	1	2	3		5		7	9		10	11		6	8		4				MABBUTT	BROWN			
30/11/1963	MANSFIELD TOWN	H	3	2	9104	1	2	3		5		7	9		10		4	6	8	11					HILLARD	BIGGS	BRADFORD		
14/12/1963	BRISTOL CITY	H	4	0	19451	1	2	3		5		7	9		10		4	6	8	11					GIBSON og	JARMAN	BIGGS	BRADFORD	
21/12/1963	OLDHAM ATHLETIC	A	2	2	8312	1	2	3		5		7	9		10		4	6	8	11					HAMILTON	JARMAN			
26/12/1963	PORT VALE	A	0	1	11442	1	2	3		5		7	9	11	10		4	6	8										
28/12/1963	PORT VALE	H	4	4	12945	1	2	3		5		7	9		10		4	6	8	11					HAMILTON 2	BIGGS	BROWN		
11/01/1964	PETERBOROUGH UNITED	H	2	2	11009	1	2	3		5		7	9		10		4	6	8	11					JARMAN	OLDFIELD			
18/01/1964	SOUTHEND UNITED	A	4	3	6774	1	2	3		5		7	9		10		4	6	8	11					BIGGS	HAMILTON	BROWN	WATSON og	
01/02/1964	WATFORD	H	1	2	10698	1	2	3		5		7	9		10		4	6	8	11					BIGGS				
08/02/1964	COLCHESTER UNITED	A	3	2	4747	1	2	3		5		7	9		10	11	4	6	8						HAMILTON	JARMAN	BROWN		
15/02/1964	MILLWALL	H	2	2	9486	1	2	3		5		7	9		10	11	4	6	8						JARMAN	BIGGS			
22/02/1964	BRENTFORD	H	3	1	8703	1	2	3				7	9		10	11	4	6	8		5				JARMAN	BIGGS 2-1pen			
26/02/1964	HULL CITY	A	2	0	3907	1	2	3				7	9	11	10		4	6	8		5				HAMILTON	BROWN			
29/02/1964	SHREWSBURY TOWN	A	1	0	6061	1	2	3				7	9	11	10		4	6	8		5				R JONES				
07/03/1964	CRYSTAL PALACE	H	1	3	10596	1	2	3				7	9	11	10		4	6	8		5				HAMILTON				
14/03/1964	WALSALL	A	3	2	3681	1	2	3				7	9	11	10		4	6	8		5				BIGGS 2	HAMILTON			
21/03/1964	SHREWSBURY TOWN	H	7	0	8902	1	2	3				7	9	11	10		4	6	8		5				JARMAN 2	R JONES 2	BIGGS pen	BROWN	STONE
27/03/1964	AFC BOURNEMOUTH	A	0	1	17162	1	2	3		6		7	9	11	10		4		8		5								
28/03/1964	LUTON TOWN	A	2	4	6612	1	2	3		5		7	9	11	10			6	8		4				BIGGS 2-1pen				
31/03/1964	AFC BOURNEMOUTH	H	2	3	12939	1	2	3				7	9	11	10			4	8		5	6			BIGGS	R JONES			
04/04/1964	COVENTRY CITY	H	0	1	12006	1	2	3				7	9	11				4	10		5	6	8						
09/04/1964	NOTTS COUNTY	A	4	3	3883	1	2	3				7	9	11	10		4	6			5		8		R JONES	BIGGS 3			
11/04/1964	MANSFIELD TOWN	A	0	2	8317	1	2	3				7	9	11	10		4	6	8		5								
13/04/1964	LUTON TOWN	H	1	2	8254	1	2	3				7	9	11	10		4	6	8		5				R JONES				
18/04/1964	NOTTS COUNTY	H	4	0	7102	1	2					7	9	11			4	6	10		5		8	3	BIGGS 2	BROWN	OLDFIELD		
21/04/1964	READING	H	2	5	8002	1	2	3		5		7	9	11			4	6	8	10					MABBUTT	R JONES			
25/04/1964	CREWE ALEXANDRA	A	1	4	2086	1	2	3		5		7	9	11	10		4	6	8						BARNES og				
	APPEARANCES					46	46	45	3	34	3	46	46	28	40	7	38	42	39	21	16	2	3	1					
	GOALS					0	2	0	0	0	0	13	30	8	13	0	2	2	13	4	1	0	0	0	OWN GOAL 3				
	LEAGUE CUP																												
04/09/1963	SHREWSBURY TOWN	A	1	1	6950	1	2	3		5		7	9	8			4	6	10	11					BIGGS				
23/09/1963	SHREWSBURY TOWN	H	6	2	12142	1	2	3		5		7	9	8	10		4	6		11					HAMILTON 4	BIGGS 2			
25/09/1963	CRYSTAL PALACE	H	2	0	7194	1	2	3		5		7	9	8	10		4	6		11					JARMAN	BIGGS			
04/11/1963	GILLINGHAM	H	1	1	10149	1	2	3				7	9		10		4	6	8	11	5				BIGGS pen				
06/11/1963	GILLINGHAM	A	1	3	10771	1	2	3				7	9		10		4	6	8	11	5				BIGGS				
	FA CUP																												
16/11/1963	BOURNEMOUTH	A	3	1	12402	1	2	3		5		7	9		10			6	8	11	4				BROWN	BIGGSpen	STONE		
07/12/1963	COVENTRY CITY	A	2	1	26248	1	2	3		5		7	9		10		4	6	8	11					BRADFORD	JARMAN			
04/01/1964	NORWICH CITY	H	2	1	17779	1	2	3		5		7	9		10		4	6	8	11					JARMAN	BRADFORD			
25/01/1964	MANCHESTER UNITED	A	1	4	55722	1	2	3		5		7	9		10		4	6	8	11					CRERAND og				
	GLOUCESTERSHIRE CUP FINAL																												
28/04/1964	BRISTOL CITY	A	2	2	7693	1	2			3		7	9		10		4	6	8		5	11			MUNRO	BROWN			

1964/65

Date						HALL Bernard	HILLARD Douglas	JONES Gwynfor	OLDFIELD Terence	DAVIS Joseph	MABBUTT Raymond	JARMAN Harold	BROWN John	BIGGS Alfred	HAMILTON Ian	JONES Robert	McCROHAN Roy	STONE David	HURFORD David	MUNRO Alexander	HAVERTY Joseph	HUDD David	FRUDE Roger	PARSONS Lindsay				
	DIVISION 3																											
22/08/1964	MANSFIELD TOWN	H	4	1	10621	1	2	3	4	5	6	7	8	9	10	11									JARMAN	BROWN	HAMILTON	BIGGS
25/08/1964	GRIMSBY TOWN	A	1	1	10350	1	2	3	4	5	6	7	8	9	10	11									BIGGS			
29/08/1964	LUTON TOWN	A	2	0	9985	1		3	4	5	6	7	8	9	10	11	2								HAMILTON	JARMAN		
01/09/1964	GRIMSBY TOWN	H	5	3	15542	1		3	4	5	6	7	8	9	10	11	2								JARMAN 2	BROWN	BIGGS	R JONES
05/09/1964	CARLISLE UNITED	H	5	2	12580	1		3	4	5	6	7	8	9	10	11	2								BIGGS 2	JARMAN	HAMILTON	CALDWELL og
07/09/1964	PETERBOROUGH UNITED	A	1	3	14420	1		3	4	5	6	7	8	9	10	11	2								BIGGS			
12/09/1964	PORT VALE	A	1	1	7571	1		3		5	6	7	8	9	10	11	2	4							HAMILTON			
15/09/1964	PETERBOROUGH INITED	H	4	0	17415	1	2			5	6	7	8	9	10	11	3	4							BIGGS 3-1pen	R JONES		
19/09/1964	COLCHESTER UNITED	H	2	2	13211	1	2	3		5	6	7	8	9	10	11	4								BIGGS	HAMILTON		
26/09/1964	BRENTFORD	A	1	1	14150	1	2		4	5	6	7	8	9	10	11	3								McCROHAN			
30/09/1964	AFC BOURNEMOUTH	A	1	1	11487	1		3	4	5	6	7	8	9	10	11		2							BIGGS			
03/10/1964	BRISTOL CITY	H	1	1	25370	1	2	3	4	5	6	7	8	9	10	11									BIGGS			
06/10/1964	AFC BOURNEMOUTH	H	4	2	14003	1		3	4	5	6	7	8	9	10	11		2							BIGGS 2	BROWN	NELSON og	
10/10/1964	SHREWSBURY TOWN	A	1	2	7345	1		3	4	5	6	7	8	9	10	11		2							BIGGS			
14/10/1964	OLDHAM ATHLETIC	A	2	1	7777	1	2	3	4	5	6		8	9	10	11			7						HAMILTON 2			
17/10/1964	READING	H	1	0	12758	1	2	3	4	5	6	7	8	9	10	11									HAMILTON			
20/10/1964	OLDHAM ATHLETIC	H	0	0	13210	1	2	3	9	5	6	7	8		10	11		4										
24/10/1964	SOUTHEND UNITED	A	3	6	6335	1	2	3	4	5	6	7	8		10	11	9								HAMILTON 3			
27/10/1964	GILLINGHAM	H	3	0	12383	1	2	3	4	5	6	7	8		10	9				11					MABBUTT	JARMAN	BROWN	
31/10/1964	BARNSLEY	H	1	0	11773	1	2	3	4	5	6	7	8		10	9				11					MUNRO			
07/11/1964	SCUNTHORPE UNITED	A	1	1	4056	1	2	3	4	5		7	8		10	9		6		11					HAMILTON			
21/11/1964	WATFORD	A	1	1	9130	1	2	3	4	5		7	8		10	9		6		11					MUNRO			
28/11/1964	WORKINGTON	H	4	0	12029	1	2	3	4	5		7	8		10	9		6		11					JARMAN	BROWN	R JONES	MUNRO
12/12/1964	MANSFIELD TOWN	A	0	3	4784	1	2	3	4	5		7	8		10	9		6		11								
19/12/1964	LUTON TOWN	H	3	2	10624	1	2	3		5	4	7	8		10	9		6			11				HAMILTON 3			
26/12/1964	QUEENS PARK RANGERS	H	3	1	17698	1	2	3		5	4	7	8		10	9		6			11				HAMILTON 2	BROWN		
28/12/1964	QUEENS PARK RANGERS	A	1	3	5220	1	2	3		5	4	7	8		10	9		6			11				HAMILTON			
02/01/1965	CARLISLE UNITED	A	2	1	11233	1	2	3		5	4	7	8		10	9		6			11				HAMILTON	JARMAN		
16/01/1965	PORT VALE	H	4	0	10011	1	2	3		5	4	7			10	9		6			11	8			R JONES 2	HUDD	HAVERTY	
23/01/1965	COLCHESTER UNITED	A	1	1	4851	1	2	3		5		7	10		11	9		4		6		8			HAMILTON			
30/01/1965	HULL CITY	A	2	3	28399	1		3	4	5	6	7	8		10	9		2			11				R JONES 2			
06/02/1965	BRENTFORD	H	1	2	14575	1		3	4	5	6	7	10			9		2			11	8			JARMAN			
13/02/1965	BRISTOL CITY	A	1	2	23052	1		3	4	5	6	7	8		10	9		2		11					DAVIS pen			
23/02/1965	SHREWSBURY TOWN	H	0	0	13143	1	2	3		5	6	7	8	9	10	11				4								
27/02/1965	READING	A	1	1	7399	1		3	4	5	6		10	8		9		2		11		7			BIGGS			
06/03/1965	HULL CITY	H	1	1	19899	1		3	4	5	6	7	10	8		9		2		11					JARMAN			
13/03/1965	BARNSLEY	A	2	0	3026	1	2	3	4	5	6	7		9		10				11		8			R JONES 2			
16/03/1965	WALSALL	H	0	1	13717	1	2	3	4	5	6	7	8	9		10				11								
20/03/1965	SCUNTHORPE UNITED	H	2	0	6650	1	2	3	4	5	6	7	8			9				11			10		R JONES	BROWN		
27/03/1965	WALSALL	A	0	2	7509	1	2	3	4	5	6	7	8			9				11			10					
03/04/1965	WATFORD	H	1	0	6849	1		3		5	4	7	8			9				6	11		10	2	JARMAN			
09/04/1965	WORKINGTON	A	1	2	2300	1		3		5	4	7	8			9				6	11		10	2	BROWN			
16/04/1965	EXETER CITY	H	1	1	12194	1		3		5	4	7	8	9						6	11		10	2	BIGGS			
17/04/1965	SOUTHEND UNITED	H	2	2	5578	1	2	3		5	4	7	8	9						6	11		10		BIGGS	JARMAN		
19/04/1965	EXETER CITY	A	1	0	8165	1		3	4		6	7	8	9			2	5		10	11				JARMAN			
24/04/1965	GILLINGHAM	A	3	1	11167	1	2	3	4	5	6	7	8			9				10	11				JARMAN	R JONES	WESTON og	
	APPEARANCES					46	29	44	32	45	41	44	44	24	33	43	10	22	1	21	13	5	6	3				
	GOALS					0	0	0	0	1	1	14	8	18	20	11	1	0	0	3	1	1	0	0	OWN GOAL 3			
	LEAGUE CUP																											
22/09/1964	CHESTERFIELD	H	0	2	7815	1	2	3		5		7	8	9	10	11	4			6								
	FA CUP																											
14/11/1964	WALSALL	A	2	0	10576	1	2	3	4	5		7	8		10	9		6		11					STONE	R JONES		
05/12/1964	WEYMOUTH	H	4	1	12468	1	2		4	5		7	8		10	9	3	6		11					JARMAN 2	MUNRO	HAMILTON	
09/01/1965	STOCKPORT COUNTY	H	0	0	12164	1	2	3		5	4	7	8		10	9		6			11							
11/01/1965	STOCKPORT COUNTY	A	2	3	19624	1	2	3		5	4	7			10	9		6		8	11				R JONES	MABBUTT		
	GLOUCESTERSHIRE CUP FINAL																											
26/04/1965	BRISTOL CITY	H	3	2	8907	1	2	3	4	5	6	7	8		10	9				11					PARR og	R JONES	HAMILTON	

1965/66

Date	Opponent	H/A	F	A	Att	HALL Bernard	HILLARD douglas	PARSONS Lindsay	OLDFIELD Terence	DAVIS Joseph	MABBUTT Raymond	JARMAN Harold	BROWN John	BIGGS Alfred	HAMILTON Ian	JONES Robert	JONES Gwynfor	PETTS John	MUNRO Alexander	GRAYDON Raymond	STONE David	PLUMB Richard	FRUDE Roger	BRIGGS Ronald	WELLER Christopher	RONALDSON Kenneth	WATKINS Robert	TAYLOR Stuart	Scorers				
	DIVISION 3																																
21/08/1965	GRIMSBY TOWN	A	1	1	5402	1	2	3	4	5	6	7	8	9	10	11													R JONES				
24/08/1965	SHREWSBURY TOWN	H	3	2	10173	1	2	3	4	5	6	7	8	9	10	11													HAMILTON	BROWN	WRIGHT og		
28/08/1965	BRENTFORD	H	1	1	12160	1	2	3	4	5	6	7	8	9	10	11													BROWN				
04/09/1965	MANSFIELD TOWN	A	0	2	9560	1	2		4	5	6	7	8	9		11	3	10															
07/09/1965	SWINDON TOWN	H	0	1	15855	1	2		4	5	6	7	8	9	10	11	3																
10/09/1965	YORK CITY	A	5	1	8500	1	2		4	5	6	7	8	9		10	3		11										JARMAN 2	OLDFIELD	MUNRO	BIGGS	
18/09/1965	OXFORD UNITED	H	3	1	9707	1	2		4	5	6	7	8	9		10	3		11										R JONES 3				
25/09/1965	SWANSEA CITY	A	0	3	9500	1	2			5	6		8	9		10	3	4	11	7													
02/10/1965	WALSALL	H	3	0	9357	1	2			A	6A	7	8	9		10	3	4	11		5								R JONES 2	JARMAN			
05/10/1965	SWINDON TOWN	A	3	4	18065	1	2				6	11	8	9		10	3	4		7	5								JARMAN 2	R JONES			
09/10/1965	BRIGHTON & HOVE ALBION	H	0	0	10418	1	2			5	6	11	8			10	3	4		7		9											
16/10/1965	SCUNTHORPE UNITED	A	0	3	4074	1	2		4	5	6	7		8	10	11	3					9											
19/10/1965	OLDHAM ATHLETIC	H	4	0	8568	1	2		4	5	6	7		8	10	11	3					9							PLUMB 2	HAMILTON	JARMAN		
23/10/1965	WATFORD	H	1	1	8826	1	2		4A	5	6	7	8	9	10	11	3		A										R JONES				
25/10/1965	MILLWALL	A	3	3	16151	1	2			5	6	7	8	9		10	3	4	11										JARMAN	BIGGS	HILLARD		
30/10/1965	OLDHAM ATHLETIC	A	0	2	3746	1	2			5	6	7	8A	9		10	3	4	11				A										
01/11/1965	SHREWSBURY TOWN	A	0	1	4007		2	3		5	6	11A		8		10		4	A	7		9		1									
06/11/1965	GILLINGHAM	H	0	0	8422		2	3		5	6		10			11		4		7		9		1	8								
09/11/1965	WORKINGTON	H	2	2	7756		2	3		5		7	10A			11		4	6			9	8	1	A				JARMAN	PLUMB			
22/11/1965	PETERBOROUGH UNITED	H	1	1	6330	1	2		4	5	6	7	8			11	3					9			10				MABBUTT				
27/11/1965	EXETER CITY	A	0	1	5964	1	2		4	5	6	7	8	9		11A	3		A							10							
11/12/1965	HULL CITY	A	1	6	16349	1	2		4A	5	6	11					3	8	A	7			9			10			FRUDE				
27/12/1965	AFC BOURNEMOUTH	H	0	0	10031	1	2		4	5	6	7	8	9	10	11	3																
28/12/1965	AFC BOURNEMOUTH	A	0	1	6153	1	2			5	6	7		9	10	8	3		4								11						
01/01/1966	BRIGHTON & HOVE ALBION	A	3	4	14408	1	2		4	5	6	7	8	9	10	11	3												OLDFIELD	JARMAN	BROWN		
08/01/1966	MILLWALL	H	1	1	9365	1	2		4	3	6	7	8	9		11					5					10			BIGGS				
15/01/1966	WATFORD	A	0	2	4681	1	2		4	3	6	7	8			11					5	9				10							
29/01/1966	GRIMSBY TOWN	H	2	1	8303	1	2		4	3	6	7	10			11					5	9	8						FRUDE 2				
05/02/1966	BRENTFORD	A	5	0	6240	1	2		4	3	6	7	10	9		11					5		8						BIGGS 3	JARMAN	SCOTT og		
12/02/1966	SOUTHEND UNITED	A	0	2	5649	1	2		4	3	6	7	8	9		11		10			5												
19/02/1966	MANSFIELD TOWN	H	6	0	7477	1	2				6	7	8	9		11	3	4			5		10						BIGGS 2	BROWN	R JONES	PETTS	FRUDE
26/02/1966	YORK CITY	H	0	0	8946	1	2			3	6	7	8	9		11		4			5		10										
05/03/1966	SOUTHEND UNITED	H	3	1	7844	1	2			3	6	7	8	9	10	11		4			5								JARMAN	BROWN	STONE		
12/03/1966	OXFORD UNITED	A	0	1	6814	1	2			3	6	7	8	9	10	11		4			5												
19/03/1966	SWANSEA CITY	H	2	1	7491	1	2		A	3	6	7A		9		10		4	11		5		8						FRUDE	R JONES			
26/03/1966	WALSALL	A	1	1	8485	1	2			3	6			9		10		4	11	7	5		8						STONE pen				
29/03/1966	SCUNTHORPE UNITED	H	2	0	7376	1	2	3			6	7		9		10		4	11		5		8						BIGGS	BURKINSHAW og			
02/04/1966	GILLINGHAM	A	0	2	5344	1	2			3	6	7	10	9A		11		4			5		8			A							
08/04/1966	QUEENS PARK RANGERS	A	1	4	13365	1	2			3	6	7	8			10		4	11		5		9						MABBUTT				
09/04/1966	READING	H	0	0	7316	1	2	3	4		6		10			9			11	7	5		8										
12/04/1966	QUEENS PARK RANGERS	H	1	0	9203	1	2			3	6	7	8	9		10		4	11		5A					A			BROWN				
16/04/1966	PETERBOROUGH UNITED	A	2	5	4926	1	2			5	3	7	10	9		11		4	6							8			BIGGS	JARMAN			
23/04/1966	EXETER CITY	H	2	0	6803	1	2	3		5	6	7	10	9		11		4								8			RONALDSON	BROWN			
26/04/1966	WORKINGTON	A	0	0	2557	1	2			3	6	7		9		11		4	A				8A			10		5					
29/04/1966	READING	A	1	0	7314	1	2			3	6	7	10	9		11		4								8		5	JARMAN				
06/05/1966	HULL CITY	H	1	2	9234	1	2			3	6A	7	8			11		4	A				9			10		5	RONALDSON				
	APPEARANCES					43	46	9	21	41	45	42	37	36	12	45	20	27	15	8	18	9	14	3	2	9	1	3					
	SUB					0	0	0	1	1	0	0	0	0	0	0	0	0	6	0	0	0	1	0	1	2	0	0					
	GOALS					0	1	0	2	0	2	13	7	10	2	10	0	1	1	0	2	3	5	0	0	2	0	0	OWN GOAL 3				
	SUBD					0	0	0	2	0	2	2	2	1	0	1	0	0	0	0	1	0	1	0	0	0	0	0					
	LEAGUE CUP																																
21/09/1965	WEST HAM UNITED	H	3	3	18354	1	2				6	7	8	9		10	3	4	11		5								BROWN	PETTS	JARMAN		
29/09/1965	WEST HAM UNITED	A	2	3	13160	1	2				6	7	8	9		10	3	4	11		5								PETTS	R JONES			
	FA CUP																																
13/11/1965	READING	A	2	3	8873		2		6	5		7		8		9	3	4	11					1	8				HILL	R JONES			
	GLOUCESTERSHIRE CUP FINAL																																
12/05/1966	BRISTOL CITY	A	1	0	9431	1	2			3	6	7		9		10		4					8			10		5	JARMAN				

1966/67

Date	Opponent	H/A	F	A	Att	HALL Bernard	HILLARD Douglas	DAVIS Joseph	PETTS John	TAYLOR Stuart	MABBUTT Raymond	JARMAN Harold	BROWN John	BIGGS Alfred	RONALDSON Kenneth	JONES Robert	BRIGGS Ronald	PARSONS Lindsay	STONE David	PLUMB Richard	MUNRO Alexander	HAMILTON Ian	FRUDE Roger	BARNEY Victor	WILLIAMS John	TAYLOR Laurence	JONES Wayne	GRAYDON Raymond	WILLIAMS Robert	LLOYD Laurence	Scorers		
	DIVISION 3																																
20/08/1966	SWANSEA TOWN	H	3	3	7688	1	2	3	4	5	6	7	8	9	10	11															BIGGS	DAVIS pen	JARMAN
27/08/1966	MIDDLESBROUGH	A	2	1	10658		A	3	4		6	7	8			11A	1	2	5	9	10										PLUMB	JARMAN	
03/09/1966	SHREWSBURY TOWN	H	1	0	7145		2	5			6	7	8				1	3	4	9	11	10									STONE		
07/09/1966	READING	A	2	1	7724		2	5			6	7				8	1	3	4	9	11	10									PLUMB	MUNRO	
10/09/1966	COLCHESTER UNITED	A	1	3	4736		2	5			6	7				8	1	3	4	9	11	10									JARMAN		
17/09/1966	SWINDON TOWN	H	3	0	10907	1	2	3			6	7	8	9		11			5			10	4								HAMILTON	JARMAN	HILLARD
24/09/1966	OXFORD UNITED	H	2	1	8745		2	3			6	7	8	9			1		5		11	10	4								BIGGS	DAVIS pen	
27/09/1966	READING	H	2	1	10394		2	3			6	7		9	8		1		5		11	10	4								HILLARD	HAMILTON	
01/10/1966	OLDHAM ATHLETIC	A	0	3	14000		2	3			6	7		9	8		1		5		11	10	4										
04/10/1966	DARLINGTON	H	3	0	7649			3		5	6	7		9	8		1		2		11	10	4								BIGGS 2	RONALDSON	
07/10/1966	DONCASTER ROVERS	A	2	3	11614			3		5	6	7	10	9	8		1		2		11		4								FRUDE	BIGGS	
15/10/1966	MANSFIELD TOWN	H	4	4	7599	1		3		5	6	7	10	9	8				2		11		4								JARMAN 2	RONALDSON	BIGGS
18/10/1966	GILLINGHAM	H	4	1	9113	1	2	3		5	6	7	8	9	10				4		11										JARMAN 2	STONE	RONALDSON
22/10/1966	GRIMSBY TOWN	A	0	0	7341	1	2	3		5	6	7	10	9	8				4		11												
24/10/1966	SCUNTHORPE UNITED	H	1	1	11015	1	2	3		5	6	7	8	9	10				4		11										BIGGS		
29/10/1966	WALSALL	H	4	2	8963	1		3		5	6	7	8	9	10			2	4		11										BIGGS 2	JARMAN	BROWN
02/11/1966	SHREWSBURY TOWN	A	4	3	5768	1		2		5	6	7	8	9	10			3	4		11										JARMAN 2	BROWN	BIGGS
05/11/1966	PETERBOROUGH UNITED	A	1	1	7226	1		2		5	6	7	8	9	10			3	4		11										BROWN		
12/11/1966	TORQUAY UNITED	H	1	0	10902	1		2		5	6	7	8	9	10			3	4A		11			A							STONE		
16/11/1966	GILLINGHAM	A	0	1	6767	1	2	5			6	7	8	9	10			3	4		11												
19/11/1966	BRIGHTON & HOVE ALBION	A	2	3	11542	1	2	5			6	7	8					3	4	9	11	10									JARMAN	MUNRO	
03/12/1966	QUEENS PARK RANGERS	A	0	3	13312	1		2		5	6	7	10A	9	8			3	4		11		A										
10/12/1966	WATFORD	H	0	3	8227	1	A	2			6	7		9A	11			3	5	8	4		10										
17/12/1966	SWANSEA TOWN	A	2	2	6041	1	2	5			6	7	10	9				3	4	8	11										BIGGS	PLUMB	
26/12/1966	ORIENT	A	2	0	6400	1	2	5			6	7	10	9				3	4	8	11A				A						BIGGS	PLUMB	
27/12/1966	ORIENT	H	1	0	15329	1	2	5			A	7	8	9	11A			3	6	10					4						PLUMB		
31/12/1966	MIDDLESBROUGH	H	2	2	10645	1A	2	5			A	7	8	9				3	6	10	11				4						HILLARD	DAVIS pen	
14/01/1967	COLCHESTER UNITED	H	4	1	15415		2	5				7	8	9				3	6	11			10		4	1					FRUDE 2	BIGGS	JARMAN
21/01/1967	SWINDON TOWN	A	1	0	15473		2	3			6	7	8	9					5		11		10		4	1					JARMAN		
04/02/1967	OXFORD UNITED	A	1	4	7489		2	3		5	6	7		9	8						11		10		4	1					BIGGS		
11/02/1967	OLDHAM ATHLETIC	H	2	1	9482			2	6	5	3	7	8	9	11							10			4	1					JARMAN	WILLIAMS	
18/02/1967	WORKINGTON	A	2	0	2348				6		2	7	8	9	11				5		3	10			4	1					BIGGS	HAMILTON	
25/02/1967	DONCASTER ROVERS	H	4	2	9012				6		2	7	10	9					5		3				4	1	8	11			JARMAN	BROWN	BIGGS 2
04/03/1967	MANSFIELD TOWN	A	0	2	12815				6		2	7	8	9					5		3				4	1	10	11					
11/03/1967	WORKINGTON	H	0	1	8619		A		6		2	7		9	10				5	8	3				4	1		11A					
18/03/1967	GRIMSBY TOWN	H	0	0	9474				6		2	7	8	9					5		3				4	1	11		10				
24/03/1967	BOURNEMOUTH	H	1	1	13924		A		6		2	7		9A					5		3		8		4	1	11		10		MABBUTT		
25/03/1967	WALSALL	A	1	1	7408		3		6		2	7		8	10				5	9	11				4	1					JARMAN		
27/03/1967	BOURNEMOUTH	A	0	0	7350		3		6		2	7		8	10				5	9	11				4	1							
01/04/1967	PETERBOROUGH UNITED	H	1	1	9202		3		6		2	7	10	8					5	9	11				4	1					BIGGS		
08/04/1967	TORQUAY UNITED	A	1	2	14171		3		6		2	7		8					5	9	11				4	1			10		R WILLIAMS		
15/04/1967	BRIGHTON & HOVE ALBION	H	2	2	9042		3		6		2	7	8	9					5						4	1	11		10		JARMAN	BIGGS	
22/04/1967	DARLINGTON	A	3	0	5104		3		6		2	7	8	9					5		11		10		4	1					BIGGS	BROWN	JARMAN
24/04/1967	SCUNTHORPE UNITED	A	1	3	4080		3		6		2	7	8	9					5		11		10		4	1					BIGGS		
29/04/1967	QUEENS PARK RANGERS	H	2	1	17721		3		6	5	2	7	8	9							11				4	1	10				BIGGS 2		
06/05/1967	WATFORD	A	1	3	17530		3			5	2	7	8	9					6		11				4	1	10				JONES		
	APPEARANCES					18	29	31	17	16	43	46	34	41	23	5	9	17	42	16	40	11	14	0	21	19	7	3	4				
	SUB					0	4	0	0	0	2	0	0	0	0	0	0	0	0	0	0	0	1	1	1	0	0	0	0				
	GOALS					0	3	3	0	0	1	19	5	23	3	0	0	0	3	5	2	3	3	0	1	0	1	0	1				
	SUBD					1	0	0	0	0	0	0	1	2	1	1	0	0	1	0	1	0	0	0	0	0	0	1	0				
	LEAGUE CUP																																
24/08/1966	CARDIFF CITY	A	0	1	5574	1	2	3	4		6	7	8	9	10	11			5														
	FA CUP																																
26/11/1966	OXFORD CITY	A	2	2	5100	1	2			5	6	7	8	9	10			3	4		11										DAVIS pen	LAMB og	
29/11/1966	OXFORD CITY	H	4	0	9465	1	2			5	6	7	10	9	8			3	4		11										BIGGS 3	RONALDSON	
07/01/1967	LUTON TOWN	H	3	2	8408		2	5			11	7	8	9				3	6	10					4	1					J WILLIAMS	JARMAN	DAVIS
28/01/1967	ARSENAL	H	0	3	35420		2	3			6	7	8	9					5	10	11				4	1							
	GLOUCESTERSHIRE CUP FINAL																																
09/05/1967	BRISTOL CITY	H	0	3	17433						2	11		9				3			6		8		4	1	10	7		5			

1967/68

Date	Opponent					TAYLOR Laurence	MABBUTT Raymond	HILLARD Douglas	WILLIAMS John	TAYLOR Stuart	MUNRO Alexander	GRAYDON Raymond	BIGGS Alfred	PLUMB Richard	BROWN John	JARMAN Harold	FRUDE Roger	BRIGGS Ronald	PARSONS Lindsay	JONES Wayne	JONES Robert	RONALDSON Kenneth	BARNEY Victor	STONE David	WILLIAMS Robert	PETTS John	HAMILTON Ian	PRINCE Francis				
	DIVISION 3																															
19/08/1967	BOURNEMOUTH	A	1	3	6813	1	2	3	4	5	6	7	8	9A	10	11	A												BIGGS			
26/08/1967	COLCHESTER UNITED	H	1	1	8260		2		4	5	6		9			7	8	1	3	10	11								MUNRO pen			
02/09/1967	PETERBOROUGH UNITED	A	1	4	6649			2	4	5	6		9		8	7		1	3	10	11								JARMAN			
06/09/1967	OXFORD UNITED	A	2	0	6803			2	4	5	6		9			7		1	3	10	11	8							JARMAN	SHUKER og		
09/09/1967	MANSFIELD TOWN	H	2	0	7317			2	4	5	6		9			7		1	3	10	11	8							BIGGS	RONALDSON		
16/09/1967	WATFORD	A	0	4	7500			2	4	5	6		9			7		1	3	10	11	8										
23/09/1967	SOUTHPORT	H	1	3	7553			2			6		9			7		1	3	10	11	8	4	5					RONALDSON			
26/09/1967	OXFORD UNITED	H	1	1	6938			2	4		11					7		1	3	10	9	8	6	5					RONALDSON			
30/09/1967	SCUNTHORPE UNITED	A	1	1	3750			2	4	5	11		9			A		1	3	10	7	8A	6						MUNRO			
02/10/1967	BARROW	A	0	1	6380			2A	4	5	3		9			7		1		10	11	8	6	A								
07/10/1967	GRIMSBY TOWN	H	3	0	6626				4	5	3		9			7		1	2	10	11	8	6						RONALDSON	WILLIAMS	W JONES	
14/10/1967	GILLINGHAM	A	0	0	6138			2	4	5	3		9			7		1		10	11	8	6A	A								
21/10/1967	WALSALL	H	2	3	7912			2	4	5	3		9			7		1		10	11	8	6						BIGGS	R JONES		
24/10/1967	BARROW	H	1	0	7802			2	4	5	3	7	9					1		10	11		6	A	8A				GRAYDON			
28/10/1967	NORTHAMPTON TOWN	A	5	4	9126		8	2	4	5		7	9					1		10	11		6	3					WILLIAMS	R JONES	MABBUTT 3	
10/11/1967	TRANMERE ROVERS	A	3	3	6636		8	2	4	5	A	7	9					1		10	11		6A	3					R JONES	MABBUTT 2		
14/11/1967	PETERBOROUGH UNITED	H	2	1	10742		8	2	4	5	6	7	9					1		10	11			3					MABBUTT	HILLARD		
18/11/1967	STOCKPORT COUNTY	H	0	2	9539		8	2	4	5	6	7	9					1		10	11			3								
25/11/1967	BRIGHTON & HOVE ALBION	A	1	1	10373		8	2	4	5	3		9			7		1		10	11			6					BIGGS			
02/12/1967	SHREWSBURY TOWN	H	4	1	7454		8	2	4	5	3			9		7		1		10	11			6					WILLIAMS 2-1pen	R JONES	HEMSLEY og	
16/12/1967	BOURNEMOUTH	H	2	0	7080		11	2	4	5	3		9			7A		1		10				6	8	A			BIGGS	MABBUTT		
23/12/1967	COLCHESTER UNITED	A	0	2	4324		7	2	4	5	3		9					1		10	11A			6	8	A						
26/12/1967	READING	H	1	0	13374		7	2	4	5	3		9					1		8	11	10		6					WILLIAMS pen			
30/12/1967	READING	A	1	2	7459		7	2	4	5	3		9					1		8	11	10		6					RONALDSON			
20/01/1968	WATFORD	H	0	2	7702	1	7	2	4	5	3		9							10	11	8		6								
03/02/1968	SOUTHPORT	A	1	2	5282	1	8	2	4	5	3	7		9						10	11			6					MABBUTT			
10/02/1968	SCUNTHORPE UNITED	H	4	0	5666	1	8		4	5	3		9						2	10	11	7		6					RONALDSON	MABBUTT	BIGGS	R JONES
17/02/1968	OLDHAM ATHLETIC	H	4	3	6864	1	8		4	5	3		9						2	10	11	7		6					BIGGS 2	WILLIAMS 2-1pen		
24/02/1968	GRIMSBY TOWN	A	2	3	3512	1	8		4	5	3		9			A			2	10	11	7A		6					S TAYLOR	BIGGS		
27/02/1968	BURY	A	2	4	9403	1	8	2	4	5	3		9			7				10	11			6					MABBUTT	JARMAN		
02/03/1968	GILLINGHAM	H	1	1	5478	1		2	4	5	3		9			7				8	10	11		6					WILLIAMS pen			
09/03/1968	BURY	H	3	1	7154	1		2	4	5	3		9			11				8	10	7		6					BIGGS	WILLIAMS pen	R JONES	
11/03/1968	MANSFIELD TOWN	A	0	3	6377	1		2	4A	5	3		9							8	10	7		6	A	11						
16/03/1968	WALSALL	A	1	2	7314	1		2	4	5	3		9			11A				8		7		6	10	A			JONES og			
23/03/1968	NORTHAMPTON TOWN	H	2	0	5413	1			8	5	3								2	9	11	7		6	10	4			S TAYLOR 2			
30/03/1968	ORIENT	A	2	2	4261	1			8	5	3					7			2	9	11			6	10	4			JARMAN	R WILLIAMS		
06/04/1968	TRANMERE ROVERS	H	3	1	6602	1		2	8	5						7			3	9	11			6	10	4			R JONES 2	W JONES		
12/04/1968	TORQUAY UNITED	H	1	0	19470	1		2	8	5						7			3	9	11			6	10	4			S TAYLOR			
13/04/1968	STOCKPORT COUNTY	A	1	3	5158	1		2		5	3			9					A		11	7A		6	10	4	8		RONALDSON			
15/04/1968	TORQUAY UNITED	A	0	2	11401	1	9	A		5	3					7A			2	8	11			6	10	4						
20/04/1968	BRIGHTON & HOVE ALBION	H	3	1	6846	1	8	2		5	A	7		9					3A		11			6	10	4			R WILLIAMS	PLUMB	TAYLOR	
23/04/1968	SWINDON TOWN	A	1	4	11438	1	8	2		5	3	7		9							11			6	10	4			PETTS			
27/04/1968	SHREWSBURY TOWN	A	0	0	11401	1	6	2		5		7		9						8	11			3	10	4						
30/04/1968	ORIENT	H	0	2	5749	1	6	2		5		7		9		A				8	11			3	10A	4						
04/05/1968	SWINDON TOWN	H	1	2	8928	1	A	2	4	5		7A				11				9	8	10		3				6	S TAYLOR			
11/05/1968	OLDHAM ATHLETIC	A	5	3	2089	1	4			5	3			9		7			2	10	11				8			6	R JONES 2	W JONES	JARMAN	TAYLOR
	APPEARANCES					23	24	37	38	44	38	12	31	9	2	25	1	23	19	42	43	23	10	33	15	11	1	2				
	SUB					0	1	1	0	0	2	0	0	0	0	3	1	0	1	0	0	0	0	3	1	3	0	0				
	GOALS					0	10	1	9	7	2	1	10	1	0	5	0	0	0	3	10	7	0	0	2	1	0	0	OWN GOAL 3			
	SUBD					0	0	1	1	0	0	1	0	1	0	3	0	0	1	0	1	3	2	0	2	0	0	0				
	LEAGUE CUP																															
23/08/1967	READING	A	0	3	7821	1	2		4	5A	6	7	9		8	11	10		3					A								
	FA CUP																															
09/12/1967	ARNOLD	A	3	0	3390		8	2	4	5	3A		9			7		1		10	11			6		A			R JONES	JARMAN	SMITH og	
06/01/1968	WIMBLEDON	A	4	0	9536	1	7	2	4	5	3		9							8	11	10		6					BIGGS 2	W JONES	RONALDSON	
27/01/1968	BRISTOL CITY	A	0	0	37237	1	8	2	4	5	3		9			7				9	11			6								
30/01/1968	BRISTOL CITY	H	1	2	30157	1	10	2	4	5	3			9		7A				8	11	A		6					S TAYLOR			
	GLOUCESTERSHIRE CUP FINAL																															
14/05/1968	BRISTOL CITY	A	1	1	11375	1	3		8	5	3			9		7			2	10	11							6	MABBUTT			

1968/69

						TAYLOR Laurence	PARSONS Lindsay	MABBUTT Raymond	LLOYD Lawrence	TAYLOR Stuart	PRINCE Francis	GRAYDON Raymond	JONES Wayne	PLUMB Richard	JONES Robert	JARMAN Harold	GADSTON Joseph	WILLIAMS John	STANTON Thomas	RONALDSON Kenneth	WHITE Raymond	BARNEY Victor	WILLIAMS Robert	PETTS John	RHODES Trevor	BROWN Robert	HIGGINS Peter	MUNRO Alexander				
	DIVISION 3																															
10/08/1968	WATFORD	H	1	1	8077	1	2	3	4	5	6	7	8	9	10	11													PRINCE			
17/08/1968	WALSALL	A	2	2	7593	1	2	3	5	4	6		8	9	11	7	10												JARMAN	R JONES		
24/08/1968	BOURNEMOUTH	H	3	2	6671	1	2	3	5	4	6	A	8	9A	11	7	10												GADSTON 2	W JONES		
27/08/1968	SHREWSBURY TOWN	H	1	2	7817	1	2	3	5	4A	6	A	9		11	7	10	8											JARMAN			
31/08/1968	CREWE ALEXANDRA	A	1	6	6835	1	2	3	5		6	7	9		11	8	10A	4	A										W JONES			
06/09/1968	HARTLEPOOL UNITED	H	2	1	7284	1	2	3	5	4	6		9		11	7		8		10									S TAYLOR	RONALDSON		
14/09/1968	PLYMOUTH ARGYLE	A	1	3	9333	1	2	3	5	4	6		9		11	7		8		10									JARMAN			
17/09/1968	NORTHAMPTON TOWN	A	2	2	8002		2	3	5	4	6	7	10		9	11					1	8							R JONES 2			
21/09/1968	SWINDON TOWN	H	2	1	10364		2	3	5	4	6	7	10		9	11					1	8							GRAYDON	W JONES		
27/09/1968	READING	A	1	2	10218		2	3	5	4	6	7	10		9	11					1		8						R JONES pen			
05/10/1968	OLDHAM ATHLETIC	H	1	0	6225	1	2	3	5	4	6	7	10		9	11						8							S TAYLOR			
09/10/1968	SHREWSBURY TOWN	A	0	1	6209	1	2		5	4		7	10	9	8	11			3					6								
12/10/1968	ROTHERHAM UNITED	A	2	3	9693	1	2		5	4		7	10	9		11			3				8	6					WILLIAMS	JARMAN		
19/10/1968	GILLINGHAM	H	5	1	5551	1	2	9	5	4		7	10			11			3				8	6					MABBUTT 2	WILLIAMS	JARMAN	GRAYDON
26/10/1968	MANSFIELD TOWN	A	0	0	5608	1	2		5	4		7	10			11			3				8	6	9							
02/11/1968	TRANMERE ROVERS	H	0	2	6250	1	2		5	4		7	10		9	11			3				8	6								
04/11/1968	BARROW	H	4	2	4937	1	2	9	5	4		7	10A		8	11			3	A				6					R JONES 2-1pen	JARMAN	RONALDSON	
09/11/1968	BRIGHTON & HOVE ALBION	A	1	3	6395	1	2	9	5	4		7	8		11				3	10				6					R JONES			
23/11/1968	ORIENT	A	1	2	3442	1	2	9	5	4		7	10		8	11	A		3A					6					MABBUTT			
30/11/1968	SOUTHPORT	H	2	1	4768	1	2	9A	5	4		7	10		8	11			3	A				6					R JONES 2-1pen			
13/12/1968	ROTHERHAM UNITED	H	1	1	5611	1	2	9	5	4		7	10		8	11			3					6					GRAYDON			
21/12/1968	GILLINGHAM	A	2	0	4289	1	2	9	5	4		7				11			3			8		6		10			JARMAN	BROWN		
26/12/1968	OLDHAM ATHLETIC	A	1	2	6796	1	2	9	5	4		7				11			3			8		6		10			MABBUTT			
10/01/1969	TRANMERE ROVERS	A	2	1	5604	1	2		5	4		7			9	11			3			8		6		10			GRAYDON	R JONES		
18/01/1969	BRIGHTON & HOVE ALBION	H	1	1	8002	1	2		5	4		7			9	11			3			8		6		10			BARNEY			
01/02/1969	TORQUAY UNITED	A	1	0	7373	1			5A	4		7	9		2	11		A	3			8		6		10			JARMAN			
18/02/1969	BARNSLEY	H	4	2	6781	1			5	4		7	9		2	11			3			8		6		10			JARMAN 2	BARNEY	GRAYDON	
24/02/1969	ORIENT	H	0	1	10211	1			5	4		7	9		2	11			3			8		6		10						
01/03/1969	WATFORD	A	0	1	13554	1			5	4		7	9		2	11			3			8		6		10						
04/03/1969	BARNSLEY	A	2	4	7760	1	A		5	4		7	9		2	11			3			8A		6		10			GRAYDON	BROWN		
08/03/1969	WALSALL	H	0	1	7199	1	A		5	4			9		2	7			3			8		6A		10	11					
11/03/1969	TORQUAY UNITED	H	1	1	7433	1	3		5	4			9		2	11		6		7		8				10			SANDERCOCK og			
15/03/1969	BOURNEMOUTH	A	0	0	6989	1	3		5	4			9		2	11		6		7		8				10						
19/03/1969	LUTON TOWN	A	0	3	14506	1	3		5	4			9		2	11		6		7		8				10						
21/03/1969	CREWE ALEXANDRA	H	1	0	5795	1	2		5	4			9		11	7			3	8				6		10			JARMAN			
25/03/1969	MANSFIELD TOWN	H	6	2	5482	1	2		5	4			9		11	7			3	8				6		10			RONALDSON	JARMAN 2	LLOYD	BROWN
28/03/1969	HARTLEPOOL UNITED	A	0	1	3447	1			5	4			9		2	7			3	8				6		10	11					
31/03/1969	LUTON TOWN	H	0	0	8112	1			5	4			9		2	11			3	7		8		6		10						
04/04/1969	NORTHAMPTON TOWN	H	2	1	9424	1			5	4			9		2	11			3	7		8		6		10			JARMAN	BARNEY		
05/04/1969	READING	H	1	3	6704	1			5	4			9		2	11		A	3	7		8A		6		10			BROWN			
08/04/1969	STOCKPORT COUNTY	A	1	0	5486	1			5	4			9		2	7	10		3	8				6				11	GADSTON			
12/04/1969	SWINDON TOWN	A	2	2	20401	1			5	4			9		2	7	10		3	8			11	6					W JONES	GADSTON		
15/04/1969	STOCKPORT COUNTY	H	2	0	6053	1			5	4			9		2	7	10		3	8			11	6					GADSTON	W JONES		
19/04/1969	PLYMOUTH ARGYLE	H	1	1	8699	1				5			9		2	7	10		3	8			11	6	4				W JONES			
21/04/1969	BARROW	A	0	3	3178	1	2			5			9		4	7	10		3	8			11	6								
23/04/1969	SOUTHPORT	A	0	3	3506	1	2			5		7	9		4	11	10		3					6		8						
	APPEARANCES					43	32	19	43	45	11	26	42	5	41	45	10	7	32	17	3	19	9	32	2	20	2	1				
	SUB					0	2	0	0	0	0	2	0	0	0	0	1	2	1	2	0	0	0	0	0	0	0	0				
	GOALS					0	0	4	1	2	1	6	6	0	10	14	5	0	0	3	0	3	2	1	0	4	0	0	OWN GOAL 1			
	SUBD					0	0	1	1	1	0	0	1	1	0	0	1	0	1	0	0	2	0	1	0	0	0	0				
	LEAGUE CUP																															
13/08/1968	SWANSEA TOWN	H	0	2	5015	1	2	3	4	5	6	7	8	9A	10	11	A															
	FA CUP																															
16/11/1968	PETERBOROUGH UNITED	H	3	1	7108	1	2	9	5	4		7	10		8	11			3					6					STANTON	MABBUTT	GRAYDON	
07/12/1968	BOURNEMOUTH	A	0	0	10914	1	2	9	5	4		7	10		8	11			3					6								
10/12/1968	BOURNEMOUTH	H	1	0	11898	1	2	9	5	4		7	10		8	11			3					6					GRAYDON			
04/01/1969	KETTERING TOWN	H	1	1	12230	1	2	9	5	4		7	10		8	11			3					6					GRAYDON			
07/01/1969	KETTERING TOWN	A	2	1	9050	1	2		5	4		7			9	11			3	10		8		6					S TAYLOR	GAMMON og		
25/01/1969	BOLTON WANDERERS	A	2	1	16707	1	2		5	4		7	A		9A	11		9	3			8		6		10			W JONES 2			
12/02/1969	EVERTON	A	0	1	55294	1			5	4		7	9		2	11			3			8		6		10						
	GLOUCESTERSHIRE CUP FINAL																															
28/04/1969	BRISTOL CITY	H	0	5	14735	1	2			5		7			4	11		8	3	9		8A		6		10		A				

1969/70

Date		H/A	F	A	Att	SHEPPARD Richard	STANTON Thomas	MUNRO Alexander	PETTS John	TAYLOR Stuart	MARSLAND Gordon	GRAYDON Raymond	JONES Wayne	STUBBS Robin	JONES Robert	JARMAN Harold	PARSONS Lindsay	BARNEY Victor	JONES Brynley	ROBERTS Phillip	BROWN Robert	PRINCE Francis	TAYLOR Laurence	FORD Anthony	GILBERT Carl	HIGGINS Peter	ALLAN Alexander	MEGSON Donald				
	DIVISION 3																															
09/08/1969	SOUTHPORT	A	0	0	3262	1	2	3	4	5	6	7	8	9	10	11																
16/08/1969	BARNSLEY	H	3	3	7548	1		3		5	6	7	8	9	10	11	2	4A	A										GRAYDON	STUBBS	R JONES	
23/08/1969	READING	A	5	1	8105	1		6		5	4	7	8	9	10	11	3			2									GRAYDON 2	STUBBS	R JONES	MELDRUM og
27/08/1969	PLYMOUTH ARGYLE	H	3	1	11562	1		6		5	4	7	8	9	10	11	3			2									MARSLAND	STUBBS	R JONES	
31/08/1969	HALIFAX TOWN	H	2	0	11768	1		6		5	4	7	8	9	10	11	3			2									JARMAN 2-1pen			
06/09/1969	LUTON TOWN	A	0	4	15198	1		6		5	4	7	8	9	10	11	3			2												
13/09/1969	FULHAM	H	3	2	10633	1		6		5	4	7	8	9	10	11	3			2									GRAYDON	STUBBS	JARMAN	
16/09/1969	GILLINGHAM	A	0	1	5397	1		6		5	4	7A	8	9	10	11	3			2	A											
20/09/1969	MANSFIELD TOWN	A	1	1	6742	1		6		5	4	7	8	9	10	11	3			2									GRAYDON			
27/09/1969	ROCHDALE	H	3	3	8652	1		6		5		7	8	9	10	11	3			2		4							STUBBS	R JONES	JARMAN	
30/09/1969	TRANMERE ROVERS	H	3	0	9152	1	3			5	2	7		9	10	11			8	4		6							STUBBS 2	JARMAN		
04/10/1969	BRIGHTON & HOVE ALBION	A	3	0	11417	1	2	3		5		7		9	10	11			8	4		6							GRAYDON	STUBBS	R JONES	
07/10/1969	BARNSLEY	A	0	2	10008	1	2	3	A	5		7	8	9	10					4	11A	6										
11/10/1969	ROTHERHAM UNITED	H	3	0	8807	1	2	3		5		7	8	9	10	11				4		6							GRAYDON	W JONES	JARMAN	
18/10/1969	BURY	H	2	1	10002	1	2	3		5		7	8	9	10	11				4		6							GRAYDON 2			
25/10/1969	BOURNEMOUTH	A	2	2	6873	1	2A	3		5		7	8	9	10	11	A			4		6							W JONES	STUBBS		
01/11/1969	SHREWSBURY TOWN	H	1	3	10025	1	2	3A		5		7	8	9	10	11	A			4		6							R JONES			
08/11/1969	DONCASTER ROVERS	A	1	3	10065		2	A		5		7	8	9	10A	11	3			4		6	1						R JONES			
22/11/1969	BRADFORD CITY	H	1	1	8986		2			5		7	8	9	10A	11	3			4	A	6	1						JARMAN			
24/11/1969	STOCKPORT COUNTY	A	1	0	2941		2			5		7	8	9	10	11	3			4		6	1						W JONES			
29/11/1969	BARROW	A	1	1	3080		2			5		7	8	9	10	11	3			4		6	1						R JONES			
13/12/1969	FULHAM	A	1	3	6675					5		7A	8	9	A	11	3		10	4		6	1	2					JARMAN			
26/12/1969	READING	H	1	1	12035	1		3		5	4	7		9A	A	11			8			6		2	10				GILBERT			
27/12/1969	HALIFAX TOWN	A	1	1	5388	1	A	3		5	4	7A			9				8			6		2	10	11			TAYLOR			
10/01/1970	MANSFIELD TOWN	H	4	1	5986	1		3		5	4	7			9	11			8			6		2	10				PRINCE	GILBERT	JARMAN	PATE og
17/01/1970	ROCHDALE	A	0	0	6701	1		3		5	4		7A		9	11			8	A		6		2	10							
24/01/1970	TORQUAY UNITED	H	3	1	11356	1		3		5	4			9	11	7			8			6		2	10				JARMAN	STUBBS	GILBERT	
31/01/1970	BRIGHTON & HOVE ALBION	H	0	2	11820	1		3		5	4		A	9A	11	7			8			6		2	10							
07/02/1970	ROTHERHAM UNITED	A	0	0	11668	1		3		5		7	8		9				6	4				2	10	11						
10/02/1970	LUTON TOWN	H	3	0	13297	1		3		5		7	8		9				6	4				2	10	11			FORD pen	MUNRO pen	GRAYDON	
14/02/1970	SOUTHPORT	H	2	0	10834	1		3		5		7	8		9				6	4				2	10	11			GILBERT	HIGGINS		
21/02/1970	BOURNEMOUTH	H	5	2	10095	1		3		5		7	8		9				6	4				2	10	11			B JONES	GRAYDON 2	W JONES	GILBERT
28/02/1970	BURY	A	2	2	3634	1		3		5		7	8	A	9				6	4				2	10	11A			HIGGINS	STUBBS		
03/03/1970	WALSALL	H	3	1	11527	1		3		5		7A	8	9		A			6	4				2	10	11			MUNRO pen	STUBBS	ATTHEY og	
07/03/1970	BRADFORD CITY	A	4	2	9230	1		3		5		7	8	9					6	4				2	10	11			GRAYDON	STUBBS 2	GILBERT	
09/03/1970	ORIENT	A	0	0	14334	1		3		5		7	8	9					6	4				2	10	11						
14/03/1970	BARROW	H	2	1	11229	1		3		5		7	8	9					6	4				2	10	11			MUNRO pen	GILBERT		
18/03/1970	TORQUAY UNITED	A	2	1	8092	1		3		5		7	8	9					6	4				2	10	11			STUBBS	GILBERT		
21/03/1970	WALSALL	A	1	2	4442	1		3		5		7	8A	9					6	4				2	10	11	A		GILBERT			
28/03/1970	ORIENT	H	1	0	22005	1				5		7	8	9					6	4				2	10		11	3	GILBERT			
30/03/1970	SHREWSBURY TOWN	A	0	0	6178	1				5		7	8	9					6	4				2	10		11	3				
31/03/1970	DONCASTER ROVERS	H	1	1	19040	1				5		7	8	9		A			6	4				2	10		11A	3	BRANFOOT og			
04/04/1970	PLYMOUTH ARGYLE	A	2	2	11142	1				5			8A	9		7			6	4				2	A	11	10	3	ALLAN 2			
07/04/1970	STOCKPORT COUNTY	H	1	0	17559	1				5			8	9		7			6	4				2		11	10	3	ALLAN			
14/04/1970	GILLINGHAM	H	1	2	18978	1				5			8	9		7			6	4				2	A	11	10A	3	ALLAN			
17/04/1970	TRANMERE ROVERS	A	2	5	5682	1				5		7	8	9A	A		6			4				2	10	11		3	GILBERT 2			
	APPEARANCES					41	12	33	1	46	16	40	39	38	31	29	15	1	26	38	1	19	5	25	21	16	6	7				
	SUB					0	1	1	1	0	0	0	1	1	3	2	2	0	1	1	2	0	0	0	2	0	1	0				
	GOALS					0	0	3	0	1	1	13	4	15	8	10	0	0	1	0	0	1	0	1	12	2	4	0	OWN GOAL 4			
	SUBD					0	1	1	0	0	0	4	3	3	2	0	0	1	0	0	1	0	0	0	0	1	2	0				
	LEAGUE CUP																															
13/08/1969	BOURNEMOUTH	A	0	3	7478	1	2	3	4A	5	6	7	8	9	10	11	A															
	FA CUP																															
15/11/1969	TELFORD UNITED	A	3	0	4595		2			5		7	8	9	10	11	3			4		6	1						STUBBS	R JONES	GRAYDON	
06/12/1969	ALDERSHOT	A	1	3	9030		2			5		7	8	9	10A	11	3		A	4		6	1						STUBBS			
	GLOUCESTERSHIRE CUP FINAL																															
22/04/1970	BRISTOL CITY	A	1	2	12004	1				5			8		11		3		7	4		6		2	9		10		W JONES			

1970/71

Date	Opponent				Att	SHEPPARD Richard	FORD Anthony	MUNRO Alexander	ROBERTS Phillip	TAYLOR Stuart	JONES Brynley	GRAYDON Raymond	JONES Wayne	STUBBS Robin	ALLAN Alexander	JARMAN Harold	GILBERT Carl	PARSONS Lindsay	PRINCE Francis	MEGSON Donald	JONES Robert	HIGGINS Peter	STEPHENS Kenneth	BROWN Robert	FEARNLEY Gordon	STANTON Thomas	Scorers			
	DIVISION 3																													
15/08/1970	ROCHDALE	A	1	1	4496	1	2	3	4	5	6	7	8	9	10A	11	A										JARMAN			
22/08/1970	SHREWSBURY TOWN	H	2	2	8994	1	2	3A	4	5	6	7	8	9		11	10	A									STUBBS	GILBERT		
29/08/1970	PRESTON NORTH END	A	2	3	7957	1	2	3	4	5	6	7	8	10		11	9A		A								ROBERTS	GRAYDON		
01/09/1970	PORT VALE	H	3	0	7931	1			2	5	10	7		9		11		3	4	6	8						STUBBS	JARMAN	ROBERTS	
05/09/1970	WREXHAM	H	3	2	7699	1			2	5	10	7	A	9		11		3	4A	6	8						STUBBS	R JONES	JARMAN	
12/09/1970	PLYMOUTH ARGYLE	A	0	0	11268	1			2	5	4	7	10			11	9	3		6	8									
19/09/1970	WALSALL	H	3	0	8545	1			2	5	4	7	10			11	9	3		6	8						GRAYDON	GILBERT	JARMAN pen	
22/09/1970	DONCASTER ROVERS	H	2	0	11048	1			2	5	4	7	10		A	11A	9	3		6	8						GRAYDON	TAYLOR		
26/09/1970	BRIGHTON & HOVE ALBION	A	0	0	10118	1			2	5	4	7	10		A	11	9A	3		6	8									
30/09/1970	ASTON VILLA	A	1	1	32082	1			2	5		7	10	9			A	3	4	6	8	11A					GRAYDON			
03/10/1970	CHESTERFIELD	H	3	2	10669	1		3	6	5		7	10	8			9	2	4		11						W JONES	GRAYDON	PHELAN og	
10/10/1970	GILLINGHAM	A	4	1	4348	1			2	5		7A	10	9		11	A	3	4	6	8						STUBBS 4			
17/10/1970	ROCHDALE	H	2	2	11712	1			2	5		7	10	9		11A	A	3	4	6	8						STUBBS	R JONES		
20/10/1970	MANSFIELD TOWN	H	2	0	12220	1			2	5		7	10	9		11		3	4	6	8						JARMAN	R JONES		
24/10/1970	BURY	H	0	1	10928	1		A	2	5		7	10	9		11		3	4	6	8A									
31/10/1970	ROTHERHAM UNITED	A	1	1	7478	1			2	5	10	7		9		11	8	3	4	6							MEGSON			
07/11/1970	READING	H	4	0	15957	1			2	5	10	7		9		11	8	3	4	6							GRAYDON	STUBBS	JARMAN	ROBERTS
10/11/1970	BRADFORD CITY	H	4	2	13368	1			2	5	10	7		9		11	8	3	4	6							TAYLOR	JARMAN 3		
13/11/1970	TRANMERE ROVERS	A	2	0	3471	1			2	5	10	7		9		11	8A	3	4	6	A						STUBBS	GRAYDON		
28/11/1970	TORQUAY UNITED	A	1	1	9281	1			2	5	10	7	11	9	A		8A	3	4	6							ROBERTS			
05/12/1970	HALIFAX TOWN	H	1	0	12289	1			2	5	10	7		9		11	8	3	4	6							B JONES pen			
18/12/1970	SHREWSBURY TOWN	A	4	1	4546	1			2	5	10	7	4	9	11			3	6		8						GRAYDON 2	STUBBS 2		
26/12/1970	SWANSEA CITY	H	0	0	15146	1			2	5	10	7	4	9	11			3	6		8									
02/01/1971	BARNSLEY	A	4	0	8527	1			2	5	10	11	4	9				3	6		8		7				STUBBS	STEPHENS	GRAYDON	W JONES
09/01/1971	ASTON VILLA	H	1	2	25836	1			2	5	10	11	6A	9			A	3	4		8		7				STUBBS			
16/01/1971	MANSFIELD TOWN	A	1	4	6357	1			2	5	10	11A	4				9	3	6		8		7	A			W JONES			
06/02/1971	HALIFAX TOWN	A	0	0	7716	1			2	5		7	8	9		11	10	3	4	6										
13/02/1971	FULHAM	H	0	1	18875	1			2	5			8	9		11	10A	3	4	6	A		7							
20/02/1971	BRADFORD CITY	A	1	1	6073	1			2	5	A		8	9		11A	10	3	4				7	6			GILBERT			
27/02/1971	ROTHERHAM UNITED	H	0	2	11092	1			2	5			8	9	10	A		3	4		11A		7	6						
02/03/1971	FULHAM	A	1	2	15971	1			2	5	7		8	9	10			3	4				11	6			PRINCE			
06/03/1971	BURY	A	0	3	3457	1			2	5		7	8	9	10			3	4		A		11	6A						
09/03/1971	DONCASTER ROVERS	A	1	0	4000	1			2	5	8	7		9	10	11		3	4	6							ALLAN			
13/03/1971	TRANMERE ROVERS	H	0	1	9249	1			2	5	8	7A		9	10	11		3	4	6	A									
16/03/1971	BARNSLEY	H	3	0	6832	1			2	5	8	7	A	9		11A		3	4	6					10		GRAYDON	JARMAN 2		
20/03/1971	READING	A	2	0	5415	1			2	5	8	7	A	9		11A		3	4	6					10		JARMAN	W JONES		
23/03/1971	TORQUAY UNITED	H	1	1	11476	1			2	5	8	7	A	9		11		3	4	6A					10		SLEEUWENHOEK og			
27/03/1971	WREXHAM	A	0	1	6182	1			2	5	8	7	6	9				3	4		11				10					
03/04/1971	PRESTON NORTH END	H	0	0	10802	1			2	5	8A	7	6	9		A		3	4		10		11							
10/04/1971	SWANSEA CITY	A	3	1	9008	1			2	5	8	7	6	9	10			3	4				11				STUBBS	ALLAN	W JONES	
12/04/1971	CHESTERFIELD	A	0	2	8435	1			2	5	8	7	6A	9	10			3	4		A		11							
13/04/1971	PLYMOUTH ARGYLE	H	1	3	8392	1			2	5		7			9	11		3	4					8	10	6	GRAYDON			
17/04/1971	GILLINGHAM	H	2	0	5260	1			6	5		7		10	9A	11		3	4		2		8			A	STUBBS	TAYLOR		
24/04/1971	WALSALL	A	2	1	3916	1			2	5		7		10		11		3	4		9		8			6	TAYLOR	GRAYDON		
26/04/1971	PORT VALE	A	0	2	4525	1			2	5		7		10		11A		3	4		9	A	8			6				
01/05/1971	BRIGHTON & HOVE ALBION	H	1	3	5530	1			2	5		7A	A	10		11		3	4		9		8			6	STUBBS			
	APPEARANCES					46	3	4	46	46	30	42	29	40	12	31	17	43	39	24	24	1	15	5	5	4				
	SUB					0	0	1	0	0	1	0	5	0	3	2	5	1	1	0	5	1	0	1	0	1				
	GOALS					0	0	0	4	4	1	13	5	17	2	12	3	0	1	1	3	0	1	0	0	0	OWN GOAL 2			
	SUBD					0	0	1	0	0	1	4	2	0	2	6	5	0	1	1	2	1	0	1	0	0				
	LEAGUE CUP																													
08/08/1970	BRIGHTON & HOVE ALBION	H	1	0	7276	1	2	3	4	5	6	7	8	9		11	10										GRAYDON			
08/09/1970	NEWCASTLE UNITED	H	2	1	16824	1			2	5	4	7	10			11	9	3		6	8						R JONES 2			
07/10/1970	NORWICH CITY	A	1	1	11518	1			2	5		7	10	8		A	9A	3	4	6	11						R JONES			
13/10/1970	NORWICH CITY	H	3	1	19122	1			2	5		7	10			11	9	3	4	6	8						TAYLOR	MEGSON	ROBERTS	
27/10/1970	BIRMINGHAM CITY	H	3	0	21426	1			2	5	10	7		9		11	8	3	4	6							HYND og	GILBERT	STUBBS	
17/11/1970	ASTON VILLA	H	1	1	28720	1			2	5	10	7		9		11A	8	3	4	6	A						TAYLOR			
25/11/1970	ASTON VILLA	A	0	1	36482	1			2	5	10	7		9		11	8	3	4	6										
	FA CUP																													
21/11/1970	FULHAM	A	2	1	12912	1			2	5	10	7		9		11	8	3	4	6							GILBERT 2			
12/12/1970	ALDERSHOT	A	1	1	7748	1			2	5	10	7	A	9		11	8	3	4A	6							JARMAN			
15/12/1970	ALDERSHOT	H	1	3	10743	1			2	5	8A	7		9		11	A	3	4	6	10						STUBBS			
	GLOUCESTERSHIRE CUP																													
04/05/1971	BRISTOL CITY	H	1	1	12256	1			2	5	8	7	6	10	9	11A		3	4				A				STEPHENS			

1971/72

Date					Att	SHEPPARD Richard	ROBERTS Phillip	PARSONS Lindsay	GODFREY Brian	TAYLOR Stuart	PRINCE Francis	STEPHENS Kenneth	JONES Wayne	ALLAN Alexander	STUBBS Robin	JONES Brynley	GREEN Michael	JARMAN Harold	BROWN Robert	JONES Robert	CLARKE Allen (L)	FEARNLEY Gordon	STANTON Thomas	BANNISTER Bruce	HIGGINS Peter	RUDGE John	CRABTREE Richard	JOHN Malcolm	DALRYMPLE Malcolm				
	DIVISION 3																																
14/08/1971	YORK CITY	A	0	0	6360	1	2	3	4	5	6	7	8	9	10	11A	A																
21/08/1971	TRANMERE ROVERS	H	2	1	10258	1	2	3	4	5	6	7	8	9	10			11												ALLAN 2-2pens			
28/08/1971	TORQUAY UNITED	A	1	1	8635	1	2	3	4	5	6	7	8	9	10			11												W JONES			
31/08/1971	SWANSEA CITY	A	0	2	6801	1	2	3	4	5	6	7	8	9	10A			11	A														
04/09/1971	BRADFORD CITY	H	7	1	8463	1	2	3	4	5	6	7	8	9				11		10										GODFREY 3	JARMAN 2	R JONES 2	
11/09/1971	OLDHAM ATHLETIC	A	2	3	9457	1	2	3	4	5	6	7	8	9	A			11A		10										ALLAN	GODFREY		
18/09/1971	BARNSLEY	H	3	0	9278	1	2	3	4	5	6	7	8	9				11		10										ALLAN 2	GODFREY		
25/09/1971	NOTTS COUNTY	A	3	2	13101		2	3	4	5	6	7	8	9		11				10	1									R JONES 2	ALLAN		
29/09/1971	BRIGHTON & HOVE ALBION	A	1	3	12649	1	2	3	4	5	6	7A	8	9		11A			A	10										R JONES			
02/10/1971	ASTON VILLA	H	0	1	20428	1	2	3	4	5	6	7	8	9			A	11		10													
09/10/1971	MANSFIELD TOWN	A	0	0	3830	1	2A	3		5	6		8	9		4		11	A	10		7											
16/10/1971	YORK CITY	H	5	4	6876	1	4	3	8	5	6	7A	10	A				11	2	9										JARMAN 3-1pen	STEPHENS 2		
23/10/1971	ROCHDALE	A	1	3	4753	1	4	3	8	5	6	7	10	A				11	2	9A										STEPHENS			
30/10/1971	BOLTON WANDERERS	H	2	0	11532	1	2	3A	4	5	6	7	8	9				11				10	A							GODFREY	ROBERTS		
06/11/1971	WALSALL	A	0	2	3978	1	2	3	4	5	6	7A	8	9				11		10			A										
09/11/1971	ROTHERHAM UNITED	H	1	2	13081	1	2	3	4	5	6	7	8					11		9				10						JARMAN			
13/11/1971	SHREWSBURY TOWN	H	3	1	8849	1	2	3	4A	5	6	7	8		A			11		9				10						R JONES 2	FELLOWS og		
27/11/1971	PLYMOUTH ARGYLE	H	2	2	9568	1	2	3	4	5	6	7	8		9			11A		A				10						JARMAN	W JONES		
04/12/1971	WREXHAM	A	1	1	6333	1	2	3	11	5	4	7	8		9		6							10						GODFREY			
18/12/1971	BRADFORD CITY	A	1	1	5423	1	2	3	4	5	6	11	8		9							7		10						STEPHENS			
27/12/1971	PORT VALE	H	2	1	12073	1	2	3	4	5	6	11	8A		9			7		A				10						BANNISTER pen	PRINCE		
01/01/1972	BARNSLEY	A	0	0	4499	1	2	3	4	5	6	7	8	9A						A				10	11								
08/01/1972	TORQUAY UNITED	H	2	0	8344	1	2	3	6	5	4	7	8							9				10	11					PRINCE	HARRISON og		
22/01/1972	BRIGHTON & HOVE ALBION	H	2	2	9744	1	2	3	6	5	4	7	8		9									10	11					STEPHENS	HIGGINS		
29/01/1972	ROTHERHAM UNITED	A	0	0	17728	1	2	3	6	5	4	7	8		9			A						10	11A								
05/02/1972	HALIFAX TOWN	A	1	2	2021	1	2	3	6	5	4	7	8		9			A						10	11A					BANNISTER			
12/02/1972	ROCHDALE	H	5	2	7042	1	2	3	6	5	4	7	8		9									10	11					STEPHENS	W JONES	BANNISTER 2	PRINCE
19/02/1972	BOLTON WANDERERS	A	0	0	5819	1	2	3	6	5	4	7	9			9								10	11								
26/02/1972	WALSALL	H	2	1	8665	1	2	3	6	5	4	7	8											10	11	9				STEPHENS	GODFREY		
04/03/1972	SHREWSBURY TOWN	A	2	2	3001	1	2	3A	6	5	4	7	8	9			A							10	11					ALLAN 2			
08/03/1972	AFC BOURNEMOUTH	A	0	2	9151	1	2	3		5	4	7	8	9A			6							10	11	A							
11/03/1972	MANSFIELD TOWN	H	2	1	5574	1	2	3	A	5	4		8				6	11		7A				10		9				PATE og	BANNISTER		
14/03/1972	BLACKBURN ROVERS	H	3	0	7290	1	2	3	11	5	4	A	8				6	7A						10		9				BANNISTER 2-2pens	RUDGE		
17/03/1972	TRANMERE ROVERS	A	1	0	4294	1	2	3	11	5	4	7	8				6							10		9				BANNISTER			
25/03/1972	OLDHAM ATHLETIC	H	1	0	7613	1	2	3	11	5	4	7	8				6		A					10		9A				CRANSTON og			
27/03/1972	BLACKBURN ROVERS	A	2	1	5740		2	3	11	5	4	7A	8	9		A	6							10			1			W JONES	B JONES		
01/04/1972	PORT VALE	A	0	0	3823		2	3		5	4	11	8	9A		7	6						A	10			1						
03/04/1972	ASTON VILLA	A	1	2	45158		2	3	11	5	4	7A	8				6			9			A	10			1			STANTON			
04/04/1972	NOTTS COUNTY	H	0	2	11988		2	3	11A	5	4					8	6	A		9			7				1	10					
08/04/1972	HALIFAX TOWN	H	1	0	5642		2	3		5	4		7			10	6			8						9	1	11		JOHN			
15/04/1972	PLYMOUTH ARGYLE	A	1	2	8938		2	3	A	5	4	7	8			11A	6							10		9	1			RUDGE			
18/04/1972	AFC BOURNEMOUTH	H	1	2	11372		2	3	11	5	4	7	8				6							10		9	1			RUDGE			
22/04/1972	WREXHAM	H	3	1	5427		2	3	11	5	4	7	8	9			6							10					1	ALLAN	BANNISTER	STEPHENS	
25/04/1972	SWANSEA CITY	H	2	1	6881		2	3	11A	5	4	7	8	9			6	A						10					1	W JONES	BANNISTER		
29/04/1972	CHESTERFIELD	A	3	1	4542	1	2	3		5	4	7	8	9			6							10	11					ALLAN	HIGGINS	TAYLOR	
02/05/1972	CHESTERFIELD	H	3	1	8006	1	2	3		5	4	7	8	9			6							10A	11	A				ALLAN	BANNISTER 2		
	APPEARANCES					36	46	46	38	46	46	41	45	22	12	9	17	18	2	17	1	3	1	29	12	8	7	2	2				
	SUB					0	0	0	2	0	0	1	0	2	2	1	3	4	4	3	0	0	4	0	0	2	0	0	0				
	GOALS					0	1	0	8	1	3	8	5	11	0	1	0	7	0	7	0	0	1	12	2	3	0	1	0	OWN GOAL 4			
	SUBD					0	1	2	3	0	0	5	1	3	1	3	0	3	0	2	0	0	0	1	2	1	0	0	0				
	LEAGUE CUP																																
18/08/1971	EXETER CITY	A	3	0	6418	1	2	3	4	5	6	7	8	9	10			11												PRINCE	GILES og	STUBBS	
07/09/1971	SUNDERLAND	H	3	1	15262	1	2	3	4	5	6	7	8	9				11		10										JARMAN	W JONES	ALLAN pen	
05/10/1971	CHARLTON ATHLETIC	H	2	1	14649	1	2	3	4	5	6		8	9				7		10		11								TAYLOR	JARMAN		
26/10/1971	QUEENS PARK RANGERS	A	1	1	17045	1	2	3	4	5	6	7	8	9				11				10								JARMAN			
02/11/1971	QUEENS PARK RANGERS	H	1	0	24373	1	2	3	4	5	6	7	8	9				11		10										ALLAN			
23/11/1971	STOKE CITY	H	2	4	33624	1	2	3	4	5	6	7	8	9	10			11												STUBBS	GODFREY pen		
	FA CUP																																
20/11/1971	TELFORD UNITED	H	3	0	8762	1	2	3	4	5	6	7A	8		A			11		9				10						BANNISTER 2	GODFREY		
11/12/1971	CAMBRIDGE UNITED	H	3	0	8768	1	2	3	4	5	A	7	8		9		6A	11						10						TAYLOR	BANNISTER	GODFREY	
15/01/1972	LEEDS UNITED	A	1	4	33565	1	2	3	6	5	4	7	8	9A									A	10						ALLAN			
	GLOUCESTERSHIRE CUP																																
09/05/1972	BRISTOL CITY	A	1	1	13137	1	2	3	6	5	4	7A	8	9		A									11	10				ALLAN			

1972/73

						SHEPPARD Richard	ROBERTS Phillip	PARSONS Lindsay	GREEN Michael	TAYLOR Stuart	STANTON Thomas	STEPHENS Kenneth	JONES Wayne	ALLAN Alexander	BANNISTER Bruce	GODFREY Brian	JONES Brynley	FEARNLEY Gordon	AITKEN Peter	PRINCE Francis	RUDGE John	JONES Robert	JARMAN Harold	HIGGINS Peter	DALRYMPLE Malcolm	DOBSON Colin	COOMBES Jeffery	EADIE James	WARBOYS Alan				
	DIVISION 3																																
12/08/1972	BLACKBURN ROVERS	H	3	0	10744	1	2	3	4	5	6	7	8	9	10	11														BANNISTER	GODFREY	ARENTOFT og	
19/08/1972	HALIFAX TOWN	A	0	3	2812	1	2	3	4	5	6	7A	8	9	10	11	A																
26/08/1972	GRIMSBY TOWN	H	2	1	9158	1	2	3	4A	5	6	7	8	9	10	11		A												GODFREY	FEARNLEY		
29/08/1972	CHESTERFIELD	H	2	2	9409	1	2	3		5	6	7	8	9	10	11			4											GODFREY 2			
02/09/1972	PORT VALE	A	1	2	3468	1	2	3		5	6	7	8	9A	10	11		A	4											ALLAN			
09/09/1972	WREXHAM	H	2	0	8207	1	2	3	4	5	6	7A	8	9	10	11		A												W JONES	GREEN		
16/09/1972	OLDHAM ATHLETIC	A	0	3	5827	1	2	3	4	5	6	7	8	9A	10	11		A															
19/09/1972	BOLTON WANDERERS	H	1	1	9572	1	2	3	4	5	6	7	8		10	11		9												BANNISTER			
23/09/1972	PLYMOUTH ARGYLE	H	2	0	8458	1	2	3	4	5		7			8	11		10		6	9									BANNISTER	STEPHENS		
25/09/1972	BRENTFORD	A	1	2	9710	1	2	3	4	5		7			8	11		10		6	9									FEARNLEY			
30/09/1972	SWANSEA CITY	A	2	0	3711	1	2	3	4	5		7			8	11		10		6	9									RUDGE 2			
07/10/1972	YORK CITY	H	1	2	7601	1	2	3	4	5		7	8		10	11		A		6	9A									BANNISTER pen			
14/10/1972	ROTHERHAM UNITED	A	1	1	4463	1	2	3		5		7	8		10	6				4	9	11								BANNISTER pen			
21/10/1972	SHREWSBURY TOWN	H	5	1	6800	1	2	3		5			8		10	6		A		4	9A	11	7							BANNISTER 2	RUDGE	GODFREY	FEARNLEY
23/10/1972	TRANMERE ROVERS	A	1	1	3474	1	2	3		5			8	A	10	6		9		4		11	7A							W JONES			
28/10/1972	WATFORD	A	1	2	8351	1	2	3		5			8		10	6		9		4		11	7							GODFREY			
04/11/1972	BRENTFORD	H	3	1	7907	1	2	3		5		7	8A		10	6		A		4	9			11						BANNISTER 2	W JONES		
07/11/1972	NOTTS COUNTY	H	1	0	6678	1	2	3	4	5		7			10	8				6	9			11						RUDGE			
11/11/1972	BOLTON WANDERERS	A	0	2	8419	1	2	3	4	5	A	7		9	10	8A				6				11									
24/11/1972	SOUTHEND UNITED	A	0	0	5873		2	3		5	6					10A		8	4	A	9		7		1	11							
02/12/1972	SCUNTHORPE UNITED	H	5	1	5715	1	2	3		5	6							8	4	10	9A		7			11	A			TAYLOR 2	ROBERTS	RUDGE	FEARNLEY
09/12/1972	ROCHDALE	A	0	0	1791	1	2	3		5	8				10				4	6	9		7			11							
16/12/1972	AFC BOURNEMOUTH	A	0	0	11767	1	2	3		5	7			9	8	10			4	6			11										
23/12/1972	CHARLTON ATHLETIC	H	2	1	8512	1	2	3		5		7			8	10			4	6	9		11							JARMAN 2			
26/12/1972	PLYMOUTH ARGYLE	A	2	3	10399	1	2	3		5		7			8	10		A	4	6	9A		11							BANNISTER	GODFREY		
30/12/1972	HALIFAX TOWN	H	4	1	8468	1	2	3		5	A			9	8	10			4	6			7			11A				JARMAN	TAYLOR	BANNISTER	PRINCE
06/01/1973	GRIMSBY TOWN	A	0	2	8975	1	2	3		5	8			9	10	11			4	6			7										
13/01/1973	TRANMERE ROVERS	H	2	0	8909	1A	2	3		5	A				10	8			4	6	9		7			11				DOBSON	RUDGE		
27/01/1973	WREXHAM	A	2	2	3138		2	3	5A		A				10	8			4	6	9		7		1	11				BANNISTER	RUDGE		
30/01/1973	PORT VALE	H	4	1	10019		2	3			6				10	8			5	4	9		7		1	11				RUDGE	GODFREY	BANNISTER 2-1pen	
03/02/1973	NOTTS COUNTY	A	0	2	11938		2	3			6				10	8		A	5	4A	9		7		1	11							
10/02/1973	OLDHAM ATHLETIC	H	3	3	9932		2	3		5	6				10	8			4		9		7		1	11				TAYLOR	STANTON	JARMAN	
17/02/1973	BLACKBURN ROVERS	A	0	0	12378		2	3		5	6	7			10	11A	8	A	4		9							1					
24/02/1973	AFC BOURNEMOUTH	H	2	0	18344		2	3		5	6	7			10	11	8		4		9							1		JONES B	BANNISTER pen		
03/03/1973	YORK CITY	A	0	0	4202		2	3		5	6	7			10	11	8		4		9							1					
06/03/1973	ROCHDALE	H	0	0	11776		2	3		5	6	7			10	11A	8	A	4									1	9				
10/03/1973	ROTHERHAM UNITED	H	3	0	9469		2	3		5	6	7			10		8		4					11				1	9	JONES B	HIGGINS	BANNISTER pen	
16/03/1973	SHREWSBURY TOWN	A	2	4	3593		2	3		5	6	7			10		8		4		A			11A				1	9	BANNISTER	RUDGE		
19/03/1973	WALSALL	A	3	4	4595		2	3		5	6	7			10		8	A	4A		11							1	9	WARBOYS 2	BANNISTER		
27/03/1973	WATFORD	H	2	1	6798		2	3		5	6	7			10	11			4	8A	A							1	9	TAYLOR	BANNISTER		
31/03/1973	SOUTHEND UNITED	H	1	2	6374			3			2	7			10	6	8		5	4	11							1	9	RUDGE			
07/04/1973	SCUNTHORPE UNITED	A	2	0	1784			3			2	7			10	6	8A		5	4	11		A					1	9	WARBOYS	BANNISTER		
14/04/1973	WALSALL	H	2	1	6285		2	3		5	8	7			10	6				4			11					1	9	WARBOYS	BANNISTER		
20/04/1973	SWANSEA CITY	H	3	1	8348		2	3		5	8	7			10	6			4				11					1	9	TAYLOR	BANNISTER 2		
24/04/1973	CHARLTON ATHLETIC	A	3	3	4724		2	3		5		7			10	6			4		11						8	1	9	WARBOYS	BANNISTER	TUMBRIDGE og	
28/04/1973	CHESTERFIELD	A	1	0	3849		2	3		5		7			10	6				4	11						8	1	9	BANNISTER			
	APPEARANCES					27	44	46	13	41	28	32	14	11	44	41	9	8	27	27	26	4	18	5	5	9	2	14	11				
	SUB					0	0	0	0	0	4	0	0	1	0	0	1	12	0	1	2	0	1	0	0	0	1	0	0				
	GOALS					0	1	0	1	6	1	1	3	1	25	8	2	4	0	1	10	0	4	1	0	1	0	0	5	OWN GOAL 2			
	SUBD					1	0	0	2	0	0	2	1	2	0	4	1	0	1	2	4	0	1	1	0	1	0	0	0				
	WATNEY CUP																																
29/07/1972	WOLVERHAMPTON W	H	2	0	12489	1	2	3	4	5		7	8	9	10	11				6										BANNISTER pen	STEPHENS		
02/08/1972	BURNLEY	A	2	0	10589	1	2	3	4	5		7	8	9	10	11				6										PRINCE	BANNISTER		
05/08/1972	SHEFFIELD UNITED	H	0	0	19768	1	2	3	4	5		7	8	9	10	11	A			6A													
	LEAGUE CUP																																
18/08/1972	CARDIFF CITY	A	2	2	14541	1	2	3	4	5	6	7	8	9	10	11														W JONES	GODFREY		
22/08/1972	CARDIFF CITY	H	3	1	14550	1	2	3	4	5	6	7	8A	9	10	11		A												GODFREY	BANNISTER	W JONES	
05/09/1972	BRIGHTON & HOVE ALBION	H	4	0	9530	1	2	3	4	5	6	7	8A	9	10	11		A												W JONES	FEARNLEY	ALLAN	STANTON
03/10/1972	MANCHESTER UNITED	H	1	1	33597	1	2	3	4	5		7	8		10	11				6	9									RUDGE			
11/10/1972	MANCHESTER UNITED	A	2	1	29349	1	2	3		5		7	8		10	6				4	9	11								RUDGE	BANNISTER		
31/10/1972	WOLVERHAMPTON W	A	0	4	20272	1	2	3		5			7	A	8	6	10			4	9	11A											
	FA CUP																																
18/11/1972	HAYES	A	0	1	6000		2	3	4	5	8	7		9A	10					6	A			11	1								
	GLOUCESTERSHIRE CUP																																
01/05/1973	BRISTOL CITY	H	2	2	12350		2	3	4A	5		7			10	6	A				11						8	1	9	BANNISTER	WARBOYS		

1973/74

Date	Opponent	H/A	F	A	Att	EADIE James	JACOBS Trrevor	PARSONS Lindsay	GREEN Michael	TAYLOR Stuart	STANTON Thomas	STEPHENS Kenneth	JONES Brynley	WARBOYS Alan	BANNISTER Bruce	DOBSON Colin	FEARNLEY Gordon	PRINCE Francis	JOHN Malcolm	RUDGE John	AITKEN Peter	COOMBES Jeffrey	STANIFORTH David	O'BRIEN Gerald (L)	Scorers		
	DIVISION 3																										
25/08/1973	AFC BOURNEMOUTH	A	3	0	11379	1	2	3	4	5	6	7A	8	9	10	11	A								WARBOYS 2	BANNISTER	
01/09/1973	CHARLTON ATHLETIC	H	2	1	7323	1	2	3	4	5	8		7	9	10	11		6							WARBOYS	BANNISTER	
08/09/1973	GRIMSBY TOWN	A	1	1	7640	1	2	3	4	5	8		7	9	10	11		6							JONES		
11/09/1973	HEREFORD UNITED	H	1	1	12620	1	2	3	4	5	8	7A		9	10	11	A	6							TAYLOR		
15/09/1973	HALIFAX TOWN	H	2	0	7485	1	2	3	4	5	8	7		9	10	11		6							STANTON 2		
18/09/1973	SHREWSBURY TOWN	A	2	0	3016	1	2	3	4	5	8	7		9	10	11		6							PRINCE	KING og	
22/09/1973	BLACKBURN ROVERS	A	2	0	8424	1	2	3	4	5	8	7A		9	10	11	A	6							BANNISTER	WARBOYS	
29/09/1973	CAMBRIDGE UNITED	H	1	0	8919	1	2	3	4	5	8	7		9	10	11		6							DOBSON		
02/10/1973	SHREWSBURY TOWN	H	1	0	11455	1	2	3	4	5	8	7		9	10	11		6							WARBOYS		
06/10/1973	WATFORD	A	0	0	10202	1	2	3	4	5	8	7		9	10	11		6									
13/10/1973	PORT VALE	H	1	1	8882	1	2	3	4	5	8	7		9	10	11		6							BANNISTER		
20/10/1973	YORK CITY	H	0	0	8706	1	2	3	4	5	8	7		9	10	11		6									
24/10/1973	HEREFORD UNITED	A	0	0	12501	1	2	3	4	5	8	7A		9	10	11	A	6									
27/10/1973	HUDDERSFIELD TOWN	A	2	1	9532	1	2	3	4	5	8			9	10	11	7	6							WARBOYS	FEARNLEY	
03/11/1973	CHESTERFIELD	H	1	0	10198	1	2	3	4	5	8			9	10	11	7	6							FEARNLEY		
10/11/1973	WALSALL	A	0	0	6058	1	2	3	4	5	8	7		9	10	11A		6	A								
13/11/1973	SOUTHPORT	H	3	1	10472	1	2	3	4	5	8	7		9	10	11		6							WARBOYS 3		
17/11/1973	OLDHAM ATHLETIC	A	1	1	11018	1	2	3	4	5	8	7		9	10	11		6							GREEN		
01/12/1973	BRIGHTON & HOVE ALBION	A	8	2	10762	1	2	3	4	5	8			9	10	11	7	6							FEARNLEY	BANNISTER 3	WARBOYS 4
08/12/1973	SOUTHEND UNITED	H	4	0	11770	1	2	3A	4	5	8			9	10	11	7	6		A					WARBOYS 3-1pen	JACOBS	
22/12/1973	CAMBRIDGE UNITED	A	2	2	4491	1	2	3	4	5	8			9	10	11	7	6							STANTON	WARBOYS	
26/12/1973	PLYMOUTH ARGYLE	H	4	2	22353	1	2	3	4	5	8			9	10	11	7	6							TAYLOR	WARBOYS 2	BANNISTER
29/12/1973	GRIMSBY TOWN	H	1	1	14317	1	2	3	4	5	8			9	10	11	7	6							WIGGINGTON og		
01/01/1974	CHARLTON ATHLETIC	A	1	1	11414	1	2	3	4	5	8				10	11	7	6		9					RUDGE		
12/01/1974	HALIFAX TOWN	A	0	0	4507	1	2	3	4	5	8			9	10	11		6		7							
19/01/1974	AFC BOURNEMOUTH	H	3	0	21186	1	2	3	4	5	8			9	10	11		6		7					WARBOYS	RUDGE	BANNISTER pen
27/01/1974	ALDERSHOT	A	3	2	13196	1	2	3	4	5	8			9	10	11		6		7					BANNISTER 2	WARBOYS	
02/02/1974	WREXHAM	A	0	1	9883	1	2	3	4	5	8	7A			10	11	A	6		9							
17/02/1974	PORT VALE	A	1	3	8505	1A	2	3	4	5	8	7			10	11	A	6		9					RUDGE		
23/02/1974	WATFORD	H	1	0	14069	1	2	3	4	5	8	7		9	10	11A		6		A					WARBOYS		
02/03/1974	PLYMOUTH ARGYLE	A	0	1	11374	1	2	3	4	5	8	7	11		10		9	6A			A						
05/03/1974	ROCHDALE	H	1	1	11195	1	2	3	4	5	8	7			10	11	9					6			BANNISTER		
09/03/1974	HUDDERSFIELD TOWN	H	2	1	13543	1	2		4	5	8	7			10			6	11		3		9		BANNISTER	JOHN	
12/03/1974	BLACKBURN ROVERS	H	3	0	14029	1	2		4	5	8	7			10			6	11		3		9		JACOBS 2	BANNISTER	
16/03/1974	YORK CITY	A	1	2	10330	1	2		4	5	8	7			10	11		6		A	3		9A		STEPHENS		
19/03/1974	WREXHAM	H	1	0	14510	1	2		4	5	8	7			10			6			3		9	11	STANIFORTH		
23/03/1974	WALSALL	H	0	2	11370	1	2	3	4	5	8	7			10	11		6		A			9A				
25/03/1974	ROCHDALE	A	1	0	1499	1	2	3	4	5	8	11		A	10			6		9				7A	BANNISTER		
30/03/1974	CHESTERFIELD	A	0	0	11559	1	2	3	4	5	8	7			10A	11		6		9			A				
02/04/1974	ALDERSHOT	H	2	1	12746	1	2	3	4	5	8	7				11		6		9			10		STANIFORTH	RUDGE	
05/04/1974	SOUTHPORT	A	0	1	1856	1	2	3	4	5	6	7			A	11A				9			10	8			
12/04/1974	TRANMERE ROVERS	A	0	0	6290	1	2	3	4	5	8	7A		9	10	11		6		A							
13/04/1974	OLDHAM ATHLETIC	H	1	2	18692	1	2	3	4A	5	8	7		9	10	11		6		A					BANNISTER		
16/04/1974	TRANMERE ROVERS	H	1	0	16090	1	2	3		5	8	7A		9	10			6		11	4		A		BANNISTER		
19/04/1974	SOUTHEND UNITED	A	0	0	8323	1	2	3		5	8			9	10			6		11	4		7				
27/04/1974	BRIGHTON & HOVE ALBION	H	1	1	19137	1	2	3	4	5	8			9	10	11A		6		7			A		BANNISTER pen		
	APPEARANCES					46	46	42	44	46	46	31	4	32	44	39	10	43	2	13	6	1	8	3			
	SUB					0	0	0	0	0	0	0	0	1	1	0	6	0	1	6	1	0	3	0			
	GOALS					0	3	0	1	2	3	1	1	22	18	1	3	1	1	4	0	0	2	0	OWN GOAL 2		
	SUBD					1	0	1	1	0	0	7	0	1	1	3	0	1	0	0	0	0	2	1			
	LEAGUE CUP																										
29/08/1973	AFC BOURNEMOUTH	A	0	1	7520	1	2	3	4	5			8	9	10	11	7	6									
	FA CUP																										
24/11/1973	BIDEFORD	A	2	0	4800	1	2	3	4	5	8			9	10	11	7A	6	A						WARBOYS	BANNISTER	
15/12/1973	NORTHAMPTON TOWN	A	2	1	6181	1	2	3	4	5	8			9	10	11	7	6							WARBOYS	FEARNLEY	
06/01/1974	NOTTINGHAM FOREST	A	3	4	23456	1	2	3	4	5	8	A			10	11A	7	6		9					PRINCE	DOBSON	RUDGE
	GLOUCESTERSHIRE CUP																										
29/04/1974	BRISTOL CITY	A	2	0	15986	1	2	3		5	8			9	A		7A	6		10	4		11		STANIFORTH	RUDGE	

1974/75

Date	Opponent				Att	EADIE James	JACOBS Trevor	PARSONS Lindsay	AITKEN Peter	TAYLOR Stuart	STANTON Thomas	JONES Brynley	STANIFORTH David	WARBOYS Alan	BANNISTER Bruce	RUDGE John	PRINCE Francis	FEARNLEY Gordon	BATER Philip	STEPHENS Kenneth	BRITTEN Martyn	COOMBES Jeffery	SHEPPARD Richard	DOBSON Colin	DAY Graham	SMITH Wilfred S	WILLIAMS David	Scorers		
	DIVISION 2																													
17/08/1974	NOTTS COUNTY	H	0	0	14365	1	2	3	4	5	6	7	8	9	10	11														
28/08/1974	SHEFFIELD WEDNESDAY	A	1	1	14343	1	2	3	4	5	8	7	A	9	10		6	11A										FEARNLEY		
31/08/1974	HULL CITY	H	2	0	11191	1	2	3	4	5	8	7		9	10		6	11										BANNISTER pen	FEARNLEY	
07/09/1974	SUNDERLAND	A	1	5	24010	1	2	3	4	5	8	7		9	10		6	11										WARBOYS		
14/09/1974	ASTON VILLA	H	2	0	14035	1	2		4	5	8			9	10	A	6	11	3A	7								WARBOYS 2		
17/09/1974	SHEFFIELD WEDNESDAY	H	1	1	12330	1	2	3	4	5	8			9	10	A	6	11A		7								BANNISTER		
21/09/1974	MANCHESTER UNITED	A	0	2	42948	1	2	3	4	5	8			9	10	A	6	11		7A										
25/09/1974	FULHAM	A	0	0	8706	1	2A	3	4	5	8			9	10	A	6	11		7										
28/09/1974	BLACKPOOL	H	1	3	10967	1		3	4	5	8			9	10	A	6	11	2A	7								BANNISTER pen		
05/10/1974	CARDIFF CITY	H	1	0	10310	1	2A	3	4	5	8			9	10	A	6	11		7								WARBOYS		
13/10/1974	YORK CITY	A	0	3	5800	1	2	3	4	5	8			9	10	A	6	11A		7										
19/10/1974	MILLWALL	H	2	0	9173	1		3	4	5	8			9	10		6	11	2	7								BANNISTER pen	STANTON	
22/10/1974	WEST BROMWICH ALBION	H	2	1	12101	1		3	4	5	8			9	10		6	11	2	7								BANNISTER	STANTON	
26/10/1974	NOTTINGHAM FOREST	A	0	1	11495	1		3	4	5	8			9	10		6	11	2	7										
02/11/1974	SOUTHAMPTON	H	0	1	15182	1		3A	4	5	8			9	10	A	6	11	2	7										
06/11/1974	WEST BROMWICH ALBION	A	2	2	8704	1		3	4	5	8			9	10		6	11	2	7								WARBOYS	PRINCE	
09/11/1974	NORWICH CITY	A	1	0	21172	1		3A	4	5	8			9	10	A	6	11	2	7								BANNISTER		
16/11/1974	ORIENT	H	0	0	10526	1	2		4	5	8			9	10	A	6	11	3	7A										
23/11/1974	OXFORD UNITED	A	1	2	7513	1	2A		4	5	8			9	10	7	6	11	3	A								PRINCE		
30/11/1974	BOLTON WANDERERS	H	1	0	9329	1		3	4	5	8			9	10		6		2	7	11							WARBOYS		
07/12/1974	OLDHAM ATHLETIC	A	4	3	9759	1		3	4	5	8			9	10		6	11	2			7						FEARNLEY 2	WARBOYS	COOMBES
14/12/1974	NOTTS COUNTY	A	2	3	7473	1		3	4	5	8A		A	9	10		6	11	2			7						PRINCE	FEARNLEY	
21/12/1974	PORTSMOUTH	H	0	1	9262	1	2	3	4	5	8A		A	9	10		6	11			7									
26/12/1974	ASTON VILLA	A	0	1	21556	1		3	4	5	7A	A	10	9			6	11	2			8								
28/12/1974	BRISTOL CITY	H	1	4	20933			3	4	5		A	10A	9			6	7	2		11	8	1					FEARNLEY		
11/01/1975	OLDHAM ATHLETIC	H	2	1	9456	1		3	4	5			7	9	10		6	11	2			8						TAYLOR	WARBOYS	
18/01/1975	BOLTON WANDERERS	A	1	5	11432	1		3	4	5			7	9	10		6	11A	2	A		8						BANNISTER		
01/02/1975	NORWICH CITY	H	0	2	12730	1		3	4	5			A	9A	10		6	11	2	7		8								
08/02/1975	SOUTHAMPTON	A	0	3	17490	1	2	3	4	5	7		10	9	8		11		6											
15/02/1975	OXFORD UNITED	H	1	0	9667	1	2		4	5	8			9	10		6	11	3	7								TAYLOR		
22/02/1975	ORIENT	A	0	1	6503	1	2		4	5		6	A	9	10	8		11	3	7A										
01/03/1975	HULL CITY	A	0	2	6223	1	2	3	4	5A	6	8	A	9	10			7						11						
11/03/1975	FULHAM	H	1	2	11765	1	2	3	4				10	9			6	A		7				11A	5	8		PRINCE		
15/03/1975	BLACKPOOL	A	0	0	8019	1	2		4		7		10	9			6		3					11	5	8				
22/03/1975	SUNDERLAND	H	2	1	13270	1	2		4				10	9	A		6	11	3	7A					5	8		WARBOYS 2-1pen		
28/03/1975	MANCHESTER UNITED	H	1	1	19000	1	2		4				10	9	A		6	11A	3	7					5	8		BANNISTER		
29/03/1975	PORTSMOUTH	A	0	3	12261	1	2		4		7		A	9	10A		6	11	3						5	8				
01/04/1975	BRISTOL CITY	A	1	1	28953	1	2		4A		A		10	9			6		3	7				11	5	8		COLLIER og		
05/04/1975	NOTTINGHAM FOREST	H	4	2	9684	1	2		4				10	9			6		3	7				11	5	8		WARBOYS	STANIFORTH	DOBSON
12/04/1975	CARDIFF CITY	A	2	2	13928	1	2		4				10	9			6		3	7				11	5	8		PRINCE	DOBSON	
19/04/1975	YORK CITY	H	1	3	11841	1	2		4				10	9			6	A	3A	7				11	5	8		STANIFORTH		
26/04/1975	MILLWALL	A	1	1	6243	1	2		4	5			10	9			6	11	3	7						8		WARBOYS		
	APPEARANCES					41	27	28	42	33	29	6	15	42	31	3	39	33	30	26	3	7	1	7	9	10				
	SUB					0	0	0	0	0	1	2	7	0	2	10	0	2	0	2	0	0	0	0	0	0				
	GOALS					0	0	0	0	2	2	0	2	12	8	0	6	6	0	0	0	1	0	2	0	0		OWN GOAL 1		
	SUBD					0	3	2	1	1	3	0	1	1	1	0	0	5	3	4	0	0	0	1	0	0				
	LEAGUE CUP																													
20/08/1974	PLYMOUTH ARGYLE	H	0	0	8974	1	2	3	4	5	6	7	8	9	10	11														
27/08/1974	PLYMOUTH ARGYLE	A	1	0	11213	1	2	3	4	5	8	7		9	10		6	11										WARBOYS		
11/09/1974	LUTON TOWN	A	0	1	10073	1	2	3A	4	5	8			9	10	A	6	11		7										
	FA CUP																													
04/01/1975	BLACKBURN ROVERS	A	2	1	12876	1		3	4	5			7	9	10		6	11	2			8								
27/01/1975	DERBY COUNTY	A	0	2	27980	1		3A	4	5	7		A	9	10		6	11	2			8						FEARNLEY	BANNISTER	
	GLOUCESTERSHIRE CUP																													
29/04/1975	BRISTOL CITY	H	2	1	11408	1			2	5				9			6	10		7	11				4	8	3	PRINCE	WARBOYS	

1975/76

Date	Opponent				Att	EADIE James	SMITH Wilfred S	WILLIAMS David	AITKEN Peter	TAYLOR Stuart	PRINCE Francis	STEPHENS Kenneth	STANTON Thomas	WARBOYS Alan	BANNISTER Bruce	EVANS Andrew	PULIS Anthony R	FEARNLEY Gordon	DAY Graham	BATER Philip	DOBSON Colin	BRITTEN Martyn	POWELL Wayne	STANIFORTH David	PARSONS Lindsay	JACOBS Trevor	LEWIS Paul			
	DIVISION 2																													
16/08/1975	OLDHAM ATHLETIC	A	0	2	6993	1	2	3	4	5	6	7	8	9	10	11														
23/08/1975	YORK CITY	H	2	1	8142	1	2	3	4	5	6	7	8	9	10	11												BANNISTER	McMORDIE og	
30/08/1975	BRISTOL CITY	A	1	1	17918	1	2	3	4	5	6	7A		9	10	11	8	A										BANNISTER		
06/09/1975	CHARLTON ATHLETIC	H	0	0	7718	1	2	3	4	5	6	7		9	10A	11	8	A												
13/09/1975	FULHAM	A	2	0	11516	1	2	3	6	5	8	7A		9	10	11		A	4									WARBOYS 2		
20/09/1975	CARLISLE UNITED	H	0	1	8223	1	2	3A	6	5	8	7		9	10	11		A	4											
23/09/1975	BOLTON WANDERERS	H	2	2	7992	1	2	3		5	8	7		9	10	11A		A	4	6								BANNISTER	PRINCE	
26/09/1975	ORIENT	A	0	0	4978	1	2	3	6	5	8	7		9	10				4		11									
04/10/1975	NOTTINGHAM FOREST	H	4	2	7689	1	2	3	6A	5	8	7		9	10				4			11	A					PRINCE 2	BANNISTER	POWELL
11/10/1975	HULL CITY	A	0	0	5642	1	6	3		5	8	7			10				4			11A	A	9	2					
18/10/1975	SUNDERLAND	H	1	0	13577	1	6	2		5	8	7A		9	10				4			11		A	3			BANNISTER		
21/10/1975	PORTSMOUTH	A	2	1	9078	1	6	2		5	8				10			7	4		11			9	3			BANNISTER	STANIFORTH	
25/10/1975	BLACKPOOL	A	4	1	9019	1	6	2		5	8				10			7	4		11			9	3			SMITH	FEARNLEY 2	BANNISTER pen
01/11/1975	BLACKBURN ROVERS	H	1	1	10534	1	6	2		5	8				10			7	4		11A	A		9	3			STANIFORTH		
04/11/1975	WEST BROMWICH ALBION	H	1	1	13105	1	6	2		5	8			9A	10			7	4			A		11	3			FEARNLEY		
08/11/1975	NOTTS COUNTY	A	1	1	10930	1	6	2		5	8	A	7		10			11	4A					9	3			STANIFORTH		
15/11/1975	PLYMOUTH ARGYLE	H	0	0	14121	1	6	2		5	8	7		9	10			11	4						3					
22/11/1975	SUNDERLAND	A	1	1	31356	1	6	2		5	11		7	9	10			8	4	A					3			WILLIAMS		
27/11/1975	CHELSEA	H	1	2	16277	1	6	2		5	8	A	7	9A	10			11	4						3			WILLIAMS		
06/12/1975	OXFORD UNITED	A	1	2	6532	1	6	2		5	11		7A	9	10				4					8	3			BANNISTER		
13/12/1975	YORK CITY	A	0	0	3112	1	6	8		5	11			9	10			7	4	2					3					
20/12/1975	OLDHAM ATHLETIC	H	1	0	7389	1	7	11		5	6			9	10			8	4	2					3			BANNISTER		
26/12/1975	SOUTHAMPTON	A	0	3	19556	1	6	5			11		7		10			8	4	2				9	3					
27/12/1975	LUTON TOWN	H	0	1	11044	1	6	8				7		9	10	11			5	4					3	2				
10/01/1976	FULHAM	H	1	0	7863	1		6	5			7	8		A			10A	4	2	11			9	3			BANNISTER		
17/01/1976	CHARLTON ATHLETIC	A	0	3	8598	1		8	6	5		7		9A	10				4	2	11		A		3					
31/01/1976	PORTSMOUTH	H	2	0	6133	1	8	3	4	5	6	7		9	10					2		11						BANNISTER	BRITTEN	
07/02/1976	WEST BROMWICH ALBION	A	0	3	17201	1	8	3	4	5	6	7		9	10					2		11A		A						
14/02/1976	NOTTS COUNTY	H	0	0	7754	1	8	3		5	6			9					4	2	11		10	7						
21/02/1976	PLYMOUTH ARGYLE	A	0	3	11183	1	8			5	6A	7		9	10				4	3	11			A		2				
28/02/1976	BLACKPOOL	H	1	1	6686	1	8	3		5		7		9	10	11	6		4	2								TAYLOR		
06/03/1976	BLACKBURN ROVERS	A	2	1	6765	1	6	8		5				9	10	11			4					7	3	2		STANIFORTH	BANNISTER	
13/03/1976	HULL CITY	H	0	1	6236	1	6	8		5		7		A	10	11			4					9	3	2A				
20/03/1976	CHELSEA	A	0	0	16132	1	6A	11		5		7		9	10	A			4					8	3	2				
27/03/1976	OXFORD UNITED	H	0	1	6952	1	6	8		5		7			10				4A			11	A	9	3	2				
03/04/1976	ORIENT	H	1	1	5182	1	6	4		5		7A		A	8	10						11		9	3	2		BANNISTER pen		
10/04/1976	CARLISLE UNITED	A	2	4	5928	1	6	8		5		A		9		11A				4		7		10	3	2		STANIFORTH	SMITH	
16/04/1976	BRISTOL CITY	H	0	0	26430	1	8	2		5	6	7		9	10				4	3		11								
17/04/1976	SOUTHAMPTON	H	2	0	11834	1	8	2		5	6	A				11			4	10A		7		9	3			PRINCE 2-1pen		
19/04/1976	LUTON TOWN	A	1	3	7646	1	8A	2		5		A				11	6	10	4			7		9	3			BRITTEN		
24/04/1976	NOTTINGHAM FOREST	A	0	3	12127	1		8	4	5	6	7		9					A			11A		10	3	2				
28/04/1976	BOLTON WANDERERS	A	1	3	12815		7	4	11A	5	6	A		9	10					2				8	3		1	WARBOYS		
	APPEARANCES					41	39	41	14	39	31	25	8	30	36	15	4	13	32	16	8	12	1	20	27	9	1			
	SUB					0	0	0	0	0	0	6	0	2	1	1	0	5	1	1	0	2	4	3	0	0	0			
	GOALS					0	2	2	0	1	5	0	0	3	13	0	0	3	0	0	0	2	1	5	0	0	0	OWN GOAL 1		
	SUBD					0	2	1	2	0	1	4	1	3	1	2	0	1	2	1	1	3	0	0	0	1	0			
	LEAGUE CUP																													
20/08/1975	CARDIFF CITY	A	2	1	6688	1	2	3	4	5	6	7	8	9	10	11												WARBOYS	BANNISTER	
26/08/1975	CARDIFF CITY	H	1	1	7220	1	2	3	4	5	6	7	8	9	10	11												STEPHENS		
09/09/1975	SOUTHAMPTON	A	1	0	10357	1	2	3	6	5	8	7		9	10	11A		A	4									FEARNLEY		
07/10/1975	NEWCASTLE UNITED	H	1	1	17141	1	6	3		5	8	7			10			A	4			11A		9	2			STANIFORTH		
15/10/1975	NEWCASTLE UNITED	A	0	2	25835	1	6	2		5	8	7A		9	10	11		A	4						3					
	FA CUP																													
01/01/1976	CHELSEA	A	1	1	35226	1	6A	5				7	11	9	10			8	4	2				A	3			WARBOYS		
03/01/1976	CHELSEA	H	0	1	13939	1		6	4			7	11	8A	10			8	5	2				A	3					
	GLOUCESTERSHIRE CUP																													
04/05/1976	BRISTOL CITY	A	2	3	10278	1	7	4	11	5	6	9			10					2				8	3			WILLIAMS	TAYLOR	

1976/77

Date	Opponent				Att	EADIE James	SMITH Wilfred S	AITKEN Peter	DAY Graham	TAYLOR Stuart	WILLIAMS David	STEPHENS Kenneth	STANIFORTH David	WARBOYS Alan	BANNISTER Bruce	EVANS Andrew	BATER Philip	PARSONS Lindsay	PRINCE Francis	BRITTEN Martyn	FEARNLEY Gordon	POWELL Wayne	HAMILTON James	GUSCOTT Raymond	THOMAS Martin	FOREMAN William	PULIS Anthony R	JONES Vaughan	Scorers		
	DIVISION 2																														
21/08/1976	BLACKPOOL	H	1	4	5845	1	2	3	4	5	6	7	8	9	10	11													WARBOYS		
25/08/1976	CARDIFF CITY	A	2	1	12680	1	8	6	4	5	3	7		9	10	11	2												WARBOYS	BANNISTER	
28/08/1976	OLDHAM ATHLETIC	H	0	0	6345	1	8	6	4	5		7		9	10	11	2	3													
04/09/1976	FULHAM	A	0	1	21127	1	8	6A		5	4	A	7	9	10		2	3	11												
11/09/1976	ORIENT	H	1	0	5494	1	8	2	4	5		7	A	9	10		3A		6	11									WARBOYS		
18/09/1976	BLACKBURN ROVERS	A	0	0	7751	1		2	4	5		7	11	9	10			3A	6	A	8										
25/09/1976	NOTTS COUNTY	H	5	1	6238	1		2	4	5	3	7	11	9	10				6		8								FEARNLEY 2	STANIFORTH 2	WARBOYS
02/10/1976	MILLWALL	A	0	2	8205	1		2	4	5	3	7	11	9	10				6		8										
05/10/1976	CHELSEA	H	2	1	13199	1		2	4	5	3	7	11	9	10				6		8								BANNISTER	STANIFORTH	
16/10/1976	BOLTON WANDERERS	A	0	1	12771	1		2	4	5	3	7	11	9	10				6		8										
23/10/1976	PLYMOUTH ARGYLE	H	1	1	10258	1		4	2	5	3	7		9	10				6		8	11							PRINCE		
30/10/1976	CHARLTON ATHLETIC	H	1	1	8183	1		4	2	5	3	7		9	10				6		8	11							FEARNLEY		
06/11/1976	LUTON TOWN	A	2	4	7066	1		4	2	5	3	7		9	10				6		8	11							BANNISTER	WARBOYS	
13/11/1976	HEREFORD UNITED	H	2	3	8485	1			2	5	4	7		9	10	A		3	6		8A	11							WARBOYS	BANNISTER	
20/11/1976	BURNLEY	A	1	1	10271	1				5	6	7	11	9	10		2	3	4		8								WILLIAMS		
27/11/1976	HULL CITY	H	3	0	6424	1		A		5	6	7	11	9	10	8A	2	3	4										STANIFORTH	WARBOYS	EVANS
04/12/1976	NOTTINGHAM FOREST	A	2	4	16302	1		4		5	6	7	11	9A	10	A	2	3			8								WILLIAMS	FEARNLEY	
11/12/1976	CARLISLE UNITED	H	2	1	5496	1				5	6	7	11	9	10		2	3	4		8								STANIFORTH	FEARNLEY	
18/12/1976	SHEFFIELD UNITED	A	3	2	15201	1				5	6	7	11	9			2	3	4		8		10						WARBOYS 2	STANIFORTH	
27/12/1976	WOLVERHAMPTON WANDERERS	H	1	5	20660	1				5	6	7	11	9		A	2	3	4A		8		10						WILLIAMS		
29/12/1976	SOUTHAMPTON	A	1	2	19790	1		6	4	5	7			9			2	3			8		11	10					WARBOYS		
01/01/1977	LUTON TOWN	H	1	0	7185	1		4		5	6	7	10	9			2	3			8		11						AITKEN		
03/01/1977	CHARLTON ATHLETIC	A	3	4	9742			4	5		6	7	10	9		11	2	3					8		1				WILLIAMS 2	STANIFORTH	
15/01/1977	CARDIFF CITY	H	1	1	9272	1		4	6	5	8	7	10	9		A	2	3A					11						WARBOYS pen		
22/01/1977	BLACKPOOL	A	0	4	9288	1		4	6	5	8	7	10	9			2	3A				A	11								
05/02/1977	OLDHAM ATHLETIC	A	0	4	9529	1		6		5	8	7	10A	9			2	3	4		A		11								
12/02/1977	FULHAM	H	2	1	11140	1			4	5	8	7	9			11	2	3	6				10						DAY	WILLIAMS	
19/02/1977	ORIENT	A	0	2	4062	1		A	4	5	8	7	9			11	2	3	6A				10								
05/03/1977	NOTTS COUNTY	A	1	2	10058	1		6	4	5	7		9			A	2	3A			8	10	11						EVANS		
08/03/1977	BLACKBURN ROVERS	H	0	0	5628	1		10	4	5	7		9			11	2	3	6A		8					A					
12/03/1977	MILLWALL	H	0	0	6242	1		6	4	5	10	7	9			11	2	3			8										
19/03/1977	CHELSEA	A	0	2	26916	1		6		5	2	7	9			11		3	4		8		10								
02/04/1977	PLYMOUTH ARGYLE	A	1	1	10307	1		10	4	5	2	7	9A					3	6	11	8		A						WILLIAMS		
05/04/1977	WOLVERHAMPTON WANDERERS	A	0	1	19149	1		3	9	5	7	11	10A				2		6		8		A				4				
09/04/1977	SOUTHAMPTON	H	2	3	11479	1		8	4	5A	11	7	10				2		6			9	A				3		STANIFORTH	WILLIAMS pen	
11/04/1977	HEREFORD UNITED	A	1	1	7195	1		8	4	5	11	7	10				2		6			9					3		POWELL		
16/04/1977	BURNLEY	H	1	1	6373	1		8	4	5	11	7	10			A	2		6A			9					3		POWELL		
23/04/1977	HULL CITY	A	1	0	4599	1		8	4	5	11	7	10				2		6			9					3		HAIGH og		
30/04/1977	NOTTINGHAM FOREST	H	1	1	8893	1		8	4	5	11	7	10				2		6			9					3		BATER		
07/05/1977	CARLISLE UNITED	A	3	2	7396	1		8A	4	5	11	7	10				2	3				9	A				6		STANIFORTH	POWELL	HAMILTON
14/05/1977	SHEFFIELD UNITED	H	3	1	7304	1		6		5	8	7	10				2	3				9	11				4		POWELL 3		
17/05/1977	BOLTON WANDERERS	H	2	2	6991	1					8	7	10				2	3	6			9	11				4	5	WILLIAMS 2		
	APPEARANCES					41	5	33	30	40	39	38	34	26	18	10	30	26	29	2	22	13	14	1	1	0	9	1			
	SUB					0	0	2	0	0	0	1	1	0	0	6	0	0	0	1	1	1	4	0	0	1	0	0			
	GOALS					0	0	1	1	0	10	0	9	11	4	2	1	0	1	0	5	6	1	0	0	0	0	0	OWN GOAL 1		
	SUBD					0	0	2	0	1	0	0	3	1	0	1	1	4	4	0	1	0	0	0	0	0	0	0			
	LEAGUE CUP																														
14/08/1976	CARDIFF CITY	A	1	2	8496	1	2	3	4	5	8	7	11	9	10				6												
17/08/1976	CARDIFF CITY	H	4	4	5592	1	2		4	5	8	7		9A	10	11		3	5									A	WILLIAMS	BANNISTER 2-1 p	PRINCE
	FA CUP																														
06/01/1977	NOTTINGHAM FOREST	A	1	1	17700	1		4	6	5	8	7	9			10	2	3					11						WILLIAMS		
11/01/1977	NOTTINGHAM FOREST	H	1	1	12348	1		4	6	5	8	7	10	9	A		2	3					11A						WARBOYS		
18/01/1977	NOTTINGHAM FOREST	N	0	6	5736	1		4	6	5	8	7	10	9	A		2	3					11								
	GLOUCESTERSHIRE CUP																														
24/05/1977	BRISTOL CITY	H	0	1	10432	1		10			7		8				2	3	6			9	11				4	5			

1977/78

Date						THOMAS Martin	AITKEN Peter	BATER Philip	DAY Graham	TAYLOR Stuart	PRINCE Francis	STEPHENS Kenneth	WILLIAMS David	RANDALL Paul	HAMILTON James	EVANS Andrew	STANIFORTH David	TAYLOR Anthony	POWELL Wayne	PULIS Anthony R	BARRY Michael	HENDRIE Paul	JONES Glyn	GOULD Robert	HARDING Stephen	WHITE Stephen	FOREMAN William	JONES Vaughan			
	DIVISION 2																														
20/08/1977	CARDIFF CITY	A	1	1	7000	1	2	3	4	5	6	7	8	9A	10	11 A													RANDALL		
23/08/1977	NOTTS COUNTY	H	2	2	5208	1	2	3	4	5	6	7	8	9A	10	11 A													RANDALL	WILLIAMS	
27/08/1977	FULHAM	H	0	0	6426	1	2	3	4	5	6	7	8	9		11	10														
03/09/1977	BLACKPOOL	A	1	3	8219	1	4	2		5	6	7	8			11	10	3	9A	A									WILLIAMS		
10/09/1977	LUTON TOWN	H	1	2	5940	1		2	4	5	6		10	9		11	7	3			8A	A							RANDALL		
17/09/1977	ORIENT	A	1	2	5104	1		2	4	5	6		8	9		11	10	3				7							RANDALL		
24/09/1977	OLDHAM ATHLETIC	H	0	0	4550	1		2	4	5	6		10	9A		11	7	3			8 A										
30/09/1977	CHARLTON ATHLETIC	A	1	3	8412	1		2	4	5	6	7	8	9			10	3			11								BARRY		
04/10/1977	MANSFIELD TOWN	H	3	1	4980	1		2	4	5	6	7	8				10	3	9		11								WILLIAMS 2	POWELL	
08/10/1977	BURNLEY	A	1	3	7207			2	5		6	7	8				10	3	9	4	11		1						STANIFORTH		
15/10/1977	BLACKBURN ROVERS	H	4	1	6431		2		4	5	6		8A		A		10	3			11	7	1	9					GOULD 3	STANIFORTH	
22/10/1977	TOTTENHAM HOTSPUR	A	0	9	26311		8	2	4	5	6A		7			11	10	3			A		1	9							
29/10/1977	SOUTHAMPTON	H	0	0	12031	1	8	2	4	5			7 A			11A	10	3			6			9							
05/11/1977	MILLWALL	H	2	0	6205	1	6	2	4	5			7	8			10	3			11			9					WILLIAMS	KITCHENER og	
12/11/1977	SUNDERLAND	A	1	5	24633	1	6	2	4	5			7	9			8	3			11			10					STANIFORTH		
19/11/1977	BOLTON WANDERERS	H	0	1	7878	1	8	2	4	5			3				10			6	11	7		9							
26/11/1977	SHEFFIELD UNITED	A	1	1	13177	1	8	3	4	5	6		2				10		11		7			9					POWELL		
03/12/1977	HULL CITY	H	1	1	5351	1	2	3	4	5	6		8 A				10		11A		7			9					STANIFORTH		
10/12/1977	STOKE CITY	A	2	3	10613	1	2	3	4	5	6		8				10		11A		7 A			9					GOULD	STANIFORTH	
17/12/1977	SUNDERLAND	H	3	2	6516	1	2	3	4	5	6		8				10		11		7			9					TAYLOR	WILLIAMS	STANIFORTH
26/12/1977	BRIGHTON & HOVE ALBION	A	1	1	25509	1	2	3	4	5	6		8 A				10		11A		7			9					POWELL		
27/12/1977	CRYSTAL PALACE	H	3	0	11688	1	2	3	4	5	6		8	11			10				7			9					BARRY	GOULD	RANDALL
31/12/1977	NOTTS COUNTY	A	2	3	8471		2	3	4	5	6		8A	11			10			A	7		1	9					RANDALL 2		
02/01/1978	CARDIFF CITY	H	3	2	11945		2	3		5	6			11			10			8	7		1	9	4				STANIFORTH 2	RANDALL	
14/01/1978	FULHAM	A	1	1	8424	1	2	3		5	6			11			10			8	7			9	4				RANDALL		
21/01/1978	BLACKPOOL	H	2	0	7304	1	2	3	4	5	6			11			10			8	7			9					RANDALL	GOULD	
08/02/1978	LUTON TOWN	A	1	1	5913	1	2	3		5	6		7	11			10			8				9	4				HARDING		
11/02/1978	ORIENT	H	2	1	9416	1	2	3	4	5	6			11A			10	A		8	7			9					RANDALL	HOADLEY og	
25/02/1978	CHARLTON ATHLETIC	H	2	2	7740	1	2	3	4	5	6		10A	11				A		8	7			9					RANDALL	GOULD pen	
04/03/1978	BURNLEY	H	2	2	7520	1	2	3	4	5	6			11A					10	8	7 A			9					GOULD	S TAYLOR	
11/03/1978	BLACKBURN ROVERS	A	1	0	11780	1	2	3	4	5	6			11					10	8	7			9					RANDALL		
18/03/1978	TOTTENHAM HOTSPUR	H	2	3	17708	1	2	3		5	6			11A					10	8	7 A			9	4				RANDALL	DAINES og	
25/03/1978	CRYSTAL PALACE	A	0	1	13428	1	2	3		5	6		4				10A			8	11	7		9 A							
27/03/1978	SOUTHAMPTON	A	1	3	24826	1	2	3	4	5	6		11							8	7A	A		9		10			WILLIAMS		
01/04/1978	MILLWALL	A	3	1	3322	1	2	3	4	5	6		7A	11						8 A				9		10			RANDALL	WHITE	GOULD pen
04/04/1978	OLDHAM ATHLETIC	A	1	4	7192	1	2	3	4A	5			6	11						8	7			9		10 A			RANDALL		
08/04/1978	SHEFFIELD UNITED	H	4	1	7659	1	2	3	4	5	6			11						8	7			9		10			RANDALL	WHITE 2	GOULD
15/04/1978	BOLTON WANDERERS	A	0	3	20393	1	2	3	4	5	6	A		11						8	7			9		10A					
18/04/1978	BRIGHTON & HOVE ALBION	H	0	4	9789	1	2	3	4	5	6			11						8	7			9		10					
22/04/1978	STOKE CITY	H	4	1	3182	1	2	3			6		8	11						4	7			9	5	10			RANDALL 2	WILLIAMS	WHITE
24/04/1978	MANSFIELD TOWN	A	0	3	6121	1	2	3			6		8	11						4	7 A			9	5	10A					
29/04/1978	HULL CITY	A	1	0	3645	1	2	3	4	5	6		8	11						10	7			9					RANDALL		
	APPEARANCES					37	36	41	34	39	37	7	32	28	2	9	27	12	11	21	34	4	5	32	6	8	0				
	SUB					0	0	0	0	0	0	0	1	3	0	1	2	0	2	2	1	8	0	0	1	0	1				
	GOALS					0	0	0	0	2	0	0	8	20	0	0	8	0	3	0	2	0	0	10	1	4	0		OWN GOAL 3		
	SUBD					0	0	0	1	0	1	0	4	6	0	1	1	0	4	0	2	0	0	0	0	2	0				
	LEAGUE CUP																														
13/08/1977	WALSALL	H	1	2	3467	1	4	3	5		6	7	8		10	11			9								A	2A	WILLIAMS pen		
16/08/1977	WALSALL	A	0	1	5445	1	3	2		5	4	7	6		10	11			9A								8 A				
	FA CUP																														
07/01/1978	SUNDERLAND	A	1	0	26214	1	2	3	4	5	6			11A			10			8	7 A			9					GOULD		
28/01/1978	SOUTHAMPTON	H	2	0	26525	1	2	3	4	5	6			11			10			8	7			9					RANDALL 2		
18/02/1978	IPSWICH TOWN	H	2	2	23456	1	2	3	4	5	6		10	11						8	7			9					WILLIAMS 2		
28/02/1978	IPSWICH TOWN	A	0	3	29532	1	2	3	4	5	6	A		11			10A			8	7			9							
	GLOUCESTERSHIRE CUP																														
02/05/1978	BRISTOL CITY	A	0	3	10178	1	2	3		5	6		8	11					9	10	7 A				B		4				

1978/79

						THOMAS Martin	JONES Vaughan	BATER Philip	PULIS Anthony R	TAYLOR Stuart	PRINCE Francis	DENNEHY Jeremiah	WILLIAMS David	GOULD Robert	RANDALL Paul	BARRY Michael	AITKEN Peter	STANIFORTH David	DAY Graham	HENDRIE Paul	LYTHGOE Philip (L)	CLARKE Gary	WHITE Stephen	PETTS Paul	HARDING Stephen	MABBUTT Gary	EMMANUEL Gary	BROWN Keith	SHAW Martin	PALMER David	ENGLAND Michael	HOULT Alan			
	DIVISION 2																																		
19/08/1978	FULHAM	H	3	1	5950	1	2	3	4	5	6	7	8	9	10	11																	RANDALL	GOULD	BARRY
22/08/1978	OLDHAM ATHLETIC	A	1	3	6005	1	A	3	4	5	6	7A	8	9	10	11	2																GOULD		
26/08/1978	CHARLTON ATHLETIC	A	0	3	7745	1	2	3	4	5		7	8	9	10A	11	6	A																	
02/09/1978	CARDIFF CITY	H	4	2	6855	1		3		5	6	7A	8	A	10	11	2	9	4														STANIFORTH 2	RANDALL	GRAPES og
09/09/1978	LUTON TOWN	H	2	0	6508	1		3	2	5	6	7	8		10	11		9	4														RANDALL	STANIFORTH	
16/09/1978	WEST HAM UNITED	A	0	2	22189	1		3	2	5	6	7A	8		10	11		9	4	A															
23/09/1978	WREXHAM	H	2	1	7619	1		3	2	5	6	7	8		10			9	4		11												WILLIAMS	RANDALL	
30/09/1978	CAMBRIDGE UNITED	A	1	1	5513	1		3	2A	5	6	7	8		10		A	9	4		11												AITKEN		
07/10/1978	BLACKBURN ROVERS	H	4	1	7111	1		3		5	6	7	8		10		2	9	4			11											RANDALL 3	WILLIAMS	
14/10/1978	NOTTS COUNTY	A	1	2	8646	1		3		5	6	7	8		10A		2		4		11	A	9										WHITE		
21/10/1978	ORIENT	H	2	1	7234	1		3		5	6	7	8		10		2	9	4		11												STANIFORTH	PRINCE	
28/10/1978	LEICESTER CITY	A	0	0	12498	1		3		5	6	7A	8		10		2	9	4	A	11														
04/11/1978	NEWCASTLE UNITED	H	2	0	10582	1		3		5	6	7	8		10		2	9	4	A	11A												RANDALL 2		
10/11/1978	FULHAM	A	0	3	10296	1	6	3		5		7A	8		10		2	9	4	11			A												
18/11/1978	CHARLTON ATHLETIC	H	5	5	8107	1		3		5	6A	7	8		10	11	2	9	4	A													RANDALL 3	WILLIAMS 2-1pen	
25/11/1978	SHEFFIELD UNITED	H	2	1	8434	1		3A		5		7	8		10	11	2	9	4	6			A										RANDALL	STANIFORTH	
02/12/1978	SUNDERLAND	A	0	5	18864	1	3			5		7A	8		10	11	2	9	4	6			A												
09/12/1978	MILLWALL	H	0	3	7112	1		3		5	6		8		10	11	2	9	4					7											
16/12/1978	BURNLEY	A	0	2	9119	1				5	6	11	8		10		2A	9	3					7	4	A									
23/12/1978	STOKE CITY	H	0	0	7897	1	3			5	6		8		10			9	2				A	7A	4	11									
26/12/1978	CRYSTAL PALACE	A	1	0	21605	1	2			5			8		9			10	4	A			7A		3	11	6						WHITE		
30/12/1978	PRESTON NORTH END	A	1	1	12600	1	3			5		A	8					9	2	7			10		6	11A	4						HENDRIE		
16/01/1979	LUTON TOWN	A	2	3	6002	1		2		5		A	8				11	10	4A	7			9		3		6						WHITE 2		
20/01/1979	WEST HAM UNITED	H	0	1	12418	1		3		5		A	8A				6	10	2	11			9		4		7								
10/02/1979	CAMBRIDGE UNITED	H	2	0	5904	1		3		5	6	7	8						2	11			9		4		10						WHITE	PRINCE	
24/02/1979	NOTTS COUNTY	H	2	2	6887	1	2	3		5	6	7	8					A		11A			9		4		10						WILLIAMS 2		
03/03/1979	ORIENT	A	1	1	5078	1		3		5	6	7	8				4	11	2				9				10						WHITE		
10/03/1979	LEICESTER CITY	H	1	1	6381	1		3		5		7A	8				4	11	2			6	9			A	10						WILLIAMS		
20/03/1979	BRIGHTON & HOVE ALBION	H	1	2	8290	1	2	3		5		7A	8			6	4	10		11		A	9										STANIFORTH		
24/03/1979	OLDHAM ATHLETIC	H	0	0	5405	1	2	3		5			8			6A	4	10		11		A	9				7								
31/03/1979	SHEFFIELD UNITED	A	0	1	14064	1	2	3		5	6A	11	8				4	10		A			9				7								
04/04/1979	BLACKBURN ROVERS	A	2	0	8554	1	2	3		5		7	8				4	10		6			9				11						WHITE	WILLIAMS	
07/04/1979	SUNDERLAND	H	0	0	8003	1	2	3		5		7	8				4	10		6			9				11								
14/04/1979	CRYSTAL PALACE	H	0	1	10986	1	2	3		5		7	8				4	10		6A		A	9				11								
16/04/1979	BRIGHTON & HOVE ALBION	A	0	3	23024	1	2	3		5	6	7	8				4	10					9A				11	A							
17/04/1979	STOKE CITY	A	0	2	18679	1	2	3		5	6A	7	8				4	10					9	A			11								
21/04/1979	BURNLEY	H	2	0	5947	1	2			5	6		8				4						9	7	3	10	11						WHITE	JONES pen	
28/04/1979	MILLWALL	A	3	0	5266	1	2	3		5	6		8				4						10	7		9	11						WHITE 2	WILLIAMS	
02/05/1979	NEWCASTLE UNITED	A	0	3	9625	1	2	3		5			8					6					9	7	4	10	11								
05/05/1979	PRESTON NORTH END	H	0	1	5814	1	2	3		5	6		8A				4						9	7		10	11		A						
07/05/1979	CARDIFF CITY	A	0	2	10185	1	2	3		5	6		7				4						11	9		10A	8	A							
10/05/1979	WREXHAM	A	1	0	6136	1		3					8				4						9	7		A	11	10	6A		2	5	WILLIAMS		
	APPEARANCES					42	21	36	7	41	26	29	42	3	21	12	31	31	24	13	6	2	23	9	10	8	21	1	1	1	1				
	SUB					0	1	0	0	0	0	3	0	1	0	0	1	2	0	6	0	4	4	1	0	3	0	2	1	0	0				
	GOALS					0	1	0	0	0	2	0	10	2	13	1	1	6	0	1	0	0	10	0	0	0	0	0	0	0	0		OWN GOAL 1		
	SUBD					0	0	1	1	0	3	8	2	0	2	1	1	0	1	2	1	0	2	1	0	2	0	0	1	0	0				
	LEAGUE CUP																																		
12/08/1978	HEREFORD UNITED	H	2	1	5001	1		3	4	5	6	7	8		9A		2	10				A											AITKEN	STANIFORTH	
16/08/1978	HEREFORD UNITED	A	0	4	5130	1		3	4	5	6	7	8	A	9		2															10A			
	FA CUP																																		
09/01/1979	SWANSEA CITY	A	1	0	16052	1	2			5		A	8				6	10	4	7			9		3	11A							WHITE		
05/02/1979	CHARLTON ATHLETIC	H	1	0	9623	1		3		5	6	7	8					10A	2	11			9		4	A							WHITE		
26/02/1979	IPSWICH TOWN	A	1	6	23231	1	2	3		5	6	7	8					A		11A			9		4		10						WHITE		
	GLOUCESTERSHIRE CUP																																		
15/05/1979	BRISTOL CITY	H	0	2	6661	1		3		5			6				4						10	8		9	7	11		2					

1979/80

Date	Opponent				Att	THOMAS Martin	PULIS Anthony R	JONES Vaughan	AITKEN Peter	HARDING Stephen	EMMANUEL Gary	BARROWCLOUGH Stewart	WILLIAMS David	WHITE Stephen	DENNEHY Jeremiah	COOPER Terence	BATER Philip	CLARKE Gary	MABBUTT Gary	PENNY Shaun	TAYLOR Stuart	PRINCE Francis	PARKINSON Noel (L)	BROWN Keith	JONES Glyn	BATES Philip	PETTS Paul	BARRETT Michael	HUGHES Mark	GRIFFITHS Ashley	KITE Philip	Scorers		
	DIVISION 2																																	
18/08/1979	QUEENS PARK RANGERS	A	0	2	12652	1	2	3	4	5	6	7	8	9	10	11																		
21/08/1979	LUTON TOWN	H	3	2	5614	1	2		4	5	6	7	8	9	10		3	11														WHITE 2	DENNEHY	
25/08/1979	SHREWSBURY TOWN	H	2	1	5713	1	2		4	5	6	7	8	9	10A		3	11	A													DENNEHY	BARROWCLOUGH pen	
01/09/1979	BIRMINGHAM CITY	A	1	1	15330	1	2		4	5	6	7	8	9	10	11	3															BARROWCLOUGH pen		
08/09/1979	WATFORD	H	1	1	7625	1	2		4	5	6	7	8	9	10A	11	3	A														BARROWCLOUGH pen		
15/09/1979	CAMBRIDGE UNITED	A	1	4	4423	1	2		4	5		7	8	9		11	3		6	10												WILLIAMS		
22/09/1979	PRESTON NORTH END	A	2	3	7555	1			2	5	6	7	8	9		11	3		A	10	4A											TAYLOR	PENNY	
29/09/1979	CARDIFF CITY	H	1	1	8949	1			4		6		2		9	11	3		7	10	5	8										PENNY		
06/10/1979	NOTTS COUNTY	H	2	3	5372	1			4		8	7	2		9A	11	3		A	10	5	6										BARROWCLOUGH	DENNEHY	
09/10/1979	LUTON TOWN	A	1	3	8507	1			4	5	6	7			9	11	3		2	10		8										EMMANUEL		
13/10/1979	CHELSEA	A	0	1	18236	1			2	5	8	7	11	10	A		3		4	9		6A												
20/10/1979	CHARLTON ATHLETIC	H	3	0	5472	1			6	5	8	7	3	9			2	11	4	10												WHITE	PENNY	AITKEN
27/10/1979	ORIENT	A	1	2	4645	1	A		6	5	8	7	3	9			2	11A	4	10												BARROWCLOUGH pen		
03/11/1979	QUEENS PARK RANGERS	H	1	3	8531	1	11		6A			7	3		9		2		4	10	5		8	A								PULIS		
10/11/1979	WREXHAM	A	2	1	9188		11		6			7	3	10	9		2		4		5		8		1							WHITE	BATER	
17/11/1979	NEWCASTLE UNITED	H	1	1	7626		11		6			7	3	9	10		2		4		5		8		1							WHITE		
24/11/1979	SUNDERLAND	A	2	3	21793		11	A	6			2	3	9	10A		7		4		5		8		1							PARKINSON	WHITE	
01/12/1979	BURNLEY	H	0	0	5273		11		6			7A	3	9	10		2		4	A	5		8		1									
08/12/1979	WEST HAM UNITED	A	1	2	17763	1	11	A	6		8	7	3				2		4	10	5			9A								BARROWCLOUGH		
15/12/1979	OLDHAM ATHLETIC	H	2	0	4596	1	11		6		8	7	3	9	10		2		4		5											BARROWCLOUGH 2 -1pen		
26/12/1979	SWANSEA CITY	H	4	1	9230	1	11		6		8	7	3		10		2		4	9	5											DENNEHY 3	WADDLE og	
29/12/1979	SHREWSBURY TOWN	A	1	3	7097	1	11	A	6		8	7	3		10		2		4	9	5A											PENNY		
01/01/1980	LEICESTER CITY	A	0	3	21579	1	11	A	6	5	8	7	3		10A		2		4	9														
12/01/1980	BIRMINGHAM CITY	H	1	0	9351	1	11	2	6			7	8		10	3				9	5	4										PENNY		
19/01/1980	WATFORD	A	0	0	12020	1	11	2	6			7	8			3				9	5	4		10										
02/02/1980	CAMBRIDGE UNITED	H	0	0	5394	1	11	2	4			7	8			3			10	9	5	6												
16/02/1980	CARDIFF CITY	A	1	0	6810	1	11	2	4		A	7	8			3			10	9A	5	6										WILLIAMS		
23/02/1980	CHELSEA	H	3	0	14176	1	11	2	4		A	7	8			3			10	9	5	6A										PENNY 2	PULIS	
26/02/1980	FULHAM	A	1	1	4744	1	11	2	4			7	8			3			10	9	5	6										WILLIAMS		
01/03/1980	CHARLTON ATHLETIC	A	0	4	4858	1	11	2	4			7	8		A	3			10	9	5	6A												
08/03/1980	ORIENT	H	1	2	5798	1	11	2	6			7	8			3	4		10	9	5											BARROWCLOUGH pen		
11/03/1980	PRESTON NORTH END	H	3	3	6022	1	11	2	4			7	8				3		6	9	5					10						BARROWCLOUGH	PULIS	WILLIAMS
15/03/1980	NOTTS COUNTY	A	0	0	5698	1	11	2	4	5		7	8			3	6		A	9A						10								
22/03/1980	WREXHAM	H	1	0	5440	1	11	2	4	5		7	8			3	6			9						10						BARROWCLOUGH		
29/03/1980	NEWCASTLE UNITED	A	1	3	19011	1	11	2	4	5	3	7	8				6		A	9						10						PENNY		
04/04/1980	FULHAM	H	1	0	7289	1	11	2	4	5			8A			3	6		A	9						10	7					BANTON og		
05/04/1980	SWANSEA CITY	A	0	2	11730	1	11	2	4	5	8					3	6			9						10	7A	A						
12/04/1980	BURNLEY	A	1	1	5270	1		2	4	5			8			3	6		11	9						10	7					JONES pen		
19/04/1980	SUNDERLAND	H	2	2	9757	1		2	4	5		7	8			3	6		11	9						10						BATES	BARROWCLOUGH	
23/04/1980	LEICESTER CITY	H	1	1	8205	1	A	2	4	5		7	8			3	6		11A	9						10						BATES		
26/04/1980	OLDHAM ATHLETIC	A	1	2	5202	1	A	2	4	5		6	7			3	11			8A						9		10				PENNY		
03/05/1980	WEST HAM UNITED	H	0	2	9824	1	8					7	A			3	2		5	9						10		11	4A	6				
	APPEARANCES					38	31	19	41	21	19	38	39	15	18	25	34	4	27	32	21	11	5	2	4	11	3	2	1	1				
	SUB					0	3	4	0	0	2	0	1	0	2	0	0	1	6	1	0	0	0	1	0	0	0	1	0	0				
	GOALS					0	3	1	1	0	1	12	4	6	6	0	1	0	0	9	1	0	1	0	0	2	0	0	0	0		OWN GOAL 2		
	SUBD					0	0	0	1	0	0	1	0	0	5	0	0	1	1	3	2	3	0	1	0	0	3	0	1	0				
	LEAGUE CUP																																	
11/08/1979	TORQUAY UNITED	A	2	1	4506	1	2		4	5	6	7	8	9	10	11A	3										A					BARROWCLOUGH	WHITE	
14/08/1979	TORQUAY UNITED	H	1	3	3758	1	2	3	4	5	6	7	8	9A	10	11											A					EMMANUEL		
	FA CUP																																	
04/01/1980	ASTON VILLA	H	1	2	16060	1	11	2				7	6		10	3			4	9	5	8										BARROWCLOUGH		
	GLOUCESTERSHIRE CUP																																	
06/05/1980	BRISTOL CITY	A	0	1	5584		8	4	6	5		7	11			3	2			9						10					1			

1980/81

						THOMAS Martin	GILLIES Donald	BATER Philip	HUGHES Mark	MABBUTT Gary	COOPER Terence	BARROWCLOUGH Stewart	WILLIAMS David	BATES Philip	PENNY Shaun	GRIFFITHS Ashley	McCAFFERY Aiden	JONES Vaughan	LEE Robert	PULIS Anthony R	BARRETT Michael	BROWN Keith	WILLIAMS Geraint	EMMANUEL Gary	WILLIAMS Steven	KITE Philip	ROUTLEDGE Alan	RANDALL Paul	McALISTER Thomas (L)	SLATTER Neil	WESTAWAY Kevin	HOLLOWAY Ian			
	DIVISION 2																																		
16/08/1980	ORIENT	H	1	1	5831	1	2	3	4	5	6	7	8	9	10	11																	D WILLIAMS		
19/08/1980	QUEENS PARK RANGERS	A	0	4	9731	1	2	3	5	4	6	7	9A	10		11	8	A																	
23/08/1980	BRISTOL CITY	A	0	0	16937	1	2	3	5	4		8	9	10	11A		7		6	A															
30/08/1980	GRIMSBY TOWN +	H	2	2	4461	1	2	3	6	5		7A	8	9	10		4		11	A													McCAFFERY	MOORE og	
06/09/1980	BOLTON WANDERERS	A	0	2	8712	1		3	6	5			8	9		7	4	2	11	10															
13/09/1980	OLDHAM ATHLETIC *	H	0	0	3808	1	2	3	6	5			8	9A	10		4	A	11	7															
20/09/1980	CARDIFF CITY	A	1	2	6122	1	2A	3	6	5		9	8	A	10		4		11	7													LEE		
27/09/1980	NEWCASTLE UNITED +	H	0	0	5171	1		3	6	5		9A	8	A	10		4	2	11	7															
04/10/1980	CAMBRIDGE UNITED	H	0	1	5231	1		3	6	5		9	8		10	2	4A	A	11		7														
08/10/1980	CHELSEA	A	0	2	13108	1	2		6	4	3	11	8		10		5		9		7														
11/10/1980	NOTTS COUNTY	A	1	3	7292	1	7	2	6	5	3		8		10A		4		A		11	9											MABBUTT		
18/10/1980	SHEFFIELD WEDNESDAY	H	3	3	4401	1		2	6	5	3	7	8	A			4		10A		11		9										MABBUTT	BARRETT	BATES
25/10/1980	PRESTON NORTH END	A	0	0	5807	1	8	2	6	5	3	7		10			4				11		9												
01/11/1980	WEST HAM UNITED	H	0	1	6328	1	2	3	5	9	6	7A		10			4				11		8	A											
04/11/1980	WATFORD	H	3	1	5450	1	2	3	5	9	6	7		10			4				11		8										BATES	MABBUTT	McCAFFERY
08/11/1980	SHREWSBURY TOWN	A	1	3	4446	1	2	3	5	9	6	7		10			4				11		8										G WILLIAMS		
11/11/1980	QUEENS PARK RANGERS	H	1	2	6636	1	2	3	5	9	6	7		10			4				11		8										BARROWCLOUGH pen		
15/11/1980	ORIENT	A	2	2	5100	1	2	3	5	9	6A			10	7		4				11		8	A									McCAFFERY 2		
22/11/1980	DERBY COUNTY	H	1	1	6258	1	2	3	5	9	6			10	7A		4				11		8	A									McCAFFERY		
29/11/1980	BLACKBURN ROVERS	A	0	2	8025	1	2	3	5	9	6A			10			4		7		11		8	A											
06/12/1980	WREXHAM	H	0	1	4562	1	2	3		9				10			4		5		11		8	6	7										
12/12/1980	SHEFFIELD WEDNESDAY	A	1	4	14008	1		3		9	6		10				4	2	5		11		8		7								JONES pen		
19/12/1980	NOTTS COUNTY	H	1	1	3552	1				9	6	8	10				4	2	5	3	11				7								S WILLIAMS		
26/12/1980	SWANSEA CITY	A	1	2	15135	1		3		5		A	10				4	2	9	8	11			6	7A								EMMANUEL		
27/12/1980	LUTON TOWN	H	2	4	7010	1	A	3	5A	9	6	8	10					2			11			4	7								BARROWCLOUGH	MABBUTT	
10/01/1981	DERBY COUNTY	A	1	2	15018		2		5	10	A	8					4	3	9		11A		7	6		1							LEE		
17/01/1981	GRIMSBY TOWN	A	0	2	9601		2		5A	9		11				8	6	3	10				4	7		1	A								
31/01/1981	BRISTOL CITY	H	0	0	10087		2		5	11	4	7						3	9				8	6		1		10							
07/02/1981	OLDHAM ATHLETIC	A	0	1	5552		2		5	11	4	7			A			3	9A				8	6		1		10							
14/02/1981	BOLTON WANDERERS	H	2	1	5368				5	10	3	7					4	2	A				8	6A	11			9	1				RANDALL 2		
21/02/1981	NEWCASTLE UNITED	A	0	0	14180				5	10	3	7					4	2	A				8	6	11			9A	1						
28/02/1981	CARDIFF CITY	H	0	1	7525				5	10	3						4	2	A		11		8	6	7A			9	1						
07/03/1981	CAMBRIDGE UNITED	A	3	1	4050		3		5	10			11		7		4	2					8	6				9	1				RANDALL	PENNY	D WILLIAMS
14/03/1981	CHELSEA	H	1	0	7565		2		5	11			8		10		4	3					7	6				9	1				D WILLIAMS		
21/03/1981	WATFORD	A	1	3	10162		2		5	11			8		10	A	4	3					7	6				9A	1				HUGHES		
28/03/1981	PRESTON NORTH END	H	2	0	4427		2		5	11	A		8		10		4	3A					7	6				9	1				PENNY	MABBUTT	
04/04/1981	WEST HAM UNITED	A	0	2	23544		2		5	11	A		8		10		4	3					7A	6				9	1						
11/04/1981	SHREWSBURY TOWN	H	1	1	4151		2		5	11	3				10A		4				8		7	6				9	1	A			PENNY		
18/04/1981	LUTON TOWN	A	0	1	9009		2		5	11			A				4		10		8A		7	6				9	1	3					
21/04/1981	SWANSEA CITY	H	1	2	8250		2A		5	11			8		10		4				7		A	6				9	1	3			BARRETT		
25/04/1981	WREXHAM	A	1	3	3220				5A	11			8		10		4				7		6					9	1	3	2	A	BARRETT		
02/05/1981	BLACKBURN ROVERS	H	0	1	9078		2	3	5	11	8		6		10A		4						A	7				9	1						
	APPEARANCES					25	30	24	38	42	23	22	24	15	20	5	38	18	19	6	23	1	26	19	8	4	0	15	13	3	1	0			
	SUB					0	1	0	0	0	3	1	1	3	1	1	0	3	4	2	0	0	2	4	0	0	1	0	0	1	0	1			
	GOAL					0	0	0	1	5	0	2	3	2	3	0	5	1	2	0	3	0	1	1	1	0	0	3	0	0	0	0	OWN GOAL 1		
	SUBD					0	2	0	3	0	2	3	1	1	5	0	1	1	2	0	2	0	1	1	2	0	0	2	0	0	0	0			
	LEAGUE CUP																																		
09/08/1980	EXETER CITY	A	1	1	4702	1	2	3	5	4	6	7	8	10										11	9								BATES		
12/08/1980	EXETER CITY + *	H	1	1	4070	1	2	3	4	5	6	7	8	9				A			11A				10								BATES		
27/08/1980	YORK CITY	A	1	2	3405	1	2	3	11	5		7	8	9	10		4		6														McCAFFERY		
03/09/1980	YORK CITY *	H	1	0	3047	1	2	3	6	5		7A	8	9			4		10	11	A												FAULKNER og		
23/09/1980	PORTSMOUTH +**	H	0	0	6982	1		3	6	5		9	8	A	10A		4	2	11	7															
30/09/1908	PORTSMOUTH	A	0	2	18965	1		3	6	5		4	8	9	10			2	11	7															
	* AET Won on away goals rule																																		
	** AET Won 7-6 on pens																																		
	FA CUP																																		
03/01/1981	PRESTON NORTH END	A	4	3	6348		2		5	9		10					4	3	8		11		7	6		1							MABBUTT	BARROWCLOU	BARRETT
24/01/1981	SOUTHAMPTON	A	1	3	23597		2		6	8	11	7			A		5	3	9A				10	4		1							G WILLIAMS		
	GLOUCESTERSHIRE CUP																																		
05/05/1981	BRISTOL CITY	H	0	1	2558		2	3	5	11			7		A		4						11	6				10	1	8					
	AET																																		

+ Match played at Ashton Gat

1981/82

Date	Opponent	H/A	F	A	Att	KITE Philip	GILLIES Donald	SLATTER Neil	McCAFFERY Aiden	PARKIN Timothy	WILLIAMS Brian	CURLE Keith	WILLIAMS David	MABBUTT Gary	RANDALL Paul	BARRETT Michael	COOPER Terence	STEPHENS Arthur	HUGHES Mark	WILLIAMS Geraint	JONES Vaughan	THOMAS Martin	PENDREY Gary	PENNY Shaun	WESTAWAY Kevin	BAILEY Steven	KELLY Errington	HOLLOWAY Ian	SMITH David	WILLIAMS Steven			
	DIVISION 3																																
29/08/1981	CHESTER CITY	H	2	2	5554	1	2	3	4	5	6	7	8	9	10A	11	A														CURLE	D WILLIAMS	
05/09/1981	CHESTERFIELD	A	0	2	3501	1	2	3	4	5	6	7	8	9	10A		11	A															
12/09/1981	BURNLEY	H	2	1	5083	1	2	3	4	5		A	8	9		7	11	10	6A												STEPHENS 2		
19/09/1981	READING	A	3	0	4947	1	2	3	4	5		A	8	9	6	7	11A	10													STEPHENS 2	RANDALL	
23/09/1981	EXETER CITY	A	3	1	5510	1	2	3	4	5		A	8	9	6	7	11	10A													D WILLIAMS	RANDALL	McCAFFERY
26/09/1981	LINCOLN CITY	H	0	2	6112	1	2	3	4A	5		A	8	9	6	7	11	10															
29/09/1981	WIMBLEDON	H	2	2	5364	1	2	3	4	5			8	9	10	7			6	11											MABBUTT 2		
03/10/1981	PRESTON NORTH END	A	1	0	4964	1	2	3	4	5			8	9	10A	7	A	6		11											STEPHENS		
09/10/1981	SOUTHEND UNITED	A	0	1	4530	1		3	4	5			8	9	10	7		6		11	2												
17/10/1981	SWINDON TOWN	H	1	4	8779	1		3A	4	5	10		8	6		11	A	9		7	2										STEPHENS		
21/10/1981	OXFORD UNITED	A	1	1	4422	1	2		4	5	11		8	9	A			6	10A	7	3										RANDALL		
24/10/1981	HUDDERSFIELD TOWN	H	3	2	5064	1	3		4	5	6		8	10	11	A		9		7A	2										RANDALL	STEPHENS	McCAFFERY
31/10/1981	DONCASTER ROVERS	A	2	4	6694	1	3	7A	4		6	A	8	10	11			9	5		2										STEPHENS	MABBUTT	
03/11/1981	NEWPORT COUNTY	H	2	0	6464		2		4		11	7	8	6	10			9	5		3	1									D WILLIAMS	RANDALL	
07/11/1981	GILLINGHAM	H	2	0	5518		7		4		11	3	8	6	10			9	5		2	1									CURLE	RANDALL	
14/11/1981	MILLWALL	A	0	0	5970		7		4		11	3	8	6	9			10	5		2	1											
28/11/1981	WALSALL	A	1	2	4311		8		4		3	A	11	6	10A	7		9	5		2	1									BARRETT		
05/12/1981	FULHAM	H	1	2	4489		8		4	A	3		11A	6	10	7		9	5		2	1									B WILLIAMS		
17/12/1981	CARLISLE UNITED	H	0	1	3759		8				3	A	11	6		7A			4	10	2	1	5	9									
26/12/1981	PORTSMOUTH	A	0	0	11395		7	3	8	5	11		9	4		6		A			2	1		10A									
29/12/1981	BRISTOL CITY	H	1	0	12355		8	10	4	5	3		11	6		7A		A			2	1		9							McCAFFERY		
02/01/1982	PLYMOUTH ARGYLE	A	0	4	7058		3	7	4A	5	11		8	6		A		9			2	1		10									
19/01/1982	CHESTERFIELD	H	1	0	4853		A	3	4	5	11	2	8	7	10A			9			6	1									RANDALL		
23/01/1982	CHESTER CITY	A	1	1	2040		A	3	4	5	11	7A	8	6	10			9			2	1									RANDALL		
30/01/1982	READING	H	1	1	5355		9	3	4	5	11		8	6	10					7	2	1									MABBUTT		
06/02/1982	BURNLEY	A	0	4	5724		9		4A	5	11		8	6	10			A		7	2	1			3								
09/02/1982	EXETER CITY	H	3	2	4987	1				5	11		8	6	10	7		9A	3		2					4	A				PARKIN	RANDALL 2	
13/02/1982	PRESTON NORTH END	H	2	0	5003	1				5	11		8	6	10	7		9	3		2					4					STEPHENS	D WILLIAMS	
20/02/1982	WIMBLEDON	A	0	1	2408	1				4	7	A	6	5	10	8A			3							9	11	2					
27/02/1982	SOUTHEND UNITED	H	2	1	4910	1	4			5	11		8	3	10	7			6							2	9				BARRETT	D WILLIAMS	
06/03/1982	SWINDON TOWN	A	2	5	6689	1	4			5	11		8	3	10	7		9	6							2					STEPHENS	PARKIN	
13/03/1982	HUDDERSFIELD TOWN	A	2	0	6156	1		11		5	10		7	3	9	6		8			2					4					B WILLIAMS	VALENTINE og	
16/03/1982	NEWPORT COUNTY	A	1	1	5312	1		3		5	11		8		10	7		9	6		2					4					B WILLIAMS pen		
20/03/1982	DONCASTER ROVERS	H	3	0	4597	1		3		5		A	8	11	10	7		9	6		2A					4					MABBUTT	D WILLIAMS	RANDALL
22/03/1982	BRENTFORD	A	0	1	5843	1		7		5		A	8	6	10A	11		9	3		2					4							
27/03/1982	GILLINGHAM	A	0	2	5100	1		3		5	10		8	11		7		9	6		2					4A	A						
03/04/1982	MILLWALL	H	0	1	4279	1	3			5	11		8	10	A	7		9	6	4	2A												
10/04/1982	PORTSMOUTH	H	1	1	4833	1	2			5	11		8	10	3	7A		9	6					A		4					D WILLIAMS		
12/04/1982	BRISTOL CITY	A	1	2	10791	1		3	A	5	11		8	10	4	7		9A			2					6					RANDALL	D WILLIAMS	
17/04/1982	FULHAM	A	2	4	6849	1		3		5	11A		8	10	4	7				6	2					A	9				D WILLIAMS pen	SLATTER	
24/04/1982	WALSALL	H	2	1	3677			3		5	11		8	6	10A			9		4	2	1				7			A		STEPHENS	BAILEY	
01/05/1982	LINCOLN CITY	A	0	1	4024			3		5	11		8	6	10			9		4	2	1				7							
03/05/1982	BRENTFORD	H	1	2	4314			3		5	11		8	6	10	A		9		4	2	1				7A					D WILLIAMS		
08/05/1982	PLYMOUTH ARGYLE	H	2	3	4025			3	4	5	11	10	8	6	A	7A		9			2	1									D WILLIAMS	B WILLIAMS pen	
11/05/1982	OXFORD UNITED	H	1	0	4754				3	5	11	7	8	6				9		4	2	1		10							PENNY		
15/05/1982	CARLISLE UNITED	A	2	1	6653				2	5	11	7	8	6				9	10	4	3	1									HUGHES 2		
	APPEARANCES					27	26	28	28	39	37	10	46	45	34	29	5	35	22	16	34	19	1	5	1	15	3	1	0				
	SUB					0	2	0	1	1	0	10	0	0	3	3	3	4	0	0	0	0	0	1	0	1	2	0	1				
	GOALS					0	0	1	3	2	4	2	11	5	12	2	0	11	2	0	0	0	0	1	0	1	0	0	0		OWN GOAL 1		
	SUBD					0	0	2	3	0	1	1	1	0	7	5	1	3	2	1	2	0	0	1	0	2	0	0	0				
	LEAGUE CUP																																
02/09/1981	CREWE ALEXANDRA	A	1	1	2137	1	2	3	4	5	6	7A	8	9	10		11		A												MABBUTT		
15/09/1981	CREWE ALEXANDRA	H	1	0	4050	1	2	3	6	5		7	8	9		11	A	10	4A												PARKIN		
06/10/1981	NORTHAMPTON TOWN	H	1	2	4476	1	2		4	5			8	6	10A	7	3	9	11											A	STEPHENS		
27/10/1981	NORTHAMPTON TOWN	A	1	3	3543	1	3		4		10		8	6	7	11		9	5		2A			A							D WILLIAMS		
	FA CUP																																
21/11/1981	FULHAM	H	1	2	4489		8A		4		3	7	11	6	10	A		9	5		2	1									D WILLIAMS pen		
	GLOUCESTERSHIRE CUP																																
08/09/1981	BRISTOL CITY	A	1	0	4022	1	2	3	4	5	11		8	9		7		10	6												McCAFFERY		

1982/83

Date					Att	KITE Philip	STEPHENS Arthur	SLATTER Neil	WILLIAMS Geraint	HUGHES Mark	McCAFFERY Aiden	CURLE Keith	WILLIAMS David	RANDALL Paul	KELLY Errington	BARRETT Michael	WITHEY Graham	WILLIAMS Brian	PARKIN Timothy	PLATNAUER Nichol:	HOLLOWAY Ian	SHERWOOD Jeffery	CHANNON Michael	PULIS Anthony R	CARTER Roy (L)	BRADD Leslie (L)	BALL Alan	ADAMS Michael	CASHLEY Raymond					
	DIVISION 3																																	
28/08/1982	BRENTFORD	A	1	5	5542	1	2	3	4	5A	6	7	8	9	10	11	A													RANDALL				
04/09/1982	DONCASTER ROVERS	H	2	0	3617	1	9A	2	4		6	7	8	10	A	11		3	5											BARRETT	KELLY			
07/09/1982	GILLINGHAM	H	2	1	3668	1	9	2	4		6	7	8	10A	A	11		3	5											RANDALL	CURLE			
11/09/1982	CHESTERFIELD	A	0	0	1990	1	9A	3	4		6	7	8	10	A	11		2	5															
18/09/1982	LINCOLN CITY	H	1	2	4177	1	A	2	4		6		8	10	9	11		3	5	7A										RANDALL				
25/09/1982	PRESTON NORTH END	A	2	2	3880	1	10	2A	4		6		8		9	11		3	5		7	A								BARRETT	G WILLIAMS			
28/09/1982	PLYMOUTH ARGYLE	A	4	0	3543	1		2	4		6		8	10	9A	11		3	5		7	A								D WILLIAMS	RANDALL 2	KELLY		
02/10/1982	BRADFORD CITY	H	4	1	4451	1	A	2	4		6		8	10	9A	11		3	5		7									RANDALL 2	PARKIN	D WILLIAMS		
09/10/1982	NEWPORT COUNTY	A	0	2	5912	1		2	4	A	6		8	10	9A	11		3	5		7													
16/10/1982	WIGAN ATHLETIC	H	4	0	4439	1	9A	2	4		6		8	10		11	A	3	5		7									WITHEY 2	RANDALL	G WILLIAMS		
19/10/1982	MILLWALL	H	4	0	7241	1		2	4		6		8	10A		11	9	3	5		7		A							D WILLIAMS 2	HOLLOWAY	McCAFFERY		
23/10/1982	ORIENT	A	5	1	2534	1		2	4		6		8	10A		11	9	3	5		7		A							HOLLOWAY 2	D WILLIAMS pen	RANDALL	WITHEY	
30/10/1982	READING	H	3	0	7270	1			4		6		8	10		11	9A	3	5		A	2	7							D WILLIAMS 2	WITHEY			
02/11/1982	AFC BOURNEMOUTH	A	0	0	6263	1			4		6		8	10			9A	3	5	11	A	2	7											
05/11/1982	SOUTHEND UNITED	A	0	1	3480	1			4		6		8	A			9	3	5	10A	11	2	7											
13/11/1982	PORTSMOUTH	H	5	1	9389	1	9	2	4		6		8	10		11		3	5		7									D WILLIAMS	HOLLOWAY	PARKIN	McCAFFERY	STEPHENS
27/11/1982	HUDDERSFIELD TOWN	A	1	3	8251	1	9	2	4		6		8	10A		11		3	5		7		A							HOLLOWAY				
30/11/1982	AFC BOURNEMOUTH	H	1	1	4358	1	9	2	4		6			10	A	11A		3	5		7		8							PARKIN				
04/12/1982	WALSALL	H	2	0	4822	1	9	2	4		6		8		10A	11		3	5		7		A							STEPHENS	KELLY			
18/12/1982	WREXHAM	H	4	0	4607	1	9	2	4		6		8A			11	10	3	5		7		A							HOLLOWAY	D WILLIAMS	G WILLIAMS	B WILLIAMS	
27/12/1982	OXFORD UNITED	A	2	4	9551	1	9	2	4		6				10A	11		3	5	8	7			A						STEPHENS	McCAFFERY			
29/12/1982	EXETER CITY	H	4	4	8160	1	9A	2	4		6		8	10		11		3	5	A	7									HOLLOWAY	RANDALL 2	VINEY og		
01/01/1983	CARDIFF CITY	A	1	3	11050	1	A		4		6			10		11		3	5		7A	2			8	9				BRADD				
08/01/1983	DONCASTER ROVERS	A	2	1	3234	1	9				6	7A		10		A		3	5	11		2		4	8					RANDALL	STEPHENS			
15/01/1983	BRENTFORD	H	2	0	5449	1	9	3			6	7		10		11			5	A		2		4A	8					RANDALL	CARTER			
22/01/1983	LINCOLN CITY	A	1	2	5342	1		3			6	7	A	9	10A				5	11		2		4	8					PLATNAUER				
29/01/1983	CHESTERFIELD	H	3	0	6066	1		3			6		8	10		9		2	5	11	4						7			PLATNAUER 2	RANDALL			
05/02/1983	PLYMOUTH ARGYLE	H	2	0	6556	1		2			6		8	10		11		3	5	9	4						7			PLATNAUER	BALL			
12/02/1983	BRADFORD CITY	A	0	2	4261	1	A	2	4		6A		8	10		11		3	5	9							7							
19/02/1983	NEWPORT COUNTY	H	1	3	6812	1	9	2			6		8	10		11		3	5	A	4A						7			RANDALL				
26/02/1983	WIGAN ATHLETIC	A	5	0	3288	1		2	8		6			10			9	3	5	11	A			4			7A			WITHEY 2	RANDALL 2	PLATNAUER		
05/03/1983	ORIENT	H	2	1	5642	1		2	4		6			10			9	3	5	11	A			8A			7			WITHEY	RANDALL			
12/03/1983	READING	A	2	1	4270	1		2	4	8	6	11		10			9	3	5A		A						7			WITHEY 2				
13/03/1983	SOUTHEND UNITED	H	2	2	6025	1	A	2	4		6			10		11	9	3	5		8A						7			BARRETT	STEPHENS			
26/03/1983	PORTSMOUTH	A	0	1	17828	1	A		4		6			10			9	3	5	11		2		8A			7							
29/03/1983	SHEFFIELD UNITED	H	2	1	6595	1	A		4		6			10A			9	3	5	11		2		8			7			B WILLIAMS	PLATNAUER			
02/04/1983	EXETER CITY	A	1	0	5741	1	A		4		6			10			9A	3	5	11		2		8			7			RANDALL				
05/04/1983	OXFORD UNITED	H	0	1	8190	1	A		4		6			10			9A	3	5	11		2		8			7							
09/04/1983	WALSALL	A	0	5	4559	1	9			5	6			10		A		3		11	8	2		4			7A							
12/04/1983	MILLWALL	A	1	1	4873	1		5			6	7		A		11	10	3		9A	8	2		4						CURLE				
16/04/1983	PRESTON NORTH END	H	3	2	5189	1	A	2			6	7A		10		11	9	3			4	5		8						BARRETT	RANDALL	STEPHENS		
22/04/1983	WREXHAM	A	0	0	2053	1	A	2			6			10		11	9A	3			8	5		4			7							
30/04/1983	HUDDERSFIELD TOWN	H	1	0	8919	1		2						10A		11	A	3	6	9	8	5		4			7			BALL				
02/05/1983	SHEFFIELD UNITED	A	1	2	7694	1		2	7		6	A				11	9	3	5	10	8A			4						WITHEY				
07/05/1983	GILLINGHAM	A	0	1	4024	1	11	2	8		6			A			10	3	5A	9				4			7							
14/05/1983	CARDIFF CITY	H	1	1	10731	1	10	2	8		6	4		9A				3	5	11							7	A		PLATNAUER				
	APPEARANCES					46	19	36	35	3	45	11	24	38	9	32	19	43	41	21	26	16	4	16	4	1	17	0						
	SUB					0	11	0	0	1	0	1	1	3	4	2	3	0	0	3	5	2	5	1	0	0	0	1						
	GOALS					0	6	0	3	0	3	2	9	20	3	4	10	2	3	7	7	0	0	0	1	1	2	0		OWN GOAL 1				
	SUBD					0	4	1	0	1	1	2	1	7	6	1	5	0	2	3	4	0	0	3	0	0	2	0						
	MILK CUP																																	
01/09/1982	TORQUAY UNITED	H	2	2	3529	1	9	3	4	2A	6	8	7	10	A	11			5											RANDALL	D WILLIAMS			
15/09/1982	TORQUAY UNITED	A	4	0	3204	1	A	2	4		6		8	10	9	11		3	5	7A										PLATNAUER	BARRETT	RANDALL	STEPHENS	
05/10/1982	SWANSEA CITY	H	1	0	9279	1	A	2	4		6		8	10	9	11A		3	5		7									PARKIN				
26/10/1982	SWANSEA CITY	A	0	3	9775	1		2	4		6		8	10		11A	9	3	5		7		A											
	FA CUP																																	
20/11/1982	WYCOMBE WANDERERS	H	1	0	6420	1	9	2	4		6		8	10		11		3	5		7									STEPHENS				
11/12/1982	PLYMOUTH ARGYLE	H	2	2	9018	1	9A	2	4		6		8	10		11	A	3	5		7									D WILLIAMS 2				
20/12/1982	PLYMOUTH ARGYLE	A	0	1	9130	1	9	2	4		6		8A			11	10	3	5	A			7											
																		3																
	GLOUCESTERSHIRE CUP																																	
21/10/1982	BRISTOL CITY	H	2	1	4369		9				6		8	10		11			5		7	2		4					1	STEPHENS	HOLLOWAY			

1983/84

Date					Att	KITE Philip	SLATTER Neil	WILLIAMS Brian	WILLIAMS Geraint	PARKIN Timothy	McCAFFERY Aiden	HOLLOWAY Ian	WILLIAMS David	WHITE Stephen	RANDALL Paul	BARRETT Michael	STEPHENS Arthur	PULIS Anthony R	BATER Philip	CASHLEY Raymond	BANNON Paul	HUGHES Mark	CURLE Keith	VASSELL Paul	ADAMS Michael	METCALFE Carl	NOBLE Wayne				
	DIVISION 3																														
27/08/1983	NEWPORT COUNTY	A	1	2	5015	1	2	3	4	5	6	7	8A	9	10	11	A											STEPHENS			
03/09/1983	SOUTHEND UNITED	H	2	1	4410	1	2	3	4	5	6	7		9	10	11		8										RANDALL	HOLLOWAY		
06/09/1983	BRENTFORD	H	3	1	5148	1	2	3	4	5	6	7		9	10	11		8										WHITE	B WILLIAMS	BARRETT	
10/09/1983	PORT VALE	A	0	2	4308	1	2	3	4	5	6	7		9	10	11A	A	8													
17/09/1983	EXETER CITY	H	2	0	4813	1	2	3		5	6	7		9A	A	11	10	8	4									STEPHENS	PARKIN		
23/09/1983	ORIENT	A	1	0	4206	1	2	3		5	6	7		9		11	10	8	4									PULIS			
27/09/1983	AFC BOURNEMOUTH	A	1	0	3328	1	2	3	8	5	6	7		9	A	11	10A		4									WHITE			
01/10/1983	BOLTON WANDERERS	H	2	1	5621	1	2	3	8	5	6	7		9	10	11			4									BARRETT	RANDALL		
08/10/1983	WIMBLEDON	A	1	1	3462	1	2	3		5	6	7		9A	10	11	A	8	4									BARRETT			
15/10/1983	BRADFORD CITY	H	1	0	3861	1	2	3	11A	5	6	7		A	10		9	8	4									RANDALL			
18/10/1983	PLYMOUTH ARGYLE	A	1	1	4896	1	2	3	11	5	6	7		A	10		9	8	4A									G WILLIAMS			
25/10/1983	SCUNTHORPE UNITED	H	4	1	5324	1	2	3	8	5	6	7		A	10A	11	9		4									B WILLIAMS pen	STEPHENS	BARRETT	GREEN og
29/10/1983	WALSALL	A	1	2	4964	1	2	3	8	5	6	7		9	10A	11	A		4									STEPHENS			
01/11/1983	PRESTON NORTH END	H	3	1	5635	1	2	3	8	5	6	7		9	A	11	10A		4									BARRETT	RANDALL	G WILLIAMS	
05/11/1983	ROTHERHAM UNITED	A	2	2	3957	1	2	3	8	5	6	7		10	9	11			4									HOLLOWAY	B WILLIAMS pen		
12/11/1983	BURNLEY	H	2	1	7021	1	2	3	8	5	6	7		9	10	11			4									BATER	B WILLIAMS pen		
26/11/1983	LINCOLN CITY	A	0	4	3709	1	2	3	8	5	6	7		9A	10	11	A		4												
03/12/1983	SHEFFIELD UNITED	H	1	1	7472	1	2	3	8	5	6	7			10	11	9		4									B WILLIAMS			
17/12/1983	HULL CITY	H	1	3	5673	1	2	3		5	6	7A	8	A	10	11	9		4									PARKIN			
26/12/1983	OXFORD UNITED	A	2	3	12748		2	3	8	5	6		7	11			9	10	4	1								STEPHENS 2			
27/12/1983	GILLINGHAM	H	3	0	5996		2	3	8	5	6		7	11		A	9A	10	4	1								D WILLIAMS	STEPHENS	WHITE	
30/12/1983	MILLWALL	A	0	1	4885		2A	3	8	5	6		7	11		A	9	10	4	1											
09/01/1984	SOUTHEND UNITED	A	2	1	2564		2	3	8	5	6			11		7	9	10	4	1								BARRETT	B WILLIAMS		
14/01/1984	NEWPORT COUNTY	H	4	0	6041		2	3	8	5	6	7	A	10A		11	9	4		1								STEPHENS 2	G WILLIAMS 2		
21/01/1984	EXETER CITY	A	2	1	5310		2	3	8	5	6	7		10		11	9	4		1								SLATTER	WEBSTER og		
28/01/1984	PORT VALE	H	0	0	6502		2	3	8	5	6	7	A	9A	10	11		4		1											
04/02/1984	BOLTON WANDERERS	A	0	3	5399		2	3	4A	5	6	7	A	9	10	11		8		1											
11/02/1984	ORIENT	H	0	0	4741		2	3	8	5	6		7			11	9	4		1	10										
14/02/1984	PRESTON NORTH END	A	0	1	3813		2	3	A	5	6	4	7		11A		9	8		1	10										
18/02/1984	WALSALL	H	4	2	5643		2	3		5	6	8	7		A	11	9	4		1	10A							BANNON	D WILLIAMS	RANDALL	HART og
26/02/1984	SCUNTHORPE UNITED	A	2	2	2737		2	3		5	6	7		9	A	11		4	8	1	10A							WHITE 2			
03/03/1984	PLYMOUTH ARGYLE	H	2	0	5619		2	3		5	6	7	11	9	A			4	8	1	10A							BANNON	WHITE		
06/03/1984	ROTHERHAM UNITED	H	2	0	5264		2	3		5	6A	7	11	9	A			4	8	1	10							BANNON	D WILLIAMS		
10/03/1984	BURNLEY	A	0	0	6296			3		5		7	8	9	11		A	4	2	1	10A	6									
17/03/1984	WIMBLEDON	H	1	1	5383			11	7A	5	6		8	10		A	9	4	3	1		2						WHITE			
27/03/1984	WIGAN ATHLETIC	H	2	1	7072		2	11		5	6		8	9	7		A	4	3	1	10A							B WILLIAMS	WALSH og		
31/03/1984	BRENTFORD	A	2	2	4067		2	11		5	6		8	10	7		A	4	3	1	9A							WHITE	B WILLIAMS		
07/04/1984	AFC BOURNEMOUTH	H	1	3	5032		2	11		5	6		8	9A	7		A	4	3	1	10							PULIS			
14/04/1984	SHEFFIELD UNITED	A	0	4	12688		2	11	7	5	6			9		8	A	4	3	1	10A										
17/04/1984	WIGAN ATHLETIC	A	0	0	2665		2	11	4		6	7		9		8	10		3	1		5									
21/04/1984	OXFORD UNITED	H	1	1	6397		2	3	4		6	7A	8	10	A	11	9			1		5						STEPHENS			
23/04/1984	GILLINGHAM	A	2	1	3400		2	3	4		6	7	8	10		11	9			1		5						STEPHENS 2			
28/04/1984	LINCOLN CITY	H	3	1	3245		2	3	4		6	7	8	10		11	9			1		5						BARRETT 2	WHITE		
02/05/1984	BRADFORD CITY	A	1	0	3271			3	4		6	7	8	10		11	9		2	1		5						STEPHENS			
08/05/1984	MILLWALL	H	3	2	5347		2	3	4		6	7	8	9	10	11			A	1		5A						B WILLIAMS pen	RANDALL	BARRETT	
12/05/1984	HULL CITY	A	0	0	11657		2	3	4		6	7A	8	9	10	11			A	1		5									
	APPEARANCES					19	43	46	33	39	45	36	21	38	24	33	24	28	30	27	11	9									
	SUB					0	0	0	1	0	0	0	3	4	8	3	10	0	2	0	0	0									
	GOALS					0	1	9	4	2	0	2	3	9	6	9	13	2	1	0	3	0						OWN GOAL 4			
	SUBD					0	1	0	3	0	1	3	1	6	3	1	3	0	1	0	7	1									
	MILK CUP																														
30/08/1983	AFC BOURNEMOUTH	A	2	1	3473	1	2	3	4	5		7		9	10	11		8										RANDALL	HOLLOWAY		
13/09/1983	AFC BOURNEMOUTH	H	2	2	4564	1	2	3	4	5	6	7		9		11	10	8										B WILLIAMS pen	STEPHENS		
04/10/1983	BRIGHTON & HOVE ALBION	A	2	4	9417	1	2	3	8	5	6	7		9	10	11		4										BARRETT	SLATTER		
25/10/1983	BRIGHTON & HOVE ALBION	H	2	1	5324	1	2	3	4	5	6	7		8	10	11	9											BARRETT	WHITE		
	* AET: Score at 90 mins 2-0																														
	FA CUP																														
19/11/1983	BARNET	A	0	0	2650	1	2	3	8	5	6	7		9	10A	11	A		4												
22/11/1983	BARNET	H	3	1	5338	1	2	3	8	5	6	7		9	10	11			4									HOLLOOWAY	BARRETT	SLATTER	
10/12/1983	BRISTOL CITY	H	1	2	14396	1	2	3	8	5	6	7		A	10	11	9		4									STEPHENS			
	ASSOCIATE MEMBERS CUP																														
28/02/1984	NEWPORT COUNTY	A	1	0	2116		2	3		5	6	7	11	9				4		1	10							BANNON			
13/03/1984	PORT VALE	H	2	0	2558	1			4	5	6		8	A		7	9	10	3			2B		10A			B	B WILLIAMS	STEPHENS		
03/04/1984	SOUTHEND UNITED	A	2	1	1480	1	2	3	4		6A	7	8			11	9	6				5			10	A		HUGHES	ADAMS		
14/05/1984	AFC BOURNEMOUTH	A	0	1	2810		2	3		5	6	4	8	9	10	11B	B	7A	A	1		5									
	GLOUCESTERSHIRE CUP FINAL																														
20/09/1983	BRISTOL CITY *	A	3	2	6538	1		3		5	6	4		9	7A	11	10	8	2				A					McCAFFREY	WHITE	CURLE	
	* AET Score at 90 mins 1-1																														

1984/85

Date					Att	CASHLEY Raymond	SLATTER Neil	WILLIAMS Brian	WILLIAMS Geraint	PARKIN Timothy	McCAFFERY Aiden	HOLLOWAY Ian	WILLIAMS David	STEPHENS Arthur	RANDALL Paul	O'CONNOR Mark	BATER Philip	WHITE Stephen	JONES Vaughan	HALLWORTH Jonathan (L)	BANNON Paul	GREEN Ronald R (L)	RAYNOR Paul (L)	PENRICE Gary	SMITH Christopher	TAYLOR Gregory	NOBLE Wayne	BRAIN Mark	TANNER Nicholas	Scorers		
	DIVISION 3																															
25/08/1984	BOLTON WANDERERS	A	1	0	4469	1	2	3	4	5	6	7	8	9	10A	11	A													STEPHENS		
01/09/1984	PRESTON NORTH END	H	3	0	5357	1	2	3	4	5	6	7	8	9	10	11														STEPHENS 2	RANDALL	
08/09/1984	BURNLEY	A	0	0	5362	1	2	3	4	5	6	7	8	9A	10	11	A															
15/09/1984	READING	H	1	0	5197	1	2	3	4	5	6	7	8A	9	10	11	A													STEPHENS		
18/09/1984	BRADFORD CITY	H	2	0	5247	1	2	3	4	5	6	7		9	10	11	8													RANDALL	HOLLOWAY	
22/09/1984	LINCOLN CITY	A	2	1	2168	1	2	3	4	5	6	7A	A	9	10	11	8													RANDALL 2		
29/09/1984	AFC BOURNEMOUTH	H	1	0	5216	1	2	3	4	5	6	7	8		10	11		9												WHITE		
02/10/1984	YORK CITY	A	0	1	7197	1	2	3	4	5	6	7	8		10	11		9														
06/10/1984	DERBY COUNTY	H	2	1	7862	1	2	3	4	5	6	7	8		10	11		9												RANDALL 2		
13/10/1984	ROTHERHAM UNITED	A	3	3	5177	1	6	3	4	5		7	8		10	11	2	9												RANDALL	D WILLIAMS 2	
20/10/1984	DONCASTER ROVERS	H	1	1	5611	1	2	3	4	5	6	7	8		10	11	A	9A												D WILLIAMS		
23/10/1984	WIGAN ATHLETIC	A	0	1	3022	1	2	3	4	5	6	7	8A	9	10	11	A															
27/10/1984	HULL CITY	H	1	1	5438	1	2	3	4	5	6	7	8	9	10	11														STEPHENS		
03/11/1984	PLYMOUTH ARGYLE	A	2	3	5818	1	2	3	4	5	6	7	8	9	10	11														RANDALL	SLATTER	
10/11/1984	BRISTOL CITY	A	0	3	18672	1	2	3	4	5	6	7	8	9	10A	A	11															
21/11/1984	MILLWALL	H	1	1	5917	1	2	3		5	6	7	8	9	10	11	4													STEPHENS		
30/11/1984	ORIENT	A	4	1	2404	1	2	3		5	6	7	8	9	10	11	4													O'CONNOR 2	HOLLOWAY	RANDALL
15/12/1984	NEWPORT COUNTY	H	2	0	5405	1		3	2	5	6	7	8	9A	10	11	4	A												O'CONNOR	D WILLIAMS	
22/12/1984	SWANSEA CITY	H	4	2	5546	1		3	2	5	6	7	8	9	10A	11	4	A												STEPHENS 2	RANDALL	O'CONNOR
26/12/1984	BRENTFORD	A	3	0	5254	1		3	2	5	6	7	8	9	10	11A	4	A												O'CONNOR	STEPHENS	RANDALL
29/12/1984	GILLINGHAM	A	1	4	6598	1		3	2	5	6	7	8	9	10	11	4													STEPHENS		
01/01/1985	CAMBRIDGE UNITED	H	2	1	6324	1		3	2	5	6	7	8	9	10	11	4													D WILLIAMS	HOLLOWAY	
12/01/1985	PRESTON NORTH END	A	2	2	3136	1		3	2	5	6	7	8		10A	11	4	9	A											WHITE	RANDALL	
26/01/1985	READING	A	2	3	4648			3	2	5	6	7	8	A	10	11	4	9A		1										D WILLIAMS	HOLLOWAY	
29/01/1985	BOLTON WANDERERS	H	1	2	3982			3	2	5	6	7	8	A	10A	11	4	9		1										RANDALL		
02/02/1985	AFC BOURNEMOUTH	A	0	1	5000	1		3	2	5	6	7	8	10		11	4	9														
13/02/1985	BRADFORD CITY	A	0	2	5428	1	2	4		5	6	7	8	9	10A	11	3		A													
23/02/1985	PLYMOUTH ARGYLE	H	1	0	5953	1	2	3		5		7	8	9	10	11A	4		6		A									B WILLIAMS		
02/03/1985	HULL CITY	A	0	2	6380		2	6		5		7	8	9		11	3		4		10	1										
05/03/1985	WIGAN ATHLETIC	H	2	0	3883		2A	3	7	5		A	8	9		11	4		6		10	1								BANNON	HOLLOWAY	
08/03/1985	DONCASTER ROVERS	A	2	2	3651		2	4	8	5		7	A		9A	11	3		6		10	1								O'CONNOR	PARKIN	
16/03/1985	ROTHERHAM UNITED	H	1	0	4083		2A	3	8	5		7	A		9	11	4		6		10	1								RANDALL		
23/03/1985	DERBY COUNTY	A	0	0	10041		2	3	8	5		7			9	11	4		6		10	1										
30/03/1985	WALSALL	A	2	1	4829		2	3		5		7	8		9	11	4		6		10	1								RANDALL 2		
02/04/1985	LINCOLN CITY	H	0	0	4159		2	3		5		7	8A		9	11	4		6		10	1	A									
06/04/1985	BRENTFORD	H	3	0	4519		2	3		5		7	8A		9	11	4	A			10	1	6							BANNON	B WILLIAMS 2-2pens	
08/04/1985	CAMBRIDGE UNITED	A	2	0	1711		2	4		5		7			9	11	3		6		10	1	8							PARKIN	SLATTER	
13/04/1985	BRISTOL CITY	H	1	0	12957		2	3		5		7			9	11	4		6		10	1	8							HOLLOWAY		
16/04/1985	BURNLEY	H	4	0	4866		2	3		5		7			9	11	4		6		10	1	8							RANDALL 2	BANNON	PARKIN
20/04/1985	MILLWALL	A	0	1	7416		2	3		5		7			9	11	4	10	6			1	8									
23/04/1985	WALSALL	H	0	0	4040		2	3			5	7	4		9	11		10A	6		A	1	8									
27/04/1985	ORIENT	H	0	1	2549		2	3		5		7A			9	11	4		6		10	1	8	A								
04/05/1985	NEWPORT COUNTY	A	1	1	2302		2	3		5					9	11	4	7	6		10	1		8						B WILLIAMS		
07/05/1985	GILLINGHAM	H	3	2	2716		2	4		5					9	11	3	8	6		10	1		7						BANNON	O'CONNOR	WHITE
11/05/1985	SWANSEA CITY	A	2	3	5155		5	3					2		9	11	4	7	6		10	1		8						BANNON	O'CONNOR	
14/05/1985	YORK CITY	H	1	1	3692		5	4					8		9	11	3		6		10	1		7	2					PENRICE		
	APPEARANCES					26	37	46	28	43	27	41	34	22	43	45	34	14	18	2	16	18	7	4	1							
	SUB					0	0	0	0	0	0	1	3	2	0	1	5	4	2	0	2	0	1	1	0							
	GOALS					0	2	4	0	3	0	6	6	10	18	8	0	3	0	0	5	0	0	1	0							
	SUBD					0	2	0	0	0	0	2	4	2	7	2	0	3	0	0	0	0	0	0	0							
	MILK CUP																															
27/08/1984	SWINDON TOWN	A	5	1	4905	1	2	3	4	5	6	7	8	9	10	11														B WILLIAMS	RANDALL 2	D WILLIAMS 2
04/09/1984	SWINDON TOWN	H	0	1	3862	1	2	3	4	5	6	7	8A	9	10	11	A	8														
25/09/1984	ARSENAL	A	0	4	28871	1	2	3	4	5	6	7		9	10	11	8															
09/10/1984	ARSENAL	H	1	1	10408	1	2	3	4	5		7	8		10	11A		9								6	A			WHITE		
	FA CUP																															
17/11/1984	KINGS LYNN	H	2	1	3841	1	2	3		5	6	7	8	9		11	4	10												D WILLIAMS	ADAMS og	
08/12/1984	BRISTOL CITY	A	3	1	19367	1	2A	3	A	5	6	7	8	9	10	11	4	2												O'CONNOR	RANDALL 2	
05/01/1985	IPSWICH TOWN	H	1	2	12257	1		3	2	5	6	7	8	9	10	11	4													HOLLOWAY		
	FRIEIGHT ROVER TROPHY																															
22/01/1985	SWANSEA CITY	A	0	2	2648			3	2	5	6	7	8B		10	11		9		1A				B				A				
19/03/1985	SWANSEA CITY	H	0	0	2223			3B		5		7	2		9A	11	4	B			10	1		A								
	GLOUCESTERSHIRE CUP FINAL																															
21/05/1985	BRISTOL CITY *	H	3	1	4033		2	4			5				9	11	3	8	6		10	1		7	B				A	WHITE	TANNER	BANNON

* AET Score at 90 mins 1-1

1985/86

Date	Opponent	H/A	F	A	Att	GREEN Ronald R	SPRING Andrew	DAVIES Ian	STEVENSON Byron	PARKIN Timothy	JONES Vaughan	BADOCK Stephen	O'CONNOR Mark	RANDALL Paul	PENRICE Gary	TANNER Nicholas	WHITE Stephen	BATER Philip	COCKRAM Allan	VAUGHAN John (L)	OBI Anthony	SCALES John	FRANCIS Gerald	MORGAN Trevor	ENGLAND Michael	SMART Gary	MEHEW David	CARTER Timothy	NOBLE Wayne	PURNELL Philip	ILES Richard	CARR Darren	PORTCH Lee	Scorers		
	DIVISION 3																																			
18/08/1985	DARLINGTON	A	3	3	4196	1	2	3	4	5	6	7	8	9	10	11A	A																	WHITE	BADOCK	STEVENSON pen
24/08/1985	BRENTFORD	H	0	1	4140	1	2A	3	4	5	6	7	8	9	10	11	A																			
26/08/1985	READING	A	2	3	3529	1	2	3	4	5	6	7	8		10		9	11																DAVIES	PENRICE	
31/08/1985	DERBY COUNTY	H	0	0	4961	1	2	3		5	6	7	8		10		9	11	4																	
07/09/1985	NEWPORT COUNTY	A	0	3	2775		2			5	6	7	8		10	3	9	11		1	4A	A														
14/09/1985	LINCOLN CITY	H	0	0	3077		7A			5	6	11	8	9	10	A		3		1		2	4													
17/09/1985	WOLVERHAMPTON WANDERERS	A	4	3	3244					5	6	7	8	9	10		11	3		1		2	4											WHITE	RANDALL	BADOCK 2
21/09/1985	WALSALL	H	0	1	3787		2A			5	6	7	11	9	10		8	3		1			4	A												
28/09/1985	SWANSEA CITY	A	1	0	4008			A	4	5			11	9	10	7		3		1		2		8	6A									MORGAN		
01/10/1985	NOTTS COUNTY	H	1	1	3549			2	8	5		A	11	10A	7	4		3		1				9	6									PENRICE		
05/10/1985	PLYMOUTH ARGYLE	A	2	4	5662	1	8	2	4	5		7A	11	10			A	3						9	6									MORGAN 2		
12/10/1985	ROTHERHAM UNITED	H	5	2	3499	1		3	4	5			11	10A		A	7	2					8	9	6									MORGAN 3	WHITE	PARKIN
19/10/1985	DONCASTER ROVERS	A	2	0	3032	1		3	4	5			11	10		2	7						8A	9	6	A								MORGAN 2		
22/10/1985	BOLTON WANDERERS	H	2	1	4308	1		3	4	5			11	10		2	7							9	6	8								WHITE	STEVENSON	
26/10/1985	AFC BOURNEMOUTH	A	1	6	3798	1		3	4	5			11	10		2	7							9A	6	8	A							RANDALL		
02/11/1985	YORK CITY	H	0	1	4174	1		3	4A	5	6		11	A	10	2	7	8						9												
05/11/1985	BURY	H	2	1	2959	1		3	4	5	6		11		7	8	10	2						9										TANNER	WHITE	
09/11/1985	BLACKPOOL	A	2	4	4707	1		3	4	6	5		11		7	8	10	2						9										TANNER	MORGAN	
23/11/1985	CARDIFF CITY	H	2	1	4563	1				5	6		11		7	8	10	3				2	4	9										O'CONNOR	PENRICE	
14/12/1985	GILLINGHAM	H	1	0	4224	1				5	6		11		4	8	10	3				2	7	9										MORGAN		
22/12/1985	BRENTFORD	A	0	1	5742	1				6	5		11		4	8	10	3				2	7	9												
26/12/1985	WIGAN ATHLETIC	A	0	4	3711	1				5	6A		11	A	4	8	10	3				2	7	9												
28/12/1985	READING	H	0	2	7555					5			11	4		8	10	3				2	7	9	6			1								
18/01/1986	DARLINGTON	H	3	1	3395	1	2		4	5	6		11		8		10	3					7	9										WHITE 3		
01/02/1986	NEWPORT COUNTY	H	2	0	3284	1	6		4	5			11		8	3	10					2	7	9										MORGAN	O'CONNOR	
04/02/1986	BOLTON WANDERERS	A	2	0	3672	1	6		4	5			11		8	3	10					2	7A	9					A					PARKIN	WHITE	
08/02/1986	DONCASTER ROVERS	H	1	0	3894	1	6		4	5A			11		8	3	10	A				2	7	9										WHITE		
01/03/1986	SWANSEA CITY	H	0	0	3098	1	6		4	5			11	9A	8	3	10					2	7						A							
04/03/1986	NOTTS COUNTY	A	0	0	3183	1	6		4	5			11	9	8	3	10					2	7													
08/03/1986	PLYMOUTH ARGYLE	H	1	2	4667	1			4	5	6		11		8	3	10					2	7	9										MORGAN		
12/03/1986	YORK CITY	A	0	4	2857	1	A		4	5	6		11		8	3	10A					2	7	9												
15/03/1986	ROTHERHAM UNITED	A	0	2	2734	1	4			5	6	A			8	3	10					2	7A	9					11							
18/03/1986	WALSALL	A	0	6	3734	1	6				5	7	11		8	3	10	4				2		9												
22/03/1986	AFC BOURNEMOUTH	H	2	3	3928	1	6			5	2		11		8	3	10	4						9					7					PENRICE	WHITE	
25/03/1986	WOLVERHAMPTON WANDERERS	H	1	1	3378	1	6A			5	2		11		8	4	10	3				A	7	9										MORGAN pen		
29/03/1986	BRISTOL CITY	A	0	2	12171	1			11	5	6				8	4	10	3				2	7A	9						A						
01/04/1986	WIGAN ATHLETIC	H	1	1	3428	1			10	5	6	7			8	4						2		9	3		A			11A				STEVENSON		
05/04/1986	BURY	A	1	1	1866	1			11	5	6	7			8	4						2		9	3					10				MORGAN		
09/04/1986	DERBY COUNTY	A	2	0	11033	1			11	5	6				8	3	7					2		9	4					10				WHITE	MORGAN	
12/04/1986	BLACKPOOL	H	1	0	3472	1			10	5		7A			8	4						2		9	3		A			11	6			PENRICE		
15/04/1986	CHESTERFIELD	A	0	2	1800				11	5	6				8	3	7					2	9		4		A	1		10A						
19/04/1986	CARDIFF CITY	A	0	2	2735	1			10	5	6	11A			8	4	7					2	3	9						A						
22/04/1986	BRISTOL CITY	H	1	1	9926	1				5	6				8	4A	10					2	7	9	3				A	11				SCALES		
26/04/1986	CHESTERFIELD	H	1	1	3576	1			A	5A	6				8		10	2					7	9	3				4	11				MORGAN		
30/04/1986	LINCOLN CITY	A	2	2	2233	1			5		6				8		10	2				4	7	9	3					11				PURNELL 2		
03/05/1986	GILLINGHAM	A	0	2	2050	1			4		6	A					10	3				2	7	9	8					11A		5				
	APPEARANCES					38	18	13	30	43	32	14	34	15	39	35	37	26	1	6	1	27	27	35	17	2	0	2	3	9	1	1				
	SUB					0	1	1	1	0	0	3	0	2	0	2	3	1	0	0	0	2	0	1	0	1	4	0	3	2	0	0				
	GOALS					0	0	1	3	2	0	3	2	2	5	2	12	0	0	0	0	1	0	16	0	0	0	0	0	2	0	0				
	SUBD					0	4	0	1	2	1	3	0	3	0	2	1	0	0	0	1	0	4	1	1	0	0	0	0	3	0	0				
	MILK CUP																																			
20/08/1985	NEWPORT COUNTY	H	2	0	2777	1	2	3	4	5	6	7	8		10	11								9										RANDALL	BADOCK	
03/09/1985	NEWPORT COUNTY	A	0	1	2012	1	2			5	6		8	7	10		9	11	4					3												
24/09/1985	BIRMINGHAM CITY	H	2	3	4332	1			8	5	6	A	11	9	7		10	3				2	4A											O'CONNOR	RANDALL	
08/10/1985	BIRMINGHAM CITY	A	1	2	3686	1		3	4	5	6A	7	11	10			9						8	2	A									RANDALL		
	FA CUP																																			
16/11/1985	BRENTFORD	A	3	1	4716	1				5	6		11		8	4	10	3				2	7	9										PENRICE	WHITE	FRANCIS
07/12/1985	SWANSEA CITY	A	2	1	4230	1				5	6		11		7	8	10	3				2	4	9										MORGAN pen	WHITE	
04/01/1986	LEICESTER CITY	H	3	1	9392	1			4	5	6		11			8	10	3				2	7	9										STEVENSON	MORGAN 2	
25/01/1986	LUTON TOWN	A	0	4	12463	1	6		4	5			11	A	3	8	10					2A	7	9												
	FREIGHT ROVER TROPHY																																			
15/01/1986	HEREFORD UNITED	A	0	2	1770	1			4	5	6	7A	11		8		10					2		9		A							3			
21/01/1986	SWINDON TOWN	H	2	1	2335	1	6		4	5			11	A	8	7A	10	3B				2		9									B	O'CONNOR	WHITE	
	GLOUCESTERSHIRE CUP FINAL																																			
09/09/1985	BRISTOL CITY	A	0	1	4894		7			5	6		8	9	10	3		11		1		2	4													

1986/87

Date	DIVISION 3					CARTER Timothy	SCALES John	TANNER Nicholas	JONES Vaughan	SMALLEY Mark	HIBBITT Kenneth	ALEXANDER Ian	PENRICE Gary	MORGAN Trevor	MEHEW David	MICALLEF Constantinous	PURNELL Philip	TWENTYMAN Geoffrey	FRANCIS Gerald	SMART Gary	HAMMOND Nicholas (L)	JOHNS Mark	NOBLE Wayne	CARR Darren	WESTON Ian	DRYDEN Richard	TURNER Robert	CAWLEY Peter	RUSHBURY David	NEWTON Robert	YATES Stephen	CLEMENT Andrew (L)	MEACHAM Jeffrey	BRADSHAW Paul	BOYLE Martin			
23/08/1986	WALSALL	A	3	0	6269	1	2	3	4	5	6	7	8	9	10	11																				HIBBITT	MORGAN 2	
30/08/1986	BOLTON WANDERERS	H	1	0	4092	1	2	3	4	5	6	7	8	9	10		11																			MORGAN pen		
06/09/1986	YORK CITY	A	0	1	3795	1	2	3	4		6	A	8	9	10A	11		5	7																			
13/09/1986	MANSFIELD TOWN	H	0	0	2802	1	2		6	3	4	7A	8	9		11	10	5		A																		
17/09/1986	MIDDLESBROUGH	H	1	2	3768	1	2		3	6	4A	7	8	9		10	11	5		A																MICALLEF		
20/09/1986	ROTHERHAM UNITED	A	1	0	2702	1	2	11	3	6		7	8	9		10A		5	4	A																TANNER		
27/09/1986	BLACKPOOL	H	2	2	3417		2	11A	3	6		7	8	9	10			5	4	A	1															JONES	MEHEW	
30/09/1986	NOTTS COUNTY	A	0	3	3409		2	11	3	5		7	8	9	10A			6	4	A	1																	
04/10/1986	CHESTERFIELD	H	3	2	2768		A	11	3	6		7	8		10		2A	5	4		1	9														MEHEW	ALEXANDER	JOHNS
11/10/1986	WIGAN ATHLETIC	A	3	4	2438	1	11	3	2	6	4	7A	8		10			5				9	A													HIBBITT pen	MEHEW 2	
18/10/1986	PORT VALE	H	0	0	3053	1	7	2	3	6	4	11	8	9	10								5															
21/10/1986	FULHAM	A	2	2	2351	1	7	2				11	8	9	10	4		5					3	6												MORGAN	MEHEW	
25/10/1986	CARLISLE UNITED	A	0	2	2799	1	2	3	6			7	8	9	10	4		5					11A	A														
04/11/1986	SWINDON TOWN	A	2	1	9070	1	2	3	6		8	7	4	9	10A			5					11	A												MORGAN 2		
08/11/1986	BURY	H	1	1	2947	1	2	3	6		4	7	8	9	10			5					11													MEHEW		
22/11/1986	CHESTER CITY	A	1	3	2026	1	2	3	6		4	7	8	9	10A	11		5						A												MORGAN		
14/12/1986	NEWPORT COUNTY	H	2	2	2660	1		11	6		4		8	9			10	5		2			7	3												SMART	NOBLE	
19/12/1986	GILLINGHAM	A	1	4	4488	1		11	6		2	10	8	9				5		4			7	3												MORGAN		
26/12/1986	AFC BOURNEMOUTH	H	0	3	3573	1	2	11	6			7A	8	9			10	5		A			4	3														
28/12/1986	BRENTFORD	A	2	1	4510	1	2	11	6					9	10			5		8				3	4	7										SMART	MEHEW	
01/01/1987	BRISTOL CITY	A	1	0	17122	1	2	11	6					9	10	A		5		4				3	8A	7										SMART		
17/01/1987	BOLTON WANDERERS	A	2	2	4087	1	3	11	2				A			10		5		8				6	4	7A	9									SMART	PENRICE	
23/01/1987	YORK CITY	H	1	0	2597	1	3	11	2A				7			10		5		8			A	6	4		9									PENRICE		
31/01/1987	MANSFIELD TOWN	A	0	5	2718	1	2	11					10			8	A	5					3A	6	4	7	9											
07/02/1987	MIDDLESBROUGH	A	0	1	11639	1	3	11					2			10		5		8				6	4	7	9											
14/02/1987	ROTHERHAM UNITED	H	0	2	2467	1	2A	11			4		8			10	A	5		7				6		3	9											
21/02/1987	BLACKPOOL	A	1	6	3434	1	2	3			4	8	7		10	11		5		A				6			9A									MEHEW		
28/02/1987	NOTTS COUNTY	H	0	0	2978	1	2	3			A		8		10			5					11		4A			6	7	9								
03/03/1987	DARLINGTON	A	1	1	1350	1	2	3					8		10	A		5					11A		4				7	9	6					MEHEW		
11/03/1987	WALSALL	H	0	3	2282	1	2	8					7		10			5					11		4A				3	9	6	A						
14/03/1987	PORT VALE	A	1	4	2758	1	2	3					8		10		A	5					11		4				6	9A		7				PENRICE		
18/03/1987	FULHAM	H	0	0	2448	1	2	6			11		8				10	5						4					3	9		7						
21/03/1987	WIGAN ATHLETIC	H	1	0	2635	1	2	6			11	A	8				10A	5						4					3	9		7				HIBBITT		
23/03/1987	CHESTERFIELD	A	1	1	2157	1	2	10	A		4		11					5						6					3	8		7A	9			PENRICE		
04/04/1987	BURY	A	0	1	1960		2	6	10		11		8					5						4					3			7	9	1				
11/04/1987	SWINDON TOWN	H	3	4	8196		2	6			11		8				7	5						4A			9	A	3				10	1		PENRICE	TURNER	PURNELL pen
18/04/1987	BRISTOL CITY	H	0	0	4695		A	6	2		11		8				7	5									9A	4	3				10	1				
20/04/1987	AFC BOURNEMOUTH	A	0	2	10034		10	6	2			7	8				11	5									9	4	3					1				
22/04/1987	CARLISLE UNITED	H	4	0	2435		3	6	2		11		8			A	7	5									9	4					10	1A		MEACHAM	PENRICE 2	PURNELL
25/04/1987	GILLINGHAM	H	0	1	3168	1	3	6	2		11A		8				7	5									9	4	A				10					
28/04/1987	CHESTER CITY	H	3	2	2323	1	3	6	2		11		8				7	5									9	4					10			MEACHAM 2	SCALES	
30/04/1987	DARLINGTON	H	2	1	2765	1	2	6	4		11		8				7	5									9		3				10			MEACHAM	HINCHLEY og	
02/05/1987	DONCASTER ROVERS	A	0	2	1206	1	3	6A	2			8				11		5		7							9		4	A			10					
04/05/1987	BRENTFORD	H	0	1	3513	1	3	6	2		11		8				7	5									9	4	A				10A					
06/05/1987	DONCASTER ROVERS	H	2	3	3003	1	2A	6	3		11		8		A		7	5									9	4					10			MEACHAM	MEHEW	
09/05/1987	NEWPORT COUNTY	A	1	0	3160	1		6	2		11		8				7	5							9		A	4A	3				10			PURNELL		
	APPEARANCES					38	41	44	33	10	27	20	42	19	20	15	18	43	5	9	3	2	13	17	11	6	16	9	14	7	2	5	12	5				
	SUB					0	2	0	1	0	1	2	1	0	1	3	3	0	0	7	0	0	2	3	0	0	1	1	2	1	0	1	0	0				
	GOALS					0	1	1	1	0	3	1	7	8	10	1	3	0	0	4	0	1	1	0	0	0	1	0	0	0	0	0	5	0		OWN GOAL 1		
	SUBD					0	2	2	1	0	2	3	0	0	4	1	2	0	0	0	0	0	3	1	3	1	2	1	0	1	0	1	1	1				
	LITTLEWOODS CUP																																					
27/08/1986	READING	H	1	2	3790	1	2	3	4		6A	7	8	9	10		11B		A	B				5												PENRICE		
03/09/1986	READING	A	0	4	4300	1	2	3	4		6	7A	8	9	10		11B	5	A					B														
	FA CUP																																					
03/12/1987	BRENTFORD	H	0	0	3035	1	2	11	4		6	7B	8	9		10A	A	5					B	3														
06/12/1987	BRENTFORD	A	0	2	3848	1	2	11	4A		6		8	9			10	5					A	3	7B										B			
	FREIGHT ROVER TROPHY																																					
16/12/1986	BRISTOL CITY	A	0	3	6903	1	A	3	6		2	7	8	9	B		10A			4			11B	5														
07/12/1986	EXETER CITY	H	1	1	1608	1	2A	11	6				8	9	10	A		5		4				3		7B	B									MICALLEF		

GLOUCESTERSHIRE CUP FINAL

Held over until next season

1987/88

						MARTYN Nigel	ALEXANDER Ian	DRYDEN Richard	HIBBITT Kenneth	CARR Darren	JONES Vaughan	WIFFILL David	REECE Andrew	TURNER Robert	PENRICE Gary	PURNELL Philip	EATON Jason	HOLLOWAY Ian	MEACHAM Jeffrey	TWENTYMAN Geoffrey	WHITE Devon	WESTON Ian	CARTER Timothy	TANNER Nicholas	CLARK William	FRANCIS Gerald	JOSEPH Francis (L)	MEHEW David	McCLEAN Christian	YATES Stephen	HOWELLS Lee	SUGRUE Paul	STEVENS Mark	PATTERSON Nigel	BOYLE Martin	CAROTA Marco				
	DIVISION 3																																							
15/08/1987	ROTHERHAM UNITED	H	3	1	3339	1	2	3	4	5	6	7A	8	9	10	11	A																				PENRICE 2	TURNER		
22/08/1987	SUNDERLAND	A	1	1	13058	1	2	3	4	5	6		8	9A	10	11		7	A																		PENRICE			
29/08/1987	ALDERSHOT	H	3	1	3396	1	2A	3	4	5	6		8		10	11			7	A	9																MEACHAM	WHITE	PENRICE	
31/08/1987	BLACKPOOL	A	1	2	3317	1	2	3	4	5	6	8		A	10	11A			7		9																WHITE			
05/09/1987	WIGAN ATHLETIC	H	2	3	3168	1	2	3B	4	5	6			A	10	11		7		B	9	8A															WHITE	PURNELL		
12/09/1987	BRISTOL CITY	A	3	3	14746		2		4		6		8		10	11		7		5	9		1	3													REECE	JONES	HOLLOWAY	
16/09/1987	YORK CITY	H	2	1	3177		2		4		6		8	A	10	11		7		5	9A		1	3													PENRICE	JONES		
19/09/1987	NORTHAMPTON TOWN	H	0	2	3655		2		4		6		8	A	10	11		7		5	9A		1	3																
26/09/1987	FULHAM	A	1	3	4614		2		4A		6		8	A	10	11		7		5	9		1	3													WHITE			
29/09/1987	NOTTS COUNTY	A	1	1	4334		2			4	6		8		10	11		7		5	9		1	3													PENRICE			
03/10/1987	MANSFIELD TOWN	H	2	1	2980		2			4A	6		8		10	11		7	A	5	9		1	3													PENRICE	MEACHAM		
10/10/1987	GILLINGHAM	A	0	3	4399		2			4A	6		8	A	10	11		7	9	5			1	3																
17/10/1987	CHESTER CITY	H	2	2	3038	1	2				6		8		10	11		7		5	9			3	4												WHITE	PENRICE		
19/10/1987	PORT VALE	A	1	2	3598	1		3			6		8	5A	10	11		7	A		9			2	4												PENRICE			
24/10/1987	DONCASTER ROVERS	H	4	0	2817	1	2		5		6		8		10	11		7A	A		9			3	4												PURNELL 2-1pen	WHITE	JONES	
31/10/1987	BRENTFORD	A	1	1	4487	1	2		5		6		8		10	11		7			9			3	4												STANISLAUS og			
04/11/1987	PRESTON NORTH END	H	1	2	2804	1	2		5		6		8		10	11A		7	A		9			3	4												HIBBITT			
07/11/1987	CHESTERFIELD	H	2	0	2633	1	2		4A		6		A		10	11		7	8	3	9				5												MEACHAM	PURNELL pen		
21/11/1987	BURY	A	1	4	2356	1	2		4		6				10	11		7	8	3	9				5												HIBBITT			
28/11/1987	GRIMSBY TOWN	H	4	2	2787	1	2		4		6				10	11		7	8	3	9				5												MEACHAM	WHITE	PENRICE	PURNELL
12/12/1987	WALSALL	A	0	0	4234	1	2		4A		6		8		10	11		7	A		9			3	5															
19/12/1987	BRIGHTON & HOVE ALBION	H	1	2	3589	1	2		4B		6		A		10	11		7	8A	B	9			3	5												HOLLOWAY			
26/12/1987	FULHAM	H	3	1	4718	1	2		4	A	6		8		10	11		7		5A	9			3													WHITE	HOLLOWAY	PENRICE	
28/12/1987	SOUTHEND UNITED	A	2	4	4094	1	2A		4		6		8		10	11	A	7		5	9			3													WHITE	PURNELL		
01/01/1988	ALDERSHOT	A	0	3	4593	1	2		4A		6		A		10	11		7		5	9			3		8														
16/01/1988	NORTHAMPTON TOWN	A	1	2	4473	1	2A				6				10	11	A	7		5	9	8		3	4												ALEXANDER			
06/02/1988	WIGAN ATHLETIC	A	0	1	3827	1	2A		8B		6		B		10	11		7	A	5				3	4		9													
13/02/1988	SOUTHEND UNITED	H	0	0	3099	1	2		5		6		8		10	11		7		3					4		9													
20/02/1988	ROTHERHAM UNITED	A	1	1	2966	1	2		5		6				10	11		7		3	9				4		8A	A									WHITE			
24/02/1988	SUNDERLAND	H	4	0	4501	1	2		5A		6		A		10B	11		7		3	9	B			4			8									PENRICE	WHITE	MEHEW	HOLLOWAY
27/02/1988	MANSFIELD TOWN	A	0	1	3191	1	2				6		8		10	11		7		3	9				4			5												
02/03/1988	NOTTS COUNTY	H	1	1	4075	1	2				6		8		10	11		7		3	9				4			5									TWENTYMAN			
05/03/1988	CHESTER CITY	A	3	0	2067	1	2				6		8		10	11		7		3	9				4			5									WHITE	PURNELL	MEHEW	
12/03/1988	GILLINGHAM	H	2	0	3846	1	2				6		8		10	11		7		3	9				4			5									PENRICE	PURNELL		
19/03/1988	BRENTFORD	H	0	0	3380	1	2				6		8		10	11		7		3	9				4			5												
25/03/1988	DONCASTER ROVERS	A	1	0	1311	1	2				6		8		10	11		7		3	9				4			5									PENRICE			
02/04/1988	CHESTERFIELD	A	1	0	2208	1	2				6		8		10	11		7		3				A	4			5	9A								PENRICE			
04/04/1988	BURY	H	0	0	4264	1	2				6		8		10	11		7		3					4			5	9											
08/04/1988	PRESTON NORTH END	A	1	3	5386	1	2				6		8		10	11A		7		3	9				4			5	A								MEHEW			
12/04/1988	BRISTOL CITY	H	1	0	5947	1	2				6		8		10	11		7		3	9				4			5									PENRICE			
15/04/1988	YORK CITY	A	4	0	1834	1	2				6		8		10			7B		3	9A	B		11	4			5	A								MEHEW 3	WHITE		
23/04/1988	PORT VALE	H	1	0	3780	1	2				6		8		10			7		3	9			11	4			5									PENRICE			
27/04/1988	BLACKPOOL	H	2	0	3546	1	2				6		8		10			7		3	9			11	4			5									MEHEW	WHITE		
30/04/1988	GRIMSBY TOWN	A	0	0	2505	1	2				6		8		10	B		7		3	9A			11	4			5B	A											
02/05/1988	WALSALL	H	3	0	6328	1	2				6		8		10			7		3	9			11	4			5									MEHEW	HOLLOWAY	WHITE	
07/05/1988	BRIGHTON & HOVE ALBION	A	1	2	19800	1	2				6		8		10B			7		3	9	B		11A	4			5	A								CLARK			
	APPEARANCES					39	45	6	24	8	46	2	35	3	46	40	0	43	7	35	39	2	7	25	31	1	3	17	2											
	SUB					0	0	0	0	1	0	0	5	6	0	1	3	0	7	3	0	3	0	1	0	0	0	1	4											
	GOALS					0	1	0	2	0	3	0	1	1	17	8	0	5	4	1	15	0	0	0	1	0	0	8	0								OWN GOAL 1			
	SUBD					0	4	1	7	2	0	1	0	2	2	3	0	2	1	1	4	1	0	1	0	0	1	1	1											
	LITTLEWOODS CUP																																							
19/08/1987	HEREFORD UNITED	H	1	0	2796	1	2	3	4	B	6	7A	8	9	10	11			A	5B																	PENRICE			
26/08/1987	HEREFORD UNITED	A	0	2	2963	1	2	3	4	5	6	7A	8	9	10	11			A																					
	FA CUP																																							
14/11/1987	MERTHYR TYDFIL	H	6	0	4635	1	2A	A	4		6		B		10B	11		7	8	5	9			3													PENRICE 3	WHITE 2		
05/12/1987	V S RUGBY	A	1	1	3168	1	2		4		6				10	11		7	8	5	9			3													MEACHAM			
17/12/1987	V S RUGBY	H	4	0	2846	1	2	B	4A		6		A		10	11		7	8B	5	9			3													PENRICE	ALEXANDER		
09/01/1988	SHREWSBURY TOWN	A	1	2	6554	1	2			4A	6		8		10	11	A	7		5	9			3													PENRICE			
	SHERPA VAN TROPHY																																							
13/10/1987	TORQUAY UNITED	A	0	2	1513	1	2			4	6		8		10	11		7A	A	5	9			3																
28/10/1987	HEREFORD UNITED	H	0	2	2158	1	2		5		6		8A		10	11		7	A		9			3	4															
	GLOUCESTERSHIRE CUP FINAL																																							
02/12/1987	BRISTOL CITY *	H	1	2	1376			11					8	9			6					2	1	5	4					3	7	10A			A		REECE			
15/03/1988	BRISTOL CITY	A	1	3	2278			11B									6					7		5		8A		B	9	3	4		1	2	10	A	CAROTA			

* Final carried over from 1986-87

1988/89

Date	Opponent	H/A	F	A	Att	MARTYN Nigel	STAPLETON Simon	TWENTYMAN Geoffrey	CLARK William	MEHEW David	JONES Vaughan	HOLLOWAY Ian	REECE Andrew	WHITE Devon	PENRICE Gary	PURNELL Philip	ALEXANDER Ian	SMITH Paul	DRYDEN Richard	McCLEAN Christian	VINEY Keith (L)	YATES Stephen	HAZEL Ian (L)	BAILEY Dennis (L)	HIBBITT Kenneth	NIXON Paul	Scorers			
	DIVISION 3																													
27/08/1988	WIGAN ATHLETIC	H	3	2	4080	1	2	3	4	5	6	7	8	9	10	11											PENRICE 2	WHITE		
03/09/1988	SHEFFIELD UNITED	A	1	4	9586	1		3	4	5	6A	7	8	9	10	11	2	A									HOLLOWAY			
10/09/1988	ALDERSHOT	H	2	2	3382	1		3	4	5	6	7	8	9	10A	11	2	A									WHITE 2			
17/09/1988	BOLTON WANDERERS	A	1	1	4821	1		3	4	5	6	7	8	9		11A	2	10	A								TWENTYMAN			
21/09/1988	BRENTFORD	H	1	2	3836	1		3	4		6	7	8A	9	10	11	2	5		A							PENRICE			
24/09/1988	NORTHAMPTON TOWN	A	2	1	3886	1		3			6	7	8	9	10	11	2	5			4						PENRICE	SMITH		
01/10/1988	CARDIFF CITY	A	2	2	5038	1	A	3	6			7	8	9	10	11	2A	5			4						PENRICE	HOLLOWAY		
05/10/1988	PRESTON NORTH END	H	1	0	3689	1		3	4	5	6	7	8	9	10	11	2										PENRICE			
08/10/1988	MANSFIELD TOWN	A	1	2	3381	1		3	4	5	6	7	8	9	10	11	2										PENRICE			
15/10/1988	NOTTS COUNTY	H	2	0	4183	1		3		5	6	7	8	9	10	11	2				A	4A					PENRICE	JONES		
22/10/1988	CHESTER CITY	H	4	1	3811	1		3	4	5A	6	7	8	9	10	11	2			A							REECE 2	MEHEW	McCLEAN	
26/10/1988	READING	A	1	3	7150	1		3	4	5	6	7	8	9A	10	11	2			A							REECE			
29/10/1988	HUDDERSFIELD TOWN	H	5	1	4460	1		3		5	6	7	8	9	10	11	2					4					PURNELL 2	PENRICE	HOLLOWAY	REECE
05/11/1988	CHESTERFIELD	A	3	0	2480	1		3		5	6	7	8		10	11	2			9		4					PURNELL	MEHEW 2		
08/11/1988	SOUTHEND UNITED	A	2	2	2453	1		3		5	6	7	8		10	11	2			9		4					PURNELL	MEHEW		
12/11/1988	GILLINGHAM	H	2	0	4826	1	2	3		5	6	7	8		10	11				9		4					REECE	McCLEAN		
26/11/1988	BURY	H	1	3	4251	1	2	3		5A	6	7	8	9	10	11				A		4					MEHEW			
03/12/1988	FULHAM	A	2	0	4461	1	2	3		5	6	7	8	9	10	11						4					MEHEW	PENRICE		
17/12/1988	BLACKPOOL	A	1	1	3240	1		3		5	6	7	8	9A	10	11	2			A		4					PURNELL			
26/12/1988	WOLVERHAMPTON WANDERERS	H	0	0	8480	1		3			6	7	8	9	10	11	2	5				4								
31/12/1988	SWANSEA CITY	H	1	1	4803	1		3			6	7	8	9A	10	11	2	5		A		4					PURNELL			
02/01/1989	BRISTOL CITY	A	1	0	23191	1		3			6	7	8	9	10	11	2	5A		A		4					PENRICE			
14/01/1989	SHEFFIELD UNITED	H	1	1	6623	1		3			6	7	8	9	10	11	2	5A		A		4					HOLLOWAY pen			
21/01/1989	ALDERSHOT	A	3	1	3101	1		3			6	7	8	9	10	11	2	5				4					HOLLOWAY	PENRICE 2		
28/01/1989	BOLTON WANDERERS	H	2	0	5375	1		3	A		6	7	8	9		11	2A	5		10		4					REECE	WHITE		
04/02/1989	CARDIFF CITY	H	0	1	5815	1		3			6	7	8	9	10	11	2	5A		A		4								
11/02/1989	PRESTON NORTH END	A	1	1	7365	1		3			6	7	8	9	10	11	2	5				4					PENRICE			
18/02/1989	MANSFIELD TOWN	H	0	0	4669	1		3			6	7	8	9	10	11	2	5A		A		4								
25/02/1989	NOTTS COUNTY	A	0	1	5176	1		3		5A	6	7		9	10	11	2	8		A		4								
01/03/1989	READING	H	1	1	4573	1		3			6	7			10	11	2			9		4	5	8			BAILEY			
04/03/1989	CHESTER CITY	A	2	0	3082	1		3			6	7		A	10	11	2			9		4	5	8A			BAILEY	PURNELL		
11/03/1989	CHESTERFIELD	H	2	1	4684	1		3		7	6				10	11	2			9		4	5A	8	A		BAILEY	PENRICE		
14/03/1989	HUDDERSFIELD TOWN	A	3	2	4105	1		3		5	6		7		10	11	2			9		4		8			BAILEY 2	JONES pen		
25/03/1989	BRISTOL CITY	H	1	1	8676	1		3			6	7	5	A	10	11A	2			9		4		8			PENRICE			
27/03/1989	WOLVERHAMPTON WANDERERS	A	1	0	20913	1		3		11	6	7	5	A	10		2			9A		4		8			BAILEY			
01/04/1989	BLACKPOOL	H	1	0	5355	1		3		11	6	7	5	A	10		2			9A		4		8			WHITE			
05/04/1989	PORT VALE	H	2	2	6869	1		3		11A	6	7	5	9	10		2			A		4		8			PENRICE	REECE		
08/04/1989	SWANSEA CITY	A	2	1	5645	1		3		5A	6	7	11	A	10		2			9		4		8			BAILEY	PENRICE		
15/04/1989	BRENTFORD	A	1	2	7558	1		3		5	6	7	11	A	10		2			9A		4		8			BAILEY			
22/04/1989	NORTHAMPTON TOWN	H	1	1	5568	1		3		5	6	7	11	9A	10		2					4		8		A	BAILEY			
28/04/1989	GILLINGHAM	A	3	2	4004	1		3		5	6	7	11	9	10		2					4		8			PENRICE 2	HOLLOWAY pen		
01/05/1989	SOUTHEND UNITED	H	1	1	6250	1		3		5A	6	7	11	9	10	A	2					4		8			MEHEW			
03/05/1989	WIGAN ATHLETIC	A	0	3	2529	1		3		5A	6	7	11	9	10	A	2					4		8						
06/05/1989	FULHAM	H	0	0	7302	1		3		5	6	7	9	A	10		2			11A		4		8						
09/05/1989	PORT VALE	A	0	1	6136	1		3		5	6	7	9	A	10		2			11		4		8A						
13/05/1989	BURY	A	0	0	3073	1		3		5	6	7	8	A		9	2			11A		4		10						
	APPEARANCES					46	4	46	10	31	45	44	42	31	43	35	42	14	0	16	2	35	3	17	0	0				
	SUB					0	1	0	1	0	0	0	0	9	0	2	0	2	1	12	1	0	0	0	1	1				
	GOALS					0	0	1	0	7	2	6	7	5	20	7	0	1	0	2	0	0	0	9	0	0				
	SUBD					0	0	0	0	7	1	0	1	4	1	2	2	4	0	5	0	1	1	2	0	0				
	PLAY OFFS																													
21/05/1989	FULHAM	H	1	0	9029	1			3	A	6	7	9	5	10	11	2					4		8A			PENRICE			
25/05/1989	FULHAM	A	4	0	10668	1			3	8	6	7	9	5B	10A	11	2			B		4		A			CLARK	HOLLOWAY	BAILEY	REECE
31/05/1989	PORT VALE	H	1	1	9042	1			3	8	6	7A	9	5	10	11	2			A		4					PENRICE			
03/06/1989	PORT VALE	A	0	1	17353	1			3	8	6	7	9	5	10	11	2					4								
	LITTLEWOODS CUP																													
30/08/1988	AFC BOURNEMOUTH	A	0	1	4601	1		3		5A	6	7	8	9	10	11B	2	A	B			4								
07/09/1988	AFC BOURNEMOUTH	H	0	0	4057	1		3		5A	6	7	8B	9	10	11	2	A	B			4								
	FA CUP																													
20/11/1988	FISHER ATHLETIC	H	3	0	5161	1		3	A	5	6	7	8	9	10B	11	2A		B			4					JONES	PENRICE	HOLLOWAY pen	
10/12/1988	KETTERING TOWN	A	1	2	4950	1	2	3		5	6	7	8	9	10	11	2					4					REECE			
	SHERPA VAN TROPHY																													
23/11/1988	BRISTOL CITY	H	1	0	3940	1	2	3		5	6	7	8	9	10	11						4					PENRICE			
14/12/1988	EXETER CITY	H	1	1	1609	1		3		5	6	7	8	9	10	11	2					4					MEHEW			
24/01/1989	CARDIFF CITY	H	2	1	4029	1		3			6	7	8	9		11	2	5		10		4					SMITH	REECE		
22/02/1989	TORQUAY UNITED	H	0	1	4316	1		3		A	6	7	8A	9	10	11	2			5		4								
	GLOUCESTERSHIRE CUP FINAL																													
17/08/1988	BRISTOL CITY	H	3	0	1664	1	2	3	4	10	5	7	8	9		11	6										MEHEW 2	WHITE		

1989/90

Date	Opponent				Att.	MARTYN Nigel	ALEXANDER Ian	TWENTYMAN Geoffrey	YATES Stephen	MEHEW David	JONES Vaughan	HOLLOWAY Ian	REECE Andrew	WHITE Devon	PENRICE Gary	WILLMOTT Ian	HAZEL Ian	NIXON Paul	SEALY Anthony	McCLEAN Christian	PARKIN Brian	CAWLEY Peter	PURNELL Philip	BROWNING Marcus	SAUNDERS Carl	BYRNE David (L)				
	DIVISION 3																													
19/08/1989	BRENTFORD	H	1	0	5835	1	2	3	4	5	6	7	8	9	10	11											MEHEW			
26/08/1989	MANSFIELD TOWN	A	1	0	3050	1	2	3	4	5	6	7	8	9	10	11A	A										MEHEW			
02/09/1989	NOTTS COUNTY	H	3	2	4753	1	2	3	4	5	6	7	8	9	10A	11		A									PENRICE	JONES	WHITE	
09/09/1989	BOLTON WANDERERS	A	0	1	5913	1	2	3	4	5	6	7	8	9	10A	11		A												
16/09/1989	PRESTON NORTH END	H	3	0	4350	1	2	3	4	5	6	7	8A	9	10	11			A								PENRICE	WHITE	TWENTYMAN	
23/09/1989	BRISTOL CITY	A	0	0	17432	1	2	3	4	5	6	7	8	9	10	11														
26/09/1989	LEYTON ORIENT	A	1	0	4675	1	2	3	4	5	6	7	8	9	10	11											MEHEW			
30/09/1989	READING	H	0	0	6120	1	2	3	4	5	6	7	8	9	10	11														
07/10/1989	FULHAM	H	2	0	5811	1		3	4	5	6	7	8	9	10	11	A	2A									PENRICE	MEHEW		
14/10/1989	BURY	A	0	0	3969	1	2	3		5	6	7	8	9	10	11		4A	A											
17/10/1989	CARDIFF CITY	A	1	1	6372	1	2	3		5	6	7	8	9	10	11		4A	A								MEHEW			
21/10/1989	NORTHAMPTON TOWN	H	4	2	4920	1	2	3		5	6	7	8	9	10A	11		4	A								WHITE	NIXON	HOLLOWAY	QUOW og
28/10/1989	CHESTER CITY	A	0	0	2618	1	2	3	4	5	6	7	8	9				11	10											
01/11/1989	HUDDERSFIELD TOWN	H	2	2	6467	1	2	3	4	5	6	7	8	9				11	10								MEHEW	NIXON		
04/11/1989	BLACKPOOL	H	1	1	5520	1	2	3	4	5	6	7A	8	9		A		11	10								SEALY			
11/11/1989	SHREWSBURY TOWN	A	3	2	4746	1	2	3	4	5	6	7	8					11	10	9							SEALY 2	HOLLOWAY		
25/11/1989	SWANSEA CITY	H	2	0	5623		2	3	4	5	6	7	8	9			10A	11		A	1						WHITE	MEHEW		
02/12/1989	WALSALL	A	2	1	4038		2	3		5	6	7	8	9		4A		11	10		1	A					WHITE	MEHEW		
15/12/1989	CREWE ALEXANDRA	A	0	1	3473			3	4	5	6	7	8	9			A	11A	10		1	2								
26/12/1989	BIRMINGHAM CITY	H	0	0	6573		2A	3	4	5	6	7	8	9				11	10		1	A								
30/12/1989	TRANMERE ROVERS	H	2	0	6821		2	3	4	5	6	7	8	9				11A	10	A	1						NIXON	VICKERS og		
01/01/1990	ROTHERHAM UNITED	A	2	3	7750		2	3	4	5	6	7	8	9			11		10A	A	1						HOLLOWAY pen	MEHEW		
13/01/1990	MANSFIELD TOWN	H	1	1	5339		2	3	4	5	6	7	8	9				11	10A		1		A				TWENTYMAN			
20/01/1990	BRENTFORD	A	1	2	7414		2	3	4	5	6	7	8					11A	10	9	1		A				McCLEAN			
28/01/1990	BOLTON WANDERERS	H	1	1	7772		2	3	4	5	6	7	8	9				10A			1		11	A			REECE			
10/02/1990	PRESTON NORTH END	A	1	0	5956		2	3	4	5	6	7	8	9							1		11A		10	A	MEHEW			
18/02/1990	WALSALL	H	2	0	6223		2	3	4	5A	6	7	8	9							1		11		10	A	SAUNDERS 2			
24/02/1990	SWANSEA CITY	A	0	0	5664		2	3	4	5	6	7	8	9							1		11		10					
03/03/1990	WIGAN ATHLETIC	H	6	1	5169		2	3	4	5	6	7	8	9		B			A		1		11B		10A		MEHEW	SAUNDERS 3	ALEXANDER	HOLLOWAY
06/03/1990	READING	A	1	0	6147		2	3	4	5	6	7	8	9							1		11		10		MEHEW			
11/03/1990	LEYTON ORIENT	H	0	0	7018		2	3	4	5	6	7	8	9							1		11		10					
17/03/1990	FULHAM	A	2	1	5656		2	3	4	5A	6	7	8	9					A		1		11		10		WHITE 2			
21/03/1990	BURY	H	2	1	5552		2	3	4	5	6	7	8	9					A		1		11		10A		WHITE	PURNELL		
24/03/1990	CARDIFF CITY	H	2	1	4631		2	3	4	5	6	7	8	9				A	10A		1		11				NIXON	MEHEW		
31/03/1990	NORTHAMPTON TOWN	A	2	1	3774		2B	3	4	5	6	7	8			B		10A		9	1		11		A		McCLEAN	HOLLOWAY		
04/04/1990	WIGAN ATHLETIC	A	2	1	2352		2	3	4	5	6	7	8	A						9A	1		11		10		MEHEW	McCLEAN		
07/04/1990	CHESTER CITY	H	2	1	6589		2	3	4	5	6	7	8A	A						9	1		11		10		MEHEW	McCLEAN		
10/04/1990	HUDDERSFIELD TOWN	A	1	1	4359		2	3	4	5	6	7	8	A						9	1		11A		10		REECE			
14/04/1990	ROTHERHAM UNITED	H	2	0	6794		2	3	4	5	6	7		9				11A		8	1		A		10		JONES	MEHEW		
16/04/1990	BIRMINGHAM CITY	A	2	2	12438			3	4	5	6	7		9		2B	B	11A		8	1		A		10		WHITE	THOMAS og		
21/04/1990	CREWE ALEXANDRA	H	1	1	7250		2	3	4	5	6	7		9			B	11A		8B	1		A		10		WHITE			
23/04/1990	TRANMERE ROVERS	A	2	1	12723		2	3	4	5	6	7	8	9			B	11A		A	1				10B		TWENTYMAN	HOLLOWAY pen		
26/04/1990	NOTTS COUNTY	A	1	3	10142		2	3	4	5	6	7	8A	9				A		11	1				10		MEHEW			
28/04/1990	SHREWSBURY TOWN	H	1	0	7903		2	3	4	5	6	7	8	9A				B		A	1		11B		10		HOLLOWAY pen			
02/05/1990	BRISTOL CITY	H	3	0	9831		2	3	4	5	6	7	8	9							1		11		10		WHITE 2	HOLLOWAY pen		
05/05/1990	BLACKPOOL	A	3	0	6776		2	3	4	5	6	7	8	9				A			1		11A		10		MEHEW	PURNELL	NIXON	
	APPEARANCES					16	43	46	42	46	46	46	43	40	12	14	2	21	12	10	30	1	17	0	19	0				
	SUB					0	0	0	0	0	0	0	0	3	0	3	6	6	7	5	0	2	5	1	1	2				
	GOALS					0	1	3	0	18	2	8	2	12	3	0	0	5	3	4	0	0	2	0	5	0	OWN GOAL 3			
	SUBD					0	2	0	0	2	0	1	3	1	3	3	1	12	3	2	0	0	5	0	3	0				
	LITTLEWOODS CUP																													
23/08/1989	PORTSMOUTH	H	1	0	4727	1	2	3	4	5	6	7	8	9	10	11											PENRICE			
29/08/1989	PORTSMOUTH	A	0	2	5287	1	2	3	4	5	6	7	8	9	10A	11				A										
	FA CUP																													
17/11/1989	READING	H	1	1	6115		2	3	4	5	6	7	8			10A	A	11		9	1						REECE			
21/11/1989	READING	A	1	1*	6015		2	3	4	5	6	7	8			11			10	9	1						MEHEW			
27/11/1989	READING	H	0	1	6782		2	3	4	5	6	7	8A	9				11	10	A	1									
	* AET Score at 90 mins 0-0																													
	LEYLAND DAF CUP																													
07/11/1989	TORQUAY UNITED	A	1	1	2218	1	2	3	4	5	6	7	8	9				11	10								WHITE			
17/01/1990	EXETER CITY	H	3	0	3136		2	3	4	5	6	7	8					11A	10	9	1			A			HOLLOWAY pen	SEALY	MEHEW	
24/01/1990	GILLINGHAM	H	1	0	2724		2	3	4	5	6	7	8	9				A	10A		1		11				NIXON			
06/02/1990	BRENTFORD *	H	2	2	4409		2	3	4	5A	6	7	8	9							1		11		10	A	HOLLOWAY pen	SAUNDERS		
14/03/1990	WALSALL **	H	0	0	4740		2	3	4	5A	6	7	8	9					A		1		11		10					
28/03/1990	NOTTS COUNTY***	H	1	0	6480		2	3	4	5	6	7	8A	9				10		A	1		11				MEHEW			
02/04/1990	NOTTS COUNTY***	A	0	0	10857		2	3	4	5	6	7	8					A		9	1		11A		10					
20/05/1990	TRANMERE ROVERS****	N	1	2	48402		2A	3	4	5	6	7	8	9				A		B	1		11B		10		WHITE			
	* AET Score at 90 mins 1-1 Rovers won 4-3 on pens ** AET w *** Southern / **** National Final at Wembley Stadium																													
	GLOUCESTERSHIRE CUP FINAL																													
08/08/1989	BRISTOL CITY	A	2	1	6153	1	2	3	4	5	6	7	8	9	10	11A	A										WILLMOTT	PENRICE		

1990/91

Date	Opponent	H/A	F	A	Att	PARKIN Brian	ALEXANDER Ian	TWENTYMAN Geoffrey	YATES Stephen	MEHEW David	JONES Vaughan	HOLLOWAY Ian	REECE Andrew	WHITE Devon	SAUNDERS Carl	POUNDER Antony	HAZEL Ian	BLOOMER Robert	NIXON Paul	McCLEAN Christian	PURNELL Philip	KELLY Gavin	SEALY Anthony	GORDON Colin	CLARK William	WILLMOTT Ian	BOOTHROYD Adrian	BAILEY Dennis (L)	BROWNING Marcus	Scorers		
	DIVISION 2																															
25/08/1990	LEICESTER CITY	A	2	3	13648	1	2	3	4	5A	6	7	8	9	10	11	A													WHITE	JONES	
01/09/1990	CHARLTON ATHLETIC	H	2	1	5357	1	2	3	4	5A	6	7	8	9	10	11		A												WHITE	MEHEW	
08/09/1990	WOLVERHAMPTON WANDERERS	A	1	1	17912	1	2	3	4	5A	6	7	8	9	10	11	A													HOLLOWAY		
15/09/1990	HULL CITY	H	1	1	4734	1	2	3	4	5	6	7	8	9	10	11														MEHEW		
22/09/1990	IPSWICH TOWN	A	1	2	11084	1		3	4	5	6	7	8A	9	10	11	2		A											SAUNDERS		
29/09/1990	NOTTS COUNTY	A	2	3	6563	1	2	3	4	5	6	7	8	9	10A	11				A										SAUNDERS	HOLLOWAY pen	
03/10/1990	BLACKBURN ROVERS	H	1	2	5200	1	2	3	4	5A	6	7	8	9		11			10		A									WHITE		
06/10/1990	SHEFFIELD WEDNESDAY	H	0	1	6413	1	2A	3	4	5	6	7	8	9		11B			10	B	A											
13/10/1990	SWINDON TOWN	A	2	0	11494	1	B	3	4	A	6	7	8	9		10		2B	5A		11									POUNDER	HOLLOWAY pen	
20/10/1990	MIDDLESBROUGH	A	2	1	18589	1		3	4	A	6	7	8	9		10		2	5A		11									WHITE	HOLLOWAY pen	
24/10/1990	OXFORD UNITED	H	1	0	5526	1		3	4	A	6	7	8	9		10		2	5A		11									HOLLOWAY pen		
27/10/1990	PORTSMOUTH	H	1	2	6500	1	B	3	4	A	6	7	8	9		10		2B	5A		11									WHITE		
03/11/1990	WEST BROMWICH ALBION	A	1	3	10997	1		3	4	A	6	7	8	9		10A		2	5		11									WHITE		
07/11/1990	BARNSLEY	H	2	1	4563	1	2	3	4	5	6	7	8B	9		10		B	11A		A									MEHEW	POUNDER	
10/11/1990	PORT VALE	H	2	0	5661	1	2	3	4	5	6	7	8	9	A	10			11A											NIXON	MEHEW	
17/11/1990	WATFORD	A	1	1	8285	1	2	3	4	5	6	7	8	9	A	10			11A											DRYSDALE og		
24/11/1990	OLDHAM ATHLETIC	H	2	0	6542	1	2	3	4	5	6	7	8B	9	10	11A		B	A											MEHEW	WHITE	
01/12/1990	MILLWALL	A	1	1	9291	1	2	3	4	5	6	7	8	9	10	11														MEHEW		
15/12/1990	LEICESTER CITY	H	0	0	5791	1	2	3	4	5	6	7	8	9	10	11																
22/12/1990	NEWCASTLE UNITED	H	1	1	6643	1	2	3	4	5A	6	7	8	9	10	11			A											SAUNDERS		
26/12/1990	BRIGHTON & HOVE ALBION	A	1	0	6936	1	2	3	4	5	6	7	8	9	10	11A			A											SAUNDERS		
29/12/1990	PLYMOUTH ARGYLE	A	2	2	8469	1		3	4	5A	6	7	8	9	10	11		2	A											SAUNDERS 2		
01/01/1991	WEST HAM UNITED	H	0	1	7932	1		3	4	5A	6	7	8	9	10	11		2	A													
12/01/1991	CHARLTON ATHLETIC	A	2	2	5606		2A	3	4	5B	6	7	8	9	10	11		A				1	B							WHITE	SAUNDERS	
19/01/1991	WOLVERHAMPTON WANDERERS	H	1	1	6042		2	3	4	5A	6	7	8	9	10	11						1	A							SAUNDERS		
26/01/1991	BRISTOL CITY	H	3	2	7054		2A	3	4	5	6	7	8	9	10	11		A				1								MEHEW 2	SAUNDERS	
02/02/1991	HULL CITY	A	0	2	5302		2	3	4B	5A	6	7	8	9	10	11		B				1	A									
16/02/1991	WATFORD	H	3	1	5736	1	2	3	4	5A	6	7	8	9	10	11							A							HOLLOWAY	WHITE	SAUNDERS
23/02/1991	PORT VALE	A	2	3	7166	1	2	3	4	5A	6	7	8	9	10	11							A							SAUNDERS	ALEXANDER	
26/02/1991	BARNSLEY	A	0	1	6197	1	2	3	4	5A	6	7	8	9B	10	11							A	B								
02/03/1991	MILLWALL	H	1	0	5587	1	2	3	4	5	6	7	8	9	10	11A							A							SEALY		
05/03/1991	BRISTOL CITY	A	0	1	22227	1	2A	3		5	6	7	8	9	10	11									4	A						
09/03/1991	OLDHAM ATHLETIC	A	0	2	12775	1		3		B		7	8	9	10	11A	5B						A		4	6	2					
12/03/1991	BLACKBURN ROVERS	A	2	2	5969	1	2	3		5A		7	8B	9	10	11							A	B	4	6				HOLLOWAY	SAUNDERS	
16/03/1991	NOTTS COUNTY	H	1	1	4878	1	2	3		A	6	7	8	9	10	11A							5		4					CLARK		
20/03/1991	SWINDON TOWN	H	2	1	6123	1	2	3		A	6	7	8		10	11							5	9A	4					SAUNDERS	SEALY	
23/03/1991	SHEFFIELD WEDNESDAY	A	1	2	25074	1	2	3			6	7	8	9	10	11A							5	A	4					SAUNDERS		
30/03/1991	BRIGHTON & HOVE ALBION	H	1	3	6276	1	2	3		A	6	7	8	9	10	A							5A		4			11A		REECE		
01/04/1991	NEWCASTLE UNITED	A	2	0	17509	1	2	3			6	7	8	9	10	A							5		4			11A		SEALY	WHITE	
06/04/1991	PLYMOUTH ARGYLE	H	0	0	5668	1	2	3			6	7	8	9	10	A							5A		4		B	11B				
10/04/1991	IPSWICH TOWN	H	1	0	4983	1	2	3		A	6	7	8	9	10	B							5A		4			11B		SEALY		
20/04/1991	MIDDLESBROUGH	H	2	0	5722		2	3		A	6	7	8	9	10							1	5A		4			11		SAUNDERS pen	BAILEY	
27/04/1991	OXFORD UNITED	A	1	3	6744		2	3			6	7	8	9	10	A						1	5A		4			11		WHITE		
04/05/1991	PORTSMOUTH	A	1	3	9410		2	3	B	5	6	7	8	9	10	A					11A	1			4B					SAUNDERS		
08/05/1991	WEST HAM UNITED	A	0	1	23054	1	2	3	4		6	7	8	9	10	11	A										5A					
11/05/1991	WEST BROMWICH ALBION	H	1	1	7595	1	2A	3	4	5B	6	7	8	9	10	11	A								B					POUNDER		
	APPEARANCES					39	37	46	33	30	44	46	46	45	36	39	2	7	10	0	6	7	9	1	13	2	2	6				
	SUB					0	2	0	1	11	0	0	0	0	2	6	4	6	6	2	3	0	9	3	1	1	1	0				
	GOALS					0	1	0	0	8	1	7	1	11	16	3	0	0	1	0	0	0	4	0	1	0	0	1		OWN GOAL 1		
	SUBD					0	5	0	1	15	0	0	4	1	1	8	1	2	7	0	1	0	5	1	1	0	1	4				
	RUMBELOWS CUP																															
29/08/1990	TORQUAY UNITED	H	1	2	2461	1	2	3	4	5A	6	7	8	9	10	11				A										TWENTYMAN		
04/09/1990	TORQUAY UNITED	A	1	1	3533	1	2	3	4	5	6		8	9	10	11		7												ALEXANDER		
	FA CUP																															
05/01/1991	CREWE ALEXANDRA	H	0	2	6143	IA		3	4	5	6	7	8	9	10	11		2	A													
	ZENITH DATA SYSTEMS CUP																															
20/11/1990	WATFORD	A	2	1	3076	1	2	3	4	5	6	7A	8	9	10	11B			A		B									SAUNDERS	MEHEW	
18/12/1990	CRYSTAL PALACE	A	1	2	5209	1	2	3	4	5	6	7	8	9	10	11														POUNDER		
	GLOUCESTERSHIRE CUP FINAL																															
15/08/1990	BRISTOL CITY	H	1	4	4208	1	2A	3	4		6		8		10	11	5A	7		9							A		B	JONES pen		

1991/92

Date		H/A	F	A	Att	PARKIN Brian	ALEXANDER Ian	TWENTYMAN Geoffrey	YATES Stephen	MEHEW David	BOOTHROYD Adrian	EVANS Richard	REECE Andrew	WHITE Devon	STEWART Marcus	POUNDER Antony	PURNELL Philip	CLARK William	WILLMOTT Iam	WILSON David	SKINNER Justin	ARCHER Lee	SAUNDERS Carl	CROSS Stephen	BROWNING Marcus	JONES Vaughan	KELLY Gavin	MOORE Kevin	MADDISON Lee	BLOOMER Robert	TAYLOR Gareth	HOPKINS Jeffrey	TAYLOR John	HAZEL Ian	Scorers		
	DIVISION 2																																				
17/08/1991	IPSWICH TOWN	H	3	3	6444	1	2	3	4	5	6	7A	8	9	10	11	A																		STEWART	WHITE 2	
23/08/1991	TRANMERE ROVERS	A	2	2	10150	1			4	5A	2		8	9	10	11	A	3	6	7															STEWART 2-1 pen		
31/08/1991	NEWCASTLE UNITED	H	1	2	6334	1		3	4	5A	2		8	9	10	11	B		6	7B	A														SKINNER		
04/09/1991	BRISTOL CITY	A	0	1	20183	1		3	4		2		8	9	10		11	5			7A	6	A														
07/09/1991	GRIMSBY TOWN	H	2	3	4641	1	2	3	4		5	6B	8	9	10		11A				7	A	B												WHITE	EVANS	
14/09/1991	SOUTHEND UNITED	A	0	2	4670	1	2	3	4		A		8	9	10	7B					5A	11	B	6													
17/09/1991	SWINDON TOWN	A	0	1	11391	1	2	3	4					9	11			5		7A		6	10	8	A												
21/09/1991	OXFORD UNITED	H	2	1	4854	1	2	3	4		7			9B	11			5				A	10	8	B	6A									ALEXANDER	CROSS	
28/09/1991	BRIGHTON & HOVE ALBION	A	1	3	6392	1	2	3	4		7A			9		11		5			6		10	8	A										SAUNDERS		
05/10/1991	MIDDLESBROUGH	H	2	1	4936	1	2	3	4	7			8	9		11					6		10A	5	A										REECE	TWENTYMAN	
12/10/1991	CHARLTON ATHLETIC	A	0	1	5685	1	2	3	4	7			8		9	11	A				6A			5	10												
19/10/1991	PLYMOUTH ARGYLE	H	0	0	5049	1	2	3	4	7			8	9A		11	A				6			5	10												
26/10/1991	SUNDERLAND	A	1	1	14746	1	2	3	4	7			8	9	A	11					6			5	10A										REECE		
02/11/1991	PORT VALE	H	3	3	3565	1		3	4	7A	2		8	9		11	A				6		10	5											SAUNDERS 2	SKINNER	
05/11/1991	WOLVERHAMPTON WANDERERS	A	3	2	8536	1	2	3	4	7			8	9		11					6		10	5											REECE	POUNDER	SAUNDERS
09/11/1991	BARNSLEY	A	1	0	6688	1	2	3	4	7			8	9		11					6		10	5											REECE		
16/11/1991	WATFORD	H	1	1	5064	1	2	3	4	7			8	9	A	11A					6		10	5											SAUNDERS 2		
20/11/1991	LEICESTER CITY	A	1	1	10095	1	2	3	4	7			8	9	A	11					6		10	5A											WHITE		
23/11/1991	DERBY COUNTY	H	2	3	6513	1	2	3	4	7A			8	9	A	11B		B			6		10	5											CROSS	MEHEW	
30/11/1991	MILLWALL	A	1	0	7824	1	2	3	4	7A			8	9		11	A				6		10	5											MEHEW		
07/12/1991	CAMBRIDGE UNITED	H	2	2	5280		2A	3	4	7			8	9		11		A			6		10	5			1								MEHEW	WHITE	
14/12/1991	BLACKBURN ROVERS	A	0	3	12295		2	3	4	7B	B		8	9	A	11A					6		10	5			1										
21/12/1991	BRISTOL CITY	H	3	2	6306		2	3	4	7			8	9		11					6		10	5			1								WHITE	POUNDER	SAUNDERS
26/12/1991	PORTSMOUTH	A	0	2	10710	1	2	3	4	7B	B		8	9	A	11A					6		10	5													
28/12/1991	NEWCASTLE UNITED	A	1	2	19329	1	2	3	4	7			8	9	A	11					6		10	5A											WHITE		
01/01/1992	LEICESTER CITY	H	1	1	6673	1	2	3	4	7			8	9		11					6		10	5											SAUNDERS		
11/01/1992	TRANMERE ROVERS	H	1	0	7138	1	2		4				8		11		A				6		10	7	9A			3	5						STEWART		
18/01/1992	IPSWICH TOWN	A	0	1	10435	1	2		4				8		11B		A				6		10	7	9			3	5A	B							
29/01/1992	PORTSMOUTH	H	1	0	5330	1	2		4	7			8	9B	B	11		5			6A		10	A				3							WHITE		
01/02/1992	PLYMOUTH ARGYLE	A	0	0	6631	1	2		4	7			8	9		11					6		10					3	5								
08/02/1992	SUNDERLAND	H	2	1	6318	1	2			7B	B		8	9	A	11A		4			6		10	5				3							STEWART 2-1 pen		
15/02/1992	DERBY COUNTY	A	0	1	11154	1	2			7			8	9	A	11		4			6		10A	5				3									
22/02/1992	MILLWALL	H	3	2	5747	1	2			7			8	9	A	11A		4			6		10	5				3							WHITE	MEHEW	BARBER og
28/02/1992	CAMBRIDGE UNITED	A	1	6	6164	1	2			7A			8	9	B	11B		4			6		10	5					A		3				HEANEY og		
07/03/1992	BLACKBURN ROVERS	H	3	0	6313	1	2			7B			8	9	A	11A		4			6		10	5					B			3			MEHEW 2	WHITE	
11/03/1992	WOLVERHAMPTON WANDERERS	H	1	1	6968	1	2			7			8	9	A	11A		4			6		10	5								3			WHITE		
14/03/1992	PORT VALE	A	1	0	5861	1	2			7B			8	9			11	4			6		10	5					B			3			SAUNDERS		
21/03/1992	BARNSLEY	H	0	0	5665	1			2					9	A	11	7A	4			6		10	8B					5	B		3					
28/03/1992	WATFORD	A	0	1	7496	1	2		4	7			8		B	11B		3			6		10						5A	A			9				
01/04/1992	SOUTHEND UNITED	H	4	1	5375	1	2		4	7			8		10A	11		3			6		A							5			9		MEHEW	TEWART	J TAYLOR 2
04/04/1992	GRIMSBY TOWN	A	1	0	4859	1	2		4	7			8		10A	11B		3			6		A							5		B	9		J TAYLOR		
12/04/1992	SWINDON TOWN	H	1	1	6905	1	2		4	7A			8		B	11B		3			6		10							5		A	9		CLARK		
18/04/1992	OXFORD UNITED	A	2	2	6891	1	2		4	7			8		10	11		3			6A								5	A			9		J TAYLOR	POUNDER	
20/04/1992	BRIGHTON & HOVE ALBION	H	4	1	6092	1	2		4	7			8		10B	11		3			6				B				5A	A			9		POUNDER	J TAYLOR 3	
24/04/1992	MIDDLESBROUGH	A	1	2	14057	1	2		4	7	B		8		10A	11B		3			6				A					5			9		J TAYLOR		
02/05/1992	CHARLTON ATHLETIC	H	1	0	7630	1	2		4	7			8		10	11		3			6								5				9		MEHEW		
	RUMBELOWS CUP																																				
25/09/1991	BRISTOL CITY	H	1	3	5155	1	2	3	4		7			9	10A	11		5				6		8	A										LLEWELLYN og		
08/10/1991	BRISTOL CITY *	A	4	2	9880	1	2A	3	4	7B			8	9		11	B	A			6			5	10										WHITE 2	MEHEW 2	
30/10/1991	NOTTINGHAM FOREST	H	0	2	17529	1	2	3	4	7A			8	9		11	A				6		10	5													
	* AET Score at 90 mins 3-2. Rovers won on away goals																																				
	FA CUP																																				
05/01/1992	PLYMOUTH ARGYLE	H	5	0	6767	1	2	3A	4				8		11	A					6		10	7	9				5						ALEXANDER	SAUNDERS 4	
05/02/1992	LIVERPOOL	H	1	1	9464	1	2		4	7			8	9		11		3			6		10	5											SAUNDERS		
11/02/1992	LIVERPOOL	A	1	2	6782	1	2		4	7	B		8	9	A	11A		3			6		10	5B											SAUNDERS		
	ZENITH DATA SYSTEMS CUP																																				
02/10/1991	IPSWICH TOWN	A	1	3	1490	1	2	3	4			7B	8	9A	A	11					6		10	5	B										POUNDER		
	GLOUCESTERSHIRE CUP FINAL																																				
17/08/1991	BRISTOL CITY	A	2	3	6796	1	2	3	4	9	A		8			11	7		6				10B		B										PURNELL	MEHEW	

1992/93

						PARKIN Brian	ALEXANDER Ian	CLARK William	YATES Stephen	HARDYMAN Paul	SKINNER Justin	MEHEW David	REECE Andrew	TAYLOR John P	SAUNDERS Carl	POUNDER Antony	STEWART Marcus	CROSS Stephen	TWENTYMAN Geoffrey	MADDISON Lee	WILSON David	KELLY Gavin	MOORE Krevin (L)	CHANNING Justin	ARCHER Lee	TILLSON Andrew	WADDOCK Gary	BROWNING Marcus	JONES Vaughan	EVANS Richard	BEASLEY Andrew (L)	DAVIS Michael				
	DIVISION 1 (2)																																			
15/08/1992	OXFORD UNITED	A	1	2	7333	1	2	3	4	5	6	7A	8	9	10	11B	A	B															TAYLOR			
19/08/1992	SWINDON TOWN	H	3	4	6150	1	2	3	4	5	6B	7	8	9	10	11A	A	B															MEHEW	STEWART	HARDYMAN	
22/08/1992	BRENTFORD	H	2	1	5779	1	2	3	4	5	6	7A	8	9	10	11B	B	A															TAYLOR 2			
25/08/1992	CHARLTON ATHLETIC	A	1	4	4719	1	2	3	4	5	6B		8	9	10	11A	A	7	B														REECE			
28/08/1992	TRANMERE ROVERS	A	1	2	5458	1	2	B	4	5			8B	9	A	11	10A	7	3	6													STEWART			
05/09/1992	NEWCASTLE UNITED	H	1	2	7487	1	2		4		8			9	A	11A	10	7	3	6	5												TAYLOR			
12/09/1992	SWINDON TOWN	A	2	2	10006	1	2	6	4	5	8			9	A	B	10	7	3A		11B												STEWART pen	TAYLOR		
19/09/1992	GRIMSBY TOWN	H	0	3	5320	1	2		4	11	8B			9	A	7A	10	B	3	5	6															
26/09/1992	SUNDERLAND	A	1	1	15593	1	2		4	11	8		A	9			10	7	3	5	6A												STEWART			
03/10/1992	NOTTS COUNTY	H	3	3	5031	1	2		4	11		A	8	9	B	7A	10B		3	5	6												HARDYMAN 2	TAYLOR		
10/10/1992	WATFORD	A	2	4	7624	1	2		4	11		7	8	9	A		10		3	5A	6												STEWART	SAUNDERS		
17/10/1992	WEST HAM UNITED	H	0	4	6187		2	3	4	5	6	7	8	9			10	11				1														
24/10/1992	BIRMINGHAM CITY	A	1	2	9874		2		4A	5	6B	A	8	9	10	11		B				1	3	7									MOORE			
31/10/1992	MILLWALL	H	1	0	5378	1	2	4		5		A	8	9	10	11A					6		3	7									SAUNDERS			
03/11/1992	BARNSLEY	H	1	5	5019	1	2	4		5		A	8	9	10	11B					6		3	7A	B								MEHEW			
07/11/1992	WOLVERHAMPTON WANDERERS	A	1	5	12163	1	2		4A	5		A	8	9B	10								3	7		6	11	B					SAUNDERS			
14/11/1992	DERBY COUNTY	H	1	2	6668	1	2		4	5A		A		9	10									7		3	11	8	6				TAYLOR			
21/11/1992	PETERBOROUGH UNITED	A	1	1	6120	1	2		4	5		A		9	10									7A		3	11	8	6				SAUNDERS			
28/11/1992	LEICESTER CITY	A	1	0	12848	1	2A		4	5		A		9	10									7		3	11	8	6				CHANNING			
05/12/1992	LUTON TOWN	H	2	0	6245	1	2		4	5				9	10		8							7		3	11		6				SAUNDERS	CHANNING		
13/12/1992	BRISTOL CITY	H	4	0	7106	1	2		4	5				9	10		8							7		3	11	6					CHANNING	STEWART	SAUNDERS	TAYLOR
18/12/1992	CAMBRIDGE UNITED	A	1	0	4027	1	2		4	5				9	10		8							7		3	11	6					BROWNING			
26/12/1992	PORTSMOUTH	A	1	4	14268	1	2		4	5				9	10		8									3	11	7	6A	A			TAYLOR			
28/12/1992	SOUTHEND UNITED	H	0	2	7707		2		4	5		A		9	10		8					1				3	11	7		6A						
09/01/1993	GRIMSBY TOWN	A	0	2	4922		2		4	5				9A	10		8					1		6		3	11	7		A						
16/01/1993	SUNDERLAND	H	2	2	6140				4	5				9	10		8					1		2		3	11	7		6			STEWART	HARDYMAN		
27/01/1993	CHARLTON ATHLETIC	H	0	2	5096		2	3	4	5				9A	10B		A					1		8			11	7	6	B						
30/01/1993	BRENTFORD	A	3	0	7527		2	3	4	5					10		9					1		8			11		6	7			STEWART 2	ALEXANDER		
06/02/1993	OXFORD UNITED	H	0	1	5593		2		4	5					10		9					1		8		3	11	7A	6	A						
20/02/1993	TRANMERE ROVERS	H	1	0	5135		2		4	5			6A	A	10		9					1		8		3	11	7					SAUNDERS			
24/02/1993	NEWCASTLE UNITED	A	0	0	29372		2	A	4	5			6	B	10B		9					1		8A		3	11	7								
27/02/1993	WATFORD	H	0	3	5702		2	A	4A	5			8		10		9					1				3	11	7	6							
06/03/1993	NOTTS COUNTY	A	0	3	6445		2		4	5	7		8A	9			10					1				3	11	A	6							
10/03/1993	DERBY COUNTY	A	1	3	13294	1	2		4	5		7A		9	10		A									3	11	8	6				SAUNDERS pen			
13/03/1993	WOLVERHAMPTON WANDERERS	H	1	1	5982		2		4	5A		A	7		10		9					1				3	11	8	6				MEHEW			
20/03/1993	LUTON TOWN	A	1	1	7717	1	2B	B	4			7		A	10	6	9A			5						3	11	8					TAYLOR			
24/03/1993	PETERBOROUGH UNITED	H	3	1	4855	1	2	A	4			7	8	9	10	6				5A						3	11						SAUNDERS	TAYLOR	POUNDER	
27/03/1993	BARNSLEY	A	1	2	5220	1	2A	5	4			7	8	9	10	6	A									3	11						REECE			
03/04/1993	LEICESTER CITY	H	0	0	5270		2	5	4			7A	8	9	10B	6	B					1		A		3	11									
06/04/1993	BRISTOL CITY	A	1	2	21854		2	5	4			7B	8	9		6	10A					1		B		3	11			A			TAYLOR			
10/04/1993	PORTSMOUTH	H	1	2	5322		2A	5	4	A			8	9	B	6B	10							7		3	11				1		STEWART			
14/04/1993	SOUTHEND UNITED	A	0	3	6154		2	5	4	6	8			9	A		10A					1		7		3	11									
17/04/1993	CAMBRIDGE UNITED	H	1	1	3929			5	4	6A				9	10		A			2		1		7		3	11			8			SAUNDERS			
24/04/1993	WEST HAM UNITED	A	1	2	16682			5	4			6A	A	9	10		B			2		1		7B		3	11			8			CLARK			
01/05/1993	BIRMINGHAM CITY	H	3	3	5150			5	4			6	A	9	10		B			2		1		7		3	11B			8A			TAYLOR 2	SAUNDERS		
08/05/1993	MILLWALL	A	3	0	15821	1		5	4			6B	B	9			10A			2				7	8	3	11					A	ARCHER	STEWART	DAVIS	
	APPEARANCES					26	41	19	44	36	12	14	22	39	33	17	27	6	7	12	8	19	4	23	1	29	31	17	12	6	1	0				
	SUB					0	0	5	0	1	0	10	4	3	8	1	11	5	1	0	0	0	0	2	1	0	0	2	0	5	0	1				
	GOAL					0	1	1	0	4	0	3	2	14	11	1	11	0	0	0	0	0	1	3	1	0	0	1	0	0	0	1				
	SUBD					0	4	0	3	3	4	7	3	3	3	10	6	0	1	2	2	0	0	4	0	0	1	1	1	2	0	0				
	COCA- COLA CUP																																			
23/09/1992	MANCHESTER CITY	A	0	0	9967	1	2		4	11	8		A	9			10	7	3	5	6A															
07/10/1992	MANCHESTER CITY	H	1	2	7823	1	2		4	11B		7	8	9	A		10	B	3	5A	6												REECE			
	FA CUP																																			
02/01/1993	ASTON VILLA	A	1	1	27040		2		4	5		A		9	10		8A					1				3	11	7		6			BROWNING			
21/01/1993	ASTON VILLA	H	0	3	8880			3	4	5				9	8		10		A			1					11	7	2	6A						
	ANGLO-ITALIAN CUP																																			
02/09/1992	WEST HAM UNITED	A	2	2	4809	1	2	B	4	5	8			9		11A	10	7	3	6B								A					STEWART 2			
16/09/1992	SOUTHEND UNITED	H	3	0	3007	1	2		4	7	8			9	A	11A	10		3	5	6												STEWART pen	SAUNDERS	HARDYMAN	
	GLOUCESTERSHIRE CUP																																			
05/08/1992	BRISTOL CITY	H	2	1	3722		2	5	4	6	8	7		9	10	11					A	1				3							STEWART	MEHEW		

1993/94

Date	Opponent	H/A	F	A	Att	PARKIN Brian	ALEXANDER Ian	HARDYMAN Paul	WADDOCK Gary	CLARK William	YATES Stephen	STERLING Worrell	TAYLOR John P	STEWART Marcus	BROWNING Marcus	ARCHER Lee	MADDISON Lee	DAVIS Michael	CHANNING Justin	TILLSON Andrew	SKINNER Justin	SAUNDERS Carl	POUNDER Antony	McLEAN Ian	WRIGHT Ian	PAUL Martin	MARGETSON Martyn (L)	EVANS Richard	KELLY Gavin	PRITCHARD David	GURNEY Andrew	TOVEY Paul	Scorers		
	DIVISION 2 (3)																																		
14/08/1993	AFC BOURNEMOUTH	H	0	1	7234	1	2	3	4	5	6	7	8	9	10B	11A	A	B																	
21/08/1993	LEYTON ORIENT	A	0	1	4155	1			4	5		7	8A	9	A	11	3		2	6	10														
28/08/1993	FULHAM	H	2	1	5261	1	B		4	5			8	9A	7B	11	3	A	2	6	10												TAYLOR 2		
01/09/1993	BRIGHTON & HOVE ALBION	A	2	0	5675	1	A		4	5		7A	8			11	3	B	2	6	10	9B											TAYLOR 2		
04/09/1993	HULL CITY	A	0	3	5362	1	B		4	5		7	8			11	3	A	2B	6	10	9A													
11/09/1993	PORT VALE	H	2	0	4908	1	2			5		7	8		4	11A	3			6	10	9	A										TAYLOR	SKINNER	
15/09/1993	EXETER CITY	H	1	1	5001	1	2			5		7	8	A	4	11	3				10	9A		6									BROWNING		
18/09/1993	ROTHERHAM UNITED	A	1	1	4000	1	2			5		7	8	9A	4	11	3				10	A		6									ARCHER		
25/09/1993	BURNLEY	H	3	1	5732	1	2	B				7	8	9A	4	11	3				10B	A		6	5								TAYLOR	McLEAN	STERLING
02/10/1993	BARNET	A	2	1	3158	1	2		10				8	9	4	11	3					A	7A	6	5								BROWNING	TAYLOR	
09/10/1993	BRADFORD CITY	H	4	3	5323	1	2		10			7	8A	9	4	11	3	A						6	5								TAYLOR	STERLING	STEWART 2-2pens
16/10/1993	CARDIFF CITY	A	2	1	5563	1			10			7	8	9	4	11	3		2					6	5								TAYLOR 2		
23/10/1993	PLYMOUTH ARGYLE	H	0	0	7758	1			10	A		7	8	9	4	11	3		2					6	5A										
30/10/1993	HUDDERSFIELD TOWN	A	0	1	5612	1			10	A		7	8	9	4	11B	3		2		B			6A	5										
02/11/1993	YORK CITY	A	1	0	3758	1		11	10	6		7	8		4		3	9A	2		A				5								TAYLOR		
06/11/1993	HARTLEPOOL UNITED	H	1	1	5308	1			10A	5		7	8		4	11	3	A	2		9				6								SKINNER		
20/11/1993	STOCKPORT COUNTY	A	2	0	5250	1			10	5		7	8		4	11	3		2		9				6								ARCHER	TAYLOR	
27/11/1993	CAMBRIDGE UNITED	H	2	1	4477	1			10	5		7	8		4	11	3		2		9			A	6A								SKINNER	TAYLOR	
11/12/1993	LEYTON ORIENT	H	1	1	4604	1				5		7	8	9A	4	11	3			2	10				6	A							TAYLOR		
18/12/1993	AFC BOURNEMOUTH	A	0	3	4811	1			10A	5		7	8		4	11	3		2		9				6		A								
01/01/1994	SWANSEA CITY	H	1	2	6285		2			5		7A	8	10	4	11	3		A		9B				6	B	1						BROWNING		
03/01/1994	BLACKPOOL	A	1	0	3311	1	2	A	10	5			8A		4	11	3				9			B	6B			7					ARCHER		
08/01/1994	BRENTFORD	A	4	3	6841		2	A	10	5		7	8B		4	11A	3			B	9			6			1						TAYLOR 2	SKINNER	BROWNING
15/01/1994	CARDIFF CITY	H	2	1	5683	1	2	A	10	5		7	8		4	11A	3				9			6									McLEAN	TAYLOR	
22/01/1994	BRADFORD CITY	A	1	0	6122	1	2	A	10	5		7	8		4	11	3				9A			6									ARCHER		
26/01/1994	READING	H	1	1	7494	1	2	A	10	5		7	8		4	11A	3				9			6									CLARK		
29/01/1994	HUDDERSFIELD TOWN	H	0	0	5127	1	2		10	5		7	8		4	11	3				9			6											
05/02/1994	PLYMOUTH ARGYLE	A	3	3	13318	1	2B	A	10	5		7	8A	B	4	11	3				9			6									SKINNER	ARCHER	STERLING
12/02/1994	BRENTFORD	H	1	4	5685	1		B	10	5		7	8A	4		11	3	A	2		9B			6									STEWART		
19/02/1994	FULHAM	A	1	0	5063	1		4	10	5		7	8	9A		11	3		2					A	6								TAYLOR		
23/02/1994	BRIGHTON & HOVE ALBION	H	1	0	4776	1		4	10	5		7	8A	9B		11	3		2				B	A	6								TAYLOR		
26/02/1994	HULL CITY	H	1	1	5703	1		9	10	5		7	8A	A	4	11	3		2						6								TAYLOR		
05/03/1994	PORT VALE	A	0	2	8682			9	10	5		7	8		4	11	3		2						6				1						
12/03/1994	ROTHERHAM UNITED	H	0	2	4224	1		11A	10	5		7	8	9	4		3		2						6			A							
15/03/1994	EXETER CITY	A	0	1	4399	1				5		7	8	9		11B	3	A	4		10A			B	6					2					
19/03/1994	BURNLEY	A	1	3	10651	1		10	4A	5		7	8	A			3		9				11	B	6					2B			HARDYMAN		
22/03/1994	WREXHAM	A	2	3	3184	1		10	4	5		7	8	A			3		9				11A		6					2			CHANNING	WADDOCK	
26/03/1994	BARNET	H	5	2	3802	1		3	4	5		7	8	9					10				11		6					2			CHANNING 3-1pen	WALKER og	STEWART
30/03/1994	BLACKPOOL	H	1	0	4231	1		3	4	5		7	8	10					9A	6			11			A				2			STERLING		
02/04/1994	READING	A	0	2	8035	1		3	4	5		7	8	9						6	10		11A	A							2				
04/04/1994	WREXHAM	H	3	1	4702	1		3	4			7		9				8A		6	10		11B	B	5	A				2			STEWART	POUNDER 2	
09/04/1994	SWANSEA CITY	A	0	2	3961	1		3	4			7	8						9	6	10		11	A	5A					2B		B			
16/04/1994	YORK CITY	H	0	1	5007	1		3	4			7	A		8	11A			9	6	10				5					2					
23/04/1994	HARTLEPOOL UNITED	A	1	2	1409	1		3	4			7	8	A	9	11			10A	6				B	5					2B			WRIGHT		
30/04/1994	STOCKPORT COUNTY	H	1	1	4189	1		3A	4			7	8	9		11			10					6	5					2	A		STERLING		
07/05/1994	CAMBRIDGE UNITED	A	3	1	4402	1			4			7	8	9		11			10					6	5					2	3		TAYLOR 2	CHANNING	
	APPEARANCES					43	15	17	39	34	1	43	44	23	30	37	36	2	28	12	27	4	8	17	29	0	2	1	1	11	2	0			
	SUB					0	3	8	0	2	0	0	1	6	1	0	1	8	1	1	2	3	2	10	0	4	1	1	0	0	1	1			
	GOALS					0	0	1	1	1	0	5	22	5	4	5	0	0	5	0	5	0	2	2	1	0	0	0	0	0	0	0	OWN GOAL 1		
	SUBD					0	1	2	3	0	0	2	8	6	2	8	0	2	3	0	5	3	4	1	4	0	0	0	0	3	0	0			
	COCA-COLA CUP																																		
18/08/1993	WEST BROMWICH ALBION	H	1	4	4562	1	2	3	4	5		7	8A	9	A	11				6	10												STERLING		
25/08/1993	WEST BROMWICH ALBION	A	0	0	9123	1			4	5		7	8	9		11	3		2	6	10														
	FA CUP																																		
14/11/1993	WYCOMBE WANDERERS	H	1	2	6421	1				5		7	8		4	11	3		2		10	9			6								ARCHER		
	AUTOGLASS TROPHY																																		
28/09/1993	TORQUAY UNITED	A	1	0	2445	1	2		10			7	8A	9	4	11	3					A		6	5								McLEAN		
20/10/1993	CARDIFF CITY	H	3	0	2035	1				B		7	8A	9	4	11	3	A	2		10B			6	5								SKINNER	STEWART 2	
01/12/1993	FULHAM	H	2	2	2882	1			10	5		7	8		4	11	3		2A		9			A	6								BROWNING 2		
	* AET Lost 3-4 on pens																																		
	GLOUCESTERSHIRE CUP																																		
05/08/1993	BRISTOL CITY	A	1	1	6698	1		3	4	5	6	7	8A	9	10	11B	B	A	2														CLARK		
	AET Won 5-3 on pens																																		

1994/95

						PARKIN Brian	PRITCHARD David	MADDISON Lee	CHANNING Justin	CLARK William	TILLSON Andrew	STERLING Worrell	STEWART Marcus	PAUL Martin	SKINNER Justin	ARCHER Lee	TAYLOR Gareth	BROWNING Marcus	GURNEY Andrew	MILLER Paul	WADDOCK Gary	WRIGHT Ian	LAW Marcus	DAVIS Michael	McLEAN Ian	COLLETT Andrew	HARDYMAN Paul	HEGGS Carl (L)	WHITE Thomas				
	DIVISION 2 (3)																																
13/08/1994	PETERBOROUGH UNITED	A	0	0	5695	1	2	3	4	5	6	7	8B	9	10	11A	A	B															
20/08/1994	YORK CITY	H	3	1	3697	1	2		4	5	6	7	9		10	11A		A	3	8										MILLER	STEWART	CLARK	
27/08/1994	WYCOMBE WANDERERS	A	0	0	5895	1	2		4	5	6	7	9A		10	11B	A	B	3	8													
31/08/1994	BLACKPOOL	H	0	0	3762	1	2		4	5	6	7				11	9		3	8	10												
03/09/1994	STOCKPORT COUNTY	H	2	2	4263	1	2		4	5	6	7			10A	11	9	A	3	8										TILLSON	ARCHER		
10/09/1994	ROTHERHAM UNITED	A	3	0	2596	1	2		4	5	6	7		A	10	11	9A		3	8										MILLER 2	WILDER og		
13/09/1994	SWANSEA CITY	A	0	0	3226	1	2		4	5	6	7			10	11	9		3	8													
17/09/1994	WREXHAM	H	4	2	4441	1	2		4	5	6	7			10	11	9		3	8										TAYLOR	MILLER	CLARK 2	
24/09/1994	SHREWSBURY TOWN	A	0	1	4596	1	2		4B	5	6	7			10A	11	9	A	3	8		B											
01/10/1994	CREWE ALEXANDRA	H	2	2	4862	1	2	B	4	5		7			10A	11	9	A	3	8B		6								TAYLOR 2			
08/10/1994	BRENTFORD	A	0	3	5330		2	A	4	5		7		9B	10	11		8	3A			6	1	B									
15/10/1994	CARDIFF CITY	H	2	2	3936		2	3	4	5B	6	7			10A	11	9	8	A				1		B					CHANNING	CLARK		
22/10/1994	BRIGHTON & HOVE ALBION	H	3	0	4107		2		4	5	6	7	9		10		A	11	3	8A						1				STEWART	MILLER 2		
29/10/1994	BIRMINGHAM CITY	A	0	2	15886		2		4	5	6	7	9A		10B	B	A	11	3	8						1							
01/11/1994	CAMBRIDGE UNITED	A	1	1	2328		2		4	5	6	7	9		10			11	3	8						1				TILLSON			
05/11/1994	BRADFORD CITY	H	4	0	4247		2		4B	5	6	7	9		10	B	A	11	3	8A						1				BROWNING	OLIVER og	STEWART 2	
19/11/1994	HULL CITY	A	2	0	4450	1	2		4A	5	6	7	9	B	10B	A	8	11	3											STEWART 2			
26/11/1994	HUDDERSFIELD TOWN	H	1	1	5679	1	2			5	6	7	9		10	11	A	4	3	8A										MILLER			
10/12/1994	YORK CITY	A	3	0	3094	1	2			5	6	7	9		10	11A		4	3	8							A			SKINNER	STEWART 2		
17/12/1994	PETERBOROUGH UNITED	H	3	1	4635	1			2	5		7	9		10	11A		4	3	8		6					A			STEWART 2-1pen	GURNEY		
26/12/1994	AFC BOURNEMOUTH	H	2	1	6913	1		3		5		7	9		10	11B	A	4	2	8		6A					B			MILLER	STEWART		
31/12/1994	CHESTER CITY	H	3	0	5629	1	2B			5	6	7	9		10A	11	A	4	3	8							B			ARCHER 2	STEWART		
14/01/1995	OXFORD UNITED	H	3	2	5875	1			2	5	6	7	9B	B		11	A	4	3	8							10A			TAYLOR	MILLER	STEWART	
04/02/1995	HUDDERSFIELD TOWN	A	1	1	10389	1	2		11	5	6	7			10		A	4	3	8								9A		STERLING			
07/02/1995	BRADFORD CITY	A	1	2	4243	1	2		11A		6	7			10		A	4	3	8								9	5	HEGGS			
14/02/1995	BRIGHTON & HOVE ALBION	A	2	1	5316	1	2		10		6	7	9B			11	B	4	3	8A								A	5	ARCHER	STEWART		
18/02/1995	OXFORD UNITED	A	0	0	6349	1	2		10		6	7	9B			11	A	4	3	8A								B	5				
25/02/1995	CREWE ALEXANDRA	A	1	2	4222	1	2		10		6	7	9B			11	8	4A	3	B								A	5	MILLER			
01/03/1995	HULL CITY	H	0	2	3707	1	2		11A	5	6	7	9		10	A		4	3	8													
04/03/1995	SHREWSBURY TOWN	H	4	0	4338	1	2			5	6	7			10	11	9A	4	3	8				A						ARCHER	BROWNING	TAYLOR	MILLER pen
07/03/1995	STOCKPORT COUNTY	A	1	2	3580	1	2		A	5	6	7			10	11	9A	4	3	8										MILLER			
11/03/1995	WYCOMBE WANDERERS	H	1	0	5118	1	2			5	6	7			10	11	9	4	3	8										TAYLOR			
15/03/1995	CAMBRIDGE UNITED	H	2	1	3734	1	2		A	5	6	7			10	11A	9	4	3	8										MILLER	TAYLOR		
18/03/1995	BLACKPOOL	A	2	0	4484	1	2		A	5	6	7			10	11A	9	4	3	8										MILLER	SKINNER		
22/03/1995	ROTHERHAM UNITED	H	2	0	4420	1	2	3	A	5	6	7			10	11A	9	4		8										TAYLOR	CLARK		
25/03/1995	WREXHAM	A	1	1	3170	1	2	3	A	5	6	7			10	11	9A	4		8										ARCHER			
29/03/1995	BIRMINGHAM CITY	H	1	1	8010	1	2	3	4	5	6	7	9A		10	11	A			8										WHYTE og			
01/04/1995	SWANSEA CITY	H	1	0	7062	1	2	3	4	5	6	7	9B		10A	11	A	B		8										TAYLOR			
04/04/1995	PLYMOUTH ARGYLE	A	1	1	6743	1	2	3	4	5	6	7	9			11		10		8										MILLER			
08/04/1995	CHESTER CITY	A	0	0	2241	1	2	3	4	5	6	7	9			11B	A	10A	B	8													
11/04/1995	LEYTON ORIENT	A	2	1	2338	1	2	3	10	5	6A	7	9			AB	11	4	B	8										MILLER	CHANNING		
15/04/1995	PLYMOUTH ARGYLE	H	2	0	7068	1	2	3	4	5		7	9A		10B	B	11	A		8		6								TAYLOR	WRIGHT		
18/04/1995	AFC BOURNEMOUTH	A	0	2	7020	1	2	3A	11	5		7			10	A	9	4		8		6											
22/04/1995	LEYTON ORIENT	H	1	0	4838	1	2		11B	5	6	7	A		10	B	9	4A	3	8										CLARK			
29/04/1995	CARDIFF CITY	A	1	0	5462	1	2		11	5	6	7A	4		10	A	9B	B	3	8										STEWART			
06/05/1995	BRENTFORD	H	2	2	8501	1	2		11B	5	6	7	4A		10	B	9	A	3	8										TAYLOR 2			
	APPEARANCES					40	43	12	35	42	40	46	26	2	38	32	23	31	35	41	1	6	2	0	0	4	1	2	4				
	SUB					0	0	2	5	0	0	0	1	3	0	10	16	10	3	1	0	1	0	2	1	0	4	3	0				
	GOALS					0	0	0	2	6	2	1	15	0	2	6	12	2	1	16	0	1	0	0	0	0	0	1	0	OWN GOAL 3			
	SUBD					0	1	1	7	1	1	1	11	1	9	11	5	3	1	6	0	1	0	0	0	0	1	1	0				
	PLAY-OFFS																																
14/05/1995	CREWE ALEXANDRA	H	0	0	8538	1	2		A	5	6	7	4A		10	11	9		3	8													
17/05/1995	CREWE ALEXANDRA	A	1	1	6578	1	2		11B	5	6	7	4		10A	B	9	A	3	8										MILLER			
28/05/1995	HUDDERSFIELD TOWN	N	1	2	59175	1	2		11B	5	6	7	4		10	B	9A	A	3			8								STEWART			
	COCA-COLA CUP																																
17/08/1994	PORT VALE	H	1	3	3307	1	2	3	4	5	6	7	9		10	11				8										TILLSON			
23/08/1994	PORT VALE	A	1	1	4728	1	2		4B	5	6	7	9		10A	11	A	B	3	8										STEWART			
	FA CUP																																
12/11/1994	BATH CITY	A	5	0	6751	1	2		4A	5	6	7	9		10	A		11	3	8										STEWART	MILLER 4		
03/12/1994	LEYTON ORIENT	A	2	0	5071	1	2			5	6	7	9		10	11A		4	3	8							A			STEWART 2			
07/01/1995	LUTON TOWN	A	1	1	7571	1			2	5	6	7	9		10	11	A		3	8A							4			STEWART			
18/01/1995	LUTON TOWN	H	0	1	4218	1	2A		10	5	6	7				11	9	4	3	8							A						
	AUTO WINDSCREEN SHIELD																																
27/09/1994	OXFORD UNITED	A	2	2	1518	1	2			5			7		10	11	9	4	3	8		6								SKINNER pen	CLARK		
19/10/1994	AFC BOURNEMOUTH	H	1	1	1728		2	3	4	5	6B	7	9	8A	B			10	11						A	1				STEWART pen			
29/11/1994	CAMBRIDGE UNITED	H	4	2	2373	1	2			5	6	7	9		10	11		4	3	8										SKINNER	STEWART 2-1	MILLER	
10/01/1995	LEYTON ORIENT	A	0	0	1381	1		B	2	5	6	7		A	10B	11	9A		3	8							4						
	AET Lost 3-4 on pens																																
	GLOUCESTERSHIRE CUP																																
03/08/1994	BRISTOL CITY	H	0	0	3699	1	2	3	A	5	6	7	8	9B			B	10	4A		11												
	AET Rovers won 11-10 on pens																																

1995/96

Date	Opponent				Att	PARKIN Brian	PRITCHARD David	GURNEY Andrew	BROWNING Marcus	CLARK William	TILLSON Andrew	STERLING Worrell	MILLER Paul	STEWART Marcus	SKINNER Justin	TAYLOR Gareth	WRIGHT Ian	WYATT Michael	HAYFIELD Matthew	ARCHER Lee	CHANNING Justin	McLEAN Ian	PAUL Martin	COLLETT Andrew	DAVIS Michael	WHITE Thomas	FRENCH Jonathan	BEADLE Peter	TOVEY Paul	ARMSTRONG Craig (L)	MATTHEW Damian (L)	MORGAN Stephen (L)	LOW Joshua	HOPE Matthew			
	DIVISION 2 (3)																																				
12/08/1995	CARLISLE UNITED	A	2	1	8003	1	2	3	4	5	6	7	8	9	10	11																			CLARK	STEWART	
19/08/1995	SWANSEA CITY	H	2	2	6689	1	2	3	4	5	6	7	8	9	10	11																			TAYLOR 2		
26/08/1995	WALSALL	A	1	1	4851	1	2	3	4	5		7	8	9	10	11	6																		TAYLOR		
29/08/1995	BURNLEY	H	1	0	5646	1	2	3	4	5		7	8	9	10	11	6																		TAYLOR		
02/09/1995	WREXHAM	H	1	2	6031	1	2	3		5		7	8	9	10A	11	6	4	A																STEWART		
09/09/1995	YORK CITY	A	1	0	4047	1	2	3	4	5		7	8	9	10		6			11A	A														MILLER		
12/09/1995	ROTHERHAM UNITED	A	1	0	2739	1	2	3B	4	5			8	9	10	11	6	7A		A		B															
16/09/1995	SWINDON TOWN	H	1	4	7025	1	2	3	4	5			8	9	10	11	6			7															MILLER		
23/09/1995	BRENTFORD	H	2	0	5131	1	2		4	A	6		8	9	10B		5A	11	B		3		7												STEWART pen	PAUL	
30/09/1995	OXFORD UNITED	A	1	2	6091	1	2	3	4		6	7		9	10		5		A		11		8A												BROWNING	STEWART	
07/10/1995	AFC BOURNEMOUTH	H	0	2	5171	1	2A	3	4		6	7		9	10		5			A	11		8														
14/10/1995	BRADFORD CITY	A	3	2	5817			3	4		6	7		9	10		5			11	2		8A	1	A										GURNEY	STEWART	ARCHER
21/10/1995	NOTTS COUNTY	H	0	3	6078			3	4		6	7		9	10		5			11	2		8A	1	A												
28/10/1995	BRIGHTON & HOVE ALBION	A	0	2	5658			3	4		6	7		9	10		5A			11	2C	A	B	1	8B	C											
31/10/1995	BLACKPOOL	A	0	3	3877			3	4		6	7		9	10			A	2	11		5	8A	1													
04/11/1995	PETERBOROUGH UNITED	H	1	1	4241			3	4A		6	7			10		2		8	11		5		1	A		9								GURNEY		
18/11/1995	WYCOMBE WANDERERS	A	1	1	4886	1	2	3	4	5	6		A	9	10						7	11						8A							GURNEY		
25/11/1995	STOCKPORT COUNTY	H	1	3	4326	1		3	4	5	6		8	9	10				2		7	11A	A												MILLER		
09/12/1995	BRENTFORD	A	0	0	5679	1		3	4	5	6	7	8	9							2		11A					A	10								
16/12/1995	OXFORD UNITED	H	2	0	4051	1		3	4	5	6	7	8	9							2							11	10						STEWART 2		
23/12/1995	CREWE ALEXANDRA	H	1	2	4519	1		3	4	5	6	7	8		A						2		9					11A	10						BROWNING		
26/12/1995	SHREWSBURY TOWN	A	1	1	4944			3A	4	5	6	7	8	9	A						2	B		1				11	10B						BEADLE		
06/01/1996	HULL CITY	H	2	1	4267	1		3	4	5	6	7	8	9	A						2							11A	10B	B					STEWART 2		
13/01/1996	SWANSEA CITY	A	2	2	2956	1		7	4	5	6		8	9							2							11		3	10				GURNEY	BEADLE	
16/01/1996	BRISTOL CITY	A	2	0	20007	1		3	4	5	6		8	9							2							11		7	10				BEADLE 2		
20/01/1996	CARLISLE UNITED	H	1	1	5196	1			4	5	6	7	8	9							2							11		3	10				STEWART		
03/02/1996	WALSALL	H	2	0	4948				4	5	6	7	8	9							2			1				11		3	10				BEADLE	STEWART pen	
10/02/1996	HULL CITY	A	3	1	3311			3	4	5	6	7A	8	9							2		A	1				11			10				BEADLE	STEWART	BROWNING
17/02/1996	ROTHERHAM UNITED	H	1	0	5412			3	4	5	6	7	8	9							2			1				11			10				STEWART		
20/02/1996	WREXHAM	A	2	3	3235			3	4	5	6	7	8	9							2			1				11			10				BEADLE	TILLSON	
24/02/1996	SWINDON TOWN	A	1	2	11697			3	4	5	6	7	8	9							2		11	1							10				STEWART		
27/02/1996	YORK CITY	H	1	0	4013			3	4A	5	6	7	8	9							2			1			A	11	10						STEWART		
02/03/1996	SHREWSBURY TOWN	H	2	1	5004			7	4	5	6	A	8	9			B				2A			1				11	10B			3			GURNEY	STEWART pen	
06/03/1996	CREWE ALEXANDRA	A	2	1	4091			2	4A	5	6	7	8	9			B						A	1			11B		10			3			FRENCH	STEWART	
16/03/1996	BRISTOL CITY	H	2	4	8648			2	4	5	6	7	8	9							10A			1			A	11				3			GURNEY	CLARK	
23/03/1996	CHESTERFIELD	A	1	2	4748			2A	4	5		7B	8	9			6			B	10			1			A	11				3			STEWART		
26/03/1996	CHESTERFIELD	H	1	0	3513			2	4	5	6	A		9						7	10			1			8A	11				3			BEADLE		
30/03/1996	AFC BOURNEMOUTH	A	1	2	4607			2B	4	5	6		8	9			A			7	10			1			B	11		3A					MILLER		
02/04/1996	BRADFORD CITY	H	1	0	4008			3	4	5	6		8	9						7A	10			1			A	11		2					BEADLE		
06/04/1996	BRIGHTON & HOVE ALBION	H	1	0	5385			2	4	5	6		8	9	A					7	10			1				11A		3					BEADLE		
09/04/1996	NOTTS COUNTY	A	2	4	4661			2A	4	5			8	9	A		6			7	10			1				11		3					STEWART	BEADLE	
13/04/1996	BLACKPOOL	H	1	1	5626			2	4	5	6		8A	9	7					A	10			1				11		3					BEADLE		
20/04/1996	PETERBOROUGH UNITED	A	0	0	4884			2A	4	5	6		8	9	7					A	10			1				11		3							
23/04/1996	BURNLEY	A	1	0	9368			2B	4	5	6		8	9	7						10			1		B	A	11A		3					STEWART		
27/04/1996	STOCKPORT COUNTY	A	0	2	6935			2A	4	5	6		8	9	7					A	10			1				11		3							
04/05/1996	WYCOMBE WANDERERS	H	2	1	6621			A	4	5	6		8	9	7					2A	10C			1			B	11B		3			C		BROWNING	STEWART	
	APPEARANCES					20	12	42	45	38	38	28	37	44	23	7	15	3	3	13	35	4	9	26	1	0	3	26	8	13	8	5	0				
	SUB					0	0	1	0	1	0	2	1	0	5	0	3	1	3	6	1	3	4	0	3	2	7	1	0	1	0	0	1				
	GOALS					0	0	6	4	2	1	0	4	21	0	4	0	0	0	1	0	0	1	0	0	0	1	12	0	0	0	0	0				
	SUBD					0	1	8	3	0	0	2	1	0	2	0	2	1	0	3	4	2	4	0	1	0	2	6	3	1	0	0	0				
	COCA-COLA CUP																																				
15/08/1995	GILLINGHAM	A	1	1	3827	1	2	3	4	5	6	7	8	9	10	11																			STEWART		
23/08/1995	GILLINGHAM	H	4	2	3601	1	2	3	4	5	6A	7	8	9	10	11	A																		STEWART 3	MILLER	
20/09/1995	WEST HAM UNITED	H	0	1	7103	1	2	3	4		6		8	9	7	11	5	A			10A																
04/10/1995	WEST HAM UNITED	A	0	3	15375	1	2	3	4		6	7		9	10		5				11A		8		A												
	FA CUP																																				
11/11/1995	HITCHIN TOWN	A	1	2	3001		2	3			6	7		9	10		8		4A	11	A	5		1											ARCHER		
	AUTO WINDSCREEN SHIELD																																				
17/10/1995	BRIGHTON & HOVE ALBION	A	2	0	1191			3	4			7A		9B	10		5		B	11C	2	6	8	1	A									C	DAVIS	ARCHER	
07/11/1995	CAMBRIDGE UNITED	H	3	0	1805			3			6	7		9	10		2		8A	11B		5	B	1		A	4								FRENCH	STEWART 2	
28/11/1995	AFC BOURNEMOUTH	H	2	1	1979	1		3	4	5	6	7	8	9							2		11				A		10A						BROWNING	TILLSON	
09/01/1996	FULHAM *	A	2	1	3479	1		3	4	5	6	7	8	9	10A						2							11	A						STEWART 2		
13/02/1996	PETERBOROUGH UNITED	A	1	0	3761			3	4	5	6	7	8	9							2			1				11			10				STEWART pen		
05/03/1996	SHREWSBURY TOWN	A	1	1	5212			2	4	5	6	7	8	9			A							1			11A				10	3			MATTHEW		
12/03/1996	SHREWSBURY TOWN	H	0	1	7050			2	4	5	6		8	9							7			1				11	10			3					

* 1-1 at 90 mins Lost in sudden death

1996/97

Date	Opponent				Att	COLLETT Andrew	MARTIN Lee	LOCKWOOD Matthew	BROWNING Marcus	CLARK William	TILLSON Andrew	HOLLOWAY Ian	GURNEY Andrew	MILLER Paul	ARCHER Lee	BEADLE Peter	FRENCH Jonathan	PARMENTER Stephen	LOW Joshua	SKINNER Justin	POWER Graeme	CURETON Jamie	RAMASUT Thomas	WHITE Thomas	HIGGS Shane	PRITCHARD David	HAYFIELD Matthew	HARRIS Jason (L)	BENNETT Frank	ALSOP Julian	MORGAN Ryan	GAYLE Brian	CLAPHAM James (L)	ZABEK Lee			
	DIVISION 2 (3)																																				
17/08/1996	PETERBOROUGH UNITED	H	1	0	6232	1	2	3	4	5	6	7	8	9	10	11																			GURNEY		
24/08/1996	PRESTON NORTH END	A	0	0	9752	1	2	3	4	5	6	7	8	9	10	11																					
31/08/1996	STOCKPORT COUNTY	H	1	1	6380	1	2	3		5	6	7	8A	9	10	11B	4	A	B																ARCHER		
07/09/1996	MILLWALL	A	0	2	7881	1	2	3	4	5	6	7	8	9A	10	11		A																			
10/09/1996	AFC BOURNEMOUTH	H	3	2	4170	1	2	3	4	5	6	7	8B	9A	10	11		A		B															TILLSON	PARMENTER	BEADLE
14/09/1996	WATFORD	H	0	1	6256	1	2	3	4	5	6	7	8B	A	10	11		9A		B																	
17/09/1996	WREXHAM	A	0	1	2401	1	2	3	4	5	6	7A	8		10	11B	B	9		A																	
21/09/1996	PLYMOUTH ARGYLE	A	1	0	8879	1	2	3	4	5		7	8		10	A				11	6	9A													ARCHER		
28/09/1996	CHESTERFIELD	H	2	0	5008	1	2	A		5	6	7	8		10A	11				4	3	9													CURETON 2		
01/10/1996	YORK CITY	A	2	2	3714	1	2	10		5	6	7	8	A		11A				4	3	9													CURETON	BEADLE	
04/10/1996	CREWE ALEXANDRA	H	2	0	6211	1	2	A		5	6	7	8	11	10A					4	3	9													CURETON	GURNEY	
12/10/1996	NOTTS COUNTY	A	1	1	4558	1	2		4	5	6	B	8	11A	10	A				7	3	9B													BEADLE		
15/10/1996	ROTHERHAM UNITED	A	0	0	2490	1	2	10	B	5	6	7	8	A		11A				4	3	9B															
19/10/1996	BLACKPOOL	H	0	0	5823	1	2	10	A	5	6	7	8	11						4	3	9A															
26/10/1996	BURY	A	1	2	4082	1		10B	2	5	6	7	8	11		A				4A	3	9	B												MILLER		
29/10/1996	BRENTFORD	H	2	1	5163	1		A	4	5	6	7	2	8		11					3	9	10A												CURETON	BROWNING	
02/11/1996	GILLINGHAM	H	0	0	5530	1			4	5	6	7	2	8		11					3	9	10														
12/11/1996	SHREWSBURY TOWN	A	0	2	2331	1			4	5	6	7		8		11	9				3		10	2													
19/11/1996	BURNLEY	H	1	2	4123			3	4	5		7B				11	8A	B		A	6	9	10C	C	1	2									BEADLE		
23/11/1996	LUTON TOWN	A	1	2	5315	1		3	4	5			8		10	11					6	9A				2	7	A							HARRIS		
30/11/1996	BURY	H	4	3	4496	1	3		4	5	6				10	11						A				2	7	9A	8						BEADLE 3	CLARK	
03/12/1996	WALSALL	A	0	1	4084	1	3		4	5	6				10A	11						A				2	7	9	8								
15/12/1996	BRISTOL CITY	A	1	1	18674	1	3	10A	4	5C	6	7			A	11				C		B				2	8B	9							BEADLE		
21/12/1996	WYCOMBE WANDERERS	H	3	4	4465	1		3	4	5	6		A			11				8		10				2	7A	9							CURETON	HARRIS	LOCKWOOD
26/12/1996	AFC BOURNEMOUTH	A	0	1	5036	1		3	4	5	6		A			11				8		10B	B			2	7A	9									
11/01/1997	CHESTERFIELD	A	0	1	3305	1	3	10A	4	5	6		7	9		11				8B		B		A		2											
18/01/1997	YORK CITY	H	1	1	4470	1		10	4		6		7A	9	B	11				8	3B	A		5		2									BEADLE		
21/01/1997	BRENTFORD	A	0	0	4191	1		3	4		6			7	10	11				8		9		5		2											
01/02/1997	SHREWSBURY TOWN	H	2	0	4924	1		3	4		6			7	10	11				8		9		5		2									BROWNING	BEADLE	
08/02/1997	GILLINGHAM	A	0	1	6900	1		3	4		6	A		7	10A	11				8		9		5		2											
15/02/1997	LUTON TOWN	H	3	2	5612	1		3			6	7		8	10	11A				4		9B		5		2	B			A					MILLER	TILLSON	HOLLOWAY
22/02/1997	BURNLEY	A	2	2	8847	1	3	11			6	7		8	B					4		9A		5		2	10B			A					CURETON	ALSOP	
25/02/1997	PLYMOUTH ARGYLE	H	2	0	6005	1	3	10			6	7		8B		11A				4		9		5		2	B			A					CURETON 2		
01/03/1997	WALSALL	H	0	1	5891	1	3	10B			6	7	8A			11				4		9		5		2	B			A							
08/03/1997	WYCOMBE WANDERERS	A	0	2	5386	1	3	10B			6A	7	A	8		11						9		5		2	4			B							
16/03/1997	BRISTOL CITY	H	1	2	8078	1	3A				6	7		8B		11				4C	10	9		5		2	B		A	C					ALSOP		
18/03/1997	WATFORD	A	0	1	6139	1	3			C	6	7				B						9	A	5		2	4		8C	10B	11A						
23/03/1997	PRESTON NORTH END	H	1	0	6405	1		3			6	7				11				4		9	10	5		2				8					CURETON		
29/03/1997	PETERBOROUGH UNITED	A	2	1	6132	1		3			6	7				11		10		4A		9				2	A			8		5			ALSOP	BEADLE	
31/03/1997	WREXHAM	H	2	0	6225	1		3			6	7				11		10A		4		9				2			A	8		5			SKINNER	BEADLE	
05/04/1997	STOCKPORT COUNTY	A	0	1	5689	1		3B			6					11		10C		4		9		A		2	7		B	8		5A	C				
08/04/1997	MILLWALL	H	1	0	5324	1		7								11		10A		4B		9	A	6		2			B	8		5	3		SKINNER		
12/04/1997	CREWE ALEXANDRA	A	0	1	4281	1		7								11		10B		4		9	B	6		2			A	8A		5	3				
20/04/1997	NOTTS COUNTY	H	1	0	6309	1		7										10A		4		9	A	6			2		11	8		5	3		BENNETT		
26/04/1997	BLACKPOOL	A	2	3	6673	1	5	7A								A		10	B	4		9		6			2B		11	8			3		CURETON	PARMENTER	
03/05/1997	ROTHERHAM UNITED	H	1	2	5950			7B								B		10C	C	4A	3	9		6	1	2			11	8		5		A	MONINGTON og		
	APPEARANCES					44	25	36	24	26	38	29	21	22	18	36	3	10	0	29	16	33	5	18	2	26	12	5	6	10	1	7	4	0			
	SUB					0	0	3	2	1	0	2	3	3	3	6	1	4	3	5	0	5	6	3	0	0	5	1	5	6	0	0	1	1			
	GOALS					0	0	1	2	1	2	1	2	2	2	12	0	2	0	2	0	11	0	0	0	0	0	2	1	3	0	0	0	0	OWN GOAL 1		
	SUBD					0	1	8	0	1	1	2	5	5	4	6	1	7	0	6	1	8	2	0	0	0	5	1	1	2	1	1	0	0			
	COCA-COLA CUP																																				
20/08/1996	LUTON TOWN	A	0	3	2643	1	2	3	4	5	6	7	8A	9B	10	11		B	A																		
04/09/1996	LUTON TOWN	H	2	1	2320	1	2	3	4	5	6	7	8A	9	10		A	11B	B																ARCHER	GURNEY	
	FA CUP																																				
16/11/1996	EXETER CITY	H	1	2	5841	1		5C	4		6A	7		8B		11	B	C		A	3	9	10			2									PARMENTER		
	AUTO WINDSCREEN SHIELD																																				
10/12/1996	BRETFORD	H	1	2	2752	1	2	A	4	5	6		8B		10C			C		B	3A	11					7	9							HARRIS		
	GLOUCESTERSHIRE CUP																																				
17/08/1996	BRISTOL CITY	A	0	1	4932	1		11A	4	5	6	7	2	B	A	9		10B	8C	C	3																

This was the last ever final competed for between just Rovers and Bristol City

1997/98

Date	Opponent				Att	COLLETT Andrew	PERRY Jason	POWER Graeme	PARMENTER Stephen	GAYLE Brian	TILLSON Andrew	HOLLOWAY Ian	PENRICE Gary	ALSOP Julian	CURETON Jamie	HAYLES Barrington	FOSTER Stephen	RAMASUT Thomas	BEADLE Peter	WHITE Thomas	BENNETT Frank	PRITCHARD David	HIGGS Shane	ZABEK Lee	LOW Joshua	LOCKWOOD Matthew	FRENCH Jonathan	HAYFIELD Matthew	BASFORD Luke	WHYTE David	SKINNER Justin	JONES Lee	SMITH Mark	Scorers		
	DIVISION 2 (3)																																			
09/08/1997	PLYMOUTH ARGYLE	H	1	1	7386	1	2	3A	4B	5	6	7	8	9C	10	11	A	B	C															HAYLES		
16/08/1997	YORK CITY	A	1	0	3307	1	2			5	6	7	8	9	10	11		A		3	4A													HAYLES		
23/08/1997	CARLISLE UNITED	H	3	1	6044	1	2			5	6	7	4	9	10A	11			A	3	8													BENNETT	HAYLES	PENRICE
30/08/1997	BURNLEY	A	0	0	9887	1	2			5	6	7	4	9	10	11		A			8A	3														
02/09/1997	AFC BOURNEMOUTH	A	1	1	5550	1	2			5		7	4	9A	10	11		B	A	6	8B	3												CURETON pen		
09/09/1997	WALSALL	H	2	0	6225	1	2			5	6	7	4		10	11		8	9			3												RAMASUT	HAYLES	
13/09/1997	GILLINGHAM	H	1	2	6572	1	2			5	6	7	4	B	10A	11		8	9B		A	3												HAYLES		
20/09/1997	CHESTERFIELD	A	0	0	5309	1	2			5	6	7	4		10A	11		8	9		A	3														
27/09/1997	OLDHAM ATHLETIC	A	4	4	5990		2			5	6	7	4B		10A	11	B	8	9		A	3	1											BEADLE 2	HAYLES	CURETON pen
04/10/1997	WREXHAM	H	1	0	6829	1	2			5	6	7	4		10B	11	3	8	9A		A			B										RAMASUT		
14/10/1997	WATFORD	H	1	2	8110	1	2			5	6	7	4	8	10A	11	3		9						A									PENRICE		
18/10/1997	WYCOMBE WANDERERS	A	0	1	5836	1	2			5	6		4	8A	10	11	3		9							7	A									
21/10/1997	BRENTFORD	A	3	2	3967	1	2			5	6	7	4			11	3	8	9							10								HAYLES 2	BEADLE	
25/10/1997	BLACKPOOL	H	0	3	6183	1	2			5C	6	7	4	C	A	11	3	8A	9						B	10B										
01/11/1997	NORTHAMPTON TOWN	A	1	1	7264	1				5	6	7	4		A	11	3A		9			2				10	8							CURETON		
04/11/1997	BRISTOL CITY	H	1	2	7552	1				5A	6	7	4	B	10	11			9	A		2				3	8B							TILLSON		
08/11/1997	FULHAM	H	2	3	6166	1					6	7	4	9	10	11	3	A		5		2				8A								PENRICE 2		
18/11/1997	PRESTON NORTH END	A	2	1	7798	1			B		6		4	9B	A	11	3A			5		2			7	10		8						PENRICE	ALSOP	
22/11/1997	SOUTHEND UNITED	A	1	1	3653	1	A		C		6		4	9B	10A	11			B	5		2			7C	3		8						BEADLE pen		
29/11/1997	MILLWALL	H	2	1	5542	1	3				6	B	4A	A		11			9	5		2			7B	10		8						BEADLE	HAYLES	
02/12/1997	WIGAN ATHLETIC	A	0	3	2738	1	3		B		6	A	4C	C		11			9	5		2			7	10B		8A								
12/12/1997	GRIMSBY TOWN	H	0	4	4801	1					6	C	4A	A	B	11			9	5		2			7C	10		8B	3							
20/12/1997	LUTON TOWN	A	4	2	5266	1						7	4		10	11	6	8A	9	5						3		2	A					CURETON	HAYLES 2	BEADLE
26/12/1997	WALSALL	A	1	0	6634	1						7	4		10A	11	6	8	9	5		2				3		A						BEADLE		
28/12/1997	AFC BOURNEMOUTH	H	5	3	7256	1						7A	4	B	10	11B	6	8	9	5		2				3			A					BEADLE 3	HAYLES 2	
10/01/1998	PLYMOUTH ARGYLE	A	2	1	6850	1					C	7B	4		10C	11	6	8A	9	5	A	2		B		3								CURETON	HAYLES	
17/01/1998	BURNLEY	H	1	0	7208	1	2					7	4		10	11B	6		9	5	A					3		B	8A					CURETON		
24/01/1998	CARLISLE UNITED	A	1	3	5725	1	2					7	4		10	11	6		9	5	A					3B		B	8A					CURETON		
31/01/1998	GILLINGHAM	A	1	1	5593		2					7			10	11B	6		9	5	B		1	4		A		8A	3					CURETON pen		
07/02/1998	CHESTERFIELD	H	3	1	5481		2					7	A		10	11	6		9C	5	8	B	1	4A				C	3B					BENNETT	CURETON 2	
14/02/1998	WREXHAM	A	0	1	3716		2C	C					4		10	11	6			5	9A	3	1	7B		B		8		A						
21/02/1998	OLDHAM ATHLETIC	H	3	1	5789			3					4B		10	11	6	9		5	8A	2	1	B				A			7			HAYLES 2	RAMASUT	
24/02/1998	WYCOMBE WANDERERS	H	3	1	5805			3				A	4A		10	11	6	8	9	5		2	1							B	7B			HAYLES	BEADLE	RAMASUT
28/02/1998	WATFORD	A	2	3	12186			3				B	4B		10	11	6	8A	9	5		2	1							A	7			WHITE	CURETON	
03/03/1998	FULHAM	A	0	1	6843			3				4			10	11	6	8A	9	5B		2	1		B					A	7					
07/03/1998	NORTHAMPTON TOWN	H	0	2	6535			3			6	4			10	11	5	8A	9		7B	2		A	B							1				
10/03/1998	YORK CITY	H	1	2	4289	1	2	3A			6	7	4		10	11	5	8	9									A						RAMASUT		
14/03/1998	BRISTOL CITY	A	0	2	17086	1		3B			6	7	4		10		5	8	9		A	2			11A			B								
21/03/1998	PRESTON NORTH END	H	2	2	5278	1		3			6	7	4		10	11	5	A	9			2						8A						CURETON pen	HAYLES	
27/03/1998	SOUTHEND UNITED	H	2	0	5323		2				6	7	4		10B	11	5	8A	9	B		3						A				1		TILLSON	HAYLES	
04/04/1998	MILLWALL	A	1	1	5635		2				6		4		10	11	5	8A	9		A	3		7								1		ZABEK		
10/04/1998	WIGAN ATHLETIC	H	5	0	6038						6	4			10	11	5	8	9			2		7		3						1		HAYLES	RAMASUT	BEADLE 3
13/04/1998	GRIMSBY TOWN	A	2	1	5484						6	4			10	11	5	8	9			2		7		3						1		HAYLES 2		
18/04/1998	LUTON TOWN	H	2	1	8038						6	4			10	11	5	8	9			2		7		3						1		BEADLE	TILLSON	
25/04/1998	BLACKPOOL	A	0	1	7057						6	4A	A		10	11	5	8	9			2		7		3						1				
02/05/1998	BRENTFORD	H	2	1	9043						6		4		10B	11	5	8A	9		B	2		7		3		A				1		CURETON	HAYLES	
	APPEARANCES					30	24	9	1	16	32	34	38	10	39	45	32	25	36	22	8	32	8	9	6	22	2	9	5	0	4	8				
	SUB					0	1	1	3	0	1	5	2	7	4	0	2	6	4	2	11	1	0	4	4	2	1	9	2	4	0	0				
	GOALS					0	0	0	0	0	3	0	5	1	13	23	0	6	15	1	2	0	0	1	0	0	0	0	0	0	0	0				
	SUBD					0	1	3	1	2	0	3	7	5	11	3	2	9	3	1	6	0	0	2	4	4	1	4	3	0	1	0				
	PLAY-OFFS																																			
10/05/1998	NORTHAMPTON TOWN	H	3	1	9173			A			6		4			11	5	8A	9		10B	2		7		3		B				1		BEADLE pen	BENNETT	HAYLES
13/05/1998	NORTHAMPTON TOWN	A	0	3	7501			B			6		4			11	5	8A	9		10B	2		7		3		A				1				
	COCA-COLA CUP																																			
11/08/1997	BRISTOL CITY	A	0	0	9341	1	2			5	6	7	8	9	10	11	3		4A		A															
26/08/1997	BRISTOL CITY	H	1	2	5872	1	2			5	6	7	8	9A	10B	11			A		4	3				B								ALSOP		
	AET 1-1 at 90 mins																																			
	FA CUP																																			
14/11/1997	GILLINGHAM	H	2	2	4825	1					6	7	4	9B		11	3			5		2A			A	10	B	8						ALSOP	HOLLOWAY	
28/11/1997	GILLINGHAM	A	2	0	4459	1	3				6		4			11			9	5		2			7A	10	A	8						HAYLES	PENRICE	
05/12/1997	WISBECH TOWN	A	2	0	3593	1	3				6		4			11			9	5		2			7	10		8						BEADLE	HAYLES	
03/01/1998	IPSWICH TOWN	H	1	1	8610	1						7	4		10	11	6	8A	9	5	A	2				3								BEADLE		
13/01/1998	IPSWICH TOWN	A	0	1	11362	1	C					7	4		10B	11	6	8A	9	5	B	2C				3		A								
	AUTO WINDSCREENS SHIELD																																			
08/12/1997	CAMBRIDGE UNITED	H	1	0	2386		5		8B		A	4		10C	11	C			9			2	1		7	B			3				6A	CURETON		
06/01/1998	EXETER CITY	A	2	1	1851	1					5			9A		B	6				8			4	11B	10		7	3				2	BENNETT	TILLSON	
28/01/1998	WALSALL	H	0	1	4165		2					7	4		10	11	6		9A	5			1			3			8	A						
	AET 0-0 at 90 mins. Lost in sudden death 91 mins																																			

1998/99

Date	Opponent	H/A	F	A	Att	JONES Lee	TREES Robert	CHALLIS Trevor	ZABEK Lee	FOSTER Stephen	ANDREASSON Marcus	HOLLOWAY Ian	MEAKER Michael	ROBERTS Jason	CURETON Jamie	HAYLES Barrington	IPOUA Guy	BASFORD Luke	LEONI Stephane	SMITH Mark	PENRICE Gary	TILLSON Andrew	LOW Joshua	COLLETT Andrew	SHORE James	TROUGHT Michael	McKEEVER Mark (L)	LEE David	THOMSON Andrew	PRITCHARD David	PETHICK Robert	ELLINGTON Nathan	HILLIER David	PHILLIPS Martin (L)	KUIPERS Michel	ANDREWS Bradley	WILLIAMS Anthony (L)	BENNETT Frank	JOHNSTON Raymond	Scorers			
	DIVISION 2 (3)																																										
08/08/1998	BURNLEY	A	1	2	11781	1	2	3	4	5	6	7	8	9	10A	11	A																							CURETON			
15/08/1998	READING	H	4	1	7529	1	2	3	4A	5	6	7	8	9	10	11		A																						HAYLES	MEAKER	CURETON pen	ROBERTS
22/08/1998	GILLINGHAM	A	0	0	4896	1	2	3		5		7A	8C	9B	10	11	B		4	6	A	C																					
29/08/1998	WIGAN ATHLETIC	H	3	2	6140	1	2	3		5		7	8	9	10A	11	A		4			6																		HAYLES 2	IPOUA		
31/08/1998	WYCOMBE WANDERERS	A	1	1	4318	1	4			5		7		9	10B	11	A	3	2		B	6	8A																	HAYLES			
05/09/1998	PRESTON NORTH END	H	2	2	6702		4			5		7	8	A	10	11	9A	3	2B	B		6		1																HAYLES	TILLSON		
08/09/1998	CHESTERFIELD	H	0	0	5416		7			5			8C	A	10	11	9A	3	2B	B	4	6		1	C																		
12/09/1998	LUTON TOWN	A	0	2	5558		4			5		7A	8	9	10	11		3	2			6		1	A																		
19/09/1998	LINCOLN CITY	H	3	0	6091	1	4	3		5				9	10	11			2			6	7		8															CURETON	HAYLES 2		
26/09/1998	YORK CITY	A	0	1	3305	1	4C	3		5		C	A	9B	10	11	B		2			6	7A		8																		
03/10/1998	AFC BOURNEMOUTH	H	1	0	7526	1	4	3	C	5		A	8B	9	10C	11	B		2A	6					7															SHORE			
10/10/1998	NORTHAMPTON TOWN	A	1	3	6023	1	4	3	A	5		C	8	9	10B	11	B		2A	6					7C															MEAKER			
17/10/1998	WREXHAM	H	0	0	6072	1		3	4B	5		7	8		10A	11	9		2	6	B		A																				
20/10/1998	STOKE CITY	H	1	0	6752	1	A	3	4	5		7	8		10B	11	9		2A	6	B																			CURETON			
24/10/1998	NOTTS COUNTY	A	1	1	4822	1	2		4	6		7			10B		9	A	3	5	11		8A		B															SHORE			
31/10/1998	WALSALL	H	3	4	5753	1	3		4	5		7	8A	C	10C	11	9	A	2B	6					B															CURETON	HAYLES 2		
07/11/1998	FULHAM	A	0	1	11575	1	8B	3		5		7	B	A	10	11	9A		2	6	4																						
10/11/1998	BLACKPOOL	H	0	2	5361	1	2	3A	4B	5			8	C	10C	11	9		A	6	B				7																		
21/11/1998	MILLWALL	A	1	1	5755	1	2	3		5		4	8A	11	10		9B		A	6	B				7															ROBERTS			
28/11/1998	OLDHAM ATHLETIC	H	2	2	5614	1	2	3		5		4	8	11	10		A			6	9				7A															CURETON	ROBERTS		
12/12/1998	MANCHESTER CITY	A	0	0	24976	1	8	3	4	5				11C	10		9B		2	A	C				7	6A	B																
18/12/1998	MACCLESFIELD TOWN	H	0	0	5039	1	8A	3	4	5				11	10		9B		2		B				7	6	A																
28/12/1998	COLCHESTER UNITED	A	3	0	4609	1		3				4	8	11A	10		A		2						7	6	9	5												CURETON	ROBERTS	IPOUA	
09/01/1999	BURNLEY	H	3	4	7129	1		3		5		4	8	11	10				2		A				7A		9	6												CURETON	ROBERTS	LEE	
16/01/1999	READING	A	6	0	13258	1	4	3		5		7		11	10				2								9	8	6											CURETON 4	ROBERTS 2		
30/01/1999	COLCHESTER UNITED	H	1	1	6249	1	4	3		5		7		11	10						B					A	8	9B	6	2A										ROBERTS			
06/02/1999	PRESTON NORTH END	A	2	2	12170	1	4C	3		5		7A		11	10				A		B		C				9	8B	6	2A										CURETON	ROBERTS		
20/02/1999	LUTON TOWN	H	1	0	6361	1	4	3				9		11	10						A	6	8A		7				5		2									TILLSON			
23/02/1999	GILLINGHAM	H	0	1	5735	1		3		B		4		11	10C		9A				A	6			7			8B	5		2	C											
27/02/1999	LINCOLN CITY	A	0	1	4235	1	4A	3						11	10							6			7				5		2	A	8	9									
06/03/1999	YORK CITY	H	2	0	5749	1		3		6		7		11	10				4										5		2	A	8	9A						ROBERTS	ELLINGTON		
09/03/1999	AFC BOURNEMOUTH	A	0	1	7181					6		7		11	10			3	4B		9A				B				5	2		A	8		1								
12/03/1999	FULHAM	H	2	3	8011	1	4B	3		6		7		11	10										9	A			5A		2	B	8							THOMSON	ROBERTS		
20/03/1999	WALSALL	A	3	3	4967	1	A	3		6		4		11	10										7A	B			5		2B		8			9				CURETON 3-1 pen			
23/03/1999	WYCOMBE WANDERERS	H	0	2	4833	1	4A	3		6		7		11	10				2							5						A	8			9							
27/03/1999	NOTTS COUNTY	H	1	1	5899		4	3		B					10		11C		2		A	6						7	5			C	8A			9B	1			IPOUA			
30/03/1999	WIGAN ATHLETIC	A	0	1	3568	1	4A	3		2		9B			10		11				B		A			6		7	5				8										
03/04/1999	WREXHAM	A	0	1	3087		4	3		9	6	A			10		11C				B					8A		7	5	C	2B						1						
05/04/1999	NORTHAMPTON TOWN	H	1	1	6580			3		6	11	7			10						9							8	5	2	4A	A					1			PENRICE			
10/04/1999	STOKE CITY	A	4	1	17823			3		4		7		11	10				B		9A	6						A	5	2			8B				1			ROBERTS	FOSTER	CURETON 2	
13/04/1999	OLDHAM ATHLETIC	A	1	2	3913			3		4		7		11	10						9	6							5	2			8				1			ROBERTS			
20/04/1999	CHESTERFIELD	A	0	0	2621			3		4		9		11	10							6			7				5	2			8				1						
24/04/1999	BLACKPOOL	A	2	1	5033		7			4					10			3	C		9A	6			B				5	2		11B	8C				1	A		CURETON 2-1pen	ROBERTS 2		
27/04/1999	MILLWALL	H	3	0	5755		A	3		4		9		11	10							6			7B				5	2			8A				1	B		CURETON	ROBERTS 2		
01/05/1999	MANCHESTER CITY	H	2	2	8033		8A	3		4		7		11	10						9	6							5	2							1	A		ROBERTS	CURETON pen		
08/05/1999	MACCLESFIELD TOWN	A	4	3	3186		11	3		4	C		A		10				7A			6							5	8	2C	B						9B	1	CURETON 3-1pen	BENNETT		
	APPEARANCES					32	33	38	9	41	4	33	17	32	46	17	15	6	25	11	10	18	5	3	18	6	5	10	21	11	9	1	13	2	1	3	9	1	1				
	SUB					0	3	0	2	2	1	4	3	5	0	0	9	3	5	3	16	1	3	0	6	3	2	1	0	1	0	9	0	0	0	0	0	3	0				
	GOALS					0	0	0	0	1	0	0	2	16	25	9	3	0	0	0	1	2	0	0	2	0	0	1	1	0	0	1	0	0	0	0	0	1	0				
	SUBD					0	9	1	3	0	0	4	5	4	11	0	9	0	8	0	3	0	4	0	5	2	0	3	1	2	4	1	4	1	0	1	0	1	0				
	WORTHINGTON CUP																																										
11/08/1998	LEYTON ORIENT	A	1	1	2663	1	B	3	4	5	6B	7	8	9	A	11	10A			2																				CURETON			
18/08/1998	LEYTON ORIENT *	H	1	2	4235	1	2	3B	4A	5	6	7C	8	9	10	11	C		B		A																			HAYLES			
	AET 0-0 at 90 mins																																										
	THE AXA FA CUP																																										
14/11/1998	WELLING UNITED	H	3	0	5381	1	2	3		5		7	8	11	10		9A			6					A															ROBERTS 3			
05/12/1998	EXETER CITY	A	2	2	4352	1	4	3	A	5		7	8A		10		11		2	6	9																			PENRICE	CURETON		
15/12/1998	EXETER CITY	H	5	0	5093	1	8	3	4	5				11	10		9		2						7	6														ZABEK	SHORE 2	CURETON	ROBERTS
02/01/1999	ROTHERHAM UNITED	A	1	0	6056	1	9	3		5		4	8	11	10				2						7			6												LEONI			
23/01/1999	LEYTON ORIENT	H	3	0	9274	1	4	3		5		7	8A	11	10						A					6		9		2										ROBERTS 2	LEE		
13/02/19999	BARNSLEY	A	1	4	17508	1	4	3		5				11	10				9						7	6		8		2										ROBERTS			
	AUTO WINDSCREEN SHIELD																																										
08/12/1998	WALSALL	A	2	2	2210	1	8	3	4	5				11	10A		9		2						7	6				A										CURETON	SHORE		

AET score at 90 mins 22. Lost 4-5 on pens

1999/2000

	DIVISION 2 (3)					JONES Lee	PRITCHARD David	CHALLIS Trevor	FOSTER Stephen	THOMSON Andrew	TILLSON Andrew	MAUGE Ronald	HILLIER David	CURETON Jamie	ROBERTS Jason	PETHICK Robert	BENNETT Frank	ANDREASSON Marcus	ELLINGTON Nathan	BRYANT Simon	PENRICE Gary	TAYLOR Stuart J (L)	LEONI Stephane	ZABEK Lee	ZAMORA Robert	WALTERS Mark	TROUGHT Michael	WHITE Thomas	PARKIN Brian	MEAKER Michael	BYRNE Shaun (L)	TREES Robert	ASTAFJEVS Vitalijs	EVANS Rhys (L)	PIERRE Nigel	STEWART Jordan (L)	WOLLEASTON Robert (L)			
07/08/1999	BRENTFORD	H	0	0	8514	P	P	P	P	P	P	P	P	P	P	PA	A																							
14/08/1999	GILLINGHAM	A	1	0	6234	P	P	P	P		P	P	P	PA	P	PB	A	P	B																			ROBERTS		
21/08/1999	OXFORD UNITED	H	1	0	7617	P	PA	P	P	P	P	P	P	P	P	P			A																			ROBERTS		
28/08/1999	WREXHAM	A	1	2	3365	P	P	P	P	P	P		P	P	P	P			A	PA																		CURETON		
30/08/1999	BURNLEY	H	1	0	7624	P	P	P	P	P	P		P	P	P	P				PA	A																	CURETON pen		
04/09/1999	SCUNTHORPE UNITED	A	2	0	4496	P	P	P	P	P	P		P	P	P	P				PA	A																	ROBERTS 2		
11/09/1999	WIGAN ATHLETIC	A	1	3	6927	P	PB	P	P	P	P	P	P	PA	P	P	B				A																	ROBERTS		
18/09/1999	OLDHAM ATHLETIC	H	3	2	6574	P	P	P	P	P	P	P	P	P	PA	P	A																					CURETON 2	FOSTER	
25/09/1999	NOTTS COUNTY	A	2	0	6197			P	P	P	P	P	PA	P	P	P			A	P		P																CURETON pen	TILLSON	
02/10/1999	BLACKPOOL	H	3	1	7715		P	PA	P	P	P	P	PB	P	PC	P			C	B		P	A															CURETON 2-1pen	ROBERTS	
09/10/1999	CARDIFF CITY	H	1	1	7363		P	P	P	P	P	P	P	P	P	P						P																THOMSON		
17/10/1999	BRISTOL CITY	A	0	0	16011		PA	PC	P	P	P	P	P	PB	P	P			B	A		P	C																	
19/10/1999	AFC BOURNEMOUTH	A	1	0	5613	P	PA	P	P	P	P	P	P	P	P	P			A																			CURETON		
23/10/1999	NOTTS COUNTY	H	0	1	8188	P	PA	P	P	P	P	PB	P	P	P	P			A	B																				
02/11/1999	BURY	H	0	0	5397	P		P	P	P	P		P	P	P	P				P				P																
06/11/1999	WYCOMBE WANDERERS	A	1	1	5167	P	P	P	P	P	P	P	P	PB			A		P	PA					B													ELLINGTON		
20/11/1999	CHESTERFIELD	A	1	0	2875	P	P	P	P	P	P		P	PC	P	PA	A		C					PB		B												PRITCHARD		
27/11/1999	LUTON TOWN	H	3	0	7805	P	P	B	P	P	P	P	P	P	P	PA	A									PB												THOMSON	WALTERS	CURETON
04/12/1999	BRENTFORD	A	3	0	6843	P	P	B	P	P	P	P		P	P	P			A	PA						PB												ROBERTS 2	WALTERS	
11/12/1999	COLCHESTER UNITED	H	2	1	7023	P	P	B	P	P	P	P		P	P	P			A	PA						PB												ROBERTS 2		
18/12/1999	STOKE CITY	A	2	1	10379	P	P	B	P	P	P	PA	P	P	P	PB	C		A							PC												ROBERTS	WALTERS	
26/12/1999	MILLWALL	H	1	0	10077	P		P	P	P	PA		P	P	P		B		P	PB				A		PC	C											ROBERTS		
28/12/1999	PRESTON NORTH END	A	1	2	16680	P		P	P	P		P	P	P	P		B		P				A			PB		PA										WALTERS		
03/01/2000	CAMBRIDGE UNITED	H	1	0	9822	PA	P	P	P	PB	P	P	P	PC	P				B							P			A	C								ROBERTS		
08/01/2000	COLCHESTER UNITED	A	4	5	4482	P	P	P	P				P	P	P	A			B							P	P	PA			PB							ROBERTS 2	CURETON pen	ELLINGTON
15/01/2000	GILLINGHAM	H	2	1	8331			P	P	P		P		PA	P	P			A							P		P	P			P						CURETON	ROBERTS	
22/01/2000	OXFORD UNITED	A	5	0	7355	P		P	P	P	P	PA		P		P			PB				B			P					A	P						CURETON 3	PETHICK	ELLINGTON
29/01/2000	WREXHAM	H	3	1	8196	P		P		P	P	P		P	P	PA			B							PB	P					P	A					CURETON	TREES	ROBERTS
05/02/2000	BURNLEY	A	0	1	13526	P		PA	P	P	P	P		P	P				A						B	P						PB	P							
12/02/2000	SCUNTHORPE UNITED	H	1	1	8236	P			P	P	P		P	P	P	P			A							P						P	PA					WALTERS		
19/02/2000	LUTON TOWN	A	4	1	6520	P		P	P	P	P		P	P	P	P										P							P					ROBERTS 2	CURETON 2	
26/02/2000	OLDHAM ATHLETIC	A	4	1	5839			P	P	P	P		P	P	PB	P			C							PC						A	PA	P	B			CURETON 2-1pen	ASTAFJEVS	THOMSON
04/03/2000	WIGAN ATHLETIC	H	1	1	11109			P	P	P	P		P	P		P			P					PA		P						A		P				GREEN og		
07/03/2000	WYCOMBE WANDERERS	H	1	0	8053				P	P	P		P	P	P	P			P				P			PA								P	A			ELLINGTON		
11/03/2000	BURY	A	0	0	4049				P	P	P		P	P	P	P			A				B			PA							P	P	PB					
18/03/2000	CHESTERFIELD	H	3	1	8765	P		P	PA	P	P		PC	P		P			P						B	PB				A		C	P					WALTERS	CURETON	ASTAFJEVS
22/03/2000	READING	A	0	2	11707	P		P	P	P	PA		P	P	P	P			A						B	PB							P							
25/03/2000	MILLWALL	A	0	3	12858	P		P	PA	P	P			P	P	P			PB							B							P			P	A			
01/04/2000	STOKE CITY	H	3	3	9312	P		P		P	P		P	P	PB	P		P	B							P							PA				A	PETHICK	CURETON pen	WALTERS
04/04/2000	READING	H	0	1	7771	P		PB		P	P		PA	PC	P	P		P	C							P							P			B	A			
08/04/2000	CAMBRIDGE UNITED	A	1	1	4536	P		PA	P	P	P		P	P	P	P			B				C			P							PB			AC		ROBERTS		
15/04/2000	PRESTON NORTH END	H	0	2	10111	P			P	P	P		P	P		PA			P				PB			P							P			B	A			
22/04/2000	BRISTOL CITY	H	2	0	10805	P			P	P	P		P	P	P	P		P	P							P												ROBERTS	WALTERS	
24/04/2000	BLACKPOOL	A	1	2	5635	P			P	P	P		P	P	P	P		PB	PA	AC						P						C	B	6				ROBERTS		
29/04/2000	AFC BOURNEMOUTH	H	2	2	8847	P		P	P		P		PC	P	P	P		PA	A	B						PB	C						P					WALTERS	CURETON	
06/05/2000	CARDIFF CITY	A	0	1	6655			P	P	P	P		PA	P	P	PB			PC	A						P			P			C	B							
	APPEARANCES					36	21	36	43	43	43	22	39	46	41	40	0	6	12	9	0	4	2	3	0	28	2	3	2	0	1	5	13	4	1	1	0			
	SUB					0	0	4	0	0	0	0	0	0	0	1	10	0	25	6	3	0	6	1	4	2	2	0	1	2	1	5	3	0	2	3	4			
	GOALS					0	1	0	1	3	1	0	0	22	22	2	0	0	4	0	0	0	0	0	0	9	0	0	0	0	0	1	2	0	0	0	0	OWN GOAL 1		
	SUBD					1	5	5	2	1	2	3	6	8	4	8	0	2	4	8	0	0	1	2	0	13	0	2	0	0	1	1	4	0	1	1	0			
	WORTHINGTON CUP																																							
10/08/1999	LUTON TOWN	A	2	0	2984	P	P	P	P	P	P	P	P	P	P	PA																A						ROBERTS 2		
25/08/1999	LUTON TOWN	H	2	2	4414	P	P	P	P	P	P	P	P	P	P	PA				A																		ROBERTS	CURETON	
14/09/1999	BIRMINGHAM CITY	A	0	2	17457	P	PA		P	P	P	P	PB	P	P	P	B			A			P																	
21/09/1999	BIRMINGHAM CITY	H	0	1	5456	P	PA	P	P	P	P	P	PB	PC	P	P				A					B					C										
	THE AXA FA CUP																																							
21/10/1999	PRESTON NORTH END	H	0	1	6145	P		PB	P	P	P	PA	P	P	P	P			B		A			P	C															
	AUTO WINDSCREEN SHIELD																																							
11/01/2000	NORTHAMPTON TOWN *	A	0	0	2443				P			P	PB	PA	P	P			P							A	P	P	P		P	B								
24/01/2000	READING	H	1	2	4948	P	P	P	PA	P	P	P		P	P	P			A							B					PB							CURETON pen		

* AET Won 5-3 on pens

2000/01

	DIVISION 2 (3)					CULKIN Nicholas (L)	FOSTER Stephen	THOMSON Andrew	FORAN Mark	CURETON Jamie	PETHICK Robert	ASTAFJEVS Vitalijs	ELLINGTON Nathan	BIGNOT Marcus	WILSON Che	JONES Scott	CAMERON Martin	BRYANT Simon	HOGG Lewis	EVANS Michael	ELLIS Clinton	WALTERS Mark	PARKIN Brian	GLENNON Matthew (L)	ANDREASSON Marcus	CHALLIS Trevor	DAGNOGO Moussa	PLUMMER Dwayne	MEAKER Michael	ALLSOPP Daniel (L)	HILLIER David	JOHANSEN Rune	BARRETT Graham (L)	MAUGE Ronald	RICHARDS Justin	OWUSU Ansah (L)	McKEEVER Mark	PARTRIDGE Richard (L)	LEE Christian	GALL Kevin				
12/08/2000	AFC BOURNEMOUTH	H	1	1	8046	P	P	P	P	P	PA	P	PC	P	PB	P	A	B	C																						CURETON			
20/08/2000	PETERBOROUGH UNITED	A	2	2	6997	P	P	P			C	P	PA	P	P	P	A	P	PC	PB	B																				EVANS	ELLINGTON		
28/08/2000	BRENTFORD	A	6	2	5434	P	P	P				P	PB	P	P	P	BC	P	P	PA	A	C																			ASTAFJEVS 2	ELLINGTON	HOGG 2	JONES
09/09/2000	NOTTS COUNTY	A	1	1	5511	P	P	P				P	P	P	PA	P		P	P	P		A																			ELLINGTON			
12/09/2000	WYCOMBE WANDERERS	A	1	0	4718	PA	P	P				P	PB	P	P	P		P	P	P		B	A																		FOSTER			
16/09/2000	WIGAN ATHLETIC	H	0	0	8109		P		B		PB	P	PC	P	PA	P		P	P	P	C	A		P																				
23/09/2000	CAMBRIDGE UNITED	A	3	0	4624	P	P					P	PA	P	P	P		P	P	P	A				P																BRYANT	EVANS	JONES	
30/09/2000	LUTON TOWN	H	3	3	7901	P	P					P	PC	P	P	P		P	P		PA	PB				A	B	C													FOSTER	ELLINGTON 2		
06/10/2000	BURY	A	0	1	3279	PA	P		B				P	P	P	P			P		PB		A		PC	P		P	C															
14/10/2000	NORTHAMPTON TOWN	H	0	1	7704	P	P		P			P		P	PB	P			PA	P	B	P						A		P														
17/10/2000	ROTHERHAM UNITED	H	1	1	6910	P	P		P			P	P	P	PA			P		P		A				P		PB		B											EVANS			
21/10/2000	SWINDON TOWN	A	3	1	8097	P			P			P		P		P		P		PC	B	PB			P	P	C			PA	A										ANDREASSON	M WILLIAMS og	EVANS pen	
24/10/2000	COLCHESTER UNITED	A	1	2	2951	P	P				A	P				P		P	PB	P	B	PA			P	P				P											ELLIS			
28/10/2000	OLDHAM ATHLETIC	H	0	2	6110	P	P		P			P	B	P	P	P	A	P	PA	PB		C								PC														
04/11/2000	OXFORD UNITED	A	1	0	5407	P	P		P			PA	P	P	P	P		P	P	PB		A								B											FOSTER			
11/11/2000	WALSALL	H	0	0	7540	P	P	P			P	P	P		A	P		PA	PB	P		P										B												
22/11/2000	MILLWALL	H	1	2	5502	P	P	PA	P			B	PC	PB			P	P	P		C	A				P					P										CAMERON			
25/11/2000	WREXHAM	A	0	1	2575	P	P	P			P	A	B			P	PC	P	P			PB				P					PA	C												
02/12/2000	SWANSEA CITY	A	0	0	5563	P	P	P				P	P	P		P		P	PA	P		A				P																		
16/12/2000	STOKE CITY	H	0	3	6838	P	P	P	PB			P	P	P		P				P		A				PA					P		B											
22/12/2000	BRISTOL CITY	A	2	3	16696	P	P	P			PC	B	PB	P		P	P	P	P	PA									A					C							BIGNOT	CAMERON		
26/12/2000	READING	H	2	2	8029	P	P	P				PA	P	P		C	PB		P	B		PC				P			A					P							ELLINGTON	THOMSON		
13/01/2001	BRENTFORD	H	0	0	6933	P	P	P			P	P	PB		P			PA		P	B	A							P					P										
20/01/2001	READING	A	0	1	11767	P	P	P				P	P	P	P		B	PC		PA								C	PB					P	A									
03/02/2001	MILLWALL	A	0	3	10828	P	P	P				P		P	PB		B		P		A	PA						P						P	P									
10/02/2001	NOTTS COUNTY	H	0	0	6914	P	P	P					PA		P		A		P							P		P						P		P	P							
17/02/2001	WIGAN ATHLETIC	A	0	0	7271	P	P	PA				PB	C		P	A		B	P							P								P	PC	P	P							
24/02/2001	CAMBRIDGE UNITED	H	2	1	7079	P	P					P	B	PA	P	P		P	A		C					P									PB	P	PC				ASTAFJEVS	ELLINGTON		
27/02/2001	AFC BOURNEMOUTH	A	2	1	3466	P	P	A					PB	P	P	P		P	P							PA									B	P	P				ELLINGTON 2			
03/03/2001	LUTON TOWN	A	0	0	7405	P	P					A	P	P	P	P		PA			B					P		P								PB	P							
06/03/2001	NORTHAMPTON TOWN	A	1	2	4552	P	P					P	P	P	PB	P										P		P						A	B	P	PA				ELLINGTON			
10/03/2001	BURY	H	2	0	7065	P	P	P				B	P	P	PC	P			PB	A								P						P		PA	C				FOSTER	PLUMMER		
17/03/2001	ROTHERHAM UNITED	A	0	3	7098	P	P	P				P	P		P	PB				P	C					B		P						PC		PA	A							
24/03/2001	SWINDON TOWN	H	0	0	8114	P	P	P					P		P	P		P								B		P								AB	PA	P	P					
31/03/2001	STOKE CITY	A	1	4	12274	P	P	P				B	P		P	P		P										P								PB	A	PA	PC	C	GALL			
03/04/2001	BRISTOL CITY	H	1	1	9361	P	P	P					P		P	P			PA							P		P						P					P	A	LEE			
07/04/2001	SWANSEA CITY	H	1	0	6505	P	P	P			P	P	PA		P	P			P							P										B			PB	A	HOGG			
09/04/2001	PORT VALE	A	0	1	3962	P	P	P			PA	P	PB		P	P		A	PC							P									C				P	B				
11/04/2001	PETERBOROUGH UNITED	H	1	2	6540	P	P	P				P	PB		P	P			P							P								PA		B			P	A	JONES			
14/04/2001	COLCHESTER UNITED	H	2	0	6551	P	P	P				P	B		PA	P	PB	PC	P			A												P		C				P	ASTAFJEVS	ELLINGTON		
16/04/2001	OLDHAM ATHLETIC	A	0	1	6883	P	P	P				P	A		P	P	PA	PB	P			B						P								C				PC				
21/04/2001	OXFORD UNITED	H	6	2	7554	P	P	P				P	PC		PA	P	C		P			A						P						P		B			PB		LEE	ELLINGTON 2	ASTAFJEVS	WALTERS 2-1pen
28/04/2001	WALSALL	A	1	2	7130	P	P	P			P	P	P		P	PB			PA			A						P										B	PC	C	ELLINGTON			
30/04/2001	PORT VALE	H	0	3	7340	P	P	P				PA	P			PB						P						P						P		P	A	P	B					
02/05/2001	WYCOMBE WANDERERS	H	1	2	8264	P	P	P	A		P	C	P		P							P						P						P		P		P		B	GALL			
05/05/2001	WREXHAM	H	4	0	6418	P			P		PC	P	P		P	PB		PA	C			P						P									B	A		P	WALTERS 2-1pen	PARTRIDGE	ELLINGTON	
	APPEARANCES					45	44	31	9	1	11	34	36	26	36	37	6	27	31	19	2	11	0	1	4	19	0	17	2	4	3	0	0	14	3	11	7	4	8	3				
	SUB					0	0	1	3	0	2	7	6	0	1	2	8	3	3	2	13	15	2	0	0	3	2	3	3	2	1	2	1	2	4	6	5	2	1	7				
	GOALS					0	4	1	0	1	0	5	15	1	0	3	2	1	3	4	1	4	0	0	1	0	0	1	0	0	0	0	0	0	0	0	0	1	2	2	OWN GOAL 1			
	SUBD					2	0	2	1	0	5	4	16	2	10	4	5	7	10	7	2	6	0	0	1	2	0	1	1	2	1	0	0	3	2	6	3	1	4	1				
	WORTHINGTON CUP																																											
23/08/2000	PLYMOUTH ARGYLE	A	2	1	3498	P	P	PA			P	P	PB	P	P		P	P	P		B	A																			BIGNOT	CAMERON		
05/09/2000	PLYMOUTH ARGYLE	H	1	1	5228	P	P	P	B			P	P	P	P			P	P		PA	A				PB															ELLINGTON			
20/09/2000	EVERTON	A	1	1	25564	P	P					P	PB	P	P	P		P	P	PC	B	C			PA			A													HOGG			
27/09/2000	EVERTON *	H	1	1	11045	P	P					P	P	P	P	P		PC	PB		P	A			PA			B	C												BIGNOT			
31/10/2000	SUNDERLAND	H	1	2	11433	P	P		PA			P	P	P	P	P		P	P	P		A																			ELLINGTON			
	* AET; Rovers won 4-2 on pens																																											
	THE AXA FA CUP																																											
19/11/2000	CARDIFF CITY	A	1	5	8013	P	P	P				P	P	P	P	PB		P	P		B	A										PA									JORDAN og			
	LD VANS TROPHY																																											
09/12/2000	TORQUAY UNITED	A	2	0	1370	P			P			P	P	P		P		P	PA	P						P					A										ELLINGTON	EVANS		
09/01/2001	PLYMOUTH ARGYLE	H	3	0	3781	P		P	P		B	P	PA	PB	P			P		P	A								P					P							ASTAFJEVS 2	EVANS pen		
30/01/2001	SOUTHEND UNITED	A	0	1	2192	P		PA	P			P	P	PB	P	A		P		PC		B							P					P	C									

2001/02

						HOWIE Scott	CHALLIS Trevor	FOSTER Stephen	THOMSON Andrew	MAUGE Ronald	GALL Kevin	WEARE Ross	WILSON Che	ELLINGTON Nathan	BRYANT Simon	TROUGHT Michael	PRITCHARD David	CAMERON Martin	HILLIER David	JONES Scott	GILROY David	BUBB Alvin	LOPEZ Rik	HAMMOND Elvis (L)	FORAN Mark	HOGG Lewis	SMITH Mark	WALTERS Mark	PLUMMER Dwayne	ROSS Neil (L)	ASTAFJEVS Vitalijs	OMMEL Sergio	SANCHEZ-LOPEZ Carlos	McKEEVER Mark	SHORE Andrew	QUINN James (L)	THOMAS James (L)	CARLISLE Wayne	TONER Ciaran	RICHARDS Justin	ARNDALE Neil	CLARKE Ryan			
	DIVISION 3(4)																																												
11/08/2001	TORQUAY UNITED	H	1	0	10127	P	P	P	P	PA	P	P	P	P	P	P	AB	B																									FOSTER		
18/08/2001	SCUNTHORPE UNITED	A	2	1	3593	P	PA	P	P	P	P	PB	P	P		P		B	P	A																							ELLINGTON	WEARE	
25/08/2001	LUTON TOWN	H	3	2	9057	P		P	P	P	P		P	P		P		PA	P	P	A																						ELLINGTON	HILLIER	GALL
27/08/2001	DARLINGTON	A	0	1	4487	P		P	P	P	P		P			P		P	P	PB	PA	A	B																						
01/09/2001	SHREWSBURY TOWN	H	0	0	6942	P		P	P	P	P	PB	P			P		B	P	PA		A		P																					
08/09/2001	LEYTON ORIENT	A	1	3	5433	P		P	P	P	P		P	P		P		A	P	PA				P																			GALL		
15/09/2001	LINCOLN CITY	A	1	0	3204	P		P	P	P	P	PA	P	PC		B		A	P				PB	C	P																		GALL		
18/09/2001	SOUTHEND UNITED	H	2	1	5743	P		P	P	P	P	PA	P				B	A	PB				P	P	P																		FORAN	THOMSON	
25/09/2001	YORK CITY	H	2	2	6933	P		P	P	P	P		P	PC		B	A	P	PA				PB	C	P																		CAMERON	POTTER og	
29/09/2001	OXFORD UNITED	H	1	1	7678	P		P	PA		P		P	P	P		B	P		A			PB		P	P																	CAMERON		
06/10/2001	CARLISLE UNITED	A	0	1	1849	P		P			PC		P	P	P	P	PB	PA				C		A		P	P	B																	
13/10/2001	MACCLESFIELD TOWN	H	0	2	6554	P		P	P		P	P	P	PA	P	P						B		A		PB		P																	
20/10/2001	HALIFAX TOWN	A	0	0	1898	P	P	P	P		P		P		P			P							P			P	P																
23/10/2001	EXETER CITY	A	0	1	3899	P	P	P	P		P		P		PA			PB				B			P			P	P	A															
28/10/2001	PLYMOUTH ARGYLE	H	1	2	6889	P	PB	P	P		P		P		C			A		B	PA				P			PC	P	P													CAMERON		
03/11/2001	KIDDERMINSTER HARRIERS	A	0	2	3588	P	B	P	P	PA	A		P		PC			P		PB		C						P	P	P															
06/11/2001	CHELTENHAM TOWN	A	0	0	4913	P	P	P	P		P		P			P			P			PA			P				PB	A	B														
10/11/2001	ROCHDALE	H	0	2	5675	P	PB	P	P		P		P			P		A	P			PA			P					B	P														
20/11/2001	MANSFIELD TOWN	H	0	1	5043	P	PA	P	P			P	P			P		P	P			B						A	PB		P														
24/11/2001	HULL CITY	A	0	0	9680	P	P	P	P	P	P	PA				P			PB								P	B	P			A													
01/12/2001	RUSHDEN & DIAMONDS	A	1	3	4570	P	P	PA	P	P	B			P		PC		P	P						A		PB				P	C											CAMERON pen		
22/12/2001	SWANSEA CITY	A	1	2	2734	P	P		PA		A		P	P		P									P	P	P				P	P											ELLINGTON		
26/12/2001	LEYTON ORIENT	H	5	3	7458	P					PA		P	P		PB			P	B					P	P	P	A			P	P											ELLINGTON 3	ASTAFJEVS	OMMEL
29/12/2001	DARLINGTON	H	1	0	7567	P					B		P	P					PC	P			C		P	P	P	PB	A		PA	P											ELLINGTON		
12/01/2002	SCUNTHORPE UNITED	H	1	1	6691	P	P				PA			P				B	P	P					P	P	P	A	P			PB											ELLINGTON		
15/01/2002	SHREWSBURY TOWN	A	1	0	3475	P	P				PA			P				B	P	P					P	P	P	A	P			PB											OMMEL		
19/01/2002	TORQUAY UNITED	A	1	2	3493	P	PB			B	PA			P				C	P	P					P	P	P	A	P			PC											ELLINGTON		
22/01/2002	SWANSEA CITY	H	4	1	5725	P	P		P					P				B	P						P	PA	P	A	P		P	PB											ELLINGTON 3-1pen	OMMEL	
02/02/2002	OXFORD UNITED	A	0	0	7467	P			P	P				P				B	PA	P			P		P		P	A			P	PB													
09/02/2002	HALIFAX TOWN	H	2	0	6921	P			P				P	P					P	P					P	P	PA		A		P	P											OMMEL	ELLINGTON	
12/02/2002	HARTLEPOOL UNITED	H	0	1	6482	P			P	P	PB		PA					B		P					P	P		A			P	P	P												
16/02/2002	MACCLESFIELD TOWN	A	1	2	2149	P			P				P					C		P		P			P	P	A	PB	B		P	PC	PA										OMMEL		
19/02/2002	LUTON TOWN	A	0	3	5651	P		P	P				P	P						P					PA	PB	P	A	P			P		B											
23/02/2002	LINCOLN CITY	H	1	2	5741	P	P	P	P				P	P					P			B				PA		A			P	P		PB									OMMEL		
26/02/2002	SOUTHEND UNITED	A	1	2	2477	P	P	P	P				P	PB					P			A				P		B				P	P	PA									ELLINGTON		
05/03/2002	CHELTENHAM TOWN	H	1	2	5651	P	P				C		P	P		PC			PA	A						P	P	B			PB	P	P										OMMEL		
09/03/2002	HARTLEPOOL UNITED	A	1	1	3699	P	P	P				A	P	P					P						P	P	P					PA			P								ELLINGTON		
12/03/2002	CARLISLE UNITED	H	0	0	4557	P	P	P	C			PA	P	P					PC						P	P	PB	B				A			P										
16/03/2002	RUSHDEN & DIAMONDS	H	0	3	5240	P	P	P	A		B		P	P					P						P	P	PC	C				PB			PA										
23/03/2002	EXETER CITY	H	0	0	6105	P	PB	P					P	P	PA										P	P	A				B				P	P	P								
30/03/2002	PLYMOUTH ARGYLE	A	0	1	15732	P	P	P					P												P									P	P	P	P	P	P						
01/04/2002	KIDDERMINSTER HARRIERS	H	2	1	5711	P	P						P												P			A			C	B	PA	PC	P	PB	P	P	P				QUINN pen	OMMEL	
06/04/2002	MANSFIELD TOWN	A	0	2	3996	P	P	P					P												P	A		C				PB		PC	PA		P	P	P	B					
13/04/2002	HULL CITY	H	1	1	6340	P	P	PC			P		P			C									P	PA		B			A				PB	P	P		P				FORAN		
16/04/2002	YORK CITY	A	0	3	2983	P	P	P			PA		P												P							B		A	P	PB	P	P	P						
20/04/2002	ROCHDALE	A	1	2	5292	PB	P	P								P					C										P		PA	P		P	PC	P	P		A	B	THOMAS		
	APPEARANCES					46	28	33	29	14	25	9	38	27	8	17	1	10	27	14	2	3	5	3	30	22	17	7	12	2	14	18	6	6	9	6	7	5	6	0	0	0			
	SUB					0	1	0	2	1	6	1	0	0	1	3	4	15	0	5	2	9	2	4	1	1	2	19	3	3	4	5	0	2	0	0	0	0	0	1	1	1			
	GOALS					0	0	1	1	0	3	1	0	15	0	0	0	4	1	0	0	0	0	0	2	0	0	0	0	0	1	8	0	0	0	1	1	0	0	0	0	0	OWN GOAL 1		
	SUBD					1	6	2	2	2	7	6	1	4	3	3	2	3	7	4	2	2	3	0	1	5	4	3	2	0	2	9	3	4	3	2	1	0	0	0	0	0			
	WORTHINGTON CUP																																												
21/08/2001	WYCOMBE WANDERERS	A	1	0	3166	P		P	P	P	P	PA	P	P		P		A	P	P																							HILLIER		
11/09/2001	BIRMINGHAM CITY	H	0	3	5582	P		P	P	P	P	PA	P	P					PB	P				B	P																				
	THE AXA FA CUP																																												
17/11/2001	ALDERSHOT	A	0	0	5059	P		P	PA		PB		P			A		P	P			B			P		P		P		P														
27/11/2001	ALDERSHOT	H	1	0	4848	P	P	P	P	P		PB	P	P		P		B	PA										P		A												ASTAFJEVS		
08/12/2001	PLYMOUTH ARGYLE	A	1	1	6141	P	A		P	P	C		P	PC		P		P							P	P		B	PA		PB												WALTERS		
18/12/2001	PLYMOUTH ARGYLE	H	3	2	5763	P	P		P				P	P		P		PB	PA						P	P	C	AC			P	B											OMMEL	HOGG	ELLINGTON
06/01/2002	DERBY COUNTY	A	3	1	18549	P	P				PA		P	P		P			P						P	P	P	A				P											ELLINGTON 3		
05/02/2002	GILLINGHAM	A	0	1	9772	P	PB			PA			P	P						P			P			P	P	B			P	P		A											
	LD VANS TROPHY																																												
31/10/2001	YEOVIL TOWN *	H	1	1	4301	P		P	P	P	P		P					P		P					P				P	P													CAMERON pen		
05/12/2001	DAGENHAM & REDBRIDGE	H	4	1	3028	P	P		P	P				P		P		P							P	P			P		P												HOGG	ELLINGTON 2	OMMEL
09/01/2002	BRISTOL CITY	A	0	3	17367	P	P				P		P	P		P									P	P			P			P			P										

* AET Score at 90 mins 1-1. Rovers won 5-4 on pens

2002/03

Date	Opponent					HOWIE Scott	BOXALL Daniel	CHALLIS Trevor	UDDIN Anwar	BARRETT Adam	BRYANT Simon	McKEEVER Mark	QUINN Robert	TAIT Paul	GRAZIOLI Giuliano	CARLISLE Wayne	RICHARDS Justin	ASTAFJEVS Vitalijs	GILROY David	HOGG Lewis	GALL Kevin	WARREN Christer	AUSTIN Kevin	CLARKE Ryan	LEE David JF (L)	ARNDALE Neil	COOTE Adrian (L)	PLUMMER Christopher (L)	HYDE Graham	STREET Kevin	ALLEN Bradley	ROSE Richard (L)	PARKER Sonny	ANDERSON Ijah	LLEWELLYN Christopher (L)	Di PIEDI Michele (L)	HODGES Lee (L)	RAMMELL Andrew			
	DIVISION 3(4)																																								
10/08/2002	TORQUAY UNITED	A	1	2	4937	P	P	P	P	P	PA	PB	P	P	P	P	A	B																					GRAZIOLI		
13/08/2002	HULL CITY	H	1	1	7501	P	P	P	P	P	P	P	P	PB	P	PA		A	B																				GRAZIOLI		
17/08/2002	ROCHDALE	H	1	2	6478	P	P	P	P	P	PA	PB	P	P	P	P	B			A																			BRYANT		
24/08/2002	CARLISLE UNITED	A	0	0	6475	P	P	P	P	P			P	P	PA	P		P		P	A																				
27/08/2002	SWANSEA CITY	H	3	1	6644	P	P	P	P	P			P	P	P	P		P		P																			GRAZIOLI	TAIT	ASTAFJEVS
31/08/2002	SCUNTHORPE UNITED	A	2	2	3178	P	P	P	P	P	B	A	P	P	PC	P	C	PA		PB																			QUINN	CARLISLE pen	
08/09/2002	MACCLESFIELD TOWN	A	1	2	1814	P	P	P	P	P	B	PA	P	P	PC	P	C			PB		A																	CARLISLE		
14/09/2002	EXETER CITY	H	1	1	6498	P	P	P	P	P	PB		P	P	PA	P	A	P		B																			TAIT		
17/09/2002	BURY	H	2	1	5493	P	P	P	P	P	P		P	P	P	PA		P				A																	TAIT	GRAZIOLI	
21/09/2002	SHREWSBURY TOWN	A	5	2	3510	P	P	P	P	P	P	C	P	P	PA	PB		PC		A	B																		GRAZIOLI 3	ASTAFJEVS	CARLISLE
28/09/2002	KIDDERMINSTER HARRIERS	H	1	2	9447	P	PB	PC	P	P	PA	A	P	P	P	P		P		C			B																TAIT		
05/10/2002	DARLINGTON	A	0	1	2849	P	PC	P	P	P	PA		P	P	PB	P	B	P		A			C																		
12/10/2002	LINCOLN CITY	H	2	0	6135			P	P	P	B	PC	P	P	PA	P			A	PB	C		P	P															FUTCHER og	GRAZIOLI pen	
19/10/2002	YORK CITY	A	2	2	3616		A	PA	P	P	B	P	P		P	P	C	PC					PB	P	P														UDDIN	ASTAFJEVS	
26/10/2002	LEYTON ORIENT	H	1	2	6625	P	P		P	P	P	A	P		PB	P				B					P	PA	P												COOTE		
29/10/2002	HARTLEPOOL UNITED	A	0	2	3889	P	P		P	P	P		P	P	B	PA				P	A				PB		P														
02/11/2002	AFC BOURNEMOUTH	A	0	1	6924	P	P			P	P		P	P	A	P				P			PA		P		P														
09/11/2002	SOUTHEND UNITED	H	0	1	5691	P	P			P	P	P	P	P	B	A				P					PA		PB	P													
23/11/2002	WREXHAM	H	0	3	6328	P	P	P		P	P		P	P	P			P					P				A	PA													
30/11/2002	RUSHDEN & DIAMONDS	A	1	2	3960	P	P	PA		P	A		P	P	PB			P	C				P						P	PC	B								GRAZIOLI pen		
14/12/2002	OXFORD UNITED	H	0	2	5864	P	P			P					PB	PA		P	B		A		P						P	P	P	P									
21/12/2002	CAMBRIDGE UNITED	A	1	3	3701	P	P			P			P	P		B		A					P						P	PA	PB	P	P						ALLEN		
26/12/2002	SWANSEA CITY	A	1	0	5879	P	P			P			P	P		P		A			B		P						PA	P	PB	P							TAIT		
28/12/2002	BOSTON UNITED	H	1	1	8311	P	P			P		B	P	P		P		P	A				P							PB	PA	P							CARLISLE pen		
04/01/2003	HULL CITY	A	0	1	14913	P	PA		A	P			P	P	C	P		P			B		P							P	PC	PB									
14/01/2003	TORQUAY UNITED	H	1	1	6196	P	P			P			P	PB		P		PC	P	C	A		P							PA	B	P							CARLISLE pen		
18/01/2003	SCUNTHORPE UNITED	H	2	1	6617	P	P			P		B	P	P		P		P	PA				P							PB	A	P							ASTAFJEVS	CARLISLE	
25/01/2003	BOSTON UNITED	A	0	0	3209	P	P			P	B		P	P		P		PA	PB	A			P							P		P									
01/02/2003	CARLISLE UNITED	H	1	2	7527	P	P		P	P	A			P	PB	P		PA	B				P						P	P									GRAZIOLI		
08/02/2003	SOUTHEND UNITED	A	2	2	4708	P				P		B	P	P	P	PB							PA						P	P		P	A	P					BARRETT	STREET	
15/02/2003	AFC BOURNEMOUTH	H	0	0	6347	P	P			P		A	P	P	PB	P			B				P						P	PA				P							
22/02/2003	MACCLESFIELD TOWN	H	1	1	6005	P	P			P			P	P	B	PA		P					P						P					P	PB	A			LLEWELLYN		
01/03/2003	EXETER CITY	A	0	0	5759	P	P					B	P	A	P	P							P						P				P	P	PB	PA					
04/03/2003	BURY	A	1	0	2425	P	P			P			P	A	PB	P			B				P						P	P				P		PA			QUINN		
08/03/2003	SHREWSBURY TOWN	H	0	0	6839	P	PA			P			PC	B	PB	P		C					P						P				A	P	P	PA					
15/03/2003	LEYTON ORIENT	A	2	1	4081	P				P			P	P	PB	PA		A		C			P						P	B			P	P	PC				GRAZIOLI	TAIT	
18/03/2003	YORK CITY	H	0	1	8248	P				PB			PA	P	P	P		A					P						P	B			P	P	P						
22/03/2003	HARTLEPOOL UNITED	H	1	0	6557	P				P			P	PB				P					P						P	B			P	P	P	A	PA		HYDE		
29/03/2003	LINCOLN CITY	A	1	2	3550	P	B			P			PC	A		C		P					P						P				P	PB	P		PA	P	ASTAFJEVS		
05/04/2003	RUSHDEN & DIAMONDS	H	1	2	6736	P	PC			P			PB	B	A	C		P					P						P				P		PA		P	P	ASTAFJEVS		
08/04/2003	ROCHDALE	A	1	1	1658	P	P			P			P	A	P			P					P						P				P		P			PA	ASTAFJEVS		
12/04/2003	WREXHAM	A	2	3	5330	P	P			P			P		PA	B		P					P						PB				P		P		A	P	LLEWELLYN 2		
19/04/2003	CAMBRIDGE UNITED	H	3	1	7563	P	B			P			P	C				P					PB						P	A			P	P	P		PA	PC	RAMMELL 2	ASTAFJEVS	
21/04/2003	OXFORD UNITED	A	1	0	8732	P				P			P	B		C		PA					P						P	A			P	P	P		PC	PB	RAMMELL		
26/04/2003	DARLINGTON	H	2	1	9835	P	B			P	A		P			P							P						PA	C			PB	P	P		PC	P	RAMMELL	CARLISLE	
03/05/2003	KIDDERMINSTER HARRIERS	A	1	1	3872	P				P	P		P	P		PA							P							A			P	P	P		P		TAIT		
	APPEARANCES					44	35	16	17	45	14	7	44	33	28	35	0	26	3	8	0	0	31	2	5	1	4	2	21	13	5	9	13	14	14	3	7	7			
	SUB					0	4	0	1	0	8	9	0	8	6	6	7	7	8	9	8	2	2	0	0	0	1	0	0	7	3	0	2	0	0	2	1	0			
	GOALS					0	0	0	1	1	1	0	2	7	11	7	0	8	0	0	0	0	0	0	0	0	1	0	1	1	1	0	0	0	3	0	0	4	OWN GOAL 1		
	SUBD					0	5	3	0	1	5	4	4	3	16	9	0	7	2	3	0	0	3	0	2	1	1	1	3	6	4	1	1	1	4	3	5	3			
	LEAGUE CUP																																								
20/08/2002	BOSTON UNITED	H	0	2	4555	P	P	P	P	P		P	P	P	P	P				P																					
	FA CUP																																								
16/11/2002	RUNCORN & HALTON	H	0	0	4135	P	P	PA		P	B	PB	P	P	P	P		P					A					P													
26/11/2002	RUNCORN & HALTON *	A	3	1	2444	P	P	P		P	PB		P	P	P	PA		P	A	B			P																GRAZIOLI	CARLISLE	GILROY
07/12/2002	ROCHDALE	H	1	1	4369	P	P			P			PB	P	PA	P		P			B		P					P	P		A								ALLEN		
17/12/2002	ROCHDALE	A	2	3	2206	P	P			P	P		P	P				P					P						P		P		P						BARRETT	TAIT	

* AET score at 90 mins 1-1

2003/04

						MILLER Kevin	BOXALL Daniel	BARRETT Adam	EDWARDS Christian	ANDERSON Ijah	SAVAGE David	STREET Kevin	QUINN Robert	TAIT Paul	AGOGO Manuel	CARLISLE Wayne	WILLOCK Calum (L)	HODGES Lee	AUSTIN Kevin	HYDE Graham	BRYANT Simon	HALDANE Lewis	PARKER Sonny	RAMMELL Andrew	HOBBS Shane	WILLIAMS Ryan	UDDIN Anwar	GILROY David	ARNDALE Neil	MATTHEWS Lee (L)	CLARKE Ryan	THORPE Lee	TWIGG Gary (L)	GIBB Alistair	LESCOTT Aaron (L)	ANDERSON John	WILLIAMS Daniel	HENRIKSEN Bo			
	DIVISION 3(4)																																								
09/08/2003	SCUNTHORPE UNITED	A	2	1	4186	P	P	P	P	P	P	PB	P	P	PA	P	A	B																				BARRETT	HODGES	
16/08/2003	ROCHDALE	H	0	0	7575	P	P	P	P	P	P	PB	P	P	PA	PC		B	A	C																					
23/08/2003	CARLISLE UNITED	A	2	0	4764	P	P	P	P	P	P	P	P	P	PA	PB	A			B																			CARLISLE 2		
25/08/2003	MACCLESFIELD TOWN	H	2	2	7064	P	P	P	P	P	P	PB	PC	P	P	PA	B			A	C																		QUINN	TAIT	
30/08/2003	HUDDERSFIELD TOWN	A	1	2	8486	P	P		P	P	P	PA	PC	P	PB	C	B	A	P	P																			TAIT		
06/09/2003	KIDDERMINSTER HARRIERS	H	1	0	6791	P	P	P	P	P	P	PA	P	P	PB		B	A		P																			HODGES		
13/09/2003	BOSTON UNITED	H	2	0	6845	P	P	P	P	P	P	B	PA	P	P	A		PB		P																			TAIT 2		
16/09/2003	TORQUAY UNITED	A	1	2	3691	P	P	P	P	P		A	P	PA	P	P		P		P																			STREET		
20/09/2003	YORK CITY	A	1	2	3968	P	P	P	P	P	A	PB	PA	P	P	P		B		PC	C																		AGOGO		
27/09/2003	CHELTENHAM TOWN	H	2	0	8013	P	P	P	P	P	P	A	B	P	PC	P		PA		PB		C																	TAIT	CALISLE pen	
30/09/2003	MANSFIELD TOWN	H	1	3	8451	P	P	P	P	P	P	PA		P	PB		P		P	A	B																	TAIT		
04/10/2003	DONCASTER ROVERS	A	1	5	5439	P	P	P	PC	P	P	A	P	P	PB		PA		P		B	C																HALDANE		
11/10/2003	DARLINGTON	A	4	0	4268	P	P	P	P	P	P	C	P	PA		P		B	PB		PC		A															HALDANE	SAVAGE	RAMMELL 2
18/10/2003	CAMBRIDGE UNITED	H	0	2	6440	P	P	P	P	P	P		P	P		PB				P	PA		A	B																
21/10/2003	LEYTON ORIENT	H	1	1	5333	P	A	P	P	P	PC		P	P		B		P	P	C	PB	PA																	TAIT		
25/10/2003	OXFORD UNITED	A	0	0	6644	P		P	P	P	P		P	P				P	P		PA	P	A																		
01/11/2003	SWANSEA CITY	A	0	0	7536	P		P	P	P	P		P							P		P	P	P		P																
15/11/2003	BURY	H	1	2	7019	P		P	P	P	P			P		P				P		P	P			P														HALDANE		
22/11/2003	LINCOLN CITY	A	1	3	3882	P		P	P		P			P		P				P		P	P			P	P													CARLISLE		
29/11/2003	HULL CITY	H	2	1	6331	P		P	P	P	P		A		P	P				P		PA	P			P														R WILLIAMS	AGOGO	
13/12/2003	YEOVIL TOWN	H	0	1	9812	P		P	P	P	P				P	P				P		PA	P	A		P																
20/12/2003	SOUTHEND UNITED	A	1	0	3771	P	P	P	P	P	P		A		P	P				P		PA				PB		B												SAVAGE		
26/12/2003	NORTHAMPTON TOWN	H	1	2	7695	P		P	P	P	P				PA	P				P		P	P			P		A												CARLISLE pen		
28/12/2003	KIDDERMINSTER HARRIERS	A	0	1	3411	P		P	P	P	P		P		PA	P							P		A	P		P														
10/01/2004	SCUNTHORPE UNITED	H	1	0	5789	P		P		P	P		A		PA	P			P	P		PB	P			P			B											CARLISLE pen		
13/01/2004	MACCLESFIELD TOWN	A	1	2	1542	P		P		P	PB				PA	P			P	P	B	A	P			P				P										HALDANE		
17/01/2004	ROCHDALE	A	2	2	2497	P		P	P	P	P			B	A	P			PA	P		PB				P				P										DOUGHTY og	AGOGO	
24/01/2004	CARLISLE UNITED	H	1	0	8485	P	P	P	P		P		B	C	A	P			P	P		PB				PA				PC										CARLISLE pen		
07/02/2004	NORTHAMPTON TOWN	A	0	2	5068	P	P	P	P		P			P	A	P			P	P		B				PB				PA												
14/02/2004	DARLINGTON	H	0	3	6011	P	P	P	P	P	P			PA	P	P		B		P		A				PB																
17/02/2004	HUDDERSFIELD TOWN	H	1	1	6262		P	P	P	P	P				P				P	P	P	P										P									HYDE		
21/02/2004	CAMBRIDGE UNITED	A	1	3	3256	P	P	P	P	P	P				P			A	P		P	PA				P														BARRETT		
28/02/2004	OXFORD UNITED	H	1	1	6556	P	P	P		P	P		P	A	PA				P	PB	P	B								P										HALDANE		
02/03/2004	LEYTON ORIENT	A	1	1	3575	P	P	P		P	P		P	PB	B				P	P	P					A				PA										TAIT		
06/03/2004	SOUTHEND UNITED	H	1	1	5625	P	PA	P	A	P	P		P	P	B				P	P	PC	C								PB										TAIT		
13/03/2004	YEOVIL TOWN	A	0	4	8726	P		P	A	P	P		P	PB				P	P	PA					C			P	PC		B										
16/03/2004	TORQUAY UNITED	H	2	2	6461	P		P	P		P		P	P	B				P	PB			PA			C			A	P			PC							TAIT	PARKER	
20/03/2004	BOSTON UNITED	A	0	1	2450	P		P	P		P		PB	P	A		C	P	P			PC			B						PA	P									
27/03/2004	YORK CITY	H	3	0	6723	P		P	P				C	B	PA			P													PB	PC	P	P	P	P	A	D WILLIAMS	BARRETT	GIBB
03/04/2004	CHELTENHAM TOWN	A	2	1	5088	P		P	P	A			C		P			PC			B											PB	PA	P	P	P	P		BARRETT	AGOGO	
10/04/2004	DONCASTER ROVERS	H	1	2	8571	P		P	PA	A					P			P			C											PC	PB	P	P	P	P	B	AGOGO		
12/04/2004	MANSFIELD TOWN	A	0	0	4735	P		P	P	PB			B		PA			P	PC		A											P	C	P	P	P					
17/04/2004	SWANSEA CITY	H	2	1	7843	P		P	P	P			C	A	B			P	PC													PA		P	P	P		PB	HYDE	AGOGO	
24/04/2004	BURY	A	0	0	2683			P	P	PB				P	P				AC			B							P	C	PA	P	P	P	P				
01/05/2004	LINCOLN CITY	H	3	1	8562	P		P	P				P	P	A							B									PB	PA	P	P	P	P		TAIT 2	THORPE	
08/05/2004	HULL CITY	A	0	3	22562	P		P	P	PB	P		B	PC	A																	PA		P	P	P	P	C			
	APPEARANCES					44	23	45	40	37	37	8	23	28	28	22	0	5	21	33	7	16	13	1	0	15	1	1	1	9	2	8	7	8	8	8	6	1			
	SUB					0	1	0	2	2	1	5	10	5	10	3	5	8	2	4	5	11	3	4	2	4	0	2	2	0	0	2	1	0	0	0	0	3			
	GOALS					0	0	4	0	0	2	1	1	12	6	7	0	2	0	2	0	5	1	2	0	1	0	0	0	0	0	1	0	1	0	0	1	0	OWN GOAL 1		
	SUBD					0	1	0	2	3	2	7	5	6	15	4	0	3	2	8	2	11	3	0	0	4	0	0	0	5	0	7	6	0	0	0	0	1			
	CARLING CUP																																								
12/08/2003	BRIGHTON	H	0	1	5518	P	PB	P	P	P	P	P	P	P	PA	P		AC			B		C																			
	FA CUP																																								
08/11/2003	BOURNEMOUTH	A	0	1	7200	P		P	P		P		PA			A			P	P		PB	P	P		P		B														
	LDV VANS TROPHY																																								
14/10/2003	SOUTHEND UNITED	A	1	2	1714	P	PA	P	P	P	P	C	PC	P		P				P		PB		B			A													HALDANE		
	AET 1-1 at 90 mins																																								

2004/05

						MILLER Kevin	HINTON Craig	RYAN Robert	EDWARDS Christian	ANDERSON John	GIBB Alistair	TROLLOPE Paul	CAMPBELL Stuart	HUNT James	AGOGO Manuel	FORRESTER Jamie	SAVAGE David	ELLIOTT Steven	WALKER Richard	WILLIAMS Ryan	THORPE Lee	DISLEY Craig	LESCOTT Aaron	HALDANE Lewis	BURNS Liam	SINCLAIR Scott	WARD Elliott (L)	CLARKE Ryan	CASH Brian	SHAKES Ricky (L)	CARRUTHERS Christopher (L)	BASS Jonathan	JEANNIN Alexandre	LOUIS Jefferson	SOARES Louie	BESWETHERICK Jonathan				
	LEAGUE 2 (4)																																							
07/08/2004	MANSFIELD TOWN	A	2	0	5709	P	P	P	P	P	P	P	PB	P	PC	PA	A	B	C																		AGOGO 2			
10/08/2004	BURY	H	2	2	8705	P		P	P	P	P	PA	PB	P	P	PC	A	P	C	B																	FORRESTER pen	ANDERSON		
14/08/2004	NOTTS COUNTY	H	2	1	8225	P	B	P	P	P	PB	P	PC	P	P	PA	C	P			A																EDWARDS	AGOGO		
21/08/2004	DARLINGTON	A	1	0	3661	P	C	P	P	P	P	PB	P	P	PC	PA	B	P			A																AGOGO			
27/08/2004	SOUTHEND UNITED	H	2	1	9287	P	P	P	P	A	PC	P	PA	P	P	B	C	P			PB																THORPE	HUNT		
30/08/2004	RUSHDEN & DIAMONDS	A	0	0	3367	P	P	P	P	B	P	P	PB	P	P	A		P			PA																			
04/09/2004	SHREWSBURY TOWN	H	0	0	8381	P	PC	P	P	C	A	PB	P	P	P	P		P	B		PA																			
11/09/2004	LEYTON ORIENT	A	2	4	3972	P	P	P	P		P	PA	PB	P	A	P		P	C		PC	B															FORRESTER	TROLLOPE		
18/09/2004	LINCOLN CITY	H	0	0	7004	P		P	P	P	P	PB	A	P	P	PA		P			P	B																		
25/09/2004	NORTHAMPTON TOWN	A	1	2	5645	P	P	P	P	P	PB	PC	P	P	P	PA	C				B		A														SAVAGE			
02/10/2004	OXFORD UNITED	H	2	0	8049	P	A	P	P	P	P		PA		P		P	P			P		P														AGOGO 2			
09/10/2004	CAMBRIDGE UNITED	A	0	1	2748	P	PC	PA	P	P	P	A			P	C	P	P	B		PB		P																	
16/10/2004	GRIMSBY TOWN	A	0	0	4691	P		P	P	P	P			P	PB	A	P	P	PA				P	B																
19/10/2004	YEOVIL TOWN	H	2	2	9295	P	B	P	P	P	PA		A	P	P		P	P	PB		C		PC														HUNT	AGOGO		
23/10/2004	KIDDERMINSTER HARRIERS	H	2	0	7020	P	P	P	P	P		P	PC	P	PB	B			PA		A	C	P														AGOGO 2			
30/10/2004	BOSTON UNITED	A	2	2	2723	P	P	P	P	P		P		P	P	B			PA		A	C	PB		PC												FORRESTER	AGOGO		
06/11/2004	SWANSEA CITY	A	0	1	8778	P	P	P	P		C	PC	PB	P	PA	A			B		P		P		P															
20/11/2004	SCUNTHORPE UNITED	H	0	3	7039	P	P	P	P		A	P		P	P	P		P			B	PA			PB															
27/11/2004	WYCOMBE WANDERERS	A	0	1	4999	P	P	P	P			PA	PC	P	PB	A	P	P		C	P			B																
07/12/2004	CHESTER CITY	H	4	1	5524	P	P		P			A	PA	P	B	PB	P	P			P	P	P														DISLEY	FORRESTER pe	THORPE	TROLLOPE
11/12/2004	MACCLESFIELD TOWN	H	0	0	6504	P	P		P			PA		P	A	P	P	P			P	P	P																	
18/12/2004	ROCHDALE	A	0	0	2623	P	P	A	P		C	P		P	B	PC	P	P			P	PB	PA																	
26/12/2004	LEYTON ORIENT	H	1	1	8414	P	P	P	P	B	A	P	PA	P	PC	PB	P	P								C											FORRESTER pen			
29/12/2004	CHELTENHAM TOWN	A	1	1	6954	P	P		P	P		PA	PC	P	P	PB	P	P			B	A					C										FORRESTER			
01/01/2005	SHREWSBURY TOWN	A	0	2	5043		P		P	P	A	PC	PA	P	B	PB	P	P			P			C				P												
03/01/2005	NORTHAMPTON TOWN	H	3	1	6961		P	P	P		P	P		P	A	PB	PA	P			P						C	P	BC								HUNT	EDWARDS	AGOGO	
08/01/2005	CAMBRIDGE UNITED	H	1	1	6510		P	P	P		P	P	A	PA	P	B		P			PC	PB		C				P									AGOGO pen			
15/01/2005	LINCOLN CITY	A	1	1	3929		P	P	P		PA	P	AC	P	P	PB		P			P	B					C	P									AGOGO			
22/01/2005	CHELTENHAM TOWN	H	1	1	6954		P	P	P	B		PA	P	P		PB		P		A	P	P						P									THORPE			
29/01/2005	OXFORD UNITED	A	2	3	7830		P	P		P			PC	P	P	PB	PA	P	A			P	C	B				P									AGOGO	WALKER		
05/02/2005	GRIMSBY TOWN	H	3	0	6134		C	P	P			PA	PC	P	PB			P	P	A		P	P	B				P									HUNT	WILLIAMS	WALKER	
12/02/2005	YEOVIL TOWN	A	2	4	9153		P	P	PA			P	PB	P	P				P	A		P	P	B				P									DISLEY	WALKER		
19/02/2005	BOSTON UNITED	H	1	1	5563		P	PB	P	B				P	P	A		P	P	P		PA	P					P									AGOGO			
22/02/2005	KIDDERMINSTER HARRIERS	A	1	1	2082	P	P	P	P	PA				P	P			P	PB	P		A	P	B													AGOGO			
26/02/2005	MACCLESFIELD TOWN	A	1	2	2114	P	P	P	PA	P				P	P			P	P	B		PB	P							A							ELLIOTT			
05/03/2005	ROCHDALE	H	0	0	5464	P	P	P		P				P	PA	B		P	P	PB		P	P	A																
12/03/2005	BURY	A	1	1	2132	P	P	P	A	P				P	P		PA	P	P			PB	P	B													DISLEY			
19/03/2005	MANSFIELD TOWN	H	4	4	5294		PB	P		P				P	P	A		P	P	P		B	P	PA				P									WILLIAMS	WALKER pen	AGOGO pen	FORRESTER
26/03/2005	NOTTS COUNTY	A	2	1	4258		P	P	A	P				P	PC		P	PA	P			PB	P	C				P			B						BAUDET og	WALKER		
28/03/2005	DARLINGTON	H	3	3	5918		PA	P	C	P				PC	P	B	P	P	P	A		PB	P					P									WALKER 2	ELLIOTT		
01/04/2005	SOUTHEND UNITED	A	0	2	7858		PC	P		P				P	PB	B	P	P	P	A		PA	P					P			C									
09/04/2005	RUSHDEN & DIAMONDS	H	3	0	5740			P	P	P					P		P	P	P	PA		P	P			A		P									WALKER 2	DISLEY		
16/04/2005	CHESTER CITY	A	2	2	2475			P	P	P				P	P		PA	P	P	P		A	P					P									WILLIAMS	AGOGO		
23/04/2005	SWANSEA CITY	H	2	0	7433			PA	P	P				P	PB	B	P	P	P	PC		C						P			A	P					WALKER	AGOGO		
30/04/2005	SCUNTHORPE UNITED	A	0	4	6925				P	P	B	A				PB	PA	P	P	P		P						P			P	P								
07/05/2005	WYCOMBE WANDERERS	H	1	0	7358				PA	P		A						P	P	PC			P	B				P			P	P	P	PB	C		WALKER			
	APPEARANCES					28	33	39	39	28	16	26	21	41	37	20	21	40	20	9	17	18	24	1	3	0	0	18	0	0	2	3	1	1	0					
	SUB					0	5	1	3	6	7	4	4	0	6	15	6	1	7	8	8	10	2	12	0	2	3	0	1	1	3	0	0	0	1					
	GOALS					0	0	0	2	1	0	2	0	4	19	7	1	2	11	3	3	4	0	0	0	0	0	0	0	0	0	0	0	0	0		OWN GOAL 1			
	SUBD					0	5	3	3	1	5	13	18	2	12	16	5	1	5	4	6	9	3	1	2	0	0	0	1	0	0	0	0	1	0					
	CARLING CUP																																							
24/08/2004	BRIGHTON	A	2	1	4217	P	P	P	P		P	P	P	P	A		B	P	PA		PB																THORPE	WALKER		
21.09/2004	NORWICH CITY	A	0	1	18658	P	P		P	P	P	PB	PC	P	P			P	C			A	B													PA				
	FA CUP CUP																																							
13/11/2004	CARLISLE UNITED	H	1	1	5658	P	P	P	P			P	PA	P	P				P			P		A	P												WALKER			
23/11/2004	CARLISLE UNITED *	A	0	1	4813	P	P	P	P		A	PC	PA	P	P		PB	P			B		P	C																
	* AET 0-0																																							
	ASSOCIATE MEMBERS CUP																																							
28/09/2004	KIDDERMINSTER HARRIERS	H	2	0	3281	P	P	P	P	P		PC	B		C	A		P	PA		P	PB	P														AGOGO 2			
03/11/2004	BARNET	H	2	0	4460	P	P	P	P	PA		PB	P			PC				B	P	P	P	C	A												FORRESTER	THORPE		
30/11/2004	WYCOMBE WANDERERS	A	1	0	3667	P	P		P			A	P	P	B	PB	PA	P			P	P	P														FORRESTER			
25/01/2005	LEYTON ORIENT	A	2	1	1846		P	P		P		P	P	P		PA		P			P	P		A				P									DISLEY	HALDANE		
15/02/2005	SOUTHEND UNITED	A	1	2	7110		P	P				PA	P	P	P			P	A	P		P	P					P									WALKER			

2005/06

Date	Opponent					SHEARER Scott	RYAN Robert	EDWARDS Christian	ELLIOTT Steven	ANDERSON John	BASS Jonathan	DISLEY Craig	CAMPBELL Stuart	LESCOTT Aaron	AGOGO Manuel	WALKER Richard	HINTON Craig	LOUIS Jefferson	WILLIAMS Ryan	CARRUTHERS Christopher	SOMNER Matthew	GIBB Alistair	HUNT James	FORRESTER Jamie	LEARY Michael	HALDANE Lewis	MULLINGS Darren	IGOE Samuel	LINES Christopher	BOOK Steven			
06/08/2005	BARNET	A	1	1	3237	P	P	P	P	PA	PC	P	P	P	P	PB	A	B	C												AGOGO		
09/08/2005	GRIMSBY TOWN	H	1	2	6300	P		P	P	P			P	PA	P	PB		B	P	P	P	A									AGOGO		
13/08/2005	PETERBOROUGH UNITED	H	2	3	5169	P	PC	P	P	PA			P		PB	P	A	B	P			P	P	C							WALKER	ELLIOTT	
20/08/2005	TORQUAY UNITED	A	3	2	3964	P	P		P	P		A	PA	P	P	B	P	PB	C			PC	P								AGOGO 2	WALKER	
27/08/2005	NOTTS COUNTY	A	0	2	4405	P	P		P	PC	C		PA	P	P	PB	P	B	A			P	P										
03/09/2005	LEYTON ORIENT	A	3	2	3481	P	P		P	P	B	PA	A		PC	PB	P	C				P	P		P						DISLEY	AGOGO 2-1pen	
10/09/2005	LINCOLN CITY	H	0	0	5057	P	P		P	P		PB			P	A	P	PA		B		P	P		P								
13/09/2005	OXFORD UNITED	H	1	1	5098	P			P	P		P			P	PA	P	A		P		P	P		P						WALKER		
17/09/2005	CHESTER CITY	A	0	4	2874	P		B	P	PB		A	PA	C	P	P	P			P		P	P		PC								
24/09/2005	DARLINGTON	H	1	0	5652	P	P		P					P	P	P	P			P		P	P		P						WALKER		
27/09/2005	BURY	A	0	1	1673	P	P		P			A		P	P	PC	P			PA		PB	P	C	P	B							
01/10/2005	CARLISLE UNITED	A	3	1	5317	P			P			P		P	P	P	P			P		P	P		P						LIVESEY og	ARANALDE og	AGOGO
07/10/2005	NORTHAMPTON TOWN	H	0	0	6912	P	P		P	P		P	A	P	P	P				PA			P		P								
15/10/2005	BOSTON UNITED	A	1	3	2469	P	P		P			A		P	PC	PB	P			PA		P	P	B	P	C					WALKER		
22/10/2005	WREXHAM	H	2	1	5730	P	P		P			P	C	P	PB	P	P			PA		PC	P	A		B					WALKER 2		
29/10/2005	MACCLESFIELD TOWN	A	1	2	1908	P	P		P			P		P	P	P	P					PA	P	A	PB	B					DISLEY		
12/11/2005	ROCHDALE	H	1	2	6042	P	P		P			P	P	P	P	PB	P			PA				A	P	B					AGOGO		
19/11/2005	NORTHAMPTON TOWN	A	0	4	5716	P	P		P			C	P	P	P	PB	P			PA		A	P		PC	B							
26/11/2005	BARNET	H	2	1	5096	P			P			PA	P	P	PB	P	P			P		P	P		A	B					WALKER 2		
06/12/2005	STOCKPORT COUNTY	A	1	0	3460	P			P			P	P	P	P	P	P			P		P	P								WALKER pen		
10/12/2005	GRIMSBY TOWN	A	1	0	4739	P			P			P	P	P	P	P	P			P		P	P								CARRUTHERS		
17/12/2005	TORQUAY UNITED	H	0	1	6061	P			P			PB	P	P	PC	P	P		A	P		PA	P	B		C							
26/12/2005	SHREWSBURY TOWN	H	2	1	7551	P			P			P	P	P	PA	P	P			P		P	P	A							DISLEY	AGOGO pen	
28/12/2005	MANSFIELD TOWN	A	3	3	2357	P			P			PC	P	P	PB	P	P		C	P		PA	P	A		B					HUNT	WALKER 2-1pen	
31/12/2005	WYCOMBE WANDERERS	H	1	2	6828	P			P			PB	P	P	PA	P	P			P		PC	P	B		A	C				WALKER		
02/01/2006	RUSHDEN & DIAMONDS	A	3	2	2720	P			P			P	P	P		P	P			P		A	P	P		PA					CAMPBELL	ELLIOTT	FORRESTER
14/01/2006	CHELTENHAM TOWN	A	3	2	6005	P		P		A		P	P	P	B	P	PA			P		PC		P		PB		C			FORRESTER	DISLEY	ANDERSON
21/01/2006	CHESTER CITY	H	2	1	6310	P		P	P			P	P	P	P	P				P						PB	A	PA	B		EDWARDS	DISLEY	
28/01/2006	LINCOLN CITY	A	0	1	4258	P		P	P			PA	P	P	P	P				P		A				P		P					
31/01/2006	LEYTON ORIENT	H	3	3	5966	P		P	P	A		P	P	PA	P	P				P			P					P			AGOGO	DISLEY	WALKER pen
04/02/2006	BURY	H	1	0	6027	P		P	P		P	P	PA		P	P				P			P	A		PB	B				AGOGO		
11/02/2006	DARLINGTON	A	1	1	4579	P		P	P		P	P	P		P	P				P			P			P					AGOGO		
14/02/2006	CHELTENHAM TOWN	H	0	1	6885	P		P	P		P	P	P		P	P				P			P	A		PA							
18/02/2006	STOCKPORT COUNTY	H	2	2	5990	P		P	P		P	P	P		P	P				P			P	PA		A					WALKER 2-1pen		
25/02/2006	PETERBOROUGH UNITED	A	2	1	4292	P			P		P	P	P		P	P	P			P			P			P					AGOGO	WALKER	
11/03/2006	NOTTS COUNTY	H	1	2	6280				P		PA	PB	P	A		P	P			P		B	P			PC	C	P		P	HALDANE		
15/03/2006	OXFORD UNITED	A	0	1	6424	P			P			P	PA	P		P	P			P		B	P	A		PB		P					
18/03/2006	SHREWSBURY TOWN	A	0	1	3641	P			P			P	PA	P		P	P			P		A	P	B		PB		P					
25/03/2006	MANSFIELD TOWN	H	2	0	5253	P			P			P		P	PA	P	P			P		A	P			P		P			IGOE	WALKER	
01/04/2006	WYCOMBE WANDERERS	A	3	1	6355	P		A	P			P	B	P	P	P	P			PA		C	P			PC		PB			AGOGO 2	WALKER	
08/04/2006	RUSHDEN & DIAMONDS	H	0	1	6432	P			P			PA	A	P	P	P	P			P		B	P			PB		P					
15/04/2006	CARLISLE UNITED	H	1	1	6181	P			P			P	A	P	P	P	P			P			P			PA		P			DISLEY		
17/04/2006	WREXHAM	A	0	1	3749	P			P			P	PB	P	P	P	P			P		A	P			PA			B				
22/04/2006	BOSTON UNITED	H	3	1	4836	P			P			P	P	P	P	P	P			P			P			P					DISLEY	WALKER pen	AGOGO
29/04/2006	ROCHDALE	A	0	2	2649	P		A	P			P	PA	P	P	P	P			PB		C	P			PC			B				
06/05/2006	MACCLESFIELD TOWN	H	2	3	6100	P		P	P			P	A	P	P	P				P			P			P			PA		HALDANE 2		
	APPEARANCES					45	14	12	45	10	7	37	31	35	41	44	34	2	2	39	1	21	40	3	12	19	0	10	1	1			
	SUB					0	0	3	0	2	2	5	7	2	1	2	2	6	5	1	0	12	0	14	1	11	4	1	3	0			
	GOALS					0	0	1	2	1	0	8	1	0	16	20	0	0	0	1	0	0	1	2	0	3	0	1	0	0	OWN GOAL 2		
	SUBD					0	1	0	0	4	2	9	8	2	10	9	1	2	0	8	0	8	0	1	3	13	0	2	1	0			
	CARLING CUP																																
23/08/2005	MILLWALL	A	0	2	3075	P	P		P	P		PC	PB	P	P	A	P	PA	B	C			P										
	FA CUP																																
05/11/2005	GRIMSBY TOWN	A	2	1	2680	P	P		P			P	A	P	P	P	P			P		PA	P								AGOGO 2		
02/12/2005	PORT VALE	A	1	1	4483	P			P			P	P	P	P	P	P		A	P		PA	P								GIBB		
13/12/2005	PORT VALE	H	0	1	5623	P			P			PB	P	P	P	PC	P		A	P		PA	P	B		C							
	ASSOCIATE MEMBERS CUP																																
18/10/2005	PETERBOROUGH UNITED*	A	1	2	1477	P	P		P			P	PA	P	P	P	P			A			P		PB	B					WALKER		

*AET after 90 mins 1-1

2006/07

Date	Opponent				Att	PHILLIPS Stephen	LESCOTT Aaron	HINTON Craig	ELLIOTT Steven	CARRUTHERS Christopher	IGOE Samuel	HUNT James	DISLEY Craig	CAMPBELL Stuart	WALKER Richard	AGOGO Manuel	SANDELL Andrew	HALDANE Lewis	GREEN Ryan	ANTHONY Byron	RIGG Sean	LAMBERT Rickie	LINES Christopher	WALKER James(L)	SHEARER Scott	EASTER Jamal(L)	NICHOLSON Stuart(L)	OJI Samuel (L)	JACOBSON Joseph (L)					
	LEAGUE 2 (4)																																	
05/08/2006	PETERBOROUGH UNITED	A	1	4	4890	P	P	P	P	PC	P	P	P	PA	P	PB	A	B	C											IGOE				
08/08/2006	WYCOMBE WANDERERS	H	1	2	5349	P	PC	P	P	P	PA	P	PB	B	P	P	A	P	C											HUNT				
12/08/2006	GRIMSBY TOWN	H	1	0	4596	P	P	P			P	P	PA	A	P	PB	P	B	P	P										SANDELL				
19/08/2006	MILTON KEYNES DONS	A	0	2	5125	P	P	P			P	P	PA	A	P		P	PB	P	P	B													
26/08/2006	SHREWSBURY TOWN	H	1	0	4774	P	P	P		B	P	P	PA	A	P		PB	PC	P	P	C									HALDANE				
03/09/2006	STOCKPORT COUNTY	A	1	2	4846	P	PC	P		C	P	P	PB	B	P		P	PA	P	P		A								R WALKER				
09/09/2006	ROCHDALE	H	0	0	4689	P	P	P	P		P	P	P		P		P	PA	P		A													
13/09/2006	TORQUAY UNITED	A	0	0	3145	P	P	P	P		P	P	P	A	PA		PB	B	P			P												
16/09/2006	DARLINGTON	A	1	1	3654	P	P	P	P	A			P	P	PB		PC	PA	P		B	P	C							HALDANE				
23/09/2006	WALSALL	H	1	2	5260	P	PC	P	P	C	P	B	PA	PB	A		P	P	P			P								SANDELL				
27/09/2006	HEREFORD UNITED	H	2	1	4975	P	P	P	P	C	PC	P	B	P	PA			P	P			PB		A						R WALKER 2				
30/09/2006	CHESTER CITY	A	0	2	2151	P	P	PA	P		PC	P	B	PB	P			C	P	A		P		P										
07/10/2006	BOSTON UNITED	H	1	0	4327	P	P		P		P	P		P	PA		PB	B	P	P		A		P						J WALKER				
14/10/2006	NOTTS COUNTY	A	2	1	5797		P	B	P	P	P		P	P	P		PA	A		P				PB	P					R WALKER	HALDANE			
21/10/2006	MACCLESFIELD TOWN	H	0	0	5130		P		P		P	B	PB	P	P		PA	P	P	P	A				P									
28/10/2006	WREXHAM	A	0	2	3803	P	P		P		PC	P	C	P	P		B	PB	P	P	PA					A								
04/11/2006	MANSFIELD TOWN	H	1	0	5044	P			P	P	P		P	P	P		PA	A	P	P	B					PB				DISLEY				
18/11/2006	BURY	A	2	0	2635	P	C		P	P	P		P	P	P		B	PB	PC	P		A					PA			HALDANE	R WALKER			
26/11/2006	BARNET	H	2	0	5351	P			P	P	P		P	P	P		B	PB	P	P		A					PA			NICHOLSON	LAMBERT			
05/12/2006	LINCOLN CITY	A	0	1	3913	P	A		P	P	P		PA	P	C		B	PB	P	P		P					PC							
09/12/2006	HARTLEPOOL UNITED	H	0	2	4906	P			P	P	P		P	P	A		C	PC	P	P		PA				B	PB							
16/12/2006	SWINDON TOWN	A	1	2	10010	P	PC	P	P	P	P		PB	P	P		A	PA	C			B					P			R WALKER				
23/12/2006	ACCRINGTON STANLEY	H	4	0	5205	P	C		P	P	PA		PC	P	PB		P		P	P		B	A				P			R WALKER 2-1pen	ELLIOTT	NICHOLSON		
26/12/2006	HEREFORD UNITED	A	0	0	5201	P			P	P	P		P	P	P		PA	A	P	P		B					PB							
30/12/2006	WALSALL	A	2	2	5941	P		A	P	P	P		P	P	P		PC	C	P	PA		B					PB			ELLIOTT 2				
01/01/2007	TORQUAY UNITED	H	1	0	6475	P		P	P	P	P		P	P	P		A	PA	P			PB					B			SANDELL				
13/01/2007	ROCHDALE	A	1	0	2547	P	P	P	P	P	P		P	P	PB		PA	A	C			PC					B			LAMBERT				
20/01/2007	CHESTER CITY	H	0	0	5694	P	P	P	P	P			P		P		P	PA			A	P	P											
03/02/2007	PETERBOROUGH UNITED	H	3	2	5700	P		P	P	P	P		P	P	P		PB	B	P			PA					A			LAMBERT	R WALKER	CAMPBELL		
06/02/2007	DARLINGTON	H	1	2	5511	P		P	P	P	PC		P	P	P		PA	A	P		C	PB					B			DISLEY				
10/02/2007	GRIMSBY TOWN	A	3	4	5883	P	A	P	P	P	P		P	P	PC		B	PB	PA			P					C			DISLEY 2	HALDANE			
17/02/2007	MILTON KEYNES DONS	H	1	1	5489	P	P	P	P	P	PB		P	P	PA		B	P				P					A			NICHOLSON				
02/03/2007	SHREWSBURY TOWN	A	0	0	4227	P	P	P	P	P	P		P	P	A		B	P				PA					PB							
06/03/2007	ACCRINGTON STANLEY	A	1	1	1302	P	P		P	P	P		P	P	PA			P				P					A	P		R WALKER				
10/03/2007	BOSTON UNITED	A	1	2	1697	P	P		P	P	P		P		PA		B	A			C	P	PC					P	PB	HALDANE				
17/03/2007	NOTTS COUNTY	H	2	0	4642	P	P	P		P			P		A			P			B	PA	P				PB	P	P	NICHOLSON 2				
20/03/2007	STOCKPORT COUNTY	H	2	1	4725	P	P	P		P	A		P		B			P			C	PB	P				P	PC	PA	LAMBERT pen	NICHOLSON			
24/03/2007	WREXHAM	H	0	1	5209	P	P	P		P	PB		P	P	A			P			B	PA					P	P						
27/03/2007	WYCOMBE WANDERERS	A	1	0	4299	P	P	P	P	P	P		P	P	PA		C	PB			B	PC							A	ELLIOTT				
07/04/2007	MANSFIELD TOWN	A	1	0	2392	P	P	P	P	P			P	P	P		A	PC		C		PB					B		PA	ELLIOTT				
09/04/2007	BURY	H	2	0	6266	P	P	P	P	P			P	P	PB		PA	P				P					B		A	LAMBERT 2				
14/04/2007	BARNET	A	1	1	2541	P	P	PC	P	P	C		P	P	PB			PA		A		P					B		P	R WALKER				
21/04/2007	LINCOLN CITY	H	0	0	6828	P			P	P	A		P	P	P			P	P	P	B	PA							PB					
24/04/2007	MACCLESFIELD TOWN	A	1	0	1940	P			P	P			P	P	P			PA	P	P	A	P							P	RIGG				
28/04/2007	SWINDON TOWN	H	1	0	9902	P			P	P	A		P	P	PC		B	PA	P	P	C	P							PB	LAMBERT				
05/05/2007	HARTLEPOOL UNITED	A	2	1	7629	P			P	PA	A		P	P	PC			PB	P	P	B	P	C						P	R WALKER pen	LAMBERT			
	APPEARANCES					44	30	28	39	33	35	12	42	35	39	3	20	32	29	20	1	28	4	3	2	1	12	5	9					
	SUB					0	4	2	0	5	5	2	3	6	7	0	16	13	4	3	17	8	3	1	0	2	10	0	2					
	GOALS					0	0	0	5	0	1	1	4	1	12	0	3	6	0	0	1	8	0	1	0	0	6	0	0					
	SUBD					0	4	2	0	2	8	0	10	3	15	2	13	20	2	1	1	13	1	1	0	1	8	1	5					
	PLAY OFFS																																	
12/05/2007	LINCOLN CITY	H	2	1	10654	P			P	P	A		P	P	P			PA	P	P	B	PB							P	DISLEY	WALKER			
17/05/2007	LINCOLN CITY	A	5	3	7694	P			P	P	A		P	P	PC			PB	P	P	C	P	B						PA	CAMPBELL	LAMBERT	R WALKER	IGOE	RIGG
26/05/2007	SHREWSBURY TOWN	N	3	1	61589	P			P	P	P		P	P	P			PA	P	P	A	P								R WALKER 2	IGOE			
	CARLING CUP																																	
26/08/2006	LUTON TOWN	H	1	1	2882	P	B		P	PB	P		P	P	P		P	PA	P	P	A									WALKER				
	AET 1-1 Lost 6-5 on pens																																	
	E.ON FA CUP																																	
11/11/2006	BARROW	A	3	2	2939	P		C	P	P	PC		P	P	P		PB	B	P	P	PA	A								R WALKER	DISLEY	ANTHONY		
02/12/2006	AFC BOURNEMOUTH	H	1	1	6252	P	P		P	P	P		P	P	P			P		P		P								R WALKER pen				
12/12/2006	AFC BOURNEMOUTH	A	1	0	4153	P	P		P	P	P		P	P	P		A	P		P		PA								R WALKER				
05/01/2007	HEREFORD UNITED	H	1	0	8978	P	P	P	P	P	P		P	P	P		P	A				PA								R WALKER pen				
27/01/2007	DERBY COUNTY	A	0	1	25033	P	P	P	P	P	PC		P	P	PA		PB	B	A		C	P												
	JPT TROPHY																																	
17/10/2006	TORQUAY UNITED	H	1	0	2672		P		P	P			P	P	P		PA	P		P	A			P	P					ANTHONY				
31/10/2006	WYCOMBE WANDERERS	A	2	0	1314	P		P		P	P		P	P	P		P		P	P	A					PA				EASTER	IGOE			
29/11/2006	PETERBOROUGH UNITED	H	1	0	3621	P			P	P	P		P	P			A	PA	P	P		P					P			NICHOLSON				
30/01/2007	SHREWSBURY TOWN	A	1	0	3199	P		P	P	P	P		P	P	P		P	A	P			PA								R WALKER				
21/02/2007	BRISTOL CITY	H	1	0	11530	P	P	P	P	P	P		P	P	PA		B	P				PB					A			LAMBERT				
01/04/2007	DONCASTER ROVERS	N	2	3	59024	P	P	P	P	P	PA		P	P	PB		A	PC				P	C				B			R WALKER pen	IGOE			

2007/08

Date	Opponent	H/A	F	A	Att	PHILLIPS Stephen	LESCOTT Aaron	CARRUTHERS Christopher	CAMPBELL Stuart	ANTHONY Byron	ELLIOTT Steven	PIPE David	DISLEY Craig	LAMBERT Rickie	WALKER Richard	JACOBSON Joseph	HALDANE Lewis	WILLIAMS Andrew	RIGG Sean	IGOE Samuel	GREEN Ryan	HINTON Craig	COLES Daniel	LINES Christopher	GROVES Matthew	KLEIN-DAVIES Joshua	REECE Charles	PULIS Anthony T	ANDREWS Wayne	CLOUGH Charles	Scorers		
	LEAGUE 1 (3)																																
11/08/2007	PORT VALE	A	1	1	6808	P	P	P	P	P	P	PA	P	PB	P	PC	B	A	C												WILLIAMS		
18/08/2007	CREWE ALEXANDRA	H	1	1	7750	P	P	PC	P	P	P	P	P	P	PB	PA	A	B		C											DISLEY		
25/08/2007	OLDHAM ATHLETIC	A	1	0	5348	P	P	P	P	P	P	PB	P	PA	P	P	B	A													JACOBSON		
01/09/2007	NOTTINGHAM FOREST	H	2	2	9080	P	P	P	P	P	P	PC	P	C	PB	B	PA	P		A											ANTHONY	WALKER pen	
08/09/2007	LUTON TOWN	A	2	1	6131	P		P	P	P	P		P	PC	B		P	PB	C	P	PA	A									LAMBERT 2		
14/09/2007	LEEDS UNITED	H	0	3	11883	P		P	P	P	P	C	P	P	B	A	P	PA		PB	PC												
22/09/2007	CARLISLE UNITED	A	1	1	6106	P		P	P	P	P		P	PB	P	PA	B	A		P	P										ELLIOTT		
29/09/2007	LEYTON ORIENT	H	2	3	7181	P		P	P	P	P	C	PC	PA	P	B	PB	A		P	P										WALKER 2-2pens		
02/10/2007	SOUTHEND UNITED	H	1	1	5762	P			P	P	P	P	PB	A	PA	P	P	PC	C	B	P										WALKER pen		
06/10/2007	BRIGHTON & HOVE ALBION	A	0	0	5820	P			P	P	P	P	P	A	P	P	PB	PA	B		P												
12/10/2007	HARTLEPOOL UNITED	A	0	1	4963	P			P		P	PA	P	P	P	P	PB	A	B		P	P											
20/10/2007	YEOVIL TOWN	H	1	1	7726	P		P	P		P	PB	P	P	PA		PC	A	C	B	P	P									ELLIOTT		
27/10/2007	GILLINGHAM	A	2	3	5333	P	P	P	P		P	P	P	P	PA	A	PB	B				P									LAMBERT	PIPE	
03/11/2007	AFC BOURNEMOUTH	H	0	2	6405	P			P		P	PB	P	P	B	P	PC	A	PA	C	P		P										
06/11/2007	NORTHAMPTON TOWN	A	1	0	5126	P		C	P		P	P	PA	P		P	PC		PB	A	P	B	P								LAMBERT		
17/11/2007	MILLWALL	H	2	1	6991	P		P	P		P	B		P			P	A	PA	PB	P		P	P							LAMBERT pen	HALDANE	
24/11/2007	SWINDON TOWN	A	0	1	9342	P			P		P	PB	P	P	C	P	PC	A	PA	B	P		P										
15/12/2007	HUDDERSFIELD TOWN	A	1	2	8118	P	P		P			PA	P	P		P	PB	P		A		P	P		B						PIPE		
22/12/2007	LEEDS UNITED	A	0	1	27863	P	P	A	P		P	P	P	P	C	PA	PC	B	PB				P										
26/12/2007	LUTON TOWN	H	1	1	7556	P	PB		P		P	P	P	P	A	P	PA	P					P	B							LAMBERT pen		
29/12/2007	CARLISLE UNITED	H	3	0	6254	P	P	A	P		P	PA		P		P		PB		PC		P		P		B	C				WILLIAMS 2	HINTON	
01/01/2008	SOUTHEND UNITED	A	1	0	7664	P	P	A	P		P	PB	B	PC	C	P		P		PA		P		P							WILLIAMS		
12/01/2008	TRANMERE ROVERS	A	2	0	5887	P	P		P		P	PB	B	PA	A	P		PC	C			P	P	P							WILLIAMS	LAMBERT	
19/01/2008	WALSALL	H	1	1	6276	P	P		P		P	PA	B	P		P		P	C	A		P	PB	PC							DISLEY		
29/01/2008	CREWE ALEXANDRA	A	1	1	3942	P	P		P			P	P	P		P		PA	A			P	P	P							WILLIAMS og		
02/02/2008	PORT VALE	H	3	2	9927	P	P		P			PA	PB	P		P	B	PC	C	A		P	P	P							COLES	LINES	LAMBERT pen
05/02/2008	CHELTENHAM TOWN	H	2	0	6780	P	P	P	P			P	P	P				PA	A			P	P	P							HINTON	LAMBERT	
09/02/2008	DONCASTER ROVERS	A	0	2	8168	P	P		P			PC	PA	P		P		P	A	B		P	P	PB				C					
12/02/2008	OLDHAM ATHLETIC	H	1	0	5778	P	P		P			P	P	PB	B	P		PA	A			P	P	P							DISLEY		
23/02/2008	TRANMERE ROVERS	H	1	1	7777	P	P		P			PA	P	PC	B	P		PB	A	C		P	P	P							DISLEY		
01/03/2008	MILLWALL	A	1	0	9202	P	P		P				P	P		P	B	PA	A	PB		P	P	P							DISLEY		
04/03/2008	DONCASTER ROVERS	H	0	1	5933	P	P		P				P	P		P	PB	PA	A	P		P	P			B							
12/03/2008	NORTHAMPTON TOWN	H	1	1	5657	P	P	P	P	P		PA	P	B	PB	C	PC		P				P	A							RIGG		
15/03/2008	CHELTENHAM TOWN	A	0	1	5187	P	P		P	P			P	P	B	P	PB	A	PA				P	P									
18/03/2008	SWANSEA CITY	H	0	2	6410	P	P		P	P			P	P	B	P	PB	A	PA				P	P									
22/03/2008	HUDDERSFIELD TOWN	H	2	3	6585	P	P		P	P		PA	P	P		P	A	B					P	P		PB					KLEIN-DAVIES	LINES	
24/03/2008	SWANSEA CITY	A	2	2	15048	P	P		P	B	P	P	P	PB			A		PA			P	PC	P		C					LAMBERT	DISLEY	
29/03/2008	YEOVIL TOWN	A	0	0	6654	P	P		P		P	P	P	P								P	P	P		A			PA				
05/04/2008	HARTLEPOOL UNITED	H	0	0	5526	P	P		P		P	P	P	P		A		B				P	PA	P		PB							
08/04/2008	NOTTINGHAM FOREST	A	1	1	15860	P	P		P		P	P	P	P		P	PA	A				P		P							ELLIOTT		
12/04/2008	AFC BOURNEMOUTH	A	1	2	6867	P	P		P		P	PB	P	P		P	PA	B	C			P		PC		A					LAMBERT		
15/04/2008	WALSALL	A	1	0	5200	P	P		P	P	P	P	P	PA		P			P			A		P							LAMBERT		
19/04/2008	GILLINGHAM	H	1	1	6614	P	P		P	P	P	PC	P	P		P	C	B	PA					PB		A					ELLIOTT		
22/04/2008	SWINDON TOWN	H	0	1	6102	P	P		P	P	P	PA	PC	P		P	A	B	PB					P		C							
26/04/2008	BRIGHTON & HOVE ALBION	H	0	2	7590	P	P		P	P	P	P	PA	P		P		A	PB					P						B			
04/05/2008	LEYTON ORIENT	A	1	3	5132	P	P		P	P	P	PA	PB	P		P		A	P					P		B					LAMBERT		
	APPEARANCES					46	34	13	46	19	33	37	41	42	12	34	22	19	14	9	12	21	24	25	0	2	0	0	1	0			
	SUB					0	0	4	0	1	0	3	3	4	12	6	10	22	17	12	0	3	0	2	1	8	1	1	0	1			
	GOALS					0	0	0	0	1	4	2	6	13	4	1	1	5	1	0	0	2	1	2	0	1	0	0	0	0	1 OWN GOAL		
	SUBD					0	1	1	0	0	0	21	8	11	6	4	18	13	11	5	2	0	3	4	0	2	0	0	1	0			
	CARLING CUP																																
14/08/2007	CRYSTAL PALACE*	H	1	1	5566	P	P	P	P	P	P	PC	P	B	P	A	PA	PB	C												DISLEY		
28/08/2007	WEST HAM UNITED	H	1	2	10831	P	P	P	P	P	P	P	PC	PB	P	PA	A	B	C												WILLIAMS		
	* Won 4-1 on pens																																
	E.ON FA CUP																																
10/11/2007	LEYTON ORIENT	A	1	1	3157	P		P	P		P			P	B	PB		A	PA	P	P	C	P	PC							LAMBERT		
27/11/2007	LEYTON ORIENT*	H	3	3	3742	P	P	PA	P			P	P	P		P	PB	P		A		P		B							HINTON	LAMBERT pen	DISLEY
06/01/2009	FULHAM	A	2	2	13634	P	P	A			P	P		PC	C	P		PB	B	PA		P	P	PC							COLES	HINTON	
22/01/2008	FULHAM **	H	0	0	11882	P	P		P		PA	P	A	P		P		PB	B			P	P	P									
16/02/2009	SOUTHAMPTON	H	1	0	11920	P	P		P			P	P	P		P		P				P	P	P							LAMBERT		
	* AET 2-2 Won 6-5 on pens																																
	** AET 0-0 Won 5-3 on pens																																
	JP TROPHY																																
09/10/2007	AFC BOURNEMOUTH	H	0	1	3313	P		P	P	PA	A	PB		PC	C		B	P	P		P	P		P									

2008/09

Date	Competition / Opponent				Att	PHILLIPS Stephen	PIPE David	LESCOTT Aaron	LINES Christopher	ANTHONY Byron	ELLIOTT Steven	CAMPBELL Stuart	DISLEY Craig	LAMBERT Rickie	DUFFY Darryl	HUGHES Jeffrey	WILLIAMS Andrew	RIGG Sean	HUNT Benjamin	OSEI-KUFFOUR Jonathan	COLES Daniel	GREEN Ryan	HINTON Craig	JACOBSON Joseph	REECE Charles				
	LEAGUE 1 (3)																												
09/08/2008	CARLISLE UNITED	H	2	3	8285	P	P	P	PA	P	P	P	P	P	P	PB	A	B								LAMBERT	WILLIAMS		
16/08/2008	BRIGHTON & HOVE ALBION	A	1	1	6210	P	PB	P	P	P	P	P	P	P	PC	PA	A		C				B			LAMBERT pen			
23/08/2008	HEREFORD UNITED	H	6	1	6735	P	P	P	P	P	P	P	P	PB	PA	P	B		A							DUFFY 2	LAMBERT 2	HUGHES	LINES
30/08/2008	LEEDS UNITED	A	2	2	21024	P	P	P	P	P	P	P	P	PB	PA	PC	A	C					B			LAMBERT	DUFFY		
06/09/2008	PETERBOROUGH UNITED	A	4	5	4876	P	P	P	PB	P	P	P	P	P	PA	P			B	A						ELLIOTT	BLACKETT og	HUGHES	LAMBERT
13/09/2008	WALSALL	H	1	3	6609	P	PC	P	PA	P	P	P	P	P	PB	P			B	A		C				ELLIOTT			
16/09/2008	CHELTENHAM TOWN	A	1	2	4546	P	P	PB	PA		P	P	A	P	B	P				P	PC	P	C			LAMBERT			
20/09/2008	YEOVIL TOWN	A	2	2	5748	P	PA	P	P		P	P	P	P	PB					A	P	P	B			LAMBERT pen	OSEI-KUFFOUR		
27/09/2008	CREWE ALEXANDRA	H	0	0	5870	P	B	P	P		PA	P	P	P	PC	P				C	P	PB	A						
04/10/2008	COLCHESTER UNITED	A	1	0	4811	P	P	P	P			P	P	P	PA	P			A		P		P			LAMBERT			
11/10/2008	LEYTON ORIENT	H	2	1	6425	P	P	P	P	B		P	P	P	PC	PA			C	A	PB		P			COLES	HINTON		
18/10/2008	HUDDERSFIELD TOWN	A	1	1	13779	P	P	P	P	P		P	P	P	PA	PB				A			P	B		LAMBERT			
21/10/2008	OLDHAM ATHLETIC	H	2	0	6379	P	P	P	P	P		P	P	P	PB	PA				A			P	B		LAMBERT	LINES		
25/10/2008	SOUTHEND UNITED	H	4	2	7055	P	P	P	P	P		P	P	P	B	PA				PB			P	A		LAMBERT 4			
01/11/2008	LEICESTER CITY	A	1	2	18981	P	PC	PA	P	P		P	P	P	C	P				P		B	P	AB		OSEI-KUFFOUR			
14/11/2008	SCUNTHORPE UNITED	H	1	2	7173	P		P	PA		P	P	P	P	A	P			B	PB		P	P			LAMBERT			
22/11/2008	SWINDON TOWN	H	2	2	8016	P		P	P		P	P	PB	P	B	PA		A		P		P	P			LAMBERT	LINES		
25/11/2008	HARTLEPOOL UNITED	A	1	1	3171	P		P		P	P	P	P	P		P				P		P		P		HUGHES			
06/12/2008	MILLWALL	A	2	3	8123	P		P	PA	P	P	P	PB	P	B	P				P		P		A		LAMBERT	OSEI-KUFFOUR		
13/12/2008	TRANMERE ROVERS	H	2	0	6217	P	P	P	P		P	P	P	P	A	P				PA			P			OSEI-KUFFOUR	LINES		
20/12/2008	STOCKPORT COUNTY	A	1	3	5364	P	P	P	P		P	P	PA	P	A	P			B	PB			P			DISLEY			
26/12/2008	MILTON KEYNES DONS	H	1	2	9002	P	PC	P	P	P	P	P	PA	P	B	PB		A		P		C				OSEI-KUFFOUR			
28/12/2008	NORTHAMPTON TOWN	A	0	0	5557	P		P	P		P	P	P	P		P				P		P	P						
17/01/2009	LEYTON ORIENT	A	2	1	4262	P	B	P	PA		P	P	P	P	A	PC				PB		P	P	C		HUGHES	DUFFY		
24/01/2009	COLCHESTER UNITED	H	0	0	6634	P	A	P	P		P	P	PA	P		PB				P		P	P	B					
27/01/2009	CHELTENHAM TOWN	H	3	2	6600	P	P	P	PB		P	P	B	P	A	PA				PC		P	P	C		LAMBERT 2	DUFFY		
31/01/2009	SOUTHEND UNITED	A	0	1	7234	P	PB	P	B		P	P	P	P	A	PA			C	PC		P	P						
14/02/2009	SCUNTHORPE UNITED	A	2	0	4156	P	P	P	P		P	P	A		PC	PA		C		PB		P	P	B		DUFFY	OSEI-KUFFOUR		
17/02/2009	YEOVIL TOWN	H	3	0	8049	P	PB	P	P		P	P	B	A	P	PC				PA		P	P	C		PIPE	DUFFY	LAMBERT	
21/02/2009	LEICESTER CITY	H	0	1	9138	P	PB	P	P		P	P	B	A	P	PA				P		P	PC	C					
24/02/2009	OLDHAM ATHLETIC	A	2	0	3745	P	P	P	P	P	P	P	C	PC	PB	PA				B		P		A		DUFFY	ANTHONY		
28/02/2009	CARLISLE UNITED	A	1	1	5343	P	P	P	P	P	P	P		P	PA	P				A		P				HUGHES			
07/03/2009	LEEDS UNITED	H	2	2	10293	P	P	PB	PC	P	P	P	C	P	P	PA				B		P		A		HUGHES	OSEI-KUFFOUR		
10/03/2009	HEREFORD UNITED	A	3	0	3199	P	PA	P	P	P	P		P	PB	PC	P		C		B		P		A		LAMBERT 3-1pen			
14/03/2009	WALSALL	A	5	0	5169	P	PA	P	P	P	P	C	PC	PB	P	P				B		P		A		DUFFY 2	DISLEY	LESCOTT 2	
17/03/2009	CREWE ALEXANDRA	A	1	1	3879	P	PA	P	P	P	P		P	P	P	P				A		P				DUFFY			
21/03/2009	PETERBOROUGH UNITED	H	0	1	7103	P	P	P	PA	P	P	A	P	P	PB	PC		C		B				P					
28/03/2009	STOCKPORT COUNTY	H	2	0	6214	P		P	P	P	P	P	A	PB	P	PA			B	P				P		ANTHONY	LAMBERT pen		
31/03/2009	HUDDERSFIELD TOWN	H	1	2	6286	P		A	P	P	P	P	P	P	P					P		P		PA		OSEI-KUFFOUR			
05/04/2009	TRANMERE ROVERS	A	0	2	8119	P	PB	PC	PA	P	P	P	A	P	P	P				B		P		C					
10/04/2009	NORTHAMPTON TOWN	H	1	0	6666	P	P	P	P	P	P	P		P	A	P				PA				P		OSEI-KUFFOUR			
13/04/2009	MILTON KEYNES DONS	A	1	2	10251	P	P	PA	P	P	P	P	A	P	B	P				PB				P		LINES			
18/04/2009	MILLWALL	H	4	2	6618	P	P		P	P	P	P	P	PA	PB	P			A	P			B			DISLEY	LAMBERT 2-1pen	OSEI-KUFFOUR	
21/04/2009	BRIGHTON & HOVE ALBION	H	1	2	6193	P	P		P	P		P	P	P	P	P				P			P			LAMBERT			
25/04/2009	SWINDON TOWN	A	1	2	10977	P	P	P	P	PA	P	P	P	P	A	P				P						DUFFY			
02/05/2009	HARTLEPOOL UNITED	H	4	1	7363	P	PA	P	P	P	P	P	A	P	P			C	B	PB					PC	OSEI KUFFOUR	DUFFY	LAMBERT	LESCOTT
	APPEARANCES					46	36	43	44	29	39	42	33	43	28	43	0	0	0	26	5	23	19	6	1				
	SUB					0	3	1	1	1	0	2	11	2	15	0	4	8	12	15	0	3	6	16	0				
	GOALS					0	1	3	5	2	2	0	3	29	13	6	1	0	0	11	1	0	1	0	0	OWN GOAL 1			
	SUBD					0	13	5	11	1	1	0	6	7	17	20	0	0	0	12	2	1	1	2	1				
	CARLING CUP																												
12/08/2008	WATFORD	H	0	1	5574	P	P	P	P	P	P	P	P	P	PA	PB	A	B											
	E.ON FA CUP																												
08/11/2008	BOURNEMOUTH	A	0	1	3935	P		P	P	P	P	P	PB	P		PA		A	B	P		PC	C						
	JP TROPHY																												
02/09/2008	BOURNEMOUTH	A	0	3	2220	P		P	PB	P		P	P	P	A	P			B	PA		P	P						

2009/10

Date	LEAGUE 1 (3)					FORSTER Fraser(L)	REGAN Carl	LESCOTT Aaron	LINES Christopher	ANTHONY Byron	COLES Daniel	CAMPBELL Stuart	PIPE David	LAMBERT Rickie	OSEI KUFFOUR Jonathan	HUGHES Jeffrey	DUFFY Darryl	BLIZZARD Dominic	HUNT Benjamin	WILLIAMS Andrew	EVANS Rhys	SWALLOW Benjamin	ANDERSEN Mikkel(L)	WRIGHT Mark	ELLIOTT Steven	DICKSON Christopher(L)	REECE Charles	BALDWIN Patrick(L)	BROWN Wayne(L)	HEFFERNAN Paul(L)	JONES Daniel(L)	RICHARDS Elliot	RIGG Sean				
08/08/2009	LEYTON ORIENT	H	1	2	7745	P	P	P	PB	P	P	P	P	P	P	PA	A	B																LAMBERT			
15/08/2009	STOCKPORT COUNTY	A	2	0	4084	P	P	P	P	P	P	P	P		P	P	PB		A															OSEI-KUFFOUR	COLES		
18/08/2009	HARTLEPOOL UNITED	A	2	1	3137	P	P	P	P	P	P	P	PB		P	P	PA	B		A														LESCOTT	OSEI-KUFFOUR		
22/08/2009	HUDDERSFIELD TOWN	H	1	0	6952	P	P	P	P	P	P	P	P		PB	P	PA	A		B														HUGHES pen			
29/08/2009	WYCOMBE WANDERERS	A	1	2	5214		P	PB	P	P	P	P	P		P	P	PA		A		P	B												LINES			
05/09/2009	MILLWALL	H	2	0	6038		P	P	P	P	P	P	B		PC	P	PA	C		A			P	PB										HUGHES pen	LINES		
12/09/2009	OLDHAM ATHLETIC	H	1	0	6674		P	P	PC	P	P	P	B		P	P	PA	C		A			P	PB										OSEI-KUFFOUR			
19/09/2009	BRENTFORD	A	3	1	6528		P	P	P	P	P	P			PB	P		B		A			P	P		PA								DICKSON 2	LESCOTT		
26/09/2009	BRIGHTON & HOVE ALBION	H	1	1	8098		P	PC	P	P	P	P			P	P	A			B		C	P	PB		PA								OSEI-KUFFOUR			
29/09/2009	SOUTHAMPTON	A	3	2	19724		P	P	P	P	P	P			PC	P	B	C		A			P	PA		PB								DICKSON	OSEI-KUFFOUR	WILLIAMS	
03/10/2009	NORWICH CITY	A	1	5	24117		P	P	PB	P	P	P			P	P	C	B		A			P	PA		PC								HUGHES pen			
17/10/2009	SOUTHEND UNITED	A	1	2	6853		P	P	P	P		P			P	PB	C			A		B	P	PA	P	PC								GRANT og			
24/10/2009	YEOVIL TOWN	H	1	2	7812		P	PC	PA	P	P	P			P	P		A		B		C	P	PB		P								DICKSON			
27/10/2009	LEEDS UNITED	H	0	4	11448		P	P		P		P			P	P	B	PA		PC		C	P	A	P	PB											
31/10/2009	MILTON KEYNES DONS	A	1	2	9711		P	P	A	P		P			P	PC	C	PB		P			P	PA	P	B								LINES			
14/11/2009	CARLISLE UNITED	H	3	2	5862		P		P	P	P	P			P	P	A	PC		B		PB	P			PA	C							OSEI-KUFFOUR	HUGHES	LINES	
21/11/2009	GILLINGHAM	H	2	1	6210				P	P	P	P			PC	P	A	PB		P		B	P	C		PA		P						LINES	HUGHES pen		
24/11/2009	CHARLTON ATHLETIC	A	2	4	15885				P	P	P	P			P	P	P	PA		PB		A	P	B				P						HUGHES pen	LINES		
01/12/2009	EXETER CITY	H	1	0	7313		P		P		P	P			P	P	PC	PB		A		B	P	PA		C		P						DUFFY			
05/12/2009	COLCHESTER UNITED	A	0	1	4942		P		P		P	P			P	PB	P	PA		C		A	P	PC	P	B											
12/12/2009	SWINDON TOWN	H	3	0	7613		P	P	P			P			PA	P	B			PB			P	PC	P	A	C	P						WILLIAMS	HUGHES	OSEI-KUFFOUR	
19/12/2009	TRANMERE ROVERS	A	0	2	4755		P	PC	P			P				P	A	C		P		B	P	PB	P	PA		P									
28/12/2009	MILLWALL	A	0	2	10014		P	PB	P		P	P			P		A	B		P		PA	P	P				P									
19/01/2010	HUDDERSFIELD TOWN	A	0	0	12624		P	P	P	P	P	P			P	P	A			PA			P	P													
23/01/2010	HARTLEPOOL UNITED	H	2	0	5794		P	P	P	P	P	P			P	PC	A			PA		C	P	PB			B							LINES	DUFFY		
30/01/2010	WYCOMBE WANDERERS	H	2	3	6688		P	PB	P	P	P	P			P	P	P			A		B	P	PA										LINES 2			
02/02/2010	LEYTON ORIENT	A	0	5	2931		P	PA	P	P	P	PC			P	P		C		P		A	P	B					PB								
06/02/2010	WALSALL	A	0	0	3886		P			P		P			P	P		P		P			P	P	P				P								
09/02/2010	WALSALL	H	0	1	5919					P		P			P	P		P		P		B	P	PB	P		A		PA	P							
15/02/2010	CHARLTON ATHLETIC	H	2	1	7624			C	PC	P	P	P			PA	P		PB		A			P		P		B			P	P			ELLIOTT	HEFFERNAN		
20/02/2010	GILLINGHAM	A	0	1	5302			P		P		P				P		P		PB	P	A			P		PA			P	P	B					
27/02/2010	COLCHESTER UNITED	H	3	2	6023		B		P	P	P	P			P	PC		PB		A		C	P		P					PA	P			BLIZZARD	OSEI-KUFFOUR	LINES	
02/03/2010	STOCKPORT COUNTY	H	1	0	5322				P	P	P	P			PB	P		PA		B	P				P		A			P	P			HUGHES			
06/03/2010	SWINDON TOWN	A	4	0	10341				P	P	P	P			P	P		P		A			P		P					PA	P			OSEI-KUFFOUR	HEFFERNAN	LINES	HUGHES
13/03/2010	TRANMERE ROVERS	H	0	0	6477				P	PA	P	P			P	P		PB		B			P		P				A	P	P						
16/03/2010	EXETER CITY	A	0	1	5269				P	P	P	P			P	PA		P		A			P		P					P	P						
20/03/2010	YEOVIL TOWN	A	3	0	5968				P	P	P	P			P	P		P		A			P		P					PA	P			OSEI KUFFOUR 2	HEFFERNAN		
27/03/2010	SOUTHEND UNITED	H	4	3	6476		B		P	PB	P	P			P	P		PA		A			P		P					P	P			OSEI-KUFFOUR	HUGHES 2-1pen	GRANT og	
02/04/2010	CARLISLE UNITED	A	1	3	5407		P		P			P			P	P		PB		PA		B	P		P		A			P	P			HEFFERNAN			
05/04/2010	MILTON KEYNES DONS	H	1	0	6406		P		P		P	P			P		PA	PB		A		P	P		P		B				P			OSEI-KUFFOUR			
10/04/2010	OLDHAM ATHLETIC	A	1	2	3769				P	P	P	P			P	P	PA	PB		A		B	P		P						P			OSEI-KUFFOUR			
13/04/2010	SOUTHAMPTON	H	1	5	8607		A		P	P	P	P			P	P		P		P			P		PA						P			HUGHES pen			
17/04/2010	BRENTFORD	H	0	0	6048		P		P		P	P			PA	P	A			P		P	P				PB				P	B					
24/04/2010	BRIGHTON & HOVE ALBION	A	1	2	6922		P		P		P	P				P	P			PB		PA	P	B			P				P	A		WILLIAMS			
01/05/2010	NORWICH CITY	H	0	3	8836		P		P			P				P	P			PA		P	P				P				P	A					
08/05/2010	LEEDS UNITED	A	1	2	38324		P		P	P	P	P			P	P	PB	P		A			P				PA				P	B		DUFFY			
	APPEARANCES					4	32	23	41	36	36	46	5	1	42	44	15	23	0	18	3	6	39	19	21	10	5	6	3	11	17	0					
	SUB					0	3	1	1	0	0	0	2	0	0	0	15	12	2	25	0	18	0	5	0	4	8	0	1	0	0	5					
	GOALS					0	0	2	11	0	1	0	0	1	14	12	3	1	0	3	0	0	0	0	1	4	0	0	0	4	0	0		OWN GOAL 2			
	SUBD					0	0	7	5	2	0	1	1	0	9	7	10	15	0	9	0	3	0	15	1	9	3	0	1	3	0	0					
	CARLING CUP																																				
11/08/2009	ALDERSHOT TOWN	H	2	1	3544		P	P	P	P		P	PA		P	P	P	A			P	C											PC	DUFFY 2-1 pen			
26/08/2009	CARDIFF CITY	A	1	3	9767		P		P	P		P	PC		P	P	PB	PA		B	P	A			P		C							ELLIOTT			
	E.ON FA CUP																																				
06/11/2009	SOUTHAMPTON	H	2	3	6446		P		P	P		P			P	P	B	PB		P	P	A		PA	P									DUFFY	HUGHES pen		
	JP TROPHY																																				
01/09/2009	HEREFORD UNITED	A	0	0	970		P	P	P			P	P			P	P	P			P	PA			P		A										
	AET Lost 4-2 on pens																																				

2010/11

Date	Opponent	H/A	F	A	Att	ANDERSEN Mikkel (L)	ANTHONY Byron	SAWYER Gary	COLES Daniel	TUNNICLIFFE James (L)	BLIZZARD Dominic	CAMPBELL Stuart	BROWN Wayne	HOSKINS William	OSEI-KUFFOUR Jonathan	HUGHES Jeffrey	LINES Christopher	DUFFY Darryl	REECE Charles	REGAN Carl	SWALLOW Benjamin	GREEN Michael J	AKINDE John (L)	RICHARDS Elliot	PELL Harry	DANIELS Luke (L)	McCRACKEN David (L)	DAVIES Scott (L)	HOWE Rene (L)	BOLGER Cian (L)	KALALA Jean-Paul	WILLIAMS Gavin	LOGAN Conrad (L)	SENDA Daniel	IFIL Jerel	THOMPSON-LAMBE Reginald	HARRISON Ellis	POWELL Lamar	CLOUGH Charles	CLARKE Oliver	GREEN Michael				
	LEAGUE 1 (3)																																												
07/08/2010	PETERBOROUGH UNITED	A	0	3	7173	P	P	P	P	P	P	P	PB	P	P	PA	A	B																											
14/08/2010	YEOVIL TOWN	H	2	1	6438	P	P	P	P	P		P	P	P	P	P	P																									OSEI-KUFFOUR	ANTHONY		
21/08/2010	EXETER CITY	A	2	2	7401	P	P	P	P	P		P	PB	PA	P	P	P	A	B																							OSEI-KUFFOUR	HOSKINS		
28/08/2010	SOUTHAMPTON	H	0	4	8226	P	P	P	P	P		P	PA	P	P	P	P	B	AB																										
04/09/2010	OLDHAM ATHLETIC	A	1	1	4039	P	P	P	P	B	PA	P		P	PB	P	P			P		P	A																			HOSKINS			
11/09/2010	BRENTFORD	H	0	0	5609	P	P	P		P		P	A	PA	P	P	P			P			P																						
18/09/2010	DAGENHAM & REDBRIDGE	A	3	0	2287	P	P		P	P		P	A	PA	P	P	P			P			P																			HUGHES 3-1pen			
25/09/2010	NOTTS COUNTY	H	2	1	5962	P	P	P	PC	C		P	A	PB	P	P	P			P			PA	B																		HOSKINS 2			
28/09/2010	TRANMERE ROVERS	H	0	1	5589	P	P	P	P			PA	A	P	P	P	P			P			P																						
02/10/2010	HUDDERSFIELD TOWN	A	1	0	12344	P	P	P	P	B		P	A	P	P	P	P			PB			PA																			HOSKINS			
11/10/2010	SWNDON TOWN	A	1	2	9065	P	P	P	P			P		P	P	P	P		A	P		P	PA																			HUGHES pen			
16/10/2010	ROCHDALE	H	2	1	5872	P	P	P	P			P	A	P	PB	P	P		PA	P			B																			HUGHES pen	LINES		
23/10/2010	HARTLEPOOL UNITED	A	2	2	2792	P	P	P	P			P	C	PC	P	PA	P		PB	P	B		A																			OSEI-KUFFOUR	ANTHONY		
30/10/2010	CARLISLE UNITED	H	1	1	6144	P	P	P	P			P		P	PA	P	P		P	P			A																			LINES			
02/11/2010	PLYMOUTH ARGYLE	A	1	3	7413	P	P	P	P			PA	A	P	P	P	P		PB	P	B																					HOSKINS			
13/11/2010	LEYTON ORIENT	H	0	3	5541	P	P	P	P	B		PC	PB		P	P	P			P			PA	A	C																				
20/11/2010	BRIGHTON & HOVE ALBION	A	2	2	7407	P	P	P	P			P	PB	A	P	P	P				P		PA	B																		ANTHONY	BENNETT og		
23/11/2010	CHARLTON ATHLETIC	A	1	1	13468	P		P	P	P		P	P	A	P	P	P				P		PA																			BROWN			
11/12/2010	SHEFFIELD WEDNESDAY	A	2	6	19242	P	P	P	P	P		P	PA	P	PC	PB	P		C		B		A																			HOSKINS 2			
01/01/2011	MILTON KEYNES DONS	A	0	2	7185	P	P	P	P			P		P	P	A	P		PA	P	PB			B																					
04/01/2011	PLYMOUTH ARGYLE	H	2	3	5943	P	P	P				P	PA	P	B	P	P		A	P	PB			P																		HOSKINS 2			
11/01/2011	WALSALL	H	2	2	4023			P	P	P	B	P		P	A	P	PB			P	P			PA		P																HOSKINS	OSEI-KUFFOUR		
15/01/2011	CARLISLE UNITED	A	0	4	4229		A	PC	P	P	C	P	B	P	PB	P	P			P	PA					P																			
18/01/2011	HARTLEPOOL UNITED	H	0	0	5285		P	P		P		P		P	P		P		A	PA	PB			B		P	P																		
22/01/2011	SWNDON TOWN	H	3	1	6972		P	P				P		P	P	P	P			P	P					P	P															HOSKINS	OSEI-KUFFOUR	HUGHES	
29/01/2011	WALSALL	A	1	6	4023		P	P			P	P		P	PB	P				PC	PA					P	P	A	B	C												HUGHES			
02/02/2011	MILTON KEYNES DONS	H	1	2	4829		P	PC				PB		P	C	P				B						P	PA	P	P	P	P	A										HUGHES pen			
05/02/2011	BRIGHTON & HOVE ALBION	H	2	4	6683		P		P					P	A	P	P				B					P		P	PA	P	PB	P										HOSKINS 2			
08/02/2011	ROCHDALE	A	1	3	2372		P	P	P				B	P		P				A						P		PA	P	P	P	PB										HOSKINS			
12/02/2011	LEYTON ORIENT	A	1	4	4913		P	P	P	P				P	B	P					A					P		PA	P		P	PB										CROWE og			
19/02/2011	OLDHAM ATHLETIC	H	1	0	5379		P	P	P					P		A	P				PA							B	P		P	PB	P	P								HOWE			
26/02/2011	BRENTFORD	A	0	1	5944			P	P					P	A	P	P		B										P		P	PB	P	PA	P										
01/03/2011	COLCHESTER UNITED	H	0	1	5181				P					PB	P	P	P							B				A	PA		P	P	P	P	P										
05/03/2011	DAGENHAM & REDBRIDGE	H	0	2	5716			P	PC			P		PB	B	P	P							C					P	A	P	PA	P		P										
08/03/2011	TRANMERE ROVERS	A	1	0	4110			P		P		P		P		P	P		PA					B	A					P		PB	P	P								LINES			
12/03/2011	HUDDERSFIELD TOWN	H	0	1	7380			P	P	P		PC		P	A	P	P		B					C	PB							PA	P	P											
19/03/2011	NOTTS COUNTY	A	1	0	5691			P	P	P		P		PB	A	P	P								PC		C		B			PA	P	P								HOSKINS			
25/03/2011	PETERBOROUGH UNITED	H	2	2	6589		P		P	P		P		P	P	P	P								PA								P	P		A						OSEI KUFFOUR	HUGHES		
02/04/2011	YEOVIL TOWN	A	1	0	6281		P		P	P		PC	C	P	PB	P	P								PA		B					A	P	P								WILLIAMS			
05/04/2011	AFC BOURNEMOUTH	H	1	0	6691		PC		P	P		PB		PA	P	P	P								B		C					P	P	P		A						HUGHES pen			
09/04/2011	EXETER CITY	H	0	2	7500			PC	P	P			C		P	P	P							B	P		A					P	P	PA		PB									
16/04/2011	SOUTHAMPTON	A	0	1	23647		P		P	P		PC			PB	P	P								PA							P	P	P		A	B	C							
23/04/2011	CHARLTON ATHLETIC	H	2	2	6586		P		PB	PC		P	C	P	P	PA	P										B					P	P	P		A						BROWN	WILLIAMS		
25/04/2011	AFC BOURNEMOUTH	A	1	2	7869		P	P				PA	PC	PB	P		P										P		C		A	P	P	P		B						BROWN			
30/04/2011	SHEFFIELD WEDNESDAY	H	1	1	8340		P	PC	PA				P	P	P		P				B								C		P	PB	P	P					A			HOSKINS pen			
07/05/2011	COLCHESTER UNITED	A	1	2	4759		P						PA	PC			P				P			A	PB						P	P	P	P		C			P	B		RICHARDS			
	APPEARANCES					21	36	37	37	21	3	37	12	41	33	40	41	0	6	19	11	2	9	2	7	9	5	4	8	4	10	17	16	15	3	1	0	0	1	0					
	SUB					0	1	0	0	4	2	0	13	2	9	2	1	3	8	2	6	0	5	11	3	0	5	3	4	2	1	2	0	0	0	6	1	1	1	1					
	GOALS					0	3	0	0	0	0	0	3	17	6	10	3	0	0	0	0	0	0	1	0	0	0	0	1	0	0	2	0	0	0	0	0	0	0	0		OWN GOAL 2			
	SUB'D					0	1	4	4	1	1	9	9	11	8	4	1	0	6	3	6	0	6	1	6	0	1	2	2	0	1	9	0	2	0	1	0	0	0	0					
	CARLING CUP																																												
10/08/2010	OXFORD UNITED	A	1	6	5008		P	P		P	PA	P		P	P	PB	P		A	P	B																				P	LINES			
	E.ON FA CUP																																												
06/11/2010	DARLINGTON	A	0	1	1602		P	P	P				PC	PA	P	P	P		PB	P	B		A	C																	P	OSEI KUFFOUR			
	JP TROPHY																																												
05/10/2010	ALDERSHOT TOWN	H	1	0	4050	P	P	P	P		PB	P	B	P	PA	P			A	P			PC	C																		HOSKINS			
09/11/2010	WYCOMBE WANDERERS	A	6	3	1591	P	P	P	PC	C		P	PA		P	P	P			P	A		PB	B																		OSEI KUFFOUR 3	LINES	HUGHES pen	SWALLOW
14/12/2010	EXETER CITY *	H	2	2	3881	P	P	P	P			P		P			P		P	P	P		PA	A																		HOSKINS	SWALLOW		

* Lost 5-4 on pens

2011/12

Date	Opponent	H/A	F	A	Att	BEVAN Scott	SMITH Michael	BROWN Lee	ANTHONY Byron	VIRGO Adam	STANLEY Craig	GILL Mattew	ANYINSAH Joseph	HARROLD Matthew	ZEBROSKI Christoher	McGLEISH Scott	LINES Christopher	KUFFOUR Joseph	CARAYOL Mustapha	BROWN Wayne	BOLGER Cian (L)	RICHARDS Eliot	CAMPBELL Stuart	WOODARDS Daniel	SAWYER Gary	RENDELL Scott (L)	NORBURN Oliver (L)	DORMAN Andrew (L)	McGLAGGON Kayne	CRONIN Lance	POKE Michael (L)	DOWNES Aaron (L)	PARKES Thomas (L)	PATERSON James	LUND Matthew (L)	GOUGH Conor	HARDING Mitch	BOATENG Michael	GODDARD Jordan	JEFFERIES Darren	SWALLOW Benjamin	Scorers		
	LEAGUE 2 (4)																																											
06/08/2011	AFC WIMBLEDON	A	3	2	4629	P	P	P	P	P	P	P	PC	P	PA	PB	A	B	C																							McGLEISH	HARROLD	VIRGO pen
13/08/2011	TORQUAY UNITED	H	1	2	8427	P	P	P	P	P	PB	P	PC	P	C	PA		A	PC	B																						ANTHONY		
16/08/2011	NORTHAMPTON TOWN	H	2	1	5812	P		P	P	P	P	P	PA	P	A	PB		P		B	P																					KUFFOUR	HARROLD	
20/08/2011	MACCLESFIELD	A	0	0	1865	P		P	P	P	P	P		P	PB	P		PA		A	P	B																						
27/08/2011	HEREFORD UNITED	H	0	0	6342	P	PB	P	P	P	PA	P		P	P	P		PC	C	B			A																					
03/09/2011	CRAWLEY TOWN	A	1	4	3693	P	A	P	P	PC		P		PB	P	B			PA	P		C	P	P																		BROWN L		
10/09/2011	BRADFORD CITY	A	2	2	10023	P		P	A	P		PA	B	P		PB				P	P	P	P	P																		HARROLD	RICHARDS	
13/09/2011	SHREWSBURY TOWN	H	1	0	5065	P	A	PA		P		PB	C	P	PC	B				P	P	P	P	P																		ZEBROSKI		
17/09/2011	ALDERSHOT TOWN	H	0	1	5640	P		P		P	B		PC		P	C			A	PB	P	PA	P	P																				
24/09/2011	MORECAMBE	A	3	2	2583	P	B	P	P		A	PA	PC	P	P	P					P	C	P	PB																		BOLGER	McLEISH	ANYINSAH
01/10/2011	CHELTENHAM TOWN	A	1	3	6108	P	A	P	P		P		P	B	PC				PB	C	P	P	P	PA																		BROWN L		
08/10/2011	OXFORD UNITED	A	0	3	9291	P	A	P	PA		P		P	B	P	PB					P		P		P	P																		
14/10/2011	ROTHERHAM UNITED	H	5	2	5395	P		P			P	P	A	PC	C	P					P		PB	P	P	P	B															McLEISH 2 -1 pen	BOLGER	BROWN L ANYINSAH
22/10/2011	BURTON ALBION	A	1	2	3094	P		P			P	PC	B	P	C	PB					P		PA	P	P	P	A															HARROLD		
25/10/2011	PORT VALE	H	0	3	5444	P		P			P	P	A	P	C	PC			B		P			PB	P	P	PA																	
29/10/2010	DAGENHAM & REDBRIDGE	H	0	2	5475	P		P			P	P	P	P		PA			P		P			P	P	A																ANYINSAH	HARROLD pen	
05/11/2011	ACCRINGTON STANLEY	A	1	2	1643	P		P			P		P	P	A	PA			P		P		P	P	P																	ANYINSAH		
19/11/2011	BARNET	A	0	2	5024	P		P			A	PA	P	P	PB	B			P		P	CB		P	P			P																
26/11/2011	SOUTHEND UNITED	A	1	1	6237	P		P	P		P	P	P	B	PB				PA			P		P	P			P														HARROLD		
10/12/2011	SWINDON TOWN	H	1	1	7726	P		P	P		P		P	P	PA				PB			A		P	P		B	P														WOODARDS		
17/12/2011	GILLINGHAM	A	1	4	7750	P		P	PA		P		PC	B	PB				P		A	P		P	P		C	P														CARAYLOL		
26/12/2011	PLYMOUTH ARGYLE	H	2	3	8090	P		P	P		P		PB	P	PA	A						P		P	P			P	B													HARROLD 2		
31/12/2011	CREWE ALEXANDRA	H	2	5	5037	PB		A	PA		P		PC	P	P	C			P			P		P	P			P		B												HARROLD	McLEISH	
02/01/2012	BARNET	A	0	2	2537						PB		B	PA	P	A			P		P	P		P	P			P			P	P												
10/01/2012	HEREFORD UNITED	A	2	1	2411			P			P		P		P	A					P	P		P	PA			P			P	P										BROWN L	McLEISH	
14/01/2012	CRAWLEY TOWN	H	0	0	5082			P	B		P		PA		P	A					P	PB		P	P			P			P	P												
21/01/2012	CHELTENHAM TOWN	A	2	0	5288			P			P		PA		P	A					P	P		P	P			P			P	P										ZEBROSKI	RICHARDS	
28/01/2012	BRADFORD CITY	H	2	1	6164		P	P			P	P			P	A					P	P		PA				P			P	P										BROWN L	RICHARDS	
11/02/2012	MORECAMBE	H	2	1	5381			P			P	P	PA	PB		P					P	A		P							P		P	P	B							BROWN L	McLEISH pen	
14/02/2012	SHREWSBURY TOWN	A	0	1	4928			PC			P	P	PB	PA		B					P	P		P				C			P		P	P	A									
18/02/2012	OXFORD UNITED	H	0	0	6512			P				P	PB		PC	C			A		P	B		P				PA			P		P	P	P									
25/02/2012	ROTHERHAM UNITED	A	1	0	3937	P		C				P	PC	A	PA				PB		P	B		P				P					P	P	P							DORMAN		
03/03/2012	MACCLESFIELD	H	0	0	5420	P	PB	P			B	P		P	A				P		P			P				PA						P	P									
06/03/2012	NORTHAMPTON TOWN	A	2	3	4028	P	A	P			P	P	PB		C				P		P	B		PA									P	P	PC							STANLEY	BROWN L pen	
10/03/2012	TORQUAY UNITED	A	2	2	3920	P					P	P	BC	PB	P				PA		P	C		P				P					P	P	A							HARROLD	ZEBROSKI	
17/03/2012	AFC WIMBLEDON	H	1	0	5828	P	A	PA			P	P		P	P				PB		P	B		P									P	P								CARAYOL		
20/03/2012	PLYMOUTH ARGYLE	A	1	1	7531	P	A	PA			P	P		P	P				PB		P			P				B					P	P								HARROLD		
24/03/2012	SOUTHEND UNITED	H	1	0	6258	P		A			P	PC		P	PA				P		P	B		P				C					P	P	PB							HARROLD pen		
27/03/2012	ALDERSHOT TOWN	A	0	1	2870	P	P	PB						P	A				B		P	PA		P	P			P						P	P									
31/03/2012	SWINDON TOWN	A	0	0	9645	P	A	B				P		P	PC				PA		P			P	PB			C					P	P	P									
06/04/2012	GILLINGHAM	H	2	2	6150	P	C				P	A		P	PB				P		P	B		PC	P								P	PA	P							RICHARDS	CARAYLOL	
09/04/2012	CREWE ALEXANDRA	A	0	3	4139	P	PB					P	A	P	B						P	P		P	PA			C				P	P		PC									
14/04/2012	BURTON ALBION	H	7	1	5353	P	C	B				P		P					PB	A	P	P		PC	P			P					P	PA								CARAYOL	RICHARDS 3	HARROLD 2 PATERSON
21/04/2012	PORT VALE	A	0	1	4066	P	A	C				P		P	B				PA		P	PB		P	P			P					P	PC										
28/04/2012	ACCRINGTON STANLEY	H	5	1	7073	P	P	A				P		P					P	C	P	PC			PA			P				P		PB	B							HARROLD 2 -1 pen	DORMAN	LUND 2
30/04/2012	DAGENHAM & REDBRIDGE	A	0	4	2377			PA				P		P					P	A	P	PC		P	B			P				P		PB		P	C							
	APPEARANCES					37	7	34	14	9	30	32	21	34	27	14	0	3	24	4	37	19	10	39	22	4	1	20	0	0	8	8	14	17	9	1	0	0	0	0	0			
	SUB					0	12	7	2	0	4	1	8	5	11	12	1	2	6	8	1	14	1	0	0	1	4	5	1	1	0	0	0	0	4	0	1	0	0	0	0			
	GOALS					0	0	7	1	1	1	0	4	15	3	7	0	1	4	0	2	7	0	1	1	0	0	2	0	0	0	0	0	1	2	0	0	0	0	0	0			
	SUB'D					1	3	6	3	1	3	6	15	6	14	9	0	2	12	1	0	7	2	6	4	0	1	2	0	0	0	0	0	5	3	0	0	0	0	0	0			
	CARLING CUP																																											
23/08/2011	WATFORD*	H	1	1	4432	P	A	P	P	P	P	P		PC	PB	P		P	B	C	PA																					HARROLD		
30/08/2011	LEYTON ORIENT	A	2	3	1881	P	P	P	P	PA	P	PB		P	P				PC	P		C	B	A																		ZEBROSKI	RICHARDS	
	* Won 4-2 on pens																																											
	JOHNSTONES PAINT TROPHY																																											
06/09/2011	WYCOMBE WANDERERS	A	1	3	771	P	P	P	P		A	PA		P		P				P		P	P	PB														B				HARROLD		
	BUDWEISER FA CUP																																											
12/11/2011	CORBY TOWN	H	3	1	3787	P		P			PB			P	P	PA			P		P	A		P	P			P											B			McLEISH pen	CARAYLOL	ZEBROSKI
04/12/2011	AFC TOTTON	A	6	1	2236	P		P	P				PC	P	P				PA			A		P	P		PB	P												B	C	ANYINSAH	CARAYLOL	WOODARDS ANTHONY
07/01/2011	ASTON VILLA	A	1	3	10883			B			P		PC		P	A			PA		P	PB		P	P			P	C		P	P										McLEISH		

2012/13

Date	LEAGUE 2 (4)	H/A	F	A	Att.	WALKER Samuel (L)	SMITH Michael	BROWN Lee	VIRGO Adam	PATERSON James	ANYINSAH Joseph	GILL Matthew	LUND Matthew (L)	BROWN Wayne	CLARKSON David	HARROLD Matthew	RICHARDS Eliot	BROGHAMMER Fabian	NORBURN Oliver	PARKES Thomas	LUCAS Seanan	BOLGER Cian (L)	KENNETH Garry	ETHERIDGE Neil (L)	EAVES Thomas (L)	RIORDAN Derek	CLARKE Oliver	WOODARDS Daniel	SANTOS Alefe	BRANSTON Guy	MILDENHALL Stephen	O'TOOLE John Joseph (L)	HITCHCOCK Thomas (L)	HARDING Mitch	McCRYSTAL Mark	HARRISON Ellis	LOCKYER Thomas	BRUNT Ryan	McDONALD Clayton (L)	TOUNKARA Oumare	GOUGH Conor	Scorers		
18/08/2012	OXFORD UNITED	H	0	2	7451	P	P	P	P	P	PB	P	PA	PC	P	P	A	B	C																									
21/08/2012	BARNET	A	1	1	1794	P	P	P	P	P		P		A	P	P	PB	B		P	PA																					HARROLD		
01/09/2012	MORECAMBE	H	0	3	5207	P	P	PB	P	P	C	P	B	PA	P	P	PC	A		P																								
08/08/2012	ALDERSHOT TOWN	H	2	2	5117	P	A	P	PA	PB		P		PC	P	P	P	B	C	P		P																				CLARKSON	BROGHAMMER	
15/09/2012	GILLINGHAM	A	0	4	4768	P	P	P	P	PB		PC	C	P	P	PA	P	A	B	P																								
18/09/2012	PLYMOUTH ARGYLE	A	1	1	6303	P	B	P	P		C	P	PA	PC	P		A	P	P	P			P																			PARKES		
22/09/2012	FLEETWOOD TOWN	H	0	0	5079		P	P			PB	P	B	PA	P		A	P	P	P			P	P																				
29/09/2012	EXETER CITY	A	2	1	5054			A	P	P			C		P		B	PA	P	P			P	P	PB	PC																CLARKSON	RICHARDS	
03/10/2012	CHELTENHAM TOWN	H	0	1	5747		B		P	PB		P	P	C	P		A	PA	PC				P	P	P	P																		
06/10/2012	NORTHAMPTON TOWN	H	3	1	5166		B	C		P			P	A	PA		P	PC	P	P			P	P	P	PB																EAVES	KENNETH	NORBURN
13/10/2012	BURTON ALBION	A	1	1	2961			A	C	PA	PC		P	B	P		P	P	PB	P			P	P	P																	CLARKSON		
20/10/2012	TORQUAY UNITED	H	3	2	6331			A		P	PB		P	B	P		P	PA	P	P			P	P	P																	EAVES 2	LUND	
23/10/2012	AFC WIMBLEDON	A	1	3	3714				PA	P	A		P	P	P		PB		P	P			P	P	P		B															EAVES		
27/10/2012	ACCRINGTON STANLEY	A	0	1	1462			P		P	B		P	P	P		P	PB	PA				P	P	P	A																		
06/11/2012	SOUTHEND UNITED	H	2	3	4721			P		PA			P	A	P		B	P	B	P	PB		P	P	PC	P																BROGHAMMER	CLARKSON pen	
10/11/2012	CHESTERFIELD	H	3	2	5491		B			P	P		P	P	P		A	PA		P			P	P	P	PB																TOGWELL og	ANYINSAH	EAVES
17/11/2012	ROCHDALE	A	1	2	2204		P			P	P			P	PA		C	A		P	B		P	P	P	PC		PB														CLARKSON pen		
20/12/2012	PORT VALE	A	0	4	4177		P	P		P		A	P	P				PC		P	PB			P	P	B		PA	C															
24/11/2012	BRADFORD CITY	H	3	3	5092	P	P			P	P			P							P		P		P	P		P		P												BRANSTON	EAVES	SMITH
01/12/2012	WYCOMBE WANDERERS	A	0	2	3740	P	PB			P		PA	P		P				A	P	C		P		P	B		PC		P														
08/12/2012	DAGENHAM & REDBRIDGE	H	0	1	4874	P				P	PC				P		A	P	PA	P	B		PB		P	C		P		P														
15/12/2012	YORK CITY	A	1	4	3109	P	B			P	P		PA		P		C	P		P	A		P		P			PB		PC												EAVES		
26/12/2012	ALDERSHOT TOWN	A	2	2	2862	P	P	A		PA	P				PB		C	P	B	P	PC	P	P		P																	CLARKSON	RICHARDS	
01/01/2013	PLYMOUTH ARGYLE	H	2	1	7332		P	P			PC		P				B	PB	PA	P	A	P									P	P	P	C								ANYINSAH	LUND	
05/01/2013	GILLINGHAM	H	0	2	6088		P	P			PB						P	PC	A	P	P		PA								P	P	B	C	P									
12/01/2013	FLEETWOOD TOWN	A	3	0	2811		P	P									PA			P	P							PA			P	P	P	A	P	PB	B					WOODARDS	RICHARDS	O'TOOLE
26/01/2013	ROTHERHAM UNITED	A	1	3	6582		P	P			PB				B		PA		P	P	P							B			P	P			P	A		PC				BROWN L pen	HARRISON	ANYINSAH
01/02/2013	BARNET	H	2	1	8527		P	P			PA				A		B	PC	PB	P	P							C			P	P			P			P				BROGHAMMER	BRUNT	
05/02/2013	CHELTENHAM TOWN	A	1	1	4436		P	P			PC						B	A	P	P	PB							PA			P	P	B		P			P				NORBURN		
09/02/2013	OXFORD UNITED	A	2	0	7608		P	P			PA				A		C	B	PC	P	P							PB			P	P			P			P				BROWN L pen	RICHARDS	
16/02/2013	WYCOMBE WANDERERS	H	1	0	7324		P	P			PB				A		B	PC	PA	P	P										P	P			P			P	C			BRUNT		
19/02/2013	ROTHERHAM UNITED	H	1	2	8646		P	P			P				B		A	PA	PC	P	P										P	P	C		P			PB				ANYINSAH		
23/02/2013	MORECAMBE	A	1	1	1736		P	P		C	P						P		A	P	PB							PA			P	P	PC		P	B						RICHARDS		
26/02/2013	NORTHAMPTON TOIWN	A	0	1	4077		P	P			P						P		P	P								P			P	P	PA		P	A								
02/03/2013	BURTON ALBION	H	3	0	6065		P	P		C	PA						P		A	P								P			P	P			P	PC		PB		B		BRUNT	O'TOOLE	RICHARDS
06/03/2013	EXETER CITY	H	2	0	7107		P	P									PB	A	P	P								PC			P	P	B		P	PA		P	C			NORBURN	BROWN L	
09/03/2013	CHESTERFIELD	A	0	2	4814		P	P			PA						P	A	P	P								PB			P	P	B		P			PC		C				
12/03/2013	PORT VALE	H	2	0	5111		P	P		P							PA		PB	P								P			P	P	A	C		PC	B	P				BRUNT 2		
16/03/2013	ROCHDALE	H	2	1	6691		P	P		PA							P			P								P			P	P	A		P	PB		P		A		HARRISON 2		
30/03/2013	YORK CITY	H	0	0	7378		P	P			P						P	A		P								P			P	P	C		P	P		P		B				
01/04/2013	DAGENHAM & REDBRIDGE	A	4	2	2082		PB	PA		A								PC		P								P				P	C		P	P	B	P		P	P	O'TOOLE	TOUNKARA 2	WOODARDS
06/04/2013	AFC WIMBLEDON	H	1	0	6881		P	P			A							PC	P									P			P		B		P	PA	C	PB	P	P		HITCHCOCK		
09/04/2013	BRADFORD CITY	A	1	4	10621		P	P			PB						B	P	P								A	PA			P		P		P			P	P			HITCHCOCK		
13/04/2013	SOUTHEND UNITED	A	0	0	4612		P	P			B						C	PC	P	P							A				P		PB		P			PA	P	P				
20/04/2013	ACCRINGTON STANLEY	H	0	1	7673		P	P			C						P	P	A	P							P				P				P	PB		B	PA	PC				
27/04/2013	TORQUAY UNITED	A	3	3	5666		P	P								B		P	P	P							P				P		PC	A	P	PA		PB		C		HITCHCOCK	JARVIS og	HARROLD
	APPEARANCES					11	32	34	9	23	24	9	14	13	21	5	21	25	25	40	14	3	18	12	16	7	2	20	0	4	22	18	7	0	21	10	0	17	4	4	1			
	SUB					0	6	5	1	3	7	1	4	5	5	1	19	11	10	0	5	0	0	0	0	4	3	2	1	0	0	0	10	5	0	3	4	1	2	5	0			
	GOALS					0	1	3	0	0	4	0	2	0	6	2	6	3	3	1	0	0	1	0	7	0	0	2	0	1	0	3	3	0	0	3	0	5	0	2	0	OWN GOALS 2		
	SUB'D					0	2	2	0	7	15	2	3	6	3	1	6	15	10	0	5	0	2	0	2	4	0	10	0	0	0	0	4	0	0	7	0	7	1	1	0			
	CAPITAL ONE CUP																																											
14/08/2012	IPSWICH TOWN	A	1	3	8645	P	P	P	P	P	PC	PA	A	P	P	P			PB		B						C															SMITH		
	JP TROPHY																																											
04/09/2012	YEOVIL TOWN	H	0	3	2810	P	P	PA	P	P		P		P	P		P	A		P		P																						
	BUDWEISER FA CUP																																											
03/11/2012	SHEFFIELD UNITED	H	1	2	4712	P	P	P		P			P	A	P		C	PC	B		PA		P		PB	P																CLARKSON		

2013/14

Date	Opponent	Venue	F	A	Att	MILDENHALL Stephen	SMITH Michael	BROWN Lee	O'TOOLE John Joseph	McCHRYSTAL Mark	PARKES Thomas	NORBURN Oliver	CLARKSON David	RICHARDS Elliot	HARDING Mitch	HARRISON Ellis	SANTOS Alefe	HUNTER Shaquille	LOCKYER Thomas	BRUNT Ryan	GILL Matthew	HARROLD Matthew	BOND Andrew (L)	CLUCAS Seanan	CLARKE Oliver	KEARY Patrick	PACKWOOD William (L)	HENSHALL Alex (L)	BEARDSLEY Christopher (L)	WOODARDS Daniel	MOHAMED Kaid (L)	GOW Alan(L)	GILLESPIE Steven	BROGHAMMER Fabian	LUCAS James	Scorers		
	LEAGUE 2 (4)																																					
03/08/2013	EXETER CITY	A	1	2	5196	P	P	P	P	P	P	P	PC	P	PA	PB	A	B	C																	RICHARDS		
10/08/2013	SCUNTHORPE UNITED	H	0	0	6259	P	P	P	P	P	PA	P	PB	P	B	PC	A	C	P																			
17/08/2013	NEWPORT COUNTY	A	0	1	5387	P	P	P	PB	P	P	P	PA	P		P	A		P	B																		
24/08/2013	YORK CITY	H	3	2	5569	P	P	P	P	P	P	PA	PB		B		P		P	P	A															CLARKSON 2	O'TOOLE	
31/08/2013	NORTHAMPTON TOWN	H	1	0	5695	P	P	P	P	P	P	P	PB	B		P			P	PA		A														LOCKYER		
07/09/2013	PLYMOUTH ARGYLE	A	0	1	8631	P	P	P	P	P	P	P	PA			PB	A	C	PC	P		B																
14/09/2013	DAGENHAM & REDBRIDGE	A	0	2	1423	P	P	P	P	P	P	PC	B	PB		PA	A		C			P	P															
21/09/2013	HARTLEPOOL UNITED	H	2	2	5579	P	P	P	P	P	P		B	PB	PA	A			P			P	P													HARROLD	O'TOOLE	
27/09/2013	SOUTHEND UNITED	A	1	1	5489	P	P	P	P	P	P	PB				A				PA		P	P	B												HARROLD		
05/10/2013	FLEETWOOD TOWN	H	1	3	5303	P	P	P	P	P	P	PA				B			P	PB		A	P	P												O'TOOLE		
12/10/2013	MANSFIELD TOWN	A	1	1	3275	P	P	PA	P		P	PB	P	B			C		P	P			PC		P	A										SANTOS		
19/10/2013	WYCOMBE WANDERERS	H	0	1	5783	P	P		P		P		P		B	PB	C		P	PA				PC	P		P	A										
22/10/2013	ACCRINGTON STANLEY	A	1	2	1101	P	P		P		P			B		P	A		P	P				P	PA		P	PB								HENSHALL		
26/10/2013	CHESTERFIELD	H	0	0	5667	P	P		P		P			P			P		P	P				P	P		P											
02/11/2013	OXFORD UNITED	A	1	0	6374	P	P		P		P			P		B	PB		P	A				P	P		P		PA							O'TOOLE pen		
16/11/2013	BURY	H	1	1	5334	P	P	P	P		P			P		B	PB		A			P			PA		P		P							O'TOOLE pen		
23/11/2013	BURTON ALBION	A	0	1	2302	P	P	P	P		P		PA	P					P			A			P		P		P									
26/11/2013	CHELTENHAM TOWN	A	0	0	3556	P	P	P			P	P	P	PA	P	A			P			P					P											
30/11/2013	AFC WIMBLEDON	H	3	0	5860	P	P	P			P	PA	P	PB	P	B			P			P			A		P									CLARKSON	PARKES	HARROLD pen
14/12/2013	MORECAMBE	A	1	2	1514	P	P	P	P		P	PB	PA	P		A			P			P			P				B							O'TOOLE		
21/12/2013	PORTSMOUTH	H	2	0	7537	P	P	P	P	P	P	P	P	P								P			P											CLARKE	CLARKSON	
26/12/2013	TORQUAY UNITED	A	1	1	3461	P	P	P	P	P	P	P	PA	PB		B	A					P			P											HARROLD		
29/12/2013	ROCHDALE	A	0	2	2576	P	P	P	P	P	P	PB	PC	A		C	PA					P			P				B									
11/01/2014	EXETER CITY	H	2	1	6674	P	P	P	P	P	P		B	PC		PB			PA			P			P				A	C						O'TOOLE 2 -1 pen		
18/01/2014	YORK CITY	A	0	0	3514	P	P	P	P	P	P			P	PB				P			PA			P				A	B								
25/01/2014	NEWPORT COUNTY	H	3	0	7288	P	P	P	P	P	P			PA	A	C			P						P				PC	B	PB					MOHAMED	RICHARDS	O'TOOLE
28/01/2014	ACCRINGTON STANLEY	H	0	0	6067	P	P	P	P	P	P			PB		B			P			PA			P				A		P							
01/02/2014	CHESTERFIELD	A	1	3	6048	P	P	P	P	P	P		B			A			P			PB			P				P		PA					BROWN		
08/02/2014	OXFORD UNITED	H	1	1	6493	P	P	P	P	P	P								P						P				P		PA	P	A			O'TOOLE		
11/02/2014	CHELTENHAM TOWN	H	1	0	5808	P	P	P	P		P		PA		B				P					P					P		P	PB	A			O'TOOLE		
21/02/2014	BURTON ALBION	H	2	0	5957	P	P	P	P	P	P		PA						P					B					P		PB	P	A			CLARKSON	O'TOOLE	
25/02/2014	SCUNTHORPE UNITED	A	1	1	3318	P	P	P	P	P	P		P						PB						A				P		P	PA	B			GILLESPIE		
01/03/2014	NORTHAMPTON TOWN	A	0	0	5058	P	P		P	P	P		PB				B		P						P				PA		P		A					
08/03/2014	PLYMOUTH ARGYLE	H	2	1	7799	P	P	P	P	P	P		PA						P			A		B	P				PB		P					BEARDSLEY	MOHAMED	
11/03/2014	DAGENHAM & REDBRIDGE	H	1	2	5761	P	P	P	P	P	P		PB				C		P			A			PA				P		PC		B			O'TOOLE		
15/03/2014	HARTLEPOOL UNITED	A	0	4	3480	P	P	P	P	P	P		PB				B					P		PA	C				A	PC	P							
21/03/2014	SOUTHEND UNITED	H	0	0	6028	P	P	P	PC	P	P		C				B		P			A			P				P		PA		PB					
25/03/2014	FLEETWOOD TOWN	A	1	3	2023	P	P	P		P	P		PA			A			P			P			P				C	PC	B		PB			HARRISON		
29/04/2014	MORECAMBE	H	1	0	5647	P	P	P		P			P			A	P		P						P				PA	P	P					MOHAMED		
01/04/2014	BURY	A	1	2	2314	P	P	P	P	P	PB						B		P			P		A	PC					PA	P		C			MOHAMED		
05/04/2014	AFC WIMBLEDON	A	0	0	4322	P	P	P	P	P	P						A		PA			P		PB	P						P		B					
12/04/2014	TORQUAY UNITED	H	1	2	6612	P	P	P	P	P			C			A	PA					B			P				P	P	P		PB			WOODARDS		
19/04/2014	PORTSMOUTH	A	2	3	17998	P	PB	P		P	P		P						P			P		A	P					PA	P			B		HARROLD 2		
21/04/2014	ROCHDALE	H	1	2	8158	P		P	P	P	PC		PA		A				P			P		P	PB						P			B	C	MOHAMED		
26/04/2014	WYCOMBE WANDERERS	A	2	1	6752	P		P	PC	P	P		P						P			PB		P	C				B		P		A	PA		BROWN	CLARKSON	
03/05/2014	MANSFIELD TOWN	H																																				
	APPEARANCES					45	43	41	40	35	43	16	36	18	5	9	6	0	35	9	0	21	5	10	28	0	8	1	14	6	19	4	3	1	0			
	SUB					0	0	0	0	0	0	0	6	4	6	16	15	3	4	2	1	8	0	5	4	1	0	1	8	3	1	0	9	2	1			
	GOALS					0	0	2	13	0	1	0	6	2	0	1	1	0	1	0	0	6	0	0	1	0	0	1	0	1	6	0	1	0	0			
	SUB'D					0	1	1	2	0	3	8	17	8	3	0	4	0	0	4	0	3	1	3	5	0	0	1	5	4	5	2	3	0	0			
	CAPITAL ONE CUP																																					
06/08/2013	WATFORD	H	1	3	4875	P	P	P	P	P	P	P	PA	PC	B	PA	A	C	PB																	RICHARDS		
	JOHNSTONE'S PAINT TROPHY																																					
04/09/2013	BRISTOL CITY	A	1	2	17888	P	P	P	P	P	P	P	PB			P	B		P	A		PA														McCHRYSTAL		
	BUDWEISER FA CUP																																					
08/11/2013	YORK CITY	H	3	3	4654	P	P	P			P	PA		P			P		P			A		P	P				P							RICHARDS	HARROLD	BEARDSLEY
19/11/2013	YORK CITY	A	3	2	2051	P	P	P	P		P	P	P	P					P			A			P				PA							O'TOOLE	NORBURN	BEARDSLEY
07/12/2013	CRAWLEY TOWN	H	0	0	4623	P	P	P			P	P	PA	P	P		A		P			P			P													
08/01/2014	CRAWLEY TOWN	A	2	1	2435	P	P	P	P	P	P		PB	P		B			PA			P			P				A							RICHARDS	O'TOOLE	
14/01/2014	BIRMINGHAM CITY	A	0	3	9914	P	P	P	P	P	P	PC	C	P		P						P			PB				A	B								